D1610523

INTERNATIONAL AND COMPARATIVE CRIMINAL JUSTICE AND URBAN GOVERNANCE

Criminal justice has traditionally been associated with the nation state, its legitimacy and its authority. The growing internationalisation of crime control raises crucial and complex questions about the future shape of justice and urban governance as these are experienced at local, national and international realms. The emergence of new international justice institutions such as the International Criminal Court, the greater movement of people and goods across national borders and the transfer of criminal justice policies between different jurisdictions all present novel challenges to criminal justice systems as well as our understandings of criminal justice.

This volume of essays explores the implications and impact of criminal justice developments in an increasingly globalised world. It offers cutting-edge conceptual contributions from leading international commentators organised around the themes of international criminal justice institutions and practices; comparative penal policies; and international and comparative urban governance and crime control.

ADAM CRAWFORD is Professor of Criminology and Criminal Justice and Director of the Centre for Criminal Justice Studies at the University of Leeds. He is a leading international specialist and has published extensively in the fields of crime prevention, policing, criminal justice policy, comparative criminology and restorative justice.

INTERNATIONAL AND COMPARATIVE CRIMINAL JUSTICE AND URBAN GOVERNANCE: CONVERGENCE AND DIVERGENCE IN GLOBAL, NATIONAL AND LOCAL SETTINGS

Edited by

ADAM CRAWFORD

CAMBRIDGE
UNIVERSITY PRESS

CAMBRIDGE UNIVERSITY PRESS
Cambridge, New York, Melbourne, Madrid, Cape Town,
Singapore, São Paulo, Delhi, Tokyo, Mexico City

Cambridge University Press
The Edinburgh Building, Cambridge CB2 8RU, UK

Published in the United States of America by Cambridge University Press, New York

www.cambridge.org
Information on this title: www.cambridge.org/9780521116442

First published 2011

Printed in the United Kingdom at the University Press, Cambridge

A catalogue record for this publication is available from the British Library

Library of Congress Cataloging-in-Publication Data

International and Comparative Criminal Justice and
Urban Governance : Convergence and Divergence in Global,
National and Local Settings / edited by Adam Crawford.
p.   cm
ISBN 978-0-521-11644-2 (Hardback)
1. Criminal law–Congresses.   2. International offenses–Congresses.   I. Crawford, Adam
Michael Crawford, editor of compilation.   II. Crawford, Adam Michael Crawford.
International and comparative criminal justice and urban governance.
K5014.8.I548 2011
345–dc22

2010044488

ISBN 978-0-521-11644-2 Hardback

CONTENTS

CONTENTS vii

FIGURES

TABLES

NOTES ON CONTRIBUTORS

KATJA FRANKO AAS is Professor of Criminology at the Department of Criminology and Sociology of Law at the University of Oslo. She studied at the University of Ljubljana where she graduated in the Faculty of Law. Subsequently she moved to Norway and has since been working at the University of Oslo.

SARAH BLANDY is a Senior Lecturer in Law at the University of Leeds. She graduated from the University of Warwick and subsequently qualified and practised as a solicitor for ten years before embarking on an academic career. She joined the University of Leeds in 2005, having previously worked at Sheffield Hallam University.

SOPHIE BODY-GENDROT is Professor of Political Science at Sorbonne-Paris IV, where she is director of the Centre for Urban Studies. She is also a CNRS researcher at CESDIP (*Centre de Recherches Sociologiques sur le Droit et les Institutions Pénales*).

HANS BOUTELLIER is the Frans Denkers Professor in Safety and Citizenship at VU University, Amsterdam. He is also director at the Verwey-Jonker Institute, Utrecht.

CHRISJE BRANTS is Professor of Criminal Law and Criminal Process at the Willem Pompe Institute for Criminal Law and Criminology, University of Utrecht. She is also a member of the *Académie Internationale de Droit Comparé* and the Association for International Criminal Justice.

MICHAEL CAVADINO is Professor of Law at the University of Central Lancashire and Research Co-ordinator for Lancashire Law School. He studied law at Oxford University and criminology and socio-legal studies at the University of Sheffield where he taught for many years before moving to his current post in 2006.

JAMES COCKAYNE is co-director of the Center on Global Counter-terrorism Cooperation in New York. He was awarded the inaugural Worldwide Universities Network (WUN) Fellowship of the 'International and Comparative Criminal Justice Network' in 2009 and held the post at Sydney University.

ADAM CRAWFORD is Professor of Criminology and Criminal Justice and director of the Centre for Criminal Justice Studies at the University of Leeds. He is the co-organiser of the WUN International and Comparative Criminal Justice Network (ICCJnet).

JAMES DIGNAN was formerly Professor of Comparative Criminology and Criminal Justice at the University of Leeds. Before moving to Leeds in 2007, he was Professor of Criminology and Restorative Justice at the University of Sheffield.

ANTHONY N. DOOB is Professor of Criminology at the University of Toronto. He served as director of the Centre of Criminology from 1979 to 1989 and was one of the members of the Canadian Sentencing Commission from 1984 to 1987.

MARK FINDLAY is the Professor of Criminal Justice, Institute of Criminology, Law Faculty at the University of Sydney. He also holds the Chair in International Criminal Justice, Centre for Criminal Justice Studies, School of Law, University of Leeds, and is an associate senior research fellow at the Institute of Advanced Legal Studies. He is the co-organiser of the WUN International and Comparative Criminal Justice Network (ICCJnet).

SUSANNE KARSTEDT is Professor of Criminology and Criminal Justice at the University of Leeds, having moved from a chair at the University of Keele in 2009. She researched and taught at the universities of Bielefeld and Hamburg in Germany.

NICOLA LACEY is Senior Research Fellow in All Souls College at Oxford University. She is a Fellow of the British Academy.

LESLEY McARA is Professor of Penology in the Law School at Edinburgh University. She is the principal co-director of the Edinburgh Study of Youth Transitions and Crime.

STEPHAN PARMENTIER is Professor of Sociology of Crime, Law and Human Rights at the University of Leuven's Institute of Criminology. He studied law and sociology at the universities of Ghent and Leuven and Minnesota – Twin Cities.

JOHN PRATT is Professor of Criminology and James Cook Research Fellow in Social Science 2009–12 at the Institute of Criminology, Victoria University of Wellington, New Zealand. During the academic year 2010–11 he holds a Straus Fellowship at the Institute for Advanced Study of Law and Justice at New York University.

JASON RALPH is Professor in International Relations in the School of Politics and International Studies at the University of Leeds. His project 'Law, War and the State of the American Exception' is funded by the Economic and Social Research Council grant number RES-000–22–3252.

JOANNA SHAPLAND is Professor of Criminal Justice and Head of the School of Law at the University of Sheffield. She is executive editor of the *International Review of Victimology*.

SONJA SNACKEN is Professor of Criminology, Penology and Sociology of Law at the Free University of Brussels. During the academic year 2010–11 she holds a Straus Fellowship at the Institute for Advanced Study of Law and Justice at New York University.

JANE B. SPROTT is Associate Professor in the Department of Criminal Justice and Criminology at Ryerson University, Toronto.

RONALD VAN STEDEN is Assistant Professor in the Department of Governance Studies at VU University, Amsterdam.

MARIANA VALVERDE is Professor of Criminology at the University of Toronto, where she is director of the Centre of Criminology.

CLIVE WALKER is Professor of Criminal Justice Studies at the University of Leeds, where he previously was the director of the Centre for Criminal Justice Studies and head of the School of Law.

CHERYL MARIE WEBSTER is an associate professor in the Department of Criminology at the University of Ottawa and a member of the Faculty of Graduate and Postdoctoral Studies.

ELMAR WEITEKAMP is Professor of Victimology and Restorative Justice at the University of Tübingen. He studied social work in Mönchen-
gladbach and at the University of Pennsylvania.

DIRK VAN ZYL SMIT is Professor of Comparative and International
Penal Law at the University of Nottingham and Emeritus Professor of
Criminology at the University of Cape Town.

ACKNOWLEDGEMENTS

This book arose out of an international colloquium held at the University of Leeds on 24–6 June 2008 under the title 'International and Comparative Criminal Justice and Urban Governance'. It was generously sponsored by the Worldwide Universities Network (WUN) and served as the inaugural meeting of the WUN International and Comparative Criminal Justice Network (ICCJnet). The international colloquium was attended by nearly forty delegates from across Europe, North America, Australasia and China. All but two of the eventual chapters in this volume were first presented at the conference and benefited from the extensive discussions that took place over the three days. On behalf of the contributors, I would like to thank all those who attended the colloquium and contributed to the various deliberations, in particular: Katja Franko Aas, Sarah Blandy, Sophie Body-Gendrot, Hans Boutellier, Chrisje Brants, Mick Cavadino, Kerry Clamp, Tony Doob, Mark Findlay, Ralph Henham, Alice Hills, Anthea Hucklesby, Susanne Karstedt, Nicola Lacey, Sam Lewis, Stuart Lister, Lesley McAra, Tim Newburn, John Pratt, Jason Ralph, Paul Seils, Joanna Shapland, Jane Sprott, Mariana Valverde, Clive Walker, David Wall, Adam White, Emma Wincup, Dirk van Zyl Smit and Miao Zhang. I am grateful to Sophie Goodeve and my colleagues at the Centre for Criminal Justice Studies in the Law School at the University of Leeds for their assistance in the organisation and hosting of the initial conference.

The ICCJnet combines WUN and non-WUN partners with interests in a range of interrelated themes that coalesce around the internationalisation of crime control, by exploring questions of comparison (both convergences and divergences) in the development of policy, norms and institutional infrastructures. The network is interested in both the development of international institutions and processes, as well as comparisons between national and sub-national developments. Questions about policy transfer, lesson-drawing and international trends in the co-ordination and delivery of modes of criminal justice and crime control are at the forefront of research concerns within this network. The ICCJnet has three main research themes which are reflected in this collected volume: (1) international criminal justice and global governance, (2) comparative penology and penal policies and (3) comparative urban governance and international policing agendas. With support from WUN, the ICCJnet funds an annual international visiting fellowship which was held by James Cockayne at the University of Sydney in 2009 and by Dr Ilaria Bottigliero (Senior Researcher at the International Development Law Organisation) jointly at the Universities Sheffield and Leeds in 2010. For further information about the ICCJnet visit the website at: www.wun.ac.uk/research/iccjnet.

I would like to thank all the contributors for their work and their forbearance in the realisation of this project. I am grateful to Sarah Blandy, Phil Hadfield and Stuart Lister for their helpful comments on drafts of some of the chapters. Many thanks to Finola O'Sullivan, at Cambridge University Press, for her patience, for believing in the ambitious idea of this volume of essays and for her – and her team's – support and encouragement in bringing this collection to fruition. Finally, I would like to dedicate this volume to my two daughters, Alex and Kirsty, whose love and honesty provide me with vital and enduring strength.

International and comparative criminal justice and urban governance

ADAM CRAWFORD

Introduction

The power to define acts as crimes and the institutionalisation of processes of criminalisation are intimately bound up with the law-making power and identity of the nation state. Similarly, the ability to enforce criminal norms through coercion is equally entwined with the state's claim to sovereignty and its monopoly over the use of legitimate force. Consequently, criminal law and criminal justice represent pre-eminent and central symbols of state sovereignty, and claims over the state's capacity to regulate populations and activities within the confines of its territorial borders. Crime control, therefore, is intrinsically tied up with questions of national identity and self-characterisation. It is infused with, and reflects, the moral, cultural and political frames of reference that inform a society and constitute membership (i.e. citizenship) for given peoples within specified geographical boundaries.

Increasingly in recent years, the capacities, competencies and legitim-ation claims of the nation state have been called into question – in the field of crime and social control as elsewhere. 'Fluidity', 'liquidity' and 'movement' appear as the defining characteristics of the contemporary age (Lash and Urry 1994; Bauman 2000; Castells 2000). In the modern era, people, goods, capital, technologies, information and communica-tions, as well as 'risks', appear to be on the move in ways that cut across territorial boundaries and question the capability of the state as the ultimate 'power-container'. The development of cross-border and inter-national political, legal and economic institutions has directly challenged the sovereignty of a nation state within its own borders in the most obvious and tangible ways. In the UK, it is the challenge presented by the progression and enlargement of the European Union that excites the most heated public and political debates about sovereignty.

However, the trends are not merely *upward* to transnational and supranational institutions under pressures of globalisation. They are also *downward* to regions, localities, communities and consumers and *outward* into the new policy networks and 'partnerships' incorporating commercial businesses, private interests and 'third sector' or charitable organisations, which are increasingly refiguring relations between centre and periphery in diverse spheres of social life – including the crime control complex. Thus, the decline of state sovereignty in the face of greater interdependencies of political economies and the globalisation of world markets only present one dimension of contemporary trends. Global pressures co-exist alongside an increasing salience of locality. The sameness of globalisation also confronts and affronts assertions of local identity. Place is at one instance 'disembedded' (Giddens 1990) – disconnected from and stretched across time and space – but also re-embedded in an increased significance accorded to locality, local social order and the local 'structures of feeling' (Taylor *et al.* 1996) that remain essential in how ordinary people interpret and make sense of the world. There appears to be an increasingly profound relationship between globalised conditions and local circumstances and outlooks. And yet, the manner in which these tensions are played out, expressed and resolved are decidedly uneven. As commentators have noted, processes of 'globalisation' and 'localisation' are not necessarily antagonistic but often are interconnected through pressures towards social integration. Giddens has insisted that 'the ever increasing abundance of global connections. . . should not be regarded as intrinsically diminishing the sovereignty' of states, but rather seen as 'in substantial part the chief condition of the world-wide extension of the nation-state system in current times' (1985: 5). As such, it may be too soon to herald the 'hollowing out of the state' (Jessop 1993; Rhodes 1994) or celebrating its premature demise. As Bayley rightly warns, we should not get carried away with 'a giddy sense at the moment among many intellectuals that the state is passé' (2001: 212). Nonetheless, a re-articulation of powers and governmental authorities across diverse aspects of social life and at different levels of governance is well under way and the challenges to traditional ways of thinking about the ambitions and capabilities of the nation state remain pre-eminent questions of our time. In different ways these are some of the key themes that animate various chapters in this volume (notably in Parts 1 and 3)

Echoing Giddens' insights into the impact of globalisation on state sovereignty, Katja Aas (in her chapter) uses the example of border controls in the EU to show how national borders are shifting under pressures of globalisation. She shows how nation states are becoming interlocked and decoupled from traditional geographic boundaries, not necessarily in ways that undermine or reduce sovereignty but rather in ways that frequently strengthen their security, working with, and through, other states and third parties. As Aas asserts: 'transnationalisation may be a way of achieving the goals of the national' (p. 407). Somewhat contradictorily, perhaps, on the one hand we see the 'de-territorialisation of the border' of nation states yet, on the other hand, we hear of the increased territorialisation of urban governance through the construction of differential 'zones' of security governance (as illustrated in the chapters by Boutellier and van Steden, and Blandy). Hence, the de-localisation of borders co-exists with the construction of new spatially defined zones and boundary formation with significant implications for policing and control (a theme developed in Crawford's contribution to this volume).

Against this background, the nation state as both an institutional and conceptual 'container' appears under threat like never before. Conceptually, in the political and social sciences, it has become something of a 'clunky' yet 'solid' term with overwhelming fixity in the face of the modernising tendencies of capitalism in which, as Marshal Berman (1983) (following Marx) noted, 'all that is solid melts into air'. Along with the nation state, fixed notions of boundaries and borders (both geographical and conceptual) have been called into question. Moreover, this traversing of borders and institutional fluidity raises important concerns about our capacity to understand social phenomena – like crime, criminal justice, social control and punishment – at different scales of analysis. The complex social production of transnational connections, city-to-city linkages, and the manner in which the 'global' and the 'local' are intertwined, destabilises taken-for-granted choices about scale and the connections between different frames of analysis. Can we deploy the same terms, vocabularies and conceptual understandings as we move between different scales (micro, mezzo, macro or local, national, global)? This is a question directly posed and explored by Mariana Valverde, in her contribution to this collection of essays. If new institutional forms and normative orderings are emerging at the intersection between flows, at the edges of traditional borders and cutting across place and scales of analysis, then what are the theoretical and empirical implications for our traditional ways of thinking about crime, law and criminology? What are the implications of the changing

relationship between political traditions and national cultures in crime
control (and elsewhere) both in relation to each other and vis-à-vis, on
the one hand, some emerging notion of international norms, standards,
procedures and legal order(s) and, on the other, local expressions of
values and sensibilities?

On the move: borders and boundaries

In keeping with the 'fluid' or 'liquid' metaphor, crime and insecurity
appear in particular to be on the move (Bauman 2006). They circulate in
novel ways, penetrating public, private and hybrid spheres, seeping
through new technologies and turning apparently benign and taken-
for-granted aspects of contemporary life – such as shopping, travel,
working and using the Internet – into potential threats. They simultaneously invade local and transnational arenas and confuse the two as
international developments inform local insecurities and vice versa.
Considerable new sources of harm – and by implication challenges of
governance – present themselves from above and beyond, as well as
below and within, the territories of the nation state. Some of these arise
as a result of the dangers and opportunities presented by new technologies, scientific innovations, the flow of information and as populations
become more mobile. The new prominence of risk connects individual
autonomy with the influence and role of scientific innovation and
technological change. We have witnessed both a growing sensitisation
to risk and the problematisation of risk itself. As Ulrich Beck (1992),
amongst others has argued, the contemporary 'risk society' constitutes a
stage of modernity in which a defining feature is the production of new
risks and harms that lie beyond the control of nation states with potential impact that transcends national territories. Global warming is the
archetypical example of such a risk. However, transnational (organised)
crimes and terrorism constitute further distinctive aspects of the types of
harms generated by the greater mobility and flow of people, goods,
capital and information facilitated by technological advances and innovations. In the process, it is argued, managing hazards (notably those that
cut across borders) has become a central preoccupation of contemporary
societies. Beck's argument has obvious implications for governments'
limited capacity to manage and assert sovereign control over contemporary risks, notably in the face of global forces. So too, it has implications for individuals and the level of micro-social interactions. The
break-up of the welfare state and the onset of neoliberal reforms – in

many advanced Western societies – have served to proliferate and disperse risks once deemed the responsibility of the nation state. Where previously contained through social insurance – public welfare provisions – risks have increasingly become individualised. In this light, a defining feature of contemporary living is the institutionalised need, on behalf of individuals, to construct and invent the 'self' and actively shape one's future in the face of contemporary risks. According to Bauman, 'Modernity replaces determination of social standing with compulsive and obligatory self-determination' (2001: xv); individuals' life trajectories become 'elective'. Here 'choice' becomes not only a meta-narrative and defining condition, but also a requirement. How one lives becomes a 'biographical solution to systemic contradictions' (Beck 1992). Despite globalising forces, the micro-social context of local order takes on a greater – not lesser – salience.

In the process, crime and insecurity have come to constitute major global and local challenges of immense contemporary significance for diverse governments (national and local), international organisations, NGOs, businesses, voluntary sector bodies and citizens alike. Security concerns inform the work and operations of numerous public, private and third-sector organisations stretching from the local to the national and the international sphere. It is now widely recognised that on the one hand policing and security measures designed to prevent and manage international threats – from terrorism and drugs or people-trafficking to inter-group conflict, for example – demand local intelligence and community-based responses whilst on the other hand the experience and salience of neighbourhood safety are informed and influenced by international trends and distant conflicts. Local crime and security concerns are interwoven with far-flung developments, global trends and experiences of injustices and inequalities in remote and sometimes far-away corners of the world. In many senses, the attacks in the USA on 11 September 2001 – as well as the subsequent bombings in Madrid, London and elsewhere – poignantly highlighted the mobile nature of security threats and allied risks and the interconnections between international conflicts and local safety, as well as problems of foresight, established methodologies for generating actionable intelligence and governmental responses to conditions of uncertainty (Zedner 2009; Crawford 2010).

Moreover, as these examples testify, the complex interpenetration of the local and the global has been unfolding (as well as having become more clearly a focus of analysis in its own right) at a time when threats to security and personal safety have come to constitute more pivotal concerns of governance. As Jonathan Simon (2007) has recently argued, in contemporary societies crime has become an intrinsic aspect of contemporary governance and an organising concept central to the exercise of authority. In his terms, societies are increasingly 'governed through crime', as a result of which the 'technologies, discourses and metaphors of crime and criminal justice have become more visible features of all kinds of institutions, where they can easily gravitate into new opportunities for governance' (Simon 2007: 4–5). In fact, as Garland (1996) has demonstrated, the very questioning of the capacity of the state to guarantee order and protect its citizenry from crime has itself prompted more volatile, contradictory and punitive expressions of punishment. As the limitations of the state have been acknowledged, at one instance, and sovereignty over crime denied – as being 'beyond the state' – so too, at another moment sovereignty is symbolically reasserted, through periodic episodes of (sometimes) hysterical and populist punitiveness. This dualistic denial and recognition produces ambivalent shifts in the state's presentation of its own capacity for effective action in crime control which subsequently generates uncertainties among on-looking anxious citizens. According to some commentators, the result-ant punitiveness, born of fear, appears to induce an obsession with rules, an insistence on uncompromising lines of demarcation between appro-priate and inappropriate behaviour, a dwindling tolerance of deviance and disorder, and a disproportionate response to rule-breaking and incivility (Young 2007; Crawford 2009a). Despite the turn-around in the long rise of (recorded) crime rates across many advanced capitalist jurisdictions in the last decade or so, and unprecedented historic reduc-tions in victimisation risks to the person, we appear to be in the grip of a pervasive preoccupation with insecurity, fear of crime and threats to safety (Boutellier 2004).

Just as crimes and insecurities appear to be shifting, so too responses to crime and insecurity are on the move. They are on the move both in the sense that the new institutions and arrangements of policing and regulation are loosened from their fixed association with the modern nation state, incorporating a diversity of actors that transcend territor-ial boundaries, and in the sense that crime control policies (at least at the level of rhetoric) are being transported – exported and imported – around the world. As crime and insecurity have become unbounded so too the governance of crime and insecurity is being refashioned through the forging of new regulatory institutions and infrastructures, as well as on the back of processes of policy diffusion and transfer (Newburn and Sparks 2004).

As a consequence, migration itself – the movement of peoples across borders – has become intimately bound up with debates about crime and its policing and punishment. Migrants and refugees, as embodiments of (uncontrolled) mobility and extraterritoriality, have become the outlet for contemporary insecurities and fears. In many ways, they constitute sitting targets upon which anxieties about the uncontrollable forces of mobility are easily projected and focused. Borders and boundaries constitute an impediment to mobility and fluidity. As such, they are key focal points that represent symbolic locations where contests are played out and new institutional apparatuses constructed. In this light, Aas describes borders as 'immobilisation strategies' that constitute an attempt at 'imposing control in world in motion'. In this regard, borders and boundaries are pivotal to processes and dynamics of both exclusion and inclusion. They reinforce the attachments of inclusion, membership and citizenship, as well as seeking to insulate these from outside, external invasion. The EU borders construct the inclusive bonds of European citizenship which give rise to human rights protections, *inter alia*, as van Zyl Smit and Snacken's analysis (in their chapter) testifies, on the one hand, but which also exclude non-citizens. In the process, such boundaries of membership create categories of aliens, 'outsiders' or internal 'non-persons' in the shape of what the French describe as '*sans papier*'. But forces of inclusion and exclusion operate outside of the territorial boundaries of the nation state or 'clubs' of member states. Sarah Blandy (in her chapter) highlights the growing salience of boundary-building as an integral tool of urban governance, in which processes of exclusion (and inclusion) are symbolically reinforced through physical 'gating'.

Just as mobility and free movement are deemed to constitute fundamental aspects of free trade – as embodied in supranational constitutional arrangements such as the EU, where the free movement of people, goods and capital are sacrosanct ideals (see Aas 2007; and this volume) – so too, they are perceived to be central to the good economic order of the city (as Crawford argues in his chapter). This prompts ambiguous attempts to differentiate between what Aas terms 'good' and 'bad' mobilities. Consequently, there is a tension between the liberality of the inclusive invitation to 'good mobilities' and governing authorities' desire to keep out 'undesirables' and 'bad mobilities'. In the context of the city, Crawford describes this as 'enticements to "good customers". . . [which] are frequently mirrored by subterranean interdictions aimed at the "unwelcome" or what Bauman describes as "flawed consumers"' (Crawford this volume: 495; Bauman 1998: 38–41 ref). As Aas argues, the intention is not to erect impenetrable borders but rather to manage the flow across boundaries and borders in an orderly and efficient manner; 'not to arrest mobility but to tame it' (Walters 2004: 248). As Crawford shows in the context of urban governance, these borders are often porous, but nevertheless have very real regulatory effects.

In urban, national and global governance, pre-emptive and preventive forms of control have become more evident (Ericson 2007). What is inferred is the need for intervention and action to occur before a threat or risk becomes an expressed and obvious 'known'. This pre-emptive governance and a focus on what Zedner (2007) calls 'pre-crime' constitute a clarion call for early intervention even before risks have expressed themselves. It proclaims the need to anticipate and forestall potential harms. Rather than acting in the present to avoid an occurrence in the future, pre-emption brings the future into the present: 'It makes present the future consequences of an eventuality that may or may not occur, indifferent to its actual occurrence' (Massumi 2005: 7–8). This focus on pre-emption and prevention is to be found informing strategies stretching across international relations – most notably the US and UK justifications for the war against Iraq – and in local community safety – especially in the UK governments' focus on 'antisocial behaviour' and the policing of incivilities in other jurisdictions. It also has implications for the blurring of disciplinary boundaries and policy fields as well as border controls, as modes of governance seek to push the policing of possible 'risks' before they express themselves, i.e. before they enter national borders and before they cross the threshold of contemporary security 'clubs' (Hope 2000; Crawford 2006). This strategy of pre-emption highlights the interconnections between internal and external dimensions of policing and security policies, and the blurring of migration policy, foreign affairs and international development and aid.

Comparisons

Comparison by necessity implies the identification of similarities and differences across spatial and temporal units of analysis; whether these are isolated variables such as imprisonment rates per capita or the more complex interactions between actors in institutions and processes, and the manner in which these are interpreted. Comparative criminal justice research, as Nelken notes, 'is both about discovering surprising differences and unexpected similarities' (2010: 32). The first issue then is the question of equivalence; do the key concepts, terms, practices, datasets, processes, actors and institutions have the same meaning in different places? Are we comparing like with like or apples with pears? At one level, this raises issues of measurement and meaning; what are we measuring and what is its meaning? Can we identify a point of comparison – a facet or variable – which can be understood in its own terms and holds constant in the process of comparison? Or, is it so implicated in, and constituted by, other factors and forces that comparing it across time and/or space is invalid or undermined? In part due to both measurement difficulties and the fact that traditionally much criminology research and teaching has maintained a decidedly domestic focus, the comparative approach in crime and criminal justice – as contrasted with some fields like economics and healthcare (Wilkinson and Pickett 2009) – remains in its infancy. Nevertheless, in the quest for comparable cross-national data, criminologists have done much in recent years both in taking official datasets as a starting point for comparison and in developing new datasets, often based on survey instruments that bypass official statistics such as international crime victims surveys (ICVS). First conducted in 1988, the ICVS has expanded to incorporate some seventy-eight countries where it has been conducted more than once. This has allowed researchers to develop 'league tables' on various types of crime and to measure public attitudes to criminal justice institutions and processes (van Dijk *et al.* 2006; van Dijk 2008). However, as well as descriptive questions about similarities and differences, comparison raises analytical questions about what accounts for difference and similarities and how differences are not only classified and explained but also interpreted.

At another level, this prompts questions about translation across time/ space. Here translation has two distinct dimensions. First, in some comparative research there is the complex task of translation from one language to another. In a European context, given the rich diversity of languages, this presents particularly acute challenges. The process of linguistic conversion, by necessity, expects the same term to carry the same meaning in each language. However, this can be a misguided assumption. Not only do practices and institutions differ considerably but the same term may carry very different meanings. What at first sight may appear to reflect the same expression may, on closer inspection, turn out to be dramatically distinct in significant and consequential ways. In some contexts, no direct translation may exist; such that a given term constitutes what Lacey and Zedner (1998) call a 'significant absence'. The interpretation and explanation of such 'absences' (and conversely 'presences') in different cultural contexts is the stuff of much innovative comparative study (Nelken 2000). In this light, Legrand argues that 'the comparativist must learn *not* to translate' (1996: 234, emphasis in original) and he chastises much comparative legal research for ignoring issues of translation and the 'foreignness of languages' (*ibid*.: 235). In this light, there may be benefits, for comparative researchers, to be derived from the quest for, and analysis of, functional equivalence (rather than similar terms or institutions) within systems of crime control rather than too hastily assuming linguistic correspondence. Such functions may be intended or unintended and therefore, take us beyond an exploration of the formal purpose (or mission statement) that institutions and processes may formally hold out. Furthermore, such an approach should beg questions about the different interests served by specified functions – in other words, for whom is it functional? And yet, the search for functional equivalence assumes that all criminal justice systems both perform the same or similar tasks and have an internal logic and coherence. The danger of such an approach, however, derives from the potential functionalism that may ensue, whereby practices are understood primarily in terms of the function they perform as a constituent element of a larger system. Research findings in criminal justice have frequently highlighted the non-system-like nature of the interactions and interrelations between the constituent parts, the incongruities and conflicts that make up crime control and the irrational dynamics that infuse criminal justice processes (Crawford 1997). Furthermore, one of the enduring lessons from (comparative) criminology is precisely that there may be a significant disjuncture between the symbolic and affective dimensions to crime control as contrasted with its instrumental or managerial functions. As Garland has noted:

> there are two contrasting visions at work in contemporary criminal justice – the passionate, morally toned desire to punish and the administrative, rationalistic, normalizing concern to manage. These visions clash in many important respects, but both are deeply embedded within the social process of punishing. It is in the conflict and tension between them that we find one of the key determinants of contemporary penal [and more broadly crime control] practice. [1990: 180]

The second sense in which translation occurs is the process whereby ideas, practices or activities are translated from one place to another. This process of contextual relocation assumes that the same practices carry the same meanings in different social and cultural contexts. There is all too often a danger within comparative criminology – as in the social sciences more generally – of analysing case studies and initiatives much like 'butterfly collecting' in which not only are selective (exotic) items displayed (often to fit into some wider narrative or advance some preconceived world view) but also the exhibits are plucked – often drawn from around the world or across time – from the very environments that they inhabit and which sustains them, and through which their lives make sense (Crawford 2002). We need to understand more, rather than less, about the differences and similarities in connections between responses to crime and cultures, as well as the manner in which such strategies derive their sense and meaning from their cultural and contextual ties. The limits to the transferability of crime control mechanisms or policies that advocates claim to be universal often derive from precisely such cultural and institutional connections; from their connectedness to the environment from which they are drawn. Hence, there is often a need for a culturally and socio-politically sensitive excavation of key defining concepts that links them to wider horizons of interpretation and searches out the meaning they may have for the participants concerned (Crawford 2000a).

Comparativists, therefore, need to be sensitive to the pitfalls of both linguistic conversion and contextual relocation. For this reason, as far as possible, contributors to this volume have sought to relate experiences to, and situate criminal justice policies and sentencing regimes within, the political and social conditions of each country. It is only on the basis of this knowledge that we can begin to understand the applicability and transferability (as well as their limitations) of given practices beyond the confines from which they emerge. As with the 'butterfly collection', the problem for the observer is that she is not provided with any sense of the settings and connections that give life to and sustain each exhibit nor how transferable any particular exhibit might be from one environment to another.

Convergence and divergence

Comparative studies inevitably run the risk of falling foul of either overly grand universal claims or slipping into a position of relativism and a celebration of (cultural) specificity. There are considerable dangers in comparative analysis in either focusing on the richness of difference and diversity of practices or – more often in criminology – rushing to hasty and misguided assumptions about the flattening of difference through policy convergence and global homogenisation. This latter tendency has been particularly evident in the recent work of those associated with the Campbell Collaboration (Farrington and Petrosino 2001) and proponents of 'crime science' (Laycock 2005).[1] David Farrington (1999; 2000), most notably, has argued for a vision of the globalisation of criminological knowledge. An explicit intention of those working within such a perspective is to use scientific claims of generalisability to influence policy and policy-makers around the world (Sherman 2009). Not only do they offer a more optimistic image of the capacity of research-informed knowledge and evidence to shape policy but, in so doing, they prioritise a particular type of knowledge that is decontextualised and largely blind to the role of culture and socio-political factors in shaping both our understandings of crime and social responses to it. It is 'butterfly collecting' par excellence. The generalisations implicit in such an approach frequently oversimplifies the interactive and constitutive relationship between crime, criminal justice and the contexts in which they operate. Too often such universal claims are infused with an ethnocentrism in which assumptions are made that (causal) links that are found to hold in familiar situations – often our own Anglo-American jurisdictions – are deemed to apply generally elsewhere (Nelken 2010). Underlying this is an implicit presumption that what is right for us should hold for others.

An emphasis on convergence in comparative studies is informed either explicitly by some notion of globalisation – through modes of connection (via markets, networks, communication systems etc.) and processes of harmonisation – or implicitly through the appropriation of conceptual lenses as ways of seeing and interpreting social and institutional change. In relation to the latter, for example, the talk of the 'risk society' – like other meta-narratives – has led many criminologists to focus on the convergence of experiences, at the expense of a sustained understanding of how these play out differently under diverse conditions and across different places. As O'Malley astutely notes:

> criminologists generally have been content – if often dismayed – to
> identify more and more examples of risk technique in the governance
> of crime, affecting more and more people. Consequently, there has been

---

[1] In very different ways this accusation can also be raised in regard of the more culturally and socially nuanced meta-narratives of commentators such as Garland (2001) and Bauman (2000; 2006).

much less emphasis on the significance of political and technical differences among risk technologies than on their unity as instances of risk.
[2004: 30]

Even where practices and technologies of control are directly influenced
by policy emulation and borrowing, this may not necessarily produce
convergence nor result in sameness. Jones and Newburn (2007: 25) note
the important symbolic and rhetorical dimension of much criminal
justice policy transfer (from the USA to the UK). Jane Sprott (in this
volume) forcefully illustrates a similar argument in relation to policy
transfer from the USA to Canada. As a consequence, there is a significant
dissonance between policy 'talk' and the activities of people – namely
those professionals and practitioners – on the ground in routine 'action';
between rhetoric and practice. Hence, claims about convergence may be
more a matter of 'talk' and symbolism than of everyday practices.

Nevertheless, undoubtedly, international pressures to standardise,
harmonise and bring into line different terminology, practices and
institutional arrangements, have grown significantly in recent years (as
the chapters in Part 1 demonstrate). Initially this developed through the
emergence of common supranational regional arrangements in the post-
Second World War period, most notably the European Union. More
recently this process has reached a crescendo with the signing and
implementation of the Rome Statute which brought into being the
International Criminal Court (ICC) a decade ago.[2] The formal preamble
to the Rome Statute emphasises a number of important themes that
inform and structure the emerging and tentative international criminal
legal order, its intentions and direction of development. First, it is
premised on the assumption that commonality is a desirable end in
itself. From the outset the *Preamble* declares that all parties to the Statute
are 'conscious that all peoples are united by common bonds, their
cultures pieced together in a shared heritage, and concerned that this
delicate mosaic may be shattered at any time' (United Nations 1999).
Difference, in this 'delicate mosaic', is to be set aside for the higher
objective of 'common bonds'. Secondly, the Statute focuses only on the
'most serious crimes of concern to the international community as a
whole' (*ibid.*), namely those crimes – war crimes, crimes against

---

[2] The Rome Statute was adopted at a diplomatic conference in Rome on 17 July 1998 and
the ICC subsequently came into force on 1 July 2002. It had been agreed under Art. 126
that the Statute would only come into force once sixty countries had ratified it. The ICC
can only prosecute crimes committed after the date that it came into force. Seven
countries voted against the original treaty, including the US, Israel and China.

humanity and genocide – that are deemed to transcend cultural and
political differences. Thirdly, at the same time as promulgating a new
international order the Statute seeks to reinforce the centrality of sovereign nation states reflected in the overarching principle of complementarity to national criminal jurisdictions which is heavily underscored
(see Brants this volume). Finally, the ICC is conceived and justified in
instrumental terms of deterrence through, in the words of the preamble,
its determination 'to put an end to impunity for the perpetrators of
these crimes and thus to contribute to the prevention of such crimes'
(*ibid.*). It may seem somewhat ironic that at a time when little faith is
accorded by most criminal justice commentators and practitioners to
notions of general deterrence in regard to national (or sub-national)
jurisdictions, it is resurrected as an article of faith at the level of the ICC.[3]

International moves towards standardisation and comparability –
such as the ongoing development of European-wide standards in
criminal justice and the elaboration of international criminal justice as
both an idea and a practice – are not neutral activities. Rather they are
part of a deliberate strategy to bring about greater similarity and harmonisation. They are, thus, an aspect of convergence. As such, they
should prompt questions about the interests they advance and the voices
they silence, as well as the assumptions and ideologies that inform them
(see Ralph this volume). Furthermore, how do uniform practices make
sense in different contexts; what are their implications and social consequences; and what may be lost, as well as gained, by changing existing
practices through standardisation; are standardisation and the erasing of
differences desirable ends in relation to given policy goals; should specificity and diversity be preserved because they are valuable in themselves
or for some additional reason(s)?

That context matters should rightly call into question the generalising
claims of 'globalising criminology' and also challenge the transferability
and replication of apparently successful criminal justice and crime control policies from one country, city or locality to another. But just as
Geertz (1983) warned against 'anti-relativism', Nelken (2000) is correct
to caution us against too hastily embracing 'anti-universalism' and
retreating into a (pessimistic) relativism in which we can never

---

[3] More so because the strongest empirical and conceptual critiques of general deterrence
theory derive from the challenges of a lack of certainty of punishment rather than any lack
of severity of the sanctions received, a point forcefully acknowledged by Right-wing
criminologists (Wilson 1975) despite the traditional association with notions of
deterrence.

discriminate what is right or provide any grounds for learning across places or times. As Nelken notes, against a backdrop of policy pressures to harmonise aspects of criminal justice, comparison becomes an intrinsic part of the activities of shaping and administering criminal justice systems: 'Thus in order to study such processes we must also explore the way others make comparisons – which will often reveal the "interested" interpretations of criminal justice practices by politicians, policy-makers, legal actors, journalists, activists, scholars and others' (2010: 2). Comparison, like standardisation, is not a neutral endeavour embarked on from some objective vantage point or a 'view from nowhere', but rather departs from specific places and understandings infused with quests to fulfil differing, sometimes very specific, purposes – be they theoretical, political or practical – and, at the same time, influenced by different methodological and epistemological approaches. In revealing the 'interested interpretations' that Nelken alludes to, we need to uncover the theoretical, political and practical purposes that inform the desire to learn from, borrow, imitate or harmonise with other approaches. For example, there are dangers in comparative criminology in implying that bad causes have bad consequences; most notably (as reflected in the debates in Part 2) that neoliberal policies and decreasing welfare provisions are responsible for higher imprisonment rates. Karstedt (in this volume) illustrates this in relation to the inverse tendency to ascribe a positive impact to democratic values and institutions in holding imprisonment rates at bay and improve prison conditions.

Decentring the nation state

Much comparative analysis – often for good and understandable reasons – has reinforced a state-centred approach by taking the nation as the unit of comparison (as largely witnessed in Part 2 of this volume). Here, especially in the field of state punishments, the nation is the logical unit of analysis, given the shared institutions, politics, constitutions and laws that inform contemporary penality. Yet, even here national policies – on sentencing and punishment amongst other things – are differently applied and interpreted, influenced as they are by local cultural traditions and political affiliations. Furthermore, much policy innovation emanates from local or regional levels and may or may not filter 'upwards'. In many fields of crime control and urban governance in particular there exist important cross-national city-to-city and region-to-region interconnections, which allow for policy travels, lesson-learning and exchange. Cities, sometimes more so than whole nations, may be the inspiration for policy developments – the examples of New York's (so-called) 'zero-tolerance policing' (Newburn and Jones 2007) and, conversely, Amsterdam's decriminalisation of cannabis and regulation of prostitution spring to mind.

Criminologists (social scientists and political scientists too!) have tended to collude with this state-centric approach, by focusing policy analysis on national government instruments and statements; notably legislation, protocols and guidance. Whilst the social sciences have shown interest in the ways in which national policies are informed by international pressures and global influences, significantly, less concern has been accorded to the manner in which formal policy pronounce-ments are shaped by local political cultures in, and through, their implementation. National policies are routinely resisted, refashioned and played out in different ways in particular locales. As a result, the expectations of national governments are modified and given positive and concrete form in different local contexts. For, as Anderson notes, 'policy is made as it is being administered and administered as it is being made' (1975: 79). To understand and make sense of what given criminal justice policies mean at specific moments in time and in particular places, we need to be sensitive to the manner in which central govern-ment edicts are refracted and reinterpreted through local traditions and political cultures, as well as appreciate the autonomous governing capacities of local institutions. For, it is in this way that policy instru-ments are brought to life 'on the ground'. Clearly, constitutional arrange-ments within given jurisdictions will influence the capacity for local variations, such that where robust systems of devolution and federalism exist the scope for local autonomy is likely to be more significant. But even in what appear as highly centralised nations such as France, the scope for distinctive local governance should not be too readily discounted (see Crawford 2000b; Body-Gendrot this volume).

That local context matters is something of a truism, particularly in the messy world of human affairs and social relations where 'people matter' and where actions and outcomes are consistently reproduced by the behaviour of individual actors. This reinforces the importance of not assuming the effectiveness of central government intentions or ambi-tions, notably those set down in formal policy statements and legislation. The history of crime control policy is especially replete with examples of weak application, implementation failure, unintended consequences and perverse effects. But as Theodore Marmor (1994) notes, in the slightly different context of healthcare reform in the USA, 'The neglect of implementation issues is more than a simple intellectual mistake: it may be a rational response to the fact that our political system confers more rewards for the shrewd deployment of symbols and generalised arguments than it does for detailed realistic analysis and forecasting.'

As well as shielding from view the messy and creative world of local policy-making and its implementation, this dominant state-centred thinking has blinded much research from understanding the governing capacities of diverse forms of 'private government', as some commentators have astutely noted (Shearing 2006; Boutellier and van Steden this volume). Criminology with its capacious interest in the sociology of deviance and social control should be well placed as a discipline to loosen the shackles of a state-centred approach, but too often it has fallen back on the study of formal state processes of control – namely criminal justice. It has been in the particular field of policing studies that the most significant strides have been made to analyse the governing capacities of diverse centres of authority (Shearing and Stenning 1981). As chapters in Part 3 of this volume testify, local social order is constituted by the governing powers and competencies of diverse, sometimes multiple, authorities, influenced by a (con)fusion of local, regional, national and supranational forces. Hence, one of the themes of this book (especially evident in the chapter by Aas) is the pressing need to develop refined conceptual tools and normative designs that better allow us to break free from the traditional embrace that state-centred thinking has held and which will enable us to understand the limitations and possibilities of different sites of governance as well as the capacity to move between these sites and their interconnections and interactional effects.

Book structure and themes

The book is organised in three loosely connected parts which come together at the tense interface between the international, the national and the local levels at which one might seek to understand and organise institutions and practices concerned with the problem of crime and its governance.

Part 1: International criminal justice

The first part focuses on questions of global governance and the internationalisation of criminal justice. It takes as its central theme the analysis, interrogation and assessment of the intensifying architecture and institutional processes that are emerging and being actively constructed above nation states at the international level. It raises questions about the purpose, legitimacy and normative basis of international criminal justice and how this departs from and connects with systems of justice attached to nation states.

The very idea of international criminal justice is both relatively novel and highly controversial. In his contribution, James Cockayne (Chapter 2) charts how during the last two decades the basic foundations of a system of international justice have emerged, somewhat tentatively, at the instigation of the United Nations Security Council. He goes on to assess its potential impact and consequences. He highlights a progressive shift from an approach based on relations between states to enforce domestic norms largely using tools of diplomacy to configurations that bear a greater resemblance to criminal justice arrangements and processes traditionally found at the level of the nation state. This movement, he argues, has seen the Security Council deploy and place greater emphasis on criminal justice tools and technologies of control, most notably evidenced through resort to and reliance on professionalised criminal investigation and trial, as well as global crime prevention strategies, in place of conventional political tools of international relations; such as political and trade sanctions. Having charted this shift towards 'judicialisation' in investigation, fact-finding and sanctioning, he goes on to examine some unintended consequences of the emergent international criminal justice apparatus. In particular, he highlights the critical response to what has been seen by some to be the selective and partisan use of the developing system of international criminal justice by Western powers. Consequently, he concludes that if the emerging system of international criminal justice is to secure widespread acceptance and legitimacy, the Security Council (and notably the five permanent members) will need to show their willingness to comply by the same system, tools and norms of regulation that hitherto they have imposed on others.

One pre-eminent feature of international criminal justice that undoubtedly clouds the political and practical authority and effectiveness of the ICC and Rome Statute has been the stance towards it adopted by the United States (and some other jurisdictions). As the self-proclaimed 'enforcers of global order', premised on a belief in certain liberal principles, the position adopted by US governments has been pivotal. This is the subject of Jason Ralph's contribution (Chapter 3). In it he sets out to interpret the US opposition to the ICC. In so doing, he contrasts the approach to international criminal justice – notably the elaboration of the institutional framework of the ICC – of European governments to that of the USA. Whilst the latter preferred unilateral state-based solutions as a means of protecting and advancing liberal causes, the former played an instrumental role in the construction of new institutions at the Rome Conference that might be premised on a broad-based multilateral consensus (detached from the constraints of the UN Security Council). Rather than there being a simple assumption that there is a trade-off between multilateralism and human rights, the former becomes a principled mechanism for securing the latter. Nevertheless, Ralph shows how the principle of sovereign consent has been deployed by US governments to attack the legitimacy of the ICC. He argues that the exception to the ICC adopted by America was motivated more by a unilateral and imperialist claim to decide independently the nature and terms of international justice than it was a principled stance in regard of how best to promote liberal ideals. Yet, Ralph points to the irony that America's own historical and constitutional make-up, with its republican influences, is premised upon the idea of delegating sovereignty to supranational institutions – namely the Constitution and federal government – in the name of protecting and promoting liberty. He concludes that a radical reading of republican security theory suggests that 'there is nothing more American than the ICC's Kantian vision'.

In Chapter 4, Chrisje Brants highlights a number of empirical and normative concerns and anomalies evident in the construction of international criminal justice that render it, in her estimation, neither universal nor able to meet its own stated aspirations. She questions whether international criminal justice can and should seek to meet the capacious expectations and goals that some hold out for it: to provide universal justice to universal crimes; to embed a culture of human rights, democracy and the rule of law; to give voice to victims in history-telling and reconciliation; and to provide deterrence and retribution. In contrast to those (like Findlay – see Chapter 5) who seek to transform the international criminal law, trial and procedure so as that it might seek to respond to the diverse demands placed upon it (notably from victims), Brants highlights the limitations of criminal law as a means of tackling either the causes or effects of crimes against humanity and genocide. But far from arguing that international criminal law has no place in responding to such acts of barbarism, she suggests that its core essence derives from its commitment to fundamental humanitarian values and providing a language – of universal human rights – that stands in contrast to arbitrary power in the hope of inculcating such values so that the conditions out of which atrocities arise become preventable. The concern is that these core values may be undermined or diluted by a broader (more all encompassing) but thinner (less principled) conception of international criminal justice.

Mark Findlay (Chapter 5), by contrast, argues that the nature of global crime and the purposes of international criminal justice require a more victim-centred trial process than the current adversarial and retributive approach, as witnessed in the examples of the international criminal courts and tribunals – notably the International Criminal Tribunal for the former Yugoslavia (ICTY). He goes on to outline the parameters and contours of what such a transformed international criminal trial might look like. These include: enhancing the 'access, inclusivity and integration to key pre-trial and trial decision-sites' of victims and those representing a victim perspective; creating and sustaining 'pathways of influence out of these crucial trial decision-sites'; and the incorporation and institutionalisation of restorative justice processes (alongside retributive justice), that are bounded by 'rights-protected' procedures of the trial. Collectively these three tenets of a transformed procedure, it is argued, will enable victims better to 'achieve their legitimate aspirations in the trial context'. Like Brants, Findlay is concerned with questions of legitimacy in relation to the emerging concept and institutions of international criminal justice. But in contrast to Brants, he sees the integration of victims as central to a more legitimate international normative order, by way of the enhanced legitimacy that the satisfaction of victim interests offers. By aligning itself more closely with 'victim communities' or at least engaging with and integrating victims' interests and needs in a more inclusive, sympathetic and systematic way, it is argued, international criminal justice may be able to free itself from the constraints of sectarian international relations and adhesion to narrow cultural norms and values. To do this requires an articulation of a concept of 'global crime victim' as somehow distinct from domestic crime victims that are the subjects of 'national' (local) rather than universal (global) justice – and therefore somehow unique.

Findlay's model appears to be appealing to a more pluralistic form of international justice that is unshackled, or at least loosened, from its universalistic claims, in the sense implied by Brants. The aspiration is for the advantages of informal, alternative and restorative processes that accord greater access, inclusivity and integration of victim interests to be drawn into the formal procedures and protections of the international trial process. The use of pre-trial processes of deliberation through mediation and conferencing, in the shadow of the procedural protections of the formal trial, should allow collective and shared notions of humanity to override the tensions of self-interest. In sum, this amounts to a call for a somewhat different conception of justice, in which the processes of deliberation and decision-making employed and the outcomes and resolutions that they achieve should be, in (large) part, determined by and through engagement with victim communities, whose aspirations will be to constitute a measure of accountability. And yet, Findlay recognises that the levels of participatory and deliberative democracy upon which his ideal of justice communities rests is rarely – if ever – evident in global governance and international relations.

The 'return of the victim' as central to (international) criminal justice policy paradoxically may allow for a bolstering of retributive sentiments and 'getting tough through restorative justice', whereby victims are drawn into 'the service of severity' within criminal processes (Ashworth 2000). The diminished emphasis on offender's rights within restorative justice, in the current punitive climate, may see 'the corruption of benevolence', a recurring theme within the history of criminal justice. Levrant et al. sagely note that recent criminal justice reforms remind us, 'Progressive sentiments are no guarantee that reforms will not be corrupted and serve punitive ends' (1999: 7). It is not by chance that the rise of the victim movement and the growth of victims' rights have coincided with a 'culture of control' (Garland 2001) and the 'return of vengeance' (Sarat 1997) at the level of domestic criminal justice. It is not only that there is the danger of the political manipulation of victim communities but also that this may be accompanied by the triumph of passion over reason, which strikes at the heart of modern legality and common morality.

Developing on the issue of victim involvement in processes of justice, Parmentier and Weitekamp (Chapter 6) explore a number of questions concerning the role and meaning of 'criminal justice' – both at international and national levels of analysis and operation – as well as truth, accountability and reparation in the context of societies in transition. They are interested in exploring the parameters, possible role and public acceptability of restorative justice values in informing alternative post-conflict dispute-resolution mechanisms in contrast to the traditional emphasis on notions of retribution and deterrence through prosecution and punishment that dominate much international jurisprudence and lay/public discourses about dealing with the crimes of the past. In contrast to the discourses of elites, that have informed much debate in this field, Parmentier and Weitekamp are keen to interrogate the experiences, understandings and values of local citizens in thinking about and devising strategies and mechanisms in response to human rights violations, mass atrocities and large-scale abuses of power, in balancing the need to account for the past whilst simultaneously reconstructing the future. They explore these challenging and wide-ranging issues through the specific case study of the former Yugoslavia and, in so doing, present the findings of a survey of citizens of Bosnia and Herzegovina conducted in 2006. The data show a tentative appetite for restorative ideals and values although, as the authors note, this is neither well-defined nor unequivocal. Even nearly some fifteen years after the end of the war in Bosnia, the survey found little inclination to embrace forgiveness amongst those who had suffered. Furthermore, the survey findings highlight the manner in which restorative mechanisms depend in large part on the ability and genuine willingness of perpetrators to acknowledge their responsibility for past crimes; a major obstacle which itself may demand certain processes or procedural inducements – such as indemnities or amnesties – that undermine wider public perceptions of holding perpetrators to account and 'doing justice'. The findings highlight the challenges for the governance of crimes and human rights violations through international criminal justice in post-conflict situations.

Developing the theme concerning the relationship between criminal justice policy developments within individual nation states and the interaction with norms, standards and principles articulated by supranational legal structures, Dirk van Zyl Smit and Sonja Snacken (Chapter 7) consider the impact of the European Court of Human Rights (ECtHR) on the development of values informing penal policies in Europe. They focus in particular on the manner in which an emerging European-level understanding of the primary purpose of sentences of imprisonment as that of reintegration and re-socialisation has influenced the interpretation of human rights provisions. They consider the implications of this developing jurisprudence for the UK where no such principle of prison law exists. The capacity of national courts to shape crime control and penal policies and practices is evident from the discussions in many chapters in this volume as are some of the limitations of judicial interventions. However, the scope for supranational and international courts to influence the values of crime control and penal policies raises further vexed issues about how differences between nation states are to be treated particularly where there are no commonly accepted standard amongst the member states. In particular, the ECtHR's concept of a 'margin of appreciation' allows nation states significant room for manoeuvre before the Court is willing to intervene.

Part 2: Comparative penal policies

In the second part of the book, the focus shifts to explore themes of comparative criminal justice through the specific analysis of forms of punishment and penal policies. In seeking to make sense of the apparent greater 'punitiveness' expressed both through the scale and intensity of punishment in many Western societies – the USA and UK in particular – scholars have looked to insights from cross-national comparisons. Whilst comparisons in modes of punishment between nation states, and between states within the USA, has a well-established history, in recent years the debate over what Bottoms (1995) termed 'populist punitiveness' has provided a significant stimulus to the analysis of, and our understanding of, comparative penal policies and their relation to political economies and social change. Part 2 engages directly with this debate, drawing together contributions by key commentators who have done much in recent years to outline and advance the study of cross-national comparative punishment.

In Chapter 8, Michael Cavadino and James Dignan open the debate by revisiting the arguments outlined in, and responding to critiques of, their recent book (Cavadino and Dignan 2006) which has become a major reference point in the study of comparative penality. Analysing prison rates (per 100,000) in twelve different countries, they offer an explanation for differences and similarities that focuses on broad families of neoliberal, conservative (and oriental) corporatist and social democratic political economies. Expanding their arguments, Cavadino and Dignan seek to explain why the connection exists between political economy and penality. They do so by reviewing five separate hypotheses: (i) punishment is driven by crime rates which are influenced by political economy; (ii) punishment is shaped by public opinion, which in turn is conditioned by a society's culture, which is linked to its political economy; (iii) political economies shape the media culture which influences political and public opinion which drives penality; (iv) political economies influence the wider political culture which helps shape political opinion, which drives punishment; and finally, (v) that the crucial factor in the link between political economies and punishment is the existence of particular sets of political institutions. They conclude their review asserting that no one of these hypotheses, on its own, appears strong enough to stand as a single explanation. Rather, they argue that the interaction between political culture and political and state institutions offers possibly the most robust account of the complex connections between political culture and punishment.

Like Cavadino and Dignan, Nicola Lacey (Chapter 9) addresses much the same sets of questions about the relationship between political economies and the scale and quality of punishment, developing upon and advancing arguments initially set out in published series of Hamlyn Lectures (Lacey 2008). Augmenting earlier work, she provides a robust defence of the explanatory value of broad (structuralist) typologies as a corrective to the (culturalist) fascination with 'the details of local particularity'. In advancing the insights to be derived from model-building in penal theory and illustrating her arguments, Lacey draws explicitly on case studies of New Zealand and the USA. She goes on to argue that political–economic forces at the macro level are mediated by cultural filters, as well as by economic, political and social institutions. It is the manner in which political and state institutions mediate cultural and structural forces, and the ways this impacts on the group interests and incentives that generate the differences across penal systems. In particular, she highlights the importance of different market economies in structuring differing types of production regimes, labour markets, education and training programmes and resultant disparities in wealth distribution. In relation to political institutions, she points to the role of different electoral arrangements – notably between proportional representation and majoritarian, two-party electoral systems – the nature of the bureaucracy and the constitutional structure of adminis-trations. She concludes noting that broad models for comparative criminology, like the one she outlines, must nevertheless be refined and investigated through close attention to local empirical research.

In developing the analysis of the experiences of punishment and penal policies across groups of similar countries, John Pratt (Chapter 10) compares and contrasts the penal trajectories of two clusters of societies: on the one hand Anglophone societies represented by England and New Zealand, and on the other Scandinavian societies represented by Finland, Norway and Sweden. Reviewing post-war developments in these coun-tries, Pratt provides an account of two phases of development. The first period, from 1945 to the 1960s, saw penal convergence. This was subsequently followed by considerable divergence across the two clusters of societies. As a result, comparative differences have become marked to such an extent that the Anglophone societies stand out for their 'penal excess', their high levels of imprisonment and poor prison conditions, whereas the Scandinavian societies are known for their 'penal exceptionalism', their low levels of imprisonment and humane prison conditions. Like Lacey and Cavadino and Dignan, Pratt advances a multifactoral explanation but stresses the importance of differing models of welfare state in shaping the respective penal developments in the countries that are the focus of his analysis. He concludes that penal policies can come to reflect the politics of exclusion and resentment that a more restrictive and selective provision of welfare encourages in neoliberal societies. This allows more punitive and intolerant values to take hold in which populist sentiments and a distrust of expertise can influence resultant policy developments. This contrasts with the more solidaristic expectations of social democratic welfare states, where penal excesses and intolerance are more generally contained.

In Chapter 11, Lesley McAra analyses the penal policy fortunes of three contrasting jurisdictions: Scotland, Spain and England and Wales. She takes issue with the methodological dualism between structuralist and culturalist accounts of penal variations which she argues has informed much debate in the sociology of punishment. This is in large part, for her, because such a duality fails adequately to capture the multi-level nature of contemporary governance both above and (more especially) below the nation state. McAra outlines an alternative methodological strategy which draws from 'systems theory' with which she interprets the divergent penal trajectories of her three case studies. She contends that penal systems – and criminal justice system more generally – are somewhat like 'fragile eco-systems' which are interdependent and interconnected with the environments in which they are located.[4] These environments exhibit complex and competing pressures with uneven effects across time. She concludes that the sustainability of particular penal policies depends, in large part, on systems establishing a form of 'cultural anchorage', which necessitates connections with, and support from, extra-systemic cultural values and processes. From this perspective, the existence of residual civic cultural support for penal–welfare values in Spain and Scotland helps explain how these jurisdictions resisted the broader, macro socio-economic pressures that

---

[4] There are obvious similarities here with my 'butterfly' analogy used earlier.

prompted change elsewhere, notably in England and Wales. Furthermore, changes to the civic cultural environment, in turn, can provide the preconditions for institutional transformations, as evidenced in Scotland over the last decade or so.

The next two chapters focus on Canadian experiences of sentencing and penal policies in the adult and youth justice systems, respectively. Canada constitutes an interesting case study because of its close proximity to and similarities with the USA. Yet Canada's penal policies reflect considerable divergences from the US 'experiment' in mass incarceration and penal populism. Given the discussion in McAra's preceding chapter, there are certain resemblances in the relationship between England and Scotland, as between the USA and Canada.

In Chapter 12, Cheryl Webster and Tony Doob seek to explain Canada's imprisonment rate, which they argue does not fit well within the framework set out by Cavadino and Dignan and, by contrast, serves as a critique of it. For all intents and purposes Canada would seem to fit within the neoliberal political economy advanced by Cavadino and Dignan, and yet its imprisonment rate is more in line with (their) conservative corporatist countries. Webster and Doob go on to explain why Canada might be an exception to this typology or has overcome the impact of neoliberal tendencies in relation to penal policies. They provide the more detailed reading of a particular jurisdiction of the type that Lacey suggest necessarily should complement (and help inform) broad typologies. Whilst Canada has not been immune to neoliberal forces it has largely been able to limit or resist the influence of these in shaping its penal response to crime. Some of the protective factors that they identify include the political culture and relations between provisional and federal jurisdictions. For them, the experiences of Canada underscore the complexity of penality and the impact of a range of structural, cultural, historical and institutional influencing factors.

Jane Sprott (Chapter 13) provides a similarly detailed analysis of the Canadian youth justice system and explains how Canada managed to reduce the use of imprisonment for young people over a period of time in which there were significant pressures from the public and political debate to 'toughen-up' penal responses to youth crime. In so doing, she uses the example of Canadian youth justice to explore the limits of policy convergence and more specifically constraints on policy transfer from the USA into Canada. She shows how justice policy in Canada is influenced more by particular social, political and cultural factors than by any direct or straightforward policy transfer from the USA. She highlights a significant dissonance between the political rhetoric around youth justice, specifically that emanating from federal politicians, on the one hand, and both the subsequent legislation and its implementation through institutional practices. With regard to policy transfer, Canadian youth justice seems to reflect more a matter of appropriating the symbols rather than the substance of punitive policies associated with the US experiences.

Susanne Karstedt (Chapter 14) concludes this part of the book with a comparative overview of differences in punishment regimes from a large sample of sixty-seven countries comprising European, Latin and Anglo-American, Asian and Pacific as well as African countries. She draws on statistical survey data on comparative values covering a twenty-year period from the 1980s to the turn of the millennium. Value patterns, she argues, generate and inform distinct status politics and practices, which impact on the regime punishment in democracies. She contends that countries with higher levels of individualistic and egalitarian values differ in their regimes of punishment from those with more collectivist, authoritarian and non-egalitarian values. The latter countries tend to exhibit harsher sentencing and punishment regimes. She goes on to show that democratic values do not correlate unambiguously with punishment but unfold (over time) in uneven patterns. She differentiates between two types of egalitarianism that express themselves in different (democratic) values: chance-oriented (or meritocratic) egalitarianism and outcome-oriented egalitarianism. The latter values when confronted with structural inequality test the inclusive capacity of democracies and produce tensions that impact on punishment regimes. According to Karstedt, this helps explain the punitiveness associated with the democracy of the USA – which clearly expresses a chance-oriented egalitarianism – as contrasted with Scandinavian and other European countries like Germany which represent more outcome-oriented egalitarianism.

Despite their different emphases and their focus on different countries, these essays collectively highlight the complexities and multifaceted nature of the social, political, cultural and institutional factors that inform and shape penal practices in their scale, form, quality and intensity. Nonetheless, the nuanced discussions should provide considerable scope to assist comparative researchers not just in the study of punishment regimes but also in the wider study of criminal justice and systems of control.

Part 3: Comparative crime control and urban governance

The third part of the book incorporates a number of themes that
coalesce around concerns for issues of comparative crime control and
security governance. It shifts the conceptual lens of study – below the
nation state – to more local, notably urban, dimensions. In so doing, it
(explicitly and implicitly) questions both the interdependence and interpenetration of local and international forces and dynamics and the
implications of moving between different scales of analysis. Do the same
criminological, sociological and political ways of thinking about and
understanding crime and responses to it operate at the various different
scales? As we move the lens of focus in and out of the international,
national, regional, city-wide and local levels do our concepts retain the
same value, relevance and force of insight? This part of the book is
therefore less concerned with specific questions about the 'flow', 'diffusion' and 'transfer' of criminological ideas and criminal justice practices
across and between nation states, which has been the subject of much
vibrant debate and analysis in recent years (Newburn and Sparks 2004;
Jones and Newburn 2007; Crawford 2009b), but rather explores the
implications of such transnational and supranational movement and
interchange for our understandings of the traditional boundaries that
they traverse. Consequently, recurring themes relate to the boundaries
and borders – both conceptual and spatial – and the scales at which we
seek to make sense of international and transnational flows. It follows
that the interwoven connections between global and local social forces
and the ways in which these impact on practices and our understandings
of urban governance and policing (broadly defined) are the prominent
concerns.

In Chapter 15, Katja Aas directly confronts a series of questions
concerning the impact of globalisation on national sovereignty in the
context of crime control. She critically explores some of the underlying
assumptions about the relationship between globalising processes and
the nation state. Using the example of European cross-border policing
she shows how justice systems are increasingly enmeshed and outlines a
conceptual framework for analysing the complex dynamics between the
national and the transnational spheres. She highlights a theme that
resonates with many of the subsequent chapters, namely the tense
relationship between on the one hand the growing significance of territory, boundaries and borders – in this instance policing controls in the
defence of the nation state (both as a conceptual entity and in terms of

its sovereign claims to govern) – and on the other hand the increased salience of international and transnational co-operation and policy convergence. Boundaries are simultaneously transcended and (re-)constructed, swept away and formulated. Extraterritoriality co-exists alongside processes of territorialisation. Given the complexity by which global and local processes are intertwined, comparing and contrasting what happens in one country with another (the traditional stuff of comparative criminology as illustrated in the chapters in Part 2) makes less sense from this perspective. As Aas argues, the Norwegian borders are being defended not only in Norway but also in Poland, Greece, Italy and Spain, in such a way that the crime control systems of the different countries are constituted and influenced by such support mechanisms and the coercive and punitive resources they imply. In other words, the relative leniency of Scandinavian countries, vis-à-vis their penal regimes, may in part be explained by the greater punitiveness of some southern and eastern European countries that bear the brunt of the burdens of managing migratory flows. The implications of these insights for comparative criminology are significant, as they demand that we understand not only a criminal justice system in terms of what happens within a nation and its boundaries but also take cross-national and global interconnections into account.

Like immigration control, security concerns relating to terrorism (most acutely since 9/11) have animated considerable policy initiative and debate at the city, national and supranational levels. The local governance of urban safety is a site in which many of these preoccupations, practices and technologies are played out and enacted. Clive Walker (Chapter 16) develops the theme of moving beyond borders in his analysis of the treatment of liberty in the face of terrorism. He uses the case study of the UK to explore internal and external dynamics concerning the law relating to how individuals suspected of terrorism are treated, particularly with regard to police detention following arrest, administrative restrictions on liberty, detention pending deportation and the incarceration of the 'enemies of the state'. He draws on notions of cosmopolitanism and the universality of human rights to advance the idea of a common shared morality that might be applied regardless of nationality and citizenship in relation to counter-terrorism policing. He defends the idea that a 'weak' version of cosmopolitanism beyond human rights doctrine holds fast in the face of contemporary terrorism. He deploys this conceptualisation both to highlight the manner in which it serves as a normative restraint within a jurisdiction upon

state-centred (national) security and to illustrate the arguments in
favour of extending mutual respect beyond jurisdictional borders.
Whilst he concludes that the current and future context is likely to
continue to reflect conditions which serve state security rather than
'cosmopolitan security', he provides a normative benchmark against
which developments in counter-terrorism at the local, national and
international spheres might be assessed.

In Chapter 17, Joanna Shapland examines the pressures – from
'below' – on national governments presented by the nature of the
relationship with their citizens and the manner in which the citizenry
engage with, and are engaged by, processes of criminal justice. She
explores how different European nation states have adapted to concerns
about public confidence and trust in systems of criminal justice. In so
doing, she uses the lens of debates about the institutionalisation of
restorative justice to analyse the 'uneasy relationship' between governments and their publics in the sphere of crime control and criminal
justice. Restorative justice constitutes a particularly interesting lens – in
the context of this book as a whole – as it appeals simultaneously, to local
diversity and context specificity but also has international relevance and
has been the subject of much cross-national policy transfer (see also the
chapters by Findlay and Parmentier and Weitekamp in this volume).
Restorative justice has received considerable global attention and been
appropriated and promoted by national governments with diverse legal
cultures and traditions, local organisations as well as supranational
institutions (including the European Union, United Nations and international peacekeeping bodies). It is believed to have relevance in guiding
the settlement of local disputes, minor infractions and serious interpersonal crimes; implications for the regulation of national political
and social conflicts including state violence and cases of mass genocide
in societies in transition; and application in international relations.
Nevertheless, the practices to which restorative justice principles have
given rise often take very different forms in different institutional
contexts (Aertsen *et al.* 2006).

Shapland argues that the resultant forms that restorative justice has
adopted in different countries tells us much about the deeply held
assumptions within different jurisdictions about the role of the state,
ideas about criminal justice and relations with the citizenry. A crucial
question, in the different reception of restorative justice across diverse
jurisdictions is understanding 'who criminal justice perceives its publics
to be'? Shapland demonstrates how the French institutionalisation

of restorative justice has tended to be shaped by a preference on the part of criminal justice professionals to avoid, and a fear of, engaging directly with the citizenry and 'difficult' citizens groups. The bottom-up, empirical (problem-solving), community-oriented and deliberative pretensions of restorative justice sit awkwardly with the normatively driven, symbolic, professionalised and top-down French legal culture (Crawford 2000a; 2000b). Consequently, as Shapland demonstrates, restorative justice in France ended up being very different from the ideal of empowering and party-centre models promoted in some Anglo-American and Australasian initiatives. It is unsurprising, she argues, that countries with a state-centred model of criminal justice, in which professionals have traditionally exerted a dominant role, have tended to prefer to create new groups of professionals as easier partners in the awkward and tentative process of reaching out in the search for greater legitimacy. By contrast, she highlights the impact of a managerialist ethos within the UK context (and other Anglophone countries), which in different ways has also served to pull restorative justice initiatives away from a primary focus on the needs of the victims, involving the lay community and increasing confidence in criminal justice processes as well as outcomes. The myopic focus of managerialist key indicators of performance has tended to narrow the criteria (and definition) of success for restorative justice initiatives to those traditionally associated with criminal justice but against which established systems have performed so poorly. The consequence has similarly been a retreat back to professionalised and formalised ways of working. And yet, if the contemporary appeal of restorative justice is that it may offer nation states ways of addressing legitimacy deficits and re-engaging with their publics in innovative ways, its enduring relevance may depend on how open judicial cultures and how willing criminal justice professionals are to relinquish a degree of control over 'doing justice' and 'entrust justice to others'.

The nature of the relationship between states, their publics and other non-state actors in the context of crime control is also the subject of Hans Boutellier and Ronald van Steden's contribution (Chapter 18). They explore the challenges presented by the multilateralisation of local security governance, notably the increasingly intermeshing and blurring of relations between the state, the market and civil society. For them, this raises questions about how security governance arrangements can be imagined and managed. In seeking to respond to such questions, they assess and evaluate concepts of 'nodal' and 'networked' governance. They do so through a case study of local security policies in the city of Eindhoven in the Netherlands. The empirical picture that emerges of the complex multi-organisational security field within this city is one that is structured and deeply infused more by governance faults, network ambiguities and policy failures than networked synergies. They acknowledge that the state is not always benign, as government bodies may serve their own professional interests and criminal justice and policing organisations sometimes struggle with solving local problems given their remoteness and their lack of local knowledge and capacity (as Shapland also argues). However, they conclude that markets, communities and citizens are still too precarious to take on these responsibilities for security alone. Consequently, they argue that governance structures need to be more 'anchored' and 'directed' than nodal theories either presuppose or imply. They offer some research-based ideas as to what this might look like.

Adam Crawford (Chapter 19) draws on empirical insights from research studies to illustrate his arguments regarding the changing face of dynamics of exclusion in the complex, multilateral governance of security in urban public space. He demonstrates the manner in which ideas, technologies and practices first developed in the policing of private space have increasingly encroached on and influenced the policing of public spaces – by both state and non-state providers of security. Public streets, he argues, are being '(re-)ordered' through the banning and dispersal of those – notably young people – who are deemed not to conform to the dominant norms of a consumer society or whose appearance jars with the prevailing vision of an ordered environment. Hence, commercially oriented strategies that combine fluid dynamics of inclusion and exclusion now routinely inform city centres and urban street corners. However, he also highlights the ambiguous nature of the relationship between order and urban consumption showing how in some contexts, the logics of security can obstruct the demands of commerce and consumption. Consequently, urban spaces – notably during the night-time economy – are informed by paradoxical forces that simultaneously seek order and moral cleansing, but also generate considerable disorder, antisocial behaviour and a loosening of normative restraint.

The themes of exclusion/inclusion and the formation of boundaries in urban spaces also inform Chapter 20 by Sarah Blandy. Her focus is on the growing role of gating and other forms of crime prevention through

environmental design in residential areas, specifically through the introduction of physical boundaries such as alley-gating. She shows how
boundaries and enclosures of all kinds are becoming established central
technique of contemporary urban governance and seeks to explore their
implications. She illustrates these by drawing on her own research
findings in relation to privately owned gated communities and the
retro-fitting of council-owned housing estates with walls and gates. She
shows how information about the spatial distribution of crime and
victimisation risks has encouraged boundaries, and the formation of
what she terms 'nomospheres'; often with differing legal powers. In
addition to physical and data-driven boundary formation, Blandy demonstrates how the law has been used to create and strengthen boundaries.
She highlights the social segmentation of residential areas at various levels
of the social hierarchy across a city (and beyond) that such boundary-
building hastens. She points to the unifying factors of fear and resentment
that inform gating in both affluent areas and stigmatised council estates,
despite the fact that there remain little other connections between these
different populations, in part due to the boundaries that are being erected.
Whilst gating presents one version of what Blandy calls the 'boundaries
spectrum', the implications of contemporary boundary-building, even
without a physical presentation, are considerable and risk not only generating bitterness around their edges but much wider social malaise.

Drawing on her own research in French cities (notably but not exclusively, Paris), Sophie Body-Gendrot (Chapter 21) explores the manner in
which large metropolitan cities seek to deal with and manage contemporary crime and security-related risks and threats that present themselves in times of global uncertainty. She analyses the manner in which
cities attempt to present themselves to (hyper-mobile) residents, visitors
and potential investors, and the way in which security risks and urban
governance are framed and mobilised in presenting places as safe and
ordered environments. In so doing, she reviews developments across
French cities in relation to experiences and trajectories of urban unrest
over the last quarter of a century and the manner in which this has been
informed by debates about migration and concerns about terrorism.
This reflects how urban governance is informed by fears, anxieties and
concerns that can be easily manipulated in the name of order and in the
exercise of authority. She shows how in France (in common with Shapland's arguments), professionals are not keen to motivate citizens to
participate in the co-production of security. She concludes that governance developments at the local rather than the national level are both

more effective and hold out greater potential, particularly in resisting securitisation and infringements on civil liberties.

In the concluding essay, Mariana Valverde (Chapter 22) addresses the question of scale in the ways in which we think about, see and describe the problem of urban safety. The issue of scale in a broad sense informs – and one might say troubles – (whether explicitly or implicitly) all the contributions to this book, as a central theme in the relationship between the local, national and international. As Valverde argues, scale effects pervade all forms of visualisation and hence our conceptions, meanings and descriptions. Consequently, she raises questions about, and explores the implications of, shifting scale in thinking about crime and urban governance and the choice that we make in selecting scales of analysis and of projection. She shows how such choices of scale can be used and misused, especially in moving from micro to macro analyses. In the context of crime, she demonstrates the manner in which social problems (and by implication their supposed solutions) are redefined – through policy, theory and research – by the device of shifting scale. She uses examples drawn from criminological depictions of 'urban disorder' from the point of view of scale (both scale effects and scale shifts) to illustrate her arguments. This includes a close reading of two influential criminological texts by Wilson and Kelling (1982) and Sampson and Raudenbush (1999) that have inspired much comparative reading and policy transfer. She illustrates the manner in which questions of scale inform these texts and their implications. She concludes that purity in choice of scale is neither possible nor desirable. However, a careful examination of scale choices can help us to better understand the limits and the constraints of methodology and terminology.

Scale also presents an additional challenge for comparative studies. Paying due attention to questions of scale and their implications might help sharpen comparative analyses. It may be that some of the policy similarities and differences across jurisdictions are due not only to political or cultural factors but also may be a product of different scales for thinking about and managing crime and disorder problems, and the manner in which assumptions about scale are made in the process of policy transfer across differing context. Hence, Valverde may be pointing to a third type of 'translation' problem that confronts comparative analysis (to add to the two discussed earlier in this chapter), namely the process of shifting between different scales and the effects of so doing.

References

Aas, K. F. (2007) *Globalization and Crime*, London: Sage.

Aertsen, I., Daems, T. and Robert, L. (2006) (eds.) *Institutionalising Restorative Justice*, Cullompton: Willan Publishing.

Anderson, J. E. (1975) *Public Policy-Making*, New York: Praeger.

Ashworth, A. (2000) 'Victim's rights, defendant's rights and criminal procedure' in A. Crawford and J. Goodey (eds.), *Integrating a Victim Perspective within Criminal Justice*, Aldershot: Ashgate, pp. 185–204.

Bauman, Z. (1998) *Work, Consumerism and the New Poor*, Buckingham: Open University Press.

(2000) *Liquid Modernity*, Cambridge: Polity.

(2001) *Community. Seeking Safety in an Insecure World*, Cambridge: Polity.

(2006) *Liquid Fear*, Cambridge: Polity.

Bayley, D. (2001) 'Security and justice for all' in H. Strang and J. Braithwaite (eds.), *Restorative Justice and Civil Society*, Cambridge: Cambridge University Press, pp. 211–21.

Beck, U. (1992) *Risk Society*, London: Sage.

Berman, M. (1983) *All That Is Solid Melts Into Air: The Experience of Modernity*, London: Verso.

Bottoms, A. E. (1995) 'The philosophy and politics of punishment and sentencing' in C. Clarkson and R. Morgan (eds.), *The Politics of Sentencing Reform*, Oxford: Clarendon, pp. 17–49.

Boutellier, H. (2004) *The Safety Utopia*, Dordrecht: Kluwer.

Castells, M. (2000) *The Rise of the Network Society*, Oxford: Blackwell.

Cavadino, M. and Dignan, J. (2006) *Penal Systems: A Comparative Approach*, London: Sage.

Crawford, A. (1997) *The Local Governance of Crime: Appeals to Community and Partnerships*, Oxford: Oxford University Press.

(2000a) 'Contrasts in victim/offender mediation and appeals to community in France and England' in D. Nelken (ed.), *Contrasting Criminal Justice*, Aldershot: Ashgate, pp. 205–29.

(2000b) 'Justice de proximité – the growth of "houses of justice" and victim/ offender mediation in France: a very unFrench legal response?', *Social and Legal Studies*, 9(1), 29–53.

(2002) 'The state, community and restorative justice: heresy, nostalgia and butterfly collecting' in L. Walgrave (ed.), *Restorative Justice and the Law*, Cullompton: Willan Publishing, pp. 101–29.

(2006) 'Policing and security as 'club goods': the new enclosures?' in J. Wood and B. Dupont (eds.), *Democracy, Society and the Governance of Security*, Cambridge: Cambridge University Press, pp. 111–38.

(2009a) 'Governing through anti-social behaviour: regulatory challenges to criminal justice', *British Journal of Criminology*, 49(6), 810–31.

(2009b) (ed.) *Crime Prevention Policies in Comparative Perspective*, Cullompton: Willan.

(2010) 'Regulating civility, governing security and policing (dis)order under conditions of uncertainty' in J. Blad, N. Rozemond, M. Hildebrandt, M. B. Schuilenburg and P. J. V. van Culster (eds.), *Governing Security under the Rule of Law*, The Hague: Eleven International Publishers, pp. 9–35.

Dijk, J. van (2008) *The World of Crime*, London: Sage.

Dijk, J. van, Manchin, R., van Kesteren, J., Nevala, S. and Hideg, G. (2006) *The Burden of Crime in the EU, Research Report: A Comparative Analysis of the European Crime and Safety Survey (EU ICS) 2005*, Turin: UNICRI.

Ericson, R. (2007) *Crime in an Insecure World*, Cambridge: Polity.

Farrington, D. (1999) 'A criminological research agenda for the next millennium', *International Journal of Offender Therapy and Comparative Criminology*, 43, 154–67.

(2000) 'Explaining and preventing crime: the globalization of knowledge', *Criminology*, 38, 1–24.

Farrington, D. and Petrosino, A. (2001) 'The Campbell Collaboration Crime and Justice Group', *Annals of the American Academy of Political and Social Science*, 578, 35–49.

Garland, D. (1990) *Punishment and Modern Society*, Oxford: Clarendon.

(1996) 'The limits of the sovereign state: strategies of crime control in contemporary society', *British Journal of Criminology*, 36(4), 445–71.

(2001) *Culture of Control*, Oxford: Oxford University Press.

Geertz, C. (1983) *Local Knowledge*, New York: Basic Books.

Giddens, A. (1985) *The Nation State and Violence*, Cambridge: Polity Press.

(1990) *The Consequences of Modernity*, Cambridge: Polity Press.

Hope, T. (2000) 'Inequality and the clubbing of private security' in T. Hope and R. Sparks (eds.), *Crime, Risk and Insecurity*, London: Routledge, pp. 83–106.

Jessop, B. (1993) 'Towards a Schumpeterian workfare state? Preliminary remarks on post-Fordist political economy', *Studies in Political Economy*, 40, 7–39.

Jones, T. and Newburn, T. (2007) *Policy Transfer and Criminal Justice*, Open University Press.

Lacey, N. (2008) *The Prisoners' Dilemma: Political Economy and Punishment in Contemporary Democracies*, Cambridge: Cambridge University Press.

Lacey, N. and Zedner, L. (1998) 'Community in German criminal justice: a significant absence', *Social and Legal Studies*, 7(1), 7–25.

Lash, S. and Urry, J. (1994) *Economies of Signs and Space*, London: Sage.

Laycock, G. (2005) 'Defining crime science' in M. J. Smith and N. Tilley (eds.), *Crime Science: New Approaches to Detecting and Preventing Crime*, Cullompton: Willan.

Legrand, P. (1996) 'How to compare now', *Legal Studies*, 16(2), 232–42.

Levrant, S., Cullen, F., Fulton, B. and Wozniak, J. (1999) 'Reconsidering restorative justice: the corruption of benevolence revisited?', *Crime & Delinquency*, 45(1), 3–27.

Marmor, T. (1994) *Understanding Health Care Reform*, New Haven: Yale University Press.

Massumi, B. (2005) *Parables for the Virtual*, Durham NC: Duke University Press.

Nelken, D. (2000) 'Telling difference: of crime and criminal justice in Italy' in D. Nelken (ed.), *Contrasting Criminal Justice*, Aldershot: Ashgate, pp. 233–64.

(2010) *Comparative Criminal Justice*, London: Sage.

Newburn, T. and Jones, T. (2007) 'Symbolising crime control: reflections on zero tolerance', *Theoretical Criminology*, 11(2), 221–43.

Newburn, T. and Sparks, R. (2004) (eds.), *Criminal Justice and Political Cultures*, Cullompton: Willan.

O'Malley, P. (2004) 'Globalising risk?' in T. Newburn and R. Sparks (eds.), *Criminal Justice and Political Cultures*, Cullompton: Willan, pp. 30–48.

Rhodes, R. A. W. (1994) 'The hollowing out of the state: the changing nature of the public service in Britain', *Political Quarterly Review*, 65, 137–51.

Sampson, R. and Raudenbush, S. (1999) 'Systematic social observation of public spaces: a new look at disorder in urban neighborhoods', *American Journal of Sociology*, 105(3), 603–51.

Sarat, A. (1997) 'Vengeance, victims and the identities of law', *Social and Legal Studies*, 6(2), 163–89.

Shearing, C. (2006) 'Reflections on the refusal to acknowledge private governments' in J. Wood and B. Dupont (eds.), *Democracy, Society and the Governance of Security*, Cambridge: Cambridge University Press, pp. 11–32.

Shearing, C. and Stenning, P. (1981) 'Modern private security: its growth and implications', *Crime & Justice*, 3, 193–245.

Sherman, L. (2009) 'Evidence and liberty: the promise of experimental criminology', *Criminology and Criminal Justice*, 9(1), 5–28.

Simon, J. (2007) *Governing through Crime*, Oxford: Oxford University Press.

Taylor, I., Evans, K. and Fraser, P. (1996) *A Tale of Two Cities: Global Change, Local Feeling and Everyday Life in the North of England, A Study of Manchester and Sheffield*, London: Routledge.

United Nations (1999) *Rome Statute of the International Criminal Court*, http://untreaty.un.org/cod/icc/statute/romefra.htm.

Walters, W. (2004) 'Secure borders, safe haven, domopolitics', *Citizenship Studies*, 8(3), 237–60.

Wilkinson, R. and Pickett, K. (2009) *The Spirit Level: Why More Equal Societies Almost Always Do Better*, London: Allen Lane.

Wilson, J. Q. (1975) *Thinking About Crime*, New York: Vintage.

Wilson, J. Q. and Kelling, G. (1982) 'Broken windows: the police and neighbourhood safety', *The Atlantic Monthly*, March, 29–37.

Young, J. (2007) *The Vertigo of Late Modernity*, London: Sage.

Zedner, L. (2007) 'Pre-crime and post-criminology', *Theoretical Criminology*, 11(2), 261–81.

(2009) 'Fixing the future? The pre-emptive turn in criminal justice' in B. McSherry, A. Norrie and S. Bronitt (eds.), *Regulating Deviance: The Redirection of Criminalisation and the Futures of Criminal Law*, Oxford: Hart Publishing.

PART 1

International criminal justice

Unintended justice: the United Nations Security Council and international criminal governance

JAMES COCKAYNE*

Introduction

In the last two decades, the United Nations (UN) Security Council has – almost accidentally – created the rudiments of a system of international criminal justice. This chapter explores the Security Council's development of these foundations of a system of international criminal justice and its unintended consequences. In both investigation and fact-finding, and in its sanctions practice, the Council's approach has moved in the last twenty years from one based on interstate and diplomatic tools towards arrangements that more closely resemble criminal justice tools found at the national level. And in each case, this has led to calls for similar procedural norms that govern criminal justice at the national level – such as due process and the need for an impartial decision-maker – to govern the use of these tools at the international level.

The relationship between the Security Council and the development of international criminal justice tools is a surprisingly under-studied question. While there have been numerous examinations in recent years of the Security Council's human rights and rule of law obligations (Clapham 2006; Chesterman 2008, 2009; Flynn 2006; Wood 2006), most of these studies are confined to theoretical examinations of the application of international law to the Council, or its subsidiary organs of the Council (see Goldstone and Smith 2008 and Zappalà 2003 on international criminal tribunals; and see Farrall 2007 on sanctions mechanisms). A separate literature has grown up around international expeditionary policing (see Dwan 2003; Hansen 2002) and post-conflict rule of law efforts (Call 2007; Chesterman 2004/5). Studies that straddle these boundaries and begin to consider the larger tapestry that these

* I am grateful for the research assistance of Alison Gurin.

separate threads form are exceptional (see Findlay 2008; also Andreas and Nadelmann 2006; Kempa 2009).

I argue that in the last two decades, the Security Council has increasingly turned to *criminal* justice tools in its quest to maintain international peace and security. I identify a movement away from a political (or 'jurying') approach (Franck 2002: 127), maximising the Council's political discretion, towards a more legalistic (or 'judicial') approach, regulating its exercise of discretion, especially where Council actions impact on individual rights. I describe this trend in the movement away from ad hoc fact-finding arrangements towards professionalised criminal investigation and trial; and in the movement away from political and trade sanctions to global crime prevention regimes. (A similar trend is evident in UN policing practices, but will not be explored here due to space constraints.) Finally, through the lens of the Darfur case in the International Criminal Court (ICC), I explore the unintended consequence of this development of international criminal justice: a growing backlash against what is perceived as selective and politicised use of criminal justice technologies.

The development of international criminal justice through the practice of the Security Council

In the past, the rhetoric of criminalisation at the international level was exactly that: rhetoric. States generally lacked the means, beyond their borders, to institutionalise that rhetoric, to put in place the classic technologies of criminal justice at the domestic level – policing, investigation, criminal trial and detention. International criminal justice was, until recently, focused on interstate co-operation to enforce domestic criminal norms, perhaps in line with some international agreement. Before the Second World War, the conduct recognised by international law as subject to criminal punishment by all states was the conduct of private, transnational actors (such as pirates and military recruiters) that states 'moved by selfish but shared interests' – as Professor Paola Gaeta (2009: 64) has put it – recognised as a common problem. Even after the depravity of the Second World War, when states agreed that there were certain extreme cases in which even the conduct of state officials warranted substantive criminalisation at the international level (such as genocide, war crimes, torture and apartheid) (*ibid.*), they left the enforcement of these international criminal norms to states – and as a result they remained largely unenforced.

This traditional approach to criminal governance in the international security system is a consequence of the close relationship between criminal justice and state sovereignty. The act of criminalisation is closely intertwined with the law-making power of the sovereign; and the ability to coercively enforce criminal norms is equally entwined with the sovereign's monopoly on the use of force. It is unsurprising, there-fore, that states have been reluctant to allow other actors – such as the Security Council and international courts – to develop similar powers to declare and enforce law, lest that dilute their own powers and prerogatives.

The Security Council's practice in the last two decades has tested that settled approach. It gives states – if they can convince the Council to act – the power to replicate these traditionally domestic control technologies at the international level. It gives the Council the power to make real what previously had been merely rhetorical: international criminal justice. But, as I explore at length below, there is an emerging perception that the Council in fact does this only selectively, and that these instruments of criminal justice and crime control are in fact used by some states (the West) to control other states (the rest). What is presented by some as a system of criminal justice thus risks being perceived by others as a system of international repression.

In this first section, I examine how the Security Council has developed international criminal justice through the adoption and adaptation of technologies of criminal justice and control found at the national level. I examine two areas of practice: (1) fact-finding in response to incidents of political violence; and (2) administrative sanctions and control regimes. In both areas, I argue that the Council's practice has increas-ingly come to resemble technologies and practices used at the national level in Western/OECD states. And in each area, I argue, those practices have been critiqued for an initial failure to respect individual rights, which has forced them to adapt towards a more 'liberal' model.

Fact-finding: from diplomatic inquiries to quasi-criminal investigations and trials

The Security Council has a long history of undertaking fact-finding missions in response to incidents of political violence, often by delegat-ing fact-finding responsibilities to subsidiary bodies and other UN organs. As I explore below, over time, the form taken by these fact-finding processes has steadily shifted from that of a diplomatic fact-finding mission to something resembling the judicially oriented investigation and trial model found in the criminal justice systems of many Western states.

The slow process of judicialisation of the Council's fact-finding function kicked off with Secretary-General Perez de Cuellar's experiment with impartial fact-finding to respond to allegations of chemical weapons use during the Iran–Iraq war. The process was perceived by the UN membership as a great success. Against that background, at the end of 1991 the General Assembly adopted a 'Declaration on Fact-finding by the United Nations in the Field of the Maintenance of International Peace and Security' (United Nations 1991a). This declaration encouraged UN organs to use fact-finding missions, setting out a range of principles that should be observed – with a significant emphasis on the use of independent and impartial fact-finders (though see Berg 1993).

At the same time, members of the Security Council were increasingly portraying its interventions – such as the response to Iraq's invasion of Kuwait in 1990 – as law enforcement actions. President George H. W. Bush (1990) called for a 'new partnership of nations . . . united by principle and the rule of law'. And US Ambassador to the UN, Jeanne Kirkpatrick, said that the USA could no longer play 'global policeman', implying that this policing role now fell to the UN (Mittelstadt 1990). Resolution 687, which set down the terms of the *post bellum* between Iraq and Kuwait, took this rhetoric seriously, creating a number of legal-regulatory mechanisms. One provision set up a system of independent international weapons inspections, to be carried out by the International Atomic Energy Agency and a newly formed multinational verification and inspections commission (UNSCOM). Another provision, now often overlooked, had the Security Council use its Chapter VII powers to set up an independent body to adjudicate compensation claims made by victims of the Iraqi military action (including legal persons – corporations),[1] which the Secretary-General recognised as playing a quasi-judicial function (United Nations 1991b: para. 20).

In 1992 the Council took another step towards incorporating criminal justice tools into its peace-maintenance repertoire, in its response to the bombing of a Pan-Am jumbo jet over Lockerbie, Scotland, on 21 December 1988, which killed 270. A similar bombing over Niger in 1989 killed 170. Western authorities quickly concluded that Libyan

---

[1] See Caron and Morris (2002).

agents had been involved in the bombings, and called for their extradition. Libya refused, and instead sought to initiate its own investigation. The matter quickly wound up before the International Court of Justice (ICJ). In 1992, before the ICJ could rule on the matter, the Western powers pushed a Chapter VII Resolution through the Security Council requiring Libya to surrender the two suspects for criminal trial, rendering the ICJ hearings moot.[2] Libya protested the Western powers' interference in the process of justice and refused to hand over the suspects. The Council retaliated by adopting Chapter VII sanctions against the Libyan regime, which were only suspended after Libya agreed to surrender the accused for trial by a Scottish criminal court sitting in the Netherlands, and only finally lifted in 2003.[3]

The Council again turned to independent fact-finding and criminal trial techniques to respond to the war in Bosnia in mid 1992. As Daphna Shraga (2009: 170) has succinctly put it: 'Disinclined to intervene militarily to stop the bloodshed, but politically and morally constrained to act and to be seen to act, the S[ecurity] C[ouncil] opted for a judicial enforcement measure.' First, the Security Council created a Commission of Experts to Investigate Violations of International Humanitarian Law in the former Yugoslavia.[4] It used a range of criminal investigation techniques such as excavation and forensic examination of a mass grave. Its final report in mid 1993 increased the pressure on the Council to take coercive enforcement action against perpetrators of atrocities in Bosnia. With military enforcement action politically and operationally difficult, the Council turned to the other coercive tool it had recently tentatively added to its repertoire: criminal trial (see O'Brien 1993: 640). The Council used its Chapter VII powers to create the International Criminal Tribunal for the former Yugoslavia (ICTY).[5] The next year, atrocities in Rwanda similarly prompted the creation of a Commission of Experts and then an International Criminal Tribunal for Rwanda (ICTR).[6]

Accounts of the development of international criminal justice often give the sense that the ad hoc International Criminal Tribunals sprang from the collective mind of the Council fully clad, like Athena springing

---

[2] *Questions of Interpretation and Application of the 1971 Montreal Convention arising from the Aerial Incident at Lockerbie (Libyan Arab Jamahiriya v. United Kingdom), Preliminary Objections*, ICJ Reports (1998) 3.

[3] See generally Plachta (2001).

[4] SC Res. 780 (1992), and see Cherif Bassiouni (1992).

[5] SC Res. 808 and 827 (1993).

[6] SC Res. 935 (1994) and 955 (1994), and see Akhavan (1996).

from the mind of Zeus. They overlook the increasing visibility of criminal justice techniques in the repertoire of the Council at the relevant
time, which made such a move conceivable – even if radical and highly
contested (see Hazan 2004).

These accounts also tend to overlook the significant role of judicial
actors as developers of – and promoters of a 'system' of – international
criminal justice. This is borne out, for example, in the manner that
international judicial actors have dealt with the question of the 'legality'
of international criminal trial (Swart 2006). As the first *international*
criminal trial process established by the Council, the ICTY and ICTR had
to deal with a number of thorny issues relating to the relationship
between the political discretion of the Council and principles of criminal
law, including the need for judicial independence. The Appeals Chamber
of the ICTY and ICTR held that it was appropriate to review whether the
trial process itself had been 'established by law' and whether the 'fair trial
guarantees' afforded by the ICTY's Statute reflected those promised in
the International Covenant on Civil and Political Rights.[7] Significantly,
in that *Tadić* case, and in others such as the *Norman* case before the
Special Court for Sierra Leone,[8] international judicial actors have determined their own jurisdiction not only by parsing the provisions of
statutes endorsed by the Security Council, but also through reference
to independent 'principles', such as the principles of legality – the notion
that individuals ought to be found culpable only for conduct which had
been criminalised by law prior to the conduct (Gallant 2009). This
reflects a specific understanding of the nature of justice, and especially
of the criminal trial process. It is a concept of justice inherently entwined
with liberal conceptions of the proper relationship between state power
and individual rights, which springs out of the historical experience
of criminal justice at the domestic – and especially Western – level
(cf. United Nations 1993: para. 106).

By promoting the concept that these trials operated according to
certain principles – such as legality – *outside* the control of the Security
Council, the criminal trial process cast a shadow back into the investigation and fact-finding processes controlled by the Security Council.
They created incentives for Council-mandated investigations and fact-
finding to be conducted in a manner that accorded with those principles,

---

[7] Judgment, *Prosecutor* v. *Tadić* (Case no. IT-94–1-AR72), AC, Jurisdiction Appeal, 2
October 1995, paras. 41–8.
[8] See Decision on Preliminary Motion based on Lack of Jurisdiction (Child Recruitment),
Prosecutor v. *Norman* (Case no. SCSL-04–14-AR72E), AC, 31 May 2004.

to ensure that their fact-finding processes would identify 'facts' and collect 'evidence' which could then be fed into an enforcement process structured according to international principles. This set in train a movement away from the diplomatic fact-finding model that had prevailed in the Council, towards a more 'judicial' model.

The early fact-finding bodies established by the Council in the 1990s differed little from the panels of experts that deal with Security Council sanctions regimes (treated in the next section). Both drew on professional lay expertise to buttress the diplomatic legitimacy of the Council, and both were sometimes criticised for their investigative methods. For example, the report of a Panel of Inquiry established by the Secretary-General, at the request of the Security Council, to examine a massacre in Liberia in 1993 never saw the light of day because of concerns about the reliability of its conclusions about which armed group committed the massacre (Wako 1993). These fact-finding bodies provided only limited-duration, part-time positions, with little administrative or research support from the UN itself. Indeed the first head of the Commission of Experts for the former Yugoslavia, Frits Kalshoven, resigned because of the lack of support the Commission was receiving.

Under the shadow of the criminal trial processes, the fact-finding bodies established by the Council, and by the Secretary-General on the recommendation of the Council, have slowly been professionalised and judicialised. Fact-finding methodologies have been compiled by the UN's Office of Legal Affairs and Office of the High Commissioner for Human Rights, drawing on past experience and experiences in the international criminal tribunals, and paying particular attention to protecting the rights of 'suspects'. And professionals from those institutions – as well as national police forces – increasingly provide research and administrative support to the international investigative mechanisms the Security Council mandates. The Independent International Investigation Commission, in Lebanon for example, has combined professional investigators and prosecutors drawn from the international criminal tribunals with experienced national police from numerous countries. And the Darfur Commission of Inquiry benefited from the expertise of professional human rights fact-finding staff with experience in the Office of the High Commissioner for Human Rights. Perhaps unsurprisingly, given the ideological and personal stakes of the personnel of such professionalised fact-finding bodies, these bodies are consistently calling for the referral of such matters to independent criminal justice mechanisms, whether at the national or international level.

Yet such proposals are not always acted upon. After all, the Council retains its political discretion over when to establish and terminate such mechanisms, or refer matters to pre-existing mechanisms (as it did in Darfur, under Article 14 of the ICC Statute); over the choice of applicable law and procedure (especially important in the Special Tribunal for Lebanon[9]); in the allocation of decision-making authority, for example through the appointment of investigators and judges; over financing arrangements; and in ensuring co-operation by other parties, including states (Shraga 2009: 168). The question is what kind of justice roles the Security Council will create and tolerate in any given situation – and in particular, what level of normative and procedural independence it will grant these mechanisms. Indeed, in one recent case – the request from the government of Pakistan for assistance in investigating the assassination of Benazir Bhutto – the Security Council specifically shied away from creating a quasi-criminal investigation, instead deliberately reverting to the old diplomatic fact-finding model, perhaps to avoid any misperception that the process would lead to referral of the matter to criminal trial.

Opponents of the ad hoc criminal tribunals have long argued that the justice roles created and tolerated by the Security Council in any given situation depend not on considerations appropriate to the impartial administration of justice, but on the interests of the Great Powers that control the Security Council. Yet the enormous expense involved in the ad hoc criminal tribunals' administration gave members of the Council a ready 'administrative' explanation for their second thoughts about reliance on international criminal justice mechanisms. The Council did authorise a variety of 'hybrid' trial processes in Kosovo, East Timor, Sierra Leone and Cambodia (see Romano *et al.* 2004; Kermani Mendez 2009), but did not again create a tribunal under Chapter VII until it created the Special Tribunal for Lebanon in 2007.[10] This gave rise to numerous warnings about the politicisation of international criminal justice. That Special Tribunal is the product of a multi-year investigation by a specially established International Independent Investigation Commission which involved highly sophisticated use of forensic and DNA analysis and intelligence sharing. The Tribunal itself has a budget in the hundreds of millions of dollars. In contrast, Burundi's

---

[9] See the symposium on the Special Tribunal for Lebanon in *Journal of International Criminal Justice* 5(5) (2007).

[10] See note 9 above.

2002 request for assistance to establish a war crimes tribunal remains unresponded to by the Council.

As Daphna Shraga (2009) has noted, the danger is that it is the politics of the Council which seems best to explain these differences in its choices relating to the administration of justice. In Sierra Leone and Lebanon, 'the political commitment of an old colonial power to its former colony drove the political process' leading to the creation of international courts (the Special Court for Sierra Leone, and the Special Tribunal for Lebanon), while in Cambodia 'it was China's thin-veiled threat to veto any S[ecurity] C[ouncil] resolution purporting to establish an international tribunal for Cambodia which barred a discussion in the Council and shifted the debate back to' the General Assembly, resulting in UN support to a domestic (rather than an international) court. By contrast, '[i]n the case of Burundi, it has been the lack of an acute political interest on the part of any Member of the Council which explains . . . the fact that five years after Burundi's request for international assistance, the negotiating process on the establishment of a [court and a truth commission] remains stalled' (*ibid.*: 170).

The 'danger' of this explanation is that it gives ammunition to those who seek to delegitimise both the trials in question, and the UN organs that created them. Time and again, we have seen high-profile defendants – Milošević, Karadžić, Seselj, Hinga Norman, Charles Taylor – seek to turn the tables on international war crimes trials by using the trial as a process of not their own ceremonial degradation, but the ceremonial degradation of those *they* cast as enemy 'others', the criminals that have violated the world order that these defendants advocate.[11]

The result of this process of development of fact-finding mechanisms, then, is what we might term 'partial judicialisation' of the Council's fact-finding processes. As a matter of law and policy, the Security Council retains complete political discretion over when to establish fact-finding bodies, and what form they will take. But as a matter of practice and habit, the Council's answers to these questions, guided by expert input from the UN Secretariat and external commentators, are increasingly shaped by the international community's experiences with international criminal investigation and trial processes. Yet the non-systematic reliance on those tools risks creating a perception that they are technically – but not politically – sophisticated technologies of control, wielded by Western powers to dominate the rest.

[11] For a detailed description of this process see Cockayne (2005).

Sanctions: from trade embargoes to global crime prevention regimes

Even as the Council has developed its fact-finding and criminal trial practices to respond to atrocities and political violence, it has carried on what has traditionally been considered a separate practice relating to economic and political sanctions. Yet it is worth considering the extent to which this aspect of the Security Council's repertoire has also contributed to the emergence of a rudimentary system of international criminal justice, not least because those who are targeted by sanctions may consider these tantamount to punishment. In this section, I argue that over the last two decades, the Security Council has altered its conception and practice of sanctions, and that they have, as a result, moved away from the classical model of trade embargoes to something that much more closely resembles crime prevention regimes – and civil preventive orders – at the domestic level.

Sanctions, explicitly authorised by Article 41 of the UN Charter, offer a form of coercive action 'between words and war' (Wallensteen and Staibano 2005). The Council has, since the end of the cold war, turned to sanctions to respond to a range of internationally deemed antisocial behaviours, including overthrows of democratic governments, abuses of human rights, terrorism and illicit trade. These sanctions have moved from blanket trade embargoes to highly targeted financial freezes, visa bans and embargoes on specific commodities including arms. Most recently, sanctions have even been used to reshape political economies not only *during* war, but also in post-conflict peace-building.

The literature on the development of Security Council sanctions is large and complex (see Farrall 2007; Cortright and Lopez 2000; 2002). It is not possible to do it justice here. One remarkable aspect of that literature is that it is almost entirely divorced from the literature on international criminal justice. The separation of these two literatures is at some level unsurprising. The Security Council and the sanctions bodies it has created have been at pains precisely to emphasise that Security Council sanctions are *not* intended to serve as penal regimes. Security Council sanctions are not intended to provide penal measures for judicially determined violations of rules or norms: they are political measures designed to serve 'as the basis for a bargaining dynamic in which the promise of lifting sanctions becomes an incentive to encourage political concessions and cooperation' (Cortright *et al.* 2008: 206).

The Guidelines of the Security Council's 1267 Committee (which deals with sanctions against members of Al-Qa'ida and the Taliban), for example, note that: 'A criminal charge is not necessary for inclusion on the Consolidated List as the sanctions are intended to be preventive in nature' (United Nations 1995: para. 66; and see *Guidelines of the Committee for the Conduct of its Work*, first adopted 7 November 2002, as amended). And the 1526 Monitoring Group has held that its sanctions are 'designed to prevent terrorist acts, rather than provide a compendium of convicted criminals . . . after all, the sanctions do not impose a criminal punishment or procedure, such as detention, arrest or extradition, but instead apply administrative measures such as freezing assets, prohibiting international travel and precluding arms sales' (United Nations 2005a: paras. 39–44). The Security Council's attempts to ring-fence its 'jurying' function in this way, keeping it free from interference by outside judicial actors, has until recently been successful. The UN Human Rights Committee has, for example, recently confirmed that '[a]lthough the sanctions regime [under Resolution 1267] has serious consequences for the individuals concerned, which could indicate that it is punitive in nature, the Committee considers that this regime does not concern a "criminal charge"' in the meaning of the International Covenant on Civil and Political Rights (Human Rights Council 2008: 25, para. 10.11).

Nevertheless, Security Council sanctions are increasingly coming to serve as globally mandated control regimes, like international versions of some states' civil preventive orders, such as the UK's 'antisocial behavioural orders' (see Crawford 2009). Like these regimes, sanctions are notionally intended both to *prevent* the worst impacts of some behaviours, and to *deter* individuals from engaging in that behaviour in the first place. They are not necessarily triggered by violation of a (criminal) norm, but rather by conduct that is considered antisocial or a threat to international public order ('peace and security'). Cessation of the conduct will – at least in theory – lead to termination of the sanction; in contrast, criminal punishment is notionally retributive and like a debt incurred and to be paid off, even after the delinquent conduct ceases. This differentiation of preventive, administrative sanctions from penal regimes is reinforced at an institutional level. Sanctions are dealt with in the UN's Department of Political Affairs, whereas tribunals and commissions of inquiry have historically been dealt with in the Office of Legal Affairs. And member states' missions often designate political officers to deal with sanctions, and legal officers to deal with tribunals and similar matters (though there are many exceptions).

But the distinction between 'civil' or 'administrative' sanctions and the broader 'punitive' aspect of the Council's work is slowly breaking down (see Bianchi 2006: 1066). The contemporary forms of Council-backed sanctions arguably interfere with individual civil liberties (such as the right to property and the freedom of movement) in ways that so resemble criminal penalties (such as criminal confiscation and detention) that similar defence or due process rights ought to be afforded sanctions targets before and after the sanctions are imposed as are afforded criminal defendants. And judicial actors increasingly see it as their role to defend these principles, bringing them into conflict with political actors.

Like the turn to criminal trial processes, the Council's turn to sanctions after the cold war quickly proved controversial. Cortright, Lopez and Gerber-Stellingwerf (2008: 206) point out that sanctions were 'imposed mostly against states which were not critical allies' of the five permanent members of the Security Council. Unsurprisingly, this quickly gave rise to resistance, which has frequently appealed to humanist values, for example through suggestions that broad trade sanctions amount to forms of collective punishment which are bad in policy, if not unlawful (see O'Connell 2002; Reinisch 2001). These criticisms led to significant reform efforts (see United Nations 2000; Wallensteen, Staibano and Eriksson 2003), and the adoption of a 'smart sanctions' by the Council in relation to Iraq in Resolution 1409 (2002), allowing humanitarian exceptions to the sanctions regime such as the lifting of travel restrictions to allow for the practice of religious freedoms. Sanctions were both 'individualised' and 'humanised'.

At the same time, the Council developed an increasingly sophisticated repertoire of monitoring and enforcement practices, relying not only on implementation by states at the national level, but also on complementary, supranational investigative and monitoring machinery. Some of these – such as the Sanctions Assistance Missions used to enforce an arms embargo against Bosnia in the mid 1990s (see Cortright *et al.* 2008: 215–7) and the Angola Sanctions Committee (Angell 2004: 179) – have specifically drawn staff from national police and customs agencies. Over time, these groups have developed detailed investigative and interview protocols, based in part on principles of natural justice drawn from domestic experiences in criminal justice (*ibid.*: 200). But resourcing of these investigators was patchy, leading human rights lawyer John Dugard as early as 2001 to point out the prospect of litigation (see Dugard 2001; van den Herik 2007). Already in 2002, monitoring reports from sanctions committees began to identify instances of misspelt or possibly improperly identified names in the information provided by states (United Nations 2002: paras. 158–9; 2004: 156). Complainants began to threaten to sue the sanctions panelists (United Nations 2005b: para. 157).

The problem was particularly grave in relation to the Al-Qa'ida/Taliban sanctions regime. Listed individuals' travel was restricted and their assets frozen, threatening them with serious personal hardship. There was no provision made for their compensation, in the event that it turned out they had been wrongly listed. Matters reached a head when it emerged that the Security Council had possibly erroneously listed two Somali-born Swedish citizens, through the 1267 Committee. It took considerable time for them to be removed from the list, because the request for their removal from the list had to be brought by their state (Sweden), and there were no protocols in place for reassessing the information brought forward by another state (the USA) which had led to their listing in the first place (Cramér 2003). With designation lists created for Liberia, Côte d'Ivoire, DRC and Sudan – more than 900 people listed by 2006 – concerns about the lack of transparency and due process across the listing system only grew (see Targeted Sanctions Project 2006).

Yet progress to address these concerns has been slow. Efforts to establish an independent body to monitor the observance of due process rights in the Council's sanctions bodies began in the early 2000s (Wallensteen, Staibano and Eriksson 2003: 22; see also Dugard 2001; Cameron 2003). At the 2005 World Summit, world leaders agreed 'to ensure that fair and clear procedures exist for placing individuals and entities on sanctions lists and for removing them, as well as for granting humanitarian exemptions' (United Nations 2005c: para. 109). But reconciling a preventive security regime and natural justice proved difficult (Fassbender 2006; Cameron 2006; and Watson Institute 2006). Eventually even the UN Secretary-General called on the Security Council to inform listing targets of the case against them, ensure their right to be heard via written submissions, and institute a system of independent, impartial and effective review (United Nations 2006b: 5).

In December 2006, the Council established a 'focal-point' within the UN Secretariat, whom individuals could petition for delisting, and clarified listing protocols. But it did not create a system of independent or impartial review of that information, or create a rebuttable presumption in favour of the target's access to the information laid against them – all of which might be said to be required on natural justice grounds.

Many found these changes wanting. The UN High Commissioner for Human Rights weighed in (2007: para. 31). And between 2005 and 2008,[12] the European Court of Justice ruled that the European Council's implementation of Security Council sanctions regimes (as required by the UN Charter) violated the claimants' *jus cogens* due process and property rights, because the lists had been compiled through procedures depriving them of their financial property without adequate opportunity to make their case. The United Nations Human Rights Committee even found that Belgium had violated the International Covenant on Civil and Political Rights in its efforts to implement UNSC Resolution 1267 (1999).[13] Three members wrote that:

> It is more than a little disturbing that the executive branches of 15 Member States appear to claim a power, with none of the consultation or checks and balances that would be applicable at the national level, to simply discard centuries of States' constitutional traditions of providing bulwarks against exorbitant and oppressive executive action.[14]

In a sole Individual opinion (concurring), Sir Nigel Rodley continued:

> It is not easy to see why nearly a decade after the first resolution 1267 (1999) and seven years after 9/11 the Council could not have evolved procedures more consistent with the human rights values of transparency, accountability and impartial, independent assessment of facts.[15]

The Security Council's failure to provide such procedures has left it open to charges of selective use of sanctions, using them as an oppressive tool

---

[12] See especially *Ahmed Ali Yusuf and Al Barakaat International Foundation* v. *Council and Commission*, ECJ, Case C-402/05 P and C-415/05, 3 September 2008; and European Court of Justice, *Yassin Abdullah Kadi* v. *Council*, Appeal against Judgment of the Court of First Instance of 21 September 2005, Case C-402/05 P, 24 November 2005. See also Sixth Report of the Analytical Support and Sanctions Monitoring Team appointed pursuant to Security Council Resolutions 1526 (2004) and 1617 (2005) concerning al Qaeda and the Taliban and associated individuals and entities, UN Doc. S/2007/132 (2007), Annex I.

[13] Human Rights Council, Communication no. 1472/2006, *Nabil Sayadi and Patricia Vinck*, UN Doc. CCPR/C/94/D/1472/2006, 29 December 2008.

[14] Individual opinion (partially dissenting) by Committee members Sir Nigel Rodley, Mr Ivan Shearer and Ms Iulia Antoanella Motoc, Appendix A to Human Rights Council, Communication no. 1472/2006, *Nabil Sayadi and Patricia Vinck*, UN Doc. CCPR/C/94/D/1472/2006, 29 December 2008, p. 27.

[15] Individual opinion of Committee member Sir Nigel Rodley (concurring), Individual opinion (partially dissenting) by Committee members Sir Nigel Rodley, Mr Ivan Shearer and Ms Iulia Antoanella Motoc, Appendix A to Human Rights Council, Communication no. 1472/2006, *Nabil Sayadi and Patricia Vinck*, UN Doc. CCPR/C/94/D/1472/2006, 29 December 2008, pp. 37–8.

to maintain the global status quo. That, in turn, has fed into an already-evident phenomenon of secondary deviance (Lemert 1967) around sanctions: even narrowly targeted sanctions can create 'increased incentives for criminal evasion [and] increased civilian dependence on criminal economic activities' (Wallensteen, Staibano and Eriksson 2003: 20). Sanctions drive their targets towards crime, to source finance, arms and other commodities. In time, they risk breaking down rather than strengthening any taboo associated with participation in those illicit trades. Sanctions thus often come to serve as a rallying point for a discourse of national victimisation and resistance (see Bolaji Akinyemi 2006). We see this pattern in South Africa, Southern Rhodesia, Iraq, Yugoslavia, Haiti and Afghanistan (Naylor 1999; Chesterman and Pouligny 2003: 511–2; Cockayne 2009). Already by 1995, the UN Secretary-General recognised that sanctions could 'defeat their own purpose by provoking a patriotic response against the international community . . . and by rallying the population behind the leaders whose behaviour the sanctions are intended to modify'.[16]

What this suggests is that the Council may be prepared to tolerate ineffective sanctions (cf. Chesterman and Pouligny 2003). Their real value may be *symbolic*, in labelling their targets as outlaws (cf. Hurd 2002; 2005). The weakness of the sanctions machinery in the UN Secretariat – especially when compared to the strength of the international fact-finding and criminal trial machinery – points to the fact that effective implementation is not a *sine qua non* of the Council's continued toleration of and reliance on these types of control regimes.

There are, however, two key exceptions to this rule of institutional weakness in sanctions regimes, which in fact tell us a lot about the politics of the development of sanctions as a system of behavioural control. Two sets of sanctions – on Al-Qa'ida and the Taliban (see Rosand 2004), and relating to counter-terrorism and non-proliferation of WMD to terrorists – have evolved over the last decade into radically different types of regimes, with global scope and a permanent implementation machinery requiring significant ongoing resource expenditure. The 1267 Committee dealing with Al-Qa'ida and the Taliban is supported by a permanent expert group in New York that conducts intensive ongoing liaison with state agencies (including intelligence and criminal law enforcement agencies), to ensure that a consolidated global list of

---

[16] This dynamic was understood already in 1995: see *Supplement to an Agenda for Peace*, UN Doc. A/50/60 – S/1995/1, 1995, para. 70.

individuals subject to the regime's control measures is kept (more or less) up to date (see Boulden 2008: 613–14). The 1373, or Counter-Terrorism, Committee and the 1540 Committee take this approach one step even further, creating committees to oversee state's implementation of obligations, imposed by the Council, to control terrorism and WMD proliferation, through the use of domestic governance mechanisms – especially criminal justice technologies.

Prior to Resolution 1373, the UN's sovereign members had dealt with terrorism by elaborating intergovernmental treaties through the General Assembly defining certain types of conduct which they would subsequently govern through domestic criminal justice systems. When the Security Council *had* been drawn into responding to terrorist attacks – which it had done almost since its inception – it rarely turned to the tools of criminal justice (with the notable Lockerbie exception) (see Luck 2004). In Resolution 1373, the Council instead laid out new substantive international criminal norms, requiring states to take specific measures within their domestic criminal justice systems to prevent, suppress, freeze and criminalise terrorist financing, and otherwise deal with and prevent terrorism (Boulden 2008: 612). State efforts were to be monitored by a Counter-Terrorism Committee, to which all states had to report within ninety days. Resolution 1540 adopts a similar approach in relation to nuclear proliferation.

Needless to say, this 'legislative' turn by the Council caused much consternation, particularly because it seemed to involve the Council arrogating to itself the legislative function traditionally performed by the General Assembly (see Szasz 2002; Happold 2003; Talmon 2005). Over time, resistance within the broader UN membership to this approach led to the General Assembly reasserting its voice on these issues, through the adoption of a Global Counter-Terrorism Strategy (United Nations 2006a).

There is also evidence of a more decentralised approach in other related areas. As with terrorism, until very recently the UN's approach to dealing with organised crime was based on intergovernmental norm-definition and operational co-operation (Madsen 2007). But recently, the Council has become involved in creating efforts to curtail organised criminal activity connected to specific conflicts, such as narco-trafficking in Afghanistan[17] and West Africa.[18] A range of UN political and

[17] S/RES/1333 (2000)S/RES/1817 (2008), 11 June 2008.
[18] See S/PRST/2009/20, 10 July 2009. See also Cockayne and Williams (2009).

peacekeeping bodies mandated by the Council are now working on preventive approaches to organised crime (see e.g. UN DPKO, Kingdom of Sweden, International Peace Institute 2008). And the Council has sponsored states' development of an elaborate naval policing, arrest, trial and crime prevention machinery to address Somali piracy (see United Nations 2009).[19]

Unintended consequences: Darfur and the growing resistance to the Security Council's experiments in international criminal justice

The somewhat illiberal nature of some of the Security Council's experiments with international criminal justice tools has slowly fuelled a growing backlash, which increasingly seeks to portray the entire system of international criminal justice as a tool manipulated by Western powers to enforce an unjust status quo. Implicit in all these criticisms is the notion that if there is to be a system of international 'justice', it must work on the basis of the principle of impartiality, treating like cases alike – and not on the basis of political considerations. But a growing body of criticism argues that the Council does not – or perhaps even cannot – allow an independent and impartial system of international justice to function independent of politics, given its mandate to maintain international peace and security. This claim, that the maintenance of international peace and the provision of international justice may be impossible to reconcile at least in the short-term, has grown particularly loud since the Security Council referred the case of Darfur to the ICC.

The events leading to the Council's referral of the Darfur situation to the ICC follow a similar pattern to those leading to the creation of the ICTY and ICTR. With strong domestic political pressure for some form of intervention, but an unwillingness to spill blood and spend treasure, the USA pushed first for an investigative commission and then, on the basis of its findings and recommendations, the activation of a criminal trial process (see United Nations 2005d).[20] Although the Security Council itself referred the case to the ICC, on the recommendation of the Darfur Commission of Inquiry (which it had established), there have been numerous calls for it to defer the proceeding (under Article 16 of the ICC Statute), in order not to interfere with peace efforts in Darfur. The request for an indictment by the prosecutor was met with jeers from

---

[19] See SC Res. 1814 (2008), 1816 (2008), 1838 (2008), 1846 (2008) and 1851 (2008).
[20] For the referral, see SC Res. 1593, 31 March 2005.

many quarters (Ciampi 2008), which grew louder when the request was approved by the Pre-Trial Chamber. The League of Arab States (2008) condemned the move. The African Union (AU) Peace and Security Council explicitly asked for an Article 16 deferral,[21] and the AU Commission appointed former South African President Thabo Mbeki to co-ordinate its response. Perhaps most explosively, the outspoken Nicaraguan President of the General Assembly in 2008–9, Miguel d'Escoto Brockmann, criticised the issuing of the warrant as 'racist' (UN News Centre 2009).

The indictment of Sudanese President al-Bashir stands out because it seems to provide something of a test case. The mechanisms and practices of international criminal justice that have emerged over the last two decades, many with the Security Council as midwife, are currently only partially systematised. In many eyes, that incomplete institutionalisation seems to align neatly with the interests of the Great Powers and risks, they fear, becoming a permanent state of affairs. The Bashir indictment thus stands as a test of whether some of those currently fearful of being targeted by international criminal justice can mount an effective rear-guard action, rolling back what they perceive as the selective application of international criminal justice. Their fear is that if the Council stops, halfway to justice, then despite its universalist, rule-of-law rhetoric, these criminal justice technologies will be deployed in a largely *symbolic* fashion, augmenting the ability of the states that control the declaratory functions of the Council to outlaw targeted individuals and groups as enemies in and of international society. Ironically, as Ian Hurd (2005) has pointed out in relation to Libya's strategy of resisting the UN sanctions imposed on it in the 1990s, the emerging resistance campaign to some extent relies on the norms of the very system of liberal internationalism – such as the need for impartiality – that the campaign seeks to resist.

It does not help that the prosecutor is the sole high-profile public face of the ICC, since there is no equivalent-rank ICC official to speak for the defence. Thus, as Göran Sluiter (2008: 874) has pointed out, the prosecutor's opinion of whether Sudan has adequately co-operated with the Court tends to stand uncontested (not withstanding his presumed partiality on this question). The stigmatising power of his announcing a mere indictment is apparently so great that he is increasingly

---

[21] AU, *Communiqué* of the 142nd meeting of the Peace and Security Council, 21 July 2008, PSecurityCouncil/MIN/Comm(CXLII).

characterised, amongst the resistance to the ICC, as an instrument of Western policy, if not Western powers.

The reality is that many of the UN's crime-control efforts *are* backed by Western states. Andreas and Nadelmann (2006: 243) claim that:

> [w]hen one digs beneath the surface of UN and many other multilateral crime control initiatives, one inevitably finds U.S. funds, personnel, model legislation, and diplomatic endeavors. Thus, far from taming and constraining U.S. power, in this policy realm international institutions extend, obscure, and legitimate it.

Security Council Resolutions 1422 (12 July 2002), 1487 (12 June 2003), 1497 (2003) and 1593 (2005) also remain fresh in the minds of many states. Those resolutions – the only uses of Article 16 of the Rome Statute to date – requested the deferral of all investigations and prosecutions of current or former members of peacekeeping operations from states not party to the ICC in various situations. They were transparently designed to shield US forces from ICC jurisdiction, creating a strong perception of double standards. Some commentators openly query why foreign peacekeeping troops in Darfur should be immune from ICC jurisdiction (Resolution 1593 (2003)), but Sudan's own head of state should not. This places the political onus on the Council to justify a decision *not* to defer the Bashir proceedings. Legally, the reverse is the case: the onus is on the Council to assemble enough votes to muster a decision *to* defer the case.

That is not just a legal nicety: it represents a key compromise in the Rome Statute between the jurying function of the Security Council and the independent judicial function of the Court. The original draft of the Rome Statute would have required a positive decision by the Security Council before the Court could bring a case in any matter relating to a situation then under consideration by the Security Council (International Law Commission 1994). The final provision reverses this, requiring a positive decision by the Council to arrest any case. This was a deliberate step taken by the negotiators to ensure the relative independence of the Court (Bergsmo and Pejic 1999: 377), while allowing the Security Council to maintain its ultimate discretion over the management of international peace and security (see Berman 1999).

How far the Security Council will allow its 'jurying' function to be curtailed by 'judicial' decision-making is hard to predict. One area that may offer insights is how the Security Council responds to proposals from the ICC on the codification of the crime of aggression. The Rome

Statute of the ICC left this crime for codification at a Review Conference, which was held in 2010. A Special Working Group of the ICC Assembly of States Parties has recently presented its final proposal.[22] One of the major challenges in codifying the crime has been precisely to find a workable balance between the jurying function of the Council – in determining, as provided for by the UN Charter, whether certain facts actually constitute an *act* of aggression by a state – and the judicial function of the Court – in determining whether that act of aggression by a state gives rise to a *crime* of aggression by one of the state's leaders. The draft proposal leaves room for both the Security Council and the ICC to have roles in activating a prosecution for a crime of aggression, giving the Council a 'red light' veto for a limited time. But it remains to be seen, at the time of writing, whether the Council will accept this approach, given how close to its core competences such a process would necessarily come.

Conclusion

Unwittingly, perhaps, the Security Council's turn to international criminal justice has unleashed forces of liberalisation by which the Council's own dealings with this emerging system of international criminal justice – and even its own working methods in some cases – are now being popularly judged. The Council's hesitance about the impacts of this system, and the extent to which it and the values it enshrines are fettering the Council's discretion are clear. That hesitance fuels concerns that the Council may prevent these tools serving the interests of justice, and instead use them as instruments to reinforce the perceived inequities and injustices of existing world order.

If the emerging system of international criminal justice is to maintain its legitimacy, it will be crucial for the members of the Council to demonstrate their willingness to subject themselves to regulation by the same system and tools that they impose on others. In the process, we can expect the 'jurying' function of the Security Council increasingly to be complemented by independent 'judicial' functions in the international system. This may not have been the kind of justice the Security Council expected to render when it began down this path a decade and

---

[22] See Report of the Special Working Group on the Crime of Aggression, ICC-ASP/7/SWGCA/2, 20 February 2009.

a half ago. But ultimately, it might prove an effective way of balancing conservative interests in maintaining world order with progressive interests in transforming it to address injustice. Justice may yet be served.

References

Akhavan, P. (1996) 'The International Criminal Tribunal for Rwanda: the politics and pragmatics of punishment', *American Journal of International Law*, 90(3), 501–10.

Andreas, P. and Nadelmann, E. (2006) *Policing the Globe: Criminalization and Crime Control in International Relations*, Oxford: Oxford University Press.

Angell, D. J. R. (2004) 'The Angola Sanctions Committee' in D. Malone (ed.), *The UN Security Council From the Cold War to the 21st Century*, Boulder, CO: Lynne Rienner, pp. 195–204.

Berg, A. (1993) 'The 1991 Declaration on Fact-finding by the United Nations', *European Journal of International Law*, 4, 1, 107–14.

Bergsmo, M. and Pejic, J. (1999) 'On Article 16' in O. Triffterer (ed.), *The Rome Statute of the International Criminal Court: Observers' Notes, Article by Article*, Baden-Baden, pp. 373–82.

Berman, F. (1999) 'The relationship between the International Criminal Court and the Security Council' in H. von Hebel, J. Lammers and J. Schukking (eds.), *Reflections on the International Criminal Court*, The Hague: T.M.C. Asser Press.

Bianchi, A. (2006) 'Security Council's anti-terror resolutions and their implementation by member states', *Journal of International Criminal Justice*, 4, 1044–73.

Bolaji Akinyemi, A. (2006) 'The Taylor saga: a clash of civilizations', *New African*, 451, 20–3.

Boulden, J. (2008) 'The Security Council and terrorism' in V. Lowe, A. Roberts, J. Welsh and D. Zaum (eds.), *The United Nations Security Council and War: The Evolution of Thought and Practice since 1945*, Oxford: Oxford University Press, pp. 608–23.

Bush, G. H. W. (1990) 'Address before the 45th Session of the United Nations General Assembly in New York', 1 October 1990.

Call, C. T. (2007) (ed.) *Constructing Justice and Security after War*, Washington DC: USIP.

Cameron, I. (2003) 'UN targeted sanctions, legal safeguards and the European Convention on Human Rights', *Nordic Journal of International Law*, 72, 159–214.
　(2006) *The European Convention on Human Rights, Due Process and United Nations Security Council Counter-terrorism Sanctions*, 6 February 2006, Council of Europe.

Caron, D. and Morris, B. (2002) 'The UN Compensation Commission: practical justice, not retribution', *European Journal of International Law*, 13, 183–99.

Cherif Bassiouni, M. (1992) 'The United Nations Commission of Experts Established Pursuant to Security Council Resolution 780 (1992)', *American Journal of International Law*, 88(4), 784–805.

Chesterman, S. (2004/5) 'Rough justice: establishing the rule of law in post-conflict territories', *Ohio State Journal on Dispute Resolution*, 20, 69–98.

(2008) 'An international rule of law?', *American Journal of Comparative Law*, 56, 331–61.

(2009) '"I'll take Manhattan": The International Rule of Law and the United Nations Security Council', *Hague Journal on the Rule of Law*, 1(1), 67–73.

Chesterman, S. and Pouligny, B. (2003) 'Are sanctions meant to work? The politics of creating and implementing sanctions through the United Nations', *Global Governance*, 9, 503–18.

Ciampi, A. (2008) 'The proceedings against President Al Bashir and the prospects of their suspension under Article 16 ICC Statute', *Journal of International Criminal Justice*, 6(5), 885–97.

Clapham, A. (2006) *The Human Rights Obligations of Non-State Actors*, Oxford: Oxford University Press.

Cockayne, J. (2005) 'Hybrids or mongrels? Internationalized war crimes tribunals as unsuccessful degradation ceremonies', *Journal of Human Rights*, 4, 1–19.

(2009) 'Winning Haiti's protection competition: organized crime and peace operations past, present and future', *International Peacekeeping*, 16(1), 77–99.

Cockayne, J. and Williams, P. (2009) *The Invisible Tide: Towards an International Strategy to Deal with Drug Trafficking through West Africa*, New York: International Peace Institute.

Cortright, D. and Lopez, G. A. (2000) *The Sanctions Decade: Assessing UN Strategies in the 1990s*, Boulder, CO: Lynne Rienner.

(2002) *Sanctions and the Search for Security: Challenges to UN Action*, Boulder, CO: Lynne Rienner.

Cortright, D., Lopez, G. A. and Gerber-Stellingwerf, L. (2008) 'The sanctions era: themes and trends in UN Security Council sanctions since 1990' in V. Lowe, A. Roberts, J. Welsh and D. Zaum (eds.), *The United Nations Security Council and War: The Evolution of Thought and Practice since 1945*, Oxford: Oxford University Press, pp. 205–25.

Cramér, P. (2003) 'Recent Swedish experiences with targeted UN sanctions: the erosion of trust in the Security Council' in E. de Wet and A. Nollkaemper (eds.), *Review of the Security Council by Member States*, Antwerp: Intersentia, pp. 91–5.

Crawford, A. (2009), 'Governing through anti-social behaviour: regulatory challenges to criminal justice', *British Journal of Criminology*, 49(6), 810–31.

Dugard, C. J. R. (2001) 'Judicial review of sanctions' in V. Gowlland-Debbas (ed.), *United Nations Sanctions and International Law*, Den Haag: Kluwer, pp. 83–91.

Dwan, R. (2003) (ed.) *Executive Policing: Enforcing the Law in Peace Operations*, Oxford: Oxford University Press.

Farrall, J. M. (2007) *United Nations Sanctions and the Rule of Law*, Cambridge: Cambridge University Press.

Fassbender, B. (2006) *Targeted Sanctions and Due Process*, 20 March 2006, UN Office of Legal Affairs.

Findlay, M. (2008) *Governing through Globalised Crime: Futures for International Criminal Justice*, Cullompton: Willan.

Flynn, E. J. (2006) 'The Security Council's Counter-Terrorism Committee and human rights', *Human Rights Law Review*, 7(2), 371–84.

Franck, T. M. (2002) *Recourse to Force: State Action Against Threats and Armed Attacks*, Cambridge: Cambridge University Press.

Gaeta, P. (2009) 'International criminalization of prohibited conduct' in A. Cassese (ed.), *The Oxford Companion to International Criminal Justice*, Oxford: Oxford University Press, pp. 63–74.

Gallant, K. S. (2009) *The Principle of Legality in International and Comparative Criminal Law*, New York: Cambridge University Press.

Goldstone, R. J. and Smith, A. M. (2008) *International Judicial Institutions: The Architecture of International Justice at Home and Abroad*, London: Routledge.

Hansen, A. S. (2002) *From Congo to Kosovo: Civilian Police in Peace Operations Adelphi Paper no. 343*, London: IISS.

Happold, M. (2003) 'Security Council Resolution 1373 and the Constitution of the United Nations', *Leiden Journal of International Law*, 16(1), 593–610.

Hazan, P. (2004) *Justice in a Time of War: The True Story Behind the International Criminal Tribunal for the Former Yugoslavia*, College Station: Texas A&M University Press.

Herik, L. van den (2007) 'The Security Council's targeted sanctions regimes: in need of better protection for the individual', *Leiden Journal of International Law*, 20, 797–807.

Human Rights Council (2008) Communication No. 1472/2006, *Nabil Sayadi and Patricia Vinck*, UN Doc. CCPR/C/94/D/1472/2006, 29 December.

Hurd, I. (2002) 'Legitimacy, power, and the symbolic life of the UN Security Council', *Global Governance*, 8(1), 35–51.

(2005) 'The strategic use of liberal internationalism: Libya and the UN sanctions, 1992–2003', *International Organization*, 59, 495–526.

International Law Commission (1994) *Report of the International Law Commission on the Work of its Forty-sixth Session*, UNGAOR 49th session, Suppl. no. 10, A/49/10.

Kempa, M. (2009) 'Politics of international policing assistance', unpublished manuscript, Ottawa, May.

Kermani Mendez, P. (2009) 'The new wave of hybrid tribunals: a sophisticated approach to enforcing international humanitarian law or an idealistic solution with empty promises?', *Criminal Law Forum*, 20, 53–95.

League of Arab States (2008) 'Statement of the extra-ordinary session of the ministerial council of the League of Arab States to examine the developments in Darfur region', 8 August 2008.

Lemert, E. (1967) *Human Deviance, Social Problems and Social Control*, Englewood Cliffs, NJ: Prentice-Hall.

Luck, E. C. (2004) 'Tackling terrorism' in D. M. Malone (ed.), *The UN Security Council: From the Cold War to the 21st Century*, Boulder, CO: Lynne Rienner, pp. 85–100.

Madsen, F. G. (2007) 'Organized crime' in T. G. Weiss and S. Daws (eds.), *The Oxford Handbook on the United Nations*, Oxford: Oxford University Press, pp. 611–19.

Mittelstadt, M. (1990) 'Kirkpatrick says U.S. cannot allow limited Iraqi withdrawal from Kuwait', Associated Press, 30 October.

Naylor, R. T. (1999) *Patriots and Profiteers: On Economic Warfare, Embargo Busting and State-Sponsored Crime*, Toronto: MacClelland & Stewart.

O'Brien, J. C. (1993) 'The International Tribunal for Violations of International Humanitarian Law in the former Yugoslavia', *American Journal of International Law*, 87(4), 639–59.

O'Connell, M. E. (2002) 'Debating the law of sanctions', *European Journal of International Law*, 13(1), 63–79.

Plachta, M. (2001) 'The Lockerbie case: the role of the Security Council in enforcing the principle *aut dedere aut judicare*', *European Journal of International Law*, 12, 125–40.

Reinisch, A. (2001) 'Developing human rights and humanitarian law accountability of the Security Council for the imposition of economic sanctions', *American Journal of International Law*, 95(4), 851–72.

Romano, C. P. R., Kleffner, J. and Nollkaemper, A. (2004) (eds.) *Internationalized Criminal Courts and Tribunals: Sierra Leone, East Timor, Kosovo and Cambodia*, Oxford: Oxford University Press.

Rosand, E. (2004) 'The Security Council's efforts to monitor the implementation of Al Qaeda/Taliban sanctions', *American Journal of International Law*, 98(4), 745–63.

Shraga, D. (2009) 'Politics and justice: the role of the Security Council' in A. Cassese (ed.), *The Oxford Companion to International Criminal Justice*, Oxford: Oxford University Press, pp. 168–74.

Sluiter, G. (2008) 'Obtaining cooperation from Sudan: where is the law?', *Journal of International Criminal Justice*, 6(5), 871–84.

Swart, M. (2006) *'Judges and Lawmaking at the International Criminal Tribunals for the former Yugoslavia and Rwanda,* Leiden University Doctoral Thesis, 2006, http://openaccess.leidenuniv.nl/bitstream/1887/5434/1/Thesis.pdf.

Szasz, P. (2002) 'The Security Council starts legislating', 96 *American Journal of International Law* (2002) 901–5.

Talmon, S. (2005) 'The Security Council as world legislature', *American Journal of International Law*, 99, 175–93.

Targeted Sanctions Project (2006) 'Strengthening targeted sanctions through fair and clear procedures', White Paper, Watson Institute for International Studies, Brown University, 20 March 2006.

United Nations (1991a) *Declaration on Fact-finding by the United Nations in the Field of the Maintenance of International Peace and Security,* UN Doc. A/RES/46/59, Annex, 9 December 1991.

(1991b) *Report of the Secretary-General Pursuant to Paragraph 19 of Security Council Resolution 687 (1991),* UN Doc. S/22559.

(1993) *Report of the Secretary-General Pursuant to Paragraph 2 of Security Council Resolution 808,* UN Doc. S/25704, 3 May 1993.

(1995) *Supplement to an Agenda for Peace,* UN Doc. A/50/60-S/1995/1.

(2000) *Note by the President of the Security Council,* UN Doc. S/2000/319, 17 April 2000.

(2002) *Report of the Panel of Experts on Liberia,* UN Doc. S/2002/470, 19 April 2002.

(2004) *Report of the Panel of Experts on Liberia,* UN Doc. S/2004/396, 1 June 2004.

(2005a) *Third Report of the Monitoring Team on Al-Qaida,* UN Doc. S/2005/572, 9 December 2005.

(2005b) *Report of the United Nations Panel of Experts on Liberia,* UN Doc. S/2005/745, 25 November 2005.

(2005c) *UN World Summit Outcome Document,* UN Doc. GA Res. 60/1, 24 October 2005.

(2005d) *Report of the International Commission of Inquiry on Darfur to the Secretary-General, Pursuant to SC Resolution 1564 (2004) of 18 September 2004,* UN Doc. S/2005/60, 1 February 2005.

(2006a) *The United Nations Global Counter-Terrorism Strategy,* UN Doc. A/RES/60/288, 8 September 2006.

(2006b) *Strengthening International Law: Rule of Law and Maintenance of International Peace and Security,* UN Doc. S/PV.5474, 22 June 2006.

(2009) *Report of the Secretary-General pursuant to Security Council Resolution 1846 (2008),* UN Doc. S/2009/146, 16 March.

United Nations Department of Peacekeeping Operations, Kingdom of Sweden, International Peace Institute, *International Policing Advisory Council, Summary Meeting Report, 26–28 August 2008*, Stockholm, Sweden.

United Nations High Commissioner for Human Rights (2007) *Report of the UN High Commissioner for Human Rights on the Protection of Human Rights and Fundamental Freedoms while Countering Terrorism*, UN Doc. A/HRC/4/88.

United Nations News Centre (2009) 'Assembly President discusses UN meeting on financial crisis with world leaders', 17 March 2009.

Wako, A. (1993) 'The Carter Camp massacre: results of an investigation by the panel of inquiry appointed by the Secretary-General into the massacre near Harbel, Liberia, on the night of 5–6 June 1993', New York: UN, 10 September 1993.

Wallensteen, P. and Staibano, C. (2005) (eds.) *International Sanctions: Between Words and Wars in the Global System*, New York: Frank Cass.

Wallensteen, P., Staibano, C. and Eriksson, M. (2003) (eds.) *Making Targeted Sanctions Effective*, Uppsala: Uppsala University.

Watson Institute (2006) *Strengthening Targeted Sanctions through Fair and Clear Procedures*, UN Doc. A/60/887 – S/2006/331.

Wood, M. (2006) 'The UN Security Council and international law', Hersch Lauterpacht Memorial Lectures, 7–9 November 2006.

Zappalà, S. (2003) *Human Rights in International Criminal Proceedings*, Oxford: Oxford University Press.

The International Criminal Court and the state of the American exception

JASON RALPH

It is almost a cliché to argue that while European governments favour a world order based on international law and organisation, Americans see international society as an epiphenomenon of American power. Robert Kagan (2003: 3) famously captured this when, at the height of the Iraq War controversy, he wrote that 'Americans are from Mars and the Europeans are from Venus'. Where the latter were 'realising Immanuel Kant's "perpetual peace"', the former was 'mired in history, exercising power in an anarchic Hobbesian world where international law and rules are unreliable, and where true security and the defense and promotion of a liberal order still depend on the possession and use of military might'. Chastened by what America found (or did not find) in Iraq, Kagan seemingly stepped back from some of the implications of this analysis. The USA, he concluded, could not and should not ignore the question of legitimacy and the role that law played in providing that. The USA must realise, moreover, that it could not claim legitimacy by acting unilaterally in its self-interest and without reference to the greater good (Kagan 2004). Yet even after recognising this, Kagan argued, the two continents would remain politically divided. That schism might not reflect the Hobbesian–Kantian divide as implied in his earlier work. Rather the post-Iraq schism reflected a division within liberalism itself; between on the one hand Europeans who (Tony Blair aside) respected the outcome of multilateral dialogue at the United Nations, and on the other hand Americans who 'generally favoured the promotion of liberal principles over the niceties of Westphalian diplomacy' (*ibid*.: 79). In this sense, America's crisis of legitimacy stemmed not from the exception it took to the rule of international law and organisation, it stemmed rather from a failure to make clear that these exceptions actually advanced the liberal cause.

The purpose of this chapter is to interpret US opposition to the International Criminal Court (ICC) in this context. In doing so, it illustrates fundamental flaws in Kagan's thesis, flaws that in turn highlight the unsustainability of the American position. The chapter first rejects Kagan's assumption that there is a trade off between multilateralism and human rights, and that European governments favour the former at the expense of the latter. In contrast to Kagan's argument, the Europeans were the revolutionaries at the Rome Conference, which met just over a decade ago to discuss the shape of the ICC. It was, in other words, the Europeans rather than the Americans who demanded that the ICC be allowed to pursue justice independently of the UN Security Council. They had recognised that the Security Council was an inappropriate forum for discussing when and where to respond to human rights abuses. Instead of turning to unilateral state-based solutions, however, European governments thought creatively about how to set up a new institution that would be founded on a broad-based multilateral consensus. Indeed, and again in contrast to Kagan's thesis, the USA insisted on Security Council approval before allowing the criminal lawyers to intervene in the sovereign affairs of another state. Furthermore, by recalling the principle of sovereign consent to attack the legitimacy of the ICC it was America and not Europe that seemed to favour the niceties of the Westphalian order. Of course, such a position did not prevent the USA from supporting international criminal processes when they were applied to situations where the USA had no particular interest. To this extent, the American exception on the ICC was motivated more by an imperial claim to decide when and where international justice is done, than it was a principled stand on the best way to promote liberal ideals. The ICC has exposed, in other words, another unresolved aspect of America's legitimacy gap. Rather than end on this pessimistic note, however, the chapter argues that a very different approach is immanent in America's own experience, one that involves delegating sovereignty to supranational institutions (i.e. the federal government) in the name of protecting and promoting liberty. Indeed, a radical reading of republican security theory suggests that there is nothing more American than the ICC's Kantian vision.

Norms and exceptions

In certain respects, the ICC transformed international criminal justice from an exception to the rule and turned it into a norm of international society. Prior to 2002, when the Court assumed jurisdiction for instance, international society was constituted with the normative goal of creating order between sovereign states in mind. To encourage comity between nations, states would tend only to prosecute non-nationals if they had a direct connection to the crime in question, e.g. if the victims of a crime committed abroad were nationals of the state. Without such a connection, states tended to respect each other's national jurisdictions. An extension of this practice was the immunity from prosecution that was granted to heads of state, their ministers and their diplomats. This institution was, and to large extent still is, considered central to the smooth functioning of international relations. Although there is now a wider consensus on the need to punish state officials for egregious violations of human rights, there remains much nervousness about the practice of universal jurisdiction. So for instance, the International Court of Justice (ICJ) insisted on the back of the Pinochet judgment that state representatives are immune from prosecution. As the president of the ICJ, Judge Gilbert Guillaume, put it in the *Arrest Warrant* case, to confer national criminal jurisdiction over the serving official of another state would 'risk creating total judicial chaos . . . Contrary to what is advocated by certain publicists', he continued, 'such a development would represent not an advance in the law but a step backward.'[1] The *Arrest Warrant* case ultimately upheld the principle of sovereign immunity from international criminal justice as practised by states. In so doing, it reinforced the idea that international criminal justice is an exception rather than a rule.

The significance of the UN Security Council's creation of the so-called ad hoc courts of the 1990s was not that they turned international criminal justice into a new norm international society. Rather, in creating such courts, the Security Council noted that in exceptional circumstances the denial of justice could be considered a threat to international peace and security. In these circumstances, international courts could be empowered to prosecute serving heads of state, as indeed the International Criminal Tribunal for the former Yugoslavia did with its indictment of Slobodan Milošević. Realists like Henry Kissinger complained that such indictments would destabilise international relations and complicate the search for peace, an argument that seemed particularly salient

---

[1] *Arrest Warrant Case*, 11 April 2000 (*Congo* v. *Belgium*), Separate Opinion of President Guillaume, para. 15 (emphasis added), 14 February 2002, www.icj-cij.org/icjwww/idocket/iCOBE/iCOBEframe.htm.

at the height of NATO's bombing campaign in the spring of 1999 (Kissinger 2001). Yet with the backing of the UN Security Council, the pursuit of criminal justice through international courts did not pose the kind of threat that Guillaume identified. To argue that the creation of such courts indicated the emergence of new norm of international criminal justice would however be mistaken. Such courts were limited in both their timeframe and jurisdiction and, more significantly, they were created only because the UN Security Council had decided that the injustices in the former Yugoslavia and Rwanda were threats to international peace and security. Under such a regime, international criminal justice was still the exception to the norm and the UN Security Council was sovereign to the extent it decided when the exception applied.[2]

This changed with the creation of the ICC. Not only is the Court permanent and notionally universal, it is also independent of the Security Council and does not need prior authorisation to prosecute.[3] The Security Council can postpone an investigation for twelve months under Article 16 of the Rome Statute, but this requires the support of at least nine Security Council members in order to pass the required resolution. A permanent member of the Security Council cannot stop the judicial process by acting unilaterally. In changing the relationship between the Security Council and justice in this way, the Rome Statute created an expectation that egregious abuses of human rights will be investigated. The victims of human rights abuses, in other words, no longer have to wait for the Security Council to decide that their sense of injustice is a threat to international peace and security. The pursuit of justice, rather than a concern for international peace and security, is now the default position for international society. Of course, a prudential concern for peace and security may lead the Security Council to impose restraint on an overzealous prosecutor. However, international society can be confident that the decision to postpone justice is justified because that decision has been made to the satisfaction of at least nine Security Council members rather than a single permanent power. The decision to postpone justice is in this respect taken because of a common concern for international peace and security rather than the particular interests of a great power.

---

[2] This formulation draws on Carl Schmitt's famous line that the '[s]overeign is he who decides the exception' (2005: 5).

[3] Art. 15 of the Rome Statute enables the prosecutor to 'initiate investigations *proprio motu* on the basis of information on crimes within the jurisdiction of the Court'. The Rome Statute is available at: http://untreaty.un.org/cod/icc/statute/romefre.htm.

Understood in this way, the ICC casts new light on the meaning and significance of American exceptionalism. The USA has opposed the ICC primarily because it sees the potential politicisation of international criminal justice (Grossman 2002). It fears that an independent prosecutor would do the bidding of America's enemies and purposefully target US service members who are, the USA has further argued, particularly exposed given their worldwide commitments. The issue for the USA therefore is not so much the practice of international criminal justice. It agrees that human rights abusers should be prosecuted when states are unwilling or unable to do so. Rather the issue is who should decide when and where justice should be done. By wrapping this issue in a concern for international peace and security, the USA has argued that the prosecutor should only be employed when the Security Council identifies an injustice in exceptional terms, i.e. as a threat to international peace and security. Behind this rhetoric, however, the USA has essentially sought to protect the great powers' veto and their de facto sovereignty over international society. Far from being a defence against the politicisation of international criminal justice, therefore, the US attack on the Court is an attempt to defend an already highly politicised system, one that privileges the great powers and their interests (see Power 2000).

The USA has made this argument against the background of strong European support for the ICC. Contrary to what Kagan suggested, it was the Europeans rather than the Americans that took a revolutionary view of human rights at the 1998 Rome Conference. Where the Europeans proposed a referral system that could bypass the UN, the USA insisted that the international criminal process should start with a Security Council resolution. Both could agree on the need for a permanent court, but they disagreed on the question of the Court's independence. This particular dispute was further played out in the summers of 2002 and 2003 when the USA disputed the Court's jurisdiction over certain UN peacekeepers. By that time the USA had realised that it was unable to stop the Court from assuming jurisdiction but it insisted that its role as 'the world's policeman' justified exempting US service personnel from the Court's jurisdiction. By threatening to withdraw its peacekeepers from Bosnia, it in effect created the threat to international peace and security that it had long claimed would be the consequence of empowering an independent prosecutor. For the most part, the Europeans opposed the US demands, arguing that it would undermine the integrity of the Rome Statute. With British help, however, the USA brokered a compromise based on an imaginative reading of Article 16 of the Rome

Statute. In the Security Council it negotiated Resolutions 1422 (2002) and 1487 (2003), both of which granted the peacekeepers of non-party states exemptions from the Court's jurisdiction (Ralph 2007: 150–79). Here was a classic case of the USA acting as the Schmittian-inspired critics of liberalism argue. That is, because the liberal state deems its cause to be just, it takes exception to the law that it otherwise applies to others (particularly see Schmitt 2003; as an example of the critique inspired by Schmitt's work see Odysseos and Petito 2007). The hypocrisy of such a position would be inconceivable for the liberal that insists on equality before the law, but for Schmitt this principle stands little chance against the politically astute liberal who demands a legal structure that prioritises the interests of his friends over and above the rights of his enemies. This view was particularly prevalent within the Bush adminis-tration, in part because it was dominated by neoconservatives sympa-thetic to this Schmittian view of law and politics (Ralph 2009). From this perspective, European liberals were naïve to believe that by delegating their sovereignty to an international court they were promoting a respect for human rights. Liberalism would only be advanced if the balance of political power favoured liberal states and that would not happen if those states consented to be bound by international law and organisation.

The point here is that while the Europeans have supported a Court that promotes respect for human rights by circumventing the politics of the Security Council, the USA maintains that the Security Council is the most appropriate body to decide these matters because it is there that its interests can be guaranteed. Contrary to Kagan's revised thesis then, the diplomacy surrounding the ICC suggests the Europeans are the proper heirs to a liberal revolutionary tradition and that the Americans appar-ently favour the niceties of Westphalian diplomacy. This is illustrated further in the manner in which the US attacked the Court's jurisdiction as specified under Article 12. Under this article, the prosecutor can only investigate situations that involve an alleged crime on the territory of a state that is party to the Rome Treaty, or where the accused is the national of a state party. Any other situation requires authorisation from the Security Council in the form of a resolution, an action that is of course vulnerable to the Great Power veto. While this narrows the exposure to the Court of citizens of non-party states, it does not rule out the possibility that they could find themselves subject to an investi-gation by the independent prosecutor. Indeed, the reason the Bush administration was so concerned about its European peacekeeping force was the fact that Bosnia was a state party and American service personnel were therefore exposed to the Court's general jurisdiction. As noted, the USA used the Security Council to address its particular concerns in Bosnia, but this did not stop a broader attack on Article 12, which was seen to be undemocratic because it applied a law to peoples that had not given their consent by ratifying the Rome Treaty.[4] By opening up the question of the source of law and the community to which politicians are accountable, this point goes to the heart of the philosophical divide within the liberal world. For the Europeans, most notably the German government, Article 12 was a regrettable political concession to encourage ratification. The default position was a pre-existing universal jurisdiction based on a strong customary understanding that individuals should be punished for the crimes contained in the Statute regardless of their particular circumstance (for the German position and related commentary see Kaul 2002). For the Americans, however, the so-called 'consent regime' set out in Article 12 did not go far enough in protecting state sovereignty. Citizens of states that had withheld their consent from the Treaty of Rome could still be prosecuted by the ICC and that, in the eyes of the American government, made the Court illegitimate.

Darfur and the continuing crisis of legitimacy

The difficulty with the American 'sovereigntist' position is that it can never be fully accepted by a political culture that sees itself, rather than Europe, as the true vanguard of a liberal revolutionary tradition (Spiro 2000). Taken to its logical conclusion, sovereigntism underpins a realist argument that relegates human rights concerns in favour of orderly relations between sovereign states and this has never sat comfortably in the US foreign policy discourse. This is because there is a persistent belief that the USA can and should intervene on behalf of the liberal ideal, which it deems to be self-evidently universal. In terms of international criminal justice, this universalism informed the creation of the Nuremberg tribunal after the Second World War as well as the ad hoc tribunals after the cold war. Indeed, while the Bush administration opposed the creation of the ICC, it never tired of reminding its detractors that the USA had been at the forefront of efforts to bring dictators to justice. In this vein, the Bush administration continued to support the work of the UN tribunals even while it rejected their progeny.

[4] This form of attack was not limited to the Bush administration (see e.g. Scheffer 1999).

The tension between the sovereigntist's rejection of the ICC and the interventionist's embrace of international criminal justice was clearly on display during the debate on Darfur. When the international community demanded that action be taken on the crimes being committed there, the USA responded by proposing the criminal prosecution of those responsible. Yet given its opposition to the ICC, it proposed further ad hoc solutions, including the extension of the mandate and jurisdiction of the International Criminal Tribunal for Rwanda (Prosper 2005).[5] The Darfur situation was very different to Rwanda however. Having invested heavily in the creation of a permanent court to overcome the various shortcomings of the ad hoc system, the states that supported the ICC refused to entertain the American alternative. Ultimately, US opposition to using the ICC in this situation was defeated by a combination of domestic and international political pressure. On the one hand, Congress would not put up additional money to finance another ad hoc court, particularly when the Bush administration had attacked them for being inefficient; and on the other hand, state supporters of the ICC challenged the USA to veto a Security Council referral by tabling a resolution inviting the prosecutor to investigate the situation in Darfur. Denied the alternative and unwilling to be cast as the state that shielded the Sudanese killers from justice, the Bush administration abstained from the vote on what became Resolution 1593 (2005) (Ralph 2007: 173–6).

The significance of Resolution 1593 is that it demonstrates the vulnerability of an exceptionalist argument that insists on remaining outside of a legal regime it applies to others. This is illustrated with reference to the following question, which was put by an anonymous reporter to the US State Department spokesperson shortly after the resolution was passed. The reporter asked why:

> the US government believes that citizens of Sudan, which signed the Rome Statute but has not ratified it and, therefore, is not a state party to it, should be subject to its jurisdiction when the crux of the American argument is that US citizens should not be subject to its jurisdiction because the United States is not a state party to it. [US State Department Press Briefing, 1 April 2005]

---

[5] Ironically, the Sudanese would propose this in an attempt to stave off the indictment of President al-Bashir, see 'Sudan may accept hybrid courts to try Darfur war crimes', *Sudan Tribune*, 2 February 2009.

US officials could respond only by stating that this was (again) an 'extraordinary situation' and that because the UN Security Council had spoken, Sudan was obliged to co-operate with the ICC even though it was not a party to the Rome Treaty (Burns 2005).[6] Of course, an inconsistent application of the law such as this may be justifiable if there was indeed a competing moral imperative that justified the American exception to the new norm. The issue surrounding the Bosnian peace-keeping force as discussed above may be one such example. Likewise, it may be appropriate to postpone a judicial process if it threatens to undermine other normative goals such as the pursuit of peace; and indeed this was an important consideration in the Sudanese case. Yet it is hard not to conclude that the inconsistency exposed by the above quote was the consequence of a peculiarly American belief, one that suggests it can remain exempt from a legal regime that it happily applies to others. In the absence of these pressing security concerns, the US exception to the new norm seems unjustifiable.

Ironically, the US commitment to justice in Sudan is in danger of prompting the kind of judicial overreach that it was concerned to avoid when arguing against the creation of an independent prosecutor. The Court's prosecutor, Louis Moreno Ocampo, initially followed up Security Council Resolution 1593 by requesting the indictment of two relatively low-level protagonists, the Sudanese Minister for Humanitarian Affairs Ahmed Mohamed Haroun, and a leader of the Janjaweed militia, Ali Kushayb. On 27 April 2007, the pre-trial chamber granted Ocampo's request and issued arrest warrants for these two men, a move that was met with contempt in Khartoum. Indeed, the government led by Omar al-Bashir responded to the charges by appointing Musa Hilal as adviser to the Federal Affairs Minister Abdel Basit Sabderat. While Hilal had not been charged by the ICC with any crime, he was described as 'the poster child for Janjaweed atrocities' and the Court's indictment did in fact refer to the fact that Hilal had spoken alongside Haroun at a militia rally in 2003. To respond in such a way clearly indicated that the ICC would not be able to rely on the co-operation of the Sudanese government. Two years after the arrest warrants were issued Haroun and Kushayb remained at large.

For its part, the US government responded to Sudan's intransigence by encouraging the prosecutor to go further. Acting as the president of the UN Security Council during the summer of 2008 for instance, the US

---

[6] US State Department Press Briefing, Under Secretary of State for Political Affairs, Nicholas Burns, 1 April 2005.

government led the diplomatic efforts to force Sudan to meet its obligations. Responding to a prosecutor's report on the situation, the Council
unanimously passed a resolution urging all parties to the conflict in Darfur
to co-operate fully with the ICC. This was a marked change in US policy,
which prior to Resolution 1593 had consistently threatened to veto the
mere mention of the ICC in Security Council resolutions. This diplomatic
encouragement was reinforced with a promise to assist the investigations in
Sudan through the supply of US intelligence if it was requested by the
prosecutor's office (Boustany 2007; see also Bellinger 2008a). The summer
of 2008 provided another reason for a push on the Darfur issue, one that
was separate from the US position. The People's Republic of China, which
had been a supporter of the al-Bashir's regime in part because of the oil and
arms deals between the two countries, desperately wished to avoid the
attention of the human rights lobby in the lead up to the Beijing Olympics.

   Against this background, Ocampo took what has been by far the most
controversial step in the Court's short history. In July 2008, he requested
that the Court issue an arrest warrant for the Sudanese head of state,
Omar al-Bashir, on charges of war crimes, crimes against humanity
and genocide. As the news broke of the prosecutor's intention, seven
soldiers in the joint UN-African Union peacekeeping mission in Darfur
(UNAMID) were killed in an ambush by Sudanese militia. This served as
an obvious illustration of why such a move was so controversial and
potentially so dangerous. UNAMID had been set up a year earlier to
support of the early and effective implementation of the Darfur Peace
Agreement, which had been signed under African Union auspices on
5 May 2006.[7] The fear was that these efforts to encourage peace would
be harmed by a deepening of the prosecutor's involvement; and while
the UN Secretary General insisted that a Sudanese peace without justice
would be unsustainable, humanitarian agencies operating under the UN
umbrella expressed deep concern that any indictment would make their
task impossible.[8] In July 2008, of course, the prosecutor had only issued

----

[7] UN Security Council had passed Res. 1769. On the African Union's call for the ICC to
   defer the indictment see 'African Union President warns of power vacuum and anarchy in
   Sudan', *Sudan Tribune*, 15 July 2008; see also Colum Lynch (2008). In a case that is often
   overlooked, the prosecutor has requested the arrest of rebel commanders who surrounded
   the Haskanita camp in September 2007 killing 12 African Union peacekeepers (see Office
   of the Prosecutor 2008).
[8] For the 'pro-justice' argument, see John Norris, David Sullivan and John Prendergast
   (2008); for the 'pro-order' argument see Julian Borger (2008) and Jonathan Steele (2008).
   The latter position included influential voices from the American aid and evangelical
   community; see respectively Andrew Natsios (2008) and Franklin Graham (2009).

a request for an indictment and states could postpone having to address the perceived dilemma between order and justice, while the pre-trial chamber considered that request. In March 2009, however, the matter became more pressing when the Court did issue an arrest warrant for al-Bashir. It dropped the initial charge of genocide but the indictment included five counts of crimes against humanity and two counts of war crimes. The implications of such a move had not fully played out at the time of writing, but the structure of the dilemma was familiar with humanitarian agencies complaining that Ocampo had exercised his discretion irresponsibly. There was an obvious concern that he had in fact overreached his mandate in a way that harmed both order and justice (de Waal 2009).

As noted, the states on the Security Council had been conscious of this particular dilemma since the summer of 2008 when Ocampo made his initial request for the indictment. During that time, the US relationship with the Court took another twist. Given the obvious concerns that Ocampo's actions were undermining the pursuit of peace in Sudan, Russia and China joined the African Union, the Arab League, the Non-Aligned Movement and Organisation of Islamic Conference in calls for a UN Security Council deferral.[9] This proposal also found support among other high-profile independent commentators who sought to chart a middle course between the seemingly extreme positions of order and justice.[10] Yet despite the concerns about the prosecutor's action, and despite hints from the British and the French that they too favoured an Article 16 resolution if Sudan took steps to co-operate, the Americans seemed happy to let the prosecutor loose, making it clear that they would veto any Security Council deferral.[11] This is not only ironic; it is potentially damaging for the Court in two ways. First, it has been argued that the prosecutor's decision to indict al-Bashir was calculated to appeal to those influential American audiences that had long opposed the Sudanese leader. Such an indictment would, it was argued, lead to a change of attitude in America and clear the way for the USA becoming a

---

[9] 'Deferral of indictment for Sudan president not on UNSC August agenda', *Sudan Tribune*, 5 August 2008.

[10] This was the position adopted by Gareth Evans, President of the International Crisis Group (see Evans 2008).

[11] 'Russia signals support to Darfur ICC deferral, UK toughens stance', *Sudan Tribune*, 14 February 2009. See also Alex Duval Smith (2008), John Ward and Betsy Pisik (2009) and Colum Lynch (2009).

state party (Gedda 2008; and on the possibility that such a strategy is working see Abromowitz and Lynch 2008). If this is the case and if the prosecutor's pursuit of al-Bashir is indeed a threat to peace and security then it is possible that by remaining outside the Court's jurisdiction the USA is in fact encouraging the kind of irresponsible prosecutorial behaviour that it initially warned against. Secondly, there may indeed be a strong case for indicting al-Bashir and the US encouragement of the prosecutor may turn out to be the correct judgement on this specific issue. Indeed, this conclusion was suggested by reports that the indictment was leading to political isolation of al-Bashir rather than a backlash against the peace and the humanitarian agencies (Glassborow 2009). Yet the irony of this situation is that it compounds the unease with America's general position on the ICC and exacerbates the impression that the Court is a tool of Western imperialism.[12] For while the USA supported the prosecutor's pursuit of al-Bashir it at no point considered reversing its policy of exempting US citizens from the Court's jurisdiction. The implication here is that if the USA is to encourage the prosecutor while avoiding the charge of liberal imperialism it must accept that it is not above the law that it readily applies to others.

Wilson, Madison and why there is nothing more American than the ICC

The US decision to abstain on the Darfur referral did therefore mark a turning point, but its ICC policy post-2005 is still problematic. Advocates of the Court may welcome the Bush administration's decision to support the prosecutor's pursuit of justice in Darfur, but they cannot accept a situation where the USA encourages the ad hoc application of a legal regime while simultaneously exempting itself from that which it applies to others. This does immense damage to the Court's credibility; it betrays the original vision, which was to overcome the charge of 'selective justice' by setting up an independent court; and it lends credence to the otherwise groundless accusations of Western liberal imperialism. Supporters of the Court, in other words, must continue to campaign for a fundamental shift in the American position, one that ultimately signals complete acceptance of the Court by becoming a state party. This will not happen with the inauguration of a new president

[12] One might expect such an argument from the accused (see Tisdall 2008), but it is by no means limited to these quarters (see de Waal 2009).

because such a step will of course require the consent of Congress; and while the Obama administration has spoken positively about co-operating with the Court and taken steps to repeal anti-ICC legislation, it has not made a commitment to sign the Rome Treaty let alone campaign for its ratification.[13]

Even if the new administration had committed itself to such a policy, it is clear that the arguments for opposing the Court are deeply embedded in an American political culture that celebrates the kind of exceptionalism described above. The argument that the US armed forces are liberalism's last best hope and should not be held back by international law, resonated strongly with neoconservatives who rode a wave of unreflective patriotism after 9–11. That may have diminished in recent years, but the claim that the US Constitution is liberalism's last best hope, and that Congress should not destroy the power of that example by delegating sovereignty to an international court, will continue to exercise a powerful influence on the debate long after Bush. It is apparent moreover that the contemporary debate on the ICC does not yet address this concern. It tends to operate only at the level of legal technicality, and while the issues at this level are important, they are not politically decisive.[14] If these issues can be resolved to the satisfaction of the Obama administration, it is still likely that Congress will draw on the exceptionalist narrative to reject the Rome Treaty just as it did when it rejected President Wilson's League of Nations. For this reason, intellectuals need to tackle head-on the Kagan-inspired perception that international organisations are somehow un-American. Intellectuals need, that is, to construct an alternative cultural narrative, one which suggests that there is nothing more American than the International Criminal Court. The

---

[13] On 12 March 2009, President Obama signed into law the annual Omnibus Appropriations Bill without including the Nethercutt Amendment, which had previously cut Economic Support Funding (ESF) to nations unwilling to enter into a so-called Art. 98 agreement with the United States. By signing these agreements states promised not to deliver US nationals to the Court. Although they did not give individuals immunity from prosecution pro-Court NGOs dubbed them Bilateral Immunity Agreements, see www.amicc.org/usinfo/administration_policy_BIAs.html.

[14] Perhaps the most notable of these is the question of how the 2010 review conference will define the act of aggression. On the outstanding issues at the end of the Bush administration, see John Bellinger III, Legal Adviser to the US Secretary of State (2008a; 2008b). For a discussion of the legal issues, including advocacy of an 'inter-agency policy review to re-examine, in light of the Court's further performance and the outcome of the 2010 Review Conference, whether the United States should become a party to the Rome Statute', see *ASIL Task Force Recommendations*, www.asil.org/pdfs/pressreleases/pr090202.pdf.

purpose of this concluding section is to suggest that the resources for that new narrative are not too far removed from the Obama administration and that they may indeed stand a good chance of informing a radical shift in policy.

This optimism is in part created by the manner in which liberals have been reflecting on the Iraq War and America's relationship to international society since then. This might seem counterintuitive because for some, like Tony Smith, the Iraq War was in many ways the liberal internationalist's war (Smith 2009). It sought, amongst other things, to overthrow a tyrannical regime, bring its leadership to justice for crimes against humanity and install a liberal democratic regime that would act as a beacon of reform in the region. It sought all this while ignoring the restraints imposed by the UN and the ICC. In this respect, there was for Smith little difference between a neoconservative policy, which is often blamed for the Iraq debacle, and a Wilsonian or 'neoliberal' policy of democracy promotion. Centre-left Democrats who embraced the liberal democratic peace theories and the *Responsibility to Protect* agenda of the 1990s were at the very least part responsible for the war. The policy implication of Smith's analysis is that the USA should drop Wilsonianism all together and should instead listen more attentively to realist internationalists like Kissinger, Scowcroft and Bush Snr. The security of a Westphalian interstate order should be prioritised over the pursuit of democracy and justice (Scowcroft 2002). Yet in response to this criticism, influential thinker-practitioners like Anne-Marie Slaughter have felt the need to defend Wilsonian liberal internationalism and, in the process, they have defined it in a way that is supportive of international law and organisation. Thus, for Slaughter (2009), a policy that ignores the 'common counsel' of the states assembled at the United Nations is not worthy of the name Wilsonianism. Indeed, had the USA and the UK listened to such counsel they would have formulated a different policy on Iraq, one that was not only legitimate but one that was ultimately better for avoiding a disastrous war.

Slaughter's defence of UN multilateralism as an essential feature of the Wilsonian tradition is significant in part because she is now at the centre of the new administration's policy-making team. Yet a key point of this chapter has been the argument that the UN Security Council is often a place where the great powers can exercise their sovereignty over the pursuit of justice. How then might Slaughter's call for a renewed emphasis on multilateralism help change US policy on the ICC? The answer to this lies in the fact that Slaughter sees a more radical implication in the Wilsonian emphasis on 'common counsel'. It requires internationalists to respond to the demands for just change in the international legal architecture and it requires nationalists to drop the insistence that they are not necessarily bound by the outcome of institutionalised multilateral dialogue. Thus, Wilsonians can and should embrace the new ideas that seek to bypass the UN Security Council but they must do so only if the new proposals have been tested in and accepted by alternative multilateral settings.

On these grounds, Wilsonians should have no qualms about support- ing the ICC even if President Wilson himself was nervous about the practice of international criminal justice. As noted above, the ICC is the product of wide-ranging multilateral processes; and if, as Slaughter insists, the USA should accept the outcome of such processes, even if its negotiating position is not fully adopted, then the USA should accept the ICC. Slaughter also insists that a proper reading of the Wilsonian tradition should recall its Madisonian and Enlightenment roots, which of course was suspicious of democracy and the leaders it promoted. In this respect, Wilsonians cannot support the American exception to the ICC because even though its leaders are democratically elected Wilsonians recognise the Kantian refrain that democracies do not always act democratically. Just as presidents need to be checked by parliaments and courts, so the Great Powers, even if they are democratic, need to be checked in similar ways. Wilsonians should insist, therefore, that dem- ocracies, including the United States, 'do not get some kind of free pass or presumption that they are complying with their international legal obligations' (Slaughter 2009: 104). Wilsonians should insist on this because they are primarily good republicans who realise the corruptibil- ity of even the most virtuous (and most American) of politicians. 'That is a premise not of neoliberalism or neoconservatism, but of the Enlightenment' (*ibid.*); and if the USA is to retrieve the beacon of the Enlightenment from the Europeans then it must change its policy.

Slaughter's recollection of the Madisonian roots of Wilsonianism is echoed by Daniel Deudney's (2007) recent account of republican secur- ity theory, an account that can also be used to construct a new narrative on America's relationship to the ICC. Deudney reminds us that American Republicans like Madison were acutely aware of the link between liberty and international (or interstate) law. The founders feared that if the newly independent states of North America did not delegate sovereignty to an interstate organisation charged with provid- ing for the common defence, then those states would be forced to adopt self-help security policies, policies that would threaten liberty by concentrating military power in the hands of the state's executive. The United States itself, Deudney argues, is an international organisation based on the principle of delegated state sovereignty and Wilsonianism in fact the true heir to this founding principle. Thus when Wilson claimed international organisation would make the world safe for democracy, he was recalling the theory that informed Madison and others when they wrote *The Federalist Papers*. Just as the original states had to delegate sovereignty to protect liberty, so in an age of security interdependence the United States had to delegate its sovereignty to achieve the goals of the enlightenment (*ibid.*: 185–9). Deudney does not directly address the question of the ICC, but the implication is clear. From the republican perspective that emerged out of the Enlighten- ment and did so much to inform the US Constitution, state sovereignty is not and should not be an obstacle to the creation of institutions that advance liberty and justice.

Conclusion

US governments have justified their opposition to the ICC by claiming that as the vanguard of a liberal world order the USA provides an example for the rest of the world to follow. To delegate sovereignty to the ICC not only threatens US democracy it attacks the very idea of the social contract and cannot possibly therefore be part of Enlightenment's political project. Yet while claiming this exception, US governments have equally claimed the right to intervene in the affairs of other sovereign states. This unilateral approach to 'democracy promotion' is in many respects echoed in the ad hoc approach to international criminal justice and indeed in the willingness to use the ICC when it suits America's interests. Advocates of the Court might welcome this flexibility in the American position, but they should not celebrate it. The judicial inter- vention in Sudan for example can be justified on its own terms, but that justification is weakened by the charge of imperialism that inevit- ably follows when the intervener elevates itself and its political allies above the law.

Ideas do not easily influence policy and it will be difficult for the arguments of Slaughter and Deudney to convince an administration that will be looking for political allies on other issues such as financial reform, healthcare and Afghanistan. Without taking their arguments on board, however, the USA will continue to be vulnerable to the charge of imperialism and it will continue to face a legitimacy crisis. It will inevitably find itself caught between a realist position keen to protect US sovereignty and the liberal position that is keen to act on universal principles. The compromise between these two positions has so far given way to an imperialist position that seeks to act on universal principles while protecting US sovereignty. What the arguments articulated by Slaughter and Deudney offer is a reading of Wilsonianism and a narrative on American identity which suggests that the delegation of sovereignty to the ICC is neither a threat to the United States nor to its role as the vanguard of the Enlightenment. Compromising US sovereignty is a sacrifice, but for these authors it is one that is consistent with America's republican spirit as articulated by the American founders and their Wilsonian heirs. In light of the alternative offered by the Bush administration, moreover, an alternative that involved a costly war in the name of regime change, criminal justice and democracy promotion, supporting the ICC is relatively small sacrifice to make.

References

Abromowitz, M. and Lynch, C. (2008) 'Darfur killings soften Bush's opposition to International Court', *Washington Post*, 12 October.

Bellinger, J. (2008a) Remarks to the DePaul University College of Law in Chicago, 25 April 2008, www.cfr.org.

(2008b) Remarks at the Fletcher School of Law and Diplomacy, 14 November 2008, www.cfr.org.

Borger, J. (2008) 'Bashir refuses to hand over suspects to ICC. Aid workers prepare for possible state backlash', *The Guardian*, 11 July.

Boustany, N. (2007) 'Official floats possibility of assistance to Hague Court', *Washington Post*, 12 June.

Burns, N. (2005) US State Department Briefing by Under Secretary of State for Political Affairs, 1 April.

Deudney, D. (2007) *Bounding Power: Republican Security Theory from the Polis to the Global Village*, Princeton: Princeton University Press.

Duval Smith, A. (2008) 'Britain blocks prosecution of Sudan's ruler', *The Guardian*, 14 September.

Evans, G. (2008) *New ICC Prosecution: Opportunities and Risks for Peace in Sudan*, International Crisis Group Press Release, 14 July 2008.

Gedda, B. (2008) 'Quo vadis, ICC?', www.ssrc.org/blogs/darfur/2008/07/04/quo-vadis-icc/.

Glassborow, K. (2009) 'Bashir "becoming burden" for Khartoum', *Institute for War and Peace Reporting*, 13 March 2009, www.iwpr.net/EN-acr-f-350918.

Graham, F. (2009) 'Put peace before justice', *New York Times*, 3 February.

Grossman, M. (2002) 'American foreign policy and the International Criminal Court', *Remarks to the Center for Strategic and International Studies*, Washington DC, 6 May 2002, www.state.gov/p/9949.htm.

Kagan, R. (2003) *Paradise and Power: American and European in the New World Order*, London: Atlantic Books.

(2004) 'America's crisis of legitimacy', *Foreign Affairs*, 83(2), 65–87.

Kaul, H.-P. (2002) 'Preconditions to the exercise of jurisdiction' in Antonio Cassese, Paola Gaeta and John R. W. D. Jones (eds.), *The Rome Statute of the International Criminal Court: A Commentary*, Oxford: Oxford University Press, pp. 583–616.

Kissinger, H. (2001) 'The pitfalls of universal jurisdiction', *Foreign Affairs*, 80, 86–96.

Lynch, C. (2008) 'Indictment of Sudanese leader seen as threat to peacekeepers', *The Washington Post*, 20 July.

(2009) 'Sudan retains clout while charges loom', *Washington Post*, 9 February.

Natsios, A. (2008) 'A disaster in the making', www.ssrc.org/blogs/darfur/2008/07/12/a-disaster-in-the-making/.

Norris, J., Sullivan, D. and Prendergast, J. (2008) *The Merits of Justice*, Enough Project, Strategy Paper 35, www.enoughproject.org/files/press_kit/action/country_analysis_specific_reports_and_papers/Sudan/The-Merits-of-Justice-7.08.pdf.

Odysseos, L. and Petito, F. (2007) (eds.) *The International Political Thought of Carl Schmitt: Terror, Liberal War and the Crisis of Global Order*, London: Routledge.

Office of the Prosecutor (2008) 'Attacks on peacekeepers will not be tolerated', Press Release, 20 November 2008, www.icc-cpi.int.

Power, S. (2000) 'The United States and genocide law' in S. B. Sewall and C. Kaysen (eds.), *The United States and the International Criminal Court*, London: Rowman and Littlefield, pp. 165–78.

Prosper, P.-R. (2005) 'Darfur, war crimes, the ICC and the quest for justice', *Brookings Briefing*, The Brookings Institute, 25 February 2005, www.brookings.edu/comm/events/20050225.pdf.

Ralph, J. (2007) *Defending the Society of States: Why America Opposes the International Criminal Court and its Vision of World Society*, Oxford: Oxford University Press.

(2009) 'The laws of war and the state of the American exception', *Review of International Studies*, 35(3), 631–49.

Scheffer, D. J. (1999) 'International Criminal Court: the challenge of jurisdiction', Address to Annual Meeting of the American Society of International Law, Washington DC, 26 March 1999, www.state.gov/documents/organization/6552.doc

Schmitt, C. (2003) *The Nomos of the Earth in the International Law of the Jus Publicum Europaeum (translated and annotated by G. L. Ulmen)*, New York: Telos Press Publishing.

(2005) *Political Theology: Four Chapters on the Concept of Sovereignty*, Chicago: University of Chicago Press.

Scowcroft, B. (2002) 'Don't attack Iraq', *Wall Street Journal*, 15 August.

Slaughter, A.-M. (2009) 'Wilsonianism in the twenty-first century' in G. J. Ikenberry, T. J. Knock, A.-M. Slaughter and T. Smith, *The Crisis of American Foreign Policy: Wilsonianism in the Twenty-first Century*, Princeton: Princeton University Press, pp. 89–117.

Smith, T. (2009) 'Wilsonianism after Iraq: The end of liberal internationalism?' in G. J. Ikenberry, T. J. Knock, A.-M. Slaughter and T. Smith, *The Crisis of American Foreign Policy. Wilsonianism in the Twenty-first Century*, Princeton: Princeton University Press, pp. 53–88.

Spiro, P. J. (2000) 'The new sovereigntists: American exceptionalism and its false prophets', *Foreign Affairs*, 79, 9–15.

Steele, J. (2008) 'The ICC should not indict Omar al-Bashir', *The Guardian*, 11 July.

Tisdall, S. (2008) 'Man blamed for Darfur says I am at peace with myself', *The Guardian*, 4 December.

Waal, A. de (2009) 'The ICC, Sudan and the crisis of human rights', *African Arguments*, March, http://africanarguments.org/.

Ward, J. and Pisik, B. (2009) 'Obama backs indictment of Sudan leader', *Washington Times*, 5 February.

4

Universal crimes, universal justice? The legitimacy of the international response to genocide, crimes against humanity and war crimes

CHRISJE BRANTS

Introduction

The title of this chapter may appear somewhat ambiguous at first sight, as it implies both an empirical and a normative question. Do universal crimes lead to universal justice? And should universal crimes lead to universal justice? However, as with all crime, the very nature of the phenomenon and any intellectual inquiry into it are normative matters and the questions as to whether we either have, or should have, universal justice cannot be regarded as separate issues. Moreover, the answer depends on many things, but most importantly on who is asking the question, who is doing the answering, and what they define as crime and as justice. In international legal-political terms, universal justice and universal crimes are equated with the definitions found in the international instruments providing procedures for judging and sanctions against specifically delineated 'core international crimes': genocide, crimes against humanity and war crimes. Logically, universal justice then becomes the reaction of the international community through ad hoc tribunals or the International Criminal Court (ICC), or the incorporation of such international definitions into national criminal law and procedure according to the universality principle of jurisdiction.

However, the fact that we have a body of international criminal law that can be institutionally upheld does not of itself mean that we have universal justice. Neither should the legitimacy of the international response be taken for granted. For, to be legitimate, any form of justice must deliver in many senses of the word – and universal justice must deliver universally. There are at least three problematic issues here. In many, if not most, respects, they are the same as those faced by any

86

national system of criminal justice, although the grave (and mass) nature of both the crimes and the breakdown of social relations in which they take place magnify their urgency.

First, it is the (international) reaction that makes such actions criminal, not the behaviour itself. Repugnant as we may find them, universal crimes are an international social and political construction that is, most especially at the time and in the place of their commission, contested (Drumbl 2005a: 567). Secondly, not only what we define as crimes, but also what we define as justice is a matter of social construction within a specific (legal) culture, so that the term 'universal' implies if not an existing universal legal culture then at least its emergence, in which what is done and seen to be done in the international reaction to genocide, crimes against humanity and war crimes is experienced as justice by all concerned. That too is contested (Drumbl 2005b; Heller 2008; Sloane 2008). Thirdly, if both the crimes and the international reaction to them are not universally accepted as uncontested social constructions, what does this say about the legitimacy of universal justice and therefore its capacity to deliver universally? What are its goals and are they attainable? What, and whose, needs does it address? What expectations does it raise, for whom, and can they be met? Big questions, to which there are no easy answers.

It is perhaps something of a heresy – certainly among many international criminal lawyers for whom these matters are often an article of faith, but also in wider social, political and academic circles in Europe and beyond – to question the legitimacy of universal justice. Indeed, it often appears to be a self-evident given in a 'world legal order': 'of course' universal crimes should lead to universal justice. But that is precisely the point. Neither universal justice nor its legitimacy is self-evident (no system of justice is), so that we must ask how it is experienced and whether it is universally accepted as justice (a variation perhaps on the old question: 'whose law, what order?'). In this chapter I want to raise some of the preliminary issues that must be addressed before we can even begin to formulate an answer to the question 'universal crimes, universal justice?' I do not use the term universal, but prefer the more neutral *international* crimes and justice,[1] for it remains to be seen

---

[1] International crimes may well, and indeed usually do, take place locally, but become international for the simple reason that they fall under the international jurisdiction of the ICC, or under the jurisdiction of national states on the basis of the universality principle – a neutral, procedural definition that also distinguishes from transnational crimes, involving by definition more than one state and the crossing of borders.

whether the ideological connotations of the adjective 'universal' are
appropriate, and in what sense.

My first concern is with a number of empirical aspects of the legal,
social and political construction of international crime and international
criminals: the principle of subsidiarity that determines the secondary
jurisdiction of the ICC, the exclusion of corporations from, and the
definition of crimes under that jurisdiction, the related principle of
individual guilt and the collective nature of crimes against humanity
and war crimes, all of which render the construction of 'universal'
criminality and justice ambiguous, selective and contested. I then turn
to the normative matter of the goals and aspirations of international
criminal justice. One of its most important manifest aims is the establishment of the rule of law in societies where it has been swept away by
dictatorship, conflict and atrocity. International justice is therefore transitional justice, but with latent political undertones (the legitimisation of
change, nation-building and the transition to democracy). There are also
inherent problems in what is required for attaining that goal: ensuring a
fair trial and developing a coherent collective memory as a means of
coming to terms with a divisive and painful past (history-telling by
means of the criminal law). At the same time, international criminal
law also aspires to deterrence, retribution and justice for victims. These
goals and aspirations, it is argued, are contradictory and in practice not
only open to abuse for political ends but unrealistic and an overstate-
ment of what 'universal' justice is, or rather, should aspire to be.

International crimes, international criminals

Criminological interest in international justice is relatively recent and
has now been incorporated into the emerging paradigm of global criminology (Roberts and McMillan 2003; Friedrichs 2006; van Swaaningen
forthcoming). Although criminologists are rarely – at least manifestly –
concerned with normative questions of legitimacy, they do question
something that is often a matter of course to legal scholars: the legal
definition of crime. If we apply to international crimes the generally
accepted but somewhat commonplace criminological insight that all
criminality is a matter of social, political and legal construction within
cultural parameters, what then are the implications for the legitimacy of
international justice? Three distinct, though related, issues may be distinguished: first, the (non-)definition under international law of crimes
and – potential – criminals; secondly, their (non-)prosecution in practice;

and thirdly, the (non-)recognition as deviance of international crimes within the societies and at the time of their commission.

The whole venture of international justice is accompanied by declarations of ideological good intent. Consider, for example, the preamble to the Statute of the ICC:

> Mindful that during this century millions of children, women and men have been victims of unimaginable atrocities that deeply shock the conscience of humanity, Recognizing that such grave crimes threaten the peace, security and well-being of the world, Affirming that the most serious crimes of concern to the international community as a whole must not go unpunished and that their effective prosecution must be ensured by taking measures at the national level and by enhancing international cooperation, Determined to put an end to impunity for the perpetrators of these crimes and thus to contribute to the prevention of such crimes . . .[2]

However, the international crimes that come under the jurisdiction of the Court are but a small selection of what threatens the peace, security and well-being of the world. Leaving aside the eventual withdrawal of the United States that somewhat undermined the ideological clout of the enterprise, the ICC or Rome Statute – that contains, for the time being, the definitive legal definition of international crimes – is, inevitably, the result of political and legal compromise (Cassese 1999; Saland 1999; Clapham 2000). Not only were parties, envisaging situations in which they themselves might wish to engage in armed conflict or could become embroiled in wars not authorised by the United Nations, unable to agree to include the (international) crime of aggression that figured so prominently at Nuremberg, they also disagreed on a number of doctrinal issues, including whether the Court should have jurisdiction over corporate actors. It does not.[3] This also therefore immediately excludes the state as a possible perpetrator of international crimes, a direct consequence of the leading principle in international law: the sovereignty of states (van der Wilt 2005: 16–20; Edlin 2006). That same principle means that, if states cannot sit in judgment of each other, then neither can the ICC take over criminal prosecutions for international crimes if that already lies within the state's own jurisdiction.

---

[2] Full text available at www.icc-cpi.int.   [3] See Art. 27 ICC Statute.

The principle of subsidiarity

The ICC Statute solves the problem of the sovereignty that all states claim in criminal matters by means of the so-called principle of complementarity or subsidiarity that governs the jurisdiction of the court. The ICC has second-ary – complementary – jurisdiction only; namely, if states are unwilling or unable to prosecute the crimes themselves in a fair and impartial manner.[4] This has important implications for the social construction of international criminality, for it produces selectivity in prosecution and affects the ideo-logical message disseminated in the practice of international criminal justice; de facto, the principle of subsidiarity determines who international criminals are and, more importantly, who they are not.

The states where armed conflict or dictatorship go hand in hand with atrocities – the international crimes with which international criminal justice is concerned – are the pariahs of the international community, the disintegrating states, failed states or rogue states unable or unwilling to prosecute the perpetrators themselves. Good states, nice democratic members of the international community, will not see their citizens and soldiers before the international court:

> In any event, some of the things that nice states do in the course of armed conflict are not crimes under the ICC Statute: just as the Nazi bombing of Rotterdam and Coventry counted as war crimes and the allied destruc-tion of Dresden did not, the use of poison gas and dum-dum bullets constitutes a war crime under article 8 of the Statute, while deploying anti-personnel mines and the use of atomic weapons are legitimate. [Brants 2007b: 326]

But leaving aside selectivity in the legal definition of such crimes, even if good states prosecute breaches of international humanitarian law under their own national statutes, the message about the perpetrators is a very different one from that implied by prosecution before the ICC.

It is true that the process of incorporating international criminal law into national legislation around the world is under way, while the United States, which did not ratify the Rome Convention, nevertheless has national legislation concerning crimes against humanity and war crimes (Ramasastry and Thompson 2006). It is also true that some national prosecutions have taken place, notably for crimes committed in Iraq. These, however, are construed as incidents committed by rogue individ-uals, while (complicity or involvement in) organised torture, the

---

[4] Art. 17 ICC Statute. I shall return to the problematic meaning of 'fair and impartial' later, being at present concerned only with the effect of the principle of subsidiarity.

systematic destruction of a country or killing of its inhabitants are not defined as criminal but as regrettable necessities or accidents of war. To name but a few examples: Guantánamo Bay and secret renditions (by the Americans), the bombing of Lebanon and Gaza and the destruction of their infrastructure (by the Israelis) and assistance in separating women from men as a prelude to mass murder – later labelled genocide by the International Criminal Tribunal for the former Yugoslavia (ICTY) – in Sbrenica (by the Dutch).

Corporate criminality

While the principle of subsidiarity produces selectivity de facto, corporate activity is explicitly excluded from the jurisdiction of the ICC and therefore *de lege* from the definition of international crime. Although there is much empirical evidence linking the activities of (legitimate) corporations to the direct or indirect financing of governments and groups engaged in internal armed conflict during which international crimes are committed (Stephens 2002; Clough 2005; Jacobson 2005),[5] corporate involvement falls outside the ambit of their definition. Partly for that reason, whether and when the activities that business enterprises engage in (such as trade in arms, chemicals and natural resources like diamonds and oil) constitute complicity in international crimes (even if in violation of UN Security Council embargoes and therefore illegal) is a neglected topic both at the political level and in academic research. Some academics and many NGOs advocate widening the concept of international crime to include violations of, for example, human rights and/ or environmental norms (Global Witness 2002; Clough 2005; Dufresne 2004). However, they inevitably come to the conclusion that:

> international law offers little systematic guidance for the qualification of harmful business behaviour as a violation of international law, let alone as an international crime. More to the point, current international law does not contain a clear overall requirement for States to regulate the business activities of corporations when they are operating abroad and committing acts that do not reach the threshold of the three 'core' international crimes. [Huisman 2008: 184]

Moreover, although the ICC Statute does allow for the prosecution of persons operating within a 'corporation' (loosely defined), the concepts

---

[5] See also *Estate of Marcos*, 25 F 3d at 1475–6; *Kadic*, 70 F 3d at 246; *Abebe-Jira*, 72 F 3d 844; *Doe I* v. *Unocal*, 963 F Supp 880, 891–2 (CD Cal 1997).

of complicity, superior responsibility and joint criminal enterprise do not cover the complexities of corporate crime, and certainly not if the corporations are legitimate and without 'criminal' intent, but engaging in activities for the simple reason that it is profitable to do so. This is notwithstanding the fact that many international crimes would be impossible without their contribution, so that they must be regarded as an often essential element of the political and economic context in which those crimes take place. In individualising the concepts of guilt and intent, international criminal law can be said to neutralise the collective element of the crimes that come under international jurisdiction, an issue that not only arises in the corporate context but in all situations of mass atrocity.

Collective crime

It is technically possible that war crimes and even the crime of genocide could be committed by one single individual, even though in their legal definition international crimes are conceived of as collective and systemic events (van Sliedregt 2003: 5; Ohlin 2006: 73): genocide only exists if there is intent to destroy, in whole or in part, a national, ethnic, racial or religious group; crimes such as rape and murder do not become crimes against humanity unless they are part of a widespread or systematic attack on a civilian population; war crimes are always part of a plan or policy.[6] However, only individuals may be prosecuted.

Yet, perpetrators of international crimes commit mass violence as part, and on behalf of, a group, and in the name of ideological values and opinions that are experienced and accepted as legitimate and imperative within the group culture. Some fulfil a leading role, while others are the 'foot soldiers' who translate ideas into collective (criminal) action. Then there are the bystanders, the majority, who simply watch and tacitly approve, or do not in any event distance themselves, let alone actively resist the acts of violence committed in their name. Equally, the victims form a collective, targeted because they too are part of a group, which is defined as hostile and dangerous. From this we may draw two conclusions. First, these crimes cannot be committed without the collective co-operation of the whole group. Secondly, an inversion of values, norms and definitions means that the criminality with which international justice is concerned, is not self-evidently regarded as deviance

---

[6] See Arts. 6–8 ICC Statute.

in the society where and at the time when it takes place, even if it deviates from international *jus cogens* and from basic notions of human decency (Drumbl 2005a: 567).

Now, 'normal' people do not usually resort to mass murder against the force of such basic notions. However, international crimes take place within a group culture of fear and violence that is rationalised and justified by neutralising techniques. The 'theory of neutralisation' – first formulated by David Matza and Gresham Sykes with regard to juvenile delinquency and later more generally applied – holds that internalised moral obligations lead those who commit illegal and/or immoral acts to employ neutralising techniques to silence the urge to follow those obligations. These include denial of responsibility, denial of injury, denial of the victim, condemnation of the condemners and appeals to higher loyalties (Sykes and Matza 1957; Matza 1964). In the context of mass violence, such group cultures can become the *culture of normality*, in which situations are redefined and individuals come to view their behaviour as legitimate.[7] In the opaque reality that is the result, violence is shorn of its criminal nature and victims of their real status (Galtung 1990: 292). A rationalising vocabulary of justification, in which the mass media play an important part, is an essential element of this process.

On the one hand, the perpetrators' appeal to higher loyalties (for example, the greater good) and need for a legitimate identity (for example as the saviours of their own group) may lead to the victims being systematically portrayed as a life-threatening plague of vermin that must be exterminated. In the Nazi press and cinema the Jews were portrayed as rats. More recently *Radio Télévision Libre des Milles Collines* in Rwanda consistently spoke of Tutsi as cockroaches.[8] On the other hand, more subtle but by no means less effective, we have the (official) vocabulary of moral neutrality that interacts with and reinforces neutralising techniques.[9] Bombing civilians becomes 'collateral damage', destroying villages and crops 'punishment' for or 'deterrence' of aid to the enemy. Likewise, removing prisoners to countries where they face certain torture and possibly death is called 'extraordinary rendition'; deporting groups of

---

[7] The concept *culture of normality* was originally used to explain corporate criminality (Box 1983; Coleman 1987). Brants (2007b: 314 ff) uses the analogy in reference to the context in which international crimes take place.

[8] See *Prosecutor v. Akayesu*, ITCR-96–4-T, T.Ch.1, 2 September 1998, § 148–9.

[9] See also Browning 1992: his research into the complicit role of 'ordinary men' in the mass murder of Jews on the eastern front as part of the 'Final Solution', demonstrates both 'moral neutrality speak' and individual and collective neutralising techniques.

the population – often the prelude to or part of genocide – does not have a neutral name but one with even positive connotations, namely 'ethnic *cleansing*' (Brants 2007b: 315–6).

Contrary to 'normal' social values, in this abnormal but normalised context, the perpetrators of mass violence are those who conform to dominant norms, while those who resist are deviant. As Drumbl notes:

> This broad participation [in atrocity], despite its catalytic role, is over-looked by the criminal law, thereby perpetuating a myth and a deception … In situations of mass violence, the assumptions of the domestic model are reversed: most people are implicated in the atrocity, and non-partici-pation – at least, open opposition – is the deviant act. [2007: 172]

Those who have expounded the collective nature of international crimes have also remarked that the principle of individual guilt that governs international criminal law, renders it singularly unsuited to deal with collective crimes in any way that is meaningful to the societies concerned – even that the prosecution of one or more individual leaders amounts to an amnesty for the rest (Drumbl 2005a: 570; cf. Fletcher 2005: 1077).

All of the above is not to say that the actions criminalised under international criminal law are not or should not be regarded as crimes or their perpetrators as criminals. However, when viewed from a crim-inological perspective, they are revealed as legal, political and social constructions that are ambiguous, selective and contested. When approached though the legal framework of goals and aspirations, similar issues emerge on the normative level of the legitimacy of international criminal justice.

The goals and aspirations of international justice

Given the limitations built into the ICC Statute in terms of jurisdiction and definitions, the goals and aspirations of international criminal justice expressed in official UN documents, by international courts and prosecutors, politicians and academics are 'as ambitious as they are contradictory' (Alvarez 2004: 321–2; see also Brants 2007a). They, and the pitfalls they imply for the legitimacy of the endeavour, are also interrelated. This section examines the problems and contradictions inherent in establishing the rule of law at an international and national level; ensuring a fair trial; history-telling by means of the criminal law; deterrence, retribution and justice for victims.

The rule of law, history-telling and fair trial

Most cases that come before the ICC emerge out of contexts that involve transitional justice, and are therefore closely associated with periods of political change in the aftermath of armed conflict. Given that ad hoc tribunals have been created precisely because the states concerned are unable or unwilling to address, through prosecution, the problems engendered by atrocities during past internal conflict, and in the light of what has already been said about the political and social construction of international crimes in relation to the principle of subsidiarity, it should come as no surprise that one of the most important manifest goals of international criminal justice, establishment of the rule of law, has latent political undertones: legitimisation of change, nation-building and the transition to democracy. Indeed, under conditions of persistent conflict governed by globally recognised and normalised 'laws of violence', international justice has become the 'new paradigm of the rule of law' (Teitel 2005: 839). Its pretensions transcend the political, even while they are shaped by political events.

As transitional justice, international criminal justice usually lacks the legitimacy deriving from a direct and uncontested link between the crime, the victims, the court and the sentence, for the simple reason that the society most affected will be in the throes of the aftermath of armed conflict and horrendous acts of violence, in a state of some chaos and confusion, and divided among and against itself about the root causes of its trouble and about how to define who are the perpetrators and who are the victors. And so, because the legitimacy of a 'just' response is necessarily contested in societies still split by past violence and injustice, the (re)writing of history with a view to establishing democracy and the rule of law becomes one of the primary legitimising aims of international criminal justice.

The ultimate aim of any criminal court's final judgment is to draw a line under past events and make the future possible; to bring closure. But, as ever in the context of international crimes the issues are magnified. The past itself is on trial in the person of its most salient figures, and with it everything that at least part of the nation believed in and is now shown to be morally wrong. In this sense, an international trial may well serve as a move towards democracy and the rule of law, but at the same time it will be 'aimed at promoting political transition, that is, to underscore the illegitimacy of the prior regime and to advance political transformation' (Teitel 2005: 846). So, however much the manifest aim may be to end the impunity of the perpetrators and so promote peace and justice, the history-telling involved in the truth-finding process that is a criminal trial will inevitably also foster normative regime change. It is but a small step from retroactive history-telling legitimising the trial of former leaders, to legitimising pro-active intervention with the humanitarian aim of stopping atrocities and making the trial possible in the first place. The legitimacy of (international) transitional justice then becomes 'irrevocably linked to the legitimacy of humanitarian intervention' (*ibid.*).

In the absence of international consensus on and authorisation for intervention, states may, for whatever reason, feel that justice should prevail over sovereignty and themselves create the conditions in which a trial becomes possible. History-telling in court then has the additional function of justifying both the trial itself and the illegality of its conception. Whether or not this is accepted is a matter of contested political morality, as demonstrated by the arguments for and against the trial of Adolf Eichmann that would never have occurred had Israel not taken the law into its own hands. More recently, there has been the case of Slobodan Milošević, to whose eventual removal and, finally, transferral to the tribunal in The Hague the intervention in Kosovo and bombing of Belgrade and Serbian positions by NATO on humanitarian grounds (the United Nations did not intervene until later) undoubtedly contributed significantly.

This is, however, a slippery slope indeed, the implication being that the end always justifies the means (consider the military action during which President Noriega of Panama was abducted to stand trial in the United States that bore the name *Operation Just Cause*). It is the point at which criminal trials may become the legitimisation for armed intervention with a view to regime change (as could be argued not only with regard to Milošević but also the demonisation, trial and execution of Saddam Hussein following the invasion of Iraq), and international criminal justice a rhetorical excuse for furthering the aims of powerful states. It is also the point at which international criminal law and genocide trials become the tools of realpolitik and risk losing their legitimacy altogether (Alvarez 1999), more likely to undermine the position of the successor regime and the likelihood of reconciliation rather than establish the rule of law.

Of course, whether or not international criminal justice has no other aim than furthering the peace and reconciliation process or is simply a sequel to armed intervention with a view to regime change, there is always something of victor's justice in the air. Does it matter? That rather depends on who the victors are, how legitimate their position and their aims, what sort of justice is meted out and, most importantly, whether that justice is accepted as such by the affected community. The great advantage of victor's justice is that it is unequivocal, expressing a relationship between law and the power from which it draws its authority. But it must also meet two criteria: its inception must not be tainted by illegitimate aims and power politics which undermine the acceptance of authority, and it must be recognisable as justice if it is to be more than simply 'punishment, revenge, spectacle' as some so-called realists maintain it always is (Mearsheimer, cited in Bass 2000: 5).

At the same time however, even if there is no reason to doubt the fundamental honesty of an international criminal trial, it is very difficult to conduct a fair trial that is accepted as justice by all concerned. Yet, only a trial that is scrupulously fair can serve to show what the rule of law can achieve, so that on its own terms the legitimacy of international criminal justice depends on illustrating that civilised values can and will prevail over barbarity. It does so partly by extending the aims of the truth-finding process beyond the question of the defendant's guilt to the much broader purpose, thus making sure that what happened goes down in the annals of history and is not forgotten. Indeed, according to Osiel (1997), the predominant purpose of such trials is to develop a coherent collective memory as a means of coming to terms with a divisive and painful history.

History-telling with a view to establishing collective memory cannot operate as a cohesive force unless the picture it paints is one with which survivors, perpetrators and victims are willing and able to identify. However, it is at worst open to abuse for political ends and is fragmentary and selective at best. In a criminal trial, victim testimony will be the primary vehicle of collective memory, so that victors and perpetrators will find themselves on opposite sides of a black and white divide that – in ignoring the problems of collaborators, bystanders and the interchangeability of perpetrator and victim in the social construction mass-atrocity – is neither a 'true' version of events nor a promising starting point for reconciliation and a tenable future. Findlay (this volume) argues for promoting the victim voice and with it the 'reconciliatory capacity' of criminal process. I have no argument with the idea of restorative justice in itself. Rather, my problem is with the notion that this can be accomplished within the context of an international criminal court without jeopardising other fundamental goals of (international) criminal process to such an extent that ensuring maximum participation for the victim as the main player and primary receptacle of 'memory' may well become self-defeating. As I shall argue later, the new paradigm of global justice and the current international legal culture – *bien ettoné de se trouver ensemble* – are simply asking too much of the criminal law and risk undermining its very legitimacy, among other things by laying too much emphasis on its reconciliatory purpose to the detriment of other goals.

Undue emphasis on (the victim's role in) history-telling is one of the factors that may compromise the fairness of a trial, although Osiel makes light of this risk by asserting that the purpose of the trial means that it is 'self-consciously designed to show the merits of liberal morality' and so should do so in 'ways consistent with its very requirements' (1997: 65). However, the way a case is constructed legally can influence historical and collective memory in several ways and, conversely, the collective memory that prosecutors seek to establish influences the legal construction of the case and the way the trial is conducted. Indeed, in some cases prosecutorial discretion allows the prosecutor to set the trial agenda to rereading the meaning of victims and justice and retelling history rather than to fair truth-finding by the court. The essence and purpose of the trial, of fairness even, then becomes the accommodation of the victim's, rather than the defendant's, day in court, which turns the truth-finding and due-process purpose of the adversarial trial on its head. (If the counter-argument were to be that it should indeed be the victim's day, then the question arises as to why we should have a trial at all and worry whether or not it is fair.)

Moreover, history-telling makes for long-drawn-out trials that then appear neither fair to the defendant nor just for the victim and risk undermining the very process of establishing a collective memory that is in any way a version of events acceptable to the community at large. Part of this was already apparent during the Eichmann trial in 1961, that failed to hold the attention of the media and the public as time went by and matters became repetitive or simply boring, with 'numbing' testimony too fragmented and contradictory to provide a solid basis for a conviction so that the court and the prosecutor had to fall back on documentary evidence (Cesarani 2005: 338). Compared to the length of current trials, however, the Eichmann case was a model of celerity, taking just over a year from the first court session to the execution of sentence and with witness testimony heard within fourteen weeks. After almost five years, the prosecutor had still not wound up the case against

Slobodan Milósoviç (who subsequently died), the main reason being that the indictment was framed so as to include the widest possible historical background and to give victims as broad a platform as they needed to bear witness to their suffering. Speaking to *The Times*, Steven Kay QC, British counsel at the Milósoviç trial, noted: '[The indictment] is like a whole chapter of a state's life, dissolution, collapse and rebirth. And to put that into the form of a trial – it's really impossible.'[10]

Another, related reason for over-long trials – evident in both the Eichmann and Milósoviç cases – is that fairness requires that the defendant be able to defend himself and be allowed at least as much time as the prosecutor to refute oral testimony and all other evidence. Adversarial debate, including witness testimony and cross-examination, is probably the ideal way to establish an acceptable version of the truth in criminal process, and the statutes of both the ad hoc tribunals and the ICC provide for an adversarial trial. However, the nature of the crimes they try and the ongoing, though possibly no longer armed, conflict in the societies where they were committed, make testifying an exceedingly traumatic and often dangerous course of action that many witnesses, for both prosecution and defence, are unwilling to undertake in open court. The only way out is to skimp on fair-trial requirements, although this is usually presented as 'finding a new balance'. The Israeli court, although generally accepted as scrupulously fair, did so by using – essentially unchallengeable – hearsay evidence of dubious reliability, while Eichmann was unable to obtain the presence of former Nazis (understandably loath to risk a journey to Israel), either to challenge them as to their motives in attributing all the blame to him, or to show extenuating circumstances (Cesarani 2005: 263). The international courts have several ways of using evidence that would not normally be acceptable in an adversarial trial, among other things allowing anonymous testimony. All of this restricts both adversarial truth-finding and adequate defence, and further muddies the historical waters.

Not only is witness testimony affected, but other evidence too. In terms of investigative powers, the defence is at a serious disadvantage compared to the prosecutor and dependent on disclosure for preparation of the defence case. However, evidence gathered on the ground, often by United Nations' officials or NGOs, may be subject to rules of secrecy and confidentiality agreements, protecting its providers in the light of the dangerous conditions under which they work.[11] Such secrecy

---

[10] *The Times*, 13 March 2006.   [11] See Art. 54(3)(e) ICC Statute.

then again endangers due process at trial, so that the option becomes either to conduct a manifestly unfair trial on the basis of undisclosed evidence, or stay the proceedings. While a stay may be the lesser of two evils, in neither case can justice be said to be done in any but a legalistic sense.

Deterrence, retribution and justice for victims

Trials can only be brought to a (reasonably) speedy and successful conclusion by reducing both the selection of defendants and of the charges to manageable proportions. Even if we were to attempt to put the past in all of its manifestations on trial and to give victims rather than perpetrators their day in court, some, probably the majority, of criminal acts against individual victims would still go unpunished. The necessary selection inevitably has the same effect as in any criminal trial: it reduces the narrative of crime to a few provable soundbites and in many ways devalues the victim's experience by taking individual culpability out of the context that was the reality of that experience. No trial of an individual murderer can ever do justice to the collective reality of genocide.

Mark Drumbl (2005b; 2007) has criticised the international legal community for failing to develop a comprehensive theory of punishment that does justice to the extraordinary nature of international criminal justice and the crimes with which it is concerned. Trials and punishment remain very much geared to ordinary concepts of individual guilt and action, ignoring the collective nature and possible normative difference of mass atrocity, for which reason international criminal justice is said to have little to offer in the way of effective punishment. That is not how the international courts view matters. The International Criminal Tribunal for Rwanda (ICTR) held that: 'Punishment dissuades for ever . . . others who may be tempted in the future to perpetrate such atrocities by showing them that the international community shall not tolerate the serious violations of international humanitarian law and human rights.'[12]

This is quite a claim by a trial chamber of the ICTR, and before we get to the retributive value of punishment per se in an international setting, a few words on the idea of deterrence, a vexed criminological question in

---

[12] *Prosecutor* v. *Rutaganda*, (ICTR-96–3-T, T.Ch. 6 December 1999), para. 456.

any system of criminal justice, for as a negative with innumerable variables it is incapable of irrefutable empirical proof in any general sense. Moreover, what *is* known about the deterrent value of criminal law and punishment shows that it depends on the rational choice to commit a certain act by weighing its illegality against the practical certainty, or at least more than mere possibility, of being caught and incurring sanctions. The prospect of (relatively swift) sanctions may, in some cases and for some crimes, serve to deter. But we may wonder whether in the case of mass atrocities the risk of punishment figures at all given the circumstances, for there is a legitimising and socialising logic in societies on the path to genocide that undercuts any rational calculation (even if the chances of standing trial for international crimes were substantial, which they are not, and certainly not in the short term).

While crimes against humanity and genocide have a certain mad and evil rationality, it is the consensus producing machinery in the society (Cottino 2003: 353) where they are committed that allows collective or individual actors to negate their own or other people's responsibility and brings 'ordinary men' to deviate from what would 'normally' be compelling social and moral norms. This is entirely irrelevant in the normative sphere of criminal guilt and the ICTY is correct in emphasising that there is 'neither merit nor logic in recognising the mere context of war itself as a factor to be considered in the mitigation of the criminal conduct of its participants'.[13] Deterrence, however, is not a normative concept but an empirical effect and its value in situations in which the abnormal has become normal is dubious, to say the least.

Deterrent effects aside, however, Drumbl has a problem with notions of retribution as a function of and justification for international criminal justice. He proceeds according to the (Kantian) definition of retribution that underlies so-called absolute theories of penalty: infliction of punishment rectifies the moral balance if it is proportionate to the nature and consequences of the crime, and goes on to note that the proportionality is seriously lacking in international criminal justice. In many cases, the punishment meted out by international courts is of only slighter higher retributive value than punishment for domestic crimes, or the punishment meted out by domestic courts for international crimes. In some cases it is, per definition, less: in Rwanda, sentences by the national courts (that include the death penalty, which the tribunals cannot impose) regularly exceed those of the ICTR for the same crimes.

---

[13] *Prosecutor v. Blaskic*, IT 95–14-A, para. 711 (ICTY Ap.Ch. 29 July 2004).

Moreover, they are imposed according to individualised guilt within a collective. This is one of the reasons why Drumbl complains that international criminal law lacks a penal theory capable of addressing the collective nature of crimes against humanity and genocide and is therefore unable to provide retribution. The very nature of such crimes and the moral stigma that they carry probably go some way to explaining why international criminal law lays such emphasis on individual immorality as the basis of criminal liability. To be sure, an essential prerequisite to mass atrocity is the silent majority of bystanders who do nothing but look the other way, who hear the politicians exhort the masses to violence but do not respond in protest. Without them, and without the little soldiers who do not question the big general's criminal orders (if they recognise them for what they are under the peculiar circumstances that generate mass atrocity), there would be no genocide. That is a sociological and psychological explanation of a social-psychological phenomenon. It does not follow that this can be translated into categories relevant to criminal procedure or that the moral guilt of the collective can serve as a basis for the retributive value that the punishment of individuals should represent, any more than it follows that under these circumstances punishment will serve as a deterrent.

Criticism of the lack of retributive value in sentencing by international criminal courts is partly connected to the concept of justice for victims. But what is meant by justice for victims and what can retribution through punishment contribute? If only because of the selectivity inherent in all criminal justice (the inevitable reality that only some evil – hopefully the 'worst' – will get punished in any system international or otherwise), retribution as a means of avenging individual victims is a symbolic, formalised and stylised expression of recognition and disproval of all the harm inflicted by punishing only a selective part of it. Its legitimacy derives from the authority of the organs of justice and the acceptance by society at large and victims in particular of that authority and the relevance and legality – in the widest sense of the term – of its actions. For that reason, neither retribution nor its contribution to a sense of justice done, also for victims, can be measured by simply looking at sentencing or at whether the criminal process and the concepts of guilt it embodies form a true mirror of empirical reality.

The problems associated with victims in international criminal justice are not that sentences are too lenient or that the very process itself reduces and deforms real experiences (which, in any event, are not the same for everyone concerned). These aspects, which some characterise as defects, are and will remain inherent unless we relinquish either the idea that crimes against humanity deserve to be punished under the criminal law, or the notion that such punishment is legitimate only after the establishment of guilt according to due process, and that there are limits to the form it may take – whatever the feelings of victims. At the same time, the community directly affected by the crimes may be, metaphorically and literally, at some distance from the court that judges them, so that its acceptance of both process and judgment is compromised from the start, regardless of how much that court takes justice for victims into account.

Universal justice?

The rule of law and the notion of fundamental human rights on which international criminal law is based, are legal cultural concepts based on Western-generated theory and philosophical discourse. The criminal procedures that the international courts follow speak to legal traditions, goals and aspirations that Western societies accept as self-evident: prosecution and sentencing by professionals on the basis of individualised guilt; highly developed principles of fair trial; and punishment through incarceration with a view to deterrence, retribution and reconciliation. These are not, however, universal aspects of justice, and do not constitute a universal legal culture. Rather there appears to be a culture of international law, driven and upheld by international lawyers and practitioners.

There is growing criticism of the self-evidence of that culture and of the way in which international criminal justice currently functions, and not without reason as this contribution has shown. International criminal law defines some acts as universal crimes and ignores others; it punishes some actors while others enjoy impunity. It pays lip service to the systemic nature of international crimes, but fails to deal with their collective context. International criminal trials are forums for selective history-telling, often politically driven and necessarily contested. Its critics call for an even more secondary place in the world legal order for international criminal jurisdiction than the ICC already occupies, advocating not justice that draws on general theories of crime and punishment in the domestic settings of countries with long-established civil or common law traditions of fair trial, but on traditional forms of retribution and reconciliation in the countries concerned (Drumbl 2007;

Waters 2008). This often involves looking to forms of restorative justice rather than to the criminal law (Findlay and Henham 2005; Braithwaite 2002), and/or placing not the perpetrators at the centre of international criminal justice but the victims (Findlay, this volume). Some have advocated collective sanctions and retribution as the only means of doing justice to the actual experience of international crimes as collective events – therefore as the only proportionate and legitimate response (Levinson 2003; Fletcher 2004; Drumbl 2005a; 2005b). While all of these solutions seek to bolster the legitimacy of the response to international crimes by questioning whether the way in which their perpetrators are tried and punished is appropriate to the communities concerned, they may be simply asking the wrong question in the context of international criminal law.

In establishing a truth that is acceptable to all, in closure and recon- ciliation, the criminal law has but a small part to play in any situation and an even smaller part when the history and social psychology of atrocities is taken into account. A criminal trial is not concerned with the collective moral guilt of a society that has allowed the culture of perverse normality to develop in which genocide becomes possible. And, however relevant the issue of bystanders and collaboration is to understanding how and why crimes against humanity and genocide occur, the criminal law requires no one to be a hero: 'it asks no more than that we muster the same courage as other reasonable, normal citizens, [and it is] abun- dantly clear how few are able to find that courage and how many turn a blind eye in the hope of getting themselves and their families through without too much hassle' (Brants 2000: 233).

Criminal justice is not a panacea for all the ills of society. Indeed, understanding the genesis of crime and the nature of the suffering it inflicts, more often than not leads to the conclusion that the criminal law is the wrong way to tackle either its causes or its effects. There can be no question that local forms of justice and reconciliation must play a role in securing the future of the societies concerned. Wanting it to be all things to all people, the culture of international criminal law has overstated its own case and led us to ask too much of international criminal law. But because universal crimes do not lead to universal justice – both the criminality and the justice are too contested to be called universal – and can be criticised for not delivering in terms of its own stated aspirations and goals, does that mean that we should not even aspire to universal justice?

I think not, for while the gradual development of international criminal law will not bring quick fixes in terms of 'justice for all', it can derive long-term discursive authority from a commitment to fundamental humanitarian values. While recognising that criminal trials may do little to humanise or even mitigate the barbaric realities of politics and war (Baxi 1998: 126–7), 'human rights languages are all that we have to interrogate the barbarism of power' (*ibid.*: 130). The language of international justice is part of exposing essential evil (Cohen 2001: 283), of the construction of 'techniques of persuasion as a means of creating awareness' (*ibid.*). This gives a new and non-instrumental meaning to deterrence that is not about dissuading through punishment those who are tempted to commit international crimes, but about the internalisation of humanitarian values so that it becomes unthinkable even to think about their commission.

The problem with international criminal justice is not so much that it does not deter because its sanctions are disproportionately lenient, that it does not equally protect the rights of victims and defendants, does not provide equal measures of deterrence, punishment and rehabilitation, and the problem is certainly not the humanitarian values that it embodies, even if these do derive in essence from western enlightenment ideals. The problem is that it so rarely stops to question whether and how its self-professed goals are achievable so that its rhetoric inevitably rings hollow, and is so often determined by Western economic and political self-interest. It is precisely because humanitarian discourse matters more than ever when material reality is determined by realpolitik that we should indeed aspire to universal justice – as a form of commitment and solidarity, no more, but also no less.

References

Alvarez, J. E. (1999) 'Crimes of states/crimes of hate: lessons from Rwanda', *Yale Journal of International Law*, 24, 365–484.
    (2004) 'Trying Hussein: between hubris and hegemony', *Journal of International Criminal Justice*, 2, 319–29.
Bass, G. J. (2000) *Stay the Hand of Vengeance: The Politics of War Crimes Tribunals*, Princeton, NJ: Princeton University Press.
Baxi, U. (1998) 'Voices of suffering and the future of human rights', *Transnational Law and Contemporary Problems*, 8, 125–69.
Box, S. (1983) *Power, Crime and Mystification*, London: Tavistock.

Braithwaite, J. (2002) *Restorative Justice and Responsive Regulation*, Oxford: Oxford University Press.

Brants, C. (2000) 'Dealing with the Holocaust and collaboration: the Dutch experience of criminal justice and accountability after World War II', *Crime, Law and Social Change*, 34, 211–36.

   (2007a) 'No man is an island: the legitimacy of international criminal process as a form of transitional justice', in R. de Lange (ed.), *Aspects of Transitional Justice and Human Rights*, Nijmegen: WLP, pp. 23–40.

   (2007b) 'Gold collar crime: the peculiar complexities and ambiguities of war crimes, crimes against humanity, and genocide', in H. N. Pontell and G. Geis (eds.), *International Handbook of White-Collar and Corporate Crime*, New York: Springer, pp. 309–26.

Browning, C. R. (1992) *Ordinary Men, Reserve Police Battalion 101 and the Final Solution in Poland*, New York: Harper Collins.

Cassese, A. (1999) 'The Statute of the International Criminal Court: some preliminary reflections', *European Journal of International Law*, 10, 144–71.

Cesarani, D. (2005) *Eichmann. His Life and Crimes*, London: Vintage.

Clapham, A. (2000) 'The question of jurisdiction under international criminal law over legal persons: lessons from the Rome Conference on an international criminal court' in M. T. Kamminga and S. Zia-Zafiri (eds.), *Liability of Multinational Corporations Under International Law*, Kluwer Law International, pp. 139–95.

Clough, J. (2005) 'Not-so-innocents abroad: corporate criminal liability for human rights abuses', *Australian Journal of Human Rights 9*, http://www.austlii.edu.au/au/journals/AJHR/2005/1.html.

Cohen, Stanley (2001) *States of Denial: Knowing about Atrocities and Suffering*, Cambridge: Polity Press.

Coleman, J. W. (1987) 'Toward an integrated theory of white collar crime', *American Journal of Sociology*, 93, 406–39.

Cottino, A. (2003) 'White-collar crime' in C. Sumner (ed.), *The Blackwell Companion to Criminology*, Oxford: Blackwell, pp. 343–58.

Cressey, D. R. (1973 [1953]) *Other People's Money. A Study in the Social Psychology of Embezzlement*, Patterson Smith.

Douglas, L. (2001) *The Memory of Judgment: Making Law and History in the Trials of the Holocaust*, New Haven: Yale University.

Drumbl, M. A. (2005a) 'Collective violence and individual punishment: the criminality of mass atrocity', *Northwestern University Law Review*, 99, 539–610.

   (2005b) 'Pluralizing international criminal justice', *Michigan Law Review*, 103, 1295–328.

   (2007) *Atrocity, Punishment and International Law*, Cambridge: Cambridge University Press.

Dufresne, R. (2004) 'The opacity of oil: oil corporations, internal violence and international law', *New York University Journal of International Law and Politics*, 36, 331–94.

Edlin, D. E. (2006) 'The anxiety of sovereignty: Britain, the United States and the International Criminal Court', *International and Comparative Law Review*, 29, 1–22.

Findlay, M. and Henham, R. (2005) *Transforming International Criminal Justice: Retributive and Restorative Justice in the Trial Process*, Cullompton: Willan Publishing.

Fletcher, G. P. (2002) 'Liberals and romantics at war: the problem of collective guilt', *Yale Law Journal*, 111, 1499–573.

(2004) 'Collective guilt and collective punishment', *Theoretical Inquiries in Law*, 5, 163–78.

Fletcher, L. E. (2005) 'From indifference to engagement: bystanders and international criminal justice', *Michigan Journal of International Law*, 26, 1013–96.

Friedrichs, D. (2006) 'Global criminology and law's ends: transcending disciplinary parochialism', Paper presented at the annual meeting of the Law and Society Association, 6 July.

Galtung, J. (1990) 'Cultural violence', *Journal of Peace Research*, 3, 291–305.

Global Witness, *Logging Off: How the Liberian Timber Industry Fuels Liberia's Humanitarian Disaster and Threatens Sierra Leone*, September 2002, http://www.globalwitness.org/reports/show.php/en.00006.html.

Heller, K. J. (2008) 'Deconstructing international criminal law', *Michigan Law Review*, 106, 975–99.

Huisman, W. (2008) 'Corporations and international crimes' in A. L. Smeulers and R. H. Haveman (eds.), *Supranational Criminology: Towards a Criminology of International Crimes*, Intersentia, Antwerpen, pp. 181–213.

Jacobson, K. R. (2005) 'Doing business with the devil: the challenges of prosecuting corporate officials whose business transactions facilitate war crimes and crimes against humanity', *Air Force Law Review*, 56, 167–231.

Levinson, D. J. (2003) 'Collective sanctions', *Stanford Law Review*, 56, 345–428.

Matza, D. (1964) *Delinquency and Drift*, New York: Wiley and Sons.

Ohlin, J. D. (2006) 'Three conceptual problems with the doctrine of joint criminal enterprise', *Journal of International Criminal Justice*, 5, 69–90.

Osiel, M. (1997) *Mass Atrocity, Collective Memory and the Law*, New Brunswick, NJ: Transaction Publishers.

Ramasastry, A. and Thompson, R. C. (2006) *Commerce, Crime and Conflict. Legal Remedies for Private Sector Liability for Grave Breaches of International Law. A Survey of Sixteen Countries*, www.fafo.no/pub/rapp/536/536.pdf.

Ratner, S. (1998) 'The schizophrenias of international criminal law', *Texas International Review*, 33, 237–56.

Roberts, P. and McMillan, N. (2003) 'For criminology in international criminal justice', *Journal of International Criminal Justice*, 1, 315–38.

Rosenburg, T. (2002) *The Year in Ideas: Peace Through Embargo*, Global Witness, December 2002, http://www.globalwitness.org/campaigns/forests.

Saland, P. (1999) 'International criminal law principles' in R. S. Lee (ed.), *The International Criminal Court. The Making of the Rome Statute. Issues, Negotiations, Results*, Kluwer Law International, pp. 189–216.

Salo, R. S. (2003) 'When the logs roll over: the need for an international convention criminalising involvement in the global illegal timber trade', *Georgetown International Environmental Law Review*, 16, 127–46.

Sliedregt, E. van (2003) *The Criminal Responsibility of Individuals for Violations of International Humanitarian Law*, The Hague: T.M.C. Asser Press.

Sloane, R. D. (2007) 'The expressive capacity of international punishment: the limits of the national law analogy and the potential of international criminal law', *Stanford Journal of International Law*, 43, 39–94.

   (2008) 'Book review of Mark. A. Drumbl, "Atrocity, Punishment and International Law"', *American Journal of International Law*, 192, 197–205.

Stephens, B. (2002) 'The amorality of profit: transnational corporations and human rights', *Berkeley Journal of International Law*, 20, 45–90.

Swaaningen, R. van (forthcoming) 'Rewriting comparative criminology's script: a cosmopolitan critique' in D. Nelken (ed.), *Comparative Criminal Justice and Globalization*, Aldershot: Ashgate/Dartmouth.

Sykes, G. M. and Matza, D. (1957) 'Techniques of neutralization: a theory of delinquency', *American Sociological Review*, 22, 664–70.

Teitel, R. (2005) 'The law and politics of contemporary transitional justice', *Cornell International Law Journal*, 38, 837–62.

Waters, T. W. (2008) 'Killing globally, punishing locally? The still-unmapped ecology of atrocity', *Buffalo Law Review*, 55, 1331–70.

Wilt, H. van der (2005) *Het kwaad in functie*, Amsterdam: Vossiuspers, UvA.

5

Locating victim communities within global justice and governance

MARK FINDLAY

The eyes of victims of past crimes and of the potential victims of future crimes are fixed firmly upon us.

Kofi Annan opening the ICC Rome Conference

Introduction

Those who would like to see the international criminal trial remain a retributive endeavour reflecting the conventional features and characteristics of domestic trials are concerned that enhancing victim constituency for the international trial process will endanger its limited potential success (Judah and Bryant 2003). Some critics declare that the International Criminal Tribunal for the former Yugoslavia (ICTY) in particular has achieved legitimacy through the effective prosecution of significant offenders important to many victim communities (Findlay and McLean 2007). In this, it is argued, lies sufficient justification for the expansion of a retributive international trial process in the form of the International Criminal Court (ICC).[1] In addition, the disclosure debacle around the first ICC indictment, which clearly divided the interests of the prosecutor and of victims heightens the challenges to conventional trial positioning if victim interests are given standing.

---

[1] This is not to suggest that the ICC has no concern for restorative, victim-centred considerations. Such considerations feature in the recent decisions to join victim's interests with the prosecution appeals against disclosure, and release of the accused in the Lubanga trial proceedings (see ICC Appeals Chamber no. ICC-01/04–01/06 0A 13 – 6 August 2008).

Despite such narrower legalist assertions the ICC, and its prosecutor, have claimed more universalist justifications in the form of the court's potential to assist in state reconstruction and peacemaking. Further, the ICC and the international tribunals which precede it have within their authorising legislation growing recognition of victim interests, even if this remains largely outside the processes of trial decision making.[2]

Today in many domestic criminal jurisdictions, the position and voice of the victim is receiving increasing attention and recognition, if only in terms of very selective participation (Schunemann 2000). Slowly it seems that the prosecution of criminal trials is moving full circle. Historically, in common law jurisdictions in particular, the prosecution of crimes was the responsibility of the victim. However, with the development of the nation state, and the institutionalisation and professionalisation of the criminal courts, as well as the establishment and monopoly of police investigation, it became more realistic for state instrumentalities to take on the prosecution role. This trend has recognised the interest of the state and the communities it protects in crime and punishment as governance tools, while tending to see the marginalisation of the victim voice to a place wherein comparable civil trials this exclusion would not be tolerated.

More recently, first with victim impact statements, and then a range of initiatives right up to victim advocacy within the trial, the necessity to recognise, consider and enunciate these victim interests in more and more formal trial scenarios has become a feature of neoconservative justice reforms (Aldana-Pindell 2002). Against this, victim advocacy groups have pushed for a repositioning of trial interests away from the conventional protection of the accused, towards victim-harm compensation (Brison 2003). The imperative for victim inclusion has progressed into the procedures governing institutional international criminal justice.

This being said, the reality of global crime victimisation and its terrible collective dimensions have found little practical trial recognition beyond the fragmentary and selective prosecution of genocide. Victim communities, and the prosecution of collective perpetration are not driving the unique jurisprudence of international criminal law or trial procedure.[3]

---

[2] For a comprehensive summary of the ICC's victim obligations see Human Rights First, 'The role of the victim in ICC proceedings', www.humanrightsfirst.org/international_justice/icc/ VICTIMS_CHART_Final.pdf.

[3] This could be seen as a reluctant reflection of the limited place for victims, particularly in common law adversarial trial traditions, and after the state assumed monopoly over prosecution on behalf of wider community interests.

Besides an emergent political utility in balancing victim interests against the protection of offenders' rights in national courts, this chapter argues that the nature of global crime, and the purposes of international criminal justice require a more victim-centred, transformed trial process (Findlay and Henham 2005; 2010). In saying this, we recognise the reservations about the domestic trends to voice victim interests and thereby to move away from the consequences of the presumption of innocence towards a more civil jurisdictional consideration of 'balance'. There is good reason for law reformers and criminal justice professionals to be suspicious of the victims' lobby when it comes to ensuring even a balanced adversarial contest. The chapter argues that the nature of international criminal justice and the global crimes it confronts, present a uniquely persuasive position for a victim constituency despite the challenging partiality of victim interests. International criminal trials are making space for such developments.

The transformed trial, as we envisage it, addresses at three levels, to better recognise victim constituency, the current failure of formal international criminal justice (Findlay and Henham 2005):

- by emphasising from the victim perspective access inclusivity and integration to key pre-trial and trial-decision sites; and as a result
- enhancing the legitimate role of victims in creating and maintaining pathways of influence out of these crucial trial-decision sites; added to which
- restorative as well as retributive processes will be available within the 'rights-protected' procedures of the trial enabling victims to better achieve their legitimate aspirations in the trial context.

Besides the necessary procedural and legislative enhancement of the trial to enable structural transformation, there is a need to reposition the normative foundations of the trial along the way (Findlay and Henham 2010). Essential for the success of trial transformation will be an enlivening of juridical discretion to manage the smooth achievement of greater victim constituency.[4]

All this must be measured against the crucial importance of accountability as an indicator of trial fairness, and the protections of the accused

---

[4] We are wrestling with the details of trial transformation, particularly in terms of a 'developed trial programme'. In particular, the analysis focuses on the repositioning of fact and evidence in the determination of responsibility, and a realignment of trial outcomes away from the limits of penalty as the consequence of adversarial argument; see Findlay and Henham (2010: Chapter 6).

which this requires. Despite active efforts by the international criminal courts and tribunals better to balance victim interests at trial and pre-trial phases, the constrictions of adversarial justice relegate the victim voice to the witness role, and compensation considerations post-sentence (Damaska 2008).

Along with accountability to a victim constituency, the pragmatic persuasion is that a heightened victim purchase over international criminal justice will generate greater legitimacy for the global justice process across a wider range of communities which it is said to serve. The legitimacy that the satisfaction of victim interests offers should not be underestimated, or over-calculated. It has already been recognised in the United States with the prosecution of those involved in the 9/11 atrocities and other mass killings (Logan 2008). Prospects for broader systemic legitimation clearly influenced the recent reform of criminal procedure laws in jurisdictions such as Italy, Russia, Japan and China where victim advocacy is provided for and greater community partici-pation in criminal justice advanced. It is not coincidental that the provisions within the ICC Rules identifying the roles of victims in its proceedings extend much further than the conventional trial limita-tions surrounding the victim witness.[5] The nature and direction of victim legitimation will be examined specifically in this chapter against a range of challenges which might tend to compromise that legitima-ting process.

In other work (Findlay 2008), we have suggested that an incapacity appropriately to confront the victimisation consequences of global crime has tended to mean that international criminal justice and the govern-ance that flows from it are unsatisfactorily entwined with sectarian international relations, and narrow cultural inclusion (Findlay 2007). Therefore, in governance terms alone, it is compelling that the concep-tualisation of global crime victims be expanded and emancipated. As a consequence the citizenship and standing necessary to enjoy inter-national criminal justice is more fairly realised.

There is no doubt that an ideologically driven campaign to prioritise victim interests in criminal justice is at risk of distorting some of the central values that criminal justice traditions have developed over cen-turies (Logan 2008; Damaska 2008).

---

[5] See e.g. r. 50 on victim witnesses, and rr. 89–91 governing the participation of victims in the trial process.

Damaska (2008: 333) goes so far as to say:

> In an ideal world, of course, there would be no reason to balance these two aspirations (accused and victim interests) – they would co-exist in harmony. But in the real world, painful trade-offs between them must often be made.

Our concluding discussion of 'communities of justice' argues for the rationalisation and distillation of common good above balancing interests. In any criminal justice resolution there may be several victims or victim communities with different victim stories exercising different interests and values. A distillation of legitimate victim interests in such a contested environment will be a challenge for the transformed criminal trial. The identification and harmonisation of legitimate victim interests is much more than an uncritical concession to the self-interested expectations, beyond retributive justice and vengeance, that victims enunciate (Albrecht *et al.* 2006; Aertsen *et al.* 2008). To swing from an accused-centred to a victim-focused trial fairness paradigm will endanger trial legitimacy if the criticism of the former is simply replaced with a new partiality. Legitimacy enhancement comes with a richer communitarian governance through international criminal justice which the constituency of humanity, rather than sectarian victim satisfaction, will achieve (Findlay 2008: Chapter 7).

Communities of justice are presented as the crucial context wherein lay and professional players will interact so that a more communitarian form of justice benefits from the application of the rule of law, and procedural fairness. As such, communities of justice become a dynamic environment where negotiation is essential and where actionable questions will be transferred into the trial decision-making framework minimising the burden of partial adversarial argument. It is assumed that if operated with a common aspiration for justice outcomes, these communities of justice will make more reasonable the victim position prior to exposure through trial interrogation (Findlay and Henham 2010: Chapter 9).

The chapter begins by confronting prevailing circumspection about why victims should be prioritised as the constituency for international criminal justice. The argument moves from the demands of legitimacy on to the anticipation that through communities of justice a sharper victim focus will require that international criminal justice be more accountable. This is a theme that prevails throughout and will link our case for transformed criminal trial process to a new age of global governance (Findlay 2008). But first it is necessary to locate the chapter's theoretical mission, against the perennial struggle between subjective and universalised analysis.

Sociocultural theorising victimisation

Providing contextual appreciations of socio-legal phenomena like victimisation within different cultures and jurisdictional boundaries is problematic (Albrecht *et al.* 2006; Aertsen *et al.* 2008; Parmentier and Weitekamp this volume). The difficulties encountered in such research are multiplied when we seek to develop understandings both within and across jurisdictional boundaries, and particularly for the comparative analysis of victim communities.

The research balance between phenomenology and social reality (i.e. what counts as an epistemologically valid explanation) lies in the extent to which there is agreement as to what constitutes the 'objectivity' of victimisation. As we say later, with the conditionality of victim legitimacy even the status of victim communities can be politically and culturally contingent (*ibid.*). Although the reality of victimisation is epistemologically conjectural, we can nevertheless postulate (depending on our theoretical persuasion) some *a priori* principles by which to measure/evaluate whether such a phenomenon 'objectively' exists. The 'politics' of victim legitimacy, we later argue, is constantly engaged in claiming such objectivity. These principles connect to:

- the nature of the harm inflicted
- the 'non-combatant' role
- the standing of victim communities against measures of political and cultural authority.

Also, if victims or victim communities are deemed resistant to these 'authorities' then the consequences of victimisation can be markedly different.

The subjectivity of the victim phenomenon is largely determined around measures of 'innocence' and hence concerned with such issues as:

- the perceived legitimacy of the causes and consequences of 'war'
- what it subjectively 'feels' like to be a victim, rather than simply having been ascribed that status
- how these intimate influences have shaped the individual attitudes of those claiming victimisation.

Thus the social reality of victimisation is a conflation of subjective and objective measures. Victimisation, particularly in its communitarian sense, is a representation of both what 'victims' claim and what they have ascribed to their status. Communitarian victimisation especially depends for its legitimacy and credibility on the consequences that flow from the community's status and behaviour.

Any social theory which seeks to address the nature and significance of victimisation must necessarily address its legal, socio-historical, economic and political dimensions. The challenge for comparative analysis (and one largely not met in many post-conflict empirical studies) involves appreciating the multilayered nature of the relationships between the values and actions which produce victimisation within particular cultures and being able to make epistemologically acceptable generalisations about them. Parmentier and Weitekamp (in this volume) employ resultant victim opinion data to in part construct a vision of justice which reflects victim aspirations. The danger in this always is to down play the diversity, and sometimes mutual inconsistency, in desires for justice which may be intensely context dependent. This chapter suggests a complex framework of indicators around which such comparative contextual analysis might be mounted.

Certain 'war victim' experience studies offering vital insights into individual perception go beyond conventional empirical victim analysis in the sense that they seek to hypothesise about observed and quantifiable 'facts' such as sentencing patterns (Fletcher 1995). In so doing, the 'victim experience and aspiration' approach applies quantitative techniques to the analysis of what is essentially an account of the subjective perception of 'facts', describing what it is like to be a victim in a particular post-conflict society and how this impacts on the perception of what constitutes justice for war crimes. The 'objectivity' of these accounts can only be evaluated, in such a subjective methodology, to the extent that we are able to understand their meaning within particular contexts. These contexts may offer micro and macro-cultural 'objectivities' outside the comprehension and daily experience of victim communities, but available for more detached comparative analysis. The comparative potential of the analysis to follow, is more universally generalised through employing community structures and functions of victimisation (collective contexts of experience) to ground the subjective appreciation and ascription of victimisation.

The repercussions of this tension between subjective methodologies and objective speculation are considerable because, both theoretically and methodologically, there is a clear distinction to be drawn between exploring the aspirational and empirical dimensions of social experience. The objectivity of any social phenomenon mirrors its subjectivity (and vice versa); the relationship is reciprocal. We can attempt to 'explain' how definitions of 'objectivity' are produced through the analysis of subjective experience, which is a recursive and constantly changing process. Hence, this approach tries to fix the meaning or contextualise social life by deconstructing the subjectivity of individual experience and making generalisations about the extent to which such experiences and understandings are held collectively. Where the collective experience is given objective form through 'community', it follows that the comparative enterprise (community to community, and aspiration to justice option) is greatly enhanced. Self-evidently, such methodologies will be culturally contextual in suggesting ways in which the objectivity of process is constructed subjectively. The challenge facing the victim 'attitude' researchers is to translate individual aspiration to community sentiment and on to normative critiques around issues such as best justice outcomes.

War victimisation should, therefore, be conceived as a social construct that involves the interplay between the causes and effects of war and the perceived appropriateness of particular forms of legal and institutional redress. The analysis of post-conflict victimisation as a comparative endeavour should benefit from community location so that the individualised and collective representation of victimisation, and its selectivity, can be critiqued and materialised in justice outcomes.

1   Why victim focus?

The first answer is simply that international criminal justice has no choice but to move towards victim constituency if its legitimacy and functional relevance are to be confirmed beyond the authority of legislative instruments and sponsor agencies, vague and contingent as these can be. It is a functional and operational shift now required by legitimate victim interests, and aspirations for pluralist justice outcomes. In its first trial, the ICC has confronted, and in a limited fashion through access and representation decisions in favour of victims, recognised this imperative.

The research carried out in victim communities affected by genocide and crimes against humanity clearly establishes that victims are not satisfied alone by the retributive justice offered through current international criminal tribunals. This is not a blanket denial that retributive justice is on the list of victim community expectations. Nor could it be said from the victim community perspectives surveyed that retribution should be marginalised in any process of trial transformation. Quite the contrary. Along with most victim communities so far studied, we endorse the importance of retributive justice (Findlay and Henham 2005: Chapter 7) in terms of current political resonance for criminal trials, and against the dissatisfaction of victims of mass harm in alternative truth and reconciliation options alone. Even the ICC's capacity for restitution and compensation may not satisfy broad restorative concerns (Barton 2003; Parmentier and Weitekamp this volume). Without a capacity for the international criminal trial to offer more than retributive justice through international penality, the potential for victims to justify and legitimate formal international criminal justice may be squandered.

It has become essential for the legitimacy of international criminal justice that a victim constituency be centrally recognised. The unavoidable justification for this rests in the nature of the international criminal jurisdiction. The types of crimes that international criminal tribunals and courts confront are all inextricably linked to victim communities. War crimes occur within jurisdictional and communitarian limits. The communities at risk and the individuals, communities and cultures that suffer harm can be clearly identified. The crimes which compose war crimes rely on the scope of victimisation for their definition. The same could be said of genocide. With genocide, however, the notion of harm extends beyond communities and into cultures and races. In fact in the case of ethnic cleansing, the purpose of military intervention and violent confrontation may be to victimise and destroy opposing cultural or racial elements. Finally, when dealing with crimes against humanity, it is the global community at risk. This community, however defined, is at least partially a community of potential victims and one for which international criminal justice is clearly constructed.

Humanity as the constituency for international criminal justice

A new moral foundation for international criminal justice with 'humanity' at its centre distinguishes the victim focus for international criminal justice from current trends to inject a higher victim profile into domestic criminal justice processes.[6] It is different for the following reasons:

---

[6] This is not to deny such a focus domestically but merely to highlight its dominance in the global criminal jurisdiction.

- Global crimes as the concern of the ICC are crimes against humanity, against communities, and against cultural integrity.
- International criminal justice agencies have declared an interest in peacemaking and conflict resolution for the benefit of communities and cultures under attack.
- The harms against which international criminal justice is directed (war, genocide and ethnic cleansing) are collectivised in their impact.
- The extent of liability for global crimes is also collectivised beyond considerations of joint criminal enterprise and superior orders, and humanity is a democratic and inclusive determinant of the global community.

To accept humanity as the natural constituency for international criminal justice does not require a rejection of 'the rule of law', 'constitutional legality' or 'the global state' as important terms of reference for the exercise of international criminal justice. It is obvious that the United Nations, and its Security Council, for instance, will play a crucial role in the interventions and priorities of the ICC. In addition, important NGOs will continue to exercise influence in the maintenance of global order. And this is as it should be. The legal professionals in the transformed trial process will be central in determining the rights and protections that the adversarial process can advance. With all this in mind, there may be natural and appropriate constraints on the inclusion of a victim's voice in the trial process but this will not deny the importance of humanity as a constituency for international criminal justice.

Collectivisation of the victim dimension

We have already argued (Findlay 2008) that international crime victimisation is a collective phenomenon. The term 'the victim community'[7] recurs throughout this chapter to emphasise the manner in which this collectivisation takes shape. Victim communities can be seen as a challenging concept to distil:

- How can victimisation be removed from individual harm?
- How are communities (in their diversity) to be conceived so as some convincing notion of victimisation can emerge?

---

[7] This concept includes collective victimisation, victim's communities, the victimisation of communities and communitarian harm.

- If it does emerge, what are legitimate interests in a community context?
- How are these interests to be revealed, and how is a community to be given access to, and voice within, criminal justice determinations?
- What particular impact should the voice of victim communities be accorded against the conventional protections for the accused in due process?

The victim dimension is collectivised because of the nature of global victimisation well beyond tribunal-based justice, and also in the legislative sense through the way the three global crimes which form the jurisdiction of the ICC are currently conceived.[8] The collectivisation of victims in a global sense from this legislative and jurisdictional foundation invites our later discussion of collective liability.

Failure of the international criminal trial on access, inclusivity and integration

Due to the failure of formal international criminal justice to incorporate fully the victim constituency,[9] many victim aspirations such as truth-telling, restoration, reconciliation and compensation have been moved into the alternative justice paradigm. Therefore, it is not surprising the mandate for conflict resolution is more acceptable and less controversial within these alternative frameworks. Truth and Reconciliation Commissions, for example, were constructed where it was thought (by post-conflict states and peacekeeping agencies) that retributive justice and its institutions could not achieve a legitimate interest of victims within transitional cultures (Freeman 2006). It is becoming clearer as international criminal justice develops and gains more significant purchase in global governance that justice for conflict resolution cannot be relegated to a second tier of truth-telling (Findlay and Henham 2010: Chapter 4).

---

[8] Crimes of aggression have been incorporated along with war crimes, crimes against humanity and genocide in 2009 as appropriate for prosecution before the ICC. Consistent with my argument as it relates to the collectivisation of victims for the already existing crime types, crimes of aggression more often than not are directed against victim communities.

[9] This is not an empirical statement as studies of that nature regarding victim inclusion are not yet available. The assertion rests on the legislative foundations of the courts and tribunals, and of the studies particularly on victim attitudes to post-verdict outreach into victim communities by the ICTY and the ICTR – see e.g. Peskin (2005) and Human Rights Watch (2008). It is also based on the relative underfunding of victim interests in the ICC – see O'Donohue 2005.

An important justification for transforming the international criminal trial is to enable victims otherwise relegated to alternative justice contexts to benefit from the procedural protections offered within the trial, contested as these may be in an adversarial environment.[10] Recognising that these protections are sometimes problematic in practice, it remains clear that the rights of victims are often ignored or mediated in local justice situations. The transformed international criminal trial is premised on commitments to expanded victim access, deeper and more genuine opportunities for inclusion and a more natural and productive integration of victim aspirations through a greater variety of resolution opportunities (Findlay and Henham 2005, 2010).

Need for conflict resolution as part of international criminal justice

Our discussion of an enhanced governance potential for international criminal justice concedes the importance of peacekeeping and conflict resolution for the legitimacy of international criminal justice (Braithwaite 2002). In much of the debate about the contemporary direction for global governance (Lederer and Muller 2005; Findlay 2008) the importance of state reconstruction is emphasised. It is assumed that post-military intervention in transitional states, conflict resolution community to community will provide an essential peacemaking function. Yet whether it is through the mechanism of Truth and Reconciliation Commissions, or the retributive outcomes of criminal tribunals and special courts, lasting peace will only emerge when communities of victims are satisfied that the governance and justice interventions on their behalf have meaning and impact. Peacemaking will be little more than political posturing when communities not at war but victimised through war remain excluded from constructive justice outcomes. Those institutions and paradigms of justice most successful in meeting the widest range of victim interests will obviously, as a consequence, enjoy greater legitimacy amongst communities that might challenge peace.

---

[10] We do not here intend to overstate trial rights' protections. If these are retained in their conventional form then the focus on accused person's rights (Art. 6 EU Convention) offers little comfort to victim participants. A feature of trial transformation, as we see it, is the actualisation of victim participant protections which do not undermine the accused.

Legitimacy of victim interests

Legitimacy for justice and governance emerging out of victim satisfaction is a crucial underpinning of international criminal justice which conciliates a liberal democratic governance model. Recognising their limited engagement with victim interests and aspirations, the international criminal tribunals and the ICC have been legislated to at least provide victims with information about the substance and impact of their determinations. This will never of itself be enough to represent democratic engagement for an emergent victim constituency. Victim communities have identified a desire to see the perpetrators of global crime brought to justice (Albrecht *et al.* 2006; Parmentier and Weitekamp in this volume). In many situations, however, this is a symbolic first stage towards addressing more restorative and community-centred considerations. The ICC has confronted the pressure for this as a feature of the emergent tension between the prosecutor's officer and the chamber in the Lubanga trial. The interests of the victim were finally in this case set free from prosecutorial imperatives.

The capacity for victims, and the satisfaction of their legitimate interests to then legitimate criminal justice service delivery, is more than an ideological attainment. With international criminal justice institutions identifying conflict resolution and peacemaking as crucial practical aims, the enjoyment of ongoing peace and good order should first be measured against the victim communities that have suffered from the global crimes in question. Where peace may be extracted along with further alienation and exclusion or consequent victimisation then the legitimacy of peacemaking institutions and processes is undermined.

An obvious problem here is to identify legitimate victim interests in situations where several victim communities contest the nature of their victimisation, its origins and what should be done in restoration. Contested victim interests will require procedural opportunities for resolution if the satisfaction of these interests is to afford legitimacy to international criminal justice (Findlay and Henham 2010: Chapters 5–7).

Capacity for victims to make global governance accountable

In our discussion of the two levels of accountability (internal and external) offered for international criminal justice through the transformed trial we identify the important contexts of 'communities of justice'. Communities of justice in each particular pre-trial incarnation will provide 'boundaries of permission' (Findlay 1994) to determine the nature of justice applied and justified within the conflicts and challenges these communities are facing. The processes of justice employed, the decision-making which they achieve and the outcomes and resolutions that they conclude will be the measures of accountability against genuine communitarian justice aspirations.

The location of justice accountability within communities takes it away from its present and, we would argue, unhealthy reliance on the sponsorship of sectarian political hegemony. This is not to say that international criminal justice accountability will not have its political dimension. Rather, a more productive place for the political aspect of accountability is grounded in the authority that communitarian justice interests and processes provide.

2   The nature of the global victim

Once the need for greater attention to a victim constituency in international criminal justice has been confirmed the next issue is to identify and describe in more detail the nature of the global victim. Collectivisation aside, the global victim presents some unique features in terms of inclusion and exclusion which make victim status not simply designated by proximity to violent harm. Even so, the harm borne by victims arising out of violent exchanges remains a critical determinant of victimisation in domestic criminal justice settings. Globally, the relativity and sectoral designation of violence which is the interest of international criminal justice means that harms to victims and communities of themselves may not alone be enough to ascribe legitimate victim status.

Problems caused by victor's justice

'Victor's justice' suggests the discrimination and exclusion initiating international criminal justice through a process of criminalisation which in the current phase of globalisation is inextricably linked to sectarian political hegemony. In terms of victimisation, victor's justice is responsible for the designation of those victims worthy of protection, imbued with the rights of citizenship and therefore standing before formal justice institutions. The flipside of this is the denial of legitimate victim status to those individuals and communities that resist the cultural, economic and political predominance of this hegemony.

Essential for discriminating between those victims worthy of justice outcomes and those not is the attribution of morality or immorality to violence applied by and against particular groups. Morality in this sense relies in part on awarding the status of innocence to some victims and perpetrators, or at the very least, that of justified collaborators to others. Concepts of risk, powerlessness, guilt, injury and blame are empowered where they are awarded on behalf of the innocent victim against those represented as unjustified perpetrators. For example, terrorist communities[11] become victims in very similar contexts as those who suffer terrorist violence, but from the perspective of victor's justice, little regard is paid to their victimisation, evolving as a necessary consequence of justice against terror.

Therefore, the subjective distinction of worthy victimisation depends on the authority of those imposing the label and the 'significant others' around whom the label rests. The process of 'meaning attribution', however, is not all one-way traffic. For any meaning to stick it must resonate in the wider audience to which it is directed. The valorised victim may retain the status accorded by our politicised process of meaning, amongst those significant others (family, friends, civic leaders etc.) who accept the authority of the labelling agency and its 'take' on the terror enterprise. Crucial to this process are the victims themselves. Those who might challenge or even modify the nature of this meaning and its authority are quickly sidelined and their valorisation denied.

The morality of the justice response (or the terrorist act for that matter) requires either community respect or superimposed violence (force) to condition its standing and ensure compliance. If the claim for standing relies on force, rather than respect through grounded authority and community consensus, then the resistance of the recipient communities is an important consideration in fashioning the response and expectations for its effectiveness. If standing is to have an essential influence over the prosecution beyond a particular version of truth or justice, then the arena within which it is claimed must be mutually respected. Particularly at this level, the morality of victor's justice is contested by terrorist violence.

---

[11] These are not to be understood as communities of terrorists. Far from it. Rather, they are communities for which the terrorist claims representative significance, and which may share common ideologies, but not necessarily common commitments to violence.

The challenge of jurisdiction and standing caused by selective citizenship[12]

Standing, even in the legal non-metaphysical sense, has largely eluded analysis in the literature on international criminal justice and global governance. A reason for this is that if standing is to have a definitive influence over the prosecution of a particular version of truth or justice then the context within which it is claimed must be mutually respected. The selective application of international criminal justice currently runs against such mutuality of interest (Findlay 2007). Particularly at this level the morality of victor's justice is constantly contested through the violence of resistant communities.

The ambiguity of violence, as both a challenge to and a confirmation of hegemonic domination, is widely apparent in the process of redefining statehood and citizenship on the 'global periphery'. Here, in transitional and separatist states, violence is transacted from the status of terrorist coercion through to legitimate armed struggle along with the transformation to legitimacy and global recognition.

In the context of the 'war on terror' crime victimisation and the legitimate claims to global citizenship are conflated. The fissures of exclusion and inclusion appear between criminality and victimisation across global communities.

Citizenship is protected through globalisation where it accords with the constructs of the global community, its market economies, liberal democratic styles of government and allegiance to the modernisation project (Bauman 1998; Findlay 1999). The nature and ramifications of global citizenship are clearer in the context of international criminal justice than they may be in other regulatory frameworks because of the triggering effect that citizenship possesses.

Humanity is represented and protected by the prosecutions before international criminal tribunals. The global community through the enabling legislation of the ICC and tribunals carries actionable responsibility for a limited range of harms caused to communities within its entity. In this regard, it is not simply individual or nation states that are

---

[12] Citizenship here is not merely referring to some as yet amorphous claim to inclusion in the 'global community'. More particularly it represents claims to legitimacy and standing within the sectarian protection of hegemonic global governance – see Findlay (2008: Chapter 9).

the subject of tribunal interest, and in fact under the terms of the ICC statute, individual liability is the focus of the justice delivered.[13]

The challenge when conceptualising and actualising global citizenship is to avoid the political partiality demonstrated in global governance as it presently operates. From the regulatory perspective of the dominant political alliance, domestic citizens are cherished if they fall within the political allegiance and jurisdictional boundaries of the alliance and supporter states. Outside these boundaries the protection of the nation state and citizenship are conditional on risk and security evaluations from the perspective of the dominant alliance, and on broader geopolitical significance. These considerations also invest the designation of legitimate victims.

Victims in both supportive and resistant communities

Resistance is often violent against the partial and discriminatory recognition of citizenship within communities where individualised rights are subservient to communitarian concerns for social harmony (Braithwaite 2002; Findlay 2007). Western governance models which promote individual autonomy over community responsibility have not received universal acceptance through globalisation, and in some contexts this has fomented violent resistance. Levi (1997) argues that citizens are more likely to comply and give active consent to imposed democratic governance when the institutions and processes that evolved are perceived as fair in decision-making and implementation. Along with this realisation, the cultural sensitivity and origination of these processes is also crucial to their acceptance (Findlay 1999). Inclusivity and community collaboration are conditions which affect the acceptance of imposed governance models. The same could be said particularly about community and cultural responses to international criminal justice as an introduced governance model where local justice is not primarily individualised.

When citizenship is more dependent on the jurisdiction of the secular state than membership of a religious culture or a cohesive community, issues on a global scale such as territoriality, sovereignty, and political authority are currently determined by the dominant economic/political alliance as risk/security contingencies. Communities which value religious culture and communitarian customary practices are over-represented

---

[13] For a critique of this position against the need to collectivise liability, see Danner and Martinez (2005).

amongst those victimised by violence internationally, but who have through their resistance to the dominant sectarian political model been denied legitimate victim status.

Collectivity and distance: who can claim victimisation?

Issues of standing for 'victims' seeking international criminal justice identify a divergence between the 'local' and the 'global' contexts of justice service delivery. The criminal justice literature is replete with cautions concerning the uncritical expansion of victim participation and influence in domestic trial deliberations (Fletcher 1995; Erez and Rogers 1999). Internationally, however, the ICC and the criminal tribunals have advanced victim interests through a range of pre-trial and trial inclusions. This is a logical consequence of the special position of victim communities in the construction of global criminality, and the jurisdiction of ICC crimes in particular. Further, the collective and communitarian contexts of global criminal victimisation defuse much of the domestic debate about distance, harm, vengeance, self-interest and legitimacy.

The experience in domestic jurisdictions of trying to identify an appropriate victim voice in homicide trials has raised the specific question of victimisation and the actionable distance from the harm caused by the substantive crime (original victim encounter). Courts have faced some difficulty in determining, in situations where the immediate victim is the deceased, to what extent family and friends intimately connected to, but removed from, the victimisation can be considered as victims for the purposes of an impact statement. The conundrum of victim status and distance from harm is likely to be moderated within global crimes like genocide, where the victim may be perceived as a community, a culture and a race as much as individuals that have suffered directly from crime perpetration.

In the situation of mass-murder trials, Logan (2008) explores the many difficulties that the use of victim statements presents in such circumstances. These include:

- demarking permissible boundaries in terms of victimisation and impact – these are issues for capital (murder) trials in general but may be exacerbated in the context of mass killings and mass victimisation
- questions of proximity to the actual victimisation, for survivors
- the forms of harm to be recognised by the court

- guarding against popular emotionalism which may affect the personal experiences of victim survivors
- a range of tactical problems in giving equal recognition or proportional weight to different victim voices depending on proximity, and how these are to be challenged.

For instance, the instrumentality of victim impact statements arising from terrorist mass killings is controversial. Should the victim voice, individual or collective, influence sentencing directly? And if so, what weight should be accorded relative to other sentencing principles such as general community protection? Further, in the context of widely feared terrorist events, how can the interests of the accused fairly be separated from victim impact and community vengeance or mob hysteria?

In terms of extending the reach of legitimate status, what are the dangers for international criminal justice in preferring victim interests and thereby compromising conventional protections for an accused person? The problems associated with this trend have been rehearsed in detail when considering the domestic jurisdiction of victim impact statements in homicide (Erez and Rogers 1999). Therein no victim voice remains, beyond the voices of secondary parties closely connected to the deceased. This issue of connection to harm is exacerbated when there is more than one voice to comprise a connected victim community. Moving up to a global location, communitarian victim contexts presuppose a more flexible and case-by-case consideration of harm 'networking'. After all, this is the essence of genocide.

3   Victim communities

Crucial to our argument in favour of repositioning the constituency of international criminal justice towards legitimate victim interests is the recognition of communitarian victimisation.[14] Communitarian incorporation assumes a level of participatory democracy not yet seen in global governance. Communitarian governance will give legitimacy to both the substantive and institutional authority of global governance so far not present beyond normative claims about themes like rights and justice (Braithwaite 2002).

---

[14] It could be argued that current victim inclusion in international criminal proceedings has focused more on participation, distribution and the balancing of stakeholder's rights, rather than confronting the unique nature and needs of global victimisation; see Trumbull (2008).

We have strategically employed the notion of 'victim communities' not only to emphasise the collective composition of global victimisation, but to identify the structures of relationships which make sense of global crime victimisation and which would be essential in the measure of appropriate restorative and reconciliatory responses. The chapter will now further develop the concept of communitarian victimisation in discussing *communities of justice*; a communitarian entity and experience for manifesting legitimate victim interests in international criminal justice resolutions. Essential to this discussion is a recognition that victim communities themselves may be in contest over the nature and legitimacy of victimisation. This is one of the principal challenges for legal professionals in the transformed international criminal trial process.

On the requirement of identifying victim communities *in action* (conflictual or otherwise), the communitarian context of victimisation engages:

- the communities of these victims which share their harm
- where wider communities or groups of victims suffer harm
- where the crime is directed at community cohesion or cultural integrity
- when violence is motivated by the destruction of what makes communities or cultures (language, art, religion, family structure etc.).

Nature of global crime and the centrality of 'mass violence'

Crimes against humanity, genocide and war crimes all have about them and within them collective composition. Global crime therefore assumes the importance of communities that comprise the 'humanity' which international criminal justice should prosecute and protect in a normative and a practical sense.

As with victim valorisation, 'humanity' has been limited as a consequence of the segregation of legitimate violence. Oppositional cultures and communities, if resisting in a violent fashion the governance of the dominant political alliance worldwide, will become the subject of criminal prosecution rather than being appreciated in any context of victimisation. Segregated cultures, therefore, are disengaged from the protection of international criminal justice through association with perpetrators rather than victims. Consequently, the notion of global victimisation from the perspective of the dominant 'global community' is selective, exclusive and discriminatory. Victimisation is not accorded as a result of violent harm alone. Violence is negotiated in terms of its legitimacy rather than its consequences.

The monopolist claims over legitimate violence (exhibited through compromised global governance) are themselves resorted to by aggressively resistant victim communities against which the violence is directed.[15] For instance, the suicide bomber gives meaning to his sacrifice (and that of his innocent victims) in terms of the discriminatory violence of oppressive cultures against which he is at war. These oppressive cultures may not be within his middle-class, detached personal experience but they remain no less 'real' as a motivation for violent resistance. The monopoly on violence is in terms of contested legitimacy and not merely the nature of its occurrence. Even victimisation cannot alone determine the legitimacy or otherwise of violence.

Violence may be a force for transition but rarely can it sustain legitimate domestic or global governance, or replace broad-based community authorisation. Whether it is resistance movements or the arms of the state against which they are directed, violent revolution may stimulate transition, but it will not ground the governability of cultures in conflict, as the Palestinian Authority recently demonstrates.

Even so, violence is all too often an essential precursor to more established styles of global governance. Legitimacy, or violently asserted legitimacy prevailing over contested political realities, is the key Benjamin (1996) sees to the 'legal ends' of violence as well. In this respect, violent responses from states in transition demonstrate a violent-response governance model against violent revolution which the state criminalises. Militarist violence claims its legality through the authority of the state but does not have legality as its principal end.

Benjamin (1996) calls the first function of violence the law-making function, and the second the law-preserving function. Violence in the context of legality and justice responses for the sake of long-standing legitimacy would replace militarism (*ibid.*), as the USA problematically claims it will in the restoration of Iraq to democratic governance. When governance itself is challenged as a consequence of a sectarian and arguably unjust or illegal

---

[15] This balancing of aggressive justice responses with violent victim reaction is not essentially causal nor universal. Violent justice can be directed against otherwise peaceful resistant communities, and violent justice is not the principal cause of terrorist resistance. However, in certain prominent examples of violent justice and resistance the relationship merits examination as much does the social and cultural factors militating against violent resistance.

application to some victim communities and not others then the limitation of violence as a regulatory capacity is clear (Arendt 1969).

The nature of global violence: conflict against states or distinguishing communities?

Violence becomes a tool for social exclusion against communities and cultures determined as living beyond and outside the realm of legitimate victimisation. When these communities and cultures become 'collateral damage' through military intervention or violent justice responses, then the experience of the ICTY shows that only the intervention of those it prefers the violence directed against will be determined as suitable for prosecution in international criminal courts.

In the setting of global governance we have discussed in detail the nature and consequences of violent regulatory responses, in the form of military intervention or formal and sometimes distorted justice incursions (Findlay 2007). There can be little doubt that the perceived danger of international terror has given the United States, and its global political alliance the opportunity to expand justifications for military intervention, and to augment traditional justice forms to segregate, contain and punish terrorist suspects.

A recurrent concern in international criminal justice, which distinguishes its scope from domestic criminal justice traditions, is conflict resolutions in transitional-state violence. In fact this objective could be refined back to more universal domestic applications of the criminal sanction to maintain social order.

The 'global community' which enjoys social order within the restored state and against cultural resistance comprises only those victims 'worthy' of justice protection. With the other 'victims and their communities' global governance is often at war.

War-based governance[16]

Traditional criminal justice protections, and even international human rights conventions can be argued away by identifying the principal threats to global security and world order in terms of war and warmaking. Like victim valorisation, the war discourse promotes a clear if questionable division between citizens who deserve the protections of international criminal justice, and the enemies who do not. On this basis

---

[16] For a discussion of the aberrant consequences of the war on terror discourse, see Fogarty (2005).

international criminal justice is co-opted into this war analogy, and even the conventional justice protections are selectively employed through this conditional citizenship. As for para-justice the discrimination and its consequences for further selective victimisation are more stark (Findlay 2008: Chapter 6).

The war discourse and its consequences for the purposes of social control as governance are not new. Jonathan Simon (2007) rightly draws our attention to the war on drugs, and even the war on cancer as policies designed to galvanise and sharpen control on regulatory potential. What makes this new phase of the war on terror interesting both in terms of governance and victimisation, is the manner in which it has justified both military intervention and the distortion of conventional criminal justice when applied to terrorist respondents. War discourse is no novelty as a language of international crime control. Whether it is a war on drugs, a war on vice, or a war on child abuse the conflictual discourse resounds through the political representation of law enforcement as military engagement. Now we are immersed in a war on terror. What distinguishes this discourse from, say, that which relates to the war on drugs is its justification for actual and extensive military intervention. This state of war is more universalised and 'honourable'.

The preference in global governance terms for 'law over war' in controlling international crimes such as terrorism may gain greater relevance as international humanitarian law plays a more important role in international criminal justice (Chadwick 2003). Modern laws of war, which evolved in the nineteenth century from reciprocal alliance pacts, were designed to ensure minimal restraint amongst civilised people. Any strict contractual approach to mutuality in restraint has been superseded in the current situation of global governance by a more rigid and delineated commitment to global security and order at whatever cost. The cost has emerged as violence to the rights of the offender and victims in the name of risk and other securities. The recent justification for the use of torture reveals that even 'law' is made subservient to the need for security and global ordering. Law becomes the victim in the new war discourse.

The violence focus of governance responses to global terror can be seen as harming the rights of offenders and communities, as much as their physical integrity. Michaelson (2003) argues that the criminal law has been 'bastardised' in the name of control and security. The perversion of human rights in the process is evidence that both law and justice have been subverted. The question is whether the terrorist threat can be

viewed legally as posing a sufficient public emergency that national
security legislation is justified in abrogating the common obligations
imposed by international human rights conventions.

Cultural victimisation

Terrorist communities worldwide currently are clearly delineated in
terms of their ideology and their political commitments. For instance,
fundamentalist Islamic predispositions now are seen as a crucial stimu-
lant to terrorist activities. Almost as it was in the time of the crusades,
Islamic culture has become the enemy of liberal democracy and Western
freedoms leading to the wholesale alienation of Muslim communities in
the West in particular.

Amongst other cultures facing simplistic terrorist designation, political
separatism may be given legitimate victim status along with credibility in
otherwise geopolitically valued states. The 'terrorist' communities are
denied the political legitimacy of rational resistance and thereby violence
against these communities is legitimated and resultant harm neutralised.

The social exclusion of whole cultures beyond claims for legitimate
global citizenship, and consequent actionable victimisation, provides
fertile opportunities for violent resistance to global governance. Devaluing
the critical components of any culture along with violent justice responses
to terrorist resistance undermines the capacity of global governance
to develop a pluralist and inclusive regulatory framework. Violence
breeds violence when cultural integrity as well as community safety is
at stake.

Hegemonic violence and sectarian exclusion

The dominant global political alliance which has assumed a crusading role
in the war on terror has consciously sponsored and promoted the emergence of violent control strategies, and their delineation (Albrecht and
Kilchling 2005). Coalescing this alliance is a hegemony of ideals, preferred
governance models, singular economic relations and cultural supremacy.
Yet this hegemony is fragile when both confirmed and challenged through
terror and violent resistance. The formation and reformation of hegemonic orders in the context of wars of any type gives disproportionate
and dangerous precedents to violence in challenging or confirming order.
Hegemony over the war on terror is no different.

It is a characteristic of political hegemonies which struggle to determine and impose a singular cultural and economic order over wide and

expanding terrain that violence becomes dominant in control strategies. Violence uniformly produces victimisation. Where violence and victim-isation become instrumental in determining the limits of a political hegemony and the nature and illegitimacy of resistance to it, then social exclusion in a community and cultural sense is a feature of that order (Tschudi 2008).

Constructive political configurations are less possible or sustainable where oppositional forces are determined through violent risks and countered with more violence than by grant of diplomacy. The security of hegemonic order becomes the overriding aspiration where order is contested and violence is the language of dominion.

At base, global hegemony is presently a political construct. As Frie-drichs (2005) observes, to provide the glue for global capitalism and ordered global community, global governance is sometimes construed as beyond and somehow above politics. That said, violence and victimisa-tion which confirm and confine world order have recently, in the global terrorist experience, exacerbated violent resistance through sectarian exclusion of communities and cultures from that order (Kay 2004).

4   Communities of justice: making victim focus work

What are communities of justice?[17] In essence they are a meeting of principal stakeholders in international criminal justice; a context wherein legitimate interests can be recognised and reconciled and features in dispute focused down with the assistance and oversight of legal professionals and the protections of a trial-justice tradition. Reverting back to our initial discussion of identifying and rationalising victim interests as the dominant commitment of international criminal justice, communities of justice will comprise:

- contesting victim interests, and their 'voices'
- perpetrators and accused persons against whom victimisation respon-sibility is charged
- juridical professionals required to manage and mediate justice reso-lutions and decision pathways onto specific trial outcomes, governed by the rule of law and procedural fairness.

---

[17] The concept is explored in the context of democratic global governance, in Findlay (2008: Chapters 7 and 9).

Because of limited access to the trial process, pre-trial communities of justice will function in an important didactic role for other communitarian justice opportunities in the less formal or alternative-justice sector of international criminal justice.

Communities of justice are more than just a place for negotiating particular or mutual interests. They are also essentially communitarian in nature, intent, discourse and diversity. As true communities, these coalesce with an eventual common purpose: the achievement of humanitarian justice. We anticipate that if the conditions for communitarian justice are ensured,[18] trust and mutual respect being essential to these, then a shared notion of humanity may override the tensions of self-interest in the trial proper. This outcome will eventuate within communities of justice provided that the rewards available through trial access, inclusivity and integration are observed and actual.

It would be naïve not to identify and confront the very different starting points for stakeholders on the road to a possible justice communion within the rationalised adversary argument of the international criminal trial. Therefore, the mechanisms which we have proposed (Findlay and Henham 2010) for the achievement of that identification and its mediation will be crucial pre-trial for establishing where possible and appropriate a common framework from which communities of justice will evolve and engage with very particularised issues in dispute for adversarial resolution in the trial.

Our trial model is a series of crucial decision sites where 'pathways of influence' are constructed by central stakeholders (victims included). Representing a vibrant and recurrent decision forum, communities of justice will centre around decision sites essential for the identification and achievement of justice outcomes. Pre-trial and trial contexts will enable the mediation of disputes which would otherwise complicate and confound the decisions that emerge progressively in this model.

These decision sites also will be influential in the type of communitarian justice resulting from the various regulatory mechanisms resorted to by any community of justice for solving its justice requirements.

---

[18] These conditions are developed in detail in Findlay and Henham (2010). Put simply, communities of justice in a trial attachment will be determined through pre-trial conferencing in a mediation format. It will be similar in process to the way in which agreed facts are settled prior to trial. The prosecutor (and where necessary victim advocates) will mediate conflicting interests in order that commonality can be passed on to the trial proper and the key issues in dispute can also progress to adversary resolution within the trial.

Outside the trial, for instance, the now peripheral process of victim compensation in the ICC framework would be significantly impacted and facilitated by the mediation of victim interests through communities of justice resolutions (pre-trial and trial). This process assumes that in a community of justice a singular regulatory model will not be appropriate and that a variety of regulatory alternatives should be on offer for negotiation and resort, even in the trial itself (Findlay and Henham 2010: Chapters 1 and 8).

A detailed contextual interrogation of how any particular community of justice reaches consensus will also require getting to know the parties and relationships from which pathways of influence to crucial decisions in the trial may evolve. In order that such an interrogation will be valuable and predictive, the obligations of trial professionals to facilitate communities of justice need to be clearly designated and uniformly required.

Communities of justice and accountability

Communities of justice, as well as providing the framework for a more conciliatory justice resolution respectful of legitimate victim interests, also act essentially as a background to test the accountability of international criminal justice. How then does the community of justice promote international justice as an accountability pillar in global governance?

- As with all communities it provides 'boundaries of permission' (Findlay 1994) within which discretion can be exercised and decisions have their acceptable reach.
- These boundaries are qualified by the same normative framework as that confirming the justice for which the community strives.
- For this justice to be confirmed and to continue it must have legitimacy within the community.
- This legitimacy is crucially dependant on an atmosphere of peace and order which global governance is charged to ensure.
- The capacity of global governance to achieve peace and good order, and to maintain their benefits relies on the widest support of the cultures and interests which contest in any community of justice.
- Therefore good governance is only achieved when the instrumentalities and processes of governance are responsible to the legitimate interests within those communities.

Communities of justice and legitimation: the future of international criminal justice?

Concluding the analysis in *Governing through Globalised Crime* (Findlay 2008) is a recognition that communitarian justice holds out a powerful potential to legitimate international criminal justice and the governance model within which it is significantly placed. But for such legitimacy to be more than superficial and contestable, communities in dispute need at least to share a common regard for the reconciliatory capacity of international criminal justice, its institutions and agencies.

The achievement of a resounding and resilient legitimacy which is community-focused takes us back to a consideration of the normative framework for a transformed international criminal justice and the manner in which it is to be actualised. Access to justice is central to this achievement. Such access needs to be much more inclusive than is possible for victim interests in contemporary domestic criminal justice models. Inclusivity means more than appearance and much more like actual involvement.[19] To confirm the reality of access, along with inclusivity comes the need for integration at all stages of the pre-trial and trial decision-making process. If this is achieved then victim interests should be recognisable in each important pathway of influence such as any pre-trial and trial decision site within the transformed trial process.

Communities of justice will not be achieved simply by a nominal recognition of a new normative framework around access, inclusivity and integration. The reality of communitarian justice for international criminal justice within international criminal trials will rely on how and if justice professionals, prosecutors and judges in particular engage with and promote the victim voice, and confront and confound the challenges that enabling a victim voice will constantly present (Kirchengast 2006).

Even so, international tribunal-based justice will never sufficiently reflect and resound the victim voice. Because of the following, global trial justice must transform:

- the structural limitations on the number of prosecutions the ICC can mount
- the nature of global victimisation involving communities of victims, most of whom will not participate in criminal proceedings
- victims of global crimes not always sharing common interest

---

[19] For a discussion of the limits of that involvement in the courts and tribunals currently constituted, see Rohne (2003).

- procedural measures designed to advance victim inclusion adversely affecting the interests of other, as yet unrecognised, victims
- the increased cost of active victim participation and accountability frameworks further diminishing the active role of international criminal prosecutions.

Selective prosecutions will continue to be advanced largely on immeasurable aspirations to end impunity and deterrence (Trumbull 2008: 826). The transformed trial offers, in addition to expressive and didactic justice, a viable and victim-actionable 'rights-based' context for the management of truth and reconciliation as well as guilt and penalty. With this as the measure for more diverse and informal victim access, restorative justice will remain the paradigm for practical international criminal justice.

References

Aertsen, I., Arsovska, J., Rohne, H. C., Valinas, M. and Vanspauwen, K. (2008) (eds.) *Restoring Justice after Large Scale Violent Conflicts*, Cullompton: Willan.

Albrecht, H.-J. and Kilchling, M. (2005) *Victims of Terrorism: Policies and Legislation in Europe*, MPI for Foreign and International Criminal Law, European Committee on Crime Problems, Second Meeting, 18–20 May 2005.

Albrecht, H.-J., Simon, J., Rezaei, H., Rohne, H. C. and Kiza, E. (2006) *Conflict and Conflict Resolution in Middle Eastern Societies: Between Tradition and Modernity*, Berlin: Duncker & Humblot.

Aldana-Pindell, R. (2002) 'In vindication of justiciable victims' rights to truth and justice for state-sponsored crimes', *Vanderbilt Journal of Transnational Law*, 35(5), 1399–435.

Arendt, H. (1969) *On Violence*, London: Allen Lane.

Barton, C. (2003) *Restorative Justice: The Empowerment Model*, Sydney: Hawkins Press.

Bauman, Z. (1998) *Globalisation: The Human Consequences*, Cambridge: Polity Press.

Benjamin W. (1996) 'Critique of violence, reflections: essays, aphorisms, autobiographical writings' as noted in Marcus Bullock and Michael Jennings (eds.) *Walter Benjamin: Selected Writings, volume 1: 1913–1926*, Cambridge, Massachusetts and London: The Belknap Press of Harvard University Press, pp. 236–53.

Braithwaite, J. (2002) *Restorative Justice and Responsive Regulation*, Oxford: Oxford University Press.

Brison, S. (2002) *Aftermath: Violence and the Remaking of Self*, Princeton: Princeton University Press.

Chadwick, E. (2003) 'It's war Jim but not as we know it: a reality check for international laws of war?' *Crime, Law and Social Change*, 39(3), 239–62.

Damaska, M. (2008) 'What is the point of international criminal justice', *Chicago-Kent Law Review*, 83(1), 329–65.

Danner A. and Martinez, J. (2005) 'Guilty associations: joint criminal enterprise, command responsibility, and the development of international criminal law', *California Law Review*, 93(75), 77–169.

Erez, E. and Rogers, L. (1999) 'Victim impact statements and sentencing outcomes and processes: the perspectives of legal professionals', *British Journal of Criminology*, 39(2), 216–39.

Findlay, M. (1994) 'The ambiguity of accountability: deaths in custody and regulation of police power', *Current Issues in Criminal Justice*, 6(2), 234–51.

  (1999) *The Globalisation of Crime: Understanding Transitional Relationships in Context*, Cambridge: Cambridge University Press.

  (2007) 'Terrorism and Relative Justice', *Crime, Law and Social Change*, 47, 57–89.

  (2008) *Governing through Globalised Crime: Futures of International Criminal Justice*, Cullompton: Willan.

Findlay, M. and Henham, R. (2005) *Transforming International Criminal Justice: Retributive and Restorative Justice in the Trial Process*, Cullompton: Willan.

  (2010) *Beyond Punishment: Achieving International Criminal Justice?* Basingstoke: Palgrave Macmillan.

Findlay, M. and McLean, C. (2007) 'Emerging international criminal justice', *Current Issues in Criminal Justice*, 18(3), 457–80.

Fletcher, G. (1995) *With Justice for Some: Victim's Rights in Criminal Trials*, New York: Addison Wesley.

Fogarty, G. (2005) 'Is Guantánamo Bay undermining the global war on terror?', *Parameters*, 35(3), 59–72.

Freeman, M. (2006) *Truth Commissions and Procedural Frameworks*, New York: Cambridge University Press.

Friedrichs, J. (2005) 'Global governance and the hegemonic project of transatlantic civil society' in M. Lederer and P. Muller (eds.), *Criticising Global Governance*, New York: Palgrave Macmillan, pp. 45–68.

Human Rights Watch (2008) *Still Waiting: Bringing Justice for War Crimes, Crimes against Humanity and Genocide in Bosnia and Herzegovina's Cantonal and District Courts*, New York: Human Rights Watch.

Judah, E. and Bryant, M. (2003) (eds.) *Criminal Justice: Retribution* v. *Restoration*, New York: The Hayworth Social Work Press.

Kay, J. (2004) 'Redefining the terrorist', *The National Interest*, 7, 87.

Kirchengast, T. (2006) *The Victim in Criminal Justice*, Basingstoke: Palgrave Macmillan.

Lederer, M. and Muller, P. (2005) (eds.) *Criticising Global Governance*, New York: Palgrave Macmillan.

Levi, M. (1997) *Consent and Dissent in Patriotism*, Cambridge: Cambridge University Press.

Linton, S. (2002) 'New approaches to international justice in Cambodia and East Timor', *International Review of the Red Cross*, 845, 93–119.

Logan, W. (2008) 'Confronting evil: victim's rights in an age of terror', *Georgetown Law Journal*, 96(3), 721–76.

Michaelson, C. (2003) 'International human rights on trial: the United Kingdom's and Australia's response', *Sydney Law Review*, 21(3), 275.

O'Donohue, J. (2005) 'The 2005 budget of the International Criminal Court: contingency, insufficient funding in key areas and the recurring question of the independence of the prosecutor', *Leiden Journal of International Law*, 18, 591–603.

Peskin, V. (2005) 'Rwanda: the promise and pitfalls of the ICTR outreach programme', *International Journal of Criminal Justice*, 3, 950–61.

Rohne, H. C. (2003) *The Victims and Witnesses Section at the ICTY*, MPI for Foreign and International Criminal Law: Freiburg.

Schunemann, B. (2000) 'The role of the victim within the criminal justice system: A three tiered concept', *Buffalo Law Journal*, 3, 33–64.

Simon, J. (2007) *Governing through Crime: How the War on Crime Transformed American Democracy and Created a Culture of Fear*, Oxford: Oxford University Press.

Trumbull, C. (2008) 'The victims of victim participation in international criminal proceedings', *Michigan Journal of International Law*, 29, 777–826.

Tschudi, F. (2008) 'Dealing with violent conflict and mass victimisation: a human dignity approach' in I. Aertsen, J. Arsovska, H. C. Rohne, M. Valinas and K. Vanspauwen (eds.), *Restoring Justice after Large Scale Violent Conflicts*, Cullompton: Willan, pp. 46–70.

6

Dealing with war crimes in Bosnia: retributive and restorative options through the eyes of the population

STEPHAN PARMENTIER AND ELMAR WEITEKAMP*

1   Introduction

The entry into force of the Rome Statute, on 1 July 2002, has been heralded by many observers as the final start of a new era, the era of international justice. The importance of the International Criminal Court (ICC) can indeed hardly be overstated. It is the first permanent international court in the world's history that is competent to judge individuals for having committed crimes in various parts of the globe. Some go even further and see it as the ultimate panacea that will not only react to crimes but also deter future crimes, promote reconciliation between former enemies and bring peace to the world. Both perspectives strongly rely on the ICC, and international criminal justice as a whole, as a new form of governance.

Notwithstanding the importance of the ICC and other institutions of criminal justice, some cautionary remarks seem warranted. First of all, the creation of the ICC is the result of a lengthy process that was far from linear, but was instead fraught with piecemeal changes and huge leaps, full of strange coincidences and even stranger alliances. This long and curving road to The Hague has displayed little coherence, let alone convergence, and it remains to be seen if and how convergence may come about. Furthermore, it should be noted that the ICC and international criminal justice as a whole reflect one particular form of governing crime, i.e. through criminal law and through the prosecution

* The authors gratefully acknowledge the financial support of the Research Fund of the K. U. Leuven for the four-year research project (2004–8) of which the Bosnian survey was a part, as well as the Flemish Academic Centre (VLAC) in Brussels for providing the ideal environment to prepare this contribution.

of persons suspected of having committed crimes by action or by omission. Other forms of dealing with the past exist but they tend to remain in the shadow. Finally, international criminal justice as a model to deal with international crimes is the creation of powerful elites, political and ethical, state and non-state. They have strongly pushed forward the agenda of the ICC and some other tribunals as a worthy cause for mankind, without paying too much attention to the viewpoints of local communities and individuals.

What are the underlying trends in international criminal justice and what are the links with the governance of crime? These are the main issues addressed in this chapter. We aim to illustrate these issues by means of a case study of dealing with war crimes in Bosnia, one part of the former Yugoslavia severely hit by crimes and human rights violations back in the early 1990s. In the following paragraphs, we will briefly sketch the development and the main features of international criminal justice, and explore alternative models of justice, mostly restorative. Then we look in more detail at the case of Bosnia and we report on the findings of an empirical survey about the attitudes and opinions of the population in relation to post-conflict justice.

2 International criminal justice: main features and some perspectives

One of the most important features of the ICC Statute lies in the enumeration of international crimes in four categories, namely: genocide, crimes against humanity, war crimes, and the crime of aggression (the latter not yet defined). Step by step, the essential aspects of these crimes are interpreted at the international level and the crimes are incorporated in the national legal orders of the states parties.

2.1 Shifting boundaries of criminal prosecutions

For decades the handling of serious human rights violations and the prosecution of serious crimes committed in the past were left to the discretion of the political and the criminal justice authorities of the country where they had taken place. Not until the fall of the Berlin wall in 1989 was the awareness created in academia and in policy-making that situations of political transition create a new space to discuss and to design policies for tackling human rights violations and crimes of the former regimes. This question of 'dealing with the past' (Huyse 1996) became rapidly coined as 'transitional justice', meaning 'the study of the choices made and the quality of justice rendered when states are replacing authoritarian regimes by democratic state institutions' (Siegel 1998: 431). More recently the latter notion has been expanded to include 'the full range of processes and mechanisms associated with a society's attempts to come to terms with a legacy of large-scale past abuses, in order to ensure accountability, serve justice and achieve reconciliation' (United Nations 2004: 4).

In view of the many challenges to address the violations and crimes of the past, we have argued elsewhere that two important shifts have taken place over the last twenty years (Parmentier *et al.* 2008). The first shift relates to the development of so-called 'universal jurisdiction' legislation in a number of countries. Such legislation allows third countries to prosecute and to try the suspects of international crimes, without the existence of a link between the third country and the place where the crimes have been committed, the nationality of the offender or the nationality of the victim. The main rationale lies in the fact that international crimes are considered so heinous that they not only affect the victims and the criminal justice system of the country where they took place, but also affect humanity as such, for which reason also third countries put their criminal justice system at the disposal of the world community. Such cases of 'pure' universal jurisdiction are in fact rare in today's world, the former Spanish and Belgian legislation being among the exceptions (Reydams 2004). In fact, a number of countries – mostly European – have a limited form of universal jurisdiction, and require at least one specific link with the crime in order to prosecute and try it. While welcomed by some as an ethical triumph for humanity (Brussels Group 2002), events of the last decade in Western Europe suggest that the efforts to establish genuine systems of universal jurisdiction are often subject to the realpolitik of international relations. The second major shift in responses to mass atrocity lies precisely in the establishment of criminal justice institutions at the international level. The immediate precursors of this movement were the two ad hoc international criminal tribunals, for the former Yugoslavia (ICTY) and for Rwanda (ICTR), set up by the Security Council of the United Nations in 1993 and 1994 respectively, for a limited period of time and with a limited territorial jurisdiction. The far-away forerunners, however, go back to the end of the Second World War with the establishment of the military tribunals of Nuremberg and Tokyo to judge the high-level officials of Germany and Japan. Furthermore, the early origins of the ICC can actually be traced back to the debates to judge the German emperor after the end of the First World War (Bassiouni 1997). While the two ad hoc tribunals have a primary competence to deal with serious human rights violations, the ICC has a complementary task to prosecute and try international crimes when states parties are 'unwilling or unable' to do so, thus leaving the prime locus at the national level (Kittichaisaree 2001). In between these developments, and even following the establishment of the ICC, several mixed or hybrid tribunals were set up to deal with a limited number of crimes, e.g. in Sierra Leone, East Timor, Kosovo and Cambodia.

Given the many developments in international criminal justice over the last decades, the whole construction was far from linear or logical, but resembles more of a patchwork of occasional and idiosyncratic elements. The coherence is far from present, and it is therefore to be regarded as a weak form of governance.

2.2   The dominant model: criminal prosecutions and retributive justice

This brings us to a second aspect. Calls to bring the presumed offenders to a criminal court usually ring loud after a regime change has taken place, and the old authoritarian leaders have been replaced by a more or less democratic form of government. Such developments rarely take shape overnight but may continue to gestate and emerge after longer periods of time as illustrated by the cases of Pinochet and other regimes in South America (Roht-Arriaza 2005). The strong focus on criminal prosecutions fits within a retributive justice approach, which according to Ashworth means that 'punishment is justified as the morally appropriate response to crime: those who commit offences deserve punishment, it is claimed, and the amount of punishment should be proportionate to the degree of wrongdoing' (Ashworth 1997: 1096–7).

As the strong and weak points of criminal prosecutions for international crimes have been documented elsewhere, it may suffice here to briefly recall them. Basic arguments in favour of criminal prosecutions include: reconstructing the moral order of society and satisfying its desire for justice (Huyse 1998); strengthening the new and fragile democracy by confirming the 'rule of law' and human rights protection; and, last but not least, complying with the legal duty to prosecute in international human rights law (Orentlicher 2005).

However, criminal prosecutions are not without problems or risks: they may undermine the 'rule of law' if they violate the principle of non-retroactivity of criminal law or if they cannot guarantee the independence and the impartiality of the criminal justice system (Huyse 1998); they may provoke the former and powerful elites to destabilise the country or to seize power again (Orentlicher 1991); they may be confronted with limited capacities of the criminal justice systems; and they tend to have a strong focus on the offenders and the accused at the expense of the victims and the harm inflicted upon them (Findlay and Henham 2005; Zehr 2003).

2.3   *What about restorative justice?*

Given the many problems with prosecutions and retributive justice in general, recent years have seen an increasing interest for other institutions and other models to deal with serious human rights violations and international crimes. The more than thirty truth commissions that have been established since the last quarter of the twentieth century are the best-known examples of 'second-best' solutions (Hayner 2002). Truth commissions have become strongly associated with restorative justice principles (Llewellyn 2007) and some, like the South African one, are among the few transitional justice mechanisms to be explicitly labelled as a restorative justice mechanism (Villa-Vicencio 2001). As a result there is increasing interest for the model of restorative justice, and particularly for the applicability of restorative justice in situations of mass victimisation and post-conflict justice (Aertsen *et al.* 2008; Weitekamp *et al.* 2006). Such approach requires 'changing lenses', as aptly put by Zehr (1991) in his seminal work on restorative justice for common crimes.

To assert that restorative justice is of growing importance inside and outside the criminal justice system of many countries is nothing less than a truism. Although no commonly accepted definition seems to exist, the literature makes frequent reference to two types of definitions. Marshall defines restorative justice as 'a process whereby parties with a stake in a specific offence resolve collectively how to deal with the aftermath of the offence and its implications for the future' (Marshall 1996: 37); whereas Bazemore and Walgrave are goal-oriented as they formulate restorative justice as 'every action that is primarily oriented towards doing justice by repairing the harm that has been caused by the crime' (Bazemore and Walgrave 1999: 48). In our view, it is more important to identify the key principles of restorative justice, which following Roche (2003), we have proposed elsewhere (Parmentier *et al.* 2008: 344) as including the following: (1) *personalism*: crime is a violation of people and their relationships rather than a violation of (criminal) law; (2) *reparation*:

the primary goal is to repair the harm of the victim rather than to punish the perpetrator; (3) *reintegration*: the aim is to finally reintegrate the perpetrator into society rather than to alienate and isolate him/her from society; and (4) *participation*: the objective is to encourage the involvement of all direct and possibly also indirect stakeholders to deal with the crime collectively.

The bottom line of restorative justice is to view crime as a violation of people and relations, thereby creating an obligation to make things right. This process should be facilitated by bringing victims and offenders together on a voluntary basis, such as in victim–offender mediation programmes, and possibly also with the other stakeholders, for example in restorative justice conferences. In these forums, room is made for dialogue and for creating an opportunity, with the help of a mediator, to restore the harm done and to reconcile the relationship. It is striking that developments in restorative justice are almost exclusively focused on less serious property crimes and on juvenile crime, with a limited number of isolated examples of victim–offender programmes for serious interpersonal crimes (e.g. Umbreit *et al.* 2003). But thus far very little attention has been paid to restorative justice for crimes of a political nature, sometimes reaching the level of mass violence and mass victimisation (Christie 2001). However, viewing restorative justice in such a way that it may complement retributive mechanisms in dealing with mass violence allows for an extension of the concept of governance of international crimes.

2.4 Broadening the top-down approach to transitional justice

The many academic discussions and policy decisions in the fields of 'transitional justice' or 'post-conflict justice' (Bassiouni 2002) are for the most part managed by elites, both at a national and international level. The views and expectations of the local populations are rarely taken into account, yet population-based research can yield unique insights into the strategies and mechanisms for dealing with the crimes of the past and for reconstructing the future.

The last couple of years have seen a rapid development in this field, with a number of empirical researches being conducted in post-conflict situations and sometimes even during ongoing conflicts (i.e. ICTJ 2004; ICTJ 2006; ICTJ 2007). Such research goes hand in hand with the newly emerging concept of 'transitional justice from below' that emphasises the spaces where struggles take place with the active involvement of organisations and individuals (McEvoy and McGregor 2008).

3   'Doing justice' through the eyes of the Bosnian population

The argument that discussions about transitional justice tend to be managed by national and international elites also applies to the case of Bosnia. The input of local organisations and the population at large seems to have been limited, and only a handful of empirical studies on transitional justice issues in the country have been conducted over the last few years (Biro *et al.* 2004; UNDP 2005; Kiza *et al.* 2006). For these reasons a Leuven research team has designed and conducted an empirical survey on various issues of post-conflict justice with the wider population in the territory of Bosnia in 2006.[1] The following paragraphs report on some findings of this population-based survey, particularly in relation to the issues of accountability and reconciliation for the crimes of the past. Before presenting the main findings we briefly introduce the background, the objectives and the design of the survey.

3.1   *Background to the situation in Bosnia*

One of the violent conflicts that gave rise to fierce debates about transitional and post-conflict justice, and about the role of international and national criminal justice, is that which raged through the countries of ex-Yugoslavia some years after the fall of the Berlin wall in 1989. In early 1992, following the break-up of Yugoslavia, Bosnia and Herzegovina (hereafter referred to as Bosnia or BiH) plunged into a devastating war that would last for almost four years and would take an enormous toll on its population, infrastructure and cultural heritage. Recent estimates point to around 100,000 deaths and 2.2 million displaced people.[2] Atrocities such as mass murders, extrajudicial executions, torture, rape,

---

[1] The Leuven research team was composed of the current authors working in close co-operation with a local consultant in Bosnia, Almir Maljevic. The authors would like to express their gratitude to Marta Valiñas for her efforts in preparing the research report (Valiñas, Parmentier and Weitekamp 2009) and to Almir Maljevic who served as their local project consultant in Bosnia. They also like to thank Uwe Ewald, Johan Goethals, Manfred Nowak and Julian Roberts for their careful reading and insightful comments on previous versions of the empirical part of the survey.

[2] The Demographic Unit of the Office of the Prosecutor of the ICTY has proposed a '*minimum estimate* of war-related deaths' of 67,530 and an overall estimate of 102,622 deaths (of which 46% were military victims and 54% civilian victims) (see Tabeau and Bijak 2005: 192 and 196). As to the number of displaced people, these are the estimates of the United Nations High Commissioner for Refugees (data available from *The State of the World's Refugees* 2000).

illegal detention, forced displacement, looting and destruction of religious and cultural sites are fairly well documented though responsibilities for them continue to be contested. As reports of such wanton
destruction and humanitarian crisis became widespread, the concern of
the international community grew over the situation in Bosnia. However, it would not be until December 1995 that the Dayton Peace
Agreements would be signed, officially ending the war in Bosnia. The
agreements created a complex political and territorial structure in order
to respond to the parties' demands. They divided the country into two
entities: the Federation of Bosnia and Herzegovina, inhabited predominantly by a Bosniak and Bosnian Croat population, and the Republika
Srpska, inhabited predominantly by Bosnian Serbs. The agreements also
provided for a far-reaching intervention of the international community
in both civilian and military affairs in post-war Bosnia. The involvement
of the international community in transitional justice issues began even
before the end of the war, with the creation in 1993 of the International
Criminal Tribunal for the former Yugoslavia (ICTY) by Resolution 827
of the United Nations Security Council.

The complexity surrounding the causes and nature of the war, as well
as the involvement of a multiplicity of internal and external actors in the
war and the post-war period, complicate the Bosnian transitional justice
context. Thirteen years after the official end of the war in Bosnia the
country is still struggling to find the best way(s) to address the atrocities
that occurred in the past and their consequences and to rebuild trust
among its members. The debate on how to deal with the past in Bosnia is
ongoing, and seems to have gained a new momentum in the recent
years. New mechanisms have recently been put in place, such as the War
Crimes Chamber at the State Court in Sarajevo, and other transitional
justice approaches, such as a truth commission for the region or specific
reparation programmes (Buyse 2008), continue to be discussed. Therefore this debate remains of high relevance to the people, organisations
and institutions of Bosnia.

3.2   Objectives and design

Through our research survey we have aimed at contributing to a
better understanding of the opinions and attitudes of citizens of
Bosnia and Herzegovina on how the past should be dealt with. The
survey forms part of the broader research project entitled 'Mass
victimisation and restorative justice: in search of the position of

restorative justice in an integrated approach to mass victimisation in post-conflict situations'. The project was conducted from the Leuven Institute of Criminology, between 2004 and 2008. This project sought to explore what the role and applicability of restorative justice principles might be in the process of dealing with post-conflict situations that include mass victimisation, taking Serbia and Bosnia and Herzegovina as two case studies.

The aim of the survey reported here was to inquire into the attitudes and opinions of individuals about the process of dealing with the past (or transitional justice) in Bosnia, with a particular focus on the opportunities for, and the potential of, a restorative approach to such processes. As a general framework we used the TARR model originally developed by Parmentier and composed of four building blocks that correspond to four key issues in the process of dealing with the past by new regimes, namely: to search for *truth* about the past (T), to ensure *accountability* of the offenders (A), to provide some form of *reparation* for the victims (R) and to promote *reconciliation* between former enemies (R) (Parmentier 2003; Parmentier and Weitekamp 2007). This model provides a useful framework to analyse the various relations between two or more of its building blocks, it allows us to examine specific institutions and mechanisms of dealing with the past in relation to each of these issues, and finally it suggests that transitional justice approaches will result from the interplay between these four building blocks.

The research method used in this study was a self-administered survey carried out through written questionnaires distributed to 900 respondents across Bosnia. The methodology comprised four key steps and has been described at length elsewhere (Parmentier *et al.* 2009; Valiñas *et al.* 2009). These included first creating an instrument of data-gathering, whereby the research team developed a questionnaire making use of a variety of written and oral sources. A second stage entailed determining an adequate sampling method. Here, the team opted for a 'quota sampling method',[3] by dividing the target population – the citizens and residents of Bosnia – into subgroups or strata according to four criteria of particular interest, namely geographical distribution (with respondents from both the Federation of

---

[3] As explained by Bryman (2008: 102), the difference between quota sampling (a non-probability method) and stratified random sampling (a probability method) is that in the former 'the sampling of individuals is not carried out randomly, since the final selection of people is left to the interviewer'.

Bosnia and Herzegovina and the Republika Srpska, and the Brčko District), religious affiliation (Muslims, Catholics and Orthodox), age (aiming at a large majority of persons between twenty-six and sixty-four years old and smaller groups of other age categories), and gender (equal groups of men and women). In relation to the religious affiliation of the respondents equal weight was given to the voices of each of the three religious groups and therefore a 'disproportionate sample' with an under-representation of Muslims (Bosniaks) and Orthodox (Serbs) and an over-representation of Catholics (Croats) in relation to the estimate composition of the country was drawn.[4] The third step involved the collection of the data through the distribution of the questionnaire. In May and June 2006 students of the University of Sarajevo distributed the questionnaires in their home towns or villages all over Bosnia to persons fitting the selection criteria. Of the total number of 900 questionnaires distributed 855 were returned duly filled. The final stage saw the analysis of the data gathered. All data were entered and processed using SPSS software, performing various analyses and tests. All figures presented in what follows are the result of this four-step process of data-gathering and analysis.

The questionnaire was organised around thirty-eight questions and was subdivided into two main parts. The first part contained questions about forms of direct victimisation (e.g. physical injuries on the respondent) and indirect victimisation (e.g. having lost family members). Respondents were asked about their perceived suffering in three categories (physical, material and psychological) and in two time periods (during and after the war). The second part of the questionnaire asked various questions under five different headings: seeking truth, establishing accountability, providing reparation, promoting reconciliation and the meaning of restorative justice.

3.3   Major research findings

In the following paragraphs we only report on some issues of accountability and restorative justice, which are part of the larger survey

---

[4] According to the CIA Factbook, Bosnia and Herzegovina, 2006, the population of the country is composed of 48% Bosniaks, 37% Serbs and 15% Croats (data from 2000 available at *https://www.cia.gov/cia/publications/factbook/geos/bk.html*).

conducted in Bosnia. The results of a similar population-based survey in Serbia are reported elsewhere (Parmentier *et al.* forthcoming).

3.3.1   Accountability and prosecutions for war crimes in Bosnia

One of the central questions that arise after the end of a violent and large-scale conflict is how to deal with those responsible for the massive human rights violations that took place. In the former Yugoslavia, the decision by the UN Security Council in 1993 to create the ICTY set the precedent of how the past human right violations were going to be dealt with at the international level and how it was suggested they should be dealt with at the national level: through criminal prosecutions. Since then, the prosecution of war crimes, genocide and crimes against humanity has been at the centre of international efforts in supporting the process of dealing with the past in the region. Prosecution in general has also been put very little into question by human rights organisations, victim organisations and the international community. The establishment of the War Crimes Chamber at the State Court of Bosnia has been another step towards accountability through criminal justice and it has been regarded as a very important development in the fight against impunity in the country. There are, however, certain questions surrounding prosecutions in the criminal courts that have been less often debated. For example, in a country in which such a large part of the population was involved actively in the war, which criteria determine who should be subject to criminal prosecution and who should not? In addition, what else should be considered as accountability measures either in parallel with criminal prosecution or as a replacement when prosecution does not take place? The survey aimed at exploring some of these questions and tried to get a better understanding of what 'accountability' means in Bosnia.

The respondents were asked who they thought should be held responsible for the things that happened during the war in Bosnia, and they were given the possibility of choosing more than one option (Table 6.1). The aim was to understand at whom accountability measures should be targeted. The option most frequently chosen was 'political leaders' (72 per cent), followed by 'direct perpetrators' (46 per cent) and by the 'international community' (41 per cent). Military or police leaders were chosen by 29 per cent of respondents, religious leaders by 24 per cent, and members of ethnic groups other than that of the respondent by 22 per cent. The media was only attributed responsibility by 18 per cent of respondents. Finally, 13 per cent of respondents attributed responsibility to the whole society.

Table 6.1 *Targets of accountability*

	n	% cases
Political leaders	615	72
Direct perpetrators	393	46
The international community	352	41
Military or police leaders	246	29
Religious leaders	205	24
Members of other ethnic groups	186	22
The media	152	18
The whole society	109	13
Don't know	13	2
Total	2271	267

Missing cases: Political leaders 28.1%; Perpetrators 52.5%; IC 58.8%; Military leaders 71.2%; Religious leaders 76%; Other ethnicity 78.2%; Media 82.2%; Society 87.3%.

Question: Who do you think should be held responsible for the things that happened during the war in Bosnia and Herzegovina? (You can choose more than one answer)

A few variations in the answers given according to religion are worth noting (Table 6.2). For example, among those who think that direct perpetrators should be held responsible there was a larger percentage of Muslim respondents (39 per cent) in comparison to the Orthodox respondents (24 per cent). In relation to the 'military and political leaders' both Catholics (40 per cent) and Muslims (39 per cent) seemed to attribute a greater degree of responsibility to them than Orthodox respondents do (20 per cent). It is also interesting that Muslims (49 per cent) attributed more responsibility to 'members of other ethnic groups' than either Catholics (20 per cent) or Orthodox (29 per cent) do. And finally, it is also worth noting that the 'international community' and the 'media' were thought to be responsible mostly by Orthodox respondents (respectively: 41 per cent of Orthodox, 26 per cent Muslims and 32 per cent Catholic in relation to the international community; and 51 per cent of Orthodox, 24 per cent Muslims and 21 per cent Catholics in relation to the media).

Then, the survey asked what should happen to the persons responsible for the things that happened to the respondent *during* the war – with the explanation that what was meant here were the persons who committed acts described earlier in the questionnaire on victimisation experiences

Table 6.2 *Targets of accountability and religious affiliation*

	Catholic	Muslim	Orthodox
Political leaders	34	33	31
Direct perpetrators	34	39	24
The international community	32	26	41
Military or police leaders	40	39	20
Religious leaders	32	34	31
Members of other ethnic groups than your own	20	49	29
The media	21	24	51
The whole society	33	28	37
Don't know	15	31	39

Values shown are for % within each option on the left column.
Question: Who should be held responsible for the things that happened in Bosnia during the war?

directly against the respondent him/herself. Among the given options were included both processes and measures that would be implemented regardless of the will of the perpetrator, and also actions that would be more intrinsically linked to the perpetrator's will and attitude. The reason behind this was to understand whether measures of accountability imposed from the outside are preferred as against measures that seek to elicit so-called 'active responsibility', meaning that the offender must contribute actively 'to repairing the negative consequences of the offence' (Walgrave 2008: 45). This presupposes a certain degree of acknowledgement of responsibility and the readiness to take steps to make up for what happened in the (best) possible way. Table 6.3 describes the accountability measures or actions favoured by respondents, ranging from those favoured more to those favoured less. A vast majority of respondents gave priority to measures of restitution (return of property and material goods) and to confession. Some 80 per cent of the respondents agreed or strongly agreed that perpetrators should return material goods, 80 per cent that perpetrators should confess, 68 per cent thought perpetrators should apologise, 66 per cent thought they should be obliged to pay compensation to the victims, and 62 per cent thought they should do community work when compensation or restitution would not be possible. All in all, the issue of restitution of property seemed to have been very important in Bosnia and Herzegovina given that enforced displacement was often accompanied by the loss of property.

Table 6.3 *Preferred measures of accountability for the harm inflicted during the war (%)*

	Strongly disagree	Disagree	Agree	Strongly agree	Don't know
Restitution of property or other stolen material goods	4	7	8	73	10
Confession	6	2	6	75	12
Prosecution in a criminal court in Bosnia-Herzegovina	12	7	10	60	10
Apologies	12	4	5	63	17
Monetary compensation to the victims	14	8	10	56	12
Work for the community or for the victim (e.g. reconstruct houses) when material compensation or restitution not possible	15	8	12	50	15
Prosecution in a criminal court outside Bosnia-Herzegovina	23	6	10	51	10
Prosecution only of those with the highest responsibility for the violence (political and military leaders)	23	8	11	48	10

Question: What should happen to the persons responsible for the things that happened to you *during the war (i.e. the persons who committed directly against you the things you have described in question no. 8)?*

Prosecutions were also valued, but generally speaking at a lower level. Some 70 per cent of the respondents thought that those responsible should be prosecuted before a criminal court in BiH and 61 per cent considered a court outside of Bosnia, while 59 per cent thought only those with highest responsibility should be prosecuted. Another interesting observation is that prosecution both outside and inside Bosnia seems to be valued higher by Muslims (70 per cent and 76 per cent

Table 6.4 *Measures of accountability and religious affiliation (%)*

	Catholic	Muslim	Orthodox
Prosecution in a criminal court outside Bosnia-Herzegovina	64	70	48
Prosecution in a criminal court in Bosnia-Herzegovina	70	76	63
Prosecution only of those with the highest responsibility for the violence (political and military leaders)	66	52	60
Monetary compensation to the victims	68	66	62
Restitution of property or other stolen material goods	79	80	83
Work for the community or for the victim (e.g. reconstruct houses) when material compensation or restitution not possible	59	61	65
Confession	79	85	76
Apologies	67	77	59

Values shown are for % within religious affiliation and for responses 'agree' and 'strongly agree' together.
Question: What should happen to the persons responsible for the things that happened *to you during the war (i.e. the persons who committed directly against you the things you have described in question no. 8)?*

respectively) and by Catholics (64 per cent and 70 per cent) rather than by Orthodox respondents (48 per cent and 63 per cent) (Table 6.4).

Given the dominant role that prosecution tends to assume in the public debate on how to deal with the past violations, it is important to understand what were the reasons given by respondents who thought that prosecutions should indeed take place (Table 6.5). A vast majority of the respondents agreed or strongly agreed that prosecutions should take place 'so that it will not happen again' (94 per cent); a great number also believe that prosecutions should take place 'for the truth to be established in the court' (89 per cent) and 'for justice to be done' (88 per cent). When asked whether the reason behind prosecution is 'to take revenge' 64 per cent said they disagreed/strongly disagreed and only 26 per cent said they agreed/strongly agreed. Among these, there was a minority of Orthodox respondents (4 per cent against 11 per cent Muslims and 10 per cent Catholics) (Table 6.6).

Table 6.5 *Reasons for prosecution*

	Strongly disagree	Disagree	Agree	Strongly agree
So that it will not happen again	2	1	4	90
For the truth to be established in the court	3	2	10	80
For justice to be done	4	3	9	79
To take revenge	53	11	8	17

Missing cases: Prevention 8.3%; Truth 12.3%; Justice 10.5%; Revenge 16.5%.
Question: If you think that they should be prosecuted, what are the reasons for your answer?

Table 6.6 *Reasons for prosecution and religious affiliation*

	Catholic	Muslim	Orthodox
To take revenge	30	32	24
For justice to be done	89	89	83
For the truth to be established in the court	91	91	85
So that it will not happen again	96	92	93

Values shown are for % within ethnicity for responses 'agree' and 'strongly agree' together.
Question: If you think that they should be prosecuted, what are the reasons for your answer?

From these data we can conclude that the main function attributed to prosecutions in a criminal court is that of prevention and/or deterrence – which are normally translated into common language as 'for it not to happen again'. This reflects the widespread belief that prosecutions bear the potential of preventing future violations from taking place through the existence of a real threat of punishment. In other words, people seemed to believe that if there is a very real possibility of criminals being tried and punished, and if some actually are, in the future other potential criminals will be discouraged from committing crimes because they can foresee a real possibility that they as well will be held to account.

Deterrence as one of the consequences of criminal prosecutions has gradually become a more controversial issue in the area of criminal justice. Some authors have argued that there are no sufficient empirical findings to support the assumption that, especially in cases of gross and massive human rights violations, prosecution effectively has a deterrent effect (Villa-Vicencio 2000). Nonetheless, our survey seems to demonstrate how such belief has penetrated people's minds as well as the public discourse, regardless of whether there is a credible empirical evidence-base to support it or not. This is also in accordance with the data collected from interviews with local NGOs working on transitional justice issues and who emphasise the need to deal with the past (understood to a great extent as through criminal prosecutions) in order to avoid violence from taking place again in the future. In any case it is interesting that individuals primarily attributed to prosecutions a forward-looking function, namely to prevent the same violations from happening again in the future. This might be related to the history of the region which was ravaged by previous conflicts, and to people's wish that history will not repeat itself once again.

3.3.2   A place for restorative justice?

Given the aim of the larger research project to explore the possibilities of applying restorative justice principles in the process of dealing with the past in Bosnia, specific questions about restorative justice were included in the survey. They related inter alia to encounter with the offender and forgiveness by the victim. The responses give us a better understanding of how important those restorative elements are for the respondents and also tell us about their *comparative* importance, namely in relation to other alternatives included in the same question.

According to the process-oriented definitions of restorative justice, the different parties to a conflict should 'resolve collectively' that same conflict (Marshall 2003). This formulation can be deconstructed into the following principles: inclusion, active participation and encounter. Encounter, in a more or less mediated form, has been considered central to restorative justice processes (van Ness and Strong 1997). Experiences of encounters between those responsible for the violence and those who were victims of it have taken place in other post-conflict settings such as South Africa, East-Timor and Northern Ireland. In this survey, respondents were asked whether they would like to meet with those who had victimised them (the so-called 'direct perpetrators') (Table 6.7). The majority (56 per cent) of those who responded to this question said 'no', 23 per cent said they did not know and 21 per cent said 'yes'. It is important to mention in this context that respondents had primarily reported direct victimisation in terms of material harm (61 per cent loss of income and 54 per cent loss of property) and that direct physical harm

Table 6.7 *Meeting with the perpetrator*

	n	%
Yes	175	21
No	459	56
I don't know	191	23

Missing cases: 3.5%
Question: Would you like to meet with those who did to you the things described in question no. 8 (i.e. the persons who victimised you)?

Table 6.8 *Meeting the perpetrator and religious affiliation*

	Catholic	Muslim	Orthodox
Yes	23	25	15
No	56	52	60
I don't know	21	22	26

Values shown are for % within religious affiliation.
Pearson Chi-square 17.639 (8 cells (44.4%) have expected count less than 5. The minimum expected count is .42).
Question: Would you like to meet with those who did to you the things described in question no. 8 (i.e. the persons who victimised you)?

was far less reported (24 per cent attempted killings and 19 per cent physical injuries). Furthermore, 86 per cent of those who responded to the question about meeting the perpetrator did not know personally the people who victimised them, while 15 per cent did. The figures show that, although there was an absolute majority that was not ready for such an encounter, it was far from being a sweeping majority. And the answer most frequently chosen was followed by the option 'I don't know' in a slightly higher degree than the opposite answer 'no'. This suggests that opinions were far from clear and a considerable group of people had more volatile opinions or were simply more vulnerable to be influenced.

As Table 6.8 shows, most of those who expressed a desire to meet their 'direct perpetrators' were either Catholic or Muslim. Among the Orthodox respondents a great majority did not want to meet with their direct perpetrators, and a considerable number remained undecided.

Respondents who said that they would like to meet those who victimised them were asked about their reasons (Table 6.9). Of the total number of

Table 6.9 *Reasons for meeting the perpetrator*

	n	% of cases
To ask why they did what they did	102	59
To see if they regret what they have done	74	43
To see if they would apologise	54	31
To have a chance to tell about one's suffering	47	27
To ask information about missing relatives and friends	32	19
To ask them to repair the damage suffered	13	8
I don't know	9	5

Missing cases: Chance to tell 87%; Ask why 86%; Ask info 95%; Ask reparation 97%; Seek regret 90%; Seek apologies 92%.
Question: Why would you like to meet with those who did to you the things described above in question no. 8 (in case you have experienced any of those things)?

respondents who replied to this question, more than half (59 per cent) said they wanted to ask the perpetrator(s) why they did what they did, as at least one of their reasons. By contrast, less than half (43 per cent) said they wanted to see if the perpetrators regretted what they had done, about a third were seeking apologies, and 27 per cent wanted to have a chance to tell the perpetrators what they had suffered. Only 19 per cent said they wanted to ask information about missing relatives or friends and finally 8 per cent said they wanted to ask the perpetrators for reparation.

The primary reason given by respondents as to why they would like to meet those who caused them harm seemed to be quite common in other instances of encounter between victim and offender. The two other main reasons given by respondents, to see if the perpetrators would regret or apologise, were also predictable and understandable motivations for such encounters. But they may pose greater difficulties as they indicate that there might be unrealistic expectations on the side of the victims which may lead to frustration and disillusionment during and after the encounter. In fact, a combination of showing regret and apologising for the deeds of the past coming from the perpetrator would probably represent the greatest form of acknowledgement to the victims and bear the greatest reparative potential. However, it is necessary to bear in mind that such an ideal outcome cannot be guaranteed to the victims (Braithwaite 2003). In such context the extensive training of mediators as well as the preparation of the parties involved in such encounters seem indispensable to avoid possible negative effects.

Table 6.10 *Reasons not to meet the perpetrator*

	n	% of cases
It would cause suffering again	86	19
Desire to forget about what happened	166	38
Not wanting to see that/those person/s again	193	44
Being scared of him/her/them	27	6
Hating him/her/them	81	18
Don't know	36	8

Missing cases: Renewed suffering 83%; To forget 78%; Not seeing person again 76%; Fear 97%; Hate 89%.
Question: Why would you not like to meet with those who did to you the things described above in question no. 8 (in case you have experienced any of those things)?

The respondents who answered that they did not want to meet with those people who had victimised them were also asked for their reasons (Table 6.10). Nearly half of these respondents (44 per cent) said they simply did not want to see the person(s) again and 38 per cent said they wanted to forget what had happened. Fear of re-victimisation was the third most common reason given (19 per cent), followed by feelings of hatred towards the perpetrator (18 per cent). Surprisingly, only 6 per cent of the respondents said that they were scared of those who victimised them. It seems, thus, that avoiding contact or meeting with the perpetrator was associated with avoiding renewed suffering or at least feelings of discomfort. Interestingly, however, the two stronger feelings here presented as possible reasons to refuse such encounter – fear and hate – were less frequently chosen by respondents.

Forgiveness is a recurrent and controversial topic in the debate on reconciliation and also in the literature of restorative justice. Although reconciliation as a concept per se is not frequently mentioned in restorative justice theories, the process of dialogue and exchange that the parties engage in is regarded as potentially fostering empathy between them, and ultimately forgiveness from the victims. For some restorative justice proponents, forgiveness is a central element of the outcome of a restorative process, but many others contend that forgiveness cannot be seen as a goal of restorative justice, although it may be one of its positive side-results (e.g. Braithwaite (2003: 12–13) who places forgiveness, as well as remorse, apology, censure of the act and mercy, among the 'emergent' values of restorative justice that 'we should not urge participants to

Table 6.11 *Forgiving the perpetrator*

	n	%
No	68	39
Yes	54	31
I do not know	52	30

Missing cases: 65%. Values shown are for the respondents who had answered previously that they would like to meet with the perpetrator. Question: If in such an encounter [between the respondent and those who victimized him/her] the person who did to you the things described in question no. 8 would acknowledge and show regret, do you think you would be able to forgive him/her?

manifest', and Zehr (2002: 8) who states that 'forgiveness or reconciliation is not a primary principle or focus of restorative justice'). However, forgiveness has become a highly controversial issue in societies in transition facing a past of gross human rights violations and it has many times been associated with disguised impunity. But even when it accompanies a process of accountability, such as in South Africa, forgiveness may sometimes be seen as the imposition of a new burden on those who were already seriously victimised. Despite the controversy, forgiveness continues to be a central issue in countries struggling to come to terms with horrendous atrocities and to move on.

The respondents in our survey who said they would be ready to meet with those who victimised them were asked whether they would be able to forgive their perpetrator(s) *if* during such an encounter the perpetrator(s) acknowledged and showed regret for their actions (Table 6.11). Most respondents (39 per cent) said they would *not* be able to forgive, while 31 per cent said they would. A similar proportion of respondents (30 per cent) said they did not know whether they would be able to forgive or not.

It is worth noting that the question asked on forgiveness contemplates what one might call a 'conditional forgiveness' – namely, only if certain conditions are fulfilled; in this case, if the perpetrator would acknowledge and show regret. Taking into consideration that these conditions are difficult to fulfil and that the respondents had in previous questions given a great deal of importance to apologies, regret and the admission of guilt, there was still a high percentage of respondents who were not

Table 6.12 *Forgiving the perpetrator and religious affiliation*

	Catholic	Muslim	Orthodox
Yes	40	14	22
No	26	54	40
I don't know	34	33	37

Values shown are % within ethnicity.
Pearson Chi-square 35.806 (15 cells (62.5%) have expected count less than 5).
Question: Could you forgive the offender if he would acknowledge your suffering and show regret?

ready to forgive. This demonstrates how the issue of forgiveness was and continues to be a very sensitive one in Bosnia and that the views of respondents in this regard were very mixed and uncertain.

In terms of religious background, there was a considerably higher proportion of Catholics ready to forgive in the circumstances explained above. In fact, contrary to Muslim and Orthodox respondents, among the Catholics a majority would be ready to forgive. Muslims seem to be the ones least ready to forgive (Table 6.12).

4   By way of conclusion

Although the survey results only relate to a limited number of issues of post-conflict justice in Bosnia, it is worthwhile trying to draw some conclusions.

In relation to the issue of accountability it should be noted that the debate in Bosnia has been dominated by the role of prosecutions first at the international (ICTY) and subsequently at the national level (ordinary courts and the War Crimes Chamber). These institutions have primarily targeted senior political and military/police leaders. In terms of the criminal justice system, the so-called 'direct perpetrators' pose the greatest challenge due to their overwhelming number and some controversies around the convictions of those only acting under orders. The results of our population-based survey of 2006 raise interesting questions. While prosecution – particularly at the national level – is considered important by over two-thirds of our respondents, the two means of ensuring accountability selected by most respondents have not been associated with criminal justice proceedings, but relate to the return of property or material goods on the one hand and confessions on the other. The return of property can be imposed by an institution or authority dealing with claims in an individual or collective manner, but confessions or apologies (the fourth most frequently chosen option) cannot be imposed – only facilitated – and are more related to processes of acknowledgement by individuals. Moreover, compensation, a part of the internationally recognised rights of victims of gross human rights violations, also figures among the needs or wishes of the respondents. These findings seem to suggest that the relevance of criminal accountability in Bosnia should not close the doors to the debate on complementary forms of accountability; the more so because significant differences can be observed across religious affiliations.

As to the understanding of restorative justice, the survey results are far from unequivocal. First of all, we focused on the possibility of encounters between the conflicting parties as one of the central elements of restorative justice programmes. Most respondents answered that they were not willing to meet with those who directly 'victimised' them. Interestingly, those who said they would be willing to meet their perpetrator, together with those who (at least) did not know, made up an almost equal number as those who said they did not want to engage in such process. The exact reasons are not fully known. One of them might be that a great majority did not know personally those who victimised them, another that encounters from a restorative justice perspective imply a degree of preparation and involvement of all parties and that was obviously not present for the respondents in the context of a survey. The main reasons informing respondents' declared desire to meet their perpetrator were first to ask why they did what they did, and then to seek an apology or regret. Out of those who said they would be willing to meet with their perpetrators, most said they would not be able to forgive them even if their perpetrator was willing to acknowledge responsibility and apologise. This reveals in other words that in 2006 there was little readiness to forgive.

Obviously all of these findings and interpretations require much more analysis and further research. It is clear that nearly fifteen years after the end of the war in Bosnia many key issues in the process of dealing with the past are regarded as important by the respondents and are still very present in the current debate on how to move forward. Our survey clearly demonstrates that controversial and sensitive issues generate opinions that are far more divided than that which is usually portrayed in public discourses. Attitudes towards prosecutions and reparations, encounter and forgiveness and retributive and restorative justice models, are less clear-cut than what one would be led to believe by such discourses. This also implies that a broader and more informative debate on these issues could be very useful for the country and the whole region of the Balkans. This is of course impossible without new methods to gauge public opinion, which marks the importance of population-based surveys on issues of post-conflict justice, for Bosnia and every country in transitional situations. Such surveys, if designed and administered in a methodologically sound way, are likely to provide a wealth of additional information about issues and debates that otherwise hardly come to the surface in post-conflict settings. This is not to argue that quantitative surveys provide a fully reliable picture of reality, partly because they force respondents to give simple answers to difficult questions, and partly because questions and concepts may be interpreted in different ways (Bryman, 2008: 78, citing Cicourel). But despite the many limitations inherent to quantitative research, it can be argued that the results still generate additional insights and contribute to further debate, both scientific and policy-oriented.

Moreover, the case study of Bosnia reveals the complex nature of governance through international criminal justice in post-conflict situations. Not only are there more than one model (retributive justice) or one type of institution (international criminal tribunals or courts) apt to deal with the crimes of the past. Other institutions, such as truth commissions and other community-based mechanisms, may add their value to tackle the large degree of distrust and trauma and the strong need for truth and reparations. Furthermore, the very concepts of truth, accountability, reparation and reconciliation are not straightforward notions but are subject to manifold interpretations by the people on the ground in a post-conflict situation. Both elements should warn us against too-quick and too-one-sided solutions in transitional justice.

References

Aertsen, I., Arsovska, J., Rohne, H.-C., Valiñas, M. and Vanspauwen, K. (2008) (eds.) *Restoring Justice after Large-scale Violent Conflicts: Kosovo, Israel-Palestine and Congo*, Cullompton: Willan Publishing.

Ashworth, A. (1997) 'Sentencing' in M. Maguire, R. Morgan and R. Reiner (eds.), *The Oxford Handbook of Criminology*, 2nd edition, Oxford: Oxford University Press, 1095–135.

Bassiouni, M. C. (1997) 'From Versailles to Rwanda in seventy-five years: the need to establish a permanent international criminal court', *Harvard Human Rights Journal*, 10, 11–62.

(2002) (ed.) *Post-Conflict Justice*, Ardsley: Transnational Publishers.

Bazemore, G. and Walgrave, L. (1999) 'Restorative juvenile justice: in search for fundamentals and an outline for systematic reform' in G. Bazemore and L. Walgrave (eds.), *Restorative Juvenile Justice: Repairing the Harm of Youth Crime*, Monsey: Criminal Justice Press, pp. 45–74.

Biro, M., Ajdukovic, D., Corkalo, D., Djipa, D., Milin, P., and Weinstein, H. M. (2004) 'Attitudes toward justice and social reconstruction in Bosnia and Herzegovina and Croatia' in E. Stover and H. M. Weinstein (eds.), *My Neighbor, My Enemy: Justice and Community in the Aftermath of Mass Atrocity*, Cambridge: Cambridge University Press.

Braithwaite, J. (2002) *Restorative Justice and Responsive Regulation*, Oxford: Oxford University Press.

(2003) 'Principles of restorative justice' in A. von Hirsch, J. Roberts, A. E. Bottoms, K. Roach and M. Schiff (eds.), *Restorative Justice and Criminal Justice: Competing or Reconcilable Paradigms?*, Oxford: Hart Publishing, pp. 1–20.

Brussels Group for International Justice (2002) (ed.) *Combating Impunity: Proceedings of the Symposium Held in Brussels from 11 to 13 March 2002, Followed by the Brussels Principles against Impunity and for International Justice*, Brussels: Bruylant.

Bryman, A. (2008) *Social Research Methods*, Oxford: Oxford University Press.

Buyse, A. (2008) *Post-Conflict Housing Restitution: The European Human Rights Perspective, with a Case Study on Bosnia and Herzegovina*, Antwerp: Intersentia Publishers.

Christie, N. (2001) 'Answers to atrocities: restorative justice in extreme situations' in E. Fattah and S. Parmentier (eds.), *Victim Policies and Criminal Justice on the Road to Restorative Justice: Essays in Honour of Tony Peters*, Leuven: Leuven University Press, pp. 379–92.

Drumbl, M. (2000) 'Punishment, postgenocide: from guilt to shame to civis in Rwanda', *New York University Law Review*, 75, 1221–326.

(2007) *Atrocity, Punishment and International Law*, Cambridge: Cambridge University Press.

Findlay, M. and Henham, R. (2005) *Transforming International Criminal Justice: Retributive and Restorative Justice in the Trial Process*, Cullompton: Willan Publishing.

Hayner, P. (2002) *Unspeakable Truths: Confronting State Terror and Atrocity: Preface by Timothy Garton Ash*, New York: Routledge.

Huyse, L. (1996) 'Justice after transition: on the choices successor elites make in dealing with the past' in A. Jongman (ed.), *Contemporary Genocides*, Leiden: PIOOM.

(1998) *Young Democracies and the Choice between Amnesty, Truth Commissions and Prosecution*, Brussels: Directorate-General Development Aid, pp. 13–21.

International Centre for Transitional Justice (2004) *Iraqi Voices: Attitudes Towards Transitional Justice and Social Reconstruction*, New York: Human Rights Centre, University of Berkeley California/International Centre for Transitional Justice.

(2006) *Colombian Perceptions and Opinions on Justice, Truth, Reparations, and Reconciliation*, New York: International Centre for Transitional Justice.

(2007) *When the War Ends: A Population-based Survey of Attitudes about Peace, Justice, and Social Reconstruction in Northern Uganda*, New York: Human Rights Centre, University of Berkeley California/International Centre for Transitional Justice.

Kittichaisaree, K. (2001) *International Criminal Law*, Oxford: Oxford University Press.

Kiza, E., Rathgeber, C. and Rohne, H.-C. (2006) *Victims of War: An Empirical Study on War Victimisation and Victims' Attitudes Towards Addressing Atrocities*, Hamburg: Hamburger Edition, www.his-online.de/Download/Forschungsberichte/978-3-936096-73-6.pdf.

Kritz, N. (1995) (ed.) *Transitional Justice: How Emerging Democracies Reckon with Former Regimes*, 3 vols., Washington DC: United States Institute of Peace Press.

Llewellyn, J. (2007) 'Truth commissions and restorative justice' in G. Johnstone and D. van Ness (eds.), *Handbook of Restorative Justice*, Cullompton: Willan Publishing, pp. 351–71.

Marshall, T. (1996) 'The evolution of restorative justice in Britain', *European Journal on Criminal Policy and Research*, 4(4), 21–43.

Marshall, T. F. (2003) 'Restorative justice: an overview' in G. Johnstone (ed.), *A Restorative Justice Reader: Texts, Sources, Context*, Cullompton: Willan Publishing, pp. 28–45.

McEvoy, K. and McGregor, L. (2008) (eds.) *Transitional Justice from Below: Grassroots Activism and the Struggle for Change*, Oxford: Hart Publishing.

Ness, D. van and Strong, K. H. (1997) *Restoring Justice*, Cincinnati: Anderson Publishing.

Orentlicher, D. (1991) 'Settling accounts: the duty to prosecute human rights violations of a prior regime', *Yale Law Journal*, 100, 2537–615.

(2005) *Report of the Independent Expert to Update the Set of Principles to Combat Impunity*, UN Doc. E/CN.4/2005/102 18 Feb. 2005.

Parmentier, S. (2003) 'Global justice in the aftermath of mass violence: the role of the International Criminal Court in dealing with political crimes', *International Annals of Criminology*, 41(1–2), 203–24.

Parmentier, S. and Weitekamp, E. (2007) 'Political crimes and serious violations of human rights: towards a criminology of international crimes' in

S. Parmentier and E. Weitekamp (eds.), *Crime and Human Rights*, Series in Sociology of Crime, Law and Deviance, vol. 9, Amsterdam/Oxford: Elsevier/JAI Press, pp. 109–44.

Parmentier, S., Valiñas, M. and Weitekamp, E. (2009) 'How to repair the harm after violent conflict in Bosnia? Results of a population-based survey', *Netherlands Quarterly of Human Rights*, 27(1), 27–44.

(forthcoming) 'How to restore justice in Serbia? A closer look at people's opinions about reconciliation' in D. Rothe and C. Mullins (eds.), *Crimes of State: Current Perspectives*, Piscataway, NJ: Rutgers University Press.

Parmentier, S., Vanspauwen, K. and Weitekamp, E. (2008) 'Dealing with the legacy of mass violence: changing lenses to restorative justice' in A. Smeulers and R. Haveman (eds.), *Supranational Criminology: Towards a Criminology of International Crimes*, Antwerp/Oxford: Intersentia, pp. 335–56.

Reydams, L. (2004) *Universal Jurisdiction: International and Municipal Legal Perspectives*, Oxford: Oxford University Press.

Roche, D. (2003) *Accountability in Restorative Justice*, Oxford: Oxford University Press.

Roht-Arriaza, N. (2005) *The Pinochet Effect: Transnational Justice in the Age of Human Rights*, Philadelphia: University of Pennsylvania, p. 272.

Siegel, R. L. (1998) 'Transitional justice: a decade of debate and experience', *Human Rights Quarterly*, 20, 431–54.

Tabeau, E. and Bijak, J. (2005) 'War-related deaths in the 1992–1995 armed conflicts in Bosnia and Herzegovina: a critique of previous estimates and recent results', *European Journal of Population*, 21, 187–215.

Umbreit, M., Bradshaw, W. and Coates, R. (2003) 'Victims of severe violence in dialogue with the offender: key principles, practices, outcomes and implications' in E. Weitekamp and H.-J. Kerner (eds.), *Restorative Justice in Context: International Practice and Directions*, Cullompton: Willan Publishing, pp. 123–44.

United Nations Development Programme (2005) *Justice and Truth in Bosnia and Herzegovina: Public Perceptions*, Early Warning System Special Edition, Sarajevo: UNDP.

United Nations Security Council (2004) *The Rule of Law and Transitional Justice in Conflict and Post-conflict Societies*, Report of the Secretary-General to the Security Council, 23 August 2004, S/2004/616.

Valiñas, M., Parmentier, S. and Weitekamp, E. (2009) *Restoring Justice in Bosnia and Herzegovina: Results of a Population-based Survey*, Working Paper 31, Leuven: Centre for Global Governance Studies, www.globalgovernancestudies.eu.

Villa-Vicencio, C. (2000) 'Why perpetrators should not always be prosecuted: where the International Criminal Court and truth commissions meet', *Emory Law Journal*, 49, 101–18.

(2001) 'Restorative justice in social context: the South African Truth and Reconciliation Commission' in N. Biggar (ed.), *Burying the Past: Making Peace and Doing Justice after Civil Conflict*, Washington DC: Georgetown University Press, pp. 207–22.

(2003) 'Restorative justice: ambiguities and limitations of a theory' in C. Villa-Vicencio and E. Doxtader (eds.), *The Provocations of Amnesty: Memory, Justice and Impunity*, Claremont, South Africa: David Philip Publishers, pp. 30–50.

Walgrave, L. (2008) 'Restorative justice: an alternative for responding to crime?' in S. Shoham, O. Beck and M. Kett (eds.), *International Handbook of Penology and Criminal Justice*, Boca Raton/London: CRC Press, pp. 613–89.

Weitekamp, E., Parmentier, S., Vanspauwen, K., Valiñas, M. and Gerits, R. (2006) 'How to deal with mass victimization and gross human rights violations. A restorative justice approach' in U. Ewald and K. Turkovic (eds.), *Large-Scale Victimization as a Potential Source of Terrorist Activities: Importance of Regaining Security in Post-conflict Societies*, NATO Security through Science Series, vol. 13, Amsterdam: IOS Press, pp. 217–41.

Zehr, H. (1991) *Changing Lenses: A New Focus for Crime and Justice*, Scottdale, PA: Herald Press.

(2002) *The Little Book of Restorative Justice*, Intercourse, PA: Good Books.

(2003) 'Retributive justice, restorative justice' in G. Johnstone (ed.), *A Restorative Justice Reader: Texts, Sources, Context*, Cullompton: Willan Publishing, pp. 69–82.

7

Shaping penal policy from above? The role of the Grand Chamber of the European Court of Human Rights

DIRK VAN ZYL SMIT AND SONJA SNACKEN

Since 2005 the Grand Chamber of the European Court of Human Rights (ECtHR) has given a series of ground-breaking judgments in which it has addressed the difficult question of the purpose of imprisonment while seeking to resolve complex practical issues, such as prisoners' rights to vote, artificial insemination by prisoners and the acceptability of whole life sentences. This chapter analyses some of these judgments closely. It points out that, while the judges often come to radical conclusions, they sometimes attempt to soften the blow by allowing states a margin of appreciation in instances where it is arguably inappropriate to do so. The chapter reflects on whether this is merely a short-term political strategy or whether this approach may undermine the considerable potential of the Grand Chamber to set a conceptual framework for prison law and policy applicable throughout Europe. It does so by considering the impact of these judgments on the penal reform process in England and Wales.

Introduction

It is the point of departure of this chapter – one that is regarded as obvious by human rights lawyers (who sometimes exaggerate its significance) – that courts applying general human rights standards can shape penal policy in crucial ways. Social scientists conversely, often do not pay sufficient attention to the subtleties of the judicial development of penal values, but they are more sensitive to the difference between the pronouncements of the courts and actual changes to penal policies and practices.

Dramatic examples of judicial interventions that have succeeded in shaping penal policies by linking their innovations directly to fundamental human rights can be found where ultimate penalties are concerned. The decisions of the Hungarian[1] and South African[2] constitutional courts abolishing capital punishment in their respective countries in the 1990s are highly significant, not only because they set aside the death sentence in the cases before them, but also because they proclaimed that capital punishment was inimical to the fundamental human rights norms enshrined in their constitutions. In contrast, the US Supreme Court, which in the early 1970s also had the opportunity to abolish the death penalty, decided the key case of *Furman* v. *Georgia*[3] on narrow procedural grounds, thus allowing the death penalty to be re-established in a way which has made it legally almost impossible to challenge directly for many decades.

Not all judicial value choices have as clear penal policy implications. However, in the area of prisons it is possible to identify judicial interventions which to a greater or lesser extent have shaped policy and others which have the potential to do so. A dramatic example is that of the German Constitutional Court which in the 1970s struck down the existing German prison legislation as unconstitutional. What was important was that it did so not only on the technical basis that the existing provision infringed prisoners' human rights because it did not set the limits on them in the way the Constitution required. The Constitutional Court went further and in a series of judgments specified that the state had a constitutional duty to adopt policies in prison that would meet the human rights guarantees of the Constitution. And the court was not shy in spelling these out. The result was that the German government was forced to enact prison legislation that not only protected the rights of prisoners against interference but which adopted a positive policy of 're-socialisation'. This gave prisoners a claim to a much wider range of rights than would otherwise have been the case. One question addressed in this chapter is whether European prison law, as developed by the Grand Chamber of the ECtHR, has reached the same conclusions and is likely to have a similar impact.

Liora Lazarus (2004; 2006) has compared the case law of the German Constitutional Court concerning the protection of prisoners' rights with

---

[1] Constitutional Court of Hungary (23/9/1990 ×31).
[2] *S* v. *Makwanyane* 1995 (3) 391 (CC).   [3] *Furman* v. *Georgia* 408 US 238 (1972).

that of the English courts[4] on the one hand and with the ECtHR on the other. She has argued that the explicit recognition by the German Constitutional Court of re-socialisation as the primary aim of the implementation of sentences, independently of the aims of sentencing, allows for a much stronger protection of prisoners' rights than that offered by the English courts or the ECtHR.

Lazarus has demonstrated convincingly how, since the 1970s, all three systems have rejected the theory of the inherent limitations of rights following deprivation of liberty. The offender's liberty is therefore no longer considered indivisible. A distinction is accepted between the 'personal' liberty and human rights, which are restricted as a consequence of the sentence to a custodial sanction, and the 'residual' liberty and human rights which are left for the prisoner, but which can be further restricted as a consequence of the administration of prisons. However, she has argued that, in the absence of a clear statement of the aims of the implementation of imprisonment in England and Wales and by the ECtHR, the scope of these restrictions and their consequences are opaque and vague, and therefore open to diverse interpretations.

In England and Wales, it has been accepted that 'a convicted prisoner, in spite of his imprisonment, retains all the civil rights which are not taken away expressly or by necessary implication'.[5] However, in the absence of a clear objective for the administration of prisons, these 'necessary implications' have been interpreted in varying ways: from a strict approach in which restrictions had to respond to a 'self-evident and pressing need' and constitute a 'minimum interference' with prisoners' rights, to a more punitive approach in which limitations to fundamental rights and liberties, such as freedom of speech, were seen as part of 'the punitive object of deprivation of liberty' (Lazarus 2006: 754–9) and could be carried over from the sentence to the manner in which it was implemented.

Lazarus contends that the ECtHR has been equally vague, and refers to the leading early case of *Golder* v. *United Kingdom*, in which the ECtHR for the first time rejected the theory of inherent limitations.[6] In *Golder* the Court argued that restrictions of rights were to be assessed 'having regard to the ordinary and reasonable requirements of imprisonment',

---

[4] Here, reference to English courts is a shorthand for the courts of England and Wales.
[5] *Raymond* v. *Honey* [1983] 1 AC 1 (HL(E)) 10.
[6] *Golder* v. *United Kingdom* 21 February 1975.

that they had to be 'stipulated by law' and should be in accordance with the proportionality test – that is, 'necessary in a democratic society' and for the attainment of a 'legitimate aim' stipulated in the Convention. The prevention of disorder and crime was accepted by the Court as such a legitimate aim, but the restrictions imposed as a result could not be greater than was necessary to address a 'pressing social need'. The Court added that it was not its function to elaborate a general theory of the limitations admissible, as it could only deal with individual petitions (Lazarus 2006: 753).

Lazarus contrasts this vagueness with the German conception of the prisoner's legal status, which recognises that different purposes of punishment predominate at the distinct stages of the criminal law: general deterrence at the level of legislation; retribution at the level of sentencing; and special prevention, with a particular emphasis on prisoner re-socialisation, at the level of execution of sentences (Kaiser *et al.* 1991: 19). The German Federal Constitutional Court has en-shrined the constitutional re-socialisation principle as the primary purpose of prison administration, against which restrictions imposed on prisoners will be evaluated. As a consequence, the German court has developed a legal position for prisoners made of negative funda-mental rights against state infringements and positive rights to state action. The negative rights status recognises prisoners as full and equal bearers of basic rights, which can only be limited by law and in pursuance of a constitutional purpose. The positive rights status refers to the right to social integration of prisoners, which is seen as an inherent element of human dignity and an essential value in a 'social state'. In the face of institutional obstacles to prisoners' rights enforce-ment, such as a formalistic approach by prison courts, resistance by prison officials, and insufficient legal advice and support, the German Federal Constitutional Court has consistently reiterated and developed the constitutional re-socialisation principle and the prisoner's positive rights status. This has led to case law recognising the right to adequate remuneration for prison work, the right to a sentence plan that fulfils the re-socialisation purpose and a qualified right to home leave and other forms of relaxation of the prison regime (Lazarus 2006: 744–52).

We have no disagreements with Lazarus' overall analysis and her depiction of English law in this respect is clearly correct. However, the jurisprudence of the ECtHR has developed since the *Golder* case. A consensus is beginning to emerge at the European level, clearly in recommendations of the Council of Europe[7] and in the standards set by the Committee for the Prevention of Torture (CPT),[8] and more haltingly in the judgments of the ECtHR, about both the relative autonomy of the implementation of sentences from the purposes of their imposition and the importance of re-socialisation, or reintegration as some European sources refer to it,[9] as a primary aim of the implementation of a prison sentence. This shift in emphasis is derived from and closely linked to the growing recognition of prisoners' human rights.

As examples of these developments, we focus on three major judgments of the Grand Chamber of the ECtHR. The first two both involved the United Kingdom directly. *Hirst*,[10] decided in 2005, dealt with sentenced prisoners' right to vote, and *Dickson*,[11] decided in December 2007, dealt with the artificial insemination by a prisoner of his wife. In both instances the English courts that had considered the matters had initially ruled against the prisoners concerned. The third case, that of *Kafkaris*,[12] decided in February 2008, originated in Cyprus but has also had a clear impact in the United Kingdom. In each instance we first focus directly on the judgment of the Grand Chamber to identify not only its key findings but also the room for manoeuvre it left for national authorities. We then turn, in a separate section, to the reaction at the national level to the individual decisions, before attempting to draw some brief conclusions about the interaction between the decisions of the Grand Chamber and penal policy in the United Kingdom.

---

[7] See for example, r. 6 European Prison Rules (Rec(2006)2 Recommendation of the Committee of Ministers to Member States on the European Prison Rules (EPR) adopted by the Committee of Ministers on 11 January 2006 at the 952nd meeting of the Ministers' Deputies); § 2 of Recommendation Rec(2003)23 of the Committee of Ministers to Member States on the Management by Prison Administrations of Life Sentence and other Long-term Prisoners adopted by the Committee of Ministers on 9 October 2003 at the 855th meeting of the Ministers' Deputies; § 3 of Recommendation Rec(2003) 22 of the Committee of Ministers to Member States on Conditional Release (Parole) adopted by the Committee of Ministers on 24 September 2003 at the 853rd meeting of the Ministers' Deputies.

[8] The CPT, which was established by the European Convention for the Prevention of Torture and Inhuman or Degrading Treatment or Punishment (CETS 126), has combined extracts from its annual reports to create the CPT Standards. The Standards are updated regularly and are an important source of European penal policy.

[9] The case for using the term reintegration, rather than re-socialisation, is made by van Zyl Smit and Snacken (2009: 83–4 and 105–8).

[10] *Hirst* v. *United Kingdom (no. 2)* [GC] 6 October 2005.

[11] *Dickson* v. *United Kingdom* [GC] 4 December 2007.

[12] *Kafkaris* v. *Cyprus* [GC] 12 February 2008.

The jurisprudence of the Grand Chamber

Hirst

Should prisoners be allowed to vote? This question was first raised in England in the case of *Pearson and Martinez*,[13] which directly preceded the case of *Hirst* that was eventually to reach the Grand Chamber.[14] The Divisional Court hearing the matter of *Pearson and Martinez* held that it was open to the state to impose the additional punishment of loss of the right to vote on sentenced prisoners: Judge Kennedy found that there was more to punishment than forcible detention and noted loss of the 'privilege' to vote could be a further element of punishment (at para. 41). The judge was quite happy to leave it to the state to decide what the purpose of such a restriction was, remarking rather weakly that the aim of the restriction 'may not be easy to articulate' and suggesting that the 'true nature of disenfranchisement' should be 'left to the philosophers to decide' (*ibid.*).

This way of avoiding the issue was resoundingly dismissed by the ECtHR.[15] In its judgment in *Hirst* the Grand Chamber restated and expanded the basis for prisoners' rights at the European level:

> [P]risoners in general continue to enjoy all the fundamental rights and freedoms guaranteed under the [European Convention on Human Rights] save for the right to liberty, where lawfully imposed detention expressly falls within the scope of Art. 5 of the Convention. For example, prisoners may not be ill-treated, subjected to inhuman or degrading punishment or conditions contrary to Art. 3 of the Convention; they continue to enjoy the right to respect for family life, the right to freedom of expression, the right to practise their religion, the right of effective access to a lawyer or to court for the purposes of Art. 6, the right to respect for correspondence and the right to marry. Any restrictions on these other rights require to be justified . . .[16]

From this basis it was easy for the Grand Chamber to argue that the right to vote, protected by Article 3 of Protocol 1 of the European Convention on Human Rights (ECHR), was a fundamental right that should be

---

[13] R (Pearson and Martinez) v. *Secretary of State for the Home Department* [2001] HRLR 39.

[14] John Hirst, in whose name the case was brought to the ECtHR, was one of the parties in *Pearson and Martinez*.

[15] Hirst first succeeded before a chamber of seven judges of the ECtHR who found unanimously in his favour in *Hirst v. United Kingdom (no. 2)* 30 March 2004. The government of the United Kingdom appealed against this decision to the Grand Chamber of the ECtHR.

[16] *Hirst v. United Kingdom (no. 2)* [GC] 6 October 2005, § 69, internal references omitted.

recognised in the same way as those mentioned in this passage, and that it too could be restricted only if it was justified to do so. The Grand Chamber remarked confidently:

> There is . . . no question that a prisoner forfeits his Convention rights merely because of his status as a person detained following conviction. Nor is there any place under the Convention system, where tolerance and broadmindedness are the acknowledged hallmarks of democratic society, for automatic disenfranchisement based purely on what might offend public opinion.' [para. 70]

But could a limitation of some prisoners' right to vote be justified? The right to vote as recognised by the Convention belongs to a class of rights that may be limited as long as the limitation is provided in law, the essence of the right is not impaired and the limitation is imposed with a legitimate aim in mind and is proportionate.

On the facts of the *Hirst* case though, the majority of the Grand Chamber had no difficulties. It described the current English legislation[17] on prisoners' right to vote as a 'blunt instrument' and explained:

> It strips of their Convention right to vote a significant category of persons and it does so in a way which is indiscriminate. The provision imposes a blanket restriction on all convicted prisoners in prison. It applies automatically to such prisoners, irrespective of the length of their sentence and irrespective of the nature or gravity of their offence and their individual circumstances. [para. 83]

The conclusion followed immediately:

> Such a general, automatic and indiscriminate restriction on a vitally important Convention right must be seen as falling outside any acceptable margin of appreciation, however wide that margin might be, and as being incompatible with Article 3 of Protocol No. 1. [*Ibid.*]

In as far as it went, this was a brave conclusion. Not only was it based on a clear assertion of prisoners' rights but the Court was also prepared to hold that the action of the UK government was disproportionate, because it applied indiscriminately to virtually all sentenced prisoners serving terms of imprisonment, notwithstanding the fact that several other European states had similar or even greater restrictions on their prisoners. This proved, as Judge Caflisch explained in his concurring judgment, that a

---

[17] s. 3 Representation of the People Act 1983.

state could not simply decide democratically what was in its best interests but that it was always subject to European control.[18]

A particular strength of the majority judgment in the *Hirst* case is that it dismissed the argument of the UK government that it should not intervene because there was no consensus amongst European states on whether prisoners should be able to vote, as there was a sizeable minority not allowing any prisoners to vote at all. This argument, which did find favour with a minority of the judges, was based on the notion that states should be allowed a 'margin of appreciation' in making their own arrangements and that the Court should only intervene if states go beyond that limitation. Close analysis of the concept of margin of appreciation shows the Court has applied it in two ways (Letsas 2006). First, it is used substantively by the Court to designate matters which it believes that national authorities are better placed to judge than the ECtHR and where decisions of such authorities need to be reviewed bearing this in mind. Secondly, it is applied more structurally in cases where the Court decides not to overturn the action taken by the state against which the complaint is brought, not because it believes that a national authority is better placed to make a judgment but because there is not a consensus or even a strongly dominant view on a particular matter amongst the states that are parties to the ECHR.

Of these, the former, the substantive margin of appreciation, is relatively unproblematic and has been applied in several prisoners' rights cases, which, precisely because of their routine nature, have not reached the Grand Chamber.[19] These decisions can be contrasted to cases in which the structural aspect of the margin of appreciation has been introduced, not in respect of the facts of an individual case, but by reference to divergent practice across European countries. An example of this is the way in which the Court has dealt with the denial of conjugal visits to prisoners.[20] Although

[18] At § 3 of the concurring opinion of Judge Caflisch.

[19] Examples of where a substantive margin of appreciation was analysed include the cases on access to correspondence, such as *Silver and ors* v. *United Kingdom* 25 March 1983; legal advice, *Campbell* v. *United Kingdom* 25 March 1992; marriage, *Hamer* v. *United Kingdom* [EComHR] 13 December 1979; searching of prisoners, *Van der Ven* v. *the Netherlands* 4 February 2003; humanitarian leave, *Płoski* v. *Poland* 12 March 2003; visits by a spouse, *Klamecki* v. *Poland (no. 2)* 3 April 2003; and searching of visitors, *Wainwright* v. *United Kingdom* 29 September 2006. Some of these preceded the creation of the Grand Chamber.

[20] See *ELH and PBH* v. *United Kingdom* 21 October 1997; *GS and RS* v. *United Kingdom* 10 July 1991; *Kalashnikov* v. *Russia* 18 September 2001 § 7; *Aliev* v. *Ukraine* 29 April 2003 § 188. The same approach has been adopted when both spouses are prisoners: *X and Y* v. *Switzerland* 3 October 1978.

an increasing number of European countries allow such visits, countries that prohibit them in all cases have claimed that a blanket prohibition is necessary in the interests of security. When considering the question in recent years the Court has not only accepted the desirability of such visits, it has recognised that denying them means restricting a right of (married) prisoners that is recognised by the ECHR. Nevertheless, the analysis that it has conducted has been very truncated. Because of the 'margin of appreciation' it has not enquired into whether in individual cases the strategy of outlawing such visits is a proportionate intervention when balanced against security concerns or indeed whether it remains proportionate when a prisoner is detained for a long period. The result is that the margin of appreciation applied in this way has served to inhibit the Court from examining closely whether a fundamental right is being infringed by the application of a particular law or policy in an individual case. It follows that the margin of appreciation, when used in this 'structural' sense, can inhibit severely the development of prison law by the ECtHR even where, as in this example, there are clear policies at the European level developed by the CPT and others in favour of a particular course of action.

In *Hirst* the structural trap was avoided. The Court did not simply say, as it was urged to do by the government of the United Kingdom, that as there was no consensus on whether prisoners could vote, the United Kingdom could regulate the matter as it saw fit. This step meant that prisoners were recognised as having the basic right to vote. Any future limitations of the right to vote would be judged on whether they met the substantive criteria.

Unfortunately, when it comes to determining the acceptability of any future limitations the Grand Chamber judgment had some shortcomings, which would allow the UK government to argue that significant limitations are still justified. First, while it found the UK law to be disproportionate, the Grand Chamber refused to follow the initial Chamber of the ECtHR in expressing its reservations about the legitimacy of the aims put forward by the UK government of restricting the right to vote of virtually all sentenced prisoners. The UK government had claimed that the aim of increasing the punishment of sentenced prisoners in this way was legitimate and also that forfeiting the right to vote would be an incentive to prisoners to citizen-like conduct in the future. Both of these should have been rejected out of hand. As the concurring opinion of Judges Tulkens and Zagrebelksy emphasised, the logic of the former was a return to the old idea that prisoners suffered a 'civic death' and their rights could be removed at will. This is the exact opposite of the well-known aphorism that people are sent to prison as punishment not for punishment. As to the latter, it beggars empirical belief that prisoners could be trained in citizenship by removing the right to vote. This had been recognised by the Canadian Supreme Court in the leading case of *Sauvé* v. *Canada*,[21] which explicitly dismissed the Canadian government's claim that disenfranchisement would '"educate" and rehabilitate inmates' (para. 38). The Canadian Court concluded that, on the contrary, 'to deny prisoners the right to vote is to lose an important means of teaching them democratic values and social responsibility' (*ibid.*).[22]

The second ill-conceived concession that the Grand Chamber made was to suggest that a problem with the UK legislation was that, when passing the Representation of the People Act 1983, Parliament had not had a substantive debate on whether there was a continued justification in the light of modern-day penal policy and of current human rights standards for maintaining such a general restriction on the right of prisoners to vote. Leaving aside the doubt one may have about whether it was factually correct that Parliament had not applied its collective mind to the matter and the wider question of whether parliamentary legislation should be questioned on this basis (Lewis 2006), it ostensibly left open the possibility that, if Parliament were to have such a debate and then come to the conclusion that the law should be substantially unaltered, that would somehow make the current general restriction compatible with the Convention.

The conclusion therefore is that, notwithstanding the important strides made in *Hirst*, the Grand Chamber had still not thought through fully what the purpose of imprisonment was; what, to use its own words, 'modern day penal policy and current human rights standards' (para. 79) required in the implementation of imprisonment. The Court was therefore unable to give principled guidance about the reform that it had required to be undertaken in this area.[23] As we explain below, this

---

[21] *Sauvé* v. *Canada (Chief Electoral Officer)* 2002 SCC 68.

[22] See also the concurring opinion of Judge Caflisch in *Hirst* v. *United Kingdom (no. 2)* [GC] 6 October 2005 § O-5: 'The United Kingdom Government further contended that disenfranchisement in the present case was in harmony with the objectives of preventing crime and punishing offenders, thereby enhancing civic responsibility. I doubt that very much. I believe, on the contrary, that participation in the democratic process may serve as a first step toward resocialisation.'

[23] This point was recognised by Judge Caflisch, who, in his concurring opinion, rejected the punishment justification and outlined general parameters within which restrictions of the right to vote could be developed.

vacillation has had real consequences expressed in the limited reforms that the British government is proposing as being all that it regards as necessary to meet the minimum standard it believes the Court to have set.

Dickson

In *Dickson* v. *United Kingdom*,[24] there was a change of emphasis when the Grand Chamber decided to consider directly the human rights basis of the purpose of imprisonment. This case involved an application by a prisoner serving a life sentence and his wife that the prison authorities should allow the prisoner to send his sperm out of prison to his wife so that she could be artificially inseminated. Unsupervised 'conjugal visits' are not allowed in the United Kingdom and the applicants had no other way of founding a family. The right to found a family is recognised by Articles 8 and 12 of the ECHR. The case was made more pressing by the fact that the wife most probably would not have been able to have children by the time the husband qualified for release. The English Prison Rules allowed for artificial insemination only in exceptional circumstances, and in this instance the authorities had refused to give permission for it. The government of the United Kingdom had argued that loss of the right to procreate could be seen as an inevitable conse- quence of imprisonment and therefore claimed a virtually unfettered discretion to decide whether or not to grant permission. It relied on the leading English case on the subject, *Mellor*, in which loss of the right to procreate was regarded as an inevitable part of imprisonment that was designed to punish and deter.[25] In *Mellor* the English court had no objection against a policy which would allow the transmission of sperm only in 'exceptional circumstances'.

In contrast, the Grand Chamber in *Dickson* embarked on an analysis of the underlying approach to the implementation of imprisonment in European law. As in *Hirst*, it dismissed the argument that this was an area in which, because there was no consensus, states should be allowed a wide (structural) margin of appreciation, which would enable states not to allow artificial insemination at all, or if they did, to regulate it as they saw fit. However, the Grand Chamber went further. It emphasised the

---

[24] *Dickson* v. *United Kingdom* [GC] 4 December 2007. For an excellent analysis of this case see Codd (2008).
[25] *R (Mellor)* v. *Secretary of State for the Home Department* [2001] 3 WLR 533.

legal significance of 'the evolution in European prison policy towards the
increasing relative importance of the rehabilitative aim of imprisonment'
(para. 28). More specifically, it noted that what it called the Council of
Europe's 'legal instruments' had clarified the European approach in this
regard commenting that 'while rehabilitation was recognised as a means
of preventing recidivism, more recently and more positively, it constitutes rather the idea of re-socialisation through the fostering of personal
responsibility' (*ibid.*). Amongst the European legal instruments that it
quoted fully in this regard were the new 2006 European Prison Rules
which provide in Rule 6:

> All detention shall be managed so as to facilitate the reintegration into
> free society of persons who have been deprived of their liberty.

And in Rule 102:

> 102.1 In addition to the rules that apply to all prisoners, the regime for
> sentenced prisoners shall be designed to enable them to lead a responsible
> and crime-free life.
> 102.2 Imprisonment is by the deprivation of liberty a punishment in
> itself and therefore the regime for sentenced prisoners shall not aggravate
> the suffering inherent in imprisonment.

In respect of Rule 102 the Grand Chamber even quoted extensively and
with approval from the official commentary to the European Prison
Rules:

> [Rule 102] states the objectives of the regime for prisoners in simple,
> positive terms. The emphasis is on measures and programmes for
> sentenced prisoners that will encourage and develop individual responsi-
> bility rather than focussing narrowly on the prevention of recidivism . . .
> The new Rule is in line with the requirements of key international
> instruments including Article 10(3) of the [International Covenant of
> Civil and Political Rights (ICCPR)]. . . However, unlike the ICCPR, the
> formulation here deliberately avoids the use of the term, 'rehabilitation',
> which carries with it the connotation of forced treatment. Instead, it
> highlights the importance of providing sentenced prisoners, who often
> come from socially deprived backgrounds, the opportunity to develop in
> a way that will enable them to choose to lead law-abiding lives.

The effect of this careful laying of foundations was that the Grand
Chamber recognised a purpose of imprisonment remarkably like the
purpose that the German Constitutional Court had identified two
decades earlier. It then set about applying it to the substantive administrative decision by the UK authorities not to allow the artificial

insemination requested by the Dicksons. The Grand Chamber provided the basis for this evaluation by referring to the basic approach to prisoners' rights set out in *Hirst* quoted above, but it combined it with the requirement that the authorities take into account the positive purpose of imprisonment that it had identified. In a key passage it set out the difference between its approach and that of the UK government:

> The Government also appeared to maintain that the restriction [on artificial insemination], of itself, contributed to the overall punitive objective of imprisonment. However, and while accepting that punishment remains one of the aims of imprisonment, the Court would also underline the evolution in European penal policy towards the increasing relative importance of the rehabilitative aim of imprisonment, particularly towards the end of a long prison sentence. [para. 75]

This difference of emphasis was crucial to the final outcome. The conclusion of the Grand Chamber was that the English Prison Rules, which allowed artificial insemination to be facilitated only in 'exceptional circumstances', did not allow adequate emphasis to be placed on the Convention-based right of individuals to found a family and thus to take their place as responsible members of the community. The structural balance was wrong because those administering the prison service had lost sight of the true purpose of the implementation of the prison sentence. This meant also that the Grand Chamber could dismiss the claim of the UK authorities that an unacceptable positive obligation to do something, that is to convey sperm out of prison, was being placed on them as a diversion from the primary issue of whether a fair balance was being struck.

Kafkaris

A prisoner seeking to artificially inseminate his wife in the circumstances that arose in *Dickson* may be a relatively unusual set of facts, but the approach taken to it by the Grand Chamber has profound implications for other cases. A clear recognition of the purpose of the implementation of a sentence of imprisonment is likely to lead the Court to hold sooner rather than later that an irreducible life sentence – that is, one from which a prisoner has no genuine prospect of release – infringes the ECHR because it makes a nonsense of the objective of reintegration. Such an opportunity arose in February 2008 in the case of *Kafkaris* v. *Cyprus*.[26] In this case the applicant had been sentenced to life

---

[26] *Kafkaris* v. *Cyprus* [GC] 12 February 2008.

imprisonment under Cypriot law, which at the time had granted him a genuine prospect of early release. After Kafkaris had been sentenced, the law changed and the previously clear release procedures were abolished. In this instance the Court only went half-way to grasp the opportunity that the case presented to develop this aspect of the law governing imprisonment. It found that the prohibition on torture and inhuman or degrading treatment or punishment, contained in Article 3 of the ECHR, would not be infringed if it were *de jure* and de facto that there was a prospect that an offender could be released. However, the Court made it clear that it did not wish to lay down any criteria for release procedures and reiterated:

> that matters relating to early release policies including the manner of their implementation fall within the power member States have in the sphere of criminal justice and penal policy. . . In this connection, the Court observes that at the present time there is not yet a clear and commonly accepted standard amongst the member States of the Council of Europe concerning life sentences and, in particular, their review and method of adjustment. Moreover, no clear tendency can be ascertained with regard to the system and procedures implemented in respect of early release. [para. 151]

In the end, the majority of the Grand Chamber, although it quoted the Council of Europe instruments to which reference was made in *Dickson*, as well as further recommendations on conditional release[27] and the treatment of lifers,[28] found on the facts that the applicant, Kafkaris, did have a prospect of release.[29]

The dissenting opinion of the minority, which did not find on the facts that Kafkaris had a genuine prospect of release, analysed the

---

[27] Recommendation Rec(2003)22 of the Committee of Ministers to Member States on Conditional Release (Parole) adopted by the Committee of Ministers on 24 September 2003 at the 853rd meeting of the Ministers' Deputies.

[28] Recommendation Rec(2003)23 of the Committee of Ministers to Member States on the Management by Prison Administrations of Life Sentence and other Long-term Prisoners adopted by the Committee of Ministers on 9 October 2003 at the 855th meeting of the Ministers' Deputies.

[29] The case could also have been determined on another basis. Judge Bratza, who agreed on the facts, commented in his concurring opinion that 'the time has come when the Court should clearly affirm that the imposition of an irreducible life sentence, even on an adult offender, is in principle inconsistent with Article 3 of the Convention'. Denial of the possibility of re-socialisation is what makes these sentences inhuman and degrading. When the appropriate case comes to the Grand Chamber the only question is likely to be what procedures for considering the release of lifers will meet the requirements of both Arts. 3 and 5(4) ECHR.

requirements of Article 3 somewhat differently. It emphasised that all prisoners, including those sentenced to life imprisonment should have a genuine prospect of release and that the procedures governing the consideration of their release should not be arbitrary. If there were not such procedures the resulting arbitrariness in their view would infringe Article 3. It based this conclusion on the various instruments of the Council of Europe quoted by the majority and criticised it for failing to recognise the significance of these instruments, which 'on a European and universal scale, have contributed and are still contributing to forming a genuine body of law on sentences and prisoners in advanced democratic societies' (para. 4). The minority opinion emphasised that the importance of the social reintegration of prisoners was 'commonly accepted'. From this it drew the wide conclusion that:

> once it is accepted that the 'legitimate requirements of the sentence' entail reintegration, questions may be asked as to whether a term of imprison-ment that jeopardises that aim is not in itself capable of constituting inhuman and degrading treatment. [para. 5]

On this basis they associated themselves with the separate concurring judgment of Judge Bratza, who agreed with the majority on the facts but nevertheless concluded that: 'the time has come when the Court should clearly affirm that the imposition of an irreducible life sentence, even on an adult offender, is in principle inconsistent with Article 3 of the Convention'.

The legal reality remains that the majority judgment in *Kafkaris* is similar to that in *Hirst*. The similarity is that it recognised the key question, in this instance that all prisoners, including those serving life sentences, should have a prospect of release. The majority stated this, even though there was no consensus on this amongst European states. However, the majority in *Kafkaris*, as in *Hirst*, was so concerned about the different practices of states that it failed to apply fully the notion to which it is increasingly paying lip service, namely, the importance of prisoners' eventual reintegration into society.[30]

---

[30] In *Léger* v. *France* (30 March 2009) the Grand Chamber again missed an opportunity to clarify the law. A majority of the Court declined, because of the death of the applicant before a final ruling could be given, to give a judgment on the merits of the case. In an unusual dissenting opinion on a procedural ruling, Judge Spielmann with whom judges Bratza, Gyulumyan and Jebens agreed, argued that the case raised major human rights concerns and should therefore nevertheless have been considered.

Impact of the jurisprudence in the United Kingdom

In the United Kingdom, where the ECHR and, in particular, its application by the ECtHR are under sustained attack, not only from the popular press but also from significant sections of the judiciary (see Hoffmann 2009), these subtleties have materially affected legal and policy developments flowing from the judgments of the Grand Chamber. These developments have manifested themselves in various ways in the application of these judgments.

Dickson

The careful reasoning of the Grand Chamber in the case of *Dickson* left the government of the United Kingdom with little option but to change its policy with regard to artificial insemination. It had to do so in the face of considerable media hostility. 'The perversion of human rights as jail thug is allowed to become a dad' was the headline of a particularly intemperate piece by A. N. Wilson (2007) in the *Daily Mail,* which reported, in highly emotional language that 'the European Court of Human Rights decreed that the British Government was wrong to prevent this murderous cretin [Dickson] from reproducing himself'.

The government's strategy was to deal with the matter administratively. It quietly dropped the requirement of 'exceptional circumstances', but it left other requirements largely intact, including the interest of the unborn child and the public interest which the Grand Chamber had criticised as factors which should not have been taken into account.

It remains to be seen whether this strategy will be adequate to prevent further legal challenges in the future. Certainly, the Parliamentary Joint Committee on Human Rights (2008: para. 43) has warned that the ECtHR may not uphold them. However, the reality seems to be that new procedures are being publicised and that prisoners are determined to make use of them (Doward 2009).

Kafkaris

The situation regarding the *Kafkaris* judgment is somewhat different because the case had not been brought directly against the United Kingdom. Nevertheless, British prisoners have sought to rely on it in attempts to overturn whole life sentences – that is, life sentences for which no minimum period is set. Most prominent of these has been the case of David Bieber, who was sentenced to life imprisonment without a minimum period for the brutal killing of a policeman.[31] On appeal, his counsel argued vigorously that, in the light of the decision in *Kafkaris*, his whole life sentence should be overturned. In the end it was overturned by the Court of Appeal and replaced with life imprisonment with a minimum period of thirty-seven years. Nevertheless, the Lord Chief Justice, Lord Phillips, who gave the judgment of the Court of Appeal, went out of his way to analyse the European jurisprudence and the *Kafkaris* case in particular. He sought to demonstrate that a close reading of the judgment of the majority in that case indicated it did *not* prevent a court from imposing an 'irreducible sentence'; it meant only that unjustifiably long detention of a lifer could possibly infringe Article 3.

In our view this distinction is without merit. If the sentence is 'irreducible' as a matter of law when it is imposed, then it cannot logically be reduced at a future date without an amendment to the law. At the time of imposition there is therefore no prospect of *de jure* or de facto release and the sentence can be held to create a situation in which the requirements of the ECHR cannot be met. The logic must be that the imposition of a whole life sentence only meets the minimal criteria set by *Kafkaris* if it is clear as a matter of law and practice that it is reducible in the future. Lord Phillips makes allowance for this conclusion, remarking that 'there seems to be a tide in Europe that is setting against the imposition of very long terms of imprisonment that are irreducible' (para. 46). Nevertheless, he chooses to ignore it and holds that the unfettered and very rarely used discretion that a Minister of State retains to 'release a life prisoner on licence if he is satisfied that exceptional circumstances exist which justify the prisoner's release on compassionate grounds'[32] is sufficient to meet the requirements of *Kafkaris*.

Two things are striking about this analysis. The first is that it was unnecessary to undertake it. Bieber's case was decided on other grounds and it is therefore simply a diversion, an *obiter dictum* in lawyers' terms. Secondly, the explanation, that reliance was not being placed on European human rights law, did not mollify critics of the decision in the slightest. A large number of newspapers, not only tabloids but also the

---

[31] *R* v. *Bieber* [2008] ECWA Crim 1601. See also the decision of the House of Lords in the case of *Wellington*, in which the applicant made an unsuccessful attempt to rely on *Kafkaris* in order to prevent extradition to the United States of America, where he faced a whole life sentence with very limited, if any, prospect of release (*R (on the application of Wellington)* v. *Secretary of State for the Home Department* [2008] UKHL 72).

[32] s. 30 Crimes (Sentences) Act 1997.

provincial press, condemned the judgment because of the recognition it gave to the human rights of the offender and linked this 'softness' to the ECHR.[33] The negative reporting of the case was further fuelled by a notably intemperate statement by the chairman of the Police Federation who commented that the 'decision to surrender to the appeal of the cold-blooded murderer' left the 'judiciary with blood on its hands';[34] this not withstanding the fact that Bieber will serve at least thirty-seven years and not even be considered for release before he turns eighty. The same statement condemned the fact that the appeal was initially lodged on the grounds that the offender's human rights had been contravened by the whole life sentence as 'ludicrous'. An earlier statement[35] by the mother of the deceased policeman, that offenders should not be allowed to invoke the Human Rights Act in such cases, was widely reported again.

The overall effect of *Bieber's* case and others like it has been to discredit the impact of the ECHR in the area of whole life sentences without even applying it. If the jurisprudence of the Grand Chamber develops to outlaw whole life sentences more clearly and to require a proper procedure for the consideration of the release of all lifers, it would mean that, if a case such as that of Myra Hindley were to reach the ECtHR in the future, her whole life sentence would be struck down and procedures for considering the release of such prisoners would have to be developed. Stoked by the tabloids, that would be even more controversial and the reluctance of the UK courts to adopt more progressive interpretations of the ECHR when it had the opportunity to do so would simply increase the concern that human rights were being imposed directly from 'Europe'.

Hirst

Of the three major cases considered in this chapter, the decision in *Hirst* presents the largest challenge in terms of implementation. The majority judgment could be read as suggesting that the margin of appreciation

---

[33] See e.g. 'Police killer Bieber gets term cut', *The Mirror*, 4 August 2008, p. 21; 'Judges who prove the law is an ass', *Liverpool Daily Echo*, 7 August 2008, p. 10; 'Travesty of justice', *The Mirror*, 4 August 2008, p. 8.

[34] 'Police rage as judges cut life jail term for PC's killer', *Daily Mail* (London), 4 August 2008, p. 8.

[35] 'Mother of murdered police officer Ian Broadhurst in plea for justice', *Daily Telegraph*, 19 May 2008.

that is allowed governments is dependent on their legislative processes
rather than on an objective judgment by the Court on whether the
restriction is reasonable in terms of the standards of the ECHR.[36]
A better reading would be that the Grand Chamber expects the legislature of the United Kingdom to reconsider the ban on prisoners' right to
vote in the light of 'modern penal policy and current human rights
standards' as articulated in the European legal instruments and subsequently followed in *Dickson.*

Unfortunately the reaction of the government of the United Kingdom
has been to adopt an extremely tardy consultation process.[37] In the first
round of its consultation the government proceeded from the clear
assumption that, since it continued to support the loss of the right to
vote for sentenced prisoners as a form of additional punishment, it
would wish to retain it to the extent that European law would allow it
to do so.[38] In March 2008 the government was called upon to explain to
the Council of Ministers of the Council of Europe why it had not yet
amended the law governing prisoners' right to vote. The government
affirmed that it still intended to do so but pointed immediately to the
room for manoeuver that the *Hirst* judgment had allowed it. It noted
that:

> As the Grand Chamber emphasised at paragraph 82 of its judgment, the
> margin of appreciation afforded to member states in this regard, while
> not all-embracing, remains wide. The Government carefully notes too the
> observation at paragraph 82 of the judgment that in the Court's view
> there has not been a 'substantive debate by members of the legislature on
> the continued justification in light of modern day penal policy and of
> current human rights standards for maintaining such a general restric-
> tion on the right of prisoners to vote'.[39]

The government used these passages in the judgment to explain that it
had combined its review of prisoners' right to vote with a much wider

---

[36] See in this regard the concurring opinion of Judge Caflisch at O-I 2.
[37] This delay has resulted in the Registration Appeal Court in Scotland making a formal
     declaration that the unrepealed provision preventing sentenced prisoners from voting,
     that is s. 3(1) Representation of the People Act 1983, is incompatible with the ECHR:
     Smith v. *Scott* [2007] CSIH 9 XA33/04 §§ 50–8.
[38] Department of Constitutional Affairs, Voting Rights of Convicted Prisoners Detained
     within the United Kingdom – the UK Government's Response to the Grand Chamber of
     the ECtHR Judgment in the Case of *Hirst* v. *United Kingdom* [CP 29/06] 14 December
     2006.
[39] *Hirst* v. *United Kingdom (no. 2)*: Note to Committee of Ministers for the Government of
     the United Kingdom: Written Ministerial Declaration of 2 February 2006.

inquiry into citizenship in the UK, which could not be fitted into its original timetable for reforming the law relating to prisoners' voting rights.

Finally, and after considerable pressure,[40] including a threat from prisoners to approach the courts,[41] in April 2009 the government did issue a second consultation paper on prisoners' right to vote (Ministry of Justice 2009), quite independently of its wider inquiry into citizenship. In practical terms this may be a further delaying tactic because it is unlikely that legislation enabling prisoners to vote will be passed before the next general election.

The most recent consultation paper is interesting nevertheless, for it recognises that the government of the United Kingdom will have to concede the right of at least some prisoners to vote. However, the proposals on what should be included are very limited. It excludes the possibility of allowing all prisoners to vote (which the majority of all respondents to the first consultation favoured) and also, with minor exceptions, the possibility of making the decision on withdrawing the right to vote primarily a judicial one to be taken at the stage of the imposition of sentence. Instead, respondents are invited to comment on whether sentenced prisoners serving sentences of less than one, two or four years should be allowed to vote. There is also a complicated fourth option that would restrict the right to vote to prisoners serving more than two years, but allow those serving between two and four years to have their right to vote restored. For all options the government reserved the right to exclude offenders convicted of certain classes of offences.

Even these very limited proposals met with considerable protest in the media. 'Rapists, paedophiles and burglars get the vote as Government prepares to lift prisoners' election ban' was the headline in the *Daily Mail* (Slack 2009), while the *Daily Express* commented in an editorial that 'our country is being imprisoned by Europe'.[42] Support for the government's specific proposals was almost entirely absent (but see White 2009), with supporters of prisoners' right to vote continuing to argue that as a matter of principle all prisoners should have the right to vote (Prison Reform Trust 2009). Nevertheless, it is clear that the government is trying to find a compromise between a principled recognition of prisoners' right to vote and the opposition to it expressed by the tabloids.

---

[40] 'Prisoner rights group lodges formal complaint over voting ban', *The Guardian*, 30 March 2009.

[41] 'Prisoners to be able to vote at next election', *Daily Telegraph*, 29 March 2009.

[42] 'Prisoners should not be given the vote by Europe', *Daily Express*, 9 April 2009.

At this stage it is impossible to know for certain what the outcome of the consultation process will be, but the likelihood is that the government will adopt one of the more restricted versions of its proposals, allowing only prisoners serving less than one or two years to vote. If that happens, the stage will be set for a further case before the ECtHR. The government of the United Kingdom is likely to argue that it has met the requirement of a legislative debate on the issue. Whether it will be able to justify its substantive decision is doubtful. It should be noted that in the *Sauvé* case, on which the ECtHR relied heavily in *Hirst*, the Supreme Court of Canada set aside as an unconstitutional limit on the franchise a blanket ban on voting by sentenced prisoners serving more than two years. Its decision was based on the notion that such a ban was arbitrary and did not serve a legitimate purpose. In the view of the Canadian court additionally punishing some prisoners because of their status was unacceptable and withdrawing the right to vote was not a rational means for re-socialising them. If the ECtHR follows this line of reasoning, the proposed reforms will not meet European standards concerning the issue of prisoners' right to vote.

Conclusion

There can be no doubt that the three major decisions of the Grand Chamber of the ECtHR, which we have discussed, have broadened the scope of prisoners' rights at the European level. The recognition of the right to artificial insemination, the right to vote and the right to *de jure* and de facto consideration of release for all prisoners are important rights. There is also no doubt that they have had an impact on the recognition of prisoners' rights in the United Kingdom. In all three instances there has been engagement with the decisions. In all three cases the Grand Chamber has moved the debate in the United Kingdom forward.

What close analysis shows, however, is that the detailed reasoning in these decisions is important. In a country such as the United Kingdom where, as Lazarus recognised, the reintegrative purpose of the implementation of the sentences of imprisonment has not been clearly accepted as a principle of prison law, it is essential for the ECtHR to emphasise its own developing thinking in this regard in every decision it takes. If this is not done explicitly, it remains open to both the executive and the courts at the national level to interpret these decisions more restrictively than judges in Strasbourg probably intended. In respect of prisoners' right to vote and, to a lesser extent, their right to procreate, it is the executive that has adopted a restrictive interpretation while, in the case of whole life sentences, the judiciary has sought to pre-empt the full recognition of a right of all prisoners to be considered for release.

Nevertheless, there is reason for cautious optimism. For several years now prison law and prison policy have been shaped by an interaction between the ECtHR and the British authorities. For the foreseeable future this pattern is likely to be repeated, as half-hearted responses by the government of the United Kingdom and narrow interpretations of the ECHR by English courts continue to be challenged in Strasbourg. In 1999 in *Selmouni* v. *France*,[43] the Grand Chamber of the ECtHR expressed the view that 'the increasingly high standard being required in the area of the protection of human rights and fundamental liberties correspondingly and inevitably requires greater firmness in assessing breaches of the fundamental values of democratic societies' (para. 101). It will be up to the ECtHR to continue to adopt this approach and for reformers in the United Kingdom and elsewhere to make full use of the leverage that these judgments provide.

[43] *Selmouni* v. *France* [GC] 28 July 1999.

References

Codd, H. (2008) *In the Shadow of the Prison: Families, Imprisonment and Criminal Justice*, Cullompton: Willan.

Doward, J. (2009) 'Prisoners Demand Right to Be Fathers', *The Observer*, 8 February.

Hoffmann, Lord L. (2009) 'The universality of human rights', Judicial Studies Board Annual Lecture, www.jsboard.co.uk/downloads/Hoffmann_2009_JSB_Annual_Lecture_Universality_of_Human_Rights.doc.

Kaiser, G., Kerner, H.-J. and Schöch, H. (1991) *Strafvollzug*, 4th edn, Heidelberg: C. F. Müller.

Lazarus, L. (2004) *Contrasting Prisoners' Rights: A Comparative Examination of England and Germany*, Oxford: Oxford University Press.

(2006) 'Conceptions of liberty deprivation', *Modern Law Review*, 69, 738–69.

Letsas, G. (2006) 'Two concepts of the margin of appreciation', *Oxford Journal of Legal Studies*, 26, 705–32.

Lewis, T. (2006) '"Difficult and slippery terrain": Hansard, human rights and *Hirst* v. *UK*', *Public Law*, 209–18.

Ministry of Justice (2009) *Voting Rights of Convicted Prisoners Detained within the United Kingdom, Second Stage Consultation*, Paper CP6/09, London: Ministry of Justice.

Parliamentary Joint Committee on Human Rights (2008) *Thirty-First Report, Session 2007–08*, London: HMSO.

Prison Reform Trust (2009) 'PRT responds to publication of government's second consultation on prisoners' votes', 8 April 2009, www.prisonreformtrust.org. uk/standard.asp?id=1736.

Slack, J. (2009) 'Rapists, paedophiles and burglars get the vote as Government prepares to lift prisoners' election ban', *Daily Mail*, 9 April.

White, M. (2009) 'Should prisoners get the vote?' *Guardian Blog*, 9 April 2009, www.guardian.co.uk/politics/blog/2009/apr/09/should-prisoners-get-vote.

Wilson, A. N. (2007) 'The perversion of human rights as jail thug is allowed to become a dad', *Daily Mail*, 6 December.

Zyl Smit, D. van and Snacken, S. (2009) *Principles of European Prison Law and Policy: Penology and Human Rights*, Oxford: Oxford University Press.

PART 2

Comparative penal policies

8

Penal comparisons: puzzling relations

MICHAEL CAVADINO AND JAMES DIGNAN

In retrospect, it seems surprising that it had attracted so little attention before. It is hardly news – it was hardly news when Durkheim considered the matter at the end of the nineteenth century – that punishment and ideas about punishment vary between different societies, and that these variations can be related to larger social and political differences. Several theorists had postulated or investigated a possible connection (some kind of inverse relationship) between a society's welfare provision and the severity of its punishments (see for example Greenberg 1999; Downes and Hansen 2006; Beckett and Western 2001). Certainly, some had spotted a link between the advance of neoliberalism in the United States and the spectacular rise in US punishment levels from the early 1970s onwards (e.g. Downes 2001). And some had made use or mention of Esping-Andersen's (1990) typology of modern capitalist welfare states in the penal context (Kilcommins *et al.* 2004: Chapter 7; Beckett and Western 2001). But we flatter ourselves that our 2006 work *Penal Systems: A Comparative Approach* (Cavadino and Dignan 2006) demonstrated just how illuminating was the Esping-Andersen schema when applied to comparative penology.

To recapitulate briefly: Esping-Andersen[1] delineated three types of contemporary capitalist political economy: the free-market *neoliberal* polity (exemplified archetypally by the United States of America); the more communitarian *conservative corporatism* (exemplified by Germany) and the *social democratic* corporatism found in the Nordic countries (the prime example being Sweden). To these we added what we call the *oriental corporatism* of Japan. Comparing twelve countries, we found that these four types of political economy exhibited significantly different penal tendencies. In particular, overall levels of 'punitiveness' (as imperfectly measured by the countries' 'imprisonment rates' proportionate

---

[1] Esping-Andersen employed slightly different terms for the first two types ('liberal' and 'conservative').

Table 8.1 *Political economy and imprisonment rates*

	IMPRISONMENT RATE (per 100,000 population)	Year
NEOLIBERAL COUNTRIES		
USA	756	2007
South Africa	335	2008
New Zealand	185	2008
England and Wales	153	2008
Australia	129	2008
CONSERVATIVE CORPORATIST COUNTRIES		
Netherlands	100	2008
France	96	2008
Italy	92	2008
Germany	89	2008
SOCIAL DEMOCRACIES		
Sweden	74	2007
Finland	64	2008
ORIENTAL CORPORATISM		
Japan	63	2006

Source: Walmsley (2008)[2]

to their population) were highest in neoliberal countries, lower in conservative corporatist nations, lower still in social democracies and lowest of all in Japan (see Table 8.1). Other variations between countries in their penal practices and ideologies (such as juvenile justice policy, openness to penal privatisation and emphasis on the rehabilitation and re-socialisation of offenders) were also associated with these variations in political economy.

The question we left hanging, however, was *why* exactly does this connection exist between political economy and penality? There are a number of possibilities, not necessarily mutually exclusive, which we shall proceed to discuss in turn.

---

[2] See www.kcl.ac.uk/depsta/law/research/icps/worldbrief/wpb_stats.php for regularly updated statistics.

Hypothesis One: crime-driven punishment?

Political economy → Crime rate → Punishment

The association between political economy and punishment could be explained as follows. Certain political economies could be more criminogenic than others. If there is more crime then there will be more criminals to be caught and sent to prison, leading to higher rates of imprisonment. (Note that the convenient measure typically used to assess a country's punitiveness is the number of persons in prison *per 100,000 of the general population*, so if there are more criminals one might expect this rate to be higher.)

The first link in this chain of explanation seems both plausible and supported by evidence. To start with its plausibility, the individualism and inequality of neoliberal societies could well reduce social cohesion, excluding and marginalising many individuals (and indeed large groups), engendering anomie and alienation, with increased crime as a result. On the other hand, the more inclusive, cohesive communities of corporatist countries could help to minimise anomie and alienation, leading its citizens to feel more at one with their society and thus engendering more pro-social and law-abiding attitudes and hence less crime. In part this could work because the more developed welfare states[3] to be found in corporatist societies and especially in social democratic societies could both help individuals feel more cared for by society and also reduce the relative deprivation which is one spur to the commission of crime. In other words, the more unequal a society, the more crime it is likely to engender.

And there is indeed mounting empirical evidence that unequal societies with weak community relationships do suffer from worse rates of crime compared with those where more citizens have a sense of belonging and where strong community ties allow for more effective informal social control (see for example Ormerod 1997; Wilkinson 2005). Interestingly, and perhaps counterintuitively, this link between inequality and crime is much better established in relation to violent crime (including homicide) than in relation to property offences. Wilkinson (2005: Chapter 5) summarises both the evidence for the link

---

[3] The welfare *state* is not so well developed in Japan. However, this is a society in which securing the welfare of others is seen as a strong obligation lying on others in the same social group – including capitalist employers. See further Cavadino and Dignan (2006: 19–21 and 173–4).

between inequality and violence and the likely reasons for it, which include a greater tendency for have-nots to use violence – typically, sadly, against other disadvantaged people – in the struggle to attain the social respect which they are denied by their unequal society.

However, the second link in the purported causal chain – the link between crime rates and imprisonment rates – seems much weaker. For, perhaps remarkably, there is not much good evidence of a strong association between these two rates.[4] It must be admitted that the evidence is inconsistent, and that studies have tended to find more evidence of a positive relationship between imprisonment rates and rates of *violent* crime – which as we have seen does tend to be higher in more unequal societies. But as Young and Brown (1993: 33) concluded, 'only a small measure of the differences in prison populations . . . seem to be related to crime rates'. Moreover, as Young and Brown (*ibid.*) point out, 'to the extent that there is a relationship, we cannot be certain that it is a causal one'. It could be that the relationship is 'spurious' generated by the fact that unequal, more criminogenic societies are also more likely to be punitive, for reasons explained by one of our other hypotheses.

Hypothesis One has an affinity with the idea that there is some kind of 'trade-off between welfare and incarceration' (Beckett and Western 2001: 51), or that welfare and punishment are in some way 'functional equivalents'. It is true that, generally speaking,[5] countries which spend less on welfare resort most to imprisonment and other harsh penalties. The conclusion could be drawn that welfare and punishment are alternative methods for the social control of those who live on the margins of society (and hence are potentially deviant). On the one hand, potential deviants on the margin can be managed by the informal social controls provided by the 'soft machine' of the welfare state, which removes or alleviates some of the hardships that lead to crime, and provides incentives to good behaviour in the form of benefits which may be in various ways jeopardised by criminal behaviour. The result of these informal controls may be that fewer people offend and so there is less need for the formal control of criminal justice sanctions. Alternatively, a society

---

[4] See e.g. Young and Brown (1993: 23–33); Beckett and Western (2001: 49–50) and works cited therein.

[5] Thus, social democratic countries have high levels of welfare spending but low imprisonment rates; neoliberal countries are the opposite; and conservative corporatist countries occupy an intermediate position on both measures. An exception is Japan, which has relatively low state spending on welfare but a low imprisonment rate: but see note 2 above.

could spend less on welfare and rely instead on harsh punishments to deter marginalised potential deviants and to lock away those who do offend. Different countries will therefore opt for different balances between the 'carrot' of welfare and the 'stick' of punishment.

We are generally sceptical about functionalist 'explanations' for social phenomena. But leaving that aside, this particular functionalist explanation would surely be a great deal more plausible if there were more evidence that punishment was actually an *effective* method of social control – or (more precisely) that the differences between different countries in how much they punish made much difference to their crime rates. Such evidence is largely lacking. Criminal sanctions seem in general to be a peculiarly inefficient method of crime control (Cavadino and Dignan 2007: 37–43; Cavadino *et al.* 1999: 37–40), and in particular there is little evidence that countries with harsh levels of sentencing derive any benefit in reduced crime rates (von Hirsch *et al.* 1999: Chapter 6). It is hard to see how something can be a functional equivalent if it does not actually work.[6]

There may be more plausible variations of this explanation, however. Perhaps, whether or not harsh punishment actually works, it has been employed in the *belief* that it is a better bet than welfare for keeping crime under control. Welfare and punishment may not be so much functional equivalents as alternative *strategies* for social control. Or perhaps, but rather differently, if a neoliberal government believes that welfare expenditure needs to be reduced (for economic and/or political reasons), such a government is also for some reason likely to believe that punishment needs to be made tougher to keep crime under control, whether or not anyone in government perceives any link between the two policies. But such an explanation no longer fits well under Hypothesis One. We shall return to it when we discuss Hypotheses Four and Five.

Hypothesis Two: public-driven punishment?

Political economy ↔ *general culture* → *public opinion* → *punishment*

Perhaps punishment is driven by public opinion, with public opinion in turn being conditioned by the society's culture, which is linked to its

---

[6] Welfare spending, on the other hand, may well keep crime levels down: see e.g. Downes and Hansen (2006). A word of clarification: 'welfare' here means generalised welfare services provided to all those who need them. 'Penal welfarism' – criminal sanctions which are intended to *reform offenders* by attending to their welfare – do not in general seem to work so well (see e.g. Cavadino and Dignan 2007: 41–3).

political economy. A society's cultural attitudes towards its deviant and marginalised fellow citizens will be both *embodied* and *embedded* in the political economy: a society whose culture encourages certain attitudes is likely to create a political economy which both expresses that attitude and tends to reinforce and 'reproduce' it over time, assisting it to persist across generations.[7] The opinions of the public about how deviants should be treated will be moulded by this culture, and these public opinions (more or less punitive) will influence what is done with offenders.

It is not difficult to make plausible suggestions about how the different families of political economy might well be associated with cultures which foster different public attitudes towards offenders. The key element is an *exclusive* approach towards the marginalised, the deviant, the loser. The neoliberal exclusion both of those who fail in the economic marketplace and of those who fail to abide by the law is no coincidence. Both are associated with a highly individualistic social ethos. In neoliberal society, economic failure is seen as being the fault of the atomised, free-willed individual, not any responsibility of society – hence the minimal, safety-net welfare state. Crime is likewise seen as entirely the responsibility of the offending individual. The social soil is fertile ground for a harsh 'law-and-order ideology' with its high levels of punishment. On the other hand, the more communitarian[8] cultures of conservative corporatism and social dem-ocracy encourage a greater social solidarity with the deviant, leading to the impulse to keep the marginalised *included* within the community and not pushed off the margins into the outer darkness. There will be greater emphasis on the rehabilitation and re-socialisation of offenders, seeking to reintegrate and re-include them in the community – just as welfare is applied to other economic and social failures to keep them included. Ordinary citizens in countries with a more individualistic, exclusive culture will hold views favouring more exclusive, harsher penal policies. These more punitive public opinions will influence

---

[7] This analysis is in line with our general 'radical pluralist' approach (for which see further Cavadino and Dignan 2007: 81–4). Whereas Marxism sees the 'economic base' of society as being what ultimately determines a society's prevailing ideologies, and a Durkheimian perspective might suggest that the causal relationship is the other way around, radical pluralism sees culture and economy as mutually determining, with neither being more 'basic' than the other.

[8] Communitarianism is of course a hotly contested concept, but one which it is unnecessary to explore here. We use the term broadly to mean the opposite of individualism, referring to cultures which afford a relatively high recognition and value to community vis-à-vis the individual.

politicians, other policy-makers and criminal justice practitioners (most importantly sentencers) and ultimately lead to harsher punishment. And conversely, in countries with a more communitarian and inclusive culture, public opinion would similarly bring about more lenient punishment.

One problem with this hypothesis is that when attempts have been made to measure the punitiveness of public opinion in different countries the results have not come out like that at all. A 'league table' of punitiveness in public opinion constructed from the findings of the International Crime Victims Survey (ICVS) would bear little relationship either to our typology of political economies or to a league table of imprisonment rates (see van Dijk *et al.* 2007: 149; Reiner 2007). Although the neoliberal countries again come out as more punitive than conservative corporatist or social democratic countries, English public opinion appears more punitive than the USA instead of much less so, while Swedish and (especially) Japanese public opinion seems remarkably pro-imprisonment and completely out of line with these countries' actual imprisonment rates. It could well be that, for a variety of reasons, the ICVS's methodology is inadequate to provide a comparative measure of public punitiveness (see Reiner 2007) – but they certainly provide no support for Hypothesis Two.

Another piece of evidence against is provided by Katherine Beckett's (1997) study of the politics of law and order in the USA, which demonstrated that it was politicians and the media who gave the lead to the public rather than the other way round. Public anxiety over crime rose as a consequence, not of real rises in crime rates, but of media and political campaigns on the subject. Thus it would appear that there is far from being a perfect one-way Durkheimian transmission of public sentiment into penal policy via the innocent medium of politics.

Hypothesis Two may be partially correct. Penal policies and practices in democracies must to a large extent be constrained and influenced by public sentiments, which in turn are likely to be related to political economy. But, we say advisedly, they are 'constrained' and 'influenced', not necessarily *driven* let alone entirely *determined* by public opinion. The realms of penal politics and penal practices may well (in the light of research such as Beckett's) exhibit a degree of autonomy from the sentiments of public opinion, and it can be politics that drives public opinion rather than the reverse. Again, politics is starting to look crucial. But we must still wait in suspense for Hypotheses Four and Five to make their appearance.

Hypothesis Three: media-driven punishment?

Political economy → Media culture → Political & public opinion → punishment

The mass media surely play a role in moulding our perceptions of the world around us, including our perceptions and beliefs about crime and punishment (see for example Pfeiffer *et al.* 2005) – although nor do they fully determine what we perceive and believe. Equally surely, the media do not simply reflect the opinions of their consumers. 'Tabloid' newspapers (and the associated phenomenon of 'tabloid television') are far more likely to embody punitive attitudes and favour punitive policies.[9] And tabloid-type media with this punitive agenda are significantly more common in neoliberal polities than in corporatist and social democratic ones. So perhaps it is these media which create the harsher penality in neoliberal societies by making the public, politicians and sentencers more punitive. The public's attitudes are made more punitive by the media they consume. Politicians also consume some of the same media and are also influenced by them; they also believe that the media either represent or successfully condition public opinion and therefore – especially in an age where politicians are obsessed with publicity and 'spin' – that their electoral prospects depend on portraying themselves as 'tough on crime'. Sentencers too are influenced by the media, both directly as malleable consumers themselves, and also because they, like the politicians, assume that the media speak for a public opinion which demands harsh sentences from them.

Why is it that neoliberal societies are more likely to have sensationalist tabloid media pushing a punitive agenda? There are doubtless several reasons. The freer market conditions of neoliberalism make for freer markets in journalism and entertainment, into which media entrepreneurs (Rupert Murdoch being an obvious example) will find it easier to enter. Pursuing profits, they will use this market freedom to produce the tabloid commodities which are most profitable, and – working on the theory that they will rarely go bust underestimating the sophistication or penal humaneness of their target readership – they will by accident even if not by design promote populist punitiveness. Crime, especially if sensationalised, makes an easy dramatic story for the media. Corporatist and social democratic political economies tend to place greater

---

[9] But not invariably: compare the British left-of-centre tabloid *The Mirror* with the right-wing broadsheet *The Daily Telegraph*.

restrictions on media ownership and control partly for reasons dictated by national communitarian ideology: unregulated capitalist press and (especially) broadcasting is avoided to ensure that it does not damage the national interest.

Another possible reason for the lesser prominence of tabloid media outside neoliberal polities could be simply that corporatist and social democratic countries, thanks to more and better public investment in education, have a better-educated populace and therefore provide less of a profitable market for such media. Thus, potential tabloid entrepreneurs (many of whom, again like Murdoch, operate on an international playing field) are more likely to concentrate their investments in the neoliberal countries.

The evidence is thin to date. We would speculate that Hypothesis Three has some validity, but is only one component in a much larger picture. Essentially we see the effect of the media as a *compounding factor* which *magnifies* the differences in penality between the different political economies – but does not create them.

Hypothesis Four: political culture-driven punishment?

Political economy → Political culture → Political opinion → punishment

Perhaps *public* opinion has little to do with it. Hypothesis Two (and indeed one facet of Hypothesis Three) concentrated on public opinion as a vital link between political economy and punishment. But are 'the people' really so powerful? Or is Marx's dictum more apt, that 'the ruling ideas of each age have ever been the ideas of its ruling class' (Marx 1977: 236)? Perhaps, for example, a harsh neoliberalism and a harsh penality tend to go together because *those with power* – the socio-political elite and the penal elite – have similar ideas and attitudes, and it is they who can do most to shape both the political economy itself and the nation's penality. They do not necessarily take the populace with them all the way on either score. Perhaps – as political systems currently work – both political economy and punishment are largely the result of the beliefs and sentiments of those people whose wishes count for most. It is *the ideologies of the powerful* that are crucial.

There have been some general trends in these ideologies in recent decades. Since the 1970s, most countries have seen a trend towards neoliberalism as markets have been made freer, rates of progressive taxation reduced and welfare spending restricted, none of which would have happened had political elites not been persuaded that such changes were desirable or necessary. Similarly, and with a similar temporal trajectory, governments now seem to have very different ideas about criminal justice than those which were most salient in the late 1960s and early 1970s. Governmental ideologies do not just change on their own: the ideas come from somewhere. But they are only likely to be taken up by governments if they are perceived as both acceptable and as providing a solution to the problems of government. As regards economic ideologies, the beginnings of these ideological changes can be traced back at least as far as the first 'oil shock' in the 1970s combined with a decline in the 'Fordist' method of production to pose economic problems which were perceived to be insoluble by the social democratic and Keynesian conventional wisdoms which had previously ruled. Governments increasingly adopted the nostrums of neoliberalism proffered by such apostles as Milton Friedman, especially in the Anglophone countries which make up the neoliberal world of today.[10]

A parallel development occurred in the sphere of criminal justice ideology. In the United States, influential 'right realists'[11] such as James Q. Wilson (1975) started to convince policy-makers that the answer to crime (which was rising significantly in the 1970s) was tougher sanctions. The fact that such prescriptions promised to be electorally popular – and therefore a solution to problems of electability as well as crime – will also naturally have been seen as an advantage by many politicians. The UK has hardly been teeming with its own home-grown right-wing criminologists,[12] but UK politicians have to a large extent imitated what they perceive to be strategies successful in the United States, and have in their turn been followed by politicians elsewhere. Thus, Tony Blair (UK Prime Minister 1997–2007) followed the 'Third Way' approach of Bill Clinton (US President 1993–2001) in accepting neoliberalism and 'tough' policies on crime despite leading a traditionally left-of-centre party. Blair was in turn consciously imitated by social democratic

---

[10] It will of course be interesting to observe the future fortunes of neoliberal ideology following its monumental failure in the global financial sector leading to the 'credit crunch' of the late 2000s.

[11] For the influence of the American criminological 'new right' on the UK's New Labour government, see Young (2003: 39–41).

[12] Although in recent years we have witnessed the rise of pressure groups advocating harsher criminal justice policies such as Civitas, which employs some academics (albeit mostly not criminologists by background).

politicians in a variety of countries (Cavadino and Dignan 2006: 11, 54, 68, 79, 88, 102, 121, 135).

The result has been a long series of governmental policies loudly trumpeted as 'tough on crime', while opposition politicians have sought to put forward policies which they portray as even tougher. This 'bidding war' has maintained a high profile for the issue of crime and punishment in public discourse and propagated the impression that everyone agrees on the need for tougher sanctions. The harsher punishment which has ensued was not merely brought about by the concrete policies and legislation introduced by governments' law-and-order programmes. Probably more potent has been the effect of this constant political rhetoric on the minds of criminal justice practitioners, notably sentencers (see Cavadino and Dignan 2007: 28; cf. Cavadino and Dignan 2006: 338).

When discussing Hypothesis One, we rejected the notion that welfare spending and punishment can be seen as genuine 'functional equivalents' in achieving social control, on the ground that punishment is in reality an extremely inefficient method of crime control. But, as we then asked, even if it doesn't actually work, could punishment form an (attempted) *alternative strategy* of social control to the welfare state? As Beckett and Western (2001: 55) put it, have we seen 'the emergence of an alternative mode of governance that is replacing, to varying degrees, the modernist strategy based on rehabilitation and welfare'? This might make a certain amount of sense – especially since one plank of 'right realism' is the claim that welfare, far from helping to control crime, has served to worsen it by producing a dependent work-shy underclass and a generation of fatherless feral children, whereas tough deterrent sanctions actually work. Beliefs which, as we noted earlier, may well be just about the opposite of the truth on the available evidence (Downes and Hansen 2006), but which have nevertheless determined policy. Consequently, policies of reducing welfare and increasing punishment have been deliberately pursued simultaneously as countries have taken a neoliberal turn.

But there are at least two problems with this scenario. One is the lack of evidence, and maybe the implausibility, of politicians actually thinking in quite this joined-up, macro-overview manner. Are politicians supposed to have *consciously* thought and agreed, 'In order to control crime we will reduce spending on welfare and increase spending on prisons'? Or perhaps, 'We have to cut spending on welfare for economic reasons; this may cause more crime but we will deal with that by locking up more people'? We know politicians can be insincere, cynical and Machiavellian, but do they really *strategise* in quite this way? A second problem relates to the actual trajectories over time of crime rates and penal policies, as can be clearly seen in both the United States and Britain (and doubtless elsewhere as well). If increasing the harshness of punishment is a conscious *strategy to cope with the problem of rising crime*, then why has this strategy been pursued at times when crime has been *falling* significantly? In the USA, crime rates fell in the early 1980s and then again since 1993; in England and Wales, crime has fallen by around 40 per cent since 1995 (Nicholas *et al.* 2007), times when the numbers of prisoners in both countries have risen enormously.[13] Perhaps increased penal harshness could have been a conscious strategy to cope with rising crime when crime actually was rising, but why has the strategy persisted since?

No doubt politicians possess a measure of sincerity and generally believe in the correctness of their policies. They may well still believe that the old liberal approach to criminal justice failed and that a tougher approach is still required. Referring back to a theme of Hypothesis Two, there is again an affinity between the mindset that accepts the failure of Keynesianism and social democratic welfarism and the need for a more individualistic and unforgiving economic system, and that which accepts the failure of liberal penal welfarism and the need for a more individualistic and unforgiving criminal justice system. On the other hand, members of the political class in a different nation who retain faith in a more communitarian economic system may well also be more likely to retain faith in a more inclusive approach to criminal justice. The economic and penal ideologies are both homologous and symbiotic, bespeaking similar attitudes towards fellow citizens. Politicians who hold the economic doctrine are likely to be predisposed in favour of the penal doctrine. Hence – perhaps, to some extent – the association between political economy and punishment.

Vitally however, the problems faced by politicians are not only those of governance but also those of electoral politics. Bearing this in mind and studying the history of the matter, it seems overwhelmingly likely that the main attraction of harsh penal policies to politicians is electoral rather than governmental. For some reason, this attractiveness is greater in more neoliberal societies, lower in corporatist ones and lower still in social democracies. And this, it seems likely, is only partly because such

---

[13] The England and Wales prison population was 51,047 in 1995; on 13 June 2008 it was 83,171 (a rise of 63%). In the US, the prison population rose from 1,369,185 in 1993 to 2,293,157 in 2007 (up 67%).

policies are indeed more likely to appeal to a neoliberal electorate (Hypothesis Two), or because of the greater influence of populist media in neoliberal societies (Hypothesis Three). There is something else afoot.

Hypothesis Five: political institution-driven punishment?

Political economy ↔ *Political institutions* → *punishment*

Nicola Lacey's 2007 Hamlyn Lectures, *The Prisoners' Dilemma* (Lacey 2008), advances a fifth hypothesis to explain the link between political economy and punishment. Her thesis is that punitive populism in the politics of law and order is much more likely to thrive in countries with particular sets of political institutions. And these political institutions are associated with the neoliberal political economy. She provides some good evidence for both of these links – but are they the whole story?

The first link first. Lacey (2008: Chapter 2) draws on the work of Hall and Soskice (2003) in distinguishing between 'co-ordinated market economies' (CMEs) on the one hand, and 'liberal market economies' (LMEs) on the other. In terms of our modified Esping-Andersen typology of political economies, LMEs equate to neoliberal countries, while CMEs are corporatist and thus embrace conservative corporatist countries and the oriental corporatism of Japan, as well as the Nordic social democracies. (The fact that these three types are lumped together in Lacey's schema is a point to which we will return.) A co-ordinated market economy depends on a high degree of skills among its workforce. The economy invests in its workers with education and training, and requires stability in the labour market over time, as the skills of its workers are not highly transferable between jobs. Providing this stability requires co-ordinating institutions which regulate and run the market and provide more security for workers, both in the sense that they are less likely to lose their jobs and also in that if they do the welfare state will maintain them well until they are redeployed. A liberal market economy, on the other hand, relies on 'flexibility' in the labour market; thus there is less job security, less social security for the unemployed and less regulation of the market in general. In the LME, individual workers are more dispensable (being less skilled); the system is also more likely to generate periods of high unemployment, when large numbers of potential workers are surplus to requirements.

One result of this, says Lacey, is that a CME 'may be more likely to generate incentives for the relevant decision-makers to opt for a relatively inclusionary criminal justice system. For it is a system which is premised on incorporation, and hence on the need to reintegrate offenders into society and economy' (Lacey 2008: 58). Exactly what these 'incentives' are, however, is not so clear to us. Again, are we talking about strategies or functions? Do politicians in a CME really reason that we need to rehabilitate offenders because the economy needs them as workers? Conversely, do those in a LME think to themselves that rehabilitation is unnecessary because if they weren't in prison they would be unemployed anyway? Or is some mysterious hidden hand at work, so that an economy gets the criminal justice it needs via some invisible mechanism of the society's subconscious?

Less enigmatically, Lacey points to the different types of political arrangements that tend to hold sway in CMEs on the one hand and LMEs on the other. In particular, CMEs have proportional representation systems which normally lead to coalitions of parties representing the interests of a number of different sections of society, while LMEs (apart from New Zealand, of which more shortly) have 'first past the post' 'winner takes all' systems which are much more likely to lead to single-party majority governments relatively untrammeled by the need to seek alliances and compromises with other parties. In CMEs this process of negotiation and compromise over governmental programmes creates an insulating layer between governments and the immediate, unmediated expressed wishes of the electorate, making populist policy-making less viable and increasing the influence of the country's permanent professional bureaucracy. For example, in a first-past-the-post system a party might propose populist policies aimed at appealing to floating voters, be elected with a majority sufficient to govern alone and then duly enact such vote-grabbing but unwise measures, whereas in a proportional representation (PR) system the policy might get negotiated out during post-election coalition building.

But PR is not the magic key to our puzzle. Lacey herself (this volume) points to the example of New Zealand, a LME where PR was introduced in 1996, followed by an *increase* in penal populism. Lacey explains this as the result of PR being grafted onto a LME with its pre-existing traditions, culture and politics. It would seem therefore that PR does not in itself lead to a milder penality; it is more that in the right circumstances PR can assist in the retention of a more corporatist economy and society (see Lacey, this volume), which is associated with a more lenient penality. In other words, it is the political economy that affects punishment, not the political arrangement (PR). A blow for Hypothesis 5, perhaps.

But here we need to note that when we speak of 'political economy', and of *types* of political economy, we are speaking of a complex phenomenon. A type of political economy is a constellation of national characteristics which is partly economy, partly political institutions and arrangements, partly popular culture, partly political culture. If PR is not fundamental, there is a range of other political arrangements and institutions which are more or less associated with different types of political economy. Notably, in corporatist countries (or CMEs) different interest groups and sections of society are integrated and bound into frameworks of accommodation in a variety of ways which tend not to exist (or to exist only in very weak forms) in neoliberal/LME polities. This can involve political parties which represent different communities of interest negotiating to form governments or policy; or it can, for example, consist of the Swedish system whereby unemployment insurance is funded by government but administered by trade unions. There may be something about this whole tradition of reasonable accommodation of differing interests that discourages too much shrill penal populism among the political class.

One vital factor may be the role and status of the professional bureaucracy in the practice of government. In more corporatist countries, the permanent civil service is respected and politically neutral, and it plays a powerful role in the formation of governmental policies and practices. To a large extent[14] it acts rather like 'state as honest broker' between different interest groups as portrayed in pluralist political theory (see Cavadino and Dignan 2007: 81–3). While doing so it acts as a carrier of the prevailing conventional wisdom of the state, which in a corporatist nation will tend towards policies which seek to combine rational management of criminal justice with a humane and rehabilitationist approach. As Lacey (2008: Chapter 2) explains, however, in neoliberal countries the civil service has become more politicised, less respected and less powerful in the face of populist politics, especially in the field of criminal justice. To judge from British experience, it would also seem that the civil service's resistance to punitive criminal justice policies has weakened at the same time, and doubtless as a result the political culture of the bureaucracy and the conventional wisdoms it espouses and carries have altered. It is notable that the classic BBC comedy of the late 1970s and 1980s *Yes Minister* portrayed British

---

[14] But not entirely, as it or its members may have their own agendas: see Cavadino and Dignan (2007: 82).

politicians as being manipulated and out-manoeuvred by civil servants, whereas the more recent comedy *The Thick of It* instead showed politicians at the mercy of their own spin doctors intent on populist publicity. Also of note is that Margaret Thatcher (who liked *Yes Minister*) saw the civil service as an obstacle to creating neoliberalism in the UK. In order to change society in a neoliberal direction it was necessary to alter the role, status and culture of the civil service; hence the correlation noted by Lacey between these and different types of political economy.

This would help to explain why populist politics and in particular 'bidding wars' on toughness in criminal justice are much more likely to take flight in neoliberal rather than corporatist countries. However, we now seem to be back to something more like Hypothesis Four, with the emphasis more on political culture than on political institutions and arrangements. Perhaps we should amend Hypothesis Four so that it is about *political and state culture* (with state culture including the culture of the civil service, and political culture including politicians' attitudes towards the permanent bureaucracy).

Returning to political arrangements, Lacey (this volume) discusses some particular, exceptional arrangements to be found in the USA, which she (surely rightly) sees as relevant to the phenomenon of penal populist politics. In many ways American democracy is extremely *decentralised* (Savelsberg 1999), with much political power residing at state, district and county levels, and this could be said to be particularly the case in the realm of the politics of criminal justice, with many judges, district attorneys and county sheriffs being directly elected, and often achieving election on extreme punitive platforms. (An example which came to me recently in a round-robin email originating in the USA – complete with smiley faces – concerned Joe Arpaio, the popular Sheriff of Maricopa County, Arizona, whose practices include reintroducing chain gangs and banning coffee for prisoners.) Such arrangements are not common to neoliberal political economies, so they presumably cannot be attributed simply to the USA's membership of the neoliberal family of nations.[15] Lacey's argument is that these arrangements help explain why the USA's penality is so exceptional even among neoliberal countries.

Her analysis is similar to an argument put forward by Michael Tonry (2004; see also Cavadino 2005). Tonry's prescriptions for the US system

---

[15] Although it could be argued that they would not exist in a corporatist system. In which case, neoliberalism or something like it might be a necessary but not sufficient condition for such arrangements.

include abolishing direct elections for such officials and moving towards a more European system whereby they are more like career civil servants than politicians, along with delegation of the task of making penal policies and rules to administrative agencies such as sentencing commissions. To paraphrase, punishment should be kept more insulated from the world of electoral politics and kept in a semi-autonomous realm in which rational *thinking about crime*[16] has a chance to predominate over short-term emotionalism and unthinking beliefs engendered by contingent sensibilities ('knee-jerk reactions', in other words). Similarly, Lacey (2008: Chapter 4) suggests that the UK should establish an expert body responsible for criminal justice policy which is independent of the party political process,[17] along the lines of the Bank of England's Monetary Policy Committee, to provide a similar kind of insulation. (Shades of such an approach may be detectable in the current UK government's favouring of a new-style sentencing commission or council.[18]) Whether or not this is the right way forward for those who want to see a more rational humane criminal justice – and we are not totally convinced (see further Cavadino and Dignan 2006: 341–2) – there is no doubt that the extraordinarily uninsulated American system is no help either to humane penal reformers or to the practice of civilised democracy. Political arrangements do indeed matter. However, some of the ones that matter – like direct election of judges and sheriffs – are at least to some extent, as we have just seen, seemingly independent of the general type of political economy in which they subsist. So yes, different political economies are associated with different types of political institutions; and yes, political institutions can affect penality – but the causative chain does not seem to run neatly all the way through.

There may be other problems with Hypothesis Five, as formulated by Lacey. As we noted previously, her analysis is based on the Hall/Soskice dichotomy between liberal and co-ordinated market economies (or neoliberalism versus corporatism, the latter including the Nordic social democracies). It can therefore provide no explanation of why social democratic countries exhibit a markedly more lenient penality than conservative corporatist nations, since the Nordic social democracies are lumped together with the other corporatist countries as CMEs.

---

[16] The title of Tonry's (2004) book, cheekily purloined from James Q. Wilson (1975).

[17] A previous body, the Advisory Council on the Penal System, was abolished by the Thatcher government in 1980.

[18] As recommended by Carter (2007), and included in the Coroners and Justice Act 2009.

Another complication is this. As it happens, the Nordic social democracies are corporatist (and CMEs), but not all social democracy necessarily has this flavour. We have previously suggested elsewhere that prior to the 1980s countries like the UK, New Zealand and Australia could be characterised as *social democracies without corporatism* (Cavadino and Dignan 2006: 73) – not CMEs, but hardly liberal market economies either. The social democratic periods in these countries were associated with relatively lenient penality, certainly compared with the neoliberalism that was to follow. This seems to point towards a possible limitation of Lacey's thesis, or a need to supplement it.[19]

Conclusion: nothing works?

Do none of these hypotheses work well enough to explain the link between political economy and penality? Is it there but inexplicable? Was the link just an optical illusion all along?

We would take some convincing that the link was never there. Although we have never claimed that the association between types of political economy and types of penality is any kind of iron law, the correlation seems undoubtedly robust. Something is causing it, but none of these five hypotheses seems strong enough on its own to explain it.

As we noted previously, political economy is a complex phenomenon, so it should be no surprise that any explanation of the political economy–penality link might also turn out to be complex. Having no great fear of the explanatory eclecticism which some theorists abhor (see also Cavadino and Dignan 2007: 83), we are currently inclined to believe that the explanation for the link lies in a combination of Hypotheses Two to Five. On the empirical evidence, Hypothesis One (crime-driven punishment) seems to have little if any explanatory power. Hypothesis Two (public opinion-driven punishment) lies under the shadow of the ICVS findings, but we strongly suspect that public opinion is influenced by the political economy which shapes the lives of the public, and that it does play a part at least in restricting the possibilities for punishment (including, unfortunately, limiting the immediate scope for humanitarian penal reform in many countries). Hypothesis Three (media-driven punishment) we judge to be a compounding factor but not the fundamental cause of the link. Hypothesis Four (political culture-driven punishment)

---

[19] For some suggestions as to why social democratic countries may be particularly lenient, see Cavadino and Dignan (2006: 26).

and Hypothesis Five (political institution-driven punishment) are perhaps the two most interesting hypotheses, especially if taken in combination. It is, we suspect, primarily the interaction between political culture and political and state institutions – including, vitally, the relationship between politicians and the permanent state bureaucracy and the culture of the latter – which can go a long way to solving the puzzle we set ourselves. However, we should not expect that any such theory can ever go all the way and provide us with a total, determining explanation of penality. For within this cultural, economic and institutional framework, humans act and interact – and punish.

If we are right about this, it may have important implications for the future prospects of punishment. The key to penality lies in the political realm, broadly defined – within an area of contest and struggle whose outcomes are not totally pre-determined or entirely bounded by unchangeable social facts. The neoliberal world, with its accompanying harsh penality, was created by the struggles of human beings – to some extent led by, but by no means entirely consisting of, personages such as Ronald Reagan, Margaret Thatcher and their successors – making their own history, albeit to some extent constrained by circumstances not of their own making. In the past, corporatist and social democratic polities and penalities were likewise created by people. Even today they can still be defended, or rebuilt, by people, and it is not unthinkable that the massive market failure which brought us the 'credit crunch' could create openings for just such developments. The pursuit of penal justice and social justice are interlinked. Neither is unattainable.

References

Beckett, K. (1997) *Making Crime Pay: Law and Order in Contemporary American Politics*, Oxford: Oxford University Press.

Beckett, K. and Western, B. (2001) 'Governing social marginality: welfare, incarceration, and the transformation of state policy', *Punishment and Society*, 3, 43–59.

Carter, P. (2007) *Securing the Future: Proposals for the Efficient and Sustainable Use of Custody in England and Wales*, London: Ministry of Justice, www.justice.gov.uk/publications/securing-the-future.htm.

Cavadino, M. (2005) 'Review of Tonry, "Thinking about crime"', *Crime, Media, Culture*, 1, 124–7.

Cavadino, M. and Dignan, J. (2006) *Penal Systems: A Comparative Approach*, London: Sage.

(2007) *The Penal System: An Introduction*, 4th edn, London: Sage.

Cavadino, M., Crow, I. and Dignan, J. (1999) *Criminal Justice 2000*, Winchester: Waterside Press.

Dijk, J. van, Kesteren, J. van and Smit, P. (2007) *Criminal Victimisation in International Perspective: Key Findings from the 2004–2005 ICVS and EU ICS*, Den Haag: WODC.

Downes, D. (2001) 'The *Macho* penal economy: mass incarceration in the United States: a European perspective', *Punishment and Society*, 3, 61–80.

Downes, D. and Hansen, K. (2006) 'Welfare and punishment in comparative context' in S. Armstrong and L. McAra (eds.), *Perspectives on Punishment: The Contours of Control*, Oxford: Oxford University Press, pp. 133–54.

Esping-Andersen, G. (1990) *The Three Worlds of Welfare Capitalism*, Cambridge: Polity Press.

Greenberg, D. (1999) 'Punishment, division of labor, and social solidarity' in W. S. Laufer and F. Adler (eds.), *The Criminology of Criminal Law, Advances in Criminological Theory*, vol. 8, New Brunswick: Transaction Books, pp. 283–361.

Hall, P. A. and Soskice, D. (2003) 'An introduction to the varieties of capitalism' in P. A. Hall and D. Soskice (eds.), *Varieties of Capitalism*, Oxford: Oxford University Press, pp. 1–68.

Hirsch, A. von, Bottoms, A. E., Burney, E. and Wikström, P.-O. (1999) *Criminal Deterrence and Sentence Severity: An Analysis of Recent Research*, Oxford: Hart Publishing.

Kilcommins, S., O'Donnell, I., O'Sullivan, E. and Vaughan, B. (2004) *Crime, Punishment and the Search for Order in Ireland*, Dublin: Institute of Public Administration.

Lacey, N. (2008) *The Prisoners' Dilemma: Political Economy and Punishment in Contemporary Democracies*, Cambridge: Cambridge University Press.

Marx, K. (1977) *Selected Writings*, ed. D. McLellan, Oxford: Oxford University Press.

Nicholas, S., Kershaw, C. and Walker, A. (2007) *Crime in England and Wales 2006/07*, 4th edn, Home Office Statistical Bulletin 11/07, London: Home Office, www.homeoffice.gov.uk/rds/pubsstatistical.html.

Ormerod, P. (1997) 'Stopping crime spreading', *New Economy*, 4, 83–8.

Pfeiffer, C., Windzio, M. and Kleimann, M. (2005) 'Media use and its impacts on crime perception, sentencing attitudes and crime policy', *European Journal of Criminology*, 2, 259–85.

Reiner, R. (2007) 'Political economy, crime, and criminal justice' in M. Maguire, R. Morgan and R. Reiner (eds.), *The Oxford Handbook of Criminology*, 4th edn, Oxford: Oxford University Press, pp. 341–80.

Savelsberg, J. J. (1999) 'Knowledge, domination and criminal punishment revisited: incorporating state socialism', *Punishment and Society*, 1, 45–70.

Tonry, M. (2004) *Thinking about Crime: Sense and Sensibility in American Penal Culture*, Oxford: Oxford University Press.

Walmsley, R. (2008) *World Prison Population List*, 8th edn, London: International Centre for Prison Studies, King's College London, www.kcl.ac.uk/depsta/law/research/icps/downloads/wppl-8th_41.pdf.

Wilkinson, R. (2005) *The Impact of Inequality: How to Make Sick Societies Healthier*, London: Routledge.

Wilson, J. Q. (1975) *Thinking About Crime*, New York: Basic Books.

Young, J. (2003) 'Winning the fight against crime? New Labour, populism and lost opportunities' in R. Matthews and J. Young (eds.), *The New Politics of Crime and Punishment* Cullompton: Willan, pp. 33–47.

Young, W. and Brown, M. (1993) 'Cross-national comparisons of imprisonment' in M. Tonry (ed.), *Crime and Justice: A Review of Research*, vol. 17, Chicago: University of Chicago Press, pp. 1–49.

9

Why globalisation doesn't spell convergence: models of institutional variation and the comparative political economy of punishment

NICOLA LACEY[*]

> [W]e are confronted with results in comparative political economy which undermine the assumptions of mainstream comparative law about 'convergence' and 'functional equivalence'. . . Against all expectations that globalization of the markets and computerization of the economy will lead to a convergence of legal regimes and to a functional equivalence of legal norms in responding to their identical problems, the opposite has turned out to be the case. Against all talk of 'regulatory competition' which is supposed to wipe out institutional differences, legal regimes under advanced capitalism have not converged.
>
> Teubner 2001: 433

In the last decade, there has been a welcome revival of criminal justice scholarship which engages with the macro-level political–economic forces which are shaping criminal justice policy in western democracies. Many of these accounts are rooted in the global economic changes which began in the 1970s – recession, the contraction or even collapse of manufacturing industries, the growth of unemployment and the creation of a large sector of people either long-term unemployed or employed in insecure forms of work. These changes, it is argued, have eroded the consensus which sustained post-war penal welfarism.

[*] The first part of this chapter draws on material from within Lacey (2008: Chapter 2), which has been adapted with permission. My thanks go to David Soskice for extensive discussion of the argument; to him and to Jan Perskalla for help in tracing regional data from the US; and to Alejandro Chehtman, Bob Hancké, John Pratt, other contributors to this volume and members of the LSE Criminal Law and Social Theory Group for helpful feedback. Unless otherwise indicated, imprisonment rate figures are taken from the *World Prison Brief* produced by the International Centre for Prison Studies, www.kcl.ac.uk/depsta/law/research/icps/worldbrief/.

As significantly rising recorded crime across Western countries gradually produced a situation in which the experience of criminal victimisation, and of managing the risk and fear of crime, became normal features of everyday life for the economically secure, crime became an increasingly politicised issue, generating a 'penal populism' which brought in its wake a combination of repressive and managerial criminal justice strategies.

In making this argument, scholars like David Garland (2001), Alessandro de Giorgi (2006) and Jock Young (1999) have refined the classical Marxist political–economic account deriving from Rusche and Kirchheimer (1969) with an analysis of broadly cultural factors, thus avoiding the pitfalls of economic reductionism. Yet in each case, the fundamental explanatory hypothesis rests at the level of political–economic changes characterised in terms of 'late modern society' or 'post-Fordism'. This emphasis on macro-level structural forces tends to direct attention away from differences attendant on variations in the institutional framework through which those forces are mediated in different countries. While each of these accounts, therefore, suggests hypotheses which are ripe for comparative investigation, a comparative focus on the significance of persisting differences among countries does not feature prominently in their analyses (however, see Garland 2007).

Ironically, the other main tendency in contemporary penology – the move to focus on very detailed elaborations of the internal dynamics of penal arrangements – is equally inhospitable to comparative approaches. We have learnt a tremendous amount from the micro-analysis of penal dynamics in important works such as Cohen's (1985) *Visions of Social Control* or Carlen's (1983) *Women's Imprisonment*. This has not been in any sense atheoretical work: much of it has contributed to, and has been inspired by, some of the most interesting developments in social theory, notably Michel Foucault's diagnosis and characterisation of the operations of disciplinary power in a number of social practices, the penal system not least among them. But its fruitful focus on the underlying dynamics and radiating implications of micro-practices has generally precluded systematic analysis of differences at national or regional levels.

In this chapter, I argue that there is strong reason to regret this non-comparative tendency in analyses of the political economy and local realities of punishment. For there are in fact striking differences in the extent to which even countries fitting most closely Garland's, de Giorgi's or Young's accounts have responded in terms of a severe penal populism; and the forces which produce these macro-differences do not exist in a separate social universe, but rather might be expected to have some

impact on the micro-dynamics of punishment which have been so
meticulously charted in other genres of penological research. Even
as between Britain and the USA, the differences in terms of the overall
scale and quality of punishment are striking. Countries like Denmark,
Germany or Sweden fulfil the prophecy of penal populism yet less
accurately. Not all 'late modern', 'post-Fordist' democracies have
plumped for a neoliberal politics. Many have managed to sustain relatively moderate, inclusionary criminal justice systems through the
period in which the British and American systems have, albeit at different speeds and to different degrees, been moving towards ever-greater
penal severity.

Comparative research is clearly central to any attempt to grasp the
significance of these differences. Cavadino and Dignan's (2006) recent
analysis of imprisonment rates, youth justice arrangements and privatisation policies in twelve countries sharpens our sense of the relevant
differences and helpfully moves the argument on by developing a fourfold typology of criminal justice systems, nested within different kinds of
political economy: the neoliberal, the conservative-corporatist, the
oriental-corporatist and the social democratic. They show that the social
democratic Nordic countries have succeeded in sustaining relatively
humane and moderate penal policies in the period during which some
of the neoliberal countries – notably the United States – have been
moving in the direction of mass incarceration, with the different
kinds of corporatist economy also showing striking differences from
the neoliberal cases.

But how, precisely, do political–economic and institutional variables
coalesce to produce family resemblances at the level of punishment?
Without some sense of why these family resemblances across types of
political economy persist over time, and of why they produce systematically different patterns of punishment, we are not in a good position to
address the crucial question of whether these differences are likely to
survive the increasing internationalisation of economic and social relations, nor to come to an assessment of how they are likely to affect the
micro-dynamics of penal practices.

In a recent book (Lacey 2008), I have argued that we can make some
progress towards a genuinely explanatory model by drawing on recent
political–economic analysis of comparative institutional advantage, and
of the capacities for strategic co-ordination inherent in differently
ordered systems. My analysis builds on structural theories inspired
by Marxism, but moves beyond the 'structurist' approach criticised

by McAra (this volume)[1] in arguing that political–economic forces at the
macro level are mediated not only by cultural filters, but also by economic, political and social institutions. I argue, moreover, that it is this
institutional stabilisation and mediation of cultural and structural
forces, and its impact on the interests, incentives and indeed identities
of relevant groups of social actors, which produce the significant and
persistent variety which, notwithstanding globalisation, we see across
systems at similar stages of capitalist development.

   In the first section of this chapter, I sketch the model which
I elaborated in that book, in an effort to put further explanatory flesh
on the structure of Cavadino and Dignan's typology. In the second
section, I develop the argument by addressing an obvious objection to
this sort of comparative method – and one which I take it will resonate
particularly with contributors to what we might think of as the broadly
culturalist strain in contemporary sociological penology. In the reaction,
across many disciplines, against the determinist character of Marxism
and variants of post-Marxist structuralism, there has developed a
marked distrust of the deployment of standardised typologies or
explanatory models in our attempts to understand social phenomena
such as punishment. In a world rich in the insights of detailed ethnographic and other forms of empirical research – research which now
travels freely across the globe thanks to rapidly developing media of
communication – we are strongly in the grip of a sense of the extraordinary variety among local practices such as punishment. Moreover, our
recognition of the power of actors well beyond the state in shaping these
practices – indeed our recognition of the ways in which certain practices
sometimes seem to take on a life of their own, transcending the interests
or instrumental directive capacities of those who might be seen in a
different ontology as their controlling agents – has lent to a strong sense
of not merely the variety but also the contingency of penal developments. So while Marxian accounts have remained influential in the field
of penal theory, a more salient focus in recent years has been this vision

---

[1] It follows that I do not accept McAra's categorisation of my position as 'structurist'.
Rather, I see it as fundamentally similar to her own systems theoretic view that
'the characteristics and evolution of a particular system lies in the relationships that exist
between the elements which constitute its physical and conceptual architecture and
between the system as a whole and the environment within which it is located' (this
volume, p. 291). Indeed my deployment in this chapter of the US and New Zealand cases
engages in just the kind of revision invited by her argument about the Scottish and
Spanish cases; the identification of cases which do not fit the preliminary model is a
provocation to further analysis.

of variety and contingency – epitomised, perhaps, by Foucault's famous maxim that power calls forth resistance; and by Roberto Unger's notion of the 'plasticity of power', articulated within his Marxisant, yet stead-fastly anti-determinist, *Social Theory* (1987).

In this context, a long-running but regrettable tendency within comparative penological research has been exacerbated. This is the tendency to become mesmerised by the fascinating details of local particularity. Comparative research has understandably, and properly, concerned itself with 'local knowledge' (Geertz 1983) and the 'pursuit of the vernacular' (Zedner 1995; see also Nelken 1995; 1997) – an attempt to render particular practices, à la anthropology, in the terms in which local participants themselves understand them. From this point of view, typologies such as that of Cavadino and Dignan, and explanatory models like the one sketched in the next section of this chapter, seem inadequate; their generalisations flatten out significant differences between national or regional systems displaying superficial similarities. But if the meticulous charting and characterisation of systems is where comparative research not only starts, but ends, the enterprise is arguably not truly comparative. Rather, it reduces to a study of the particular and, in its less sophisticated forms, the 'exotic', with comparativists either marvelling at the diversity of practices or – more usually in the context of criminal justice – rushing to unwarranted assumptions about possible transnational learning and policy transfer.

The problem of transporting policies and arrangements which inter-act decisively with a wide array of local institutions is just part of a larger problem here. Policy inspiration may, certainly, be one of the most obvious pay-offs from comparative research, as well as one of the most salient preoccupations in a world in which diffusion of policy ideas is facilitated by new technologies and transnational networks. But policy design must itself be premised on a deep understanding of the interact-ing institutional dynamics of particular systems, whether regional or national, whose power Sprott's analysis of the Canadian case (this volume) demonstrates. If our purchase on this broader context has to be exclusively through detailed ethnographic research, the task comes to seem utterly daunting; and even if we can undertake it, how we are to address the further task of making sense of its findings remains obscure. This, I shall argue, is where models can come into their own.

The distrust of models, in short, proceeds from some legitimate concerns, but it is nonetheless obstructive to the capacity of comparative research to achieve its full explanatory potential. In the second part of the chapter, accordingly, I explore the objections to typology or model-building in penal theory. I do so by drawing on the case studies of New Zealand and the USA – countries which present difficulties for the model I sketch. I argue that the objections to model-building may be more readily overcome than is usually recognised and that the apparently different enterprises of model-building or theoretical generalisation on the one hand and detailed empirical research on the other are linked in a number of ways. Indeed, I shall argue that they are interdependent.

Comparative political economy and criminal justice: an explanatory model

The comparative institutional analysis which I elaborated in *The Prisoners' Dilemma*,[2] and which I sketch in this section, takes off from the distinction between 'liberal' and 'co-ordinated' market economies developed by political scientists Peter Hall and David Soskice (2001).[3] A 'co-ordinated market economy' (CME) functions in terms of long-term relationships and stable structures of investment, not least in education and training oriented to company- or sector-specific skills, and incorporates a wide range of social groups and institutions into a highly co-ordinated governmental structure. Such a system, I argue, is more likely to generate incentives for the relevant decision-makers to opt for a relatively inclusionary criminal justice system. For it is a system which is premised on incorporation, and hence on the need to reintegrate offenders into society and economy. Such a system is, I hypothesise, structurally less likely to opt for exclusionary stigmatisation in punishment. Typically, moreover, the interlocking and diffused institutions of co-ordination of the CME's conduce to an environment of relatively extensive informal social controls, and this in turn supports the cultural mentalities which underpin and help to stabilise a moderated approach to formal punishment.

---

[2] See also Sutton (2004), finding that criteria such as degree of union strength, low levels of partisanship, employment growth and corporatist labour market institutions were strong predictors of moderation in punishment across a large number of democracies; see also Tonry (2007).

[3] The varieties of capitalism framework was developed specifically in relation to the 'advanced economies' which made up the original group of OECD countries. Its hypotheses would require adaptation in relation to the countries of Southern Europe – Spain, Portugal, Greece and Turkey – and *a fortiori* in relation to other regions such as Latin America. My analysis is accordingly restricted to the 'advanced economies'.

220   NICOLA LACEY

Imprisonment Rate
(per 100,000)

	2002–3	2008–9
Neo-liberal countries (Liberal Market Economies)		
USA	701	760
New Zealand	155	196
England and Wales	141	153
Australia	115	129
Conservative corporatist countries (Co-ordinated or hybrid market economies)		
Netherlands	100	100
Italy	100	97
Germany	98	90
France	93	96
Social democracies (Co-ordinated market economies)		
Sweden	73	74
Denmark	58	63
Finland	70	67
Norway	58	70
Oriental corporatist (Co-ordinated market economy)		
Japan	53	63

Sources: Adapted from Hall and Soskice (2001);
Cavadino and Dignan (2006); International Centre for Prison Studies
(August 2009).

Figure 9.1   Political economy, imprisonment and homicide.

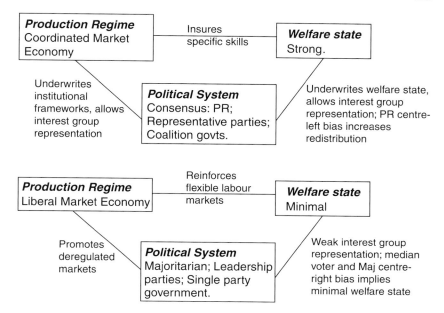

Figure 9.2   Table summarising main institutional linkages in different varieties of political system.

A 'liberal market economy' (LME) – of which the extreme case, significantly for any argument about criminal justice, is the USA – is typically more individualistic in structure, is less interventionist in regulatory stance, and depends far less strongly on the sorts of co-ordinating institutions which are needed to sustain long-term economic and social relations (see Figure 9.2). In these economies, flexibility and innovation, rather than stability and investment, form the backbone of comparative institutional advantage. It follows that, particularly under conditions of surplus unskilled labour – conditions which liberal market economies are also more likely to produce – the costs of a harsh, exclusionary criminal justice system are less than they would be in a co-ordinated market economy.[4]

The distinction between different varieties of advanced capitalist political economy is, I shall argue, a powerful tool in building an understanding of

[4] As Figure 9.1 illustrates, the liberal/co-ordinated market economy distinction maps neatly onto Cavadino and Dignan's (2006) fourfold typology: their social democratic and (most of their) corporatist systems are, in these terms, co-ordinated market economies, while their neoliberal countries are liberal market economies.

the inclusionary and exclusionary dynamics of different criminal justice systems. For, particularly as developed in the most recent political economy literature, which explores the relationship between the regime of economic production and labour-market-based institutions and a cluster of social and political institutions, the distinction has an analytic reach into a wide range of interrelated political and economic variables. In the remainder of this section, I sketch the features of the distinction between liberal and co-ordinated market economies which appear to be of greatest relevance to criminal justice. The various factors which characterise co-ordinated and liberal systems are closely intertwined, and the number of variables further implies that there may be paradigm and less central cases of each type of system. The following schematic account, summarised in Figure 9.2, should however give an idea of the sorts of issues which an analysis of comparative political economy would put on the agenda of scholars interested in the relationship between criminal justice and different varieties of political economy and democratic system.

1   The structure of the economy: production regimes, labour markets, education and training, disparities of wealth

The departure point for an analysis of two main varieties of capitalism lies in the changing nature of economic relations. But whereas in Marxism the focus is on the ownership of the means of production and distinctive modes of production in particular historical epochs, contemporary political economy draws on an analysis of a wider range of institutions to sketch two main forms of contemporary capitalist economy: an individualistic liberal model whose comparative advantage lies in flexibility, and a co-ordinated model in which comparative advantage depends on long term investment in workers and their skills. In Britain, the dynamics of a liberal market economy have accelerated markedly over the last thirty years, as many of the attitudes and values which sustained the post-war welfare state settlement have come to be eroded by a more aggressively market-oriented culture (Reiner 2006). This culture is itself premised in part on the imperative of high performance amid increasing global economic competition, with the collapse of Fordist production regimes and the availability of cheap manufactured goods from countries like South Korea, China and India. The inevitable upshot is structural economic insecurity for low-skilled workers. In a short-term economic culture, the bottom third of the workforce risks becoming a socially as well as economically excluded group (Hale 2005).

In the co-ordinated market economies, by contrast, a longer-term economic culture appears to have survived increased international competition and the collapse of Fordism. Within the political economy of comparative advantage, this is seen as a function of several interlocking factors: the nature of the economic activities in which these countries have concentrated their efforts; the close incorporation of employers as well as unions in the management of the economy; and the implications of each of these factors for the structure of education and training. Unlike the increasingly flexibilised economies of the liberal market countries, many co-ordinated market economies excel in producing high-quality goods which depend on industry-specific, non-transferable skills. In this context, employers have strong reason to invest in education, training and apprenticeship systems. They also have strong reason to use their considerable bargaining power with government to press for generous welfare provision for workers who are temporarily unemployed but whose skills remain necessary to the economy. With the higher levels of investment in education and training typical of these economies, which also demonstrate lower disparities of wealth and higher literacy rates,[5] the costs of pursuing socially exclusionary policies in areas such as criminal justice are relatively high. This implies that many of the general theories of increasing penal severity are based on an account primarily applicable to liberal as opposed to co-ordinated market economies, whose high-skill production regimes were less strongly affected by the collapse of Fordism.

In the liberal market economies, increasing relative deprivation consequent on flexibilisation of labour markets and growing disparities of both income and skills pose a huge challenge for inclusionary criminal justice policies (Young 1999; Reiner, 2006, 2007: Chapter 3; Cavadino and Dignan, and Pratt, this volume), particularly in a world in which mass communications and increased levels of education imply the cultural inclusion of the relatively deprived within the individualistic values of a consumer society from which they are economically excluded. What is more, this relative deprivation has increased along a number of dimensions, accentuating both differences between the richest and the poorest, and the difficulty of moving from a position in the bottom one-third or so into the relatively advantaged majority. In this context,

[5] Iversen and Soskice (2009) have recently traced the roots of varieties of capitalism back to the distinctive structures of political and economic organization in the nineteenth century.

prisons have, unfortunately, become a mechanism for 'warehousing' those excluded from the legitimate economy. It is therefore no surprise that during this period we have seen a large increase in the absolute and relative size of the harsher end of the American and, to a lesser extent, British criminal justice systems. In Britain, the imprisonment rate virtually doubled – from 79 to 151 per 100,000 – between 1970 and 2007; while in the USA, it quintupled – from 153 to 756 per 100,000 – between 1974 and 2007. This is reflected not only in the scale of imprisonment and policies such as mandatory minimum sentences, but also in a weakening of political sensibilities in favour of human rights and decent conditions for prisoners. There comes a point, we might suggest, at which both the absolute situation of the disadvantaged and disparities of wealth between rich and poor – disparities which are markedly greater in liberal than in co-ordinated market economies – become so acute as to amount in themselves to a form of status distinction.

To sum up, in the face of political–economic imperatives leading to ever-increasing disparities of wealth and de facto status distinctions in the liberal, Anglo-Saxon economies, underlying economic dynamics feed into the political and social forces favouring harsh and extensive punishment. But in countries whose economic and political arrangements have sustained a consensus-oriented system, and where social inequality has remained much less acute, penal dynamics are different. Features of political–economic organisation which conduce to lower disparities of wealth and investment in long term skills make it easier for governments to pursue inclusionary criminal justice policies.

2 Political systems: electoral arrangements and the bureaucracy

Thus far, my account is vulnerable to much the same charge of economic reductionism levelled at Marxian criminological theory. But the analysis of two systematically different variants of contemporary capitalist economy deploys not only economic variables but also a variety of other institutional variables. Among the most important of these to our understanding of criminal justice is electoral politics. Given the increasing salience in many countries of criminal justice to politics, and the force of electoral discipline on democratic governments, it seems obvious that contrasts in popular attitudes to punishment constitute an important variable in any attempt to understand the differences between contemporary penal systems in relatively similar societies. This is the case even if popular attitudes conducing to fear of crime and to penal severity are on occasion accidentally or deliberately stimulated by government rhetoric and policy (Beckett 1997; Beckett and Sasson 2004; Roberts and Hough 2002; Cavadino and Dignan, this volume). Whatever the causation here – and it seems likely that it moves in both directions – once certain popular attitudes and expectations are created, they in turn create significant electoral constraints. How directly these are reflected in the electoral system, and hence exert discipline on governing parties, is therefore likely to be an important factor in explaining the institutional capacity of different systems to sustain moderate criminal justice policies.

In this context, it is significant that there is, empirically, an association between co-ordinated market economies and proportionally representative (PR) electoral systems, whereas liberal market economies tend to have first-past-the-post, winner-takes-all systems.[6] The policy-making autonomy of co-ordinated market economies is constrained by the need to negotiate with groups incorporated in the governmental process. In this sense, we might say that co-ordinated market economies with PR systems are more oriented to effective participation in and contribution to policy-making – at least for groups integrated within subsisting socio-political structures – than are liberal market economies whose electorate gets a one-shot say in policy-making at election time. But this consensus-building dynamic may make the co-ordinated market economies less heteronymous in the light of swings of popular opinion. While decisive winners of first-past-the-post elections in liberal market economies may feel relatively unconstrained by popular opinion early on in their terms, their unmediated accountability at the ballot box makes them highly sensitive to public opinion as elections loom.

What is more, as party affiliations among the electorate weaken, governments' increasing dependence on the approval of a large number of 'floating' median voters, who regard crime as a threat to their well-being, may feed into the political salience of criminal justice (cf. Chevigny 2003; Useem et al. 2003; Ryan 2003; Pratt et al. 2005). Under the conditions attendant on the collapse of Fordism since the 1970s, and in the light of the salience of increasing relative deprivation to the scale and the perceived seriousness of crime problems, there may thus be a stronger association between the politicisation of criminal justice and the impact

---

[6] A key exception here is New Zealand, a liberal market economy which moved from a first-past-the-post system to PR in 1996. The New Zealand case is discussed in greater detail in the next section.

of penal populism in majoritarian, two-party liberal market economies such as the USA, with decisive implications for the harshness of punishment. In this context, the further empirical fact that PR-based co-ordinated market democracies are more likely to elect left-of-centre governments and to display lower disparities between the best and worst off, is highly significant (see Iversen and Soskice 2006). Electoral structure, in other words, has implications for both partisanship and the substance of political, social and economic outcomes.

There is further reason to think that this difference in the electoral structure of liberal and co-ordinated market economies may have some important implications for upward pressure on punishment. As many commentators have observed, one of the developments which has fed the trend towards penal populism in several neoliberal countries is the emergence of well-organised single-issue pressure groups, notably those representing the interests of victims of crime.[7] The genesis, for example, of 'Megan's law', instituting harsher treatment for those convicted of paedophile offences, stemmed from just such a single-issue campaign.

On the face of it, one would expect single-issue political groups to find it harder to get their voices heard in a majoritarian, two-party system than in a PR system which incorporates a number of smaller parties. The exception to this expectation that single-issue groups would do better in PR than in majoritarian systems, however, is the situation where a particular single issue appeals widely to floating, median voters. Such has been the situation of crime in the USA over the last thirty years.[8] As Simon (2007: 26 ff; 159 ff) has shown, both the popularity of harsh criminal policy among median voters and the relative simplicity of enacting such policy – the lack of need, for example, to develop complex new bureaucracies to administer or implement increased criminalisation – has proved a potent temptation to US politicians and other elected officials.

Furthermore, while concerns about crime reflected in victims' movements may well find a footing in the PR environment, particularly among smaller parties who may hold the balance of power, their adoption and implementation will ultimately have to be negotiated out in the complex bargaining process typical of PR systems, and will hence tend to

---

[7] To the 'single issue politics' variable, Chevigny (2003) persuasively adds an observation of the relevance of high inequality and strong competition for offices. See also Pratt and Clark (2005) and Pratt (2007: Chapter 3).

[8] On the resulting role of both 'conservative' and 'progressive' social movements in the acceleration of American imprisonment, see Gottschalk (2007: Chapters 5–7).

be more insulated in their realisation from the dynamics of emotive campaigns than is typical in the majoritarian systems. What we see in the latter is a vicious cycle of mutual reinforcement, grounded in a set of incentives conducing to politicians' focus on single issues such as criminal justice which are, superficially, easy to demonstrate that they have acted upon, such action in turn leading to heightened public identification of the salience of crime problems and to heightened expectations of governmental capacity to resolve them through tough criminal policy. The scale and impact of this sort of cycle is vividly illustrated by the fact that, in addition to its unplanned expansion of the prison system, the British Labour government has been estimated to have enacted no fewer than 3,000 additional criminal offences in the mere eight years between its election and the end of 2005 (Morris 2006; Ashworth 2009).

It is also worth noting a further difference between the political systems to be found in liberal and co-ordinated market economies, itself correlated with the PR/majoritarian distinction. In most co-ordinated market economies, deference to the expertise of the professional bureaucracy – namely the civil service, often including not only policy advisers, penal system officials and prosecutors but also judges – tends to be high. This is in part because the coalition politics typical of PR systems implies a less polarized political environment in which governments feel less need to retain total control of policy-making. By contrast, particularly in recent years, the tendency in majoritarian systems has been for governments to prefer to work with their own, politically appointed advisers, and to ignore the advice of technically neutral civil servants wherever it interferes with political expediency.[9] Particularly in the UK, the increasing domination of parties by their leaders has fed this dynamic. This not infrequently leads to a situation in which pressure groups such as those representing victims of crime are constructed as the relevant 'experts' for the purposes of consultation in the development of policy, weakening both an important constraint on

[9] Joachim Savelsberg (1994) was among the first to note the importance of the power of professional bureaucracies; see also Michael Tonry (2004a: 63–4; 2007: 31–2) and Ian Loader (2006). Loader argues that a culture of strong reliance on expertise is itself 'anti-democratic' – a claim which is questioned by Tonry. A more perplexing question is whether such a culture is a genuinely independent variable, or rather itself a product of the broader factors conducing to consensus politics and penal moderation. Recently, Barker (2009) has questioned the status of reliance on bureaucratic expertise as a factor protecting against penal populism, at least in the US, where she argues that such reliance has been associated with a decline in civic participation and engagement which has contributed to a more volatile politics of law and order.

ad hoc policy making and co-ordination with criminal justice professionals (Pratt 2007: Chapter 3; Simon 2007: Chapter 3). In LMEs, this feeds
into a dynamic in which politicians' decisions become ever-less insulated
from the flow of perceived public opinion – a factor which has been a
crucial driver of penal harshness in several countries (Tonry 2004b; 2007).
In CMEs, by contrast, the strength of a professional bureaucracy, along
with deference to expertise, have been identified by a number of scholars
as conditions key to the maintenance of moderate criminal justice policies
(Cavadino and Dignan 2006: 35–6; Savelsberg 1999).

  To sum up, in liberal market economies with majoritarian electoral
systems, particularly under conditions of relatively low trust in politicians, relatively low deference to the expertise of criminal justice professionals and a weakening of the ideological divide between political
parties as they become increasingly focused on the median voter, the
unmediated responsiveness of politics to popular opinion in the adversarial context of the two-party system makes it harder for governments
to resist a ratcheting up of penal severity. These dynamics become
particularly strong where both parties take up a law-and-order agenda
(Newburn 2007: 450 ff). In PR systems, where negotiation and consensus are central, and where incorporated groups can have greater confidence that their interests will be effectively represented in the bargaining
process which characterises coalition politics, the dynamics of penal
populism may be easier to resist. And due to the discipline of coalition
politics typical of PR systems, in which bargains have to be struck before
elections, voters can be more confident about what policy slate they are
voting for – a striking difference from majoritarian systems, where a
party with a comfortable majority is more or less unconstrained by its
own manifesto once elected.

3   The welfare state

Another key difference between contemporary capitalist democracies lies
in their welfare regimes (Esping-Andersen 1990; 1996).[10] Here again, to
paint with very broad brush strokes, political economies at relatively
similar levels of development, characterised by broadly liberal democratic

---

[10] The 'liberal', 'social democratic' and 'continental' typology is drawn from Esping-
Andersen. The main differences between social-democratic and continental systems are
the tendency of the former to fund welfare provision from general taxation rather than
payroll taxes; the size of the public sector; and the low involvement of private bodies in
providing public services.

political structures, have taken markedly different paths. In terms of Esping-Andersen's famous typology, while countries with liberal welfare regimes like the USA and Britain have adopted neoliberal policies committed to 'rolling back the state' and curtailing public expenditure (Hillyard and Tombs 2005), the Scandinavian, 'social democratic' countries have maintained their welfare states more or less intact (Pratt 2008a; 2008b; this volume), with European 'Continental' countries such as Germany adopting a pattern closer, in terms of generosity of provision and scope of coverage, to their Scandinavian than to their British neighbours.

Among variables in political–economic structure, the welfare state is the institutional feature which has received most sustained attention from comparative penologists (see e.g. Cavadino and Dignan, this volume). It is, of course, highly plausible that the impact of generous welfare provision on the reduction of both absolute and relative poverty would have a knock-on effect on crime. Less obviously, there is evidence that it is also associated with levels of punishment. Downes and Hansen (2006) have shown, in a study covering eighteen countries, that those spending a higher proportion of their GDP on welfare have lower imprisonment rates – a relationship which has grown stronger over the last fifteen years. Similarly, Beckett and Western (2001: 44, 48, 55; Western 2006) have demonstrated systematic differences among states within the USA, in which those with relatively low social welfare spending are also those with relatively high prison populations.

But the precise causal mechanisms are not very clear. Sometimes the argument takes a cultural form: the generous and inclusionary instincts represented in welfare state policies are likely to be reflected in criminal justice policy. Beckett and Western, for example, argue that welfare regimes vary according to their commitment to including or excluding marginal groups: the more inclusive systems exhibit both higher welfare spending and lower imprisonment rates. Albeit making some observations about the relationship between the welfare state settlement and the structure of the economy and consensus-oriented political system, Pratt (2008a), in his recent analysis of 'Scandinavian exceptionalism', attributes the generosity of the Scandinavian welfare systems primarily to a 'culture of equality' with long historical roots. But what explains this varying commitment to egalitarianism and inclusion? What are the factors which predispose countries or regions towards inclusivity or exclusivity in both penal and welfare arrangements, and which underpin the necessary political support? (cf. Greenberg 2001).

It would be nice to be able to attribute the persistence of decent welfare provision and penal moderation exclusively to humane sensibilities. Clearly, long-standing institutional arrangements are typically articulated with, and stabilised by, distinctive cultural attitudes such as the strong Scandinavian commitment to social solidarity and equality (Cavadino and Dignan 2006: Chapter 10; Bondeson 2005: 189). But there is also evidence that the distinctive structures of welfare states are articulated with the political and economic dynamics already discussed. In other words, there are political–economic explanations of why it is possible – indeed sensible – for some countries to maintain generous welfare provision even in the face of increasing competition from countries who are not investing public resources in this way. Certain economic and other structural arrangements, in short, themselves foster a culture of solidarity or support for the welfare state – a culture which is in its turn important in sustaining the political support needed to sustain generous welfare institutions.

A range of explanations has focused on precisely such an articulation of the welfare state to the structure of the economy, and I canvassed some of them in my discussion of production regimes. Within a liberal market system in a flexible economy, governments have chosen to maximise incentives to rejoin the labour market – a strategy that has had sufficient plausibility with a critical mass of the electorate because of the high degree of transferable skills within the workforce. Within the labour markets of countries with less flexibility, where long-term investment in less transferable skills (as in the social democratic and corporatist systems), or an extensive public sector providing employment for women and services for dual-career families (as in the social democratic systems of Scandinavia), are still key to comparative advantage, it makes sense to give relatively generous support to workers who experience periods of unemployment, rather than encouraging them to retrain or to find work in new sectors of the economy. Contrary to the neoliberal view, generosity of welfare provision and relatively secure employment relations are, under certain conditions, just as good a basis for economic success and stability as flexibilisation and welfare cuts. For, though there has been some recent reduction of welfare benefits in several of the European and, to a lesser extent, Nordic countries (Gilbert 2002), with generosity of provision in the corporatist countries depending heavily on status as an insider to the high-skills economy, the remaining differences

between even corporatist and neoliberal welfare regimes remain significant and seem unlikely to be eroded in the near future.[11]

4   Constitutional structure: decision-makers, veto points, and constraints on criminalisation

So far, our discussion has encompassed a range of political and economic institutions, but has had little to say about specifically legal or
constitutional structure. Yet the constitutional structure of a country
provides parameters for the institutional environment already considered, and for the legal system through which much criminal policy
is implemented. Here I touch on just three constitutional and legal
variables which might be thought to entail systematic differences in
countries' capacities to develop and sustain moderate penal practices.
These are the distribution of decision-making power among different
actors; the structure of legal institutions, and in particular of the tenure
and selection of the judiciary and prosecutors; and the impact of constitutional framework on the definition of what conduct may be
criminalised.

   In our discussion of political systems, we saw that one important
variable in shaping the reception of popular concern about crime into
criminal justice policy was the degree to which political decision-making
was insulated from the flow of electoral opinion. But beyond the electoral arrangements canvassed in that section, another variable seems
likely to be important here. This is the distribution of veto points across
the system, with consequent potential for checks and balances to be
invoked, and for reactive policies to be blocked or delayed, thus leading
to a more reflective and, possibly, negotiated style of policy-making.

   On the face of it, such veto points might be taken to be correlated with
federal as opposed to unitary systems, and with unicameral as opposed
to bi- or multi-cameral legislatures. But this is not inevitably the case.
For example, in the USA, most criminal justice policy is developed at
state level or even at city or county level, so that the federal structure
cannot exert the sort of inhibiting power which has been noted to be the

---

[11] Downes' and Hansen's figures for 1998 reveal the scale of the difference, with the
proportion of GDP spent on welfare ranging from 31% in Sweden to less than half that
level – 14.6% – in the US. Again, the figures arrange themselves on co-ordinated/liberal
market economy lines, with the exception of Japan, which has a level of welfare spending
similar to that of the US. On the general tendency for distinctive systems to evolve and
adapt without necessarily converging, see Hall (2007: 39) and Iversen (2007: 278).

case, for example, in Germany or Canada.[12] And in the bicameral legislature of the UK, the constitutionally privileged place of the House of Commons restricts the degree to which the upper house can act as a serious block on policy formation. This is not to say that, for example, US federalism has been unimportant to the way in which criminal policy has developed (Miller 2008; Stuntz 2001). The need to address multiple constituencies can, as in the case of campaigns to abolish capital punishment, place barriers in the path of criminal justice reform, while the highly decentralised form of US government allows local politicians to emphasise popular issues, the costs of which their own constituents will not have to bear (Soskice 2009). And the creation of federal structures can itself feed upward trends in punishment: this appears to have been the case in the USA through both direct and indirect (via state imitation) effects of the federal Uniform Determinate Sentencing Act and, in Europe, in recent EU initiatives arguing for cross-Union statutory minima for certain serious crimes (Pratt 2007: 169).[13]

There is scope here for a careful empirical analysis of the ways in which systems with more and less diffused structures for criminal justice decision-making have responded to external pressures towards penal severity. *A priori*, the distribution of veto points and the need to co-ordinate decision-making points in federal systems where key aspects of criminal justice policy have to be centrally or constitutionally determined would appear to be important variables. It would also be worth adding in to this set of variables that of the size or scale of the system. In relatively small jurisdictions like the Netherlands (Cavadino and Dignan 2006: 123) or Scotland (McAra 2005: 293, 296), both the capacities for central negotiation and the intensity and influence of elite policy networks may also constitute important structural differences between systems. They are differences which may favour either the stabilisation of moderate policies via co-ordination between elite networks, as in the 1970s in the Netherlands, or rapid shifts of policy through precisely the same mechanism, as in that country in the late 1980s. Leaving the question of scale aside, however, the orientation to negotiation across

---

[12] On federalism and checks and balances, see Cavadino and Dignan (2006: 108) on Germany; Tonry (2004b) on Germany and Canada; and Pratt (2007: 157) on Canada; see also Savelsberg (1999) on centralisation.

[13] This is not to say that sentencing guidelines lead inevitably to upward pressure on punishment: under certain conditions, they in fact appear to have the opposite effect, not least through their capacity to act as a buffer between political pressure and criminal justice decision-making: see Marvell (1995) and Reitz (2005). I am grateful to Maximo Langer for alerting me to this research.

groups, typical of PR systems, is likely to conduce to a wider distribution of veto or delaying points, and hence underpins an association between CMEs and checks on the politicisation of criminal justice.

Secondly, it seems plausible to hypothesise that the selection, training and tenure of judges and other key criminal justice officials will be likely to have implications for the environment in which penal policy is developed and implemented. To take only the most obvious example, a system like that of the USA, in which many judges are elected, is one in which a key barrier between popular demands for punishment and sentencing is, if not removed, seriously weakened. This becomes important under conditions in which criminal justice is highly politicised. We might draw an analogy here between the election of many US judges and the fact that the vast bulk of criminal cases in Britain is heard by lay magistrates. This arrangement would be unthinkable in the highly professionalised systems of Continental Europe. While magistrates are not answerable to popular opinion in the style of elected officials, they are less buffered by a professional expertise and culture. Their place in the administration of criminal justice suggests that the relatively low importance attached to expertise already noted may find its roots deep in the history of British socio-political arrangements rather than merely being a product of the recent dynamics of criminal policy.

In many Northern European and Nordic co-ordinated market countries, the judiciary continues to be regarded as a key partner in the development as well as the implementation of criminal justice policy. In liberal market countries like the USA and the UK, by contrast, the rise of penal populism has seen an increasingly unstable relationship between government and judiciary. The judiciary conceives their independence as inconsistent with any overt incorporation in governmental negotiations, and the government is accordingly inclined to regard the judiciary as an irksome and even irresponsible thorn in the flesh of its criminal justice policy. Though constitutional or human rights structures such as the European Convention or the US Constitution may provide judges with some tools to resist certain government excesses of punishment or criminalisation, these have tended to be relatively weak in the face of a determined executive with a clear legislative majority (Lacey 2009). While British judges still have considerable influence behind the scenes, their public criticism tends to be met with denigration of judges as 'out of touch with reality' – a move which politicians see as likely to command considerable public sympathy. In this context it is interesting that judiciaries in the Anglo-Saxon, common law, liberal market countries

with strong traditions of judicial independence appear to have suffered a
decline in public status and authority in recent years (see Simon (2007:
Chapter 4) on the USA and Pratt and Clark (2005: 307) on New
Zealand); while their European, civilian cousins, traditionally of lower
status and more intimately linked to the state bureaucracy, appear so far
to have escaped a similar fate.

Thirdly, systems exhibit markedly variable constitutional constraints
on both the content of criminal law and the conduct of criminalisation
and punishment. And these constraints have deep historical roots.
Whereas in most European countries, the process of constitutional
modernisation entailed a clear differentiation between criminal justice
and administrative 'police power', in common law systems such as
Britain and the USA no such differentiation has ever been fully institutionalised in the constitutional system (Dubber 2005; Whitman 2003;
Stuntz 2006). Legal and constitutional constraints on both criminalisation and punishment are, accordingly, on average weaker in these
systems. Again, there is an association between this variable and the
liberal/co-ordinated market economy distinction.

5   Institutional capacity to integrate 'outsiders'

Another key feature of contemporary societies is the increasing mobility
of the social world from the late 1960s on. In a wealth-valuing culture
and flexible economy, with relatively high levels of education, there may
be more mobility between social classes;[14] in a globalising economy
characterised by transnational political structures like the EU, relatively
cheap international travel and mass communications, there is more
geographical mobility. These developments have added new layers of
complexity to one of the central challenges for any democratic system of
criminal justice: that of 'reintegrating' offenders into society and economy (Crawford 1998; Young 2002).

This is far too complex an issue to be susceptible of even a preliminary
analysis here. But it is an important corrective to what might be seen as
the temptation to think that the highly co-ordinated systems of Europe
and Scandinavia are necessarily better placed to sustain democratically
acceptable levels of penal moderation than their liberal market Anglo-
Saxon counterparts. For the structure of this problem is significantly

---

[14] Though the recent evidence on social mobility in Britain suggests that this change has
been exaggerated (see Blanden *et al.* 2005).

different in the two sorts of system. While the laissez-faire and individualistic culture typical of liberal market economies may well make it
relatively easy to integrate geographical or 'cultural outsiders' like recent
immigrants wherever they find access to the labour market, the more
intensively group- and skills-based system of the co-ordinated market
economies may well pose significant challenges in terms of integrating
newcomers into the representative and decision-making structures
which have helped to sustain a relatively moderate criminal justice policy
with relatively high institutional capacity for reintegration. Co-ordinated
market economies are, in short, good places to be incorporated insiders,
but hard systems to enter from the outside.[15]

The utility of models

I have now sketched a model of two families of political economy,
themselves articulated with distinctive penal dynamics. In each case,
the model includes a number of different institutional and cultural
variables, and hypothesises significant interaction effects, many of them
reinforcing the dynamics set up by the other variables. But how useful is
such a generalised account? Are there really only two families of criminal
justice political economy? And how do these models account for variations among systems within their respective family types? Furthermore,
how does this sort of model-building relate to the empirical research on
particular systems which has formed the core of criminological and
penological scholarship – including comparative research? As we saw
in the introduction, criminal justice scholars in recent decades have
shown a marked distrust of such models, raising a number of objections
to their utility; and the chapters by McAra and by Cavadino and Dignan
in this volume raise questions about the specific model which I have
defended. How, if at all, can these objections be met? In what follows,
I demonstrate that a model underpinned by a theoretical framework
explaining the dynamic linkages between its various criteria – even when

---

[15] This issue, and in particular the impact of migration, is taken up in greater detail in
Chapter 3 of my *The Prisoners' Dilemma*, where I discuss in particular the over-
representation of foreign nationals in the prison systems of many European countries.
This issue of course has a particular relevance for the politics of race and ethnicity. To take
just one example, it has recently been noted that between 60% and 70% of the French
prison population is Muslim, as compared with 12% of the French population as a whole:
in Britain, 11% of prisoners have been estimated to be Muslim, as compared with about
3% of the general population: see *Washington Post*, 29 April 2008. I am grateful to Daniel
Richman for alerting me to this article.

based on an initially very simple, twofold classification – can be appropriately sensitive to local environment, and hence to intra-model differences, while preserving its explanatory power.

To get a purchase on how the obvious pitfalls of model-building can
be minimised, and their undoubted strengths in comparative research
maximised, let us take an obvious objection to the framework sketched
in the previous section. Let us accept, for the sake of argument, that the
characterisation of co-ordinated and liberal market systems has some
plausibility at a high level of generality; and that I am right in thinking
that these political–economic types also map onto systematic differences
in criminal justice. Even granting this, it is evident that large differences
exist among criminal justice systems nested within, respectively, the two
models. Recent increases in Dutch levels of punishment (Downes 2010)
contrast, for example, with the relative stability of the German prison
system; while the dualisation of the labour market which has characterised both the Netherlands and Germany in recent years, and which on
my argument would be expected to lead to significant differences in
penality, has not so far characterised the Nordic countries to anything
like the same degree. Yet more spectacularly – and even using the
relatively crude indicator of imprisonment rates as our primary comparative indicator – it might be objected that levels of punishment in the
UK, Australia, Canada and New Zealand are far closer to those in the co-
ordinated market economies of Northern Europe and Scandinavia than
they are to the perhaps extreme case of their fellow liberal market
economy, the USA. In the rest of this section, I want to focus on the
examples of two liberal market economies, New Zealand and the USA –
two of the most troubling cases for any argument about the utility of a
'varieties of capitalism' model in comparative criminal justice – to show
why, and how, the model in fact allows us to deepen our analysis in a way
which recognises and attributes real significance and meaning to local
differences. Furthermore, I shall show how that deepened analysis acts as
a provocation, in turn, to more refined model-building. The extent to
which the generalisation implied by models is intellectually damaging
depends, in short, on how the model is constructed, and on how it is put
to use.

PR: exogenous or endogenous variable? The case of New Zealand

In terms of the model which I have sketched, New Zealand presents an
obvious difficulty. The liberal/co-ordinated market economy model

predicts that a proportionally representative political system will be associated with more stable levels of punishment, with a higher status professional bureaucracy, and with less highly politicised criminal justice. In New Zealand, by contrast, the adoption of proportional representation in 1996 has gone hand in hand with an acceleration of 'law-and-order politics' (Pratt and Clark 2005; Pratt 2007; Pratt, this volume) and with an increase in levels of punishment: the imprisonment rate has risen substantially, from 128 per 100,000 of the population in 1995 to 197 in 2007. This is the case notwithstanding the fact that PR has been associated with stronger electoral performance by left-of-centre parties, and by consequently longer tenure for Labour governments. A lazy use of the model might lead us to gloss over this uncomfortable fact that PR in New Zealand has been associated with penal populism as an anomaly. But a more intelligent approach – itself inspired by the intellectual framework underpinning the model, with its focus on interlocking institutions – should prompt us to look more closely at this case. If our overall account shows that proportionally representative electoral systems are, in a large number of systems, associated with a more moderate penal politics, what is it about the New Zealand case which is different? And what does this tell us about how the model itself should be refined?

The starting point for our reflections here should be the fact that PR is itself articulated in the explanatory model with key economic and cultural features of co-ordinated market economies: with a tradition of bargaining in which a diversity of economic interests – within both unions and management – are incorporated; with a long-running multi-party system in which negotiated political compromises are the order of the day; and with production arrangements which depend on long-term investments in education and training. This alone might give us reason to think that PR electoral arrangements, when grafted onto a substantially different set of economic, social and political institutions, would have a somewhat different impact on criminal justice. A closer look at the recent history of criminal justice politics in New Zealand confirms this surmise. While New Zealand conforms to the left-of-centre pattern of partisanship predicted by the model, the power which PR systems accord to small parties appears to have enhanced the political influence of groups advancing a 'law-and-order agenda', by giving such groups bargaining power vis-à-vis larger parties unable to command sufficient support to form a government (Pratt 2007). Single-issue parties tend to be attractive coalition partners to larger parties, because their specific focus means that a bargain can be struck with them without the larger party having to tie its hands across a range of policy issues. The New Zealand case therefore suggests that the dynamics set up by the electoral system are rather different in a country in which PR is grafted onto a society otherwise organised on 'liberal market' lines than in one in which a long-standing PR system reflects established class interests articulated with the production regime and embedded social identities represented by political parties (Iversen and Soskice 2009). This example further shows that particular features such as electoral arrangements interact strongly with other institutional factors. In the case of both liberal and co-ordinated economies, we find paradigmatic and penumbral cases, according to how strongly the constellation of co-ordinated or liberal market economy institutions is present.

The move from a basically two-party, majoritarian system in New Zealand generated, as one would expect, a proliferation of small political parties. But instead of being articulated with long-standing economic, religious or regional interests – as in, say, Germany – many of the emerging small parties in New Zealand were single-issue parties. And given the salience of 'law and order' to the pre-existing majoritarian political system and the relatively polarised social and economic relations and levels of inequality typical of liberal market economies, it is hardly surprising that several of these parties focused on criminal justice interests such as victims' rights. Add to this equation the fact that single-issue parties are attractive coalition partners for larger parties, in that they do not tie the hands of the larger parties in relation to the economic issues which are those parties' key electoral platform, and it begins to become clear why PR, instead of moderating 'law-and-order politics', gave them a new spin.

Does this imply the failure of the explanatory model? Quite the contrary, for two reasons. First, the model has already pointed us to features of recent New Zealand developments which turn out to be of significance – features moreover which have not received much sustained attention in criminological analysis thus far. Secondly, models properly understood are not static, but are answerable to empirical findings; and we can now take the insights from the New Zealand case back in order to refine the model itself. For this case study tells us that PR is not in itself an exogenous factor in explaining penal policy: rather, its impact depends on its articulation with a further set of institutional and cultural arrangements. Within a co-ordinated market economy cluster of institutions, PR serves to stabilise punishment; within a liberal market economy cluster, notwithstanding its orientation to the electoral success of the left, it can serve to accentuate dynamics towards penal severity by consolidating the electoral influence of single-issue interests.

Federalism and the diffusion of electoral politics: the case of the USA

The case of the USA presents a different sort of puzzle for the liberal market economy model. On the face of it, the US criminal justice system conforms to all the predictions associated with the model. But, with an imprisonment rate three and a half times higher than that of the next most punitive liberal market economy, New Zealand, there is clearly something to be explained about why the USA presents such an extreme case – as well as to justify its inclusion in a family of systems within which it undoubtedly constitutes a penal outlier.

The most obvious way forward here would simply be to review each of the institutional variables which characterise a liberal market system, see whether the USA presents extreme forms of some or all of these and to assess whether it does so to an extent consistent with its distinctively costly and punitive practices in criminal justice. And certainly, this takes us some way. The US majoritarian system has a particularly weak system of party discipline; its bureaucracy has become highly politicised; and its constitutional controls are oriented to due process rather than the substance of punishment or criminalisation. Moreover the US economy is marked by particularly low levels of unionisation, of employment protections and of industry/union/government co-ordination and investment in training; it experienced a particularly catastrophic collapse of Fordist industrial production; its welfare system is particularly ungenerous, and this conduces – notwithstanding its reputation as a classless society – to especially high levels of social inequality and polarisation, most vividly along lines of race (see Western and Pettit 2000; Western 2006; Stuntz 2008).

Indeed race may count as one important contributor to America's distinctive mass imprisonment. For while the over-representation of certain ethnic groups, notably young black men, is a marked phenomenon in the criminal justice systems of many countries, with the disproportion in the UK for example corresponding to that in the USA, the much larger population of African-Americans in the USA than of Black Britons in the UK entails a much larger impact on overall prison numbers. In 2006, the incarceration rate for men in the USA was 943 per 100,000; disaggregating by race, this drops to 487 for White males, rising to 1,261 for Hispanic and Latino males and to a staggering 3,042 for Black males (US Department of Justice 2006: 8). These factors, it might be argued, are in themselves sufficient to lead us to expect that the USA would display especially acute features of 'the culture of control', notably in its politicisation of criminal justice and increasing penal severity.

But this explanation is not entirely satisfactory. For a start, the huge penal disparity between the USA and other liberal market economies at similar levels of economic and political development has become markedly greater over the last thirty years, while in the earlier part of the twentieth century its penal practices equated much more closely to those of, say, the UK. Until the mid 1970s, the US imprisonment rate was relatively stable, ranging from a low of 119 in 1925 to 153 in 1974, with moderate fluctuations, and breaching the 200 mark only in a single year – 1939.[16] In the early 1970s, the US imprisonment rate was about one and a half times higher than that of England and Wales; today, notwithstanding that the English rate has itself almost doubled during this time, the US imprisonment is almost five times higher than its English/Welsh counterpart. And while some of the model's explanatory factors – notably the collapse of Fordism – relate specifically to the more recent period in which those disparities have grown, many of the salient features of the US system – including its relatively high Black and Hispanic population and its practices of institutional discrimination – have a much longer history.

Secondly, even granting the relevance of the argument that the USA amounts to an 'extreme case' of a liberal market economy type, the scale of the penal disparities is such as to invite a more careful look at the way in which the model applies. Western and his colleagues have argued (Western and Pettit 2000; Western 2006) that there is a persuasive case for the proposition that increasing social inequality in the USA is strongly associated with the rise in punishment, with prisons gradually replacing, in many states, social welfare as the dominant strategy for 'governing social marginality'. Yet this sort of analysis displays a problematic functionalism (Cavadino and Dignan, this volume) and begs the question of why these dynamics should have become so extraordinarily marked in the USA – and in certain states of the USA in particular. In 2001, the imprisonment rate ranged from a high of 1,398 per 100,000 in Louisiana to a low of 288 in Maine, with average rates in the South

---

[16] www.angelfire.com/rnb/y/rates.htim.

(1,052) one and a half times those in the North-East (646), as compared with an overall US rate of 688.[17] This variation also applies to racial disparities in incarceration: the rate of Black imprisonment in the USA in 2006 ranged from highs of 4,710 and 4,416 per 100,000 in, respectively, South Dakota and Wisconsin, to 'lows' of 851 in Hawaii, 1,065 in Washington DC and 1,579 in Maryland (Mauer and King 2007: 8). And analogous differences can be seen in patterns of capital punishment: since the re-legalisation of the death penalty in 1976, more than 70 per cent of all executions have been carried out by the Southern states, with Texas alone accounting for more than a third of the executions which took place in the thirty years from 1976 (Garland 2008). Can the model give us any help in tracing the relevant institutional and causal relationships here?

This is a large subject, and I can do no more here than to point out some promising lines of inquiry which are suggested by the contours of the explanatory model. The two lines of inquiry which I shall mark out have to do with what is perhaps the least obvious distinguishing mark of the USA. They concern not its minimal welfare system, its racial politics or its staggering (though regionally variable) record of social inequality but rather its political system. Features of political institutional structure are beginning to attract some very fruitful criminological analysis. Marie Gottschalk (2007) has traced the shifting role of criminal politics in American history, pointing up a gradual accretion of institutional capacity which ultimately underpinned the prison expansion of the late twentieth century, and a political structure in which the preferences of a distinctively punitive victims' movement registered strongly. Vanessa Barker's (2009) recent study of California, New York and Washington has shown the way in which the different structure and culture of state politics has fed into large regional disparities in patterns of punishment. And Lisa Miller (2008) has illuminated the shaping force of the differently constituted policy-making environments at national, state and local levels, diagnosing a distortion of political representation at the national and state levels, and one which has been of great significance in the upswing in punishment as a result of the increasing federalisation of criminal policy (see also Stuntz 2001, 2008; Husak 2008). In the rest of this section, I focus in particular on the nature of the US party system and the highly decentralised nature of its electoral democracy.

---

[17] www.ojp.usdoj.gov.bjs.pdf.pjim01.

Let us take the party system first. The conventional wisdom in much of the literature on the USA has long been that voter affiliation to the two main parties is organised along lines which link very weakly, if at all, with stable ideological positions. And while a weakening of left–right ideological affiliation and an increased emphasis on political leaders has marked other countries' party systems too, this has tended to be both more recent and less extreme than in the USA. Voter affiliations – and hence the strategies which candidates for office use in seeking election – tend therefore to be defined rather in terms of the policies and even personalities of current office-seekers or office-holders. In this context, policies likely to secure independent votes by appealing to median voter interests have become a key preoccupation for political leaders – not least in a system equally characterised by weak party discipline, and in which it therefore pays leaders, and particularly presidents, who are less constrained than are members of Congress by the need to answer to local constituents, to appeal direct to voters as individual candidates for office. Unfortunately, criminal justice has often been identified by political leaders as just such an issue, setting up what I have called, loosely speaking, a 'prisoners' dilemma' in which both main parties risk becoming locked into a costly strategy which they dare not abandon because of the electoral advantage, particularly vis-à-vis 'floating voters', which they fear would accrue to the other party. A key example at the national level would be President Nixon's policy of 'the war on drugs'. In the context of a majoritarian, two-party system, the fact that this dynamic has also been associated with a general move towards the ideological right is also of significance here.

However, there is some reason to think that, at the federal level, this conventional analysis has become outdated. For in recent years, particularly in relation to economic issues, the two main parties have in fact become significantly more ideologically polarised, albeit that voters' ideological preferences have remained more fluid. In a recent analysis tracking ideological, party and constituency interests in congress members' voting records, McCarty, Poole and Rosenthal (2006: Chapters 1–2) have shown that the two parties have come over the last thirty years to occupy quite distinct ideological positions, with Republicans, broadly speaking, becoming more conservative, and Democrats more liberal. Moreover they demonstrate that this party polarisation correlates closely with accentuating economic inequality across America – a phenomenon itself accelerated by immigration (*ibid.*: Chapters 3–4). In this context, until the 2008 presidential election, the majority of states had become stably 'red' or 'blue', with Democrat strongholds increasingly concentrated in the North-East, and moderate Republicans replacing conservative Democrats in many areas of the South. This sort of development is of undoubted importance for criminal justice policy, and may help to explain the relatively low-key approach to general law-and-order issues (as opposed to terrorism and drug policy) in federal elections in recent years.

Electoral politics and the structure of party systems, in other words, set up dynamics which are of key importance to criminal justice. But these dynamics vary significantly as between different levels of electoral competition. And, crucially, these levels are much more numerous and differentiated in the USA than in almost any other advanced democracy. At the presidential level, weak party discipline gives candidates extraordinary power to define their own electoral platform. In the context of a large body of voters who are unattached to either party, either formally or in terms of general allegiance, this entails the huge importance of independents in several recent presidential elections, particularly given the arrangements which in some states allow independents to vote for party nominees in presidential primary contests. In the case of candidates for Congress, the situation is somewhat different, and more akin to that of members of Parliament in the UK; they experience more acutely than presidents the need to balance appeal to voters and constituents with allegiance to party lines in Congress, albeit that weaker party discipline than in the UK somewhat dilutes this effect. The key impact of the electoral 'prisoners' dilemma' dynamic in the USA seems, however, likely to be at the state and local levels.[18]

This brings us to the second dimension of the American political system which would be worth exploring. This is the radically extensive and decentralised character of electoral politics. First, the extraordinarily

---

[18] My argument here is somewhat at odds with Miller's (2008) finding that local politics in Philadelphia evinced a markedly more complex, less straightforwardly punitive analysis of crime than that which pertained at national or state levels. Miller's argument is that the distance of state and national politicians from constituents' concerns, in which *both* criminal victimisation *and* the deleterious social impact of mass imprisonment register rather strongly, and the influence of prosecutors and other pro-victim lobbies, has had a decisive impact on the acceleration of punitiveness at those levels. This is persuasive, and an excellent example of the ways in which both the size and the fragmentation of the US system have affected its penal policy. But the electoral studies which I cite below nonetheless suggest that in the competition for office, law and order bidding wars also feature strongly at the local level.

decentralised quality of American democracy sets up a situation in which
the prisoners' dilemma is reproduced through very frequent elections at
state, county and municipal levels, significantly increasing its impact.
Secondly, individuals seeking election at local level have an interest in
advocating popular policies the costs of which do not necessarily fall on
the electoral constituency (Soskice 2009; see also Boggess and Bound
1993; Stuntz 2001, 2008). Increased resort to imprisonment would be a
key example.

These points are of particular importance in any attempt to explain
American penal harshness. This is not least because 'law and order' in
national politics has tended in recent years to be, if anything, less salient
than it has been in the UK, Australia or New Zealand, with national
preoccupations focusing quite specifically on issues like terrorism, drugs
policy and capital punishment rather than on overall issues of prison
capacity and extent – a matter which is in any case largely in the hands of
individual states.

But the dynamics of state-level politics are just the beginning
of American political decentralisation and, though state politics have
undoubtedly been of great importance in underpinning the move to
mass imprisonment, the local level of the county or city – far more costly
to research, and hence much less fully understood – has almost certainly
been of equal or even greater significance. If weak party discipline
and leader/personality domination has characterised even national and
state-level politics, this is probably yet more true of local politics, where
actors with key roles in the criminal process – mayors, judges,
district attorneys, sheriffs, to name only the most obvious – are often
elected, and hence subject to direct electoral discipline, and where their
electoral campaigns depend on an extensive practice of radio and television advertising focused on individual record or policy commitments
rather than on party platforms. Even beyond this, the American
practice of electing officials – County Commissioners, School Boards,
Treasurers and so on – reaches deep into institutions at one or more
remove from the criminal justice system, yet in which a median-voter
orientation will be likely to bring the 'governing through crime' agenda
into play.

A sense of the impact of such elections on criminal justice policy is
suggested by recent empirical research. For example, Levitt (1997: 271)
has demonstrated that the electoral cycle across fifty-nine large US cities
had a significant impact on police hiring, with increases in the size
of the police force 'disproportionately concentrated in mayoral and

gubernatorial election years', and a 'mean percentage change in sworn police officers for the cities in the sample [at] 2.1 percent in gubernatorial election years, 2.0 percent in mayoral election years, and 0.0 percent in nonelection years'. This relationship held when demographic, socio-economic and other factors were controlled for. As Levitt claims, this specific finding has much broader potential implications than merely for policing levels.

In a recent paper, Dyke (2007) has demonstrated a yet more striking effect of electoral cycles on criminal justice in a study of the impact of district-attorney elections on criminal case outcomes, using a very complete data set from North Carolina. Defendants turned out to face a higher probability of conviction and a lower probability of having all charges dismissed in an election year, suggesting that in the run-up to an electoral contest, sitting district attorneys are more reluctant to dismiss cases and more concerned to assert their 'tough on crime' credentials. At each level, then, the opportunities for an exacerbation of the 'prisoners' dilemma' dynamic are more extensive in the American system than in other liberal market economies with lower levels of political decentralisation, stronger systems of party discipline and fewer electoral offices of relevance to criminal justice.

Note, finally, one particularly important feature of these American electoral dynamics. Crime ranks among the most important issues identified in national opinion surveys, and is seen as an especially salient electoral issue when the economy is performing well (Levitt 1997: 274). Local officials like district attorneys and mayors therefore stand to gain electorally by promising tougher measures on crime. Yet, crucially, they may either not have themselves to fund the costs of such measures, or, if they do have to fund them, may not face the full political costs of their economic choices. Mayors for example are not responsible for most aspects of a city's economic performance. And Levitt (1997: 274) cites research by Chubb finding that even state governors are rarely regarded by voters as importantly responsible for the state of the economy, whose management is seen as lying primarily at a federal level. In this context, tough law-and-order policies are electorally attractive – and politically costless. This is a powerful recipe for, loosely speaking, a prisoners' dilemma, in which competing political actors – including voters – become locked into policy choices which it would be in their individual, and the overall social, interest to avoid.

Conclusion

Models, like maps, inevitably simplify the terrain which they chart. But without their orienting framework, we cannot interpret the local data which we are collecting. Nor are we well equipped to decide which data is worthy of our attention. Even our relatively simple, two-families model has already drawn attention to the potential relevance of a number of areas thus far barely addressed by criminal justice scholars: the nature of political decentralisation; the dynamics of different electoral systems and the impact of electoral cycles at local as well as national levels; and the relevance of education and training to a system's capacity for integration. Moreover it illuminates the flaws in one of the most persistent generalisations in contemporary penology: the assumption that globalisation is leading to a convergence in criminal justice policy. The obvious problems with the use of models – the problems of over-simplification, of attendant reductivism and of undue determinism – are, I have argued, resolvable within an appropriately flexible and reflective use of this method, a deployment which uses a model rooted in an explanatory theory which underpins its component variables; which posits dynamic relationships between both the analytic components of the model, and between these variables and their environment; and which moves back and forth between model and data, revising and refining the model in the light of further findings. And this in turn will open up new and fruitful fields of local empirical inquiry for criminologists and others.

Models are in short, answerable to local knowledge; but they are not in opposition to it. They are, on the contrary, one of its preconditions.

References

Ashworth, A. (2009) 'The contours of English criminal law' in B. McSherry, A. Norrie and S. Bronitt (eds.), *Regulating Deviance: The Redirection of Criminalisation and the Futures of Criminal Law*, Oxford: Hart Publishing.

Barker, V. (2009) *The Politics of Punishment: How the Democratic Process Shapes the Way America Punishes Offenders*, New York: Oxford University Press.

Beckett, K. (1997) *Making Crime Pay*, New York: Oxford University Press.

Beckett, K. and Sasson, T. (2004) *The Politics of Injustice: Crime and Punishment in America*, 2nd edn, Thousand Oaks, CA: Sage.

Beckett, K. and Western, B. (2001) 'Governing social marginality' in D. Garland (ed.), *Mass Imprisonment: Social Causes and Consequences*, London: Sage, pp. 35–50.

Blanden, J., Gregg, P. and Machin, S. (2005) *Social Mobility in Britain: Low and Falling*, Centre for Economic Performance Working Paper CP172, London: LSE.

Boggess, S. and Bound, J. (1993) 'Did criminal activity increase during the 1980s? Comparisons across data sources', National Bureau of Economic Research Working Paper no. 443.

Bondeson, U. (2005) 'Levels of punitiveness in Scandinavia: descriptions and explanations' in J. Pratt, D. Brown, M. Brown, S. Hallsworth and W. Morrison (eds.), *The New Punitiveness*, Cullompton, Willan Publishing.

Carlen, P. (1983) *Women's Imprisonment*, London: Routledge & Kegan Paul.

Cavadino, M. and Dignan, J. (2006) *Penal Systems: A Comparative Approach*, London: Sage.

Chevigny, P. (2003) 'The populism of fear: politics of crime in the Americas', *Punishment and Society*, 5(1), 77–96.

Cohen, S. (1985) *Visions of Social Control*, Oxford: Polity Press.

Crawford, A. (1998) 'Community safety and the quest for security: holding back the dynamics of social exclusion', *Policy Studies*, 19, 237–53.

Downes, D. (1988) *Contrasts in Tolerance*, Oxford: Oxford University Press.
    (2010) 'Comparative criminology, globalisation and the "punitive turn"' in D. Nelken (ed.), *Comparative Criminal Justice and Globalisation*, Aldershot: Ashgate.

Downes, D. and Hansen, K. (2006) 'Welfare and punishment in comparative perspective' in S. Armstrong and L. McAra (eds.), *Perspectives on Punishment*, Oxford: Oxford University Press.

Dubber, M. D. (2005) *Police Power*, Columbia University Press.

Dyke, A. (2007) 'Electoral cycles in the administration of criminal justice', *Public Choice*, 133, 417–37.

Esping-Andersen, G. (1990) *The Three Worlds of Welfare Capitalism*, Cambridge: Polity Press.
    (1996) *Welfare States in Transition*, London: Sage.

Garland, D. (2001) *The Culture of Control*, Oxford: Oxford University Press.
    (2007) 'High crime societies and cultures of control' in L. Ostermeier and B. Paul (eds.), Special Issue, *Kriminologisches Journal*.
    (2008) 'A peculiar institution: capital punishment and American society', paper delivered to the Harvard Criminal Justice Forum, May.

Geertz, C. (1983) *Local Knowledge*, New York: Basic Books.

Gilbert, N. (2002) *The Transformation of the Welfare State: The Silent Surrender of Public Responsibility*, Oxford: Oxford University Press.

Giorgi, A. de (2006) *Rethinking the Political Economy of Punishment*, Aldershot: Ashgate.

Gottschalk, M. (2007) *The Prison and the Gallows*, Cambridge: Cambridge University Press.

Greenberg, D. (2001) 'Novus ordo saeclorum: a comment on Downes, and on Beckett and Western', *Punishment and Society*, 3, 81–93.

Hale, C. (2005) 'Economic marginalisation, social exclusion and crime' in C. Hale, K. Hayward, A. Wahidin and E. Wincup (eds.), *Criminology*, Oxford: Oxford University Press, pp. 325–43.

Hall, P. A. (2007) 'The evolution of varieties of capitalism in Europe' in B. Hancké, M. Rhodes and M. Thatcher (eds.), *Beyond Varieties of Capitalism*, Oxford: Oxford University Press.

Hall, P. A. and Soskice, D. (2001) 'An introduction to the varieties of capitalism' in P. A. Hall and D. Soskice (eds.), *Varieties of Capitalism*, Oxford: Oxford University Press, pp. 1–68.

Hillyard, P. and Tombs, S. (2005) 'Towards a political economy of harm: states, corporations and the production of inequality' in P. Hillyard, C. Pantazis, S. Tombs and D. Gordon (eds.), *Beyond Criminology: Taking Harm Seriously*, London: Pluto Press, pp. 30–54.

Husak, D. (2008) *Overcriminalization: The Limits of the Criminal Law*, Oxford and New York: Oxford University Press.

Iversen, T. (2007) 'Economic shocks and varieties of government responses' in B. Hancké, M. Rhodes and M. Thatcher (eds.), *Beyond Varieties of Capitalism*, Oxford: Oxford University Press.

Iversen, T. and Soskice, D. (2006) 'Electoral institutions and the politics of coalitions: why some democracies redistribute more than others', *American Political Science Review*, 100, 165–81.

  (2009) 'Distribution and redistribution: the shadow of the nineteenth century', *World Politics*, 61(3), 438–86.

Lacey, N. (2008) *The Prisoners' Dilemma: Political Economy and Punishment in Contemporary Democracies*, Cambridge: Cambridge University Press.

  (2009) 'Historicising criminalisation: conceptual and empirical issues', *Modern Law Review*, 72(6), 936–60.

Levitt, S. D. (1997) 'Using electoral cycles in police hiring to estimate the effect of police on crime', *The American Economic Review*, 87, 270–90.

Loader, I. (2006) 'Fall of the Platonic guardians: liberalism, criminology and political responses to crime in England and Wales', *British Journal of Criminology*, 46, 561–86.

McAra, L. (2005) 'Modelling penal transformation', *Punishment and Society*, 7, 277–302.

McCarty, N., Poole, K. T. and Rosenthal, H. (2006) *Polarized America: The Dance of Ideology and Unequal Riches*, Cambridge, MA: MIT Press.

Marvell, T. B. (1995) 'Sentencing guidelines and prison population growth', *Criminal Law and Criminology*, 85, 696–709.

Mauer, M. and King, R. S. (2007) *Uneven Justice: State Rates of Incarceration by Race and Ethnicity*, Washington: The Sentencing Project.

Miller, L. L. (2008) *The Perils of Federalism: Race, Poverty, and the Politics of Crime Control*, New York: Oxford University Press.

Morris, N. (2006) 'Blair's "frenzied law-making"', *The Independent*, 16 August.

Nelken, D. (1995) 'Disclosing/invoking legal culture', *Social and Legal Studies*, 4, 435–52.

(1997) (ed.) *Comparing Legal Cultures*, Aldershot: Dartmouth.

Newburn, T. (2007) '"Tough on crime": penal policy in England and Wales' in M. Tonry (ed.), *Crime, Punishment and Politics in Comparative Perspective: Crime and Justice: A Review of Research*, vol. 36, Chicago: University of Chicago Press, pp. 425–70.

Pratt, J. (2007) *Penal Populism*, London: Routledge.

(2008a) 'Scandinavian exceptionalism in an era of penal excess, Part I: The nature and roots of Scandinavian exceptionalism', *British Journal of Criminology*, 48, 119–37.

(2008b) 'Scandinavian exceptionalism in an era of penal excess, Part II: Does Scandinavian exceptionalism have a future?', *British Journal of Criminology*, 48, 275–92.

Pratt, J., and Clark, M. C. (2005) 'Penal populism in New Zealand', *Punishment and Society*, 7(4), 303–22.

Pratt, J., Brown, D., Brown, M., Hallsworth, S. and Morrison, W. (2005) (eds.) *The New Punitiveness*, Cullompton: Willan Publishing.

Reiner, R. (2006) 'Beyond risk: a lament for social democratic criminology' in T. Newburn and P. Rock (eds.), *The Politics of Crime Control*, Oxford: Clarendon Press, pp. 7–49.

(2007) *Law and Order: An Honest Citizen's Guide to Crime and Control*, Oxford: Polity Press.

Reitz, K. (2005) 'The enforceability of sentencing guidelines', *Stanford Law Review*, 58, 155–73.

Roberts, J. and Hough, M. (2002) (eds.) *Changing Attitudes to Punishment: Public Opinion, Crime and Justice*, Cullompton: Willan Publishing.

Rusche, G. and Kirchheimer, O. (1969) *Punishment and Social Structure* (first published in German, 1939), New York: Russell Sage.

Ryan, M. (2003) *Penal Policy and Political Culture in England and Wales*, Winchester: Waterside.

Savelsberg, J. J. (1994) 'Knowledge, domination, and criminal punishment', *American Journal of Sociology*, 99, 911–43.

(1999) 'Knowledge, domination and criminal punishment revisited', *Punishment and Society*, 1, 45–70.

Simon, J. (2007) *Governing through Crime: How the War on Crime Transformed American Democracy and Created a Culture of Fear*, New York: Oxford University Press.

Soskice, D. (2009) 'American exceptionalism and comparative political economy' in C. Brown, B. Eichengreen and M. Reich (eds.), *Labor in the Era of Globalization*, New York: Cambridge University Press, pp. 51–93.

Stuntz, W. J. (2001) 'The pathological politics of criminal law', *Michigan Law Review*, 100, 505–600.

(2006) 'The political constitution of criminal justice', *Harvard Law Review*, 119, 780–851.

(2008) 'Unequal justice', *Harvard Law Review*, 121, 1969–2040.

Sutton, J. (2004) 'The political economy of imprisonment in affluent Western democracies, 1960–1990', *American Sociological Review*, 69, 170–89.

Teubner, G. (2001) 'Legal irritants: how unifying law ends up in new divergences' in Hall and Soskice (eds.), *Varieties of Capitalism*, Oxford: Oxford University Press, pp. 417–41.

Tonry, M. (2004a) *Punishment and Politics: Evidence and Emulation in the Making of English Crime Control Policy*, Cullompton: Willan.

(2004b) 'Why aren't German penal policies harsher and imprisonment rates higher?', *German Law Review*, 5, 1187–206.

(2007) 'Determinants of penal policies' in M. Tonry (ed.), *Crime and Justice: A Review of Research*, vol. 36, Chicago: University of Chicago Press, pp. 1–48.

Unger, R. M. (1987) *Social Theory: Its Situation and Task*, Cambridge: Cambridge University Press.

US Department of Justice (2006) *Prisoners in 2006*, Bureau of Justice Statistics, US Department of Justice.

Useem, B., Liedka, R. V. and Morrison Piehl, A. (2003) 'Popular support for the prison build-up', *Punishment and Society*, 5(1), 5–32.

Western, B. (2006) *Punishment and Inequality in America*, New York: Russell Sage.

Western, B. and Pettit, B. (2000) 'Incarceration and racial inequality in men's employment', *Industrial and Labour Relations Review*, 54, 3–16.

Whitman, J. Q. (2003) *Harsh Justice*, Oxford: Oxford University Press.

Young, J. (1999) *The Exclusive Society*, London: Sage.

(2002) 'Crime and social exclusion' in M. Maguire, R. Morgan and R. Reiner (eds.), *The Oxford Handbook of Criminology*, 3rd edn, Oxford: Oxford University Press, pp. 457–90.

Zedner, L. (1995) 'In pursuit of the vernacular: comparing law and order discourse in Britain and Germany', *Social and Legal Studies*, 4, 517–35.

10

Penal excess and penal exceptionalism: welfare and imprisonment in Anglophone and Scandinavian societies

JOHN PRATT

This chapter is about penal convergence which was then followed by divergence between two clusters of societies: England and New Zealand on the one hand, Finland, Norway and Sweden on the other. First it examines and explains initial post-1945 convergences between them in relation to prison rates and prison development. Secondly, it traces and explains the divergences that have since occurred between them. While these divergences begin around 1960, their pace has quickened, as Figure 10.1 illustrates in relation to prison rates (although Finland did not follow the same course as the other Scandinavian societies until the late 1960s).[1] Indeed, the differences have become so marked that the Anglophone societies are now known for their *penal excess* (very high levels of imprisonment[2] and deteriorating prison conditions), while the Scandinavian societies are known for their *penal exceptionalism* (very low levels of imprisonment and humane prison conditions).

What lies behind these moves from convergence to divergence? Any full account will involve a multi-factored explanatory framework, as recent research in comparative penology suggests.[3] In this chapter, however, I want to give attention to the way in which the differing models of welfare state in these two clusters impacted on respective penal developments. The chapter thus draws on Esping-Andersen's (1990) typologies: the 'liberal welfare state' of the Anglophone countries that involved modest, means-tested benefits usually targeted

---

[1] See Lappi-Seppälä (2000) on the transformation of Finnish penal policy at this time.

[2] At a rate of 203 per 100,000 of population, New Zealand has the second highest rate of imprisonment amongst Western societies. At a rate of 155, England has the highest in Western Europe.

[3] See variously Green (2008), Cavadino and Dignan (2006), Lacey (2008), Downes (1988).

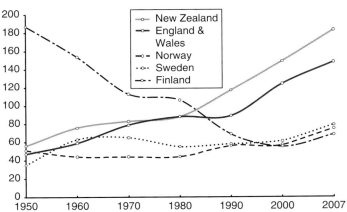

Figure 10.1   Prison rate per 100,000 total population 1950–2007.

at low-income dependents; and the 'social democratic welfare state' of the Scandinavian countries that involved universal provision and high rather than subsistence levels of benefit. The argument will be that the Scandinavian model, by generating *a politics of acceptance and inclusion*, helped to act as a barrier against the tendencies towards penal excess that became so pronounced in these Anglophone countries. The Anglophone model, in contrast, has helped to make such excess possible by generating *a politics of resentment and exclusion*.

Post-war convergences

In the immediate post-war period, prison conditions as well as imprisonment rates were very similar between these two clusters. In both we find more extensive development of 1930s reforms that had included open prisons, prison farms and more specialist penal institutions (see variously, Lingard 1936; Goransson 1938; Grunhut 1948; Lahti 1977). Across these societies there was a common emphasis on the following:

(i)   Rehabilitation

In England in 1949 the new Prison Rules (no. 6) stipulated that 'the purposes of training and treatment of . . . prisoners shall be to establish in them the will to lead a good and useful life on discharge and to fit them to do so'. In New Zealand, the Report of the Controller-General of

Prisons (1947: 8) explained that 'the aim of penal administration is not to punish . . . the primary objective is to effect the rehabilitation of the offender through a carefully devised individualized programme of treatment and training'. In Sweden, the treatment and rehabilitation of offenders was formalised in the provisions of the Implementation of Sentences Act (1945). In Norway, under the provisions of the Prison Act 1958 (based on the recommendations of the Prison Reform Committee 1951) 'the potential for adjustment to society is to be fostered and encouraged. The harmful consequences of the loss of freedom shall as far as possible be prevented or counteracted' (Evenson 1958: 70).

(ii)   Expert knowledge and research

In England, the Advisory Committee on the Treatment of Offenders (ACTO) was established in 1944. As Home Secretary Butler later explained, 'research may sound academic, but I am quite certain that in this field of crime it is the absolutely vital basis without which we cannot work' (*Hansard* 1958, vol. 594, 31 October: 505). In New Zealand, a Department of Justice Advisory Council was established in 1954. In Sweden, standing committees worked on redrafting the Criminal Code (1953) and the Protection Code (1956), which dealt with criminal sanctions. In Norway, a Penal Code Commission was constituted as a permanent advisory body: 'the Commission has four permanent members (a judge, the Attorney-General, a professor of criminal law and a barrister) but experts from different fields such as social welfare and psychiatry [can be] called on' (Andenaes 1954: 21).

There were high expectations of this investment in expertise. In Sweden, Myrdal (1945: 1) claimed that crime could be eliminated 'like other contagious diseases'. In England, it was recognised that 'delinquency cannot be dealt with effectively without more knowledge of its causes and a more accurate measurement than we have at present of the success of the various forms of treatment. It is now widely recognised that in this field research is as essential in the fields of science and technology' (Home Office 1959: 5). In New Zealand, it was thought 'indisputable that research in the form of scientific analysis of penal methods is a necessary and vital part of penal work' (Ministry of Justice 1962: 18). Similarly in Norway, it was anticipated that the Institute of Criminology, opened at the University of Oslo in 1954, 'would be able to offer considerable assistance in the field of criminal legislation' (Olaussen and Sorensen 1980: 4).

(iii)   Optimism about what prison might achieve

Prison is the only sanction discussed in the section on penal methods in the iconic English document of the period, *Penal Practice in a Changing Society* (Home Office 1959). It claimed that 'methods of training have been progressively extended and improved, notably in the application of psychiatry and psychology, in the development of skilled industrial training, in getting prisoners out of their cells into associated activities, in the establishment in all prisons of evening education institutes staffed by local education authority teachers and in preparation for release through pre-release courses' (*ibid.*: 12). Similarly, the New Zealand Ministry of Justice (1954: 17) explained that:

> prisoners should not only be detained, they should also be trained . . . if no personal training is given or interest shown, the tedium of prison life and the lack of any need to think, or make major decisions, will eventually result in the mental and moral deterioration of the prisoners, and the release of men and women unfitted to take their place in the community.

In Sweden, Strode (1949: 225) noted that the prison regimes now in existence 'do not try and break a prisoner's spirit, but work to restore his self-confidence'. As regards Norwegian prisons, Andenaes (1954: 29) observed that 'post-war years have seen the introduction of special social workers in the Prison Service, and psychological and social examination of prisoners on reception in institutions'. This belief in the positive possibilities of imprisonment, given the injection of treatment and rehabilitation to prison administration, may help to explain the growth of imprisonment in the 1950s in these countries. At this stage, in both clusters, the commitment to welfare was meant to provide appropriate *curative* responses to crime, which might thus include imprisonment, rather than actually *reduce* imprisonment. This is very clearly reflected in the comments of Torsten Erikkson, director of the Swedish Prison Commission, in 1950: 'if we treat offenders, we must have the same liberties in criminal care as they do in medical health care and this means we have the power to free a person immediately if the treatment requires or keep him in an institution for any length of time if it seems appropriate' (Finnish Kriminalist Society 1951: 67).

(iv)   Public security as a secondary issue

In England, the Report of the Director of Penal Services (1957: 8) stated that 'the public should accept something less than one hundred per cent security . . . if society wants to develop the positive and redemptive side of prison work, it must face the fact that the occasional prisoner may escape and do damage'. Similarly in New Zealand, the Ministry of Justice (1954: 16) noted that 'it is in our ultimate interests that a reasonable degree of calculated risk should be taken in the process of reformation. It is better that a very small percentage of prisoners should escape than that society should be continually burdened with men unprepared and unfitted for release.' In Norway, a training school for young male offenders provided for 'lectures and entertainment, and the boys can occupy themselves with hobbies and sports. They may be allowed short leave of absence as a part of their treatment . . . [they] may also be allowed to work in factories outside the institution. *The school has neither wall nor fence*' (Halvorsen 1954: 28, my italics). In Sweden, Strode (1949: 225, my italics) observed that 'in the open prisons, guards are not armed, windows not barred, *and nothing prevents a prisoner from quietly strolling away over the fields*'.

These convergences were one segment of the broader post-war welfare reforms taking place across these societies. In both clusters, it was envisaged that their developing welfare states would not only alleviate the material hardships of the poor but also *bring about a greater sense of social solidarity and inclusion*. In relation to the Anglophone model, T. H. Marshall (1950: 56), the most renowned British sociologist of the period, wrote that 'the extension of the social services is not primarily a means of equalising incomes . . . What matters is that there is a general enrichment of the concrete substance of civilised life, a general reduction of risk and insecurity, an equalisation between the more or less fortunate at all levels.' Similarly, Nelson (1953: 502) writing of Scandinavian developments in social welfare, noted that '[their] importance must to an equal extent be found on the plane of social psychology, in the reduction of social tensions and in the promotion of social solidarity'. Hence the shared developments in penal policy at this time. Societies built around solidarity and inclusion could provide opportunities for the rehabilitation of prisoners rather than for their incapacitation. Equally, concerns about escaping prisoners were relaxed – in inclusive societies they posed no incipient menace to the rest of the community. In addition, expert knowledge and planning had become an integral feature of penal policy development, as in other sectors of the welfare state. One speaker in the parliamentary debate on New Zealand's 1938 Social Security Bill had thus stated that: 'security can only be purchased by conscious planning and by the utilization of the best brains in the country so that we may evolve a system which will embrace every one of our citizens' (NZPD 1938, vol. 252: 369).

Thereafter, however, the penal arrangements of these clusters begin to diverge and follow routes that ultimately led to penal excess in the Anglophone societies, penal exceptionalism in the Scandinavian.

The Anglophone route to penal excess

This increasingly took on the following characteristics:

(i) Deteriorating prison conditions

Prison conditions never reached post-war expectations of them. Even in the 1950s, shortage of staff, dilapidated buildings and lack of political interest negated the intents of the prison authorities: 'in spite of the development of specialised prisons and of an extensive open prison system, the great majority of men sentenced to imprisonment who are not serving a first sentence have to serve their sentences in the general local prisons – in grossly overcrowded conditions and without adequate facilities for work or training' (Home Office 1959: 13). These substandard conditions were then exacerbated by the growth of the prison population in these countries and, in the mid 1960s, the intensification of security after a series of high-profile escapes. These changes in prison administration alongside the deteriorating conditions have since provoked periodic disturbances. Subsequent inquiries (e.g. Woolf and Tumin 1991) may have temporarily reinvigorated prison administration, only for it to be quickly overwhelmed by further security issues and overcrowding.

(ii) The declining influence of criminal justice experts

By the 1960s the news media had begun to challenge the criminal justice experts' monopoly of knowledge and control of penal affairs (Morris 1989). Feeding on perennial anxieties about rising crime statistics, it provided a different framework of knowledge through which crime and punishment issues could be understood. Public opinion polls then began to show regular expressions of public support for greater penal severity and at the same time scepticism and mistrust of the experts who, despite all the expectations of them, seemed to have no answer to rising crime (Roberts *et al.* 2003).

As this has happened, both Conservative and Labour governments have variously undermined or distanced themselves from the criminal justice elites in whom the power to determine penal policy had previously been vested. One of the first actions of the Thatcher government on coming to power in 1979, for example, was to abolish ACTO. Two decades later, the New Labour Home Secretary justified his government's hybrid antisocial behaviour legislation as 'a triumph for democratic politics – in truth a victory for local communities over detached metropolitan elites' (*Hansard*, 8 April 1998, col. 370). In addition, the power and authority of the civil service has been steadily eroded by restructuring, recourse to private sector think tanks for advice and the appointment of 'special advisers' within the civil service to ensure that it more readily acted in line with government aspirations (Rock 1995).

(iii)   Populism and the importance of public security

One of the consequences of these changes was that policy began to be driven more by common sense than research, became more ad hoc than planned, more emotive than objective. Representations of public opinion, public mood and sentiment have become influential on policy development as the power of experts has declined. One of the most dramatic and far-reaching examples of this populism has been the 1999 citizen's initiated (non-binding) referendum in New Zealand (which attracted the support of 92 per cent of the electorate). Voters were asked the following question: 'Should there be a reform of our justice system placing greater emphasis on the needs of victims, providing restitution, and compensation for them and imposing minimum sentences and hard labour for all serious violent offences?' Irrespective of its manifest contradictions and inconsistencies, the Ministry of Justice (2002: 1) acknowledged that the 2002 Sentencing Act was prompted by the need to 'respond to the 1999 Referendum which revealed public concern over the sentencing of serious violent offenders. New Zealanders also expressed a desire for better protection from dangerous offenders.' As a result of such influences, public security rather than prisoner rehabilitation has come to be of paramount importance in policy development. The New Zealand Parole Act (2002), for example, stipulates that the sole criterion for parole eligibility is *risk to the public*.

(iv)   Deterrence and incapacitation

Deterrence and incapacitation have become increasingly significant features of sentencing policy, amidst a growing sense of pessimism about any reformative capabilities that prison might have. This was assisted by the collapse of the rehabilitative ideal in the 1970s and the limited impact thereafter of the 'justice model' in these clusters. As such, recidivist offenders especially have been transformed from the weak-willed, usually psychologically or socially damaged individuals, that rehabilitation would nourish, into calculating predators, only able to be stopped from offending by the intensity of pain that punishment brings them – hence the longer prison terms and proliferation of indeterminate sentence provisions in both England (Criminal Justice Act 2003) and New Zealand (Sentencing Act 2002). As this has happened, it has been argued that the increasing level of imprisonment is an indicator of the success, not failure, of government policy. Legitimated in this way, further growth in the prison population is then built into policy and planning. The New Zealand Justice Minister thus explained that 'the number of criminals in jail is expected to increase by 20 per cent in the next seven years – proof that the government is tough on crime . . . the public referendum in 1999 showed New Zealanders wanted tougher measures taken against criminals and the government has acted on that. These figures are the proof' (*Dominion Post*, 10 March 2004: A11).

The Scandinavian route to penal exceptionalism

In contrast, over the same period, penal arrangements in Scandinavia have come to be associated with the following characteristics:

(i)   Humane prison conditions

Issues of security have not been allowed to dominate prison administration to anything like the same extent as in the Anglophone world. Even as concerns about prison escapers were beginning to fundamentally change the administration of Anglophone prisons, Connery (1966: 409–10) wrote of Sweden as follows: 'I asked [the governor] what was done about escaping prisoners, since none of the guards had guns and the [prison] walls were not exactly formidable. He replied, "it is better to let the man go than to put a hole in him . . . we can always catch him later."' As a consequence, it became possible to introduce 'experiments in family living' to some Swedish prisons (*New York Times*, 29 August 1966: 2): 'the experiment will be made at two small prisons . . . At one, wives and fiancées will be allowed to "live in" for a few days. At the other, wives and children will live in prison apartments with the convicts for their entire sentence' (*ibid.*). Thereafter, Marnell (1974: 11) observed that 'local community prisons are planned to be open or semi-open for at most 40–60 inmates'. Again, as maximum security conditions were becoming central to prison development in the Anglophone world, the Swedish Correctional Treatment in Institutions Act (1974) put prisoners' rights on the same level of those of other citizens: 'every prisoner had the same right as whichever Swede to get the support from government authorities to get a job, a place to live, medical care, the right to vote in elections etc.' (Ekbom 2003: 8). In other words, prisons were being 'normalised' – it was recognised that going to prison itself was punishment enough, without the further privations and restrictions characteristic of Anglophone prisons.

While there has since been some periodic tightening of security arrangements in the Scandinavian prisons, Sweden especially in the aftermath of escapes and murders in 2005, their conditions remain dramatically different from those in the Anglophone countries, as the following description intimates: 'Look in on Finland's penal institutions, whether those the system categorizes as "open" or "closed", and it is hard to tell when you've entered the world of custody . . . [in one closed institution] walls and fences have been removed in favour of unobtrusive camera surveillance and electronic networks. Instead of clanging iron gates, metal passageways and grim cells, there are linoleum-floored hallways lined with living spaces for inmates that resemble dormitory rooms more than lock ups in a slammer. Guards are unarmed and wear either civilian clothes or uniforms free of emblems like chevrons and epaulettes' (*New York Times*, 2 January 2003: 1).

These differences become even more dramatic when account is taken of such matters as the provision of solarium facilities in some Norwegian and Swedish prisons, unsupervised contact visits, even in maximum security institutions, and car parks for prisoners in some open institutions so they may commute to work (Pratt 2008a).

(ii) The absence of public involvement in penal affairs

The authority of criminal justice experts has not been undermined by the press to anything like the same extent as has occurred in the

Anglophone countries (Green 2008). And although the growth of satellite television has led to changes in news presentation in this region, to a large extent state television still maintains a significant public information and education role. For example, 'the Finnish version of Police-TV is more like an education programme with criminal justice officials explaining the contents and functions of the criminal justice system' (Lappi-Seppälä 2007: 64). Extra-parliamentary law-and-order groups campaigning for tougher sentences and demanding greater public influence on policy making are largely non-existent in Scandinavia and do not generate the kind of sensational headlines that have become commonplace in the Anglophone world (Pratt 2008b). There has, accordingly, been little public pressure for harsher sentences: 'a search from the Finnish supreme court case register covering the years 1980–2004 did not find a single case with the words "public opinion" or "general sense of justice" cited in the decision' (Lappi-Seppälä 2007: 70).

(iii) The continuing importance of criminal justice expertise

At the same time, for much of the post-1950s period, policy-making remained much more expert dominated than in the Anglophone world. In contrast to the plethora of criminal justice legislation and the speed at which this has been made in recent years in England (Tonry 2004), policy-making in Scandinavia is more likely to be planned and long considered. Jareborg (1995: 99) wrote in relation to penal policy-making in Sweden that 'a legislative committee typically works for a number of years. All this serves to make the process as rational as possible. The issue is "cooled down" and political difficulties are normally solved within the committee whose members continually consult important persons in their respective political parties.' Similarly Lappi-Seppälä (2007: 69–70) refers to the revision of the Finnish penal code that commenced in 1972. After four years, 'the Committee . . . laid down its principal paper. Again, after four years of preparation a specific Task-Force for criminal law reform was established . . . practically all key figures stayed active from the start to the closing of the project (1980–1999) and some remained in the work from their initial start in 1972 till the last official sub-reform in 1999'.

(iv) Just deserts/proportionality

Here, too, the rehabilitative ideal lost credibility in the 1970s. However, just deserts and proportionality became central features of sentencing policy, with little recourse to deterrence and incapacitation. In Sweden, the National Council for Crime Prevention (1977) proposed that punishment should be awarded on a 'deserts' and 'least restrictive intervention' basis. In Norway, the Ministry of Justice (1978: 31) proclaimed that 'the demand for justice is a more secure penal foundation than theories which are grounded in the view that punishments are meant to achieve other goals'. Finland, too, pursued a policy of 'humane neoclassicism' from the late 1960s, stressing 'both legal safeguards against coercive care and the goal of less repressive measures in general' (Lappi-Seppälä 2007: 11). These inscribed limits to punishment meant reducing the size of the prison population became a paramount penal objective – the Swedish Minister of Justice even predicting that there would only be a mere 600 prisoners in that country by 1980 (Ministry of Justice 1974). While such utopianism never eventuated, the overarching intent to develop sentencing policy that would restrict imprisonment and limit the size of the prison estate (e.g. the use of the prison 'queue' in Norway) has meant that Sweden and Norway have remained at the bottom end of the European imprisonment spectrum, while Finland began its dramatic imprisonment descent from the late 1960s.

Welfare, imprisonment and penal policy

How, though, did the differing models of welfare contribute to these diverging patterns of penal development?

(i)   The liberal welfare state and the politics of resentment and exclusion

Let us first examine the relationship between penal development and the liberal model of welfare in the Anglophone world. Despite the initial political commitment to it in these societies, the liberal welfare state quickly became subject to economic restraints (see Kynaston 2008: 535–59). Thereafter, the election of Conservative governments in the Anglophone countries for long periods from the early 1950s led to policies that emphasised individual resilience rather than universal welfare entitlements. As a consequence, the liberal welfare state lost the political momentum it had initially enjoyed. For example: 'New Zealand was one of the few countries in the world where social security spending had decreased since the 1950s. By any kind of measure the downhill slide through the sixties was marked. The proportion of GNP allocated to social security was 7.21 per cent in 1961 and 5.51 per cent in 1971'

(Sutch 1971: 160). Instead of the broader purposes of generating social cohesion and unity, it came to have a more minimalist role – preventing destitution, as Finlay (1943: 46) had earlier specified in relation to New Zealand: 'nothing not strictly necessary is promised – no frills, no luxuries, no more than healthy subsistence'.

As such, its discretionary means-tested benefits designed to provide subsistence living only might routinely involve the interrogation and investigation of claimants, bringing fear and distrust. On the other hand, those not in receipt of benefits were increasingly likely to regard welfare as a burden unfairly borne by them, something that never seemed commensurate with their insurance and taxation contributions, while provoking anger and resentment at those who it seemed to unduly favour. As Rothstein and Uslaner (2005: 59) explain:

> if a state is going to tax the rich and give to the poor, the rich (especially the middle classes) will not agree to pay high taxes because they perceive that they do not get enough in return. They will perceive such [welfare] programmes as policies 'only for the poor', and the middle classes in particular will turn away from political parties that argue for increasing taxes and social policies.

While, from the 1970s, economic pressures and political dissatisfaction led to the liberal welfare state becoming increasingly selective in relation to benefit provisions, the divisions it made between worthy and unworthy beneficiaries generated new social divisions and tensions (see Deacon 1978; Golding and Middleton 1979). Indeed, as its public and political support declined, rather than being seen as the solution to social problems, the liberal welfare state came to be seen as the cause of them. As a consequence, from the Thatcher governments of the 1980s to those of New Labour from the 1990s, *the capabilities of the welfare state to provide inclusion and solidarity* were further undermined by benefit cuts and new restrictions to entitlements. At the same time, citizens were encouraged to make use of the private sector to provide security in areas such as health, pensions and so on. As Tony Blair later explained, 'we need to put behind us . . . the 1945 "big state" that wrongly believed it could solve every social problem [and instead build] an enabling state founded on the liberation of individual potential' (Harris 2004: 306). In effect, the security that the welfare state had intended to provide for all has become a commodity to be purchased (Garland 2001). Those not able to do so find themselves, at best, reliant on the minimal levels of state assistance that are still provided; at worst, simply cut adrift from the rest of society.

What, then, have been the consequences of this? We need to note that welfare restructuring in both England and New Zealand has not brought an end to the liberal welfare state but rather refined and sharpened the focus it had come to have after the post-1945 welfare euphoria on dividing worthy from unworthy claimants and acting as a more deliberate instrument of coercion against particularly problematic groups. In these respects, it still pursues its social-engineering responsibilities – raising the life prospects and potential of the worthy: in Britain, for example, the investments made by the Blair governments in primary and secondary education since 1997; in New Zealand, increases in benefits and some reintroduction of free healthcare for poor families by successive Labour-led coalition governments since 1999. Yet at the same time, there have been sharper distinctions and divisions amongst the claimant population as the worthy are separated out from the unworthy. Indeed, these divisions have even been applied to those administering welfare, with the publication of 'league tables' and 'ratings' by which their performance can be judged. In these ways, the trust and status of both groups is likely to be further diminished. In addition, in Britain particularly, it is able to synthesise separate sectors of welfare – benefits, job training, education and social work with offenders – to build a more coercive machinery of control in which to encase problematic groups such as the young unemployed and the long-term unemployed. In effect, anticipated reductions in welfare expenditure never materialised in the Anglophone countries. All that happened, by and large, was the transfer of welfare sources from assistantial sectors to more coercive sectors of governance, leaving the liberal welfare state at some kind of midway point between the Scandinavian welfare state and the USA penal state.

As such, the restructuring of the liberal welfare state has only increased the sense of citizen vulnerability, with anxiety and insecurity becoming more deeply embedded features of these societies: the liberal welfare state itself is not able to remedy these sentiments. There are also high levels of mistrust and suspicion of existing political processes and the institutions of government as government itself has downgraded its own responsibilities to its citizens (European Commission 2006). In these respects, fear of crime has become one of the most evocative and instrumental expressions of these concerns. At this most elemental level of security, the liberal welfare state seemed to have failed law-abiding citizens while its 'bureaucrats' – the pejorative expression now regularly used to describe its civil servants, planners and experts – seem to indulge lawbreakers by not being punitive enough. At the same time, the articulation of such sentiments in the media especially has generated support for populist politicians with tough law-and-order agendas, politicians who are prepared to increase the penal resources of the state while limiting its welfare obligations. Their common-sense solutions to crime – promises of deterrent and incapacitatory sentencing – become the means to restore cohesion, and consensus (Tyler and Boeckmann 1997) and a way to gain political power: speaking to the interests of the 'ordinary people' whom the liberal welfare state had failed and taking power away from the ineffective and elitist bureaucrats who had administered it according to their own interests rather than those of 'the people'. The report by Louise Casey (2008), former head of the government's Respect Taskforce, for the British Cabinet Office provides a very clear illustration of this matter. The report, a review of the co-operation between the public and the criminal justice authorities, is based mainly on public representations that were made to her, some 13,000 in all (through questionnaires, community meetings etc.). This is because it wanted to reposition the role played by 'the public' in the administration of justice: 'too often there is a sense that the public can't be trusted to take a view on their policing and criminal justice system. During this review I have tried to redress that balance by putting at its heart the voice of the public' (Casey 2008: 2). While it is recognised that this repositioning will not be welcomed by some, their concerns are dismissed. The repositioning is a political imperative that will also strengthen social cohesion:

> there are some who argue that the Government and the Criminal Justice System must not allow itself to be swayed by public opinion; that pandering to public opinion leads to 'mob rule' and an uncivilized society. But, currently, the system is so far away from pandering to public opinion that this seems the remotest of risks . . . Radical change is needed to get the public more engaged in tackling crime and to stop the erosion of community spirit. [Casey 2008: 7]

Again, then, if governing through welfare is now unable to provide social cohesion, 'governing through crime' becomes a way of doing so.

As a consequence, crime and insecurity have become central issues of governance in these societies, marking the end of the 'solidarity project' with which the liberal welfare state had initially been associated (Simon 2007; Garland 2001). Lawbreakers have become irredeemable enemies of society, the only legitimate responses to them being punishment and exclusion. As Tony Blair has explained:

crime, anti-social behaviour, racial intolerance, drug abuse, destroy families and communities. They destroy the very respect on which society is
founded . . . Fail to confront this evil and we will never build a Britain
where everyone can succeed . . . by acknowledging the duty to care, we
earn the right to be tough on crime . . . it is time for zero tolerance of yob
culture. [*The Guardian*, 27 September 2006: 6]

This politics of resentment is also directed at prison conditions. Reports
of any 'privileges' prisoners might receive – ranging from free Christmas
lunches to access to higher-education courses – provoke public outrage.
The 'otherness' now associated with prisoners justifies rigorous deprivation and exclusion rather than tolerance and inclusion. Risks can no
longer be taken regarding their security. Instead, the rest of society has to
be protected from them, whatever the effects on the prison environment,
whatever the economic costs to the rest of society.

(ii)   The social democratic welfare state and the politics of acceptance and inclusion

In contrast to the Anglophone societies, the post-war dominance of
social democratic and centre parties in Scandinavia ensured that the
political commitment to welfare in this region was largely unchallenged
from the 1940s to the 1980s. This allowed the social democratic welfare
state to become more deeply embedded in the fabric of these societies.
And, from the mid 1950s, its scope became far more extensive.
Administered on a universal rather than a needs basis, flat-rate benefits
were introduced in Sweden, guaranteeing 'normal' living standards
divorced from market criteria (Esping-Andersen and Korpi 1987: 53).
For example, those who became unemployed would receive 80 to 90
per cent of their previous salary in earnings-related benefits (the rate is
currently 75 per cent). Child welfare services in particular were
expanded to allow women to enjoy a fuller role in society: 'in order
to provide satisfactory conditions for children both of whose parents
are gainfully employed outside the home to supplement the home
upbringing of children whose parents consider it desirable for educational purposes, a considerable number of preschool institutions have
been established in the Scandinavian countries' (Friis 1950: 166).
Similarly, Shirer (1955: 71) wrote that, in Norway, in addition to free
holidays for the children of working women, 'vacations for housewives
are encouraged too. Various private organizations devote themselves to
this objective and are helped by the public authorities. Free vacations

are now given to thousands of housewives and their children at special seashore and mountain camps.'

Apart from the relatively small numbers who were dependent on means-tested social assistance (e.g. immigrants, the young unemployed), the comprehensive and largely universal social democratic welfare systems in Scandinavia meant that there was much less stigma in becoming a beneficiary than in the Anglophone world: for the most part, these were entitlements rather than discretionary awards. As such, they could be advertised rather than hidden away under layers of impenetrable bureaucracy, as we see in the following example from the early 1970s: 'if a Swedish mother is away from Sweden while her child allowance is due, she receives a notice from the Department of Social Security which says "don't forget that, even if you are abroad, you can still enjoy your social benefits. Fill in the enclosed form, and we will send your children's allowance to you wherever you may be"' (Huntford 1971: 201). In these ways, the provisions of the social democratic welfare state became means to achieving full, rather than tainted citizenship: 'from its origins, Swedish social democracy has been committed to creating a society where first industrial workers and then employees in general participated on equal terms in the organization and governance of society' (Tilton 1990: 257). State intervention and regulation were thus more likely to be a normal, taken-for-granted feature of Scandinavian political life rather than something that was feared or that seemed unwarranted in the Anglophone societies. Rosenthal (1967: 159) observed that 'there is little question that most Swedish citizens expect rather than fear the provision of service activities by the government agencies'.

Rothstein and Uslaner (2005) have since argued that the establishment of these universal welfare arrangements programmes led to increased solidarity between citizens and more social trust – both of other citizens who are not regarded as potential 'cheats', getting any unfair advantage that they do not deserve from the state; and of the state itself because of the tangible benefits it provides for most of its citizens. The same authors further claim that this model of welfare helped to build high levels of social capital and civic responsibility (Putnam 2000). In such ways it also helped to generate *a politics of acceptance and inclusion*. The very different approach that began to be taken to prison conditions in Scandinavia from the 1960s in comparison to the Anglophone world is one example of this politics at work. Rather than being seen as dangerous outsiders, which is what they had become in the latter societies, prisoners were instead more likely to be seen as just another group of welfare clients.

As such, neither they nor their conditions of confinement possessed any inherent newsworthiness: 'if one should be sentenced to a work camp for driving under the influence of alcohol, it will not be in the newspaper even if one is well known' (Tomasson 1970: 276).

The way in which penal differences between these two clusters have then become much starker from the 1970s is indicative of the way in which the social democratic model of welfare has become a barrier against the populist excesses characteristics of the Anglophone societies; this is in spite of some reshaping of the Scandinavian welfare state since the 1980s, particularly in Sweden. Here, too, there has also been disenchantment with the apparatus of the welfare state (too much regulation) and what it has seemed unable to provide (control over crime and criminals in particular, see Tham 1995). As this has happened, the power of expert knowledge to influence penal policy has declined – Swedish drug laws provide some of the clearest examples of this (see Tham 2005). More generally, Lindvall and Rothstein (2006: 58) detect 'a widespread critique of knowledge and research as a base for social steering'. Other patterns of development, more usually associated with the Anglophone countries can also be discerned: a relatively low level of trust in government (by Scandinavian standards) – 41 per cent against the EU average of 34 per cent (European Commission 2006);[4] an increasing mood of punitiveness (van Dijk et al. 2007); an untroubled acceptance by government and the penal bureaucracy that the Swedish prison population will increase (Ministry of Justice, Sweden 2008); and the increased emphasis on prison security noted earlier. We can also add to these qualificatory comments that in Norway, the rise of the Progress Party, pursuing a populist programme of law and order (at least by Scandinavian standards) and anti-immigration, has not only won considerable electoral support but to some extent has begun to shift the terms of penal debate. Here, too, there is now a political consensus, articulated in a new White Paper (Ministry of Justice, Norway 2008) that punishments for serious violent crime should increase.

Do not such developments thus weaken the argument that the Scandinavian welfare state acts as a barrier to penal excess? On the contrary, they actually support it in two ways. First, negatively: that we can now discern traces of Anglophone excess in these two countries (some of these quite well defined now in Sweden) illustrates what can happen when the barrier to them that this model of welfare had provided is weakened, or when the social cohesion that it helped to bring about is

---

[4] That for England was thirty, while for Finland it was fifty-five.

undermined. Secondly, positively: that we can only discern traces and that stark differences remain in relation to their prison levels and prison conditions and those in the Anglophone countries is indicative of the way in which the extensive still-existing welfare arrangements of the Scandinavian countries help to limit penal excess tendencies.

In these respects, it is important not to overstate the changes that have been made to the Scandinavian welfare state. There has been some redrawing of its boundaries but none of the wholesale restructuring that has taken place in the Anglophone countries. There is no 'user pays' as in New Zealand nor has there been any major shift from public to private provision, as in England (there are no private prisons in Scandinavia). Benefit levels remain dramatically more extensive and generous. Ahn and Olsson-Hort (2003: 108) thus argue that 'the Swedish welfare system has been reformed and somewhat downsized but is still basically the same institutional system based on citizenship and social rights'. In other words, much of the infrastructure of the social democratic welfare state is still in place, with no political intent to dismantle it further. The vast majority of Swedes, particularly women who make up the majority of public sector workers as well as benefiting most from its levels of child care, have a great investment in maintaining it. Levels of trust between citizens, at least, remains high. Public attitudes to immigration are more positive than the European norm (European Commission 2006). And if there has been a decline in confidence in government, this has not been sufficient to generate significant political support for anti-establishment populist politics.

However, it still has to be recognised that Sweden is becoming increasingly marked by social tension and dissonance. Concerns about violent crime are perhaps the most public expression of these matters, helping to provide a sense of solidarity in this way while also masking deep-rooted concerns about racism and social division. In a policy statement prior to their 2006 election victory, the Alliance of Centre-Right Parties (Allians for Sverige 2006: 1) claimed that:

> Sweden is no longer the safe country we are used to. Criminality is spreading and the violence is getting more brutal. Crimes of violence are steadily increasing. The number of reported rapes and cases of assault is becoming higher and higher and contributes to the view of a rougher, dehumanized society. Along with the increase in criminality, people's feeling of being unsafe increases too.

This shift in public mood is reflected in the public response to the murder of ten-year-old Engla Hoglund in 2008. In contrast to the murder of seven-year-old Silje Redergard in Norway in 1994, where 'there was no mass outpouring of anger or outrage from the family, the community, or the press, no cries for vigilante justice, and no political manoeuvring by any party's politicians to politicize the incident' (Green 2008: 7), in Sweden, the grief spread out from the girl's home town where 'community members gathered at Stjarnsund Church . . . to share their grief and seek support from another' to become a national event, and the girl's funeral was televised on state television (www.thelocal.se/11090/ 20080414/). Now the circumstances of the two murders are not identical: the Norwegian child was killed by two other seven-year-olds; Engla Hoglund was a little older and was murdered by a 42-year-old truck driver with a history of violence. In addition, it may well be that in the ensuing time since 1994 such a murder, if repeated in the same way in Norway, may no longer be met with such objective and rational responses. What does seem clear from the Swedish incident in 2008, however, is that the social constraints that might previously have prevented such outlets of anger and emotion no longer function in that country as they used to do. In the aftermath of this case, but also amidst more general concerns about violent crime (even if their recorded levels show no increase), longer prison terms for violent crime have been introduced or are on the penal agenda.

Even so, the Alliance document above, while trying to refashion penal responses to crime, could still acknowledge that 'many inmates at [penal] institutions are parents . . . Children's possibilities to create and maintain a good relationship to the parents during the time at the institution must be facilitated. Visiting rooms and visiting apartments that are adjusted to children's needs must therefore be available at more institutions' (Allians for Sverige 2006: 21). Now we have moved back to a more familiar Scandinavian world and one that is incomprehensible to the Anglophone societies; a world where apartments are provided in prison for inmates to enjoy unsupervised visits from their families, rather than having to experience the noise, surveillance and lack of privacy of common 'visiting rooms' characterstic of Anglophone prisons – rooms where tables and chairs are nailed to the floor, where inmates have to sit in an appointed chair painted in a different colour from the rest, while wearing brightly coloured 'clown suits' to make them distinctive to the watching prison officers. In contrast, 'conjugal relations' are actively encouraged in Sweden and the other Scandinavian countries. This is part of the policy of prison normalisation that has been pursued in this region since the 1970s and which remains largely unchallenged despite more heightened awareness of crime problems. In effect, even though the pillars on which the Swedish welfare state had been built have been shaking (certainly more so than in the other Scandinavian countries in this study), this has not yet been sufficient to drain away the high levels of social capital that had accumulated and the corresponding levels of trust and tolerance associated with this (Halpern 2005). For the most part, social problems are still more likely to be addressed and managed through the social democratic welfare-state mode of governance in Sweden, rather than the more exclusionary and intolerant liberal welfare-state mode.

Similarly, in Norway, the welfare state has maintained its popularity. Any plans for economic restructuring would meet widespread opposition; 30 per cent of the work force are in public sector employment, compared to 17 per cent in New Zealand and 20 per cent in England in 2007. Here, too, governance is through welfare and security rather than crime and insecurity. We find this exemplified in the Norwegian Labour Party's *Crime Policy* (2006):

> with good welfare services for everyone, crime can be prevented and many of the initial incentives for a life of crime can be removed. Given that 60 per cent of violent crime is committed under the influence of alcohol, it is important to adhere to a restrictive drug and alcohol policy. Good psychiatric health care services and an active labour market policy are important for comprehensive crime fighting.

In Finland, where the welfare state has not been discredited (Kvist 1999) and social democratic values are still spread across its political spectrum, we find the strongest support for the argument that the social democratic welfare state acts as a barrier to penal excess. In this country, the expertise associated with welfarism remains very influential. Indeed, it has been the power and status of experts that lies behind the dramatic decline in the Finnish prison population from the late 1960s. Lappi-Seppälä (2000: 37) writes that Finnish society is 'exceptionally expert-oriented. Reforms have been prepared and conducted by a relatively small group of experts whose thinking on crime policy . . . has followed similar lines.'

At the same time, rather than acting as one of the sharpest of reminders of the way in which the welfare state seemed to ignore the worthy and favour the unworthy, crime victims here have also become another group of welfare clients. The state acts on their behalf rather than leaving them to be exploited by law-and-order lobby groups. In the Finnish

Victims Compensation Act (1973) and subsequent provisions, they are given material compensation rather than spurious rights of representation in courts and parole hearings that may lead to them only being revictimised with no material or psychological closure, as in the Anglophone countries. Their claims are dealt with at the same time as conviction is secured. In unproblematic cases, they need not appear at all – the prosecutor claims damages on their behalf. Victim impact statements are thus unknown, allowing sentencing to be administered on the basis of objective rationality rather than subjective emotion. As such, by being able to maintain cohesion and solidarity, the Finnish state in particular does not need to use symbolic, expressive punishments to reinforce its authority and has thus been able to maintain humane prison conditions and relatively low levels of imprisonment. Indeed, the 2006 Prison Act (itself the product of a committee which began its deliberations in 1998) inscribes prisoners' rights in the Finnish Constitution, while at the same time is designed to try and curtail any further inflation of the prison population.[5]

Conclusion

There is a bigger research programme underlying this chapter, of course: one that examines *what it was* about these clusters of societies that set them on their differing welfare and penal courses. Here, I have only been able to show the connections and parallels between the respective welfare and penal developments in them. In these respects, the clusters initially shared similar welfare goals and expectations. Governing through welfare, it was thought, would provide solidarity and inclusion in addition to relieving material hardships. These ideals were reflected in their post-war converging penal programmes. Hence the emphasis given to the rehabilitation and training of prisoners, even if this came at the expense of security. Furthermore, expertise and planning had a central role to play in penal administration as in other welfare sectors. Thereafter, however, the liberal welfare state, because of its innate limitations and eventual lack of political and public support, began to lose its solidifying capabilities and became more restrictive and selective. Penal policies mirrored the

[5] For example, s.1: 3.1 states that 'the enforcement of imprisonment may not restrict the rights or circumstances of a prisoner in any other manner than that provided in the law or is necessary due to the punishment itself'. As regards prison restrictions, the legislation is intended e.g. to bring about minimal use of imprisonment for fine default (see Lappi-Seppälä 2008).

politics of exclusion and resentment that this model of welfare generated – becoming more punitive and intolerant, distrusting expertise, abandoning planning and allowing populist sentiment, anecdote and personal experience to play a leading role in policy development.

In contrast, the social democratic welfare state, with its universalism that guaranteed a 'normal' rather than subsistence standard of living, was able to maintain the solidaristic expectations. As a result, the Scandinavian societies have been provided with high levels of immunity against the social unravelling and penal excesses characteristic of the Anglophone countries. For much of this period, the politics of acceptance and inclusion that the social democratic welfare state helped to generate were reflected in penal development with more trust and tolerance of prisoners, less emphasis on security and control. There was also a larger role for penal expertise in policy development in Scandinavia than in the Anglophone countries, which was much more considered and deliberated, with long-term objectives. Whatever modifications there have been to the social democratic welfare state in recent years, these do not seem to have caused sufficient damage to its infrastructure and its *zeitgeist* to now allow the penal excesses characteristic of the Anglophone countries to flourish in Scandinavia.

References

Ahn, S.-H. and Olsson-Hort, S. (2003) 'The welfare state in Sweden' in C. Aspalter (ed.), *Welfare Capitalism Around the World*, Taichung City, Taiwan: Casa Verde Publishing, pp. 87–111.

Allians for Sverige (2006) *Ett tryggare Sverige* [*A Safer Sweden*], Stockholm: Allians for Sverige. maktskifte06.se

Andenaes, J. (1954) 'Recent trends in the criminal law and penal system in Norway, Part I: The Criminal Law', *British Journal of Delinquency*, 5, 21–6.

Casey, L. (2008) *Engaging Communities and Fighting Crime*, London: Cabinet Office.

Cavadino, M. and Dignan, J. (2006) *Penal Systems*, London: Sage.

Connery, D. (1966) *The Scandinavians*, London: Eyre & Spottiswoode.

Deacon, A. (1978) 'The scrounging controversy: public attitudes towards the unemployed in contemporary Britain', *Social Policy and Administration*, 12(2), 120–35.

Dijk, J. van, Manchin, R., Kesteren, J. van, Nevala, S. and Hidig, G. (2007) *A Comparative Analysis of the European Crime and Safety Survey (EU ICS) 2005*, Brussels: European Community.

Director of Penal Services (1957) *Annual Report to Parliament*, London: HMSO.

Downes, D. (1988) *Contrasts in Tolerance*, Oxford: Oxford University Press.

Ekbom, T. (2003) *Swedish Prisons: Seminar given to the Polish Ministry of Justice*, Warsaw.

Esping-Andersen, G. (1990) *The Three Worlds of Welfare Capitalism*, Princeton, NJ: Princeton University Press.

Esping-Andersen G. and Korpi, W. (1987) 'From poor relief to institutional welfare states: the development of Scandinavian social policy' in R. Erikson, R. J. Hansen and H. Uusitalo (eds.), *The Scandinavian Model: Welfare States and Welfare Research*, New York: M. E. Sharpe, Inc, pp. 39–74.

European Commission (2006) *Standard Eurobarometer 63, Brussels*: Public Opinion Analysis Sector, European Commission.

Evenson, A. (1958) *Social Defence in Norway*, Oslo; Ministry of Social Affairs.

Finlay, A. (1943) *Social Security in New Zealand*, Auckland: Whitcombe and Tombs Ltd.

Finnish Kriminalist Society (1951) *Annual Journal of the Finnish Kriminalist Society*, Helsinki: National Research Institute of Legal Policy.

Friis, H. K. (1950) *Scandinavia: Between East and West*, Ithaca: Cornell University Press.

Garland, D. (2001) *The Culture of Control*, New York: Oxford University Press.

Golding, P. and Middleton, S. (1979) 'Making claims: news media and the welfare state', *Media, Culture and Society*, 1, 5–21.

Goransson, H. (1938) 'Treatment of criminals and other asocial individuals', *Annals of the American Academy of Political and Social Science*, 197, 120–33.

Green, D. (2008) *When Children Kill Children*, Oxford: Clarendon Press.

Grunhut, M. (1948) *Penal reform: A Comparative Study*, Oxford: Clarendon Press.

Halpern, D. (2005) *Social Capital*, Cambridge: Polity Press.

Halvorsen, J. (1954) 'Post-war development in the prison system', *British Journal of Delinquency*, 5, 26–9.

Harris, B. (2004) *The Origins of the British Welfare State*, London: Palgrave.

Home Office (1959) *Penal Practice in a Changing Society*, London: HMSO.

Huntford, R. (1971) *The New Totalitarians*, London: Allen Lane.

Jareborg, N. (1995) 'The Swedish sentencing reform' in C. M. V. Clarkson and R. Morgan (eds.), *The Politics of Sentencing Reform*, Oxford: Oxford University Press, pp. 95–124.

Kvist, J. (1999) 'Welfare reform in the Nordic countries in the 1990s: using fuzzy-set theory to assess conformity to ideal types', *Journal of European Social Policy*, 9(3), 231–52.

Kynaston, D. (2008) *Austerity Britain 1945–51*, London: Bloomsbury.

Lacey, N. (2008) *The Prisoners' Dilemma*, Cambridge: Cambridge University Press.

Lahti, R. (1977) 'Criminal sanctions in Finland: a system in transition', *Scandinavian Studies in Law*, 21, 119–57.

Lappi-Seppälä, T. (2000) 'The fall of the Finnish prison population', *Journal of Scandinavian Studies in Criminology and Crime Prevention*, 1(1), 27–40.

— (2007) 'Penal policy in Scandinavia', *Crime and Justice: An Annual Review of Research*, 34, 1–81.

— (2008) *Imprisonment and Penal Policy in Finland*, Helsinki: National Research Institute of Legal Policy.

Lindvall, J. and Rothstein, B. (2006) 'Sweden: the fall of the strong state', *Scandinavian Political Studies*, 29, 47–63.

Lingard, F. (1936) *Prison Labour in New Zealand: A Historical, Statistical, and Analytical Survey*, Wellington, NZ: G. H. Loney, Government Printer.

Marnell, G. (1974) 'Penal reform: a Swedish viewpoint', *Howard Journal*, 14, 8–21.

Marshall, T. H. (1950) *Citizenship and Social Class*, Cambridge: Cambridge University Press.

Ministry of Justice (New Zealand) (1954) *A Penal Policy for New Zealand*, Wellington, NZ: Government Printer.

— (1962) *Annual Report to Parliament*, Wellington, NZ: Government Printer.

— (2002) *Reforming the Criminal Justice System*, Wellington, NZ: Ministry of Justice.

Ministry of Justice (Norway) (1978) *On Crime Policy*, Oslo: Ministry of Justice.

— (2008) *Punishment that Works*, Oslo: Ministry of Justice.

Ministry of Justice (Sweden) (1974) *Depopulate the Prisons*, Stockholm: Ministry of Justice.

— (2008) *Straff I proportion till brollets allvar*, Stockholm: Riksdag, SOU: 85.

Morris, T. (1989) *Crime and Criminal Justice Since 1945*, Oxford: Basil Blackwell.

Myrdal, A. (1945; 1968) *Nation and Family: The Swedish Experiment in Democratic Family and Population Policy*, Cambridge, MA: M.I.T. Press.

National Council for Crime Prevention (1977) *A New Penal System: Ideas and Proposals*, Stockholm: BRA.

Nelson, G. R. (1953) *Social Welfare in Scandinavia*, Copenhagen: Danish Ministry of Labour and Social Affairs.

Norwegian Labour Party (2006) *Crime Policy*, Oslo: Norwegian Labour Party.

Olaussen, L. and Sorensen, R. (1980) *Norwegian Criminology and Changes in the Political and Social Structure in Norway*, Oslo: Institute of Criminology, University of Oslo.

Pratt, J. (2008a) 'Scandinavian exceptionalism in an era of penal excess, Part I: The roots of Scandinavian exceptionalism', *British Journal of Criminology*, 48, 119–37.

— (2008b) 'When penal populism stops: legitimacy, scandal and the power to punish in New Zealand', *Australian and New Zealand Journal of Criminology*, 41, 364–83.

Putnam, R. (2000) *Bowling Alone: The Collapse and Revival of American Community*, New York: Simon and Schuster.

Report of the Controller-General of Prisons (1947) *Annual Report to Parliament*, Wellington, NZ: Government Printer.

Roberts, J. V., Stalans, L., Indermaur, D. and Hough, M. (2003) *Penal Populism and Public Opinion*, New York: Oxford University Press.

Rock, P. (1995) *Helping Victims of Crime*, Oxford: Clarendon Press.

Rosenthal, A. H. (1967) *The Social Programs of Sweden: A Search for Security in a Free Society*, Minneapolis: University of Minnesota Press.

Rothstein, B. and Uslaner, E. (2005) 'All for all. Equality, corruption and social trust', *World Politics*, 58, 41–72.

Shirer, W. L. (1955) *The Challenge of Scandinavia*, Boston: Little, Brown.

Simon, J. (2007) *Governing Through Crime*, New York: Oxford University Press.

Strode, H. (1949) *Sweden, Model for a World*, New York: Harcourt, Brace.

Sutch, W. B. (1971) *The Responsible Society in New Zealand*, Christchurch: Whitcombe and Tombs.

Tham, H. (1995) 'From treatment to just deserts in a changing welfare state' in A. Snare (ed.), *Beware of Punishment*, Oslo: Pax Forlag, pp. 89–122.

(2005) 'Swedish drug policy and the vision of the good society', *Journal of Scandinavian Studies in Criminology and Crime Prevention*, 6, 57–73.

Tilton, T. (1990) *The Political Theory of Swedish Social Democracy*, New York: Oxford University Press.

Tomasson, R. (1970) *Sweden: Prototype of Modern Society*, New York: Random House.

Tonry, M. (2004) *Punishment and Politics: Evidence and Emulation in the Making of English Crime Control Policy*, Cullompton: Willan Publishing.

Tyler, T. and Boeckmann, R. (1997) 'Three strikes and you are out, but why? The psychology of public support for punishing rule breakers', *Law and Society Review*, 31, 237–65.

Woolf, H. and Tumin, S. (1991) *Prison Disturbances April 1990*, London: HMSO.

11

The impact of multi-level governance on crime control and punishment

LESLEY MCARA

Introduction

Within the sociology of punishment, a veritable industry has built up both charting and theorising changes in the nature and function of crime control and penal practice in the context of late modernity (Garland 2001; Feeley and Simon 1992; O'Malley 1992). In this chapter, I will suggest that this field of scholarship has become dominated by a methodological dualism between accounts which lay emphasis on structural factors and those which lay emphasis on cultural factors. I will argue that this dualism constrains our capacity to understand the *variations* in crime control and penal policy which are evident across many Western jurisdictions, principally because it fails adequately to capture the multi-level nature of contemporary modes of governance both above, but, more particularly, below the nation state. A key aim of the chapter is to set out an alternative methodological strategy with which to interrogate recent developments; a strategy which draws on the vocabulary of systems theory.[1] The chapter is built around a case study comparing Scotland and Spain with England and it comprises four interrelated parts. Part 1 overviews key variations in crime control and penal policy within my selected jurisdictions as they have evolved over the past forty years. Part 2 describes the methodological dualism within the sociology of punishment and highlights its limitations in terms of this case study. Part 3 sets out an alternative methodological strategy. Finally, Part 4 implements this strategy, offering a rereading of the case study within its own terms.

---

[1] This chapter expands on arguments relating to systematicity in the penal realm, first set out in McAra 2005.

Part 1:   The case study

Scotland and Spain rarely feature in scholarly work which is attempting to theorise the shifting nature of crime control and punishment in late modernity (see for example Cavadino and Dignan 2006; Lacey 2008). Far from being marginal to debate, I would argue that these jurisdictions merit close attention because they have followed slightly different trajectories from many other Western penal systems by embracing penal-welfarism in the 1970s and 1980s at a time when it was being undermined in England and the USA, and only latterly, in the early years of the twenty-first century, taking a more punitive turn (which, in the case of Scotland, may yet prove to be short-lived, see McAra 2008).[2] As such, Scotland and Spain confound most dominant theories of penal change.

Divergent trajectories

(i)   Scottish divergence

Pre-devolution, Scottish policy on crime control and penal practice was administered through the Home and Health Department of then Scottish Office (a UK Department of State).[3] Major policy divergence from England was set in train by the Social Work (Scotland) Act 1968. This Act abolished the existing juvenile courts and established the children's hearings system. It also abolished the probation service and transferred its functions to newly created local authority social work departments, whose principal duty was to promote social welfare (McAra 2008).

The new children's hearing system formed a paradigm example of a welfare-based system. It aimed to take a holistic approach to child offenders and those in need of care and protection, with the best interests of the child to be paramount in decision-making. Key features of the new system were involvement of ordinary members of the public (via the lay panel) and the emphasis placed on consensual and participatory decision-making. The system aimed to avoid the criminalisation of children and to be as non-stigmatising as possible. All interventions

---

[2] Note that this chapter does not cover policy developments post 2007. Within Scotland, a minority Scottish National Party administration took power in May of that year. There are some signs that the punitiveness, which characterised the Labour–Liberal democratic-coalition years, may now be on the wane. It will be interesting to observe whether such a minority administration can resist a more populist turn as it nears a general election.

[3] The Scottish Parliament was reinstated in 1999 after a period of almost 300 years (enabled by the Scotland Act 1998).

Table 11.1 *Divergence*

	England	Scotland	Spain
1970s	Retreat from welfarism ↓	Full-flowering welfarism ↓	Post Franco – penal-welfarism plus 'rights talk' ↓
1980s	Punishment and systems management ↓	↓	↓
Early mid 1990s	'The darkness'	↓	↓

were to be framed by the principles of early and minimal intervention, based on a social educational model of care (see McAra 2006 for a detailed overview). The children's hearing system remained largely unchanged during the 1970s and 1980s, a period in which there was a major *retreat* from welfarist principles in a range of other Western juvenile justice systems, including the system south of the border in England (see Crawford 2002).

A review of youth justice in England (conducted by the Ingleby and Longford committees respectively in late 1950s and early 1960s) had recommended a similar commitment to welfare principles as in Scotland, a commitment which was enshrined in the subsequent Children and Young Persons Act 1969. However, this Act was never fully implemented. Key welfare-based provisions were dropped, including mandatory care proceedings for the under-fourteens instead of prosecution and planned restrictions on magistrates powers to use custody (Newburn 1997). Indeed the 1970s saw a major *increase* in custody for young offenders in England and a shift in the balance of power within the system away from social work in favour of the judiciary (Cavadino and Dignan 2007).

During the 1980s a more complex set of values began to frame the English juvenile justice system. On the one hand, the punitive edge continued, in the wake of the election of the Thatcher government, with greater emphasis on the 'short, sharp, shock'. On the other hand, practitioners challenged these values from below, introducing a form of systems management, aimed at diverting youngsters out of the system, or minimising levels of intervention (Newburn 1997). However, systems management was largely abandoned in the early 1990s, with a further lurch towards greater punitiveness. In Table 11.1, this period has been designated 'the darkness' in tribute to Michael Howard, the then Home Secretary (famously described by Ann Widdecombe, a fellow Conservative MP, as 'having something of the night about him'). Howard's dictum that 'prison works' flowed into both adult and youth justice policy.

Turning more specifically to the adult criminal justice system, the shift from specialist probation to generic social work in Scotland, again heralded an enhanced commitment to welfarism. As with juvenile justice, social work criminal justice services remained largely unchanged during the 1970s and early 1980s, a period which saw the gradual erosion of social work values in other jurisdictions (including England, see McWilliams 1987). These services did, however, come under increased scrutiny during the mid to late 1980s; fuelled by concerns about effectiveness, tensions between central and local government over service funding and a growing prisons crisis linked to overcrowding, riots and industrial unrest (Wozniak 1994). The policy response to these concerns was the introduction of 100 per cent central government funding of certain specified social work criminal justice services (on implementation of the Law Reform Miscellaneous Provisions (Scotland) Act 1990) and the accompanying National Objectives and Standards (implemented from 1991). This policy introduced managerialism into social work for the first time as well as risk assessment. However, far from supplanting penal-welfarism, these developments were intended primarily to *facilitate* effective work with offenders (McAra 2005). The model of social work practice set out in the national standards was premised on the view that higher-risk offenders should be placed back into the community (rather than being dealt with in prison), precisely because reform and rehabilitation were more likely to be effected in a community-based setting. In contrast to England in the early 1990s, there was an acceptance that generally prison did *not* work (being useful only as a means of incapacitating the most dangerous offenders) and there was an explicit statement in the national standards document, that punitive measures were particularly ineffective in respect of young adult offenders (the key policy target group). Moreover, the impact of national standards implementation was to re-professionalise social work (McAra 2005), in contrast to policy developments south of the border which (over the same timeframe) were threatening to undermine the professionalism of the probation service, by removing the need for social-work training and encouraging recruitment from ex-army and ex-police officers (Nellis 1996).

(ii)   Spanish divergence

Although having a very different constitutional history from Scotland, Spain did share a similar commitment to penal-welfarism over the 1980s up to the mid 1990s. However, as indicated in Table 11.1 above, within Spain this was accompanied by a more explicit policy focus on the rights of the offender.

In the wake of the death of General Franco (1975), Spain made the transition from dictatorship to democracy. The Constitution of 1978 included provision for a constitutional monarchy and the disestablish-ment of the Catholic Church. It also set in train the process of devolu-tion to the autonomous communities (Basque and Catalan autonomy was implemented in 1980 but there are now seventeen such commu-nities).[4] In terms of penal-welfarism, the new Constitution abolished capital punishment and declared that rehabilitation should be the goal of custodial punishment (subsequently reinforced by the Penitentiary Act 1979 which was based on the premise that prisons had a duty to transform and re-educate individual offenders, Varona 2000). In a simi-lar vein, the Law of Social Dangerousness which formerly had criminal-ised homosexuality, political dissidence, homelessness and other special categories (including antisocial behaviour) was abolished (in 1978).

With regard to rights discourse, a key aim of the constitutional settlement was to shift away from the repressive authoritarian regimes of the past, through an emphasis on legality and proportionality. A key objective was to combat the highly discretionary nature of law enforce-ment during the Franco era (which lurched between extreme punitive-ness and mass pardonings, Barberet 2005), with a commitment to greater certainty in sentencing. Furthermore, the Constitution contained provisions which explicitly shifted the goals of policing away from public order to public safety.

The twin themes of welfarism and rights are evident within the variant penal codes which were enacted in the first two decades of the democ-racy. Indeed the Penal Code of the Democracy (1995) aimed to balance the need to re-socialise the offender with the principle of minimum intervention (Varona 2000). Similarly, the paternalistic and protectionist

---

[4] While criminal justice has always been a reserved matter, both the Basque country and Catalonia have their own police force.

model of juvenile justice, which the new democracy had inherited, underwent reform in the early 1990s. The aim was to balance the extant rehabilitative framework with a set of procedural guarantees, including the presumption of innocence, the right to legal representation and greater determinacy in sentencing (Guasch 1995).

In contrast to England, during the 1980s and 1990s (a period during which the Spanish Socialist Party was in power) crime control did not feature in mainstream political discourse (Varona 2000). The only exception was terrorism, linked to ETA and the campaign for Basque separatism. Importantly, the causes and consequences of terrorism were regarded as being completely distinct from normal street crime. The latter was principally attributed to social and economic factors (including unemployment, poverty and social inequalities) rather than moral blameworthiness (Barberet 2005; Medina-Ariza 2006). As a consequence, many of the major criminal justice reforms in the early years of the democracy (including the 1995 Penal Code as well as the Law for the Criminal Responsibility of Minors 2000) were developed behind closed doors by experts, with only limited public debate (Medina-Ariza 2006).

Convergent trajectories

The divergence exhibited in both Scotland and Spain from England diminished over the course of the mid to late 1990s, with greater commonalities between the jurisdictions evident by the early years of the new century (as summarised in Table 11.2).

(i)   Scottish convergent trends

Within Scotland from the mid to late 1990s onwards, core aspects of penal-welfarism were abandoned and a whole raft of new institutions and procedures were grafted onto the adult and juvenile justice systems (such as the national Criminal Justice Board, community safety partnerships and specialist drug and domestic violence courts). Whilst the roots of some of the changes can be traced to the period immediately prior to devolution, the pace of change has gathered momentum in the post-devolutionary era. Somewhat ironically the changes which were made, rather than reinforcing the distinctiveness of Scotland led to a degree of 'de-tartanisation' (McAra 2006: 142).

Convergence is exemplified by the exponential increase in managerialism in both England and Scotland: strategic planning, target setting,

Table 11.2 *Convergence*

	England	Scotland	Spain
Late 1990s–2000s		Politicisation	Politicisation
		New punitiveness	New punitiveness
		Moral panic over youth crime	Moral panics over immigration and domestic abuse
	Increased managerialism	Increased managerialism	Increased managerialism
	Risk management, effective practice	Risk management, effective practice	Risk management, effective practice
	Social inclusion elided with crime prevention, communities as stakeholders	Social inclusion elided with crime prevention, communities as stakeholders	Social inclusion elided with crime prevention, communities as stakeholders
	Individual rights and responsibilisation	Individual rights and responsibilisation	
	Restorative justice, victims as stakeholders	Restorative justice, victims as stakeholders	Restorative justice, victims as stakeholders

efficiency, effectiveness, monitoring and evaluating became key watch words in criminal justice. New forms of vertical and horizontal account-ability permeated each system premised on multi-agency working and the development of cross-institutional cultures.[5] As a corollary to this, public protection, risk management and effective, evidence-based prac-tice increasingly framed both adult and youth justice interventions. There was also a gradual elision between the social exclusion, crime prevention and criminal justice policy frameworks – with communities increasingly being seen as key stakeholders in criminal justice. Rights talk permeated each system, a process given particular momentum by the

---

[5] Examples include the introduction of: Multi-agency Public Protection Arrangements for serious sexual and violent offenders in both jurisdictions, the National Offender Manage-ment Service in England; and Community Justice Authorities in Scotland (see Cavadino and Dignan 2007; McAra 2008).

incorporation of the European Convention for Human Rights (ECHR) into domestic law. Furthermore both systems became equally in thrall to the promises held out by restorative justice (as exemplified by the mushrooming of victim offender mediation schemes, conferencing and police restorative cautioning initiatives), with victims also attaining stakeholder status (see Crawford and Burden 2005). Finally, a key policy aim in both jurisdictions was to reduce persistent offending and tackle antisocial behaviour and both jurisdictions legislated to enable the use of civil orders to tackle low-level crime and disorder (notably Anti-Social Behaviour Orders and parenting orders). Youth courts for sixteen- and seventeen-year-old offenders were also piloted in Scotland, with the Scottish government stoking up a moral panic about youth crime which ran counter to all published indicators (the latter of which showed that youth crime rates were either stable or falling) (McAra 2006).

These convergent themes led to a degree of tension within Scottish and English criminal justice policy. Some elements of the policy frame were underpinned by a desire to promote social inclusion, to reintegrate and to enhance citizenship (as exemplified by much of the community safety agenda); other elements by contrast were aimed at exclusion, dispersal and punishment (as exemplified by core aspects of the antisocial behaviour agenda). Indeed, at the launch of the youth court pilots in 2003 the then Scottish Minister for Justice commented that 'punishment is a key part of the youth justice process' (Scottish Executive 2003), a statement that would have been unthinkable twenty years ago in Scotland.

(ii) Spanish convergent trends

The convergent trends outlined above, are also evident within Spain. Over the turn of the century, there was increased politicisation of street crime, and increased punitiveness within political discourse, both from the Conservative governments (1996–2004) and the Socialist government (2004 onwards), with a concomitant decline in the power and influence of expert groups.

As with Scotland, this new punitiveness has been accompanied by moral panic, such that concerns about public order are increasingly in conflict with the liberal guarantees enshrined in the Constitution. In the case of Spain key issues linked to the panic were immigration (Calavita 2003) and domestic violence (Barberet 2005).

In respect of immigration, Spain experienced a massive influx of immigrants over the mid to late 1990s and early 2000s, particularly from Latin America and Africa (mostly Morocco) (Miller *et al.* 2008).

Although there is limited evidence that immigrants were in practice
fuelling increases in crime, Medina-Ariza (2006: 196) cites figures
which show that the proportion of the population who believed that
there was such a link rose from 20 per cent in 1991 to 75 per cent by
2006. While ethnic minorities are now over-represented in the criminal
justice system (foreign nationals were estimated as being around 9 per
cent of the general population in 2006, but made up around 31 per
cent of those arrested: Miller *et al.* 2008), this has been attributed to
biases in criminal justice decision-making (rather than increased crime
levels). Research by Miller *et al.* (2008) found that police stops of
individuals simply because they looked like foreigners had become
accepted operational policy. Concerns about the links between immigration, crime and terrorism also resulted in a project (in 2001) to
place advanced military surveillance technology along 900 km of Anda-
lusian coastline (the so-called 'Wall of Aznar', named after the then
prime minister).

In respect of domestic violence, a moral panic was given initial
momentum in 1997 by the case of Ana Orantes who was tied to a chair
and burned alive by her husband after appearing on a television show in
which she talked about her forty-year history of abuse (see Barberet
2005). Crime statistics showed that in the late 1990s there was a major
rise in gendered violence. Although much of this rise can be attributed to
legal changes subsequent to the Orantes case, which served to encourage
the reporting of domestic violence, the crime rise was utilised by political
parties (most notably the Conservatives) to create what Medina-Ariza
has termed (2006: 195) an 'emotional context' for greater punitiveness in
policy discourse.

Punitiveness was also reflected in the reforms made to the penal code
in the mid to late 1990s and early 2000s, with concerns about public
order and security increasingly trumping formerly progressive and
democratic impulsions. For example, in 1996 remission from prison
was abolished and minimum sentences for property offences were introduced (see Cid and Larrauri 1998). In 2003, criminal code reforms
included a commitment to *truth in sentencing*, stronger penalties for
recidivism akin to the US three-strikes policy and restrictions to the
granting of parole (Barberet 2005). Moreover in 2003 and 2004, reforms
were made to community service which both increased the length of
orders and stressed their 'punitive credentials' (Blay 2008: 246). Importantly Blay (2008) has tracked the ways in which the nothing-works
discourse has installed itself within Spain, and hampered efforts to

develop community sentences more generally as credible alternatives to custody.

As with Scotland and England, there has also been an increased focus on victims within Spain and a mushrooming of restorative justice at local levels particularly in juvenile justice (Alberola and Molina 2003). For example, the Juvenile Criminal Act 2000 was strongly oriented towards victims, with s. 2 of the Act containing an explicit statement that restorative justice should be a main objective of youth justice. Again as with Scotland and England, the language of new public management has seeped into the system, with politicians promising a speedier and more efficient penal system (see especially Varona 2000). Similarly commitments were made to enhance community participation in crime prevention initiatives, with communities again attaining stakeholder status.

Taken together, the convergent trends outlined above suggest that Spanish crime control, and penal practice too, is framed by a conflicted policy framework, beset by tension between inclusionary and exclusionary impulses.

Part 2: Accounts of transformation and their limitations

Having set out the parameters of the case study, the chapter now turns to accounts of institutional transformation and their limitations. I will argue that two paradigms have come to dominate scholarship within the sociology of punishment, neither of which adequately captures the variant trajectories demonstrated by the case study. For the purposes of this chapter, I have termed these the 'structurist' and 'culturist' paradigms.

The 'structurist' paradigm

One set of commentators – including Garland (1996; 2001), Lacey (2008), Feeley and Simon (1992) – claim that the more punitive, actuarial and managerialist impulses that are evident in Western criminal justice penal systems have occurred primarily in response to the social, economic and political processes associated with late modernity. Key drivers of change include: (i) the emergence of the so-called 'risk society' in which fear has become a primary mechanism in the promotion of social solidarity (Beck 1992); (ii) a crisis of governance and state sovereignty provoked by the forces of globalisation, increasing pressures to develop international networks for the control and prosecution of crime, and the pernicious consequences of macro-economic transformation (with rising numbers of, what Sparks (1997) has termed, 'structurally redundant populations'); and (iii) persistently high crime rates, deep social divisions and increased opportunities for crime which have become endemic features of advanced liberal societies (Garland 2001).

Importantly not all structurist accounts accord equal weight to these drivers of change. For example, in her recent book, Lacey (2008) argues that political economy should be the *focal* point of analysis. According to Lacey (see this volume), neoliberal market economies with first-past-the-post electoral systems (e.g. UK and USA) provide a context favourable to more punitive and exclusionary penal policies; by contrast co-ordinated market economies with electoral systems based on proportional representation (e.g. Germany) provide a structural context within which more inclusionary and welfarist policies can flourish.

These variations notwithstanding, a key characteristic of all work within the structurist paradigm lies in its functionalist account of penality, one in which macro-level (top-down) processes beyond the criminal justice and penal system shape its institutional infrastructure and internal dynamics.

My case study poses a conundrum for the structurist paradigm principally because the criminal justice and penal systems in Scotland and Spain remained wedded to penal-welfare values for around two decades in the face of the *same* macro socio-economic transformations which it is claimed prompted change elsewhere and only recently appear to be shifting in their trajectory. Scotland, in common with other Western societies (including England), underwent major structural changes over the last decades of the twentieth century. Subject to the aggressive neoliberal market policies of the UK Thatcher and Major governments during the 1980s and early 1990s, there was a massive decline in traditional heavy industries such as steel-making and mining and an increase in service industries and more insecure and de-skilled forms of labour. While there was some major inward investment from multinational enterprise (particularly in respect of information technology), this sector of the economy became increasingly fragile in the wake of uncertainties in the market and global recession (and indeed has now collapsed). This was accompanied by increased social polarisation, with the top income earners becoming richer and those at the lower end of the social spectrum becoming even poorer. Research indicates that the number of people living in poverty has increased dramatically in recent years. At the turn of the twenty-first century, one-fifth of households with adults of working age had no one in work and around one-third of children lived in low-income households. Moreover, lone parents were disproportionately represented amongst those who faced poverty, reflecting a growth in divorce and separation rates as well as a more general disembedding of social relationships away from intermediate groups (McAra 2005). Despite these broader structural pressures, however, Scotland clung on to its penal-welfarist framework until at least the mid 1990s.

Spain too was buffeted by the vagaries of market forces over the 1980s and early 1990s and yet retained its commitment to penal-welfarism. Importantly, Spain underwent a relatively late and rapid transformation from an agricultural to an industrial and service economy (with a massive increase in industrialisation in the wake of the death of Franco). From round 1975 to the mid 1980s, however, unemployment rocketed (from 3 per cent of the workforce in early 1970s to 21 per cent by 1985–6) and there was a major increase in inflation during the very early post-Franco years (standing at 24 per cent in 1977) (United Nations 2000). As in the UK, the Spanish government (ironically under the tutelage of the Socialists) pursued aggressive neoliberal policies between 1986 and 1996, including privatisation and deregulation, in an attempt to reform the labour market (Muñoz de Bustillo Llorente 2002). The international economic crisis in the 1980s brought home groups of workers who formerly had sought employment outside Spain (in both Europe and South America), leading to further increases in unemployment and an expanding pool of surplus labour (Muñoz de Bustillo Llorente 2002). Over the same timeframe, Spain too experienced a gradual disembedding of social relationships (although it should be noted that this started from a much lower baseline and continued at a far lower level than most other Northern and Central European countries (Kiernan 2001)). For example, there were increases in the number of single-parent families, with a high proportion of divorced and widowed women living in poverty (Kiernan 2001). In 1984, there were 8 million poor (living on less than 50 per cent of the income mean), which included a high proportion of socially excluded young people (Arriba and Moreno 2002).

Given these macro-level transformative processes, adherents of the structurist paradigm would predict that both Scotland and Spain should have adopted a more punitive and exclusionary set of penal policies at least twenty years before they did. No explanation is proffered as to why the impact of such processes might be lagged and/or resisted.

The 'culturist' paradigm

A second dominant paradigm within the sociology of punishment privileges culture over structure and offers a bottom-up approach to the analysis of penal change (Armstrong and McAra 2006). Here, I use the work of Dario Melossi (2001) as a key exemplar. Melossi has criticised the structurist approach, arguing that theories linking penal change to factors such as economic development or social stratification can only account for diachronic variation internal to a particular society and not cross-cultural variation (or indeed cross-cultural similarity) at any point in time and space. This is because criminal justice and punishment are so deeply enmeshed in the national and cultural specificity of the locale within which they are produced. His 2001 article is based on a comparison between the USA and Italy, and argues that the variations in penal practice between these jurisdictions can be accounted for by their distinctive religious traditions: the more punitive culture in the USA stemming from Protestantism, the more merciful penal culture in Italy stemming from Catholicism. Although valorising culture, Melossi's reading of penality is also highly functionalist in orientation, with extra-systemic impulsions shaping the nature and operation of criminal justice institutions and penal practice.

Again the jurisdictions in my case study pose a conundrum for this account. If punishment is so culturally embedded in the manner suggested by Melossi, then why did the system in Scotland shed its Scottish identity at the very time when the extant political structures (the devolved settlement) ought to have nurtured all things Scottish? And why too the belated politicisation of crime in Spain, where a defining characteristic of Spanish democratic nationhood was the shedding of its older repressive/punitive baggage? Spain is also a predominantly Catholic country and in Melossi's terms, should have a more merciful penal culture. Although there is now religious freedom within Spain, a very high proportion of the population remain Catholic and the Church continues to have high status as a cultural lodestone as well as having a significant role in the provision of social services and support at local levels. Given such continuities, adherents of the culturist paradigm would anticipate that Spain should remain committed to welfarism, rather than embracing the more punitive and exclusionary set of values which leeched into policy in the early years of the new century.

Core limitations

Although the structurist and culturist paradigms give primacy to very different factors in their analysis of penality, they share a number of characteristics (in addition to their functionalist orientation). It is these very characteristics which, I would suggest, limit their capacity to explain the variant trajectories within my case study.

First, the nation state is the principal actor and primary unit of analysis in both paradigms. As a consequence, substate dynamics are largely overlooked, in particular the potential for the myriad forms of governance below the nation state to shape more localised responses to crime and punishment. This is of key importance when researching jurisdictions which have strong regional forms of governance such as Spain and the UK more generally.

A second commonality is that each paradigm paints a very passive picture of crime control and penal institutions. There is a tendency to analyse institutions as if they were empty boxes. In reality, however, criminal justice and penal institutions are inhabited by a range of competing actors through which external impulsions for change are mediated.

Finally both paradigms play down the complexity of the pressures to which criminal justice and penal systems are subject. The structural and cultural factors identified in each paradigm for the most part contain competing impulsions which may work against each other in complex ways and have differential rather than uniform effects.

As I aim to demonstrate in the following sections of the chapter, the above limitations can be addressed by adopting an alternative vocabulary for analysing penality, one linked to a systems analytical framework.

Part 3: Towards an alternative methodological strategy

Although there have been few attempts to theorise systematicity in the penal realm, there is a much broader tradition of 'systems theory' within both social science and legal philosophy. Although this tradition itself encompasses a variety of competing models of systemic functioning,[6] at a more abstract level it is possible to discern a number of core features of systems which inhere in all accounts, namely boundary mechanisms,

---

[6] This ranges from the structure-functionalist approach of Parsons (1951) to autopoietic accounts of systems found in the work of Luhmann (1986).

internal linkage mechanisms, and mechanisms for systemic reproduction. It is these particular features which provide a useful starting point for understanding the dynamics of my case-study jurisdictions.

All systems require a boundary to enable their status *qua* system to be recognised from an internal and external point of view. Such boundaries may take a variety of forms including a legal framework, a physical or environmental location, and/or modes of cognition which undergird perceptions of systematicity (see respectively King and Trowell 1992; Parsons 1951; Hejl 1984). Importantly in variant forms of systems theory, boundaries are conceptualised as either open (rendering the system subject to the influence of external processes) or closed (rendering the system distinct from, and impermeable to, environmental pressure).

Social and legal systems also require mechanisms which hold together the internal elements of the system. One such mechanism is a conceptual vocabulary shared between different elements of the system: a network of meanings to which each aspect of the system adheres (Canaris 1969). Linkage may also be provided by function, with systemic connections being sustained by the aims and purposes of the individuals and institutions inhabiting the system or by what Merton (1968) has termed the 'manifest function' of the system.

According to most exponents of systems theory, social and/or legal systems are dynamic rather than static in nature, a core feature being a mechanism for systemic reproduction. From an internal point of view, shared vocabularies may be an important way in which a system is able to retain a degree of dynamism and, reproductive potential. This is a particular feature of autopoietic theory which claims that systems become self-reflexive and self-perpetuating, reproducing themselves and achieving some form of dynamic equilibrium by constantly reconstructing the social world within their own terms (see Luhmann 1986).

From an external point of view, both the overt and also latent functioning of a system may be linked to its reproductive capabilities. This is a particular feature of structure-functionalist theories, whereby the function of a system is over-determined by broader cultural or social processes. Systemic dynamism is, thereby, provided by external stimuli, with the very survival of the system resting on its ability to adapt to environmental pressure (achieving dynamic equilibrium either through modifying or completely altering its internal modes of operation).

Taken together, the features described above suggest that the key to understanding the characteristics and evolution of a particular system lies in the relationships that exist between the elements which constitute its physical and conceptual architecture and between the system as a whole and the environment within which it is located. As such, a systems analytical framework cuts across the structural/cultural dualism which has beset the sociology of punishment and can be used to provide a fresh take on the nature and development of penal forms.

Part 4:   Rereading the case study

The final section of the chapter now turns to a re-analysis of the case-study jurisdictions, viewed through the lens of systematicity.

Taken as a whole, the divergent and convergent phases within my case study suggest that criminal justice and penal systems are rather like fragile ecosystems inhabiting a multi-level and increasingly complex environment. The environment contains competing pressures which stem from a range of supra-state and substate dynamics to which systems require to react. The permeability of system boundaries means that intra-systemic vocabularies and modes of working (internal linkages) are constantly adjusting to such environmental turbulence in ways which render systems both coherent and viable (the search for dynamic equilibrium), but also in ways which accord with the interests of key intra-systemic actors. Crucially, dynamic equilibrium is achieved where there is cultural anchorage, namely commonality or accommodation between intra- and extra-systemic cultures. Strain between such cultures, by contrast, produces a critical juncture presaging penal transformation.

Divergent trajectories

As indicated in Table 11.3, during the period of divergence each of the case-study jurisdictions was subject to a complex range of environmental pressures. While there were similarities in respect of macro socio-economic transformation (as set out in Part 2 above), the key difference between England and the dyad of Scotland and Spain lay in the nature of civic culture. Within England, environmental processes worked in tandem to produce overwhelming pressure for criminal justice and penal transformation; by contrast, in Scotland and Spain environmental pressures were conflicted, with the civic cultural context providing sufficient anchorage for continuities in the penal-welfare frame.

Table 11.3 *Rereading divergence*

England	Scotland	Spain
Environment	*Environment*	*Environment*
Macro-economic and social transformation	Macro-economic and social transformation	Macro-economic and social transformation
Increased political polarisation	Increased political tension (constitutional crisis)	Political capacity building, constructing a democratic polity (crime control not used to mobilise communities)
Civic culture (rightwards movement)	Civic culture (welfarist, Scottish identity as 'other-to-England')	Civic culture (welfarist and paternalistic, dual local/national identities but nurtured as 'other-to Franco-ism')
Internal culture	*Internal culture*	*Internal culture*
Policy networks increased fragmentation (power struggle)	Policy networks strong coherence	Policy elites increased coherence
Punitive (top-down and wins through)	Penal-welfare values	Penal-welfare values and rights
Systems management plus residual welfarism (bottom-up and loses out)		

(i)   England

England over the period of divergence experienced what Hall (1979) has termed the 'great moving right show'. Structural pressures linked to late modernity led to a breakdown in the post war consensus on issues such as welfare, the economy and crime. This resulted in a major political realignment in England, with skilled working-class voters shifting allegiance from predominantly traditional Labour Party politics to new conservatism and a rightwards drift for members of the middle classes who became increasingly disenchanted with high taxes, stop/start economic policy, and the 'undeserving' beneficiaries of the welfare state. Clear blue water emerged between the major political parties within the UK as the Conservative Party (elected to office in 1979) abandoned its traditional one-nation, paternalistic ethos, with a firm commitment to neoliberal economic policy. As a consequence 'authoritarian populism' began to dominate at both a civic and political level, becoming a source of both identity and pride for certain key groups (see Hall *et al.* 1978).

Importantly, within England macro socio-economic and civic cultural pressures became mutually constitutive, providing a turbulent environment for criminal justice and penal institutions, one in which extant penal-welfare values rapidly lost cultural anchorage. The strain that developed between extra- and intra-systemic cultures shattered the unity of the system leading to increased competition between key actors (McAra 2005). McWilliams (1987), for example, has charted the ways in which struggles for domination took place within the probation service between an older cadre of practitioners clinging on to welfarist traditions and a new managerialist generation, with the latter winning through. Similarly within juvenile justice, the systems-management approach which had evolved in the 1980s (although contributing to a major reduction in youth custody: Newburn 1997), could not be sustained. In the wake of all this turbulence (by the early 1990s) a new more punitive dynamic equilibrium was reached.

(ii)   Scotland

Turning to Scottish developments, in the period prior to devolution, one of the reasons why the criminal justice and penal system north of the border was able to sustain a commitment to welfarism was because of the distinctive nature of Scottish civic and political culture, with its greater emphasis on communitarian values, public provision of welfare and mutual support (see Brown *et al.* 1996; McAra 2005).

Historically, Scotland has enjoyed a more democratic tradition within key civic institutions such as education and the Scottish Presbyterian Church, as well as a long-standing, increasingly powerful socialist tradition, particularly at local government level (Curtis *et al.* 2002). Despite being subject to the same social and economic transformations as England, there was no major political realignment, with skilled working-class voters and the middle classes in Scotland continuing to support left-of-centre or nationalist parties (see Brown *et al.* 1996). Indeed, during the 1980s and early 1990s, the strident right-wing

ideologies of the Thatcher and Major governments at Westminster
became increasingly out of kilter with these values. The disjuncture that
developed between Scottish and Westminster politics threw the
distinctiveness of Scottish cultural identity into sharper relief and contributed to a growing constitutional crisis, with an increasing clamour for
home rule.

Unlike England, macro socio-economic and civic cultural pressures
within Scotland were in *conflict* rather than self-reinforcing, and it is the
very continuities in civic culture which provided an environmental locus
in which penal-welfare values could be sustained. The criminal justice
and penal system therefore retained cultural anchorage. Of key significance was the manner in which elite policy networks (comprising
civil servants, directors of social work, the judiciary, crown office and
key academics) were able to shape a field of expertise on crime and
punishment and connect it meaningfully to mainstream discourse on
Scottishness; and part of that Scottish identity was based on being
'other-to-England' (McAra 2008).

(iii)   Spain

As with Scotland, the Spanish criminal justice and penal system was
subject to conflicted and competing environmental pressures in the
1980s and early 1990s, with the macro socio-economic impulsions
associated with late modernity running alongside civic cultural dynamics more conducive to welfarist penal policy.

In the Franco era, Spanish civic culture was characterised by social
networking, patronage and clientelism (Arriba and Moreno 2002). The
early decades of the post-Franco period saw efforts made at both the
national and substate levels (namely the autonomous communities) to
build more democratic political and civic identities based on inclusion,
mutual support and equitable treatment (Martinez-Herrera 2002; Giordano and Roller 2004). As noted earlier, the Catholic Church was an
important source of continuity at grass-roots level in the context of the
emergent and embryonic civic institutions of the new democracy.

This cultural context provided anchorage for a reborn criminal justice
and penal system which advocated welfarism over punitiveness, and
valorised rights and greater certainty of treatment over repression and
inconsistency. As with Scotland, policy elites controlled knowledge production, such that debate over crime and justice was de-politicised. It
was in these ways that Spanish criminal justice and penal system attained
a degree of dynamic equilibrium during the 1980s and early 1990s.

Convergent trajectories

In respect of convergent trajectories, these occurred in the context of a marked ratcheting-up of environmental pressures as the full impact of globalisation (flows of capital, information and people) and other macro socio-economic trends were felt in each jurisdiction. This included the fall-out from events such as the terrorist atrocities in the USA (9/11), Madrid (3/11), London (7/7) and Glasgow (7/7). Such pressures contributed to shifts in extant civic and political cultures. This, in turn, led to loss of cultural anchorage for welfarist criminal justice and penal institutions in both Scotland and Spain and the emergence of a more conflicted penal framework (as summarised in Table 11.4).

(i)   England

In England over the period of convergence, political polarisation diminished. The Labour Party underwent a process of modernisation, ditching its more radical left-wing elements and shifting to occupy the centre-right ground. The New Labour government of 1997 placed social inclusion, urban regeneration and social justice at the heart of its agenda at the same time as trying to win the support of floating voters with promises of rigorous economic management and being tough on crime. Blair's 'third way' did mark a significant shift from the crude individualism which had characterised previous Conservative administrations, whilst at the same attempting to transcend older-style social democracy. The aim was to enhance equal opportunity, mutual responsibility and empower citizens to act for themselves (see Giddens 1998). The effect of all of these changes was to eradicate the clear blue water between Labour and the Conservatives that was evident in earlier decades.

The promises of 1997, however, slowly turned into disillusionment and civic culture within England underwent a process of increased fragmentation. Major schisms arose over issues such as the war in Iraq; asylum seekers and terrorist suspects; and immigration and race relations. There were also debates over the nature of English identity and Britishness (Clarke 2008). All of this took place against the backdrop of moral panic. A range of political and criminological commentators have highlighted the ways in which there was a gradual convergence of moral panics resulting in an exclusionary continuum from the global to the local. Sparks (2006) in particular has highlighted the elision that occurred between popular and political discourse on low-level forms of disorder (such as vandalism, graffiti and other aspects of antisocial

Table 11.4 *Rereading convergence*

England	Scotland	Spain
Environment	*Environment*	*Environment*
Exponential growth in trans/supranational institutional forms and pressures	Exponential growth in trans/supranational institutional forms and pressures	Exponential growth in trans/supranational institutional forms and pressures
Full impact of globalisation	Full impact of globalisation	Full impact of globalisation
Cosmopolitanism	Cosmopolitanism	Cosmopolitanism
9/11, 7/7	9/11, 7/7	9/11, 3/11
Diminished political polarisation (the third way?)	Resolution of constitutional crisis (the devolved settlement)	Political polarisation
Civic culture (attempts to remobilise communities and embrace multi-culturalism: increased schisms?)	Civic culture (drift?)	Crime control key role in political capacity building for first time
The 'politics of fear'	Political capacity building in context of devolution	The politics of race
	The 'politics of fear'	The 'politics of fear' Strengthening regional identities
Internal culture	*Internal culture*	*Internal culture*
Policy networks: increased coherence?	Policy networks increased fragmentation and struggles for power	Policy networks diminished capacity
Hyper-institutionalisation	Hyper-institutionalisation	Punitive, managerialist, (top down)
Punitive, managerialist, restorative, preventative, rehabilitative	Punitive, managerialist, restorative and preventative (top-down and initially won through)	Restorative, preventative and penal-welfarism (bottom-up)
	Penal-welfare values (bottom-up and losing out)	

behaviour) and discourse on more spectacular terrorist atrocities, which resulted in an exponential increase in collective fears.

At the same time, supranational impulsions in the form of international conventions and transnational regulatory mechanisms began to imprint themselves on popular consciousness, in somewhat conflicted ways. On the one hand such impulsions introduced a degree of cosmopolitanism, in the form of rights discourse. On the other hand they led to the emergence of a set of transnational penal cultures and identities floating somewhere above the nation state, driven for the most part by exclusionary imperatives. Wacquant (2006: 100) has highlighted the ways in which the punitive treatment of migrant workers and non-white foreigners across the European Union, served to construct 'the trans-national personhood of Europeans': defining insider status through the process of 'othering'.

The context just described paved the way for a more complex and contradictory penal framework to gain anchorage within England; one in which inclusionary imperatives (linked to restoration, prevention and rehabilitation) jostled with more exclusionary and punitive imperatives, with the latter once more increasingly trumping the former (see Muncie and Goldson 2006; Moore 2008). The massive increase in institutional infrastructure over the turn of the century also led to a reconstruction of professional identity, as practitioners sought to negotiate their way through a more complex penal architecture.

(ii)   Scotland

In respect of Scotland, in the period immediately after devolution welfarist institutions found it increasingly difficult to achieve cultural anchorage. Arguably civic culture in Scotland went into a period of drift. Greater ideological congruence between the Labour–Liberal democratic coalition government in Scotland (which dominated until May 2007) and the Blairite New Labour government at Westminster diminished political tensions and weakened a sense of Scottish political identity based on 'other-to-England'. This in turn weakened the purchase of welfarism as the principal framework for debates on criminal justice, opening up a conceptual space for other, more visceral, penal discourses to leech in (McAra 2008).

A further compounding factor, which increased the *strain* between older penal cultures and their environmental locale, was the need for post-devolutionary institutions to build political capacity. Somewhat surprisingly, the new Parliament did not immediately enjoy a great deal of public support (a focal point of dissatisfaction being the spiralling costs of a controversial new Parliament building). As is well-documented (see Hall *et al.* 1978), weak governments often turn to crime control as a ready mechanism through which to whip up public support and to be seen to be in control. Efforts to build capacity were evident in the hyper-institutionalisation that characterised the first decade of devolution; the attempts to construct community solidarities principally via a crime control agenda; and in the harder-edged populist rhetoric which drove debates on crime and justice.

Practitioners and former policy elites attempted to resist many of the more exclusionary policies (especially the antisocial behaviour strategy). Their capacity to effect policy change was, however, undermined by the logic of managerialism which reinforced centralised political control over the system. It was also undermined by the new institutional infrastructure which served to reconstruct the role of policy networks at national level into one of advice and reformulated such networks at the local level as partnerships (by introducing a range of new and competing players such as local community representatives, victim support groups and representatives from education and health). As a consequence the grip of such networks over the strategic direction of policy has been loosened (McAra 2008: 494).

More broadly, Scotland too has felt the full force of globalisation and has mirrored the experience of England in respect of the politics of fear and the complex interplay between supra-state impulses and penal sensibilities. These have served to feed the more punitive turn in policy within Scotland and reinforce the post-devolutionary convergent trajectory.

(iii)   Spain

Turning finally to Spain, from the mid 1990s onwards there has been increased political polarisation and concerted efforts by successive national governments (both Conservative and Socialist) and the autonomous communities to use crime control as a mechanism to build political capacity.

As with England and Scotland, Spain has now experienced the full force of globalisation particularly in relation to migratory patterns. Spain's geographical location has given it a singular role as the guarantor of the southern border of 'Fortress Europe' (Varona 2000) which, as indicated in Parts 1 and 2, has played into more exclusionary discourses linking immigration with crime. Again as with Scotland, the politics of

THE IMPACT OF MULTI-LEVEL GOVERNANCE

fear (underpinned by moral panics and reinforced by the Madrid bomb-ings) has allowed more punitive imperatives to work their way into mainstream national political debate.

Against this backdrop penal-welfarism has gradually lost cultural anchorage at the national level, and, as noted in Part 2, there are tensions between elements of the new, more conflicted, policy framework and the rights guarantees enshrined in the Constitution. The role of elite policy networks is also in the process of transformation as professional know-ledge about offender management and intervention has been opened up to public debate and scrutiny, with a concomitant loss of power amongst these groups to shape the crime control agenda.

As a counterweight to transformations at the national level, however, crime control and youth justice initiatives are being increasingly used at the regional level as part of the drive to construct distinctive policy identities and carve out a broader sphere of influence. Barberet (2005) has tracked the ways in which policing, crime prevention and responding to needs of victims have become predominantly local responsibilities. Moreover, lacking a national probation service, much community-based offender work has become dependent on local social workers, psycholo-gists and lawyers, as well as the Catholic Church. Welfarist and more inclusionary penal values are thus becoming a small but important aspect of regional identity. As the power of the autonomous commu-nities continues to grow, so too penal-welfarism may continue to find anchorage in more localised cultures.

Conclusion

In this chapter I have argued that contemporary scholarship within the sociology of punishment is beset by a methodological dualism which limits its capacity to understand the impact of multi-level governance on crime control and penal practice. I have suggested that a vocabulary drawn from systems theory provides a more useful analytical framework with which to study divergent and convergent penal trends.

The case study of Scotland, Spain and England suggests that the environments which criminal justice and penal systems inhabit are complex and turbulent phenomena, containing a range of competing pressures often with differential rather than uniform effects. It also suggests that the sustainability of criminal justice and penal policy is dependent upon systems finding some form of cultural anchorage, with dynamic equilibrium being achieved where such anchorage exists. The case study further indicates that strain between intra- and extra-systemic cultures forms one of the preconditions for institutional transformation. Residual civic cultural support for penal-welfare values in Scotland and Spain meant that the macro socio-economic pressures which led to change elsewhere could be resisted. In the wake of transformations in the civic cultural environment itself in the late 1990s/2000s, such support diminished, leading to the fracturing and remaking of older networks and a more conflicted discursive framework.

Taken together the divergent and convergent trajectories of the case study jurisdictions indicate that criminal justice and penal systems are akin to fragile ecosystems which are functionally interdependent with the environment within which they are located. They also indicate that contemporary accounts of penality require greater critical awareness of the myriad of pressures to which systems are subject, both above and below the nation-state level, through the development of a multi-level systems theory of penality.

References

Alberola, C. and Molina, E. (2003) 'Juvenile justice in Spain', *Journal of Contemporary Criminal Justice*, 19(4), 384–412.

Armstrong, S. and McAra, L. (2006) 'Audience, borders, architecture: the contours of control' in S. Armstrong and L. McAra (eds.), *Perspectives on Punishment: The Contours of Control*, Oxford: Oxford University Press, pp. 1–30.

Arriba, A. and Moreno, L. (2002) '*Spain: poverty, social exclusion and "safety nets"*', *Unidad de Politicas Comparadas 02–10*, Research Directorate European Commission.

Barberet, R. (2005) 'Spain', *European Journal of Criminology*, 2(3), 341–68.

Beck, U. (1992) *Risk Society*, London: Sage.

Blay, E. (2008) 'Community work as a criminal sanction in Spain', *Probation Journal*, 55(3), 245–57.

Brown, A., McCrone, D. and Paterson, L. (eds.) (1996) *Politics and Society in Scotland*, Basingstoke: Macmillan.

Calavita, K. (2003) 'A reserve army of delinquents: the criminalisation and economic punishment of immigrants in Spain', *Punishment and Society*, 5(4), 399–413.

Canaris, C. (1969) *Systemdenkenund Systembegriff im der Jurisprudenz*, Berlin: Duncker and Humblot.

Cavadino, M. and Dignan, J. (2006) 'Penal policy and political economy', *Criminology and Criminal Justice*, 6(4): 435–56.

(2007) *The Penal System: An Introduction*, 4th edn, London: Sage.

Cid, J. and Larrauri, E. (1998) 'Prisons and alternatives to prison in Spain' in V. Ruggerio, N. South and I. Taylor (eds.), *The New European Criminology*, London: Routledge, pp. 146–55.

Clarke, J. (2008) 'Still policing the crisis?', *Crime, Media, Culture*, 4(1), 123–9.

Crawford, A. (2002) 'La réforme de la justice des mineurs en Angleterre et au Pays de Galles', *Déviance et Société*, 26(4), 387–402.

Crawford, A. and Burden, T. (2005) *Integrating Victims in Restorative Youth Justice*, Bristol: Policy Press.

Curtis, J., McCrone, D., Park, A. and Paterson, L. (2002) *New Scotland, New Society?: Are Social and Political Ties Fragmenting?*, Edinburgh: Polygon.

Feeley, M. and Simon, J. (1992) 'The new penology', *Criminology*, 39(4), 449–74.

Garland, D. (1996) 'The limits of the sovereign state: strategies of crime control in contemporary society', *British Journal of Criminology*, 36(4), 445–71.

—— (2001) *The Culture of Control*, Oxford: Oxford University Press.

Giddens, A. (1998) *The Third Way: The Renewal of Social Democracy*, Cambridge: Polity Press.

Giordano, B. and Roller, E. (2004) '"Té para todos"? (Tea for everyone) A comparison of the processes of devolution in Spain and the UK', *Environment and Planning*, 36(12), 2163–81.

Guasch, M. (1995) 'Juvenile justice in Spain. Catalonia: at the vanguard in social-educative intervention for young offenders', *British Journal Social Work*, 25, 499–511.

Hall, S. (1979) 'The great moving right show', *Marxism Today*, 23, 14–20.

Hall, S., Clarke, J., Critcher, C., Jefferson, T. and Roberts, B. (1978) *Policing the Crisis: Mugging, the State and Law and Order*, London: Macmillan.

Hejl, P. (1984) 'Towards a theory of social systems: self-organisation and self-maintenance, self-reference and syn-reference', H. Ulrich and G. Probst (eds.), *Self-Organisation and Management of Social Systems*, Berlin: Springer, pp. 60–78.

Kiernan, K. (2001) 'The rise of cohabitation and childbearing outside marriage in Western Europe', *International Journal of Law, Policy and the Family*, 15, 1–21.

King, M. and Trowell, J. (1992) *Children's Welfare and the Law: The Limits of Legal Intervention*, London: Sage.

Lacey, N. (2008) *The Prisoners' Dilemma: Political Economy and Punishment in Contemporary Democracies*, Cambridge: Cambridge University Press.

Luhmann, N. (1986) 'The autopoiesis of social systems' in F. Geyer, and J. van der Zouwen (eds.), *Sociocybernetic Paradoxes: Observation, Control and Evolution of Self-Steering Systems*, Beverly Hills, California: Sage, pp. 172–92.

McAra, L. (2005) 'Modelling penal transformation', *Punishment and Society*, 7(3), 277–302.

McAra, L. (2006) 'Welfare in crisis? Youth justice in Scotland' in J. Muncie and B. Goldson (eds.), *Comparative Youth Justice*, London: Sage, pp. 127–45.

(2008) 'Crime, criminal justice and criminology in Scotland', *European Journal of Criminology*, 5(4), 481–504.

McWilliams, W. (1987) 'Probation, pragmatism and policy', *Howard Journal*, 26, 257–74.

Martinez-Herrera, E. (2002) 'From nation-building to building identification with political communities. consequences of political decentralisation in Spain, the Basque country, Catalonia and Galicia, 1978–2001', *European Journal of Political Research*, 41(4), 421–53.

Medina-Ariza, J. (2006) 'Politics of crime in Spain', *Punishment and Society*, 8(2), 183–201.

Melossi, D. (2001) 'The cultural embeddedness of social control: reflections on the comparison of Italian and North-American cultures concerning punishment', *Theoretical Criminology*, 5, 403–25.

Merton, R. (1968) *Social Theory and Social Structure*, Toronto and Ontario: Collier-Macmillan.

Miller, J., Gounev, P., Pap, A., Wagman, D., Balogi, A., Bezlov, T., Simonovits, B. and Vargha, L. (2008) 'Racism and police stops', *European Journal of Criminology*, 5(2), 161–91.

Moore, S. (2008) 'Neighbourhood policing and the punitive community', *Crime Prevention and Community Safety*, 10, 190–202.

Muncie, J. and Goldson, B. (2006) 'England and Wales: the new correctionalism' in J. Muncie and B. Goldson (eds.), *Comparative Youth Justice*, London: Sage, pp. 34–47.

Muñoz de Bustillo Llorente, R. (2002) *Spain and the Neo-liberal Paradigm*, CEPA Working Paper, New York: Center for Economic Policy Analysis.

Nellis, M. (1996) 'Probation training: the links with social work' in T. May and A. Vass (eds.), *Working with Offenders, Issues, Contexts and Outcomes*. London: Sage, pp. 7–30.

Newburn, T. (1997) 'Youth, crime and justice' in M. Maguire, R. Morgan, R. Reiner (eds.), *The Oxford Handbook of Criminology*, 2nd edn, Oxford: Clarendon, pp. 613–60.

O'Malley, P. (1992) 'Risk, power and crime prevention', *Economy and Society*, 21(3), 252–75.

Parsons, T. (1951) *Social Systems*, London: Routledge and Kegan Paul.

Scottish Executive (2003) 'Scotland's first youth court opens', *Press Release*, www.scotland.gov.uk/pages/news.

Sparks, R. (1997) 'Recent social theory and the study of crime and punishment' in M. Maguire, R. Morgan and R. Reiner (eds.), *The Oxford Handbook of Criminology*, 2nd edn, Oxford: Clarendon, pp. 409–36.

(2006) 'Ordinary anxieties and states of emergency: statecraft and spectatorship in the new politics of insecurity' in S. Armstrong and L. McAra (eds.),

Perspectives on Punishment: The Contours of Control, Oxford: Oxford University Press, pp. 31–48.

United Nations (2000) *Human Development Reports 2000: Trends in Human Development and Per Capita Income*, http://hdr.undp.org/en/.

Varona, G. (2000) '"Spain is different": beyond an invisible criminal policy' in P. Green and A. Rutherford (eds.), *Criminal Policy in Transition*, Oxford: Hart Publishing, pp. 241–2.

Wacquant, L. (2006) 'Penalization, depoliticization, racialization: on the over-incarceration of immigrants' in S. Armstrong and L. McAra (eds.), *Perspectives on Punishment: The Contours of Control*, Oxford: Oxford University Press, pp. 83–100.

Wozniak, E. (1994) 'A customer focused prison service in Scotland' in A. Duff, S. Marshall, R. Dobash and R. Dobash (eds.), *Penal Theory and Practice: Tradition and Innovation in Criminal Justice*, Manchester: Manchester University Press, pp. 146–60.

12

Explaining Canada's imprisonment rate: the inadequacy of simple explanations

CHERYL MARIE WEBSTER AND ANTHONY N. DOOB

Introduction

Canada does not fit easily into the typology of political economies and their penal tendencies proposed by Cavadino and Dignan (2006a; 2006b). Based on a study of penal systems in twelve contemporary capitalist countries (not including Canada), these scholars demonstrate a relationship between a nation's political economy on the one hand and the punitiveness of its penal culture (particularly as expressed by its rate of imprisonment) on the other hand. Indeed, they suggest that certain political regimes (e.g. neoliberalism, conservative corporatism, etc.) have distinct penal landscapes (i.e. more or less punitive penal policies).

In terms of penal policies, most observers would probably assume that Canada would fit neatly within those nations described as having political economies and penal tendencies that could be categorised as neoliberal. This placement would certainly seem obvious given geographic, economic and cultural proximity to the country highlighted by Cavadino and Dignan as the 'archetypical example' of this group (USA). In addition, it would seem natural that Canada would be grouped with the 'other examples' of the neoliberal political economy listed by these scholars – England and Wales, Australia, New Zealand and South Africa – given their historical (e.g. as members of the Commonwealth) and institutional (similar legal systems) ties.

The most obvious problem with this categorisation of Canada is that in 2008 – when this paper was written – its imprisonment rate (of 112 per 100,000 in the general population) would place it more closely among the countries described by Cavadino and Dignan as 'conservative corporatist' in their political economies and penal tendencies rather than those of a neoliberal persuasion. More important, perhaps, is the fact that the Canadian imprisonment rate – unlike that of the USA or England and Wales – has been relatively stable for the past half-century.

There are at least two possible explanations for Canada's anomalous status. First is the possibility that Canada – as a country – has greater similarities to those countries classified as part of a conservative corporatist political economy (e.g. Italy, Germany, France and the Netherlands) than it does to those categorised as neoliberal (e.g. Australia, New Zealand, England and Wales and the United States). Having said this, we would argue that the multidimensional affinities – particularly among Canada, the USA and England and Wales – of a historical, cultural, economic, geographic and institutional nature preclude the likelihood of this hypothesis. The second explanation is that because of specific characteristics of the country itself, Canada either is an exception to this typology or has overcome neoliberal tendencies in the area of their impact on penal policies.

This chapter explores this latter hypothesis. To this end, we begin by describing the trends in Canadian imprisonment rates, highlighting their problematic nature in terms of Cavadino and Dignan's description of a neoliberal regime. These patterns of incarceration are subsequently considered in light of Canada's long history of resistance to punitive forces that have impacted on imprisonment rates elsewhere. This discussion highlights several factors which may be contributing to Canada's stable imprisonment rates, undermining the singular nature of Cavadino and Dignan's model for understanding penal policy.

We conclude with an examination of a number of recent changes in the political use of penal policy in Canada's federal Parliament. These shifts corroborate the notion that there may be forces – beyond those described by Cavadino and Dignan – that have been important in shaping Canada's penal response to crime. Specifically, while Canada has clearly not been immune to wider (neoliberal) pressures leading to more punitive responses toward crime and offenders, it has been able to largely limit or resist them.

Trends in Canadian imprisonment rates

One of the least discussed aspects of the Canadian criminal justice system is the fact that imprisonment rates in Canada have been relatively stable for at least the past fifty years. Although counts, and sometimes rates, of people in Canada's prisons are regularly published, our guess is that most Canadians – including many criminologists – would assume that levels of incarceration in Canada have followed those of the United States, albeit in a less dramatic way. Obviously the cultural and economic similarities as well as the geographic proximity of Canada and the USA would encourage this view of shared 'harsh criminal justice policies' – policies leading to high imprisonment rates and other punitive outcomes. However, the reality is quite different.

In the mid 1970s, Al Blumstein and his colleagues (Blumstein and Cohen 1973; Blumstein, *et al.* 1976) attempted to explain why it was that certain countries – including the United States and Canada – had apparently experienced stability in their levels of imprisonment over a number of decades. The titles of their two papers – 'A theory of the stability of punishment' and 'The dynamics of a homeostatic punishment process' – are instructive in the context of recent concern about rising imprisonment rates. Relatively stable imprisonment rates in the United States, Norway and Canada were pictured, and it appeared to be assumed that stability over time would be the rule. Stability was explained in a manner that had little to do with the nature of the country being described.

Ironically though, these papers can be seen as marking the beginning of a period of unprecedented growth in imprisonment rates in the United States. Few would blame Blumstein and his colleagues for bringing about the end of a period of *relative* moderation in American imprisonment rates. However, their 1970s description of Canada (Doob and Webster 2006; Webster and Doob 2007) and Norway (Pratt 2008a: 133, Figure 1; Lappi-Seppälä 2007) would appear to be reasonably good even today. In Figure 12.1, we have presented Canadian imprisonment rates for most of the past half-century.

Looking at the top curve – total imprisonment – we see that despite some variation across time, there is no obvious overall trend. However, rates are *not* stable. It could legitimately be stated that between 1974 and 1994 the rate increased by about 40 per cent (from 83 in 1974 to 116 in 1994). Had we been writing this paper in 1994 rather than in 2009, we might have been confident that Canada fit into the list of countries described by Cavadino and Dignan as having neoliberal regimes and, consequently, (relatively) high imprisonment rates. However, a broader perspective arguably undermines this classification.

Understanding Canadian stability in imprisonment

To understand another aspect of Canadian imprisonment policy, one needs to comprehend the other two lines in Figure 12.1. Canada's

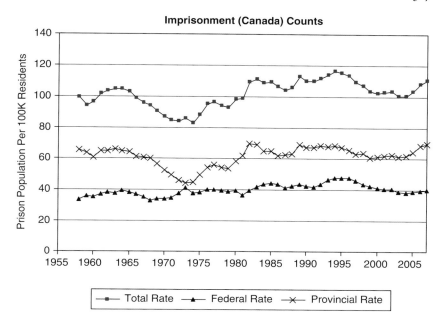

Figure 12.1 Federal and provincial imprisonment rates (counts per 100,000 residents) 1958–2007.

imprisonment rate consists of two separate types of imprisonment. Offenders sentenced to two years or more are sent to federally operated penitentiaries. Release decisions concerning these offenders are made by a parole board consisting of people appointed by the federal government. Further, these inmates – when released – are supervised by federally employed parole officers.

In contrast, those sentenced to less than two years are housed in provincially operated prisons. Decisions about release are made by provincially appointed parole boards in some provinces, although the majority of provinces delegate this responsibility to the National Parole Board. In addition, the provincial prisons include prisoners who are not serving a sentence – largely those who are awaiting trial. Notably, provincial prisons are paid for by provincial governments, not by the federal government.

For criminologists, one of the few advantages of this 'split' jurisdiction on imprisonment is that we can easily differentiate between the population of those serving relatively long sentences (the federal penitentiary population) and those serving relatively short sentences, or who are in prison without having been sentenced (the provincial prison population). For our current purposes, this federal–provincial distinction also calls attention to another relevant factor. Although Canada is a federal state (with ten provinces and three territories), criminal law is solely a federal responsibility. As such, the laws which are ultimately responsible for determining who is in prison and for how long are the responsibility of the federal government. However, the administration of justice – police, courts and part of corrections – is a provincial responsibility.

Within this context, most prosecutors are appointed by the provincial governments (although federally appointed prosecutors are responsible for the prosecution of drug and other federal offences not included in the Criminal Code). In addition, the judges who are appointed to the *provincial* courts are appointed by the provinces. The federally appointed superior court (and appeals court judges) deals with only a tiny portion of criminal cases (estimated to be approximately 1.5 per cent to 5 per cent, depending on the province). Although the overall criminal caseload of the superior court is largely made up of more serious cases, the vast majority of the most serious cases (e.g. serious violence), are dealt with in provincial courts (Webster and Doob 2003). This apparent contradiction is explained by a simple fact: most cases of *all* types are completed in provincial courts.

As we have argued elsewhere (Webster and Doob 2007), it is important to note that this constitutional structure is unlike that in England with its unitary criminal justice jurisdiction, nor is it similar to that in the United States with its fifty-one separate criminal justice jurisdictions. The Canadian provincial governments have no direct power to modify the criminal law despite the fact that they play the largest role in the administration of justice. This historical distinction is crucial in creating and maintaining a two-tiered political structure which distances the federal government (which has the power to increase punitiveness within criminal justice legislation) from not only provincial demands but also, to some extent, from demands of the general public.

Indeed, provincial governments have no legislative power over sentencing. Hence it is safe for provincial politicians to 'talk tough' about criminal law matters. They can achieve the political benefits of being 'tough on crime' knowing that the federal government will typically see them as simply deflecting responsibility for crime onto a higher level of government. Further, since all appeals court judges (the provincial appeals courts, and the Supreme Court of Canada) are appointed by the federal government, no structural mechanism is available for local (grass-roots) citizens' groups to have a direct influence in the creation of laws. In this way, 'public' pressure toward increased punitiveness can have no direct impact on imprisonment policies as has been the case in such US states as California (e.g. its introduction of three-strikes legislation; see Vitiello 1997).

Even when examining issues directly pertaining to specific citizens' groups or advocacy organisations, the Canadian government has generally limited the degree of influence of these bodies over criminal policy. Illustratively, Petrunik (2003: 59) notes that although both Canada and the USA established government-sponsored task forces on crime victims in the 1980s, the level of participation of victims' advocacy groups as well as the composition of these task forces were substantially different. In the USA, the President's Task Force on the Victims of Crime was composed largely of victims' advocates and representatives of the religious and ideological right. In striking contrast, federal and provincial bureaucrats made up the Canadian Federal–Provincial Task Force on Justice for Victims of Crime (Roach 1999: 281–3). Not surprisingly, the American Victims Task Force took a punitive, confrontational approach – undoubtedly spurred on by a well-developed populist victims' movement – while the Canadian task force focused largely on 'nuts and bolts' matters (Petrunik 2003: 59).

Of equal note, Canadian politics have consistently shown a broadly based disinclination by (federal or provincial) governments to support referenda on any subject (Lipset 1989). Hence, the issue of sentencing policies is left in the hands of the federal Parliament (which is typically responding to government initiatives crafted by career civil servants) and to federal governments through their appointment of judges of all appeals courts. In fact, Friedland (2004: 472) argues that the result of this latter arrangement is clearly one in which 'the judiciary has – perhaps with the federal government's tacit approval – become the dominant player in the development of the criminal justice system'.

Now we can return to Figure 12.1. Our point in this little excursion is that the overall growth in Canadian imprisonment between 1974 and 1994 was largely a growth in the kind of imprisonment paid for by the provinces. Provincial average prisoner counts increased during this 20-year period by 9,824 (from 9,987 to 19,811) or by 98 per cent and the provincial imprisonment rate (per 100,000 residents) increased by 51 per cent (from 45 to 68). In contrast, the number of prisoners being housed in federal penitentiaries only increased by 5,449 prisoners (from 8,499 to 13,948) or 64 per cent and the federal rate (per 100,000 residents) increased by 'only' 26 per cent (from 38 to 48).

In considering what happened in Canada, one should recall what was occurring in England and Wales and in the United States at this time. Prisons were said to 'work' in England and Wales in the early 1990s. In the United States after 1992, the Democratic president had successfully kept to the right of his right-wing critics on criminal justice policy. In contrast to this widespread support for the increased use of incarceration, the rise in provincial imprisonment in Canada was perceived as a serious problem. As is often the case in problem areas such as the one seen as emerging in the first half of the 1990s, the governments (federal, provincial and territorial) commissioned a joint report. The original report was released publicly in 1996. In a 1997 progress report, a *Historical Review* was provided which, in the context of imprisonment policies in other countries, is quite instructive:

> At the January 1995 meeting . . . [the justice] Ministers asked . . . [their] Deputy Ministers and Heads of Corrections . . . to identify options to deal effectively with growing prison populations. . . . [Their report was] presented to Ministers at their May, 1996 meeting. It reported that most jurisdictions were experiencing growing correctional populations and concern was expressed that this growth threatened to outstrip available capacity and resources during a time when government resources continued to decline. The paper provided an overview of federal, provincial and territorial activities, either planned or under way, that would assist in managing and countering the pressures of prison population growth. In addition, eleven recommendations were presented . . .

> The eleven recommendations . . . were endorsed by all . . . Ministers in May 1996, and a Progress Report . . . was requested in one year's time . . .

> In summary, the . . . [progress] report demonstrates the efforts that have been made by all jurisdictions, individually and in collaboration with various criminal justice partners, to achieve results. All of the eleven recommendations are being implemented by various jurisdictions. [*Correctional Population Growth: First Report on Progress*, February 1997, p. i]

In May 1996, the committee noted that certain 'objectives that are held in common . . . could be made explicit and endorsed', including the suggestion that 'Incarceration should in most cases be used only where public safety so requires, and we should seek alternatives to incarceration if safe and more effective community sanctions are available' (*Correctional Population Growth*, 1996: 7). Not surprisingly, their eleven recommendations included: 'De-incarcerate low-risk offenders', 'Increased use of restorative and mediation approaches' and 'Make more use of diversion programs and other alternative measures' (*Ibid.*: 8–9).

By quoting from these reports which were (then) publicly available, we are not suggesting that any – or all – of the various recommendations were effective and fully implemented or that what came from these deliberations was responsible for the reduction in Canada's rate of imprisonment in the latter years of the last century. Rather, we are suggesting that governments in Canada have attempted – at least until recently – to limit the growth of imprisonment. As such, these reports should be read as cultural indicators, not as prescriptions for operational policies. It should also be noted that the provincial governments were quite varied in terms of their political attitudes. For example, Ontario (Canada's most populous province) acquired a very hard line right-wing government in 1995. Despite this political orientation though, it apparently endorsed – in 1996 – a 'control imprisonment' policy. It seems that none of the provinces were enthusiastic about the rate of growth of imprisonment in their jurisdiction.

Indeed, high imprisonment has not been traditionally seen as a useful policy to pursue in Canada. For instance, a 1988 report of a House of Commons Committee chaired by a Conservative Member of Parliament (who subsequently, under a Liberal government, was hired as a civil servant and made responsible for sentencing policy) suggested not only that 'imprisonment should be used with restraint' (Daubney 1988: 54) but that 'greater use [should be made] of community alternatives to incarceration' (p. 6). In fact, it was concluded that the use of incarceration for non-violent offenders 'is clearly too expensive in both financial and social terms' (p. 49) and consequently '[e]xpensive prison resources should be reserved for the most serious cases' (p. 50).

A more highly cited instance of Conservative Canadians' scepticism about high imprisonment policies comes from another Conservative-dominated House of Commons Standing Committee. It noted in 1993 that '[i]f locking up those who violate the law contributed to safer societies, then the United States should be the safest country in the world. In fact, the United States affords a glaring example of the limited impact that criminal justice responses may have on crime' (Canada 1993: 2). Elsewhere (Doob and Webster 2006; Webster and Doob 2007), we have cited numerous government reports over the past forty years that have echoed this same theme, underlining the historically entrenched 'culture of restraint' in the use of imprisonment in Canada.

Canada within typologies of political economies and their penal tendencies

The problem with this Canadian context – we would argue – is that it appears to largely undermine Cavadino and Dignan's typology of 'regime types'. Indeed, we are uncertain which 'type' best categorises Canada. Although the typology suggested by these scholars (2006b: 15, Table 1.1) may be useful for the countries that were analysed as part of that particular exercise, it is possible that Canada is truly anomalous and that the forces shaping punishment policy in Canada are different from those shaping policy in the countries which they studied. Part of the problem, we would argue, is that certain dimensions are more difficult to analyse in a federal state in which the responsibility for criminal justice and other matters is split between levels of government.

An illustrative example resides in the difficulties rooted in the characterisation of Canada's political regime. At the federal level, there has been some variability in the party in power over the past fifty years. Looking at the period covered by Figure 12.1, political power continually flip-flopped between the two principal parties (Conservatives and Liberals) over this entire timeframe.[1] Notably though, imprisonment rates did not change dramatically over this same period. Indeed, the nature of the federal government has appeared to be – at least until recently – relatively independent of those penal policies impacting on levels of incarceration. In fact, our historically engrained 'culture of restraint' in the use of imprisonment has been supported by both principal political parties while in power.

The situation is only exacerbated when one considers the various political orientations of the provinces. For instance, Canada had a centrist Liberal government at the federal level during the time of the federal–provincial–territorial meetings to which we previously referred. However, several provinces had (very) conservative governments over the same period, most notably the most populous province (Ontario) and the wealthiest province (Alberta). Indeed, Ontario's Conservative government during the period 1995–2003 was generally seen (even by the government itself) as a hard-line 'tough' government on many dimensions (crime, education, welfare etc.). One of its more telling moves was to pass regulations banning welfare payments for life for anyone found guilty of fraud against the welfare system – a policy that

---

[1] Specifically, the Conservatives were in power from 1958 to 1963 as well as from 1984 until 1993. Further, they have been in power – as a minority government – since early 2006.

was quietly rescinded after the next provincial election by a Liberal government. Clearly if one were looking for stable characterisations of regimes, it would seem that Canada's largest province has been relatively unstable in the past twenty to twenty-five years, despite relative stability in its imprisonment rates.

Similar difficulties with the typology proposed by Cavadino and Dignan arise when one carefully considers their penal index of 'imprisonment rate'. Specifically, the term 'high imprisonment' as a descriptor of their 'neoliberal' regime types is obviously an issue of comparison. In Figure 12.2, we have plotted the imprisonment rates of the USA, Canada, and England and Wales. The question, of course, is whether the values and the trends for these three countries (or perhaps only for the USA and England and Wales) is the result of the same forces.

The data contained in Figure 12.2 – particularly those of the USA and England and Wales – have been examined numerous times by numerous people. However, by putting them in the same figure with the same scale,

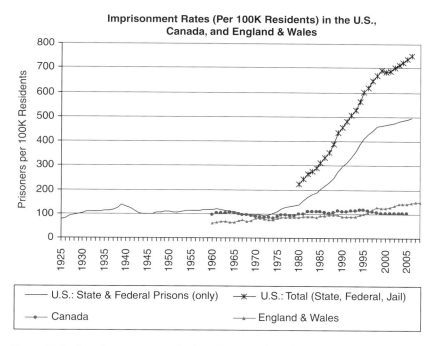

Figure 12.2   Imprisonment rates in the USA, Canada and England and Wales (per 100,000).

we wish to make two obvious points. First, American rates of imprisonment prior to the mid 1970s were – in terms of comparison with other Western countries – high, but not ridiculously high. We would estimate that if one were to have included short-sentenced prisoners and the remand population, the American rate would have been approximately 140–150 per 100,000 residents. Canada's rate was roughly 100 during the same time period.

Second, the two countries that look alike after approximately 1980 (when the American rate is allowed to distort the scale) are not – as Cavadino and Dignan's typology would suggest – the United States and England and Wales. While the pattern in England and Wales shows a substantial increase beginning in the mid 1990s which is absent from the trend in Canada, this graph clearly suggests that the two nations most alike are Canada and England and Wales. In fact, Frank Zimring (personal communication) has argued that to suggest that the growth of imprisonment in the United States is comparable to the growth in England and Wales is like comparing a beheading to a haircut.

Unfortunately, this difficulty with the application of Cavadino and Dignan's typology to Canada merely foreshadows the problematic nature of yet other dimensions that they used to classify nations. Most obviously, additional problems arise with the index 'receptiveness to prison privatization'. Specifically, Canada distanced itself from both the USA and England and Wales on this dimension. Further, it would also fit badly within those countries classified by Cavadino and Dignan as having political economies and penal tendencies described as conservative corporatist. In the first 'regime' typology, 'receptiveness to prison privatization' is 'high' and in the second typology it is moderate. In contrast to both of them, Canada no longer has – as far as we know – any private prisons for adults (although numerous youth facilities are operated by private not-for-profit agencies).

Even historically, the recourse to prison privatisation within Canada has not borne fruit. As an illustrative case study, the same right-wing government in Ontario as described earlier made one significant attempt to bring the private sector prison industry into Canada. Shortly after it took power in 1995, this Conservative government announced its intent to close many smaller correctional facilities in various parts of the province and replace them with two large (approximately 1,000 prisoners each) facilities in central Ontario. The argument was one of efficiency. The small facilities were seen as expensive and difficult to run. Centralisation was seen as the solution.

It was determined that one of these two facilities was to be run by the public sector while the other would be run by the winner of a competition among private companies. It was to be Canada's first privately operated prison. Ultimately important in this decision was that the province would build and own the physical facility. At the end of the first five years of operation of the two facilities an evaluation would take place (comparing the operation of the new privately run facility with its publicly run counterpart) to determine whether the management contract should be renewed.

By the time that the first five-year contract was coming to a close, the American company running the private facility was faced with a new (Liberal) provincial government (although it did not appear to be ideologically tied to any particular outcome). A review was ordered and detailed empirical studies comparing the two institutions were carried out. Based on the findings, the government decided – without fanfare – to return the operation of the facility to the public sector.

Similarly, the privatisation of federal prisoners has never progressed very far. A former commissioner of Correctional Service of Canada told one of us that this agency had been approached by the private sector prison companies during this commissioner's tenure as head. These companies wanted to determine whether the federal correctional service was interested in having privately run prisons. Correctional Service of Canada has, for decades, prided itself for its research-based approach to rehabilitative programmes. Consequently, the Commissioner told us that the private sector companies were informed that as soon as they were able to demonstrate that they could match the recidivism rates of Canada's penitentiaries, discussions could take place. We were told that this 'condition' generally closed off discussion.

As a final difficulty with the application of Cavadino and Dignan's typology to the Canadian context, we return to their index of 'imprisonment rate' as a measure of the punitiveness of a nation's penal culture. In addition to our prior concerns surrounding the common 'neoliberal' categorisation of the United States and England and Wales – despite the relative dissimilarity in their patterns of incarceration over the past several decades – we raise yet another. Potentially of a more methodological nature, we would argue that Canada's imprisonment rate, as a measure of a country's degree of punitiveness, may hide more than it reveals, rendering it a poor descriptor of the complexities of the Canadian penal landscape.

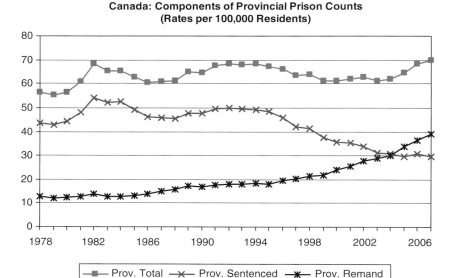

Figure 12.3   Provincial imprisonment rates (1978–2007).

As Figures 12.1 and 12.2 (above) clearly suggest, Canada's imprisonment pattern is relatively stable. However, the overall incarceration rates mask a number of significant changes in the nature of Canadian imprisonment. One of the most obvious shifts – and a concern in a number of provinces – is the growth in the pre-trial remand population over the past several decades. This increase is shown in the bottom line of Figure 12.3.

What is interesting about Figure 12.3 is that although the number of people being held in pre-trial detention rose dramatically in the period presented in this graph (going from 15 per 100,000 residents in 1987 to almost 40 per 100,000 in 2007), this increase was largely 'compensated' for by a decrease in the size of the sentenced population in provincial correctional institutions. Canadian judges are permitted by legislation to take into account the amount of time which an offender spent in pre-trial detention when determining the appropriate sentence. Given that they traditionally compensate for the difference between sentence length and time that they might expect an offender to actually serve in prison, it is not particularly surprising that the overall rate of imprisonment in provincial institutions did not change.

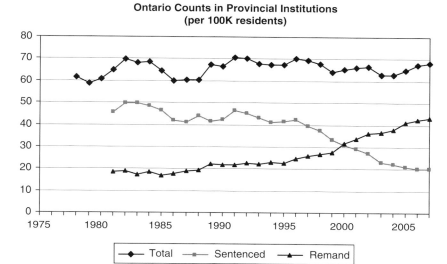

Figure 12.4   Ontario imprisonment rates (total,[2] sentenced and remand) per 100,000 residents (1978–2007).

However, the relative stability of levels of provincial imprisonment over the past fifty years hides a substantial shift in punitiveness vis-à-vis prisoners being held in pre-trial detention. Specifically, the growth in the remand population has created an important change in the legal status of a significant number of Canadian prisoners. In fact, there are currently more prisoners 'serving time' *before* rather than *after* being sentenced in the correctional institutions of some provinces. Figure 12.4 presents an example of this shift in legal status of the prisoners in Ontario. Clearly, the stability of the top line in Figure 12.4 hides a rather disturbing trend shown by the growth in the pre-trial remand population in this Canadian province.

Unfortunately, the problem with this measure of punitiveness is not limited to 'misleading' assumptions about consistency in the nature of imprisonment. Indeed, stability also implies 'sameness'. This second assumption would also prove wrong within Canada as a federal state. Specifically, an examination of the levels of incarceration across Canada's ten provinces and three territories quickly reveals enormous variability.

---

[2] The 'total' also includes a small number of 'other' inmates – typically those being held for immigration purposes. Hence the remand + sentenced is often very slightly less than the 'total'.

To understand provincial variation in imprisonment levels, one has to understand one of the large – and officially recognised[3] – problems of Canadian imprisonment policy. For various reasons, Canada's aboriginal people have a higher incarceration rate than that of non-aboriginal people. Because the Canadian territories have large aboriginal populations, their imprisonment rates are very high. The reasons for the high aboriginal incarceration rate are complex. It is almost certainly not a *simple* function of differential sentencing practices. For instance, rates of violence within the aboriginal community are high, as are recidivism rates. Further, alternatives to imprisonment appear to be structured in such a manner that aboriginal offenders are unlikely to be good candidates for certain non-custodial sentences. For these reasons – and because the territories are so different from the provinces – we will largely be discussing the variation across provinces.

The difficulty in this task is rooted in the fact that *overall* incarceration rates for the provinces and territories are not normally available. Indeed, the roughly 40 per cent of Canada's prisoners who are in (federal) penitentiaries are not normally described in terms of the province in which they were (last) sentenced. Given this limitation, examinations of inter-jurisdictional variation in imprisonment rates can be carried out in two different ways.

Most obviously, levels of imprisonment can be measured strictly at the provincial level. This approach was recently adopted by Tucker (2009). In her comparative study of inter-provincial incarceration rates (i.e. exclusively inmates in provincial institutions), she presented count and admissions data for each Canadian jurisdiction from 1978 to 2004. Overall, significant variability was found to exist across provinces. For either measure, five of Canada's provinces saw increases in their imprisonment rates across time while the five other provinces witnessed decreases over the same period. Notably, the five provinces showing increases/decreases were not always the same when one considered count versus admissions data.

Alternatively, levels of imprisonment can be described by an aggregate measure which includes both federal and provincial institutions. However, given the limitation of publicly available data (i.e. the absence of information relative to the province in which federal prisoners were

---

[3] E.g. the Criminal Code states that 'All available sanctions other than imprisonment that are reasonable in the circumstances should be considered for all offenders, *with particular attention to the circumstances of aboriginal offenders*' (s. 718.2(e), emphasis added).

sentenced), the only option of which we were aware was to use more detailed information to which we had unique access directly from Correctional Service Canada. While these data permitted an accurate description of all (federal and provincial) prisoners by jurisdiction, they were only available for two recent years: 1995 (see Sprott and Doob 1998)[4] and 2003.[5]

These data corroborated the same variation in imprisonment rates across Canadian provinces described by Tucker (2009). For instance, while Ontario and Quebec (the two largest provinces) each had imprisonment rates of 104 per 100,000 residents in 1995, Nova Scotia and Saskatchewan had rates of 156 and 212 (respectively). These findings suggest, once again, that the overall imprisonment rate of a federal state like Canada may not be a good descriptor of internal levels of punitiveness.

We also examined the correlation of imprisonment rates between the two temporal data points for each of the jurisdictions under study. A fair amount of stability was found across the ten provinces between 1995 and 2003. Notably, the correlation between the overall provincial rates for these two years was strongly positive ($r = +0.77$), suggesting that provinces with high incarceration rates in 1995 continued to have high levels in 2003 and those with low rates of imprisonment in 1995 also tended to be low in 2003.

Given that provincial institutions only house remand prisoners and sentenced prisoners who have received sentences of less than two years, this correlation cannot be simply attributed to the same people being in prison over this eight-year period. Rather, it reflects forces leading to stability within the criminal justice systems of each province. Indeed, it would seem that while Canada – as a whole – has huge variation across its provinces in its use of imprisonment, this variability appears to be stable over time within each jurisdiction.

The obvious caveat to this conclusion is the relatively short time period (eight years) under analysis. Having said this, it is notable that

---

[4] Sprott and Doob (1998) reported only *sentenced* imprisonment at the provincial level. Since the current paper deals with *overall* rates of imprisonment, we have used overall figures when calculating the provincial rate of imprisonment.

[5] For a number of inmates (733 of 12,927 in 2003 and 2,053 of 14,274 in 1995), the province of sentencing was not available. As such, these cases were allocated proportionally to those whose province of sentencing was known. We obviously do not know whether this decision is appropriate. However, we could not determine any other available course of action. We wish to thank Correctional Service of Canada, and in particular, Roger Boe, for making these data available to us.

this 'Canadian stability' finds its parallel in the United States. Specifically, we also examined the stability of *state prison*[6] incarceration rates in
the United States for this same period. Using states as the unit of
analysis, the correlation between the incarceration rates in the various
states in 1995 and 2003 was 0.89.

More importantly for our current purposes, this correlation of state
prison imprisonment rates across the relatively short time period between
1995 and 2003 is less interesting, we would suggest, than the correlation
between the incarceration rates across states over a longer time frame. As
such, we also examined the correlation of state levels of imprisonment in
the United States in 1973 – just prior to the beginning of the increase in
incarceration rates that has continued into this century – and those
in 2006. This correlation was also quite large: r = 0.60. States which had
high levels of imprisonment in 1973 continued to have high levels in 2006,
just as those states with low incarceration rates in 1973 were also low in
2006.

When looking at state prison incarceration rates alone for 1973
(i.e. without considering federal and jail populations),[7] the range is
impressive. At the bottom end with state prison (only) rates of 25–37
per 100,000 were North Dakota, Massachusetts, New Hampshire,
South Dakota, Minnesota and Hawaii. At the top, with state prison
(only) rates in the range of 144 to 184 were North Carolina, Georgia,
Texas, and Maryland. By any standard, the rates for the first set of
states were low, just as the rates for the second set were high. The fact
that there is such a high correlation across such a substantial period of
time and with such dramatic differences across states would suggest to
us that each state constitutes, in effect, a separate culture. Superimposed on that (state) culture, there was clearly a change (or, more
likely, a set of changes) that affected all states. This can be easily seen
in Table 12.1.

One is immediately struck by the massive increases over time across
states. For instance, the lowest state prison imprisonment rate in 2006

---

[6] By using state prison incarceration rates, we ignored 'jail' populations (those in pre-trial
remand and those serving short sentences) as well as federal prisoners.

[7] The overall federal incarceration rate in the US in 1973 was roughly 11 per hundred
thousand. Jail populations might be estimated to constitute an additional 50% of the
combined federal and state prison populations. The overall state incarceration rate for the
US as a whole was about 98 per hundred thousand. Hence one could estimate very
roughly that the total incarceration rate in 1973 was approximately 164 – clearly high by
any standards of the day.

Table 12.1 *Relationship between US incarceration rates in 1973 and 2006*

			2006 State Prison Imprisonment Rate			
			Low, 151 thru 338	Medium, 350–469	High, 475–846	Total
1973 State Prison Imprisonment Rate	Low, 25 thru 55	Count	10 58.8%	6 35.3%	1 5.9%	17 100.0%
	Medium, 56 thru 79	Count	7 43.8%	6 37.5%	3 18.8%	16 100.0%
	High, 81 thru 184	Count	0 0%	4 23.5%	13 76.5%	17 100.0%
	Total	Count	17 34.0%	16 32.0%	17 34.0%	50 100.0%

was that for Maine, with a rate of 151. In 1973, forty-eight of the fifty states (the exceptions being North Carolina and Georgia) had imprisonment rates lower than this value. Indeed, every one of the fifty states increased its imprisonment rate between 1973 and 2006. Further, the size of these increases was large. However, the states that were *relatively* low in 1973 tended to be *relatively* low in 2006 and the states that were *relatively* high in 1973 tended to be *relatively* high in 2006.

Others have either carried out detailed studies of individual states (e.g. Barker 2006) or have tried to explain what happened in the mid 1970s that led to the beginning of the increase in American incarceration (e.g. Tonry 1999; 2004; Ruth and Reitz 2003). We are not confident that we can add much to this debate. However, we would, in the current context, raise the question as to whether it makes sense to speculate about whether there was a change in the political–economic makeup of each state such that increased imprisonment (at the state level) became an inevitability. Elsewhere (Webster and Doob 2007: 352, Table 1), we have demonstrated that the value structure of the residents of individual American states correlated with their 1999 imprisonment rates. Those states with residents whose values were closest to those of Canadians had the lowest imprisonment rates while those states with residents least like Canadians had high imprisonment rates. We would argue that this relationship suggests – at a minimum – that multiple factors are at play.

Returning to the limited Canadian data that we have, one could similarly suggest that there are quite different punishment 'cultures', even among the thirteen Canadian jurisdictions. The territories and the two provinces with the highest imprisonment rates in 2003 (Manitoba and Saskatchewan) all have relatively high aboriginal populations (between 23 and 85 per cent for the territories and 14 per cent for Manitoba and Saskatchewan in 2003). Although in terms of rhetoric – in particular, rhetoric about the treatment of youth – Quebec is seen as being more thoughtful and moderate on crime policy issues, Quebec's overall imprisonment rate is more or less the same as that of its neighbour Ontario. The difference it would seem is that Quebec has apparently placed more of its residents in federal institutions, and fewer in provincial institutions than has Ontario.

These details of the Canadian variation are not important. What is important, we believe, is the fact that there is a certain amount of consistency. The consistency for provincial imprisonment across time ($r = 0.88$) and federal imprisonment across time ($r = 0.54$) is considerably higher than the correlations of the two 'types' of imprisonment at either of the time periods ($r = 0.01$ in 1995 and $r = 0.30$ in 2003). Indeed, it would seem that provinces have their own local penal cultures which have their own unique impact on provincial imprisonment rates.

Canada within neoliberal tendencies

Arguably, the typology proposed by Cavadino and Dignan has a number of serious limitations within the Canadian context. Most obviously, the natural inclusion of Canada within their neoliberal regime largely fails to explain many of the penal practices in this country, particularly from a longitudinal perspective. However, this conclusion by no means suggests that Cavadino and Dignan's emphasis on a nation's political economy has absolutely no application or explanatory power in Canada.

On the contrary, Canada has clearly not been immune to wider pressures toward increased punitiveness in its response to crime and criminals. Rather, many of the forces at the root of higher incarceration levels in other countries have also affected Canadians. Illustratively, one simply needs a cursory glance at the recent shift in orientation of our political landscape toward an explicit 'tough-on-crime' mentality. Ending eleven years of

EXPLAINING CANADA'S IMPRISONMENT RATE

Liberal majority rule and a short Liberal minority government, the election in January 2006 of a minority Conservative federal government and its re-election (as a minority) in October 2008 introduced a new era. Specifically, all three national parties had platforms in the 2006 election that could be characterised as reflecting law-and-order politics. Most notably, the New Democratic Party – Canada's self-styled social democratic party – developed punishment policies that were at least as 'high imprisonment' in their orientation as either of the two major parties. In contrast, Quebec's separatist party for the most part ignored the crime issue.

Given the fact that three of the four parties represented in Parliament had 'tough on crime' platforms, it is not surprising that Canada's thirty-ninth Parliament had numerous government-sponsored crime bills. Further, these bills clearly have the potential of increasing Canada's rates of imprisonment. However, they also demonstrate, we would argue, something important about the nature of Canada's 'tough on crime' movement at the legislative level. Specifically, it would appear that the current pressures toward increased punitiveness are playing out differ-ently within the Canadian context from elsewhere.

As illustrative examples, soon after the new parliamentary session opened in 2006, the government fulfilled its promise to demonstrate a 'toughening up' of sentencing by introducing two sentencing bills. The first of these bills (Bill C-9, 39th Parliament, First session) would have dramatically restricted the use of what is known in Canada as the 'conditional sentence of imprisonment' – a sanction introduced into the Criminal Code in the mid 1990s (largely as the federal government's response to provincial concerns, described earlier in this chapter, having to do with rising imprisonment rates). The theory of conditional sen-tences is that an offender who normally would receive a prison sentence can, instead, be ordered to serve the sentence in the community. The complexities, as well as the logical problems with the sanction, need not concern us in this context, except to say that 'conditional sentences' were controversial from the start and were seen as yet another way in which judges were encouraged to be 'soft on crime'.

As it was first introduced, this bill would have disallowed the use of this sanction for any indictable offence punishable by a maximum sentence of ten years or more. Canada's sentencing structure has very high maximum sentences. As such, many ordinary offences not involv-ing violence (e.g. thefts or frauds involving more than $5,000; break-ins) as well as more serious offences would no longer be eligible for a conditional sentence of imprisonment.

Not surprisingly, the bill was framed in terms of public safety. Indeed, the Justice Minister was quoted as saying in the Department press release dated 4 May 2006: 'Our new government has made safe streets and communities a key priority. This legislation meets the commitment we made to Canadians.' The Minister of Public Safety was quoted in this same press release as suggesting: 'Front-line officers, especially the police, have stated loudly and clearly that rethinking conditional sentences is necessary to make our communities safer.' Further, the press release focused largely on serious crime. In fact, it was stated: 'Those convicted of serious violent and sexual offences, as well as other significant crimes, such as major drug offences, would be ineligible to receive a conditional sentence.' Both ministers failed to mention that other crimes – such as welfare frauds – would also no longer be eligible for this sanction.

More importantly for our purposes, it is notable that neither minister, nor any of the press releases describing this bill, mentioned an important caveat. Specifically, in the event that a judge does not think that an offender should be sentenced to prison, the traditional sanction of a term of probation (with punitive conditions such as house arrest or curfews) could be substituted without any loss in punitive bite. Equally notable is that final amendments to the bill – also not generally reported in the press – significantly restricted those offences which would no longer be eligible for conditional sentences. For all practical purposes, the bill, as passed by Parliament, reduced the number of non-eligible offences, primarily targeting those which in all likelihood would not have been given a conditional sentence prior to this new bill (e.g. serious personal injury offences, terrorism offences or criminal organisation offences prosecuted by way of indictment).

On the same day as this Conditional Sentences of Imprisonment Bill was announced, the Minister of Justice introduced another bill (C-10, 39th Parliament, First session) described (in a press release) as proposing 'Tougher sentencing for crimes involving firearms by enhancing the mandatory minimum provisions of the Criminal Code.' The suggestion was made that these amendments, along with those put forward in the Conditional Sentences of Imprisonment Bill, 'will restore confidence in the justice system, and make our streets safer. There will be clear consequences for gun crime – prison sentences that are in keeping with the gravity of the offence. Serious crime will mean serious time.' The press release stated that:

> The use of a firearm in committing a serious offence will be subject to a significant sentence. If for example, an offence is gang related, or if a

restricted or prohibited firearm such as a handgun is used, the minimum penalty will be:

- 5 years on a first offence
- 7 years if the accused has one prior conviction involving the use of a firearm to commit an offence
- 10 years if the accused has more than one prior conviction for using a firearm to commit an offence.

Of particular note is what was left out of the press release (except by the use of the words '*enhancing* the mandatory minimum provisions of the Criminal Code'). Specifically, it was never mentioned that Canada has already had four-year mandatory minimum sentences for these firearms offences since 1996. Similarly, the fact that these 'enhanced' mandatory minimum penalties were – for inexplicable reasons – not going to be applied to 'ordinary' firearms such as shotguns and rifles was also omitted from the press release and, as far as we could tell, ignored by the media.

Indeed, two years after these mandatory minimum sentences were first introduced (and several months after they became law), many criminologists to whom we have spoken assume, incorrectly, that the existence of mandatory minimum penalties for these offences was a Conservative government invention (in 2006–8). They are unaware of the fact that a four-year minimum sentence for these same offences carried out with a firearm was made law by a Liberal majority government in the mid 1990s. Many people also appear to be unaware that these 'enhanced' mandatory minimum sentences relate only to a subset of firearms offences. Clearly, the press releases and related material created by the government to describe the bill were written in such a way as to imply that the government had introduced five-year mandatory minimum sentences for offences where there had, previously, been no mandatory minimums. Equally notable for our current purposes, the final bill – as passed by Parliament – also eliminated the 'third strike' (ten-year minimum penalty), leaving only the five- and seven-year minimums.

We could easily provide other examples of a similar nature. In fact, Sprott (this volume) discusses another relevant bill, introduced under the current Conservative government. Specifically, the original proposal would have inserted the principles of 'deterrence' and 'denunciation' in the sentencing provisions of Canada's youth legislation in such a manner that could not, logically, have affected the severity of the sentence. Indeed, even setting aside changes that were made in some of the legislation as it went through the legislative process (e.g. restricting the prohibition in conditional sentences of imprisonment to serious violent offences or removing the 'third strike' from the firearms mandatory minimum bill), bill after bill introduced into Parliament by a very conservative federal government appeared to us to be designed to look tough but have little to no real effect.

The American President Teddy Roosevelt used what is described as a West African proverb to characterise (or perhaps guide) his foreign policy during his time as president (1901–9): 'Speak softly but carry a big stick.' We would suggest that the current Conservative Canadian federal government – at least during its first three legislative years – has turned this proverb on its head when dealing with criminal justice policy. Indeed, we would argue that 'It spoke loudly, but carried a twig.' This practice should not surprise anyone who is familiar with Jones and Newburn (2007). As these scholars note, the clearest evidence of the successful importation of American crime policies in the past several decades has come in the form of political rhetoric, not concrete policies.

Hence we appear to be witnessing a process in Canada (at least until the present day) by which wider punitive trends have only been given muted or limited expression. Clearly, Canadians have not been immune to broader forces compelling other nations toward harsher responses to crime. Rather, Canada has simply been able to restrict or contain their impact. In our earlier work on Canadian imprisonment rates, we suggested that 'Canada's stability in levels of incarceration since the 1960s appears to be the result of two interrelated processes' (Webster and Doob 2007: 359). Using the language of developmental psychology, we suggested that:

> Canada has not only been able to escape several of the forces – or 'risk factors' – producing higher imprisonment rates in other nations. Rather, there also appear to be certain 'protective factors' that have restricted the extent to which Canada has adopted the punitive policies at the root of [other nations' high] levels of incarceration.   (*Ibid.*: 323)

Conclusion

We set out in this chapter to examine the hypothesis that Canada either is an exception to the political economy typology set out by Cavadino and Dignan or has somehow overcome neoliberal tendencies in the area of their impact on penal policies. In hindsight, both of these explanations may have been too simplistic. Rather, it may be more accurate to suggest that the real contribution of the Canadian case study is to place Cavadino and Dignan's study within a broader context.

Notably, the various provincial and federal right-wing governments that Canadians have elected over the past ten to fifteen years have clearly reminded us that Canada – like other nations – is not impervious to wider punitive forces. Clearly, a nation's political orientation would appear to be one factor affecting penal policy and practice. However, what potentially distinguishes countries in terms of the impact of this component is not only their 'regime' type but also the ways in which it plays out or interacts with other contributing factors.

Indeed, the Canadian case highlights the complexity of penality. In Canada, penal policies and practices not only reflect the impact of a multiplicity of (structural, cultural, historical and institutional) factors. Rather, Canada's penal culture is also the product of the interaction of these factors as they combine in complicated and intricate ways. Clearly, Canada's right-wing governments have tested the strengths of these other forces as they continue to jostle for voice and influence. At least until 2008, the outcome for Canada has been one of limited expression of wider pressures toward increased punitiveness. However, there is no certainty that these same factors will not – at some future point – combine in other unique and complex ways, producing a different overall effect. In a similar vein, it is unlikely that even countries of a particular political–economic persuasion and comparable levels of punitiveness arrived at their current penal culture in the same manner or through the same intricate interactions.

As Garland (1990: 287) reminds us, 'underlying any study of penality should be a determination to think of punishment as a complex social institution'. He suggests that:

> The implicit argument which runs throughout this enterprise has been that a pluralistic, multidimensional approach is needed if we are to understand the historical development and present-day operation of penality . . .

> Instead of searching for a single explanatory principle, we need to grasp the facts of multiple causality, multiple effects, and multiple meaning . . . The aim of analysis should always be to capture that variety of causes, effects, and meanings and trace their interaction, rather than to reduce them all to a single currency . . .   [p. 280]

> In the shaping of any penal event – whether it be a sentencing decision, the formation of a regime, or the legislative enactment of a penal policy – a large number of conflicting forces are at work. Broad ideological ambitions may run up against immediate financial constraints, political

> expediency may conflict with established sensibilities . . . These swarming circumstances are only ever resolved into particular outcomes by means of the struggles, negotiations, actions and decisions which are undertaken by those involved in the making and the implementation of policy, and can only be traced by detailed historical work.   [p. 285]

We read these sections from Garland (1990) as a warning against simple or single-factor explanations about imprisonment levels or changes in penal policy. We would suggest that Garland's analysis of penality implies that simple changes in the penal environment will not necessarily have simple impacts on the nature of punishment. Recent events provide, we think, an illustration of this postulate. Garland also seems to suggest that even multiple constructs such as the nature of the political economy of a nation may not adequately explain imprisonment rates for all jurisdictions. More notably, perhaps, Garland's analysis may be very important when one looks at what happens when the political economy of a nation changes.

In this context, we are not optimistic that efforts to understand imprisonment policies by focusing on a limited number of theoretically relevant factors are likely to be satisfactory. While such approaches (e.g. Cavadino and Dignan 2006a; 2006b; Lacey 2008) have their own merits in calling attention to additional factors which need to be considered when attempting to understand the final penal product, their explanatory power is inherently reduced. As Lacey (2008) herself explicitly notes, such approaches have the difficulty of explaining penal policies with a limited number of explanatory concepts.

We would add that it is not only a question of the *number* of explanatory factors which is fundamental in understanding complex phenomena such as a nation's penal culture. Rather, it is also a question of the conceptual approach to the analysis of these (multiple) factors. In particular, a simple additive model in which several different factors – each with its own independent effect – are combined together is likely to fall short of capturing (and, as such, understanding) a country's penal landscape. As we have attempted to demonstrate with the Canadian example, penal policies and practices are – as we have argued elsewhere (Webster and Doob 2008: 483) – 'a product of a range of forces which uniquely interact in their own particularities, reflecting and reproducing the defining elements of a country's specific history, culture, and politico-legal structures'. As such, it is unlikely that simple political or economic models will – in and of themselves – be sufficient to understand them.

References

Barker, V. (2006) 'The politics of punishing', *Punishment and Society*, 8(1), 5–32.

Blumstein, A. and Cohen, J. (1973) 'A theory of the stability of punishment', *Journal of Criminal Law and Criminology*, 64, 198–207.

Blumstein, A., Cohen, J. and Nagin, D. (1976) 'The dynamics of a homeostatic punishment process', *Journal of Criminal Law and Criminology*, 67, 317–34.

Canada (1993) *Crime Prevention in Canada: Toward a National Strategy*, 12th Report of the Standing Committee on Justice and the Solicitor General.

Cavadino, M. and Dignan, J. (2006a) 'Penal policy and political economy', *Criminology and Criminal Justice*, 6(4), 435–56.

(2006b) *Penal System: A Comparative Approach*, London: Sage.

Daubney, D. (Chair) (1988) *Taking Responsibility: Report of the Standing Committee on Justice and Solicitor General on its Review of Sentencing, Conditional Release and Related Aspects of Corrections*, House of Commons, Canada.

Doob, A. N. and Webster, C. M. (2006) 'Countering punitiveness: understanding stability in Canada's imprisonment rate', *Law & Society Review*, 40 (2), 325–67.

Friedland, M. L. (2004) 'Criminal justice in Canada revisited', *Criminal Law Quarterly*, 48, 419–73.

Garland, D. (1990) *Punishment and Modern Society*, Chicago: University of Chicago Press.

Horner, Dr Bob, MP, Chairman (1993) *Third Session of the 34th Parliament*, February 1993.

Jones, T. and Newburn, T. (2007) *Policy Transfer and Criminal Justice: Exploring US Influence over British Crime Control Policy*, Maidenhead, Berkshire: Open University Press/McGraw-Hill.

Lacey, N. (2008) *The Prisoner's Dilemma: Political Economy and Punishment in Contemporary Democracies*, Cambridge: Cambridge University Press.

Lappi-Seppälä, T. (2007) 'Penal policy in Scandinavia' in M. Tonry (ed.), *Crime and Justice: A Review of Research*, vol. 36, Chicago: University of Chicago Press, pp. 297–369.

Lipset, S. M. (1989) *Continental Divide: The Values and Institutions of the United States and Canada*, Toronto: Canadian-American Committee, C. D. Howe Institute.

New Democratic Party (2006) 'Jack Layton: getting results for people', *Platform 2006*.

Petrunik, M. (2003) 'The hare and the tortoise: dangerousness and sex offender policy in the United States and Canada', *Canadian Journal of Criminology and Criminal Justice*, 45, 43–72.

Pratt, J. (2008a) 'Scandinavian exceptionalism in an era of penal excess, Part I: The nature and roots of Scandinavian exceptionalism', *British Journal of Criminology*, 48, 119–37.

Pratt, J. (2008b) 'Scandinavian exceptionalism in an era of penal excess, Part II: Does Scandinavian exceptionalism have a future?', *British Journal of Criminology*, 48, 275–92.

(2008c) 'When penal populism stops: legitimacy, scandal and the power to punish in New Zealand', *Australian and New Zealand Journal of Criminology*, 41(3), 364–83.

Roach, K. (1999) *Due Process and Victims' Rights*, Toronto: University of Toronto Press.

Ruth, H. and Reitz, K. R. (2003) *The Challenge of Crime: Rethinking Our Response*, Cambridge, MA: Harvard University Press.

Sprott, J. and Doob, A. N. (1998) 'Understanding provincial variation in incarceration rates', *Canadian Journal of Criminology*, 40(3), 305–22.

Tonry, M. (1999) 'Why are U.S. incarceration rates so high?', *Crime and Delinquency*, 45, 419–37.

(2004) *Thinking about Crime: Sense and Sensibility in American Penal Culture*, New York: Oxford University Press.

Tucker, S. (2009) *Instability within Stability: Conflicting Trends beneath Canada's Aggregate Incarceration Rate*, Unpublished MA Thesis. Ottawa: Department of Criminology, University of Ottawa.

Vitiello, M. (1997) 'Three strikes: can we return to rationality?', *Journal of Criminal Law and Criminology*, 87(2), 395–481.

Webster, C. M. and Doob, A. N. (2003) 'The superior/provincial criminal court distinction: historical anachronism or empirical reality?', *Criminal Law Quarterly*, 48, 77–109.

(2007) 'Punitive trends and stable imprisonment rates in Canada' in M. Tonry (ed.), *Crime and Justice: A Review of Research*, vol. 36. Chicago: University of Chicago Press, pp. 297–369.

(2008) 'America in a larger world: the future of the penal harm movement', *Criminology and Public Policy*, 7(3), 473–87.

Working Group of Federal/Provincial/Territorial Deputy Ministers (1996) *Correctional Population Growth: Report for Federal/Provincial/Territorial Ministers Responsible for Justice*, Ottawa: Solicitor General, Canada.

(1997) *Correctional Population Growth: First Report on Progress*, February 1997.

13

US youth justice policy transfer in Canada: we'll take the symbols but not the substance*

JANE B. SPROTT

Introduction

On an average day in 1997 there were 4,687 youths in custodial facilities in Canada (a rate of 192.13 per 100,000) and by 2005–6 there were 1,987 (a rate of 77.42 per 100,000). Canada has a rather lengthy history of being concerned about the overuse of custody for youths and has struggled for some time to reduce it. In 1965 a government committee released the first report on youth justice and noted great concern about the use of court and custody for minor offences (Department of Justice 1965). Since then, most government reports have reiterated those concerns. However, during the late 1980s onwards the Canadian public became increasingly concerned about crime and wanted the government to 'toughen-up' the youth justice system. The government was therefore in a difficult position – for political reasons it felt that it should respond to the public, but there were also the persistent concerns that custody was actually being overused. How Canada managed to reduce the use of imprisonment for youths during an era where there was considerable pressure from the public to 'toughen-up' the youth justice system is the focus of this chapter. More generally, this chapter uses Canada's youth justice reforms to explore the limits of policy convergence and policy transfer between Canada and the USA. Youth justice policy in Canada appears to be driven more by social, political and cultural specificities and less by simple policy transfer from the USA.

Canada used punitive rhetoric to describe policy, but ultimately the legislation did not match the rhetoric. In order to illustrate this, the government's public depictions (through the national newspaper) of the 1990s amendments to the Young Offenders Act will be contrasted to

---

* Parts of this chapter develop upon earlier work (see Doob and Sprott 2004).

the actual amendments. The introduction of the Youth Criminal Justice
Act in 2003, along with more recent suggested amendments will also
be discussed, contrasting the public (national newspaper/press release)
discussions with what the legislation and amendments actually contained.

The Young Offenders Act

The responsibility for Canada's youth justice laws resides with Canada's
federal government though the provinces have the constitutional
responsibility to administer the law. The Young Offenders Act (YOA)
was Canada's second piece of federal youth justice legislation. It came
into force in 1984 and was replaced in 2003 with the Youth Criminal
Justice Act (YCJA). While the YOA was passed with the three political
parties supporting it, soon after it was implemented controversy
developed. During the 1980s there was a growing perception of increasing youth crime as well as some high-profile cases that were not well
explained in the media – these two issues helped to create the impression
that the YOA was 'too lenient' (for more discussion on these issues see
Doob and Sprott 2004). The public, therefore, wanted the government to
'toughen-up' the Act. Canada, it seems, responded to these desires by
using more punitive rhetoric when discussing youth justice responses to
a subset of serious violent offences. Making distinctions between serious
violence and other types of offences is obviously not a unique strategy.
Bottoms (1995) noted this 'classic' political strategy where governments
increase penalties for more serious offences for reasons of populist
punitiveness rather than substantial policy concerns.

   Moreover, Canada was not alone in the use of punitive rhetoric.
During the late 1980s and early 1990s it appears that punitive rhetoric
around criminal justice policies flourished across many, but not all,
nations (USA and UK for example) and across party lines (Newburn
and Jones 2005). A turning point, perhaps, was Michael Dukakis's loss to
George Bush in the 1988 US presidential election, in part due to the
negative campaigning from Bush's camp about issues around crime and
violence. As Newburn and Jones (2005: 77–8) argue:

> the experience of the 1988 presidential election was widely interpreted
> as having three key messages for politicians concerning crime. First,
> crime has the potential to be a key 'wedge issue' in elections . . . Second,
> candidates should at all costs not get caught being 'soft on crime'.
> Finally . . . irrespective of the substance of any policies they may endorse,
> the bottom line is that they must appear 'tough'.

Interestingly, however, while Canada emphasised punitive changes to a subset of violent offences, the law as administered did not change. Thus, throughout the 1990s Canada embarked on a strategy which publicly aimed to 'look tough' on a subset of more serious crimes. More quietly, Canada simultaneously tried to decrease the use of custody for less serious offences and in this respect it was successful, but only in 2003 when new youth justice legislation was implemented.

Amendments: rhetoric versus actual policy

During the 1990s one sees a gradually increasing use of punitive rhetoric, while other discussions and some legislative changes aimed to reduce the use of court and custody were considered more quietly. The progression began somewhat slowly with the second[1] of three sets of amendments introduced in 1989. The amendments were eventually passed in 1992 and focused on changing three things. The first entailed increasing the youth court sentence for murder from three years to five years less a day[2] and the second involved changing the test for when a youth court case could be transferred to adult court. When considering whether or not to transfer a case, the judge had to consider protection of the public and the rehabilitation of the young offender. The 1992 amendment added that where those two issues cannot be reconciled, protection of the public is the paramount issue. This change was made to (at least theoretically) make it easier to transfer a case. The third change was a lowering of the parole ineligibility periods for youths who were sentenced in adult court for murder.

Before the amendments were introduced into Parliament, the one national newspaper[3] at the time reported the likely changes, focusing on the increased sentence for murder and the lowering of parole ineligibility periods for youths sentenced in adult court. With the headline 'Minister says ire over penalties warrants changes to youth act' the article quoted the

---

[1] The first set of amendments was largely technical in nature and implemented shortly after the Act had been in place.

[2] Canada, since 1982, has had a 'Charter of Rights and Freedoms' which, not surprisingly, governs youth justice matters along with all other laws. For the most part, Charter issues do not have much impact on youth justice legislation. The exception is a requirement that any person facing a penalty lasting five years or more must have the option of a trial by jury. The government did not want to break that threshold and thus opted for just under the five-year mark in order to avoid jury trials for youths.

[3] Newspaper descriptions in this chapter are generally only gathered from the national newspapers. There was only one national newspaper (*The Globe and Mail*) until 27 October 1998, when the *National Post* began circulation across Canada.

Justice Minister as saying: 'It's a good piece of legislation in other ways, but it's in danger of losing public support unless some changes are implemented' (*Globe and Mail*, 15 October 1989: A13). The justification the minister gave to the media for reducing the parole ineligibility periods for youths sentenced in adult court was so that 'judges would be more likely to transfer cases involving youth repeat offenders'.

At second reading in the House of Commons, the Parliamentary Secretary to the Minister of Justice (Nicolson) gave a speech about the amendments and described them in much the same way as the media.[4] However, while the reduction in the parole ineligibility periods was described in the media as a mechanism to increase transfers for certain types of cases, Nicolson's speech outlined another reason: to reduce the disparity between the youth and adult systems. Before the amendments the sentences for first degree murder were a maximum of three years in custody for a youth sentenced in youth court or a life sentence if sentenced in adult court with no chance for parole until twenty-five years. The 1992 amendments changed this so the sentence in the youth court became five years less a day and if convicted in adult court, the youth would receive a life sentence, but could apply for parole in five to ten years. Clearly, then, this change could be seen as necessary in order to reduce the stark differences between the youth and adult systems. However, one could argue that the change was defended using a more punitive justification in the media (i.e. to increase the likelihood of transferring certain cases).

While some parts of the amendments may have been necessary to create greater coherence between the youth and adult systems, changing the test for when to transfer a case was clearly unnecessary and thus only done to placate the public. There was no indication that judges were unable to transfer cases where they wished to do so. Moreover, the change appeared somewhat weak given all the ways in which one could change legislation to increase the use of transfers, if that was desired.

The last set of amendments was introduced in 1994 (passed in 1995) and here one sees greater use of punitive rhetoric in the media description of the changes along with a distinction between serious violence and other offences. These amendments again increased the youth court sentence for murder (from five years less a day to ten years), and created 'presumptive transfers' for sixteen- and seventeen-year-olds whereby a youth charged

---

[4] Details from the speech came from Parliamentary Debates (Hansard): 34th Parliament, 2nd session, 30 May 1990, pp. 12066–8.

with certain serious offences (murder, manslaughter, attempted murder and aggravated sexual assault) would presumptively be tried in an adult court, unless the defence could show why the case should be kept in the youth court. In addition, however, there were also changes, again, to the parole ineligibility dates for youths convicted in the adult court and some directions for judges to use custody more sparingly.

When the amendments were first introduced the national newspaper carried stories including: 'Longer terms for young killers expected in legislation today' (*Globe and Mail*, 2 June 1994: A6) and 'Youth rehabilitation loses priority: Ottawa indicates society comes first as harsher justice proposed' (*Globe and Mail*, 3 June 1994: A1). Both stories focused on the increased sentence for murder, the creation of presumptive transfers and tended to describe the changes broadly as being quite punitive: 'Reflecting public demands for more protection and more punishment, the federal government has proposed legislation that would allow tougher treatment of young people who commit violent crimes . . . rehabilitating violent youths will no longer be considered as high a priority as protecting society' (*Globe and Mail*, 3 June 1994: A1). At the same time, however, both stories quoted the Justice Minister as being against a general increased use of custody: 'If the answer to crime was simply harsher laws, longer penalties, and bigger prisons, then the United States would be nirvana today' (*Globe and Mail*, 2 June 1992: A6). 'For young people who commit non-violent crimes, I want non-jail sentences' (*Globe and Mail*, 3 June 1992: A1).

When the Minister of Justice gave his speech about the amendments at second reading in the House of Commons the tough sounding changes were all highlighted first. Near the end of the speech, however, the Justice Minister noted that:

> the emphasis should be and must be upon non-jail sentences for young offenders who commit non-violent crimes . . . the stated expectation [from the YOA] was that the emphasis for young people caught up in the criminal justice system would be on community based . . . dispositions . . . For the most part that promise had not been fulfilled. In fact, the level and extent of custody as a sentence for young offenders are vastly higher than first expected. Over 30% of those young offenders found guilty in youth court receive a sentence involving custody. Over half those in custody are there for non-violent crimes.
>
> [Justice Minister Rock, 6 June 1994, 35th Parliament, 1st Session][5]

[5] Available online at: http://www2.parl.gc.ca/HousePublications/Publication.aspx?Language=E&Mode=1&Parl=35&Ses=1&DocId=2332333.

To that end, the minister noted that the amendments contained statements for the YOA which were designed to reduce the use of custody (e.g. statements that custody cannot be used as a substitute for child welfare, that youths who commit non-violent offences can be held accountable through non-custodial dispositions and that custody should only be imposed when all available alternatives have been considered). These changes were apparently not discussed in the national newspaper. What one sees, then, is an almost exclusive focus in the media (largely through government press releases) on punitive-sounding changes and rhetoric. These amendments were obviously discussed this way to placate the public. The government's other concern – the overuse of custody – was addressed more privately, never making it into news reports.

Interestingly, the two sets of amendments implemented during the 1990s had no effect – the number of youths transferred did not change nor did the use of custody. This was likely because the changes were weak in both cases. Telling judges that there is a presumption towards transfer still does not guarantee that it will happen, nor does telling judges simply to consider all available sanctions other than imprisonment guarantee that non-custodial sentences will be used more often.

The use of custody did start declining in Canada in the mid to late 1990s, though this probably was not due to the 1995 amendments. Rather it could have been the result of a growing consensus among those who worked in, or knew about, the operation of the YOA, that custody was being overused. Two reviews – one by a Federal–Provincial– Territorial Task Force on Youth Justice (1996) and the other by the Standing Committee on Justice and Legal Affairs (1997) of the House of Commons – reported in 1996 and 1997 respectively, and both noted an overuse of custody. Soon after, a federal election took place (1997) and a new Minister of Justice was appointed. The government had promised to respond to the reports and to change the YOA – it responded instead by developing entirely new legislation.

Youth Criminal Justice Act (2003+)

During the 1990s it appears that the Canadian government was starting to use more punitive rhetoric while backgrounding other changes designed to reduce the use of custody. The selling of the new youth justice legislation took these strategies even further. The Youth Criminal Justice Act (YCJA) was first introduced into Parliament and to the Canadian public in March 1999. In the week before the bill was introduced, stories appeared in some of the larger Canadian newspapers under headlines like: 'New act would jail parents for children's crimes' (*The National Post*, 6 March 1999); 'Young Offenders to face closer supervision – Ottawa plans mandatory probation period' (*Globe and Mail*, 6 March 1999); 'Young offenders' criminal record no longer a secret' (*The Ottawa Citizen*, 7 March 1999); 'Law would toughen youth justice: MP whose son was slain has worked hard to see changes introduced' (*Globe and Mail*, 8 March 1999); and 'Young offenders face adult sentences at 14' (*The Toronto Star*, 11 March 1999).

Whether or not these stories were, in effect, planted by the government, it is clear that the government was successful in priming the public to expect a tough bill. The news coverage after the release of the bill was slightly more 'balanced' but, nevertheless, the 'tough' parts of the bill dominated discussion. This was not surprising when one looks at the press release from the Minister's office. The first four bullet points in the press release indicated that the YCJA will include provisions that:

- allow an adult sentence for any youth 14 years old or more . . .
- expand the offences for which a young person convicted of an offence would be presumed to receive an adult sentence . . .
- lower the age for youth who are presumed to receive an adult sentence . . .
- permit the publication of names of all youth who receive an adult sentence. Publication of the names of [serious violent offenders over age 14] will also be permitted.

[Department of Justice, 1999: pp. 1–2]

The first of the points listed by the Minister's office is noteworthy because it is a statement of the law as it has *always* been in Canada. Few, however, would likely know that. Thus, it is not surprising that the bill was labelled largely as being 'tough'. Only those who had access to data on Canada's youth justice system would be able to know that these 'tough' provisions are numerically unimportant. Few, if any, cases would be affected by them.

During the second reading of the bill in the House of Commons the Justice Minister highlighted key changes which tended to follow the press release. Near the end of the speech, however, there was, once again, the recognition that Canada overuses custody:

The majority of young people who get into trouble with the law are non-violent and only commit one offence. Unfortunately there are too many examples in our current youth justice system of young people

serving time in jail for minor offences. We incarcerate youth at a rate four
times that of adults and twice that of many US states.[6]

Clearly then, with the media coverage, the press release and Minister of
Justice's speech in the House of Commons, the main message was one of
'toughness'. The secondary message was that in addition to 'cracking
down' on certain offenders, more alternatives to court and custody were
needed for non-violent offenders. The problem with the focus being
predominately on 'tough' changes, however, was that it appeased no one.
Provincial governments in Ontario and the West claimed the Act was
still not tough enough, while Quebec claimed the Act was too tough.

The culture in Quebec is distinctly different from the rest of Canada.
The province tends to have a more 'social welfare' focus, and with
respect to youths, there is a long tradition of developing and supporting
social programmes. Quebec, for example, is the only province in Canada
to have, in 1997, essentially developed universal non-profit daycare – a
network of fixed-fee services ($7 per day) for all children aged four and
under, irrespective of family income (Lefebvre *et al.* 2008).

It is not surprising, then, that Quebec also has a unique history in
terms of the treatment of juvenile offenders. Quebec implemented a
form of formal diversion of young people from the youth justice system
before the YOA was implemented in 1984 (Trépanier 1983). Thus, even
though a young person may be brought to the attention of the police
because of an offence, such a youth would be diverted from the criminal
justice stream if it was felt that the case could best be handled other than
in the youth court. In contrast, Ontario, for example, fought the necessity of having 'alternative measures' programmes for youths up to the
Supreme Court of Canada (*R. v. S.(S)* [1990] Supreme Court Reports
254). Hence, given the legislated provincial policy that youths who
offend should not necessarily be brought to court, it is not particularly
surprising to find variation between Quebec (the lowest use of court and
custody under the YOA) and the rest of Canada.

From a political perspective, then, an Act described largely in terms
of 'toughness' is doomed to fail in Quebec. However, Quebec is a large
and politically important province; therefore, politicians cannot
easily dismiss their concerns. The political party from Quebec (Bloc
Quebecois) was so upset with the bill that it attempted to block the

[6] Quotes from the Minister's speech were obtained from Parliamentary Debates (Hansard):
36th Parliament, 1st Session, 22 March 1999, www2.parl.gc.ca/HousePublications/
Publication.aspx? Language=E&Mode=1&Parl=36&Ses=1&DocId=2332908.

legislation with a committee filibuster and over 2,000 amendments. Part of the reason the Quebec government did not want the new law was because they claimed to be administering the current law (YOA) sufficiently and thus did not see the need for a new law. The new Act, therefore, became a tool for separatists in Quebec to argue that the Canadian federation does not serve Quebec's interests. Additionally, however, it is quite possible that the punitive spin placed on the Act also affected Quebec's view of the legislation. It is likely that, similar to the rest of Canada, Quebec read and believed the media and government press releases and thus felt that the bill, in various respects, was 'too punitive' (for more discussion about what, exactly, Quebec was opposed to see: Trépanier 2004).

Quebec stalled the legislative process until a new session of Parliament started, followed by a federal election in the autumn of 2000. This meant that the bill had to be reintroduced in early 2001. The reintroduction described a radically different-sounding bill. In the press release there was no mention of 'tough changes'. In fact, there were no specific changes described at all. Instead the press release talked broadly about how the Act:

> reflects a balanced approach to youth justice that aims to instill values such as accountability, responsibility and respect. The Act includes more effective, targeted measures to deal with both serious and violence offences and the vast majority of youth offences which are less serious. The *Youth Criminal Justice Act* gives provinces and territories flexibility in choosing options in some areas. [Department of Justice 2001: 1]

The media followed the press release and thus most stories focused on the 'balanced' approach and flexibility for provinces. One national newspaper ran a front-page headline: 'Ottawa to overhaul youth law: Amended bill coming today adds flexibility to provinces' (*National Post*, 5 February 2001: A1) while the other national paper simply reported that: 'Ottawa revives reform of young offender law' (*Globe and Mail*, 6 February 2001: A7). The text in both of the national newspapers highlighted the new flexibility, allowing 'provinces to opt out of one of the existing law's stricter provisions – that youth as young as 14 are presumed to face adults sentences . . . if convicted of a serious offence' (*National Post*, 5 February 2001: A1). That was obviously done to appease Quebec.

During the second reading in the House of Commons the Justice Minister once again gave a speech about the bill. Unlike the previous speech, where she focused on 'tough' changes, this time there was no mention of any of the 'tough'-sounding changes like the expansion of presumptive adult sentences or the publication of names. Instead, the bill was largely described in terms of flexibility and rehabilitation. Moreover, the overuse of custody was heavily emphasised and, in fact, exaggerated:[7]

> I will not accept the rhetoric from the benches opposite and elsewhere that this piece of legislation is too tough or that it is not tough enough. Those who seek to reduce the discussion of youth justice to such a simplistic paradigm feed misconceptions. Canadians want a system that prevents crime by addressing the circumstances underlying a young person's offending behaviour, that rehabilitates young people who commit offences and safely reintegrates them into the community, and ensures that a young person is subject to meaningful and appropriate consequences for his or her offending behaviour . . . The new legislation makes clear that the nature of the system's response to a youth's offending behaviour should reflect the needs and individual circumstances of the youth . . . The existing YOA has resulted in the highest youth incarceration rate in the western world, including our neighbours to the south, the United States.[8]

The bill, although described in radically different terms in newspapers, the government press release and by the Minister of Justice when she spoke in the House of Commons, was essentially the same as the bill first introduced in 1999. The shift in rhetoric was likely due to the complexity of Quebec feeling that the bill was 'too tough' and thus not supporting it. While the 1990 amendments to the YOA could be largely publicly discussed in terms of 'tough' changes, it appeared that developing entirely new legislation and describing it as predominately punitive went too far for Quebec (and ironically not far enough for other provinces). And thus, while the government attempted, upon reintroduction, to use 'flexibility' and 'rehabilitation' as key descriptors, the damage had been done. Quebec still felt it was too punitive and many academics also described the legislation as largely punitive (see e.g. Giles and Jackson 2003; Hogeveen 2005).

---

[7] Quotes from the Minister's speech were obtained from Parliamentary Debates (Hansard): 37th Parliament, 1st Session, 14 February 2001, www2.parl.gc.ca/HousePublications/Publication.aspx?Language=E&Mode=1&Parl=37&Ses=1&DocId=2332075.

[8] There is, in fact, no evidence for the Minister's assertion that Canada has the highest youth incarceration rate in the Western world. The only evidence suggested that for some offences, Canada may sentence youths to custody at a slightly higher rate than the US. However, there was also some evidence which suggested that the US may have longer sentences than Canada (see Sprott and Snyder 1999).

The legislation finally passed in 2002 and became law on 1 April 2003. The preamble to the bill noted, among other things, that 'Canadian society should have a justice system . . . that reserves its most serious intervention for the most serious crimes and reduces the over-reliance on incarceration for non-violent young persons.'

An important change in orientation in the Act is that the 'protection of the public' is not to be interpreted as meaning either deterrence or incapacitation. The YCJA states that the youth justice system does various things (addressing the circumstances underlying offending, rehabilitating and reintegrating offenders, ensuring meaningful conse-quences) '*in order to promote* the *long-term* protection of the public' (s. 3(1), emphasis added). Thus, the words 'protection of the public' appear, but the underlying theory appears to be that ensuring meaning-ful consequences along with rehabilitation and reintegration are means to accomplish long-term protection.

Along with these general statements are the principles designed to address the need to screen cases out of the court system. Measures outside of the formal court system ('extrajudicial' measures) such as warnings, referrals to community programmes etc., are 'presumed to be adequate to hold a young person accountable for his or her offending behaviour if the young person has committed a non-violent offence and has previously not been found guilty of an offence' (s. 4(c)). Moreover, the law further states that non-court alternatives can be used even if they have been used before, and even if the youth has been found guilty on a previous occasion (s. 4(d)(i)–(ii)).

Police are told that they 'shall' in all cases consider non-court approaches before starting judicial proceedings (s. 6(1)). However, perhaps because of the provincial, rather than federal, responsibility for the administration of justice, the failure of a police officer to consider non-court approaches does not invalidate any charge that is laid against the youth (s. 6(2)).

When a youth has been found guilty, judges are told that 'the purpose of sentencing . . . is to contribute to the protection of society by holding a youth accountable for an offence' (s. 38(1)). More specif-ically, 'the sentence must be proportionate to the seriousness of the offence and the degree of responsibility of the young person for that offence' (s. 38(2)(c)). Furthermore, subject to the proportionality requirement, 'the sentence must be the least restrictive sentence that is capable of [holding the youth accountable]' and must be 'the one that is most likely to rehabilitate the young person and reintegrate him or her into society' (s. 38(2)(e)(i)–(ii)).

While the proportionality principle sets the rules by which the relative severities of sentences are determined, the actual sentence (within the limits set by proportionality) must be the most likely sentence to rehabilitate or reintegrate. As various commentators (e.g. von Hirsch 1976) have pointed out, a proportionality principle on its own defines the *relative* severity of punishments. It does not, however, define on its own the level of punishments that should be given. Perfect proportionality, therefore, could be achieved by giving all young persons custodial sentences as long as their length was proportional to the seriousness of the offence. Thus it is necessary to set at least some standards within the proportionality framework. The YCJA chose to focus on the decision of whether a youth receives a custodial sentence. Section 39(1) of the Act states:

> A youth justice shall not commit a young person to custody . . . unless
>
> (a) the young person has committed a violent offence;
> (b) the young person has failed to comply with non-custodial sentences;
> (c) the young person has committed an indictable offence for which an adult would be liable to imprisonment for a term of more than two years and has a history that indicates a pattern of findings of guilty;
> (d) in exceptional cases where the young person has committed an . . . offence, such that the imposition of a non-custodial sentence would be inconsistent with the purpose and principles [of sentencing].

Furthermore, in cases where custody is imposed, the judge is specifically required 'to state the reasons why it has determined that a non-custodial sentence is not adequate to achieve the purpose [of sentencing] including, if applicable, the reasons why the case is an exceptional case' (s. 39(2)). The point of these and other similar requirements is clear: judges are forced to think about whether custody is really necessary.

The 'tough-sounding' measure contained in the new Act is the provision that anyone over the age of fourteen found guilty of one of the four 'presumptive offences' (murder, manslaughter, attempted murder, aggravated sexual assault) or who had a history of serious violent convictions[9] would be 'presumptively' sentenced as an adult. Another 'tough-sounding' provision was that youth court judges would be empowered to hand down adult sentences if the prosecution gave sufficient notice that it was seeking such a sentence. Two factors made it unlikely that these changes would have

---

[9] The judge must designate an offence as a 'serious violent offence' and once an offender has three such designations, he/she is presumptively sentenced as an adult. That this was not played up by the government in 1999 as a form of 'three-strikes' is curious given the desire to make the bill look 'tough'.

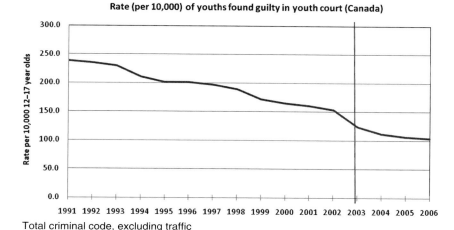

Figure 13.1   Rate of youths found guilty in youth court (per 10,000) (12–17-year-olds).

any impact. As discussed earlier, the 1996 'presumptive transfer' provisions had no apparent impact on transfer rates. Secondly, the test of whether a person should be sentenced as a youth or as an adult is the same: can a youth sentence be crafted that meets the 'proportionality' test. Most recently in May 2008, the Supreme Court of Canada struck down the use of presumptive adult sentences which obviously puts an end to any speculation about how this provision will be used. More about that Supreme Court case will be discussed shortly.

Given the wording of the legislation, there was, not surprisingly, a relatively large decline in the use of court and custody. Figure 13.1 shows the rate (per 10,000 twelve- to seventeen-year-olds) of finding youths guilty in youth court.[10] It shows a general decline from the mid 1990s onwards, but highlights a relatively large one-year reduction in 2003, the first year of the YCJA. As Table 13.1 demonstrates, reductions were seen in every province and in the three territories and in all cases the reductions in that one year were larger than any other year. Moreover, many of

[10] Data were obtained from Statistics Canada. Table 252–0050 – Youth court survey, number of guilty cases, by type of sentence, annual (table), CANSIM (database). The definition of a 'case' has changed from time to time since 1990 and 'total cases' may or may not include traffic or other federal statutes (drugs, etc.). Thus the numbers and rates presented here may differ slightly from other published numbers/rates. What is most important in this context, however, is that the same case definition and included offences were used for all data in this chapter.

Table 13.1 *Rate (per 10,000 12–17-year-olds) of finding cases guilty (total criminal code, excluding traffic)*

	5-year average (1998–2002)	2003–4 (first year of YCJA)	2004–5	2005–6	2006–7
Canada	167.56	123.27	111.85	106.36	103.33
NFL and LB	210.09	170.25	163.39	130.27	128.02
PEI	119.08	83.54	63.79	99.97	103.54
Nova Scotia	164.80	109.52	99.60	111.41	131.07
New Brunswick	198.46	138.98	141.50	150.17	140.50
Quebec	90.09	69.07	64.32	62.87	59.84
Ontario	187.11	140.26	127.38	118.51	112.64
Manitoba	212.63	163.97	152.90	158.44	157.94
Saskatchewan	328.64	234.70	244.20	208.35	223.48
Alberta	216.20	166.42	129.26	128.67	126.91
BC	123.43	74.20	67.81	63.99	61.58
Yukon	279.47	116.32	95.68	96.95	118.65
*NWT	502.75	71.04	93.61	79.25	281.15
*Nunavut	325.03	76.86	86.68	89.59	285.64

*4-year averages

Note: The Yukon, NWT and Nunavut are the three territories in Canada. They constitute roughly 40% of the landmass of Canada but have a combined population of roughly 100,000, which is approximately 0.3% of the total population. They historically have very high rates in the use of court and custody

the provinces continued to experience slight declines during the three years (2004–5, 2005–6 and 2006–7) after the YCJA was first implemented (2003–4). One may also notice the considerable variability across the provinces and territories in administrating the law (see further Doob and Webster this volume; Sprott and Doob 1998).

Figure 13.2 shows the rate (per 10,000) of youths sentenced to custody. It highlights slight increases until 1993, followed by general stability and then declines. Specifically, since 1998 there have been declines each year, with the sharpest decline in 2003. Once again every province and territory in Canada experienced declines (Table 13.2). Moreover, in the majority of provinces the declines continued after the first year of the YCJA.

The reduction in the use of custody is seen most dramatically when looking at relatively minor offences. Table 13.3 shows the change, from

Table 13.2 *Rate (per 10,000 12–17-year-olds) of sentencing cases to custody (total criminal code, excluding traffic)*

	5-year average (1998–2002)	2003–4 (First year of YCJA)	2004–5	2005–6	2006–7
Canada	45.81	27.66	24.08	19.63	17.22
NFL and LB	71.90	39.25	38.78	26.86	23.58
PEI	44.27	16.38	9.94	15.96	19.52
Nova Scotia	49.11	16.58	13.78	13.02	17.95
New Brunswick	54.84	33.34	30.91	25.98	24.56
Quebec	21.99	12.48	10.82	8.04	6.91
Ontario	54.63	38.61	33.51	28.02	23.27
Manitoba	56.42	29.23	26.29	12.51	11.35
Saskatchewan	106.52	66.89	56.45	41.40	40.38
Alberta	44.12	21.88	16.98	15.85	15.85
BC	30.99	12.99	12.91	11.37	9.79
Yukon	112.06	38.77	21.26	46.68	40.79
*NWT	239.64	71.04	93.61	79.25	69.10
*Nunavut	81.62	76.86	86.68	89.59	54.53

*4-year averages – see Note under Table 13.1

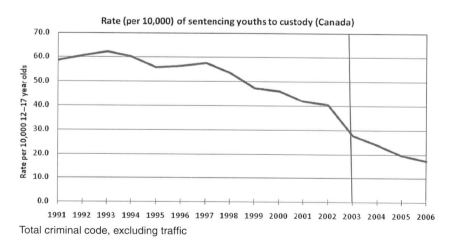

Figure 13.2   Rate of youths sentenced to custody (per 10,000) (12–17-year-olds).

Table 13.3 *Proportion (and number) of all cases sentenced to custody (Canada)*

	1991–2	2006–7
Theft	14% (1,845)	10% (423)
Breaking and entering	30% (4,024)	14% (635)
Failure to comply with disposition	8% (1,266)	19% (859)
Sub-total	*52% (7,135)*	*43% (1,917)*
Unlawfully at large	12% (1,643)	7% (338)
Possession stolen property	9% (1,232)	7% (306)
Mischief	3% (338)	4% (159)
Minor assault	5% (631)	8% (341)
Sub-total	*29% (3,791)*	*27% (1,144)*
Total of seven offences	**81% (10,926)**	**70% (3,061)**

1991–2 to 2006–7 in the custodial population. Three relatively minor offences (thefts, breaking and entering and failing to comply with a disposition) accounted for 52 per cent of the cases sentenced to custody in 1991–2. By 2006–7 these same three offences accounted for 43 per cent of the custodial population. Once adding in unlawfully at large, possession of stolen property, mischief and minor assault, 81 per cent of the custodial population was accounted for in 1991–2. By 2006–7 these seven offences accounted for 70 per cent of the custodial population. Only two offences – failing to comply with a disposition and minor assaults – accounted for a larger proportion of the custodial population in 2006–7 compared to 1991–2. The reason for the increased proportion of those two offences is that other high-volume offences declined more (see e.g. the decline in breaking and entering). Perhaps most interesting, however, is the reduction in the absolute number of cases in custody.

Figures 13.3 and 13.4 show the rate (per 10,000) of sentencing each of the seven offences to custody. Each offence saw rather dramatic reductions in 2003 and these offences have continued to decline slightly in subsequent years. These declines, we can safely presume, are due to the YCJA.

Case law and suggested amendments to the YCJA

Aside from the rhetoric, the legislation and implementation did what it was supposed to do – it reduced the use of court and custody. If one read

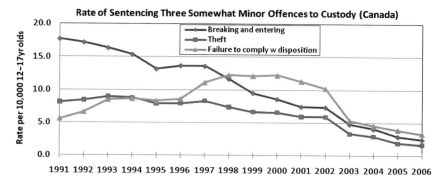

Figure 13.3 Rate of sentencing for three relatively minor offences – Part 1.

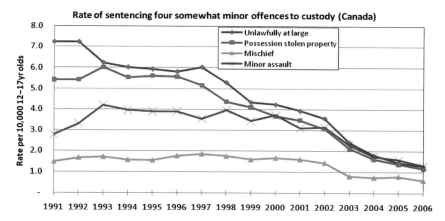

Figure 13.4 Rate of sentencing for four relatively minor offences – Part 2.

the legislation, and knew something about how the YOA had been implemented with respect to presumptive transfers, this would not be surprising. A clear goal throughout – and, in fact, since 1965 – has been to use court and custody sparingly. Fears, based primarily on the 1999 rhetoric around the bill, of an increasing use of adult sentences appear largely unfounded. Figure 13.5 shows the proportion of custodial sentences of varying lengths. It demonstrates a slight decrease in the shortest sentences (one month or less) coupled with a slight increase in sentences over one month and up to six months. This shift in sentence lengths likely reflects the fact that the minor cases were screened out. What is clear, however, is that there is no increase, after the implementation of the YCJA, in the proportion of cases that received long sentences. Also

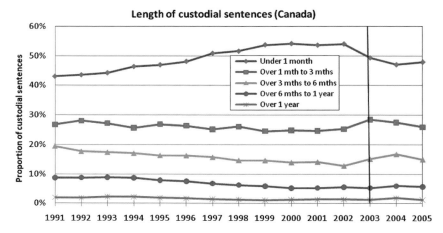

Figure 13.5   Length of custodial sentence.

clear is that the vast majority of custodial sentences are quite short (e.g. 74 per cent of custodial sentences are for three months or less).

The fact that there appears to be no increase in long sentences is perhaps not surprising given the legislation. While presumptive adult sentences could be given to more youths (those fourteen and fifteen and those who have a 'pattern of serious violent offending') we know that very few youths aged fourteen and fifteen commit serious offences in Canada. Moreover, the end decision – whether or not to impose an adult sentence – is still left to a judge to decide and is based on the principle of proportionality. The courts, to date, have been relatively restrictive[11] in deciding what violent offences qualify for the 'serious violent offence' designation (three such designations are needed in order for a youth to presumptively be sentenced as an adult). Most importantly, as already mentioned, in May 2008 the Supreme Court of Canada found presumptive adult sentences to be unconstitutional because they violate the Charter of Rights' principle of fundamental justice (*R.* v. *D.B.*, 2008 SCC 25). The court also

[11] See e.g. *R.* v. *N.(D.)*, 2007 ABCA 370 or *R.* v. *P.(D.)*, 2006 BCCA 409. On the other hand, some appeal courts have allowed SVO designations, though typically there is substantial physical harm and/or some degree of premeditation (see e.g. *R.* v. *T.(V.J.)*; *R.* v. *C.(A.B.)*, 2007 MBCA 45 or *R.* v. *G.B.*, 2008 ABCA 156). One recent Ontario Appeal Court case is perhaps more broad in its decision because it applied a serious violent offence designation based predominately on a victim impact statement and did not allow any cross-examination of the victim (*R.* v. *W.(V.)*, 2008 ONCA 55). Thanks to Charles Seto of the Youth Criminal Defence Office for bringing much of the relevant case law to my attention.

argued that for youths, the presumption is one of diminished moral blameworthiness or culpability because of their increased vulnerability and lack of maturity due to their age. Thus, while adult sentences are still allowed, there will be no more 'presumptive' adult sentences.[12]

The YCJA states that sentencing is to be determined largely by proportionality, though the sentence crafted must be one that is most likely to rehabilitate the youth, within the limits of a proportionate sentence (s. 39(2)(e)(ii)). None of the other traditional purposes of sentencing are mentioned and thus some have argued that certain goals (deterrence) should be 'read in' because they were not explicitly kept out. The Supreme Court ultimately decided that deterrence was not part of the YCJA (*R. v. B.W.P.; R. v. B.V.N.*, 2006 SCC 27). In its decision, the Court argued that:

> Parliament chose not to incorporate that principle [deterrence] in the new youth sentencing regime . . . had Parliament intended to make deterrence part of the new regime, one would reasonably expect that it would be expressly included in the detailed purpose and principles set out in the statute. Yet the words 'deter' and 'deterrence' are nowhere to be found in the *YCJA* . . . This omission is . . . of considerable significance . . . the focus throughout remains on the young person before the court. Since no basis can be found in the *YCJA* for imposing a harsher sanction than would otherwise be called for to deter others from committing crime, general deterrence is not a principle of youth sentencing under the new regime. [*R. v. B.W.P.; R. v. B.V.N.* [2006] 1 S.C.R. 941, 2006 SCC 27]

While the interpretations of the Act (e.g. adult sentences, the role of deterrence) seemed generally to fit with the intent of the legislation, the minority Conservative government was looking to amend the YCJA. In the Throne Speech on 16 October 2007 there was a promise to 'strengthen the *Youth Criminal Justice Act* to ensure that young offenders who commit serious crimes are held accountable to victims and their communities'. In November 2007 Bill C-25 was introduced which, as the press release described it, 'would allow the courts to consider deterrence and denunciation as objectives of youth sentences' along with making it 'easier to detain youths in custody prior to their trials' (Department of Justice, 19 November 2007).

[12] The reader may wonder how presumptive transfers to adult court could have existed from 1996 until 2003 without challenge. The logic appears to be that the 'transfer' to adult court was a procedural decision whereas under the YCJA, with youth court judges imposing the adult sentence, the presumption is no longer procedural (where the case should be held) but rather involves a punishment (the decision to impose an adult sentence).

Interestingly, Bill C-25 received almost no press when it was introduced. The one national newspaper (but not the other) covered the amendment, simply stating that the changes are aimed to 'get tough on youth crime' (*Globe and Mail*, 20 November 2007: A4). During the second reading of the bill, the Minister of Justice discussed the amendments in similar terms as the *Globe and Mail*. Noting that the:

> new measures [will] protect communities from young people who pose a significant risk to public safety and hold youth accountable for their criminal conduct . . . Canadians are concerned about youth crime and believe that changes to sentences can be very helpful. They want to stem the reported recent increase in violent youth crime and restore respect for the law . . .[13]

Here the 'tough' rhetoric reappears along with a coupling of how these tough measures will make people safer. Once again, however, in reading the actual bill it was unclear if there would be any effect on the administration of the law. The words 'deterrence' and 'denunciation' were indeed added in, but subject to the statement that 'the sentence must be proportionate to the seriousness of the offence and the degree of responsibility of the young person for that offence' (s. 38(2)(c)). If the overriding goal was still to craft a proportionate sentence, then it is unclear how the goal of deterrence or denunciation could significantly change sentencing. Regardless, the bill died after the second reading in Parliament because an election was called in the autumn of 2008.

During the autumn 2008 election the Conservatives proposed reforms to the YCJA which went further than then Bill C-25. The information released was somewhat vague, but in addition to adding 'deterrence' and 'denunciation' into the Act, there was also a focus on 'enhanced' youth sentencing and automatic 'enhanced' sentences for certain violent offences.[14] The media followed the press release and headlines like 'Harper calls for new young offenders law; Stiffer sentences proposed for serious crimes' (*National Post*, 23 September 2008: A4) ran throughout Canada.

While many provinces endorsed and supported the tough-sounding proposals, Quebec did not. Indeed these proposals served to alienate Quebec and soon the media focused on how the Conservatives were initially poised to win a majority government but were faltering. Thus,

---

[13] Quotes from the Minister's speech were obtained from Hansard debates, 39th Parliament, 2nd Session, 21 November 2007, www2.parl.gc.ca/HousePublications/Publication.aspx?Language=E&Mode=1&Parl=39&Ses=2&DocId=3127508.

[14] Press release, www.conservative.ca/EN/1091/106115.

much of the public debate in the newspapers focused not on the proposals themselves, but on how those proposals were alienating Quebec. In discussing the proposals, headlines like 'Social-values issues halt Harper's Momentum in Quebec City' (*Globe and Mail*, 1 October 2008: A8) and 'Majority government will likely elude Conservative grasp, analysts say' (*Globe and Mail*, 2 October 2008: A11) dominated. In the end, the Conservatives did not win a majority government because of Quebec, in part due to the suggested reforms to the YCJA.

Conclusion

Canada's strategy over the last decade or so, intentional or not, appeared to involve making a distinction between serious and less serious offences and then focusing public discussions on punitive sounding changes for the former category. Employing similar rhetoric as other countries have employed (most notably the USA), Canada focused on 'toughening up' youth justice legislation for a subset of more serious crimes. However, as Pollitt (2001) and Jones and Newburn (2007) note, public policy can operate on three different levels: rhetoric/symbols, actual legislation and implementation. Thus, 'understanding the complexity of public policy requires us to consider the analytically distinct levels of 'talk' (political rhetoric and symbolism), 'decision' (written policy statements, specific legislation, programmes, etc.) and 'action' (the actual implementation of such policies on the ground)' (Jones and Newburn 2007: 23).

Canada, it appears, was more 'talk' than 'action' when it came to 'toughening up' the youth justice system. Custody levels did not change during the 1990s; indeed if anything they started declining during the later 1990s. Moreover, there were no increases in transferring cases to adult court. Thus, with respect to 'policy transfer', although some (e.g. Cavadino and Dignan, this volume) might expect that given the proximity of Canada to the USA, along with the generally similar political economies, many of the US youth justice policies would have transferred over to Canada, this does not appear to be the case. Youth justice policy in Canada appears to be driven more by social, political and cultural specificities (e.g. institutional arrangements – namely federalism, historical federal concern about the overuse of custody, Quebec culture towards youths etc.) and less by simple policy transfer from the USA. Policy transfer appeared to be limited to the use of similar rhetoric in the two countries. Unlike the UK context, where British politicians have looked to the USA for policy ideas, Canada has remained relatively isolated from the USA. There appears to be no networking or meetings between youth justice officials in Canada and those in the USA to exchange or discuss policy ideas. Indeed, publicly it appears to be beneficial for politicians to distance themselves from American criminal justice (and other) policies.

However, it is also clear that Canada has a limit to how much punitive rhetoric it will tolerate. When trying to sell new youth justice legislation primarily through making it sound 'tough' the government seriously underestimated the effect, most notably in Quebec. Most recently that rhetoric cost the Conservative government a majority. As discussed earlier, given the culture in Quebec – in particular, concern over child welfare and social programmes for youths – Quebec tends to have a moderating influence on Canadian policies (Doob and Sprott 2004; Tonry 2007). The federal government cannot easily dismiss complaints from Quebec as complaints can turn into reasons why Quebecers will not vote for the federal party in power; or, at the extreme, complaints can turn into justifications for why Quebec should separate from the rest of Canada.

At the same time as the government was focusing on 'tough-sounding' changes, it was faced with concerns about the overuse of custody. The historical concerns about overusing custody for youths began in the 1960s and cast a long shadow. Thus, throughout the 1990s the federal government noted that custody must be reserved only for the most serious offences. That theme even made it into the broader media press releases, though obviously did not receive the same attention as the tough-sounding changes did.

It is perhaps because of this long history of being concerned about the use of custody, coupled with Quebec as a moderating influence, that the policy transfer from the USA only focused on rhetoric. Additionally, a rejection of American-style policies typically garners favour with Canadian voters. Thus, with respect to policy transfer from the USA, Canada's culture may not allow for much more than punitive rhetoric to take hold. As Newburn and Sparks (2004: 5) note, 'it is the sociopolitical and cultural context in which transfer occurs, or is attempted, that has the most profound effect on the eventual shape and style of the policy concerned'. Canada's structure of political and juridical systems, the role of non-elected bureaucrats and civil servants and role of expert opinion also likely helped to keep the punitive rhetoric from spilling over into policy (see Webster and Doob, 2007 for further discussion of what they have called 'protective factors' for Canada).

As for what the future holds for Canada, and whether the long-standing tradition of being concerned about the overuse of custody will continue, it is difficult to predict. There are signs that the current government may continue in the same vein, highlighting 'tough' changes that have no effect on the implementation of the law. Moreover, given the recent election results the Conservatives may have learned a valuable lesson about the consequence of alienating Quebec. However, there is also a chance that the hard-right minority government currently in power will begin to shift policy. Campbell (2000: 346) has suggested that there has been an increasing lack of confidence in expert opinion and that this has been extending even to civil servants who try to advise the government such that there has been an 'increase in political-style personal attacks on public servants'. Nonetheless, it is remarkable that Canada managed to reduce youth custody by a substantial amount during an era where it was politically unwise to do so. Whether Canada will continue along these lines is unclear.

References

Bottoms, A. (1995) 'Philosophy and politics of sentencing' in C. Clarkson and R. Morgan (eds.), *Politics of Sentencing Reform*, Oxford: Clarendon Press, pp. 17–49.

Campbell, M. (2000) 'Politics and public servants: observations on the current state of criminal law reform', *Canadian Journal of Criminology*, 42(3), 341–54.

Department of Justice (1965) *Juvenile Delinquency in Canada: The Report of the Department of Justice Committee on Juvenile Delinquency*, Ottawa: Government of Canada.

(1999) *Minister of Justice Introduces New Youth Justice Law*, Press release, March 11. Ottawa: Department of Justice, Canada.

(2008) Statement from the Minister of Justice concerning the Supreme Court of Canada's decision on *R. v. D.B.*, 16 May, http://www.justice.gc.ca/eng/news-nouv/nr-cp/2008/doc_32255.html.

Doob, A. N. (2001) *Youth Court Judges' Views of the Youth Justice System: The Results of a Survey*, Ottawa: Department of Justice.

Doob, A. N. and Sprott, J. B. (2004) 'Youth justice in Canada' in M. Tonry and A. Doob (eds.), *Crime and Justice: A Review of the Research*, vol. 31, Chicago: University of Chicago Press, pp. 185–242.

Federal–Provincial–Territorial Task Force on Youth Justice (1996) *A Review of the Young Offenders Act and the Youth Justice System in Canada*, Ottawa: Department of Justice.

Giles, C. and Jackson, M. (2003) 'Bill C-7: the new Youth Criminal Justice Act: a darker Young Offenders Act?', *International Journal of Comparative and Applied Criminal Justice*, 27(1), 19–38.

Hirsch, A. von (1976) *Doing Justice: The Choice of Punishments*, New York: Hill and Wang.

Hogeveen, B. (2005) 'If we are tough on crime, if we punish crime, then people get the message: constructing and governing the punishable young offender in Canada during the late 1990s', *Punishment and Society*, 7(1), 73–89.

Jones, T. and Newburn, T. (2007) *Policy Transfer and Criminal Justice: Exploring US Influence over British Crime Control Policy*, Maidenhead: Open University Press.

Lefebvre, P., Merrigan, P. and Verstraete, M. (2008) 'Dynamic labour supply effects of childcare subsidies: evidence from a Canadian natural experiment on low-fee universal child care', 6 October 2008, http://ssrn.com/abstract=1279674.

Newburn, T. and Jones, T. (2005) 'Symbolic politics and penal populism: the long shadow of Willie Horton', *Crime Media Culture*, 1(1), 72–87.

Newburn, T. and Sparks, R. (2004) 'Criminal justice and political cultures' in T. Newburn and R. Sparks (eds.), *Criminal Justice and Political Cultures: National and International Dimensions of Crime Control*, Cullompton: Willan Publishing, pp. 1–15.

Pollitt, C. (2001) 'Convergence: the useful myth?', *Public Administration*, 79(4), 933–47.

Sprott, J. B. and Doob, A. N. (1998) 'One law, ten outcomes: imprisonment in Canada', *Overcrowded Times*, 9(4), 1–9.

(2006) *Understanding Trends in the Use of Youth Court and in the Use of Custody under the Youth Criminal Justice Act*, Ottawa: Department of Justice.

Sprott, J. B. and Snyder, H. N. (1999) 'Youth crime in the U.S. and Canada, 1991 to 1996', *Overcrowded Times*, 10(5), 1, 12–19.

Standing Committee on Justice and Legal Affairs (1997) *Reviewing Youth Justice*, Shaughnessy Cohen, M.P., Chair, Thirteenth Report of the Standing Committee on Justice and Legal Affairs, House of Commons, Ottawa: House of Commons.

Tonry, M. (2007) 'Determinants of penal policies' in M. Tonry (ed.), *Crime, Punishment, and Politics in Comparative Perspective: Crime and Justice: A Review of the Research*, vol. 36, Chicago: University of Chicago Press, pp. 1–48.

Trépanier, J. (1983) 'The Quebec Youth Protection Act: institutionalized diversion' in R. R. Corrado, M. Le Blanc and J. Trépanier (eds.), *Current Issues in Juvenile Justice*, Toronto: Butterworths.

(2004) 'What did Quebec not want? Opposition to the adoption of the Youth Criminal Justice Act in Quebec', *Canadian Journal of Criminology and Criminal Justice*, 46(3), 273–99.

Webster, C. M. and Doob, A. N. (2007) 'Punitive trends and stable imprisonment rates in Canada' in M. Tonry (ed.), *Crime, Punishment, and Politics in Comparative Perspective: Crime and Justice: A Review of the Research*, vol. 36, Chicago: University of Chicago Press, pp. 297–369.

14

Liberty, equality and justice: democratic culture and punishment*

SUSANNE KARSTEDT

1 Convergence and divergence: criminal punishment in contemporary democracies

Presently, imprisonment rates in the oldest of modern democracies, the United States are at historically high levels, and by far exceed those in other democracies. Imprisonment rates in the USA are affecting the social fabric of neighbourhoods and communities, and even impact on democratic elections in a way that changes their results (Manza and Uggen 2006). Even if this has often been seen as a case of 'American exceptionalism', as the exceptional scope and velocity of the increase of imprisonment rates in the USA was not matched in other Western democracies, it raises the question whether democratic societies are particularly susceptible to 'penal excess', which might endanger the very mechanisms of rule, law and justice on which democracies are founded. The exceptional rise of imprisonment rates in the USA took place against the backdrop of a less distinct increase in Canada (Webster and Doob in this volume; Tonry 2004), and most Western as well as Eastern European countries. The trend toward decreasing imprisonment rates that had defined the early decades of the second half of the twentieth century was reversed latest in the 1980s (see Tonry 2004; Tonry and Farrington 2005; Lacey 2008; Lappi-Seppälä 2008). The trend towards higher imprisonment rates initially trailed the general increase of crime that took place in all democratic countries (Rosenfeld and Messner 2009); however, it seems that in the long run it has been largely unaffected by the ensuing 'crime drop' (van Dijk 2006), if it did not take the opposite direction (see also Tonry 2004).

* Parts of this paper are published in German in Dünkel *et al.* (2010). I am grateful to John Braithwaite, Steven Messner, Gary LaFree and Frieder Dünkel for their comments and discussions.

Notwithstanding such common trends, democracies are far from convergence in terms of penal punishment. As Cavadino and Dignan note in their careful assessment of penal policies in twelve democracies:

Even the most general trends are not all going in the same direction everywhere. And with the US imprisonment rate far exceeding that of any other country, the differences remain massive. Some convergence, yes; homogenisation – far from it.   [2006a: 440]

In fact, democratic societies differ considerably as to the frequency of prison sentences passed by courts, their actual execution and, finally, the completion of sentences. They differ according to how long offenders serve their sentences in prison, the conditions of imprisonment and the treatment of offenders in prison and after their release, even where supranational laws, and guidelines exist as in Europe (van Zyl Smit and Snacken 2009; and this volume). In 2008, the imprisonment rate in Australia (129 per 100,000 of the population) was twice as high as in Denmark (63); and in the United Kingdom (163 per 100,000) nearly twice as high as in Germany (89) and nearly three times as high as in Norway (69). However, none of these countries, who all experienced an increase of their imprisonment rates during the past decades can compete with the US imprisonment rate of 756 per 100,000 (all data, Walmsley 1999–2009).

These figures emerge at the surface of historical and deeply engrained differences between the penal systems of democracies and testify to their embeddedness within distinct institutional patterns of democratic societies (see Tonry 2004; Lacey 2008; Karstedt 2010). These institutional patterns transcend those directly related to the system of criminal justice, as they epitomise the general values and broader principles of democratic societies that impact on the penal system in contemporary societies. The process of policy-making in democracies responds to public opinion and demand for punishment, and both interact in the outcome of penal policies, though in differing ways (Tonry 2004: 1192). Democracies differ in their populations' 'taste for punishment', in the extent to which the public is willing to defer to professional expertise on crime and punishment and, finally, in adopting more consensual versus more adversarial policies of democratic government (Tonry 2004; Lacey 2008). Differences between democracies extend to specific penal policies: Manza and Uggen (2006) showed that a growing number of convicted felons are disenfranchised in the USA, resulting in particularly deprived neighbourhoods and communities being without any democratic representation proper. In contrast, sentenced offenders in European democracies mostly have the right to vote and even to stand for election, albeit considerable differences between European countries do exist (van Zyl Smit and Snacken 2009; and this volume).

From a more cursory perspective such differences between democratic societies in terms of the level and development of penal punishment do not directly suggest that democratic societies have common or built-in mechanisms that are conducive to particular types and frequency of punishment or generate particular levels of punitiveness.[1] This seems equally to apply to democratic institutional regimes and patterns (see Lacey 2008), as well as to democratic values that are widespread, accepted and held in high esteem among the public in democratic societies. The public in Denmark with low imprisonment rates can be assumed to support these penal policies as much as the public in the USA is supportive of high imprisonment rates (Useem *et al.* 2003), and in both countries democratic values are equally deeply embedded and widely accepted. As van Kesteren (2009) has recently shown, for a cross-national sample in developed countries, public support for imprisonment does not unambiguously translate into actual sentencing severity, and is in fact reversely related to an index of sentencing severity.

'We do not respect law in the abstract but the values which the laws of the community preserve', Herbert Mead wrote in 1918 (Mead 1964: 218). The classics of sociology from Durkheim to Foucault made punishment and penal systems a core element within the institutional patterns of society. Penal systems embody the spirit and the beliefs of collectives, and the contrast between good and evil, as well as between punishment and atonement, are defining and core cultural dynamics of societies. This applies in particular to democratic societies. We expect that punishment expresses and embodies the values of democratic communities, or are at least related to values held by these communities, even if they are mitigated through the process of governance in democratic societies. Intuitively, democratic values therefore should shape the regimes of criminal punishment that democratic communities and polities are willing to adopt. Popular demands that sentencing in courts should reflect the attitudes and values of the affected community are particularly pronounced in Anglo-American democracies, and the

[1] Punitiveness is a multifaceted concept, that refers to 'objective measures' like imprisonment rates, prison conditions etc. and thus to jurisdictions, as well as to 'subjective' measures of attitudes toward the punishment of criminals among social groups and total populations (see e.g. Unnever and Cullen 2010).

criminal justice system in these countries is not as 'insulated' from the impact of populist demands (see Zimring and Johnson 2006), as in countries where the penal system is embedded in civil law traditions (see Tonry 2004).

The distinct significance of penal law and criminal justice is further particularly visible in processes of democratisation (Karstedt and LaFree 2006). Establishing the rule of law within all agencies of criminal justice ranks among the most decisive steps towards democracy, and failure of the rule of law in criminal justice is generally deemed a signal for more far-reaching failures and obstacles in the process of democratisation (*ibid.*; Loader 2006). Latin American democracies have been described as 'disjunctive democracies' (Caldeira and Holston 1999) due to illegal and unrestricted use of force by the police, poor prison conditions and failing penal courts; accordingly, the failures of establishing the rule of law in the criminal justice system amount to an 'abdication of democratic authority' (Mendez 1999: 19). However, as much as we assume that the basic principles guiding criminal punishment and policing are decisive for processes of democratisation, we rarely expect that police or criminal justice can make major contributions to democratic development in established and mature democracies (Loader 2006).[2] Whilst we take for granted that the criminal justice system is decisive in the process of establishing democratic institutions, we hardly expect that severe shortcomings of criminal justice can contribute to the demise of established democracies.

Neither core values nor institutions of democracies unfold in unambiguous patterns common to all democracies. The innate tensions of democracies generate distinct differences between values and institutions of democratic countries; these differences should also become visible in criminal justice systems, levels of punishment and punitiveness among the public. The focus of this chapter will be on core democratic values – the basic culture of democracies – and their impact on penal punishment, as measured by imprisonment rates and prison conditions. Are democratic values conducive to harsher criminal justice, or are they capable of attenuating and restricting penal punishment? The nature of the question requires a comparative and international perspective (Karstedt and LaFree 2006), which as Tonry (2004: 1195) asserts 'is in its infancy'. David Nelken (2009) has recently drawn attention to pitfalls

---

[2] From a historical perspective, the rule of law precedes the establishment of modern democracies by nearly two centuries.

of comparative research on criminal justice particularly applying to the questions posed here. We tend to assume that bad causes have bad consequences; for example, that neoliberal policies and decreasing welfare are driving imprisonment rates up (although for a critique of such an assumption see Harcourt 2010).[3] Vice versa, we would tend to ascribe a positive impact to democratic values and institutions in holding imprisonment rates at bay and improve prison conditions. It is therefore of utmost importance to be aware of the distinctive value patterns and institutional regimes that dominate different democratic societies, and of mechanisms that generate convergence as well as of those that produce divergence between democracies.

This chapter contributes to a small and growing body of research on democracy and penal punishment that will be presented in the following section. The next section will explore two core democratic values – individualism and egalitarianism – and their potential impact on two indicators of penal punishment: imprisonment rates and prison conditions. The cross-national comparative study is based on a sample of sixty-seven countries, and covers the period from 1999–2005; it provides bi-variate analyses of the impact of core democratic values and related structural indicators.

2   Democracy and punishment

The huge differences between penal punishment in contemporary democracies have stimulated criminological interest in democratic regimes and mechanisms that either shield, restrict or absorb populist demands for penal sanctions and punitiveness or, on the other hand, surrender criminal justice to such demands. They each focus on one dimension of democracy – its institutional system of governance, in particular electoral systems, the relationship between the public and criminal justice and, finally, the particular embodiment of democratic values within and through the system of penal justice.

In her exploration of *The Prisoners' Dilemma* in contemporary democracies, Nicola Lacey (2008; see also this volume) focuses on those mechanisms of the institutional framework of democracies, through

---

[3] Such fallacies apply to research on the relationship between welfare expenditure and imprisonment rates, if not controlled for age of the population. In countries with ageing populations, welfare expenditures increase, in particular when pensions and costs of healthcare are included; however, ageing populations usually have decreasing crime rates, which accounts for the strong negative relationship (see Downes and Hansen 2006).

which democracies seek consensus and support, and transform these into political decision-making. Majority rule and single-party governments generate partisanship and more adversarial styles of politics, which all make crime and punishment a more salient subject in political and public discourse (Simon 2007). In contrast, democracies with proportional representation more often have coalition governments and foster more consensual styles of politics. Both these institutional frameworks produce distinct institutional outcomes in terms of penal policies and systems. In terms of the level of 'insulation' of the criminal justice system from public demands and political bodies that both systems provide, proportional representation and coalition governments seem to be more insulated from popular demands and attitudes conducive to penal severity. The combination of proportional representation and coalition governments retards and dilutes demands from small, single issue groups. In contrast, majority rule and single-party governments have a built-in dynamic towards enhancing such issues and spreading them throughout the electorate (e.g. for Germany see Karstedt 2002; 2003; Tonry 2004). Lacey thus identifies a 'comparative advantage' for democracies with proportional representation that impedes tendencies towards harsher penal policies and more generally account for a lower level of imprisonment.[4]

Lacey (2008) bases her argument mainly on a number of West and North European countries and those countries that Cavadino and Dignan (2006a) had included in their comparison of imprisonment rates and other features of the penal system. Both studies confirm the contrast between Scandinavian and Western European countries, on the one hand, and the Anglo-American world (including the United Kingdom, the USA, Australia and New Zealand) on the other, which all have majority rule in their electoral systems. Lappi-Seppälä (2008) reaches the same conclusion as Lacey by using Lijphart's (1999) classification of consensual and adversarial systems of democratic governance (see also Tonry 2004). Both authors base their observations on a small and highly selective sample of democratic countries that mainly includes European and countries influenced by the Anglo-American model; whether these results can be generalised towards a more encompassing cross-national sample is presently doubtful.

---

[4] See Karstedt (2006b) for an application of the concept of 'comparative advantages' of democracies with regard to levels of violence.

Lappi-Seppälä (2008) analysed the particular relationship between citizens and penal justice in democracies where penal punishment should take up and express collective emotions and demands for punishment. Indeed, this relationship requires that citizens trust criminal justice institutions that they are acting in accordance with such demands and emotions; consequently a lack of trust in these institutions should engender not only more punitive demands but also actually harsher crime policies and more severe sentences. In particular, Frank Zimring and his colleagues (Zimring *et al.* 2001; Zimring and Johnson 2006) and Jonathan Simon (2007) have argued that mistrust of governing institutions is decisive for communities in their demands for 'justice for the victims' and an end of what they see as inappropriate leniency of the criminal justice system and 'big government' towards criminal offenders (see Karstedt 2006a). His sample only comprises European countries, for which he shows that countries with a high level of generalised trust in others and trust in the justice system have significantly lower rates of imprisonment. The Scandinavian countries with their well-known high levels of trust rank at the lower end of the punishment scale, whilst countries like Portugal and East European countries with low levels of trust rank at the upper end of imprisonment rates. Levels of trust are generally higher in mature democracies than in those still going through a period of transition; however, it is decisive for the interpretation of his results that income inequality and ethnic differentiation and fractionalisation both reduce the level of trust, and both are factors that increase the imprisonment rate. Consequently, the relation between levels of trust and imprisonment rates could neither be confirmed for a more encompassing cross-national sample, nor for regions outside of Europe, and only for the combination of European and Anglo-American nations as used by Lappi-Seppälä (Karstedt 2008). Furthermore, Unnever and Cullen (2010) found little support for the impact of distrust in courts on punitiveness for the citizens of the USA.

In his historical study, James Whitman (2003) contrasts three democratic countries, the USA, France and Germany. He asks in which ways the pathway towards democracy has a continuous impact on contemporary penal policies, and analyses the democratic and egalitarian revolutions in these countries between the eighteenth and twentieth centuries. Democracy profoundly changes the 'politics of status' and as criminal punishment implies a change of status for those affected, and is deemed a process of degradation, both should change concomitantly. Whitman analyses the treatment of sentenced offenders and prisoners, and the conditions of incarceration. While the egalitarian USA 'levelled down' and geared the treatment of offenders toward the lowest status group, namely the slaves, both France and later Germany 'levelled up' and adjusted treatment of all prisoners to high-ranking, often political, prisoners. This accounts for the significantly harsher treatment in the USA until today as it can be traced back to the status of slaves and contemporary recent groups of immigrants. Whitman teases out the extraordinary differences in status politics in democracies, notwithstanding their general and pervading egalitarian values.

In sum, these studies suggest that the mechanisms and values of democracies are decisive factors in determining the level of punitiveness in democratic countries and, as democracies widely differ and are far from uniformity and homogeneity in terms of governance and values, this should be reflected in differential penal systems and punitiveness. It is therefore important to address these contingencies and differences when analysing the impact of democracy on the level of punishment.

3 Democratic values and punishment

3.1 Contingencies and tensions

As Alexis de Tocqueville (2000 [1835 and 1840]) noted, both the core values of democracy, individualism and egalitarianism do not unfold in an unambiguous value pattern common to all democracies; rather their built-in tensions generate very distinct patterns. In his account of the USA, the first of modern democracies, he pointed to the paradox and inconsistencies that arise out of the innate tensions between individual autonomy, egalitarianism and integration. Democracy simultaneously gives rise to individual independence and high levels of conformity: the rights of individuals are counterbalanced by strong forces towards conformity. Majority rules imply dominance and authority, and rely on submission at the same time that they provoke resistance. Tolerance and individual rights simultaneously come with strong belief and profound rejection of belief, with norm compliance and violation of norms. Democracy offers its citizens wide opportunities for deviant, licentious and dangerous behaviour, and simultaneously reduces their desire to do what democracy allows them to do by establishing common, shared values and procedures that ensure the exertion of

individual rights. Thus democracies can differ to the extent they give
way to self-expression, or put more emphasis on norm compliance.
Interestingly, de Tocqueville was convinced that the flaws and innate
tensions of democracy could be overcome by more democracy, not less
(Elster 1999). Calibrating egalitarian values with social and economic
inequality, individual autonomy with social control and cohesion could
only succeed if democracy expanded and became firmly embedded in
society. His observations further point to the potential diversity of
democratic regimes and value patterns. Democratic societies resolve
these tensions in different ways, and have developed different mechanisms to address these antagonisms; accordingly their penal regimes also
should differ widely.

De Tocqueville had identified the two defining democratic values,
individual autonomy and egalitarianism. Both values are the foundation
for democracy's practices and institutions, which in turn foster democratic values (Jaggers and Gurr 1995: 476); they guide institutions as well
as citizens. As they define democracies they distinguish them from
authoritarian and non-democratic societies.[5] Both values are vital in
shaping the regimes and institutions of punishment in democratic
communities. Imprisonment and the conditions of deprivation of liberty
in penal regimes fundamentally contradict democratic values of individual autonomy, and therefore require justification. Values of individual
autonomy and freedom should clearly restrict the power of criminal
justice institutions, support due process and also reduce restrictions of
freedom that are imposed as sanctions. Further, these values should
impact on the treatment of offenders within the criminal justice system,
which implies treating them with dignity and the respect that the
individual can expect and is afforded in democracies, by democratic
institutions, its representatives and fellow citizens.

Following Whitman's (2003) argument, egalitarian values should in
particular be important in shaping punishment regimes, and distinguish
between democracies and non-democracies, as well as between democracies, presumably even more so than values of individual autonomy.
These are the values that define practices and politics of status: how
those in power are restricted, what treatment those with lower status can
expect, the extent to which status differences shape everyday encounters

---

[5] Recent studies based on the World Values Survey demonstrated that democratic values
increase the probability of the development of democratic practices and institutions,
reach higher levels in established democracies, and develop concomitantly with the
process of democratisation (Inglehart and Welzel 2005).

and finally the extent to which any kind of debasing or degrading treatment is acceptable as an expression of status differences. Egalitarian values define the extent to which democracies are inclusive, i.e. include all citizens in the community and foster their participation in rights and values (Karstedt 2006b). Egalitarian values therefore are of eminent importance for the ways in which democratic communities treat offenders.

In this chapter, I argue that countries with higher levels of individualistic and egalitarian values differ in their regimes of punishment from those with more collectivistic and authoritarian and non-egalitarian values, the latter having generally more harsh sentencing and punishment regimes. Secondly, I argue that democratic values are not unfolding in an unambiguous pattern, but have actually developed along very different lines, that in particular affect status practices and politics. These differences should show themselves even in mature democracies and account for differences in punishment regimes between them. Finally, I argue that the precarious nature of democratic values becomes visible when confronted with structural inequality, and that the capacity of democracies for inclusion is tested here; the tensions between democratic values and structure will impact on punishment regimes. In sum, I confront three general hypotheses with data from a cross-national sample of sixty-seven countries:

- Individualistic and egalitarian values generally reduce the harshness of criminal justice.
- The specific pattern of individualistic values and status practices account for differences between punishment regimes in general and between those in mature democracies.
- The tensions between democratic values and actual status differences account for differences between punishment regimes in democracies.

3.2   Two types of egalitarianism

De Tocqueville further observed that egalitarian values co-exist with envy, status differences and social inequality.[6] Egalitarian values do not necessarily nor in the long-run coincide with social equality. Besides these tensions between value patterns and social structure,

---

[6] De Tocqueville, however, never commented on the big divide in the democracy of the United States between its African (then slave) population and white population.

others arise from the simultaneity and equal weight given to values
of individual autonomy and equality in democratic societies. Democracies handle the paradox between egalitarianism and individual
autonomy in two distinct ways, which can be termed, first, either
chance-oriented or *pure meritocratic* egalitarianism, and secondly, *outcome-oriented* egalitarianism. Chance-oriented (or pure meritocratic)
egalitarianism is focused on giving equal chances to each individual at
the start, but allows for individuals making bad choices and not
appropriately using the chances offered to them. Outcome-oriented
egalitarianism, in contrast, focuses on amending where social injustice
disadvantages people thoroughly, and attenuates possible adverse outcomes for individuals, independent of their own responsibility for
their needs.

Thus, chance-oriented or pure meritocratic egalitarianism allows
for considerable status differences, and also assigns a function to them
in terms of social order. Status differences are seen as incentives for
integration and compliance, and consequently those who made bad
choices have to suffer a loss of status. This type of value pattern allows
for the deep 'fall from grace' in case of failure, and exclusion in the
case of non-compliance. Need is seen as the result of personal failure,
not of social injustice. In contrast, outcome-oriented egalitarianism
focuses on reducing status differences and on achieving inclusion by
supporting even those who fail, thus attenuating the purely meritocratic position and its consequences. The democracy of the USA
clearly represents chance-oriented egalitarianism while Scandinavian
and other European countries like Germany represent the second
type. In contrast to what could be expected, some post-communist
countries in this sample, e.g. Poland represent the chance-oriented
and pure meritocratic type.

These value patterns generate distinct status politics and practices,
which impact on the regime of criminal punishment in democracies.
Democracies that promote normative integration more than individualistic self-expression, should adopt more severe practices of criminal
justice regimes. Where value patterns are dominated by chance-oriented
egalitarianism, penal regimes should operate in a way that increases
status differences between offenders and other, norm-abiding, citizens.
Confirming and deepening status differences are both built into the
practices of punishment regimes, and result in harsher sentencing practices and penal regimes than in countries with outcome-oriented
egalitarianism.

4 Sample and data

The following analyses are based on a cross-national sample of sixty-seven countries comprising of European, Latin and Anglo-American, Asian and Pacific as well as of African countries, for which data on penal regimes, value patterns and structural indicators were collected. Large cross-national samples like this one allow for statistical analyses and generalisation of results; however, they cannot account for the particularities of specific cases as case studies of countries do. In principle, both strategies have their merits, even if the highly selective and small sample might be the most problematic of all strategies (Karstedt 2001; Nelken 2009). This study pursues the strategy of using a comparatively large sample and a small number of quantifiable indicators. The data cover the period from the first wave of the World Values Survey in the 1980s until 2000 (European Values Study Group and World Values Survey Association (1981–2004)), which provide a number of value patterns. The Polity Index provides measurement of the type and quality of democratic institutions and regimes covering the period from 1999 to 2003. The core democratic values – individualism and egalitarianism – are available for an increasing number of countries since the 1960s. Data on penal regimes span the period from 1999 to 2005 (see Table 14.1). For all indicators mean values for the respective periods were used; this allowed for adjusting for missing values and generally higher stability of measurement. In addition it was taken care that independent variables were measured previous to the measurement period of the dependent variables in order not to confound causal ordering.

The study uses two indicators of penal regimes: the rate of imprisonment per 100,000 of the population (Walmsley 1999–2009) and 'prison conditions', which are included in the Country Reports regularly issued by the US State Department (US State Department 1999–2005).[7] This qualitative assessment is based on a number of indicators of conditions of life in the country's prisons. Neapolitano (2001) has turned these into a scale with three general categories: first, prison conditions fulfil minimum international standards; secondly, they are 'harsh' and do not fulfil these standards; and thirdly, they are harsh bordering on being 'life threatening'. This scale was used as the basis for a new scale with five categories as the first and the last of Neapolitano's categories did not seem to differentiate sufficiently between countries, and only roughly represented the qualitative categories. The new scale comprises

---

[7] This might be the reason for the exclusion of the US from these reports.

Table 14.1 *Prison population (rate of imprisonment) and prison conditions 1999–2005*

Countries	Prison population 1999–2005 (per 100.000) (mean)	Prison population 2005 (per 100.000)	Prison conditions 1999–2005 (mean)	Prison conditions 2005
Argentina (ARG)	115.3	148	3.9	5
Australia (AUSTR)	110.5	117	1.0	1
Austria (AUS)	91.0	106	1.0	1
Belgium (BEL)	84.5	88	2.0	2
Brazil (BRA)	135.2	183	4.7	5
Canada (CAN)	110.7	116	1.0	1
Chile (CHL)	235.7	212	3.0	3
China (CHN)	113.5	118	4.0	4
Colombia (COL)	142.7	152	4.0	4
Costa Rica (CRI)	208.3	177	2.1	3
Czech Republic (CZR)	198.7	184	1.9	1
Denmark (DEN)	63.8	70	1.0	1
Ecuador (ECU)	75.5	100	3.0	3
Egypt (EGY)	110.5	121	3.4	3
El Salvador (ELS)	136.8	184	3.4	4
Ethiopia (ETH)			3.0	3
Finland (FIN)	58.3	71	1.0	1
France (FRA)	88.2	91	1.9	2
Germany (GER)	95.0	96	1.0	1
Ghana (GHA)	51.8	54	4.6	5
Greece (GRE)	74.3	82	4.0	4
Guatemala (GUA)	69.2	68	4.0	4
Hong Kong (HKO)	178.0	189	1.0	
Hungary (HUN)	158.2	165	2.0	2
India (IND)	31.8	29	3.9	5
Indonesia (INO)	27.7	38	4.0	4
Iran (IRN)	199.0	194	4.0	4
Iraq (IRQ)			4.4	4
Ireland (IRE)	80.2	85	2.4	2
Israel (ISR)	170.0	209	1.7	3
Italy (ITA)	93.8	98	2.9	2
Jamaica (JAM)	167.8	176	3.0	3
Japan (JAP)	47.3	58	2.7	2
Kenya (KEN)	131.3	169	5.0	5

Countries	Prison population 1999–2005 (per 100.000) (mean)	Prison population 2005 (per 100.000)	Prison conditions 1999–2005 (mean)	Prison conditions 2005
Kuwait (KUW)	108.7	148	2.1	3
Lebanon (LEB)	181.2	145	3.0	3
Libya (LIB)	142.2	207	3.7	3
Malaysia (MAL)	129.2	174	2.9	3
Mexico (MEX)	149.8	182	3.3	5
Netherlands (NET)	96.0	123	1.0	1
New Zealand (NZE)	153.3	168	1.4	2
Nigeria (NIG)	39.7	31	5.0	5
Norway (NOR)	59.7	65	1.0	1
Pakistan (PAK)	52.5	55	4.1	4
Panama (PAN)	312.3	354	4.9	5
Peru (PER)	104.2	114	4.0	4
Philippines (PHI)	79.5	94	4.0	4
Poland (POL)	185.8	209	3.0	3
Portugal (POR)	133.5	128	3.3	4
Saudi Arabia (SAR)	77.5	110	1.0	1
Sierra Leone (SIL)			3.7	3
Singapore (SIN)	388.2	392	2.0	2
South Africa (SAF)	391.5	413	3.3	4
South Korea (SKO)	137.0	121	2.0	1
Spain (ESP)	123.2	140	1.4	4
Sweden (SWE)	66.8	75	1.3	2
Switzerland (SWI)	80.5	81	1.7	2
Taiwan (TWN)	200.2	251	2.0	2
Tanzania (TAN)	125.5	116	5.0	5
Thailand (THA)	314.5	264	3.0	3
Turkey (TUR)	97.5	95	3.0	3
United Arab Emirates (UAE)	250.0	250	2.0	1
United Kingdom (UK)	132.8	142	2.0	2
Uruguay (URU)	159.3	209	3.4	4
United States of America (USA)	687.7	714		
Venezuela (VEN)	88.5	83	4.0	4
Zambia (ZAM)	157.0	122	5.0	5

Source: Walmsley (1999–2009); US State Department (1999–2005); Marshall and Jaggers (2005); own computations
Grey shaded areas indicate mature democracies, ranked 8–10 in the Polity Index.

five categories: (1) 'fulfils minimum standards'; (2) 'fulfils standards with some deficits'; (3) 'does not fulfil minimum standards'; (4) 'harsh but not life threatening'; and (5) 'life threatening'.[8] Neither indicator is correlated and prison conditions are only related to the mean length of prison sentences. For both indicators, mean values for the period between 1999 and 2005 were calculated in order to adjust for inconsistencies in the data and reports.

Besides the core democratic values of individualism and egalitarianism the set of independent variables includes specific value patterns, the assessment of democratic regimes and institutions with the Polity Index, as well as measures of social inequality and ethnic differentiation in order to indicate the extent of integrative tensions in democratic societies. The core democratic values of individualism and egalitarianism are based on a study by Hofstede (Hofstede and Hofstede 2005), which has been extended since the 1970s to more than sixty countries. Hofstede collected these value patterns as cultural and social practices, and as such they represent 'lived values' (see Karstedt 2001; 2006b). The data are collected on the individual level and aggregated, with values for each country ranging from 0 to 100. Individualism and its opposite, collectivism, measure the detachment from traditional group, family and local bonds and the importance of values of autonomy and individual achievement, and as such the dimension of meritocratic values in democracies. Egalitarianism and its opposite, which Hofstede terms 'power distance', measure the extent to which power, domination and subordination define relationships between different status groups in society or are replaced by more egalitarian orientations; this value pattern represents the egalitarian component of democratic values and practices. High values on both scales represent individualism

---

[8] The categories were coded: (1) compliance with and fulfilment of minimum standards; (2) some deficits, in particular resulting from overcrowding; (3) prison conditions below minimum standards, in particular deficiencies of buildings and sanitary provisions due to the age of buildings; (4) harsh prison conditions, violence between inmates and violence by prison officers; and (5) reports explicitly noting threats to the lives of inmates. This results in slightly different prison conditions for Germany and Sweden, as the reports note overcrowding for Swedish prisons but not for Germany at the start of the century. As the sample includes a number of countries, where prison conditions are rated as 'life threatening', and rates of imprisonment are comparatively low (e.g. in Nigeria), prison conditions are not related to imprisonment rates in the total sample, whilst they are for a sub-sample of European countries. Other indicators of the severity of sanctions like the rate of prisoners with life sentences, or the mean length of prison sentences were only available for a small number of countries and were not used (see van Kesteren (2009) for a more differentiated indicator).

respectively egalitarianism. In all Western industrialized societies, including Australia and New Zealand, individualism is the dominating value pattern, while in Latin American and Islamic countries mostly collectivistic orientations prevail. Asian societies have medium to strong collectivistic orientations. Western industrialized countries – with the exception of Latin European countries (France and Italy) – are distinctly egalitarian, while Latin American and Asian countries are characterised by a comparably low level of egalitarian values, and are dominated by more hierarchical values and practices. Both value patterns are strongly related to the Polity Index (Marshall and Jaggers 2005) and to the Freedom House Index of Civil Liberties (1973–2009), indicating the strong interaction between democratic institutions and democratic values.

The variables indicating the specific type of democratic value pattern were collected from the four waves of the World Values Survey in 1982, 1990, 1995 and 2000. They were calculated as the mean percentage of a country's population who supported the following statements in all waves for which data were available. The statements were: 'Greater respect for authority would be a good thing'; 'Would not like to have people with criminal records as neighbours'; 'We need larger income differences as incentives'; 'Laziness or lack of willpower' is given as a 'reason why people live in need in this country'.[9] The first two items represent the importance of norm compliance and inclusive tendencies in the countries, while the latter two indicate meritocratic versus outcome-oriented egalitarianism. High levels of support indicate the chance-oriented/pure meritocratic value pattern and low levels outcome-oriented egalitarianism.

Variables indicating structural inequality are the Gini Index of income inequality (United Nations Development Program 2002) and the index of ethnic fractionalisation by Alesina and his colleagues (Alesina *et al.* 2003), which includes linguistic, religious and ethnic differentiation. The assessment of democratic regimes and institutions was based on the Polity Index (Marshall and Jaggers 2005). The Polity Index ranks countries on a scale from −10 to +10, where negative values indicate autocracies and dictatorships. Countries with values between 8 and 10 are usually classified as *mature* democracies. Table 14.1 gives an overview of

---

[9] The opposite statements were also used; e.g. 'injustice in society as a reason why people live in need'. The results are similar to those obtained with the selected item.

the sample of countries, imprisonment rates and prison conditions, and their classification as mature democracies on the Polity Index (grey shaded areas).

Analyses were conducted in three steps. First, penal regimes were compared for different levels of individualistic and egalitarian value patterns. Secondly, the impact of specific combinations of democratic values and status practice on penal regimes was analysed; to this purpose groups of countries were defined according to the median of the distribution, and contrasted by Oneway ANOVA. In a third step, value patterns and structural variables were analysed for the sub-sample of mature democracies thus controlling for democratic institutions and governance. Groups of countries above and below the median were contrasted in order to account for the distribution of the independent variables, and t-tests were used; the hypotheses allowed for one-sided tests.

5   Results

The scatter plot and the regression line in both Figures 14.1 and 14.3 demonstrate that neither of the two democratic value patterns impacts on the rate of imprisonment. Countries where individualism and individual autonomy is dominating do not differ, and even have slightly higher rates of imprisonment than countries with collectivistic value patterns. The extraordinarily high rate of imprisonment in the USA is clearly visible in both figures. However, decisive is the complete lack of any relationship. In contrast, a strong and linear relationship with both democratic values is found for prison conditions in Figures 14.2 and 14.4. Individualistic value patterns generate respect for others even under conditions of imprisonment, and egalitarian values reduce power differentials and domination, and they prevent debasing status politics even for inmates in prisons. It is important to note that measurement of these values represents 'lived values' and practices of everyday life; as such they extend into the penal systems of these countries. Countries where these democratic values dominate do not imprison less offenders, but rather treat prisoners better and provide for better conditions in prisons. Democratic values and the cultural and institutional practices that build on these values define *the way how we punish*, but not *how many we punish*.

In Tables 14.2 and 14.3 countries with high (above median) levels of individualism are analysed and their penal regimes are contrasted according to the extent to which norm compliance is stressed or way is

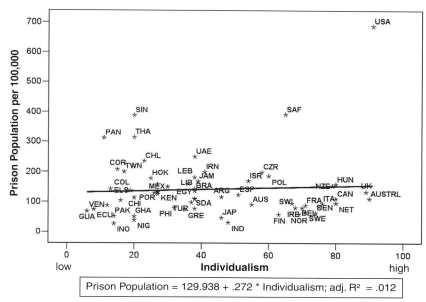

Prison Population = 129.938 + .272 * Individualism; adj. R² = .012

For countries see Table 14.1.

Figure 14.1 Individualism and prison population 1999–2005.

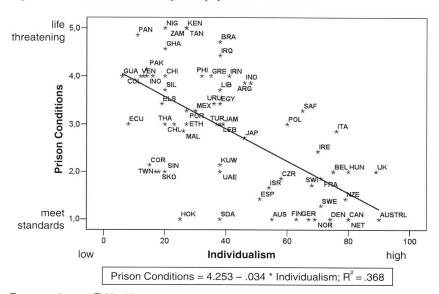

Prison Conditions = 4.253 − .034 * Individualism; R² = .368

For countries see Table 14.1.

Figure 14.2 Individualism and prison conditions 1999–2005.

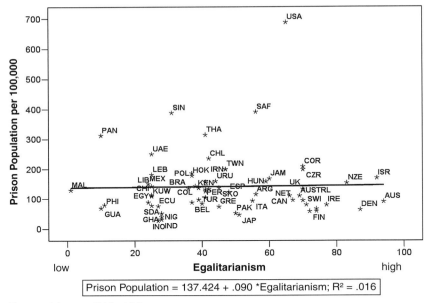

Prison Population = 137.424 + .090 *Egalitarianism; R² = .016

For countries see Table 14.1.

Figure 14.3   Egalitarianism and prison populations 1999–2005.

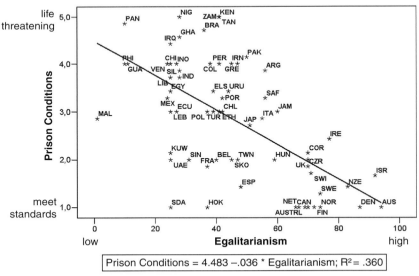

Prison Conditions = 4.483 −.036 * Egalitarianism; R²= .360

For countries see Table 14.1.

Figure 14.4   Egalitarianism and prison conditions 1999–2005.

Table 14.2 *High individualism and preference for norm compliance: prison population and prison conditions*

Value pattern	Prison population rank of four: low (1), high (4)	Sign.	Prison conditions rank of four: worst (1), best (4)	Sign.
High individualism and		**ns.**		***
→ low support for authority	lowest (1)	*	best (4)	
→ high support for authority	highest (4)	*	second best (3)	
High individualism and		**		***
→ low support for exclusion of criminals	lowest (1)	**	second best (3)	
→ high support for exclusion of criminals	second highest (3)	**	second worst (2)	

Oneway ANOVA (* p< .05; ** p< .01; *** p< .0001)

given to individual autonomy and self-expression (Table 14.2), and whether meritocratic chance-oriented egalitarianism is preferred in contrast to outcome-oriented egalitarianism (Table 14.3).[10] High levels of support indicate dominance of norm compliance and a more exclusive climate, as well as acceptance of chance-oriented/meritocratic egalitarianism. Imprisonment rates and prison conditions are represented in four groups, ranking from lowest to highest, respectively from best to worst.

As both tables demonstrate, the ensuing value patterns have a strong and significant impact on prison conditions, and are significant for rates of imprisonment only in the case of exclusionary tendencies. However, the direction of the impact on both indicators of penal regimes is unambiguous and corroborates the initial hypotheses. Where support for authority and norm compliance is high, and exclusionary tendencies are more prevalent, there is also a tendency towards higher rates of

[10] An analogous analysis for high levels of egalitarianism produced similar results, as the group includes mostly the same countries. These results are not reported here.

Table 14.3 *High individualism and support for chance-oriented versus outcome-oriented egalitarianism: prison population and prison conditions*

Value pattern	Prison population rank of four: low (1), high (4)	Sign.	Prison conditions rank of four: worst (1), best (4)	Sign.
High individualism and		**ns.**		***
→ low support for large income differences			best (4)	
→ high support for large income differences			second best (3)	
High individualism and		**ns.**		***
→ low support for laziness as reason of need	lowest (1)	*	best (4)	
→ high support for laziness as reason of need	highest (4)	*	second best (3)	

Oneway ANOVA (* p< .05; ** p< .01; *** p< .001)

imprisonment, and clearly a significant decline of prison conditions. If the population supports large income differences, and laziness is predominantly seen as a reason of need, in sum if egalitarianism is chance-oriented, prison conditions are significantly worse than for the opposite value pattern of outcome-oriented egalitarianism. However, there is no significant impact on imprisonment rates, and the predicted direction of impact is only found for one of the indicators of chance-oriented egalitarianism. It needs to be noted though that Tables 14.2 and 14.3 represent only countries with high levels of individualism respectively egalitarianism.[11] Even in these countries where prison

[11] Rankings of countries with predominantly collectivistic and non-egalitarian value patterns are not reported in Tables 14.2 and 14.3. The US were excluded from the analyses; however, if they are included the results for imprisonment rates do not change substantively.

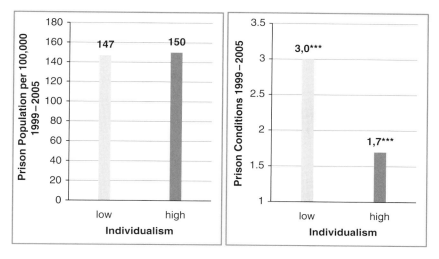

Figure 14.5   Mature democracies: individualism, prison population and prison conditions 1999–2005.

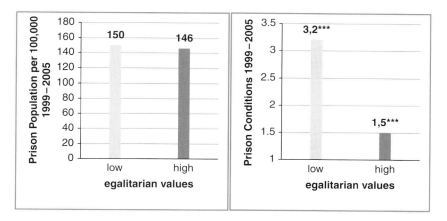

Figure 14.6   Mature democracies: egalitarianism, prison population and prison conditions 1999–2005.

conditions are generally improved, the particular pattern of chance-oriented egalitarianism makes a significant difference in terms of deteriorating prison conditions, and a tendency towards higher imprisonment rates can be found, even if it is not significant.

As democracies differ widely in terms of criminal punishment and penal regimes the question arises whether differences in value patterns

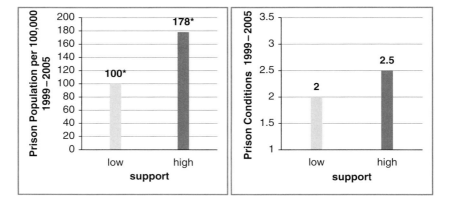

Figure 14.7   Mature democracies: support for 'respect for authority', prison population and prison conditions 1999–2005.

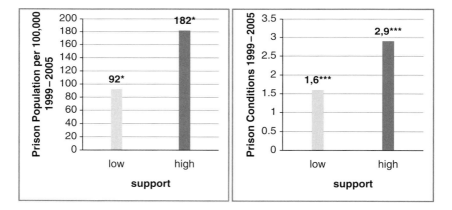

Figure 14.8   Mature democracies: support for exclusion of offenders, prison population and prison conditions 1999–2005.

and ensuing status politics still make a difference within institutionally stable and mature democratic countries, or whether stable democratic institutions reduce or mitigate the impact of value patterns. In order to answer this question the following analyses are conducted only for mature democracies, as defined by a ranking between 8 and 10 on the Polity Index Scale.

Figures 14.5 and 14.6 demonstrate that even in this group of institutionally more homogeneous democratic societies the core values of

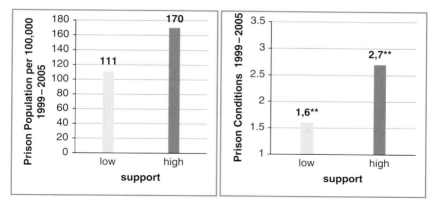

Figure 14.9 Mature democracies: support for 'income differences as incentives', prison population and prison conditions 1999–2005.

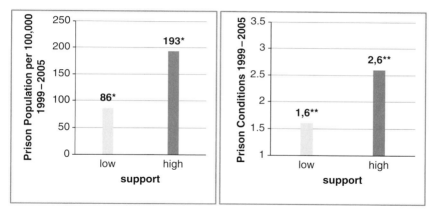

Figure 14.10 Mature democracies: support for 'laziness is reason why people live in need', prison population and prison conditions 1999–2005.

individualism and egalitarianism determine the ways how punishment is executed in prisons and prisoners are treated, but they do not have an impact on the size of the prison population. Acceptance of core democratic values defines the extent of punitiveness in the penal system itself, independent of the maturity and stability of democratic institutions. The results shown in Figures 14.7 and 14.8 corroborate the impact of value patterns in mature democracies, including imprisonment rates. In mature democracies where the population supports norm compliance in contrast to self-expression, and where exclusionary tendencies prevail, imprisonment rates are significantly higher. Results for prison conditions are mixed and, though they tend towards the predicted direction, significant differences are only found for support of exclusion of offenders.

Chance-oriented/pure meritocratic egalitarianism increases imprisonment rates and significantly contributes to deteriorating prison conditions (Figures 14.9 and 14.10). In sum, the findings indicate that the substantial differences between imprisonment rates in democratic countries hardly coincide with specific characteristics and parameters of core democratic values. In contrast, prison conditions are a distinct expression of these value patterns, and they mirror differences between them independent of democratic governance and institutions. The different indicators used in this study clearly demonstrate the far-reaching impact of status politics within the penal system itself. Hierarchy, exclusion and acceptance of chance-oriented/meritocratic egalitarianism as practised in society extend into the penal system, and the way in which people are treated 'outside' defines their treatment 'inside'.

The final analyses address the question whether tensions between structural conditions and democratic values and institutions are responsible for differences in rates of imprisonment and prison conditions. These tensions should be particularly pronounced where social inequality and ethnic fractionalisation thwart the core values of egalitarianism and the democratic ideal of equality and inclusion for all citizens. The results (Figures 14.11 and 14.12) demonstrate that there is a massive and significant impact of social inequality, measured as income inequality on both imprisonment rates and prison conditions in mature democracies, whilst none or only a weak impact is found for ethnic fractionalisation. This would suggest that social inequality confronts mature democracies with a stronger potential for tensions between values and structural conditions. In contrast, ethnic fractionalisation might induce lower levels of such tensions as individualistic values provide conditions for integrating ethnic groups.[12]

---

[12] It cannot be excluded that the indicator of social inequality includes massive discrimination of ethnic groups which is not captured by the factor of ethnic fractionalisation itself.

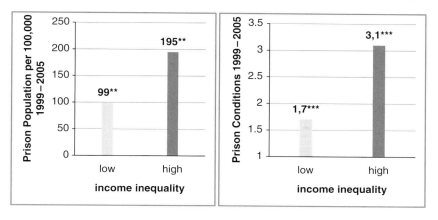

Figure 14.11 Mature democracies: income inequality, prison population and prison conditions 1999–2005.

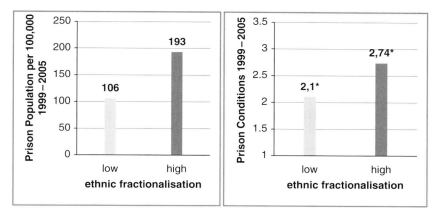

Figure 14.12 Mature democracies: ethnic fractionalisation, prison population and prison conditions 1999–2005.

6 A question of difference: democratic values and punitiveness in penal systems

The core democratic values of individual autonomy and equality are realised as specific value patterns in democratic societies. Two dividing lines set democracies apart. One line runs along the divide between pure meritocratic and chance-oriented versus outcome-oriented egalitarianism, the other one along the divide between integration and norm compliance versus value patterns that promote individual self-expression. These differences, however, do not coincide with the substantial differences in the rate of imprisonment across democratic societies. Rather, these core value patterns have a decisive and consistent impact on prison conditions. As they define status politics and practices and are experienced and practised in the everyday life of citizens, they equally define in which ways offenders and prisoners are treated, even if stable democratic institutions are in place in the criminal justice system, and prison conditions are monitored in accordance with democratic values and institutions. Higher levels of punitiveness within the penal system are finally generated by these status practices. Popular attitudes towards status differences, or towards responsibility for individual exigencies and need seem to support harsher prison conditions, even if they are not necessarily supportive of imprisonment in general (see also van Kesteren 2009). These attitudes in particular seem to approve of status degradation for offenders and prison inmates and consequently contribute to down-grading conditions for imprisoned offenders.

It is plausible to link these results to the important role that values have for welfare regimes in these countries. In the welfare states of North and West Europe, outcome-oriented egalitarianism dominates. Transitional countries like Poland, as well as the Anglo-American world, are distinctly chance-oriented and purely meritocratic, whilst Mediterranean democracies do not tend unequivocally to one or the other pattern. A cautious interpretation of these results needs to include the potential impact of welfare regimes, as Cavadino and Dignan (2006b) have demonstrated for a much smaller sample of countries. A further caveat refers to the fact that in this study, levels of imprisonment rather than increase of imprisonment was analysed. Even if democratic values do not define the level of imprisonment, in particular the meritocratic type might be vulnerable to fast increases and exponential dynamics of rates of imprisonment.

The Janus-face, built-in tensions and ambivalences of democracies which Alexis de Tocqueville was the first to observe, are reflected in their penal systems. Deeply engrained belief systems and cultural practices are difficult to change. However, democracies are adverse to uniform belief systems, and in most countries, including the USA, there is a considerable minority who hold outcome-oriented values. Democracies give voice to both. They are capable of accommodating different voices and provide flexibility for profound change. This might be the genuine comparative advantage of their penal systems.

References

Alesina, A., Devleeschauwer, A., Easterly, W., Kurlat, S. and Wacziarg, R. (2003) 'Ethnic fractionalization', *Journal of Economic Growth*, 8, 155–94.

Caldeira, T. P. R. and Holston, J. (1999) 'Democracy and violence in Brazil', *Comparative Studies in Society and History*, 41(4), 691–729.

Cavadino, M. and Dignan, J. (2006a) 'Penal policy and political economy', *Criminology and Criminal Justice*, 6(4), 435–56.

(2006b) *Penal Systems: A Comparative Approach*, London: Sage.

Dijk, J. van (2006) 'What goes up comes down: explaining falling crime rates', *Criminology in Europe*, 5, 3(3), 17–18.

Downes, D. and Hansen, K. (2006) *The Relationship between Welfare Spending and Imprisonment*, Briefing, 2nd November 2006, London: Crime and Society Foundation.

Dünkel, F., Lappi-Seppälä, T., Morgenstern, T. and Zyl Smit, D. van (2010) (eds.) *Kriminalität, Kriminalpolitik, strafrechtliche Sanktionspraxis und Gefangenenraten im europäischen Vergleich*, 2 vols., Godesberg: Forum.

Elster, J. (1999) *Deliberative Democracy*, Cambridge: Cambridge University Press.

European Values Study Group and World Values Survey Association (1981–2004) European and World Values Surveys four-wave integrated data file, 1981–2004, v.20060423, 2006, *Surveys designed and executed by the European Values Study Group and World Values Survey Association*, File Producers: ASEP/JDS, Madrid, Spain and Tilburg University, Tilburg, the Netherlands. File Distributors: ASEP/JDS and GESIS, Cologne, Germany, www.worldvaluessurvey.org.

Freedom House (1973–2009) *Freedom in the World: Country Ratings and Status by Region*, FIW 1973–2009, Aggregate Data Excel File, www.freedomhouse.org/uploads/fiw09/CompHistData/FIW_ScoresByRegion.xls.

Harcourt, B. (2010) 'Neoliberal penality: a brief genealogy', *Theoretical Criminology*, 14(1), 74–92.

Hofstede, G. and Hofstede, G. J. (2005) (eds.) *Cultures and Organizations: Software of the Mind*, 2nd edn, New York: McGraw-Hill Professional.

Inglehart, R. and Welzel, C. (2005) *Modernization, Cultural Change and Democracy: The Human Development Sequence*, Cambridge: Cambridge University Press.

Jaggers, K. and Gurr, T. (1995) 'Tracking democracy's third wave with the Polity III data', *Journal of Peace Research*, 32, 469–82.

Karstedt, S. (2001) 'Comparing cultures, comparing crime: challenges, prospects and problems for a global criminology', *Crime, Law & Social Change*, 36, 285–308.

(2002) 'Emotions and criminal justice', *Theoretical Criminology*, 6, 299–317.

(2003) 'Moral und Skandal: Die Macht der öffentlichen Moral. Ein Vergleich der Kriminalitätsdiskurse in Deutschland und Großbritannien' in M. Junge (ed.), *Macht und Moral*, Opladen: Westdeutscher Verlag, pp. 255–74.

(2006a) 'Emotions, crime and justice: exploring Durkheimian themes' in M. Deflem (ed.), *Sociological Theory and Criminological Research: Views from Europe and the United States, Sociology of Crime, Law and Deviance*, vol. 7, Oxford: Elsevier, pp. 223–48.

(2006b) 'Democracy, values and violence: paradoxes, tensions, and comparative advantages of liberal inclusion', *Annals of the American Academy of Political and Social Science*, 605, 50–81.

(2008) '*Do trusted governments imprison less? Exploring the trust-punishment nexus with a cross-national sample*', Paper presented at the European Criminology Conference, Edinburgh.

(2010) 'New institutionalism in criminology: approaches, theories and themes' in E. McLaughlin and T. Newburn (eds.), *The Sage Handbook of Criminological Theory*, London: Sage, pp. 337–59.

Karstedt, S. and LaFree, G. (2006) 'Democracy, crime and justice', *Annals of the American Academy of Political and Social Science*, 605, 6–25.

Kesteren, J. van (2009) 'Public attitudes and sentencing policies across the world', *European Journal of Criminal Policy Research*, 15, 25–46.

Lacey, N. (2008) *The Prisoners' Dilemma: Political Economy and Punishment in Contemporary Democracies*, Cambridge: Cambridge University Press.

Lappi-Seppälä, T. (2008) 'Trust, welfare and political culture: explaining differences in national penal policies' in M. Tonry (ed.), *Crime and Justice: A Review of Research*, vol. 37, Chicago: University of Chicago Press, pp. 313–87.

Lijphart, A. (1999) *Patterns of Democracy: Government Forms and Performance in Thirty-six Countries*, New Haven: Yale University Press.

Loader, I. (2006) 'Policing, recognition and belonging', *The Annals of the American Academy of Political and Social Science*, 605, 202–21.

Manza, J. and Uggen, C. (2006) *Locked Out: Felon Disenfranchisement and American Democracy*, New York: Oxford University Press.

Marshall, M. G. and Jaggers, K. (2005) *Polity IV Data Set*, Center for International Development and Conflict Management, College Park: University of Maryland, www.systemicpeace.org/inscr/inscr.htm (version: p4v2008).

Mead, H. (1964) 'The psychology of punitive justice' in A. J. Reck (ed.), *Selected Writings*, Chicago: University of Chicago Press, pp. 212–39.

Mendez, J. E. (1999) 'Problems of lawless violence: introduction' in J. E. Mendez, G. O'Donnell and P. S. Pinheiro (eds.), *The (UN) Rule of Law and the Underprivileged in Latin America*, Notre Dame: University of Notre Dame Press, pp. 1–27.

Neapolitano, J. L. (2001) 'An examination of cross-national variation in punitiveness', *International Journal of Offender Therapy and Comparative Criminology*, 45(6), 691–710.

Nelken, D. (2009) 'Comparative criminal justice: beyond ethnocentrism and relativism', *European Journal of Criminology*, 6(4), 291–312.

Rosenfeld, R. and Messner, S. F. (2009) 'The crime drop in comparative perspective: the impact of the economy and imprisonment on American and European burglary rates', *British Journal of Sociology*, 60, 445–71.

Simon, J. (2007) *Governing through Crime: How the War on Crime Transformed American Democracy and Created a Culture of Fear*, New York: Oxford University Press.

Tocqueville, A. de (2000 [1835 and 1840]) *Democracy in America*, Chicago: Chicago University Press.

Tonry, M. (2004) 'Why aren't German penal policies harsher and imprisonment rates higher?', *German Law Journal*, 5(10), 1187–206.

Tonry, M. and Farrington, D. (2005) (eds.) *Crime and Punishment in Western Countries 1980–1999 (Crime and Justice: A Review of Research)*, Chicago: University of Chicago Press.

United Nations Development Program (2002) *Human Development Report 2002: Deepening Democracy in a Fragmented World*, New York, Oxford: Oxford University Press, http://hdr.undp.org/en/media/HDR_2002_EN_Complete.pdf.

Unnever, J. D. and Cullen, F. T. (2010) 'The social sources of Americans' punitiveness: A test of three competing models', *Criminology*, 48(1), 99–130.

Useem, B., Liedka, R. V. and Piehl, A. M. (2003) 'Popular support for the prison build-up', *Punishment and Society*, 5, 5–32.

US State Department (1999–2005) *Human Rights: Country Reports*, Washington DC, www.state.gov/g/drl/rls/hrrpt.

Walmsley, R. (1999–2009) *World Prison Population List*, 1–8th edn, London: *International Centre for Prison Studies*, www.prisonstudies.org.

Whitman, J. (2003) *Harsh Justice: Criminal Punishment and the Widening Divide between America and Europe*, Oxford: Oxford University Press.

Zimring, F., Hawkins, G. and Kamin, S. (2001) *Punishment and Democracy: Three Strikes and You are Out in California*, Oxford: Oxford University Press.

Zimring, F. and Johnson, D. T. (2006) 'Public opinion and the governance of punishment in democratic political systems', *The Annals of the American Academy of Political and Social Science*, 605, 266–80.

Zyl Smit, D. van and Snacken, S. (2009) *Principles of European Prison Law and Policy*, Oxford: Oxford University Press.

PART 3

Comparative crime control and urban governance

15

Victimhood of the national? Denationalising sovereignty in crime control

KATJA FRANKO AAS[*]

> Weak states is precisely what the New World Order, all too often looking suspiciously like the new world *disorder*, needs to sustain and reproduce itself.
>
> Bauman 1998: 68

There is a growing number of academic '–isms' and '–isations' aiming to describe the trans-border interconnectedness of the contemporary social condition. Internationalisation, globalisation, transnationalisation, glocalisation – to name but some – have become increasingly popular fields of criminological inquiry. A common part of globalisation debates has been an image of failing state sovereignty, even propositions of its withering and death. While newspaper reports, political discourse and activist slogans forcefully mobilise for the rescue of the national under threat, the assumption about the 'victimhood of the national' is nevertheless also implicit in much of academic discourse about globalisation and crime. It is an assumption, seldom explicated, yet nevertheless present in various forms and, to greater or lesser extent, in many criminological narratives about globalisation. The growth of unaccountable international surveillance and policing networks and transnational legal orders is seen to be eroding the powers of nation states and, ultimately, raising the question of their survival (Mathiesen 2006). The fall of the golden age of the welfare state under the relentless attacks of neoliberalism offers yet another account of falling state sovereignty. Here, globalisation tends to be equated with its economic motor – neoliberalism – inevitably leading to more social inequality, crime, violence and insecurity and, consequently, increased levels of punitiveness.

[*] I am grateful to Helene Ingebrigtsen Gundhus and to the participants of the Leeds 2008 colloquium on international and comparative criminal justice for their comments on earlier versions of this chapter.

Even more pervasive than the equation between globalisation and neoliberalism has been the equation between globalisation and homogenisation. This is particularly relevant for the field of criminal justice studies, where global influences frequently end up in discussions about convergence, sameness, loss of national uniqueness and, ultimately, a question of the emergence of a homogenous penological landscape. And although the idea of a withered-away state, so prevalent in the 1990s, has lost much of its appeal, particularly in light of the growing security and surveillance state (Haggerty and Ericson 2006; Lyon 2003), the notion of the global eating away at the national nevertheless perseveres. Not infrequently, the narrative about the victimhood of the national is framed as an issue of political failure and surrounded by 'an aura of a natural catastrophe' (Bauman 1998: 57).

However, as much as the globalising processes have been accompanied and enhanced by political impotence on the national level – and clearly deserve to be studied as such – this chapter suggests that as an analytical framework the notion of a national versus global contest has considerable weaknesses. The chapter examines some of the assumptions about the relationship between the globalising process and the national and asks: how might we analyse it? How can we best conceptually grasp these transformations? How much and, not least, what kind of a challenge do they represent to state sovereignty? Do we have an adequate conceptual and theoretical apparatus at our disposal, or do they call for a redefinition of the criminological frame of reference?

Through an outline of European border policing strategies the chapter seeks to clarify and develop a conceptual framework for analysing the complex dynamics between the national and the transnational sphere in crime control. Border protection policies represent 'powerful expressions of order-seeking through sovereignty' (Weber and Bowling 2008: 366), yet at the same time they are a testimony of the intensity of internationalisation in the field of European security and justice. As such they can be seen as an example of an intricate dialectics between the national and the international sphere, which challenges and stretches our existing conceptual apparatus. The chapter explores two seemingly contradictory developments: on the one hand the growing significance of territory and defence of the national, and on the other hand progressive denationalisation of border control capabilities and increased salience of international and transnational co-operation and policy convergence.

The national versus global contest

However, if we are to create a greater level of conceptual precision in the debates about globalisation, one of the first steps may be to take off for a moment the normative glasses, frequently worn by academic and other observers alike, and focus first and foremost on the analytical tools at our disposal. In what follows it will be argued that the view of the national as a victim of a hostile take-over, not only leads to a blind alley of polarised and politically charged debate, but also obscures more nuanced modes of criminological investigation. Although intuitively appealing, the notion of the victimhood of the national is namely based on a problematic assumption since it envisions the global and the national as two distinct, binary opposite, master categories (Sassen 2007a). The effect of this theoretical framework is that one is necessarily losing at the expense of the other as they seem to be competing in a zero-sum game.

As such, the global versus national framework represents a reification of the national as it builds on the territorial imagination of the nation state and modernity, or what Beck (2000) terms 'the container theory of society'. In this perspective, the world society is made of smaller territorial entities, and the dividing lines between the national and the international sphere also imply an antagonistic, either/or relationship between the two: one grows at the expense of the other. The drawbacks of this approach have been amply pointed out by critics of the so-called methodological nationalism within the social sciences (Beck 2000; Sassen 2007a). The critics point out that, due to the growing global interconnectedness, the nation state and national societies no longer represent an adequate frame of reference for analysing social phenomena. Globalisation fundamentally destabilises one of the cornerstones of modernity: the nation state–society nexus. Drawing on this body of work, the dichotomy between the global and the national becomes problematic since it envisions the national and global as monolithic, rather than *hybrid* entities, shot through with diversity and movement. And although the acknowledgement that phenomena can be simultaneously global and local (i.e. 'glocal') has by now become part of conventional wisdom, the view of the national and the global as mixed is far less recognised.

The discussion below will provide several examples of the national–global hybridity. We shall see that Italian and Spanish border-guard vessels in the Mediterranean protect not only Spanish and Italian but also German, French, Norwegian and other borders from unwanted migrants. Because of international agreements the 'duty to guard what were previously only national borders becomes a duty owed to all the Schengen states' (House of Lords 2008: 12). One of the new EU member states, Slovenia, for example, reorganised its entire national police organisation and training in order to adjust to the accession to the Schengen agreement (Gasperlin, 2008). What is national policing here becomes unclear as the national and the local are shot through and through with transnational elements, yet describing these activities as simply international would be inadequate. On the other hand, UK borders and custom authorities are able to check passengers in chosen French and Belgian checkpoints. The House of Lords (2008: 17) reports that Calais, for example, identifies more forged documents than any other point of control. Although these checks take place outside the national territory, they are essentially national by nature (i.e. pertaining to the UK's right to control access to its territory). The international is thus strongly influenced by the dynamics and interests of the national.

The examples thus challenge the correspondence of national territory with the national; the assumption that 'if a process or condition is located in a national institution or in a national territory, it must be national' (Sassen 2007a: 3). According to Sassen, a sociological under-standing of globalisation demands a focus not only on self-evidently global processes and institutions, but also 'entails detecting the presence of globalizing dynamics in thick social environments that mix national and non-national elements' (*ibid.*: 5). We are therefore challenged with establishing elements of a conceptual framework which transcends the nation-state outlook and is sensitive to the complexities of the global, particularly the blurring boundaries between internal and external, and local, national and transnational phenomena.

Since the 1990s, the predominant theoretical framework for analysing transformations of the state in criminology has been that of govern-mentality. Taking up Foucault's (1980) encouragement to 'cut off the king's head' in political thinking and social sciences, this vibrant body of literature has aimed to think alternatively about the diverse ways in which neoliberal societies govern the conduct of their citizens. This narrative has seen the state transformed from a strong 'rowing' agency to the neoliberal regulatory state, where an increasing number of tasks is being relinquished to private actors and other agencies 'below' and 'above' the nation-state level, including international and supranational institutions (Shearing 2001). Transnationalisation thus represents yet another aspect of state relinquishing its responsibilities to other actors. This approach has, justifiably, had a strong hold on criminological theoretical imagination and it provides, as we shall see in the next section, a fruitful frame for understanding several developments within the field of border policing. For example, the EU, along with some other countries, has introduced legislation which penalises air carriers for transporting passengers without the required documents. The state is still involved in the process of passport control, although only indirectly and at a distance, by providing carriers with necessary instructions for carrying out the controls.[1] This model of 'policing at a distance' (Bigo and Guild 2004) effectively co-opts commercial agents and consulates into the task of carrying out EU border controls and identity checks inside third-country territories.

However, while singularly well suited to explain the neoliberal zeitgeist of 'governing through freedom' and 'governing at a distance', the governmentality theories carry far less explanatory potential when it comes to various control strategies built on more or less openly coercive measures, or at least a threat of their use, particularly in a broader geopolitical context. A question can be therefore asked whether the imagery of 'decapitated statehood' can in fact account for the interventionist *modus operandi* of contemporary politics which mixes elements of crime control and warfare, foreign policy and domestic control. Governmentality within criminology has been applied primarily as an 'inward-looking' theory, limited to what Morrison (2006) terms 'the civilised space of modernity'; that is, limited *within* the territorial boundaries of the Western state. As such we may need to examine the implicit notions of the state, more specifically of Western statehood, built into the governmentality approach. As Butler and Spivak (2007) lucidly ask, when we discuss states, what states are we in? How can we best take into account the emerging post-colonial and imperialist dynamics and can they be reconciled with the concept of governing through freedom? And if so, how? The king's head still seems to be firmly on, not least, in the imperialist projects of state-building and military intervention in the name of global crime prevention (Goldsmith and Sheptycki 2007). Furthermore, in many developing countries the Weberian model of state organisation cannot simply be assumed as a starting premise (Goldsmith

---

[1] Guild (2005: 38) reports that at busy airports, airlines may also engage services of private agencies to carry out additional passenger checks for them, thus diffusing the responsibility even further.

2003), and even in the West there is great variation in the nature of nation states. Looking at the UK developments, Crawford (2006) points out that the British state is expanding its net and repertoire of social controls and sponsors social engineering, similar to the projects that lay at the heart of the 'old style' welfare state. Instead of 'hands off' government envisaged by the neoliberal ideologists, there is increasing evidence that 'hands on' governance still seems to hold much purchase on contemporary strategies of social control (*ibid.*).

Elements of a transnational policing system: denationalising border control capabilities

Discerning between 'good' and 'bad' global mobilities has become a vital task of contemporary governance (Aas 2007). This task of border policing (in a broad sense of the word) is today performed by a rapidly growing range of actors and activities and is becoming an increasingly complex and untransparent matter. Although traditionally border controls represent an attempt to assert state sovereignty over a given territory, today border policing also reveals some of the crucial transformations in the nature of state sovereignty. Border controls are marked by a progressive *denationalisation* of state bordering capabilities and can serve as an illustration of how global governance is transcending the nation state, which is particularly evident in the case of EU mobility and border governance.

In what follows, this chapter offers an account of various elements involved in denationalisation processes, loosely based on what Eriksen (2007) lists as key features of globalisation: disembedding, acceleration, movement, standardisation, interconnectedness, vulnerability and re-embedding. These features, although by no means original or exhaustive, provide us with a useful and pedagogically friendly starting point for our discussion.

Disembedding: 'the border is everywhere'

The field of European border policing and mobility governance represents a typical example of internationalisation and transnationalisation of law. The year 1985 marked the signing of the Schengen Agreement whose objective was to dismantle the EU's internal borders while co-ordinating and strengthening its external borders, particularly through better police co-operation and exchange of information. Since then it has become apparent that international migration is increasingly subjected to legal and institutional regulation and decision-making processes on the international level – a case of 'disembedding of law from its national encasement' (Sassen 2006). Migration has been constituted as a challenge that requires trans-border, macro-regional and international responses, and policing of migratory flows is one of the central elements of European policing and its emerging structures of the Area of Freedom, Security and Justice. The trend is exemplified particularly by the recent establishment of the European border control agency, Frontex, which can be seen an as example of development of global governance and of pooling of sovereignty, where the 'transnational system developed its own bureaucracy existing "above" that of the apparatuses of nation states' (Sheptycki 2002: 216).

As such, these developments have been open to questions of accountability frequently raised by the international policing scholarship (Sheptycki 2002; Loader 2004). As Mathiesen (2006: 128) points out, national media and parliaments – the traditional guarantors of accountability – no longer have the capacity nor the time to dig deeply into these issues, accepting the premises of the executive branch and police agencies. The various European systems are increasingly becoming 'interlocked' and 'de-coupled' from the nation states, not only through formal agreements, but also through informal agreements, thus gathering an internal sociological momentum (*ibid.*).

However, the disembedding process is evident not only in the 'disembedding of law from its national encasement' but also in the de-territorialisation of the border itself. The objective of contemporary border control strategies is to act pre-emptively and to avert potentially risky individuals before they ever have a chance to enter the national territory (Aas 2005). A Third World traveller encounters the border of the EU already when trying to book an airplane ticket or contacting a travel agency. Networks of airline liaison officers, employed by a number of countries, work at international airports helping airlines in preventing *potentially* inadmissible passengers to board airplanes (Bigo 2000). Similarly, the pre-clearance systems allow immigration officials to carry out immigration checks at airports abroad, thus effectively moving the border outside national territory (Aas 2005). This system of 'governance at a distance' defies the established notion of territoriality and of borders as walls around territories. Instead, borders are constituted as intervention points outside the nation-state territory, which is reflected for example in the aforementioned expansion of the British immigration checks to certain Belgian, French and Dutch cities and ports. Rather than protecting a wall around national territory, police and customs co-operation assumes the dispersed and network-like shape of the flows of goods they are trying to control.

The emerging new immobilisation and surveillance strategies intro-duce a new logic and a new scope to border policing. As Lyon (2005) aptly puts it: 'The border is everywhere.'[2] Using a wide array of tech-nologies, these measures disperse and de-localise the border:

> [B]orders themselves become 'delocalized' as efforts are made to check travellers before they reach physical borders of ports of entry. Images and information circulate through different departments, looping back and forth in commercial, policing, and government networks. Surveillance records, once kept in fixed filing cabinets and dealing in data focused on persons in specific places, are now fluid, flowing and global. These consequences are properly 'globalized' in the sense that they signal new patterns of social activity and novel social arrangements, which are less constrained by geography. The 'delocalized border' is a prime example of globalized surveillance. [Lyon 2003: 110]

Unlike in the Westphalian sovereignty, the state thus no longer has unambiguous boundaries, with a clearly defined inside and outside. There is a proliferation of intervention points – not only in terms of plurality of actors, but also in terms of a geographic dispersal of points of control. The complex social production of transnational connections destabilises older, taken-for-granted scale choices (Valverde, this volume) and methodological approaches. Increasingly, global networks, global cities, flows and movements gain precedence over past, seemingly stable, territorialities of the national and the local (Sassen 2007a).

Acceleration: 'A positive hit is a matter of minutes'

Instantaneous communication, speed and movement are essential fea-tures of the globalising condition. And even though the aim of border control strategies is to achieve the opposite of that – they can be described as 'immobilisation strategies', as attempts at imposing control

---

[2] De-localisation of the border means that the border can essentially be 'everywhere' not only outside a given territory, but also inside it. The Schengen lands are therefore by no means a 'borderless zone' (Bigo and Guild 2004). While abolishing internal state borders, Schengen lands have intensified internal police activities and identity checks of potentially undesirable individuals, particularly in certain zones heavily populated by third-country nationals; e.g. Norwegian police operate several cars with access to the central databases, which function as mobile border control units inside state territory.

in world in motion (Aas 2007) – they are crucially dependent on speed, particularly the speed of communication afforded by contemporary information and communication technologies (ICTs). The transnationalisation of law discussed above – which by itself has a long history – is put into operation by a series of technological systems, which are essential for its efficiency. The European border security crucially depends on a variety of transnational information flows and technological zones, most notably the ones based on the Schengen Agreement as well as the so-called Dublin Convention and the Eurodac system, dealing with asylum issues. Schengen Information System (SIS) is a trans-European database which allows police and other agents from Schengen member states to access and enter a variety of data on specific individuals, vehicles and objects. SIS is in the process of expanding into SIS II, with a series of new functions and considerably expanded information capacity. Eurodac, on the other hand, authorises fingerprinting of all individuals aged over fourteen, who apply for asylum in an EU country, or who are found illegally present on the EU borders and in the EU territory (Aas 2006). The system aims to prevent so-called asylum shopping by harmonising responses to asylum claims within the EU. A 'positive hit' (i.e. fingerprint identification) can be achieved in a matter of minutes and may result in the removal of an asylum applicant from a country, solely on the basis of the fingerprint identification. The EU furthermore envisages a series of other databases such as VIS (a pan-European database with biometric identifiers of all residence holders and applicants, potentially one of the largest in the world) and an entry/exit system (allowing recording of *all* third-country nationals) (European Parliament 2007).

The field of European policing is therefore 'an almost entirely informationalised activity – a practice oriented not on-the-ground delivery of visible police functions . . . but towards supporting such practices through the generation, storage and dissemination of information' (Loader 2004: 67). The development urges us to acknowledge the centrality of technology to the reconfiguration of what one can call the space of governance. If geography and territorial boundaries before were central for defining the space of governance, now on the other hand government operates 'in relation to zones formed through the circulation of technical practices and devices' (Barry 2002: 3). Technological zones are zones of circulation where technical devices, practices and artefacts are highly connected and compatible. Living in a technological society means, as Barry (2002: 2) points out, that various technologies dominate the sense of problems which need to be addressed as well as dominating their solutions. Issues tend to be discussed in terms of technical operability, rather than in normative terms.[3] Sassen (2007a: 15) furthermore points out the centrality of ICTs in the constitution of 'strategic scalings beyond that of the national'. ICTs destabilise older hierarchies of scale, which were centred in the national, and introduce novel scalings and multi-scalar dynamics (*ibid.*). A police entity, for example, can thus continue to function in its local and national framework, but is also through some aspects of its work a part of globally scaled circuits of communication.

Through various technologically supported strategies – expressed in the official buzzwords 'integrated border management' – contemporary governance is able constantly to expand the range of actors who participate in global-risk communication networks. However, as Ericson and Haggerty (1997: 4) point out, technological risk communication systems are not simply neutral channels through which knowledge is transferred:

> Rather, they have their own logics and autonomous processes. They govern institutional relations and circumscribe what individuals and their organisations are able to accomplish.

The contemporary technological paraphernalia therefore not only enables fortification of the border, it also reshapes the border according to its own logic. These surveillance practices:

> operate by abstracting human bodies from their territorial settings, and separating them into a series of discrete flows. These flows are then reassembled in different locations as discrete and virtual 'data doubles'. [Haggerty and Ericson 2000: 605]

Through the various border surveillance practices such as airport profiling, SIS, US-VISIT programme, biometric passports etc., individuals' identities are recorded as their 'data doubles' and then communicated between various countries and agencies. The vast national and global surveillance efforts to protect the border function as a form of what Lyon (2002) terms 'social sorting' – categorising people and assessing their risk. As Lyon (2002: 14) writes:

---

[3] One recent example is the discussions about fingerprinting of migrant children in relation to the new Visa Information System (VIS) – where the lowest age seems to be determined by the unreliability of technology rather than by possible ethical objections to fingerprinting of children.

the social process occurs, as it were, on the move. Surveillance now deals in speed and mobility . . . In the desire to keep track, surveillance ebbs and flows through space.

Standardisation

Standardisation tends to be mentioned as one of the most predictable consequences of globalisation. And not unlike the McDonaldisation thesis (Ritzer 2007) usually associated with globalising processes, the area of border policing also exhibits strong tendencies towards standardisation. 'A world of standardization is a world of many common denominators and bridgeheads for communication' (Eriksen 2007: 53). ICTs as such carry a strong standardising momentum as they rely on communication of standardised items of information (although communication of 'soft' intelligence between individual police entities should by no means be underestimated). Therefore despite the fact that a lack of central monitoring and common standards is a perennial complaint of EU bureaucrats and practitioners in the justice field, one should keep in mind the level of standardisation that has already taken place.

The drive towards standardisation is perhaps most visible in the establishment of the so-called Schengen Border Code and the Practical Handbook for Border Guards (Schengen Handbook). The purpose of these documents is the uniform implementation of Community rules on border control. Member states are thus to instruct their national border control authorities to use the manuals as the main tool when performing border control tasks. Also Frontex sees education as one of its main tasks with a particular focus on establishment of common training standards and development of a Common Core Curriculum.[4] Interoperability – harmonisation for the sake of working together – is therefore one of the main challenges and tasks of Frontex.

Before the recent wave of enlargement, the new Schengen countries were subjected to comprehensive monitoring and evaluation by the Commission. Throughout the Schengen evaluation procedure (SCH-EVAL) experts groups were sent on evaluation missions to evaluate progress and the implementation of common standards. This is not to say though that the drive towards standardisation has resulted in uniformity of on-the-ground control practices. This uniformity is often

---

[4] www.frontex.europa.eu/origin_and_tasks/tasks/.

assumed in official EU documents but seldom achieved in reality. As Walker (this volume) points out, when it comes to international policing, the features which have traditionally conduced toward national structures continue to conduce against international structures and there is a deep-seated tendency to mistrust the competence of foreign policing organisations.

Interconnectedness: 'global approach to migration'

EU border controls operate under a framework of so-called 'integrated border management' and according to a four-tier access control model, which consists of:

1. inland activities
2. border controls checks
3. co-operation across the border
4. activities in third countries.

The approach reveals that the trans-border dimensions of contemporary border policing are not only evident on the macro-regional level of European co-operation (3), but also in the growing numbers of interventions and activities in third (non-EU) countries (4). The so-called 'global approach to migration' brings together migration, external relations and development policy to address the broad migration agenda in 'partnership' with third countries. The EU exerts considerable pressure on its neighbours, such as North African and Balkans states and ex-Soviet republics, to implement better border controls and ease the EU's workload. This 'circle of friends' among other things co-operates in the fight against organised crime, terrorism and migration issues. By using aid and trade as financial incentives, the EU has also signed repatriation agreements with a number of third countries, which will accept back illegal immigrants coming from or having lived in those countries. The objective of these strategies is clearly to shift the flows of unwanted migrants to zones outside the EU. Unfortunately, these zones consist mostly of countries which have considerably poorer resources and human rights records than the EU itself. The strategy of enlisting the co-operation of third countries in the task of border policing furthermore highlights the blurring boundaries between internal and external spheres of policing and security policies, and the progressive merging of foreign policy, migration management and development aid.

The global approach to migration can be read as a testimony of political awareness of global interconnectedness. According to its wording:

> The Global Approach aims to formulate comprehensive and coherent policies that address the broad range of migration-related issues, bringing together different policy areas – development, social affairs and employment, external relations and justice and home affairs – and taking both short term actions as well as a longer term vision to address the root causes of migration and forced migration. The Global Approach has a strong theme of working in partnership with countries of origin and transit: its key concepts are partnership, solidarity and shared responsibility.[5]

Since its adoption in 2005, this approach has managed to achieve an extraordinary amount of highest-level political activity, particularly with African countries, including Libya. And although it clearly contains elements of 'arm twisting', it is essentially a strategy for transferring responsibility for unwanted migratory flows to third countries. As Fekete (2001) puts it, EU policies have turned Third World governments into immigration police for Western Europe.

Returning to the discussion in the beginning of the chapter, the global approach to migration can be seen as mixing elements of governmentality and realpolitik. It also shows the extent to which policing today is implicated in, and produces effects, in countries geographically far removed from its national territories. Frontex has had for example a number of extensive maritime control operations reaching into Mauritanian and Senegalese territorial waters and a recent inquiry by the House of Lords (2008) has raised concerns about its mandate to act extraterritorially. Furthermore, a question has been asked about who has the responsibility for possible human rights violations of migrants who are sent to, or prevented from leaving, third countries such as, for example, Libya who is not even party to Refugee Convention (*ibid.*: 46). Policing in its classical sense is increasingly intertwined with issues of foreign relations, development, human rights and international security politics, and the ethical issues related to policing thus become far more complicated. For example, what responsibility do member state authorities have for the activities of international bodies in which they participate when these bodies act extraterritorially and beyond areas where the European Community law applies?

---

[5] http://europa.eu/rapid/pressReleasesAction.do?reference=MEMO/07/549.

Movement: police officers in 'global switchboards'

However, even though the above discussion seems to support pessimistic accounts of Fortress Europe and the rise of surveillance societies, an important aspect is that the immobilisation strategies presented here are far from resembling walls and fortresses, nor do they have such effects. Contemporary governments seem to be caught between two contradicting impulses: on the one hand, the urge towards increasing securitisation of borders and, on the other hand, the awareness of the importance of global mobility for sustaining the present world economic order (Aas 2007). The acknowledgement of the importance of global mobility is evident in a recent EU proposal for a directive on the admission of highly skilled migrants, which aims to offer more attractive entry and residence conditions for highly skilled migrant workers. The objective is therefore not to seal off the border but rather to manage it efficiently; 'not to arrest mobility but to tame it; not to build walls, but systems capable of utilizing mobilities and in certain cases deploying them against the sedentary and ossified elements within society' (Walters 2004: 248).

However, the issues of mobility and international travel are not only a question of distinguishing between 'good' and 'bad' mobilities, but crucially also effect the habitus of policing. Denationalisation of policing is not only a matter of legal developments, but crucially also invites investigation of the changing cultural habitus of international justice. Several observers have situated issues of autonomy of transnational policing networks from the state within the sociological context of the development of specific transnational police subcultures – a professional 'fraternity', which sees its tasks in terms of a shared mission (Sheptycki 2002). At its higher echelons, officers working with internationalisation of border controls constitute an elite who, like other EU bureaucrats, enjoy frequent flights to Brussels and Warsaw (Frontex headquarters) and meet regularly at seminars and in various committees and working groups. These venues can be described by using Ulf Hannerz' expression 'global switchboards': 'Those who meet there, originating from different societies, speak a shared language (often English) and also have other things in common; they conform to a number of cultural standards' (Eriksen 2007: 54). Like tourists, businessmen and other professionals, these groups of police officers can be seen as cosmopolitans and as examples of 'outsourcing of the nation-state' (*ibid.*: 96). As such, they raise questions about the 'detachment from the nation-state of groups that are physically located in it' (*ibid.*) and, even more importantly, that are meant to represent its democratic nature.

Vulnerability

Although the developments described so far represent a profound reconfiguration of state sovereignty, they should not be taken at face value as a sign of diminution of state control over its territory. Quite the opposite, it appears that through the extensive denationalisation of border controls EU states are relinquishing aspects of their authority in order to, ultimately, strengthen their security. Globalisation marks not only trans-border mobility of goods, money, cultural impulses, etc. but crucially also mobility and de-bounding of risk. In the emerging world 'risk society' (Beck 1999) one of the most politically contentious risks is that of illegal migration. The question of policing the border is therefore a question about vulnerability, control of access and membership. The control measures, such as SIS, are therefore an answer to the vulnerability felt by the EU member states after the abolition of the internal borders. Higher levels of internal mobility have been compensated by stricter external border controls.

Denationalisation of border policing can be thus seen as an acknowledgement that better co-operation in the police and justice sector is the best answer to the increased levels of vulnerability due to higher levels of mobility. It should be noticed though that some states (UK and Ireland) have chosen to opt out of parts of Schengen, retaining authority over border controls but participating in the police and judicial co-operation. The opt-out is mainly based on their confidence that they can protect themselves better (House of Lords 2008). Other states (Norway, Iceland, Switzerland) on the other hand, although not EU members, have been eager to join the co-operation. One could argue that being left out of international co-operation may be a risk that only strong states can afford while the sovereignty of weaker states depends to a larger extent on international support. In a world of global mobility, fears of terrorism, etc. the sovereign state's ability to identify its enemies depends not only on internal monitoring of its population, but also on the constant communication and exchange of information with its allies.

Re-embedding

The example above also indicates the complex nature of the effects of trans-border connections. They are not a unidirectional process. All of the key features listed above 'have their countervailing forces opposing them and positing alternatives' (Eriksen 2007: 9). Resistance is an essential element of the trans-border connections and the focus on disembedding in globalisation research needs to be complemented with a focus on re-embedding. EU member states for example rejected at an early stage plans for a European corps of border guards – showing that sovereignty is a sensitive issue which is often jealously guarded. The dynamics between the denationalising tendencies and their counter-forces is particularly visible in the nature and the functioning of the recently established EU external borders agency – Frontex.

Frontex – a supranational police organisation?

Frontex, the EU external borders agency, was established by way of a Council regulation[6] in October 2004 and became operational a year later. It is led by an executive director and a strategic management board which consists of 'border chiefs' of individual member states and two representatives for the Commission.[7] As an international policing actor Frontex obviously has several relatives, most notably Europol. However, it can also be distinguished by a relatively quick build-up of its capacity and, not least, its coercive powers in the three years since its inception. Its budget for 2008 was €70.4 million (expected to reach €83 million in 2009), compared to Europol's €65 million budget for 2007.[8] Although Frontex aims, like Europol, to be an intelligence-driven agency, responsible for risk analysis and co-ordination, it also has considerable possibilities for direct use of force. Its 'armada' – listed in a centralised catalogue or record of available technical equipment (CRATE)[9] – consists of, among other things, a considerable number of helicopters, airplanes, maritime vessels, vehicles, mobile radar units, thermal/infrared cameras, etc. As such, Frontex represents a hybrid between a military and police organisation and its tasks reflect the progressive merging of internal and external security in the field of international policing.

The list of the tasks Frontex is expected to perform includes risk analyses, border guard training at the European level, research and

[6] Council Regulation (EC) No. 2007/2004 of 26 October 2004 (i.e. Frontex Regulation).
[7] UK and Ireland participate but have no voting rights. The UK government has asked to join, but was not allowed by the Court of Justice. It does take part in joint operations.
[8] www.frontex.europa.eu/finance/.
[9] The word 'catalogue' refers to a list of equipment that member states are willing to make available at Frontex's disposal.

development, assistance to member states in emergencies, organisation of joint return operations of illegal migrants, and co-operation with third countries and international organisations (see Frontex Regulation). Despite the variety of tasks, most of its budget is nevertheless spent on sea operations (House of Lords 2008: 32) and their intensity is only expected to increase in the coming years. These operations represent the most visible Frontex activities, which also have been the most controversial as they embody the trend towards militarisation of the EU's and Western borders more generally.

The gist of Frontex' operative power is located in the so-called 'joint support teams', which are systematically managed pools of national experts participating in joint operations, training, pilot projects, etc. Relying on the impressive pool of equipment, on one level these teams may be seen as symptomatic of the state's loss of monopoly on the use of force. However, at a closer look the picture is far more complex. This considerable force is largely dependent on the willingness of the individual member states to actually contribute the promised experts and equipment. Joint operations are, according to its executive director, designed as a product which is 'marketed' to the member states, which contribute on voluntary basis (Laitinen 2008). The willingness of member states to participate in operations is a critical point in the effectiveness of Frontex and has been at times a serious source of concern. According to a recent report by the House of Lords (2008: 35):

> A major problem has been the failure of some Member States actually to make available the resources they have promised. In July 2007 the Central Register of Available Technical Equipment (CRATE) was impressive – on paper – and included 21 fixed wing aircraft, 27 helicopters and 117 vessels. Of these, 32 were patrol vessels pledged by Italy, yet . . . not one Italian vessel took part in operation NAUTILUS.

As an answer to the problem, the Commission has recently adopted a regulation on the creation of so-called Rapid Border Intervention Teams (RABITs). Instead of voluntary participation, these teams introduce a stronger form of solidarity – 'mandatory solidarity' – and a much higher level of commitment. RABITs are meant to be employed only in 'urgent and exceptional situations'. Nevertheless, they represent a possibility for new levels of integration and intervention.

As a supranational organisation Frontex may be seen as representing a serious challenge to nation state authority. '[T]he emergence of a supra-state policing capacity at the EU level threatens to establish a new centre of authority over which the state no longer retains even *ultimate* regulatory control' (Walker 2003: 308). This is particularly evident in the debates around the right of Frontex officers to carry arms in joint operations. The amended Frontex regulation opens for such a possibility (not just in RABITs). Yet a question arises about their right to do so in relation to the national legislation of individual member states where they are deployed, and about the liabilities of guest border guards from the use of weapons.[10]

However, the case of Frontex also reveals that even though individual states no longer have ultimate control over the new centres of policing authority, they are by no means impotent in relation to them. There are constant negotiations between the tasks of the organisation and the will of member states to contribute, which can, in extreme cases, cripple the whole organisation. On one level Frontex is seen (not least by members of management broad and its executive director) as a 'service' to member states. It needs to market its 'products' and its appeals to solidarity are not always successful, hence a move towards mandatory solidarity. The case of Frontex also reveals that internationalisation is hard work, transnationalisation perhaps even harder. The existence of transnational bodies and legal arrangements by no means automatically leads to their effectiveness. And although states have relinquished some aspects of their sovereignty they are also jealously defending it.

At the same time there is also an awareness that the loss of sovereignty in terms of new jurisdictions, international regimes, inspections, etc. also means more effective control over access to national territory. This is particularly relevant for smaller countries as they expand their scope of influence through their participation in EU bodies. Rather than representing a 'hostile take-over', Frontex is at times met with too high expectations from some states. This has prompted its director to issue a press release entitled 'Frontex – facts and myths' where he specifies:

[10] The House of Lords report (2008: 42) describes a case of a recent RABIT exercise in Portugal: 'The exercise was made as realistic as possible, and the guest officers were therefore asked to bring their service weapons with them. This raised the issue as to whether guest officers were required, as a matter of Portuguese law, to obtain a Portuguese firearms permit before the weapons could be carried in public (Portuguese border guards are required to hold such a permit). Frontex argued that the RABITs Regulation took precedence over national legislation and that guest officers could not be required to obtain these permits. After some debate this was accepted by the Portuguese authorities, but only after they had issued the national permits.' The problem becomes even more acute in jurisdictions where border guards do not wear arms.

I would like to remind that Frontex activities are *supplementary* to those undertaken by the Member States. Frontex doesn't have any monopoly on border protection and is not omnipotent. It is a *coordinator* of the operational cooperation in which the Member States show their volition. If some of our critics think it is not enough they should fix their eyes on decision takers. [Laitinen 2007; emphasis added]

This role of a co-ordinator becomes rather less plausible though when it comes to its role in international relations. Here, Frontex acts more like an independent actor, negotiating and realising agreements with authorities in third countries. A cursory look at its news releases reveals a high level of diplomatic activity, including working agreements with a series of neighbouring countries.[11]

Conclusion

In this chapter we have seen several dynamics pertaining to the relationship between the national and the transnational. We have addressed the establishment of what seem to be properly supranational institutions, exemplified by Frontex. On the other hand, we have seen denationalisation of particular aspects of police work, which nonetheless remain situated in the national institutional framework. International co-operation is for member states a prerequisite of achieving greater levels of security. And although their bordering capabilities are being denationalised and submitted to sometimes stringent international regimes, the result is a greater control over national territory and even the ability to intervene in neighbouring countries through examples such as 'hot pursuit' action and joint border police teams. The case of denationalisation of border policing reveals that transnationalisation is not a unidirectional process. A question can be also asked: are we in fact seeing two different types of transnationalisation – one strengthening and the other running against the nation state? In fine-tuning our conceptual apparatus we should therefore acknowledge the various modalities of the transnational. Rather than taking over, transnationalisation may be a way of achieving the goals of the national.[12] Debates about the global leading to less sovereignty are therefore simplistic since what we are seeing are transformations in various *aspects* of sovereignty

---

[11] www.frontex.europa.eu/newsroom/news_releases/.

[12] In a telling example, Slovene police authorities recently presented a scoreboard: Schengen 'for Slovenian security' (how member states take care of Slovene security), which in the period 1 September 2007–31 March 2008 consisted of: 21 arrested persons, 4 missing persons identified, 15 motor vehicles etc. (Gasperlin 2008).

or statehood. While some have been denationalised, others remain firmly situated in the national, yet both may be working towards the same goal (greater control of access to national territory).

The relationship between transnationalisation and the state is therefore far more complex and unpredictable than may appear at first sight. Contrary to popular representations, the global should not be seen as an emerging structure which is growing at the expense of the national, leading inevitably to a homogenous world system. While trans-border connections undoubtedly change the dynamics between the national, the local and the global, these profound processes of change have not necessarily given primacy to one at the expense of the other. It is furthermore apparent that, rather than representing a radical break with the past, the features of a supranational control system described here are the classic cornerstones of modernity (Giddens 1990). The transnational grows from the trajectory of modernity and has its preconditions and lifelines planted in the nation-state project rather than *over* it. 'Nationalism, often seen as an obstacle to globalization, is a product of the same forces that are shaping the latter' (Eriksen 2007: 25; see also Sassen 2006). Rather than inhabiting binary opposite entities, the global and the national can thus inhabit the same trajectory, marked by disembedding, standardisation and large-scale integration. Consequently, by failing to recognise the modern/national roots of the global and, not least, failing to expect novelty when exploring the global, we may be in danger of overlooking the complexity and the pervasiveness of social change actually taking place. Yet, at the same time, a question can be asked: can the process outlined in this chapter simply be seen as 'modernity at large' (Appadurai 1996), or does the disembedding, speed and scale of social control outlined above also constitute a 'critical mass' and thus represent something new?

In terms of conclusion, a question can be asked about the conceptual and methodological apparatus at our disposal when we attempt to understand these new modes of governance. This chapter has argued that clear-cut delineations between the transnational and the national may be unproductive. As Sassen (2006: 1) points out:

> The epochal transformation we call globalization is taking place inside the national to a far larger scale than is usually recognized. It is there that the most complex meanings of the global are being constituted, and the national is also often one of the key enablers and enactors of the emergent global scale.

The transnational is built through determined efforts of nation states and the transnational may furthermore also reside in the national. By treating the national and the transnational as two separate categories, we externalise the transnational and thus lose sight of the transformations happening inside the national or the local.

On a similar note I would like to suggest that the methodological challenge is not only (perhaps not even primarily) to develop comparative insights and to analyse policy transfers. Frequently, a 'test of globalisation' applied in academic and popular conversation is whether we are witnessing sameness and policy convergence. However, as Eriksen (2007: 10) points out, 'globalization does not entail the production of *global uniformity* or homogeneity. Rather, it can be seen as a way of organizing *heterogeneity*.' The expectation that globalisation leads to uniformity, and even erasure of the national, may lead to blind spots about various other forms of trans-border interconnectedness which do not confirm our expectations about homogeneity. Moreover, the international and supranational developments discussed in this chapter are creating a mesh of legal arrangements, ICT networks, joint operations and so forth, which are interlocking and integrating national systems into a functional entity which soon may not be recognisable through its individual parts – nation states. Consequently, the value of a methodological and conceptual framework essentially based on the Westphalian notion of the national (or its comparison) is questionable when it comes to understanding these emerging modes of governance. Societies today are no longer (if they ever have been) clearly delineated entities, and this is true also for their justice systems, which are increasingly enmeshed and integrated. When a system works as an integrated entity, some of its parts may be different in comparison with others, yet they produce effects together. For example, Norwegian borders are being defended not only in Norway but also in Poland, Greece, Italy and Spain. These countries take the lion's share of the migratory flows and as such contribute to the relative stability of the Norwegian asylum system. That their own resources are stretched to the limits, consequently prompts such countries to adopt more coercive and punitive policies. Simply comparing the two systems in terms of human rights standards and punitiveness may be inadequate since they, although qualitatively different, support each other. Looking at the EU as a whole, the same task is performed by its neighbouring countries. The 'humanity' of European control institutions needs to be seen in relation to the realpolitik towards its Eastern and North African neighbours.

References

Aas, K. F. (2005) '"Getting ahead of the game": border technologies and the changing space of governance' in E. Zureik and M. Salter (eds.), *Global Surveillance and Policing: Borders, Security, Identity*, Cullompton: Willan Publishing, pp. 194–214.

    (2006) 'The body does not lie; identity, risk and trust in technoculture', *Crime, Media, Culture*, 2(2), 143–58.

    (2007) *Globalization and Crime*, London: Sage.

Appadurai, A. (1996) *Modernity at Large: Cultural Dimensions of Globalization*, Minneapolis: University of Minneapolis Press.

Barry, A. (2002) *Political Machines: Governing a Technological Society*, London: Athlone Press.

Bauman, Z. (1998) *Globalization: The Human Consequences*, Cambridge: Polity Press.

Beck, U. (1999) *World Risk Society*, Cambridge: Polity Press.

    (2000) *What is Globalization?*, Cambridge: Polity Press.

Bigo, D. (2000) 'Liaison officers in Europe: new officers in the European security field' in J. Sheptycki (ed.), *Issues in Transnational Policing*, London: Routledge, pp. 67–99.

Bigo, D. and Guild, E. (2004) 'Distancering af de fremmede – logikken i Schengenvisumet', *Tidsskriftet Politikk*, 7(3), 23–33.

Butler, J. and Spivak, G. (2007) *Who Sings the Nation-State?: Language, Politics, Belonging*, London: Seagull Books.

Crawford, A. (2006) 'Networked governance and the post-regulatory state?', *Theoretical Criminology*, 10(4), 449–79.

Ericson, R. and Haggerty, K. (1997) *Policing the Risk Society*, Toronto: University of Toronto Press.

Eriksen, T. H. (2007) *Globalization: The Key Concepts*, Oxford and New York: Berg.

European Parliament (2007) *A Comparison of the Now Agreed VIS Package and the US-VISIT System*, Briefing paper, Civil Liberties, Justice and Home Affairs, www.europarl.europa.eu/activities/committees/studies/download.do?file=17239.

Fekete, L. (2001) 'The emergence of xeno-racism', *Race & Class*, 43(2): 23–40.

Foucault, M. (1980) *Power/Knowledge: Selected Interviews and Other Writings 1972–1977*, ed. C. Gordon, New York: Pantheon Books.

Gasperlin, M. (2008) 'Experiences with accession', Lecture at the 'Enlarging the Schengen Area' seminar, Trier, 3–4 April 2008.

Giddens, A. (1990) *The Consequences of Modernity*, Cambridge: Polity Press.

Goldsmith, A. (2003) 'Policing weak states: citizen safety and state responsibility', *Policing and Society*, 13(1), 3–21.

Goldsmith, A. and Sheptycki, J. (2007) (eds.) *Crafting Transnational Policing: Police Capacity-building and Global Police Reform*, Oxford: Hart Publishing.

Guild, E. (2005) 'The legal framework: who is entitled to move?' in D. Bigo and E. Guild (eds.), *Controlling Frontiers: Free Movement into and within Europe*, Aldershot: Ashgate, pp: 14–48.

Haggerty, K. and Ericson, R. (2000) 'The surveillant assemblage', *British Journal of Sociology*, 51, 605–22.

(2006) *The New Politics of Surveillance and Visibility*, Toronto: University of Toronto Press.

House of Lords (2008) *FRONTEX: The EU External Borders Agency*, Report with evidence, www.publications.parliament.uk/pa/ld200708/ldselect/ldeucom/60/60.pdf.

Laitinen, I. (2007) 'Frontex – facts and myths', www.frontex.europa.eu/newsroom/news_releases/art26.html.

(2008) 'A new EU agency to support external security: the role and tasks of FRONTEX', Presentation at the 'Enlarging the Schengen Area' seminar, Trier, 4 April 2008.

Loader, I. (2004) 'Policing, securitisation and democratisation in Europe' in T. Newburn and R. Sparks (eds.), *Criminal Justice and Political Cultures: National and International Dimensions of Crime Control*, Cullompton: Willan Publishing, pp. 49–79.

Lyon, D. (2002) 'Surveillance as social sorting: computer codes and mobile bodies' in D. Lyon (ed.), *Surveillance as Social Sorting: Privacy, Risk and Digital Discrimination*, London and New York: Routledge, pp. 13–30.

(2003) *Surveillance after September 11*, Cambridge: Polity Press.

(2005) 'The border is everywhere: ID cards, surveillance, and the other' in E. Zureik and M. Salter (eds.), *Global Surveillance and Policing: Borders, Security, Identity*, Cullompton: Willan Publishing, pp. 66–82.

Mathiesen, T. (2006) '*Lex Vigilatoria* – towards a control system without a state?' in S. Armstrong and L. McAra (eds.), *Perspectives on Punishment*, Oxford: Oxford University Press, pp. 119–31.

Morrison, W. (2006) *Criminology, Civilisation and the New World Order*, London: Routledge.

Ritzer, G. (2007) *The McDonaldization of Society*, 5th edn, Thousand Oaks: Pine Forge Press.

Sassen, S. (2006) *Territory, Authority, Rights: From Medieval to Global Assemblages*, Princeton, NJ: Princeton University Press.

(2007a) *A Sociology of Globalization*, London: W. W. Norton & Company.

(2007b) 'Introduction: deciphering the global' in S. Sassen (ed.), *Deciphering the Global: Its Scales, Spaces and Subjects*, London: Routledge, pp. 1–18.

Shearing, C. (2001) 'Punishment and the changing face of the governance', *Punishment & Society*, 3(2), 203–20.

Sheptycki, J. (2002) 'Accountability across the policing field: towards a general cartography of accountability for post-modern policing', *Policing & Society*, 12(4), 323–38.

Walker, N. (2003) 'The pattern of transnational policing' in T. Newburn (ed.), *Handbook of Policing*, Cullompton: Willan Publishing, pp. 111–35.

Walters, W. (2004) 'Secure borders, safe haven, domopolitics', *Citizenship Studies*, 8(3), 237–60.

Weber, L. and Bowling, B. (2008) 'Valiant beggars and global vagabonds: select, eject, immobilize', *Theoretical Criminology*, 12(3), 355–75.

16

Cosmopolitan liberty in the age of terrorism

CLIVE WALKER*

Introduction

Though of ancient origin, the concept of cosmopolitanism remains salient, not least within contemporary rights discourse (Anderson-Gold 2001; Tan 2004; Appiah 2006; Benhabib 2006; Fine 2007; Douzinas 2007). The concept's normative emphasis on the ideal of value being shared by all of humanity, within circles of affiliation going beyond family, the local, or even national ties (Nussbaum 1997: 9), helpfully underlines the universality of each human life 'beyond . . . the ties of kith and kin' (Appiah 2006: xv). Its institutional implications promulgate the ideal of a common community which can be viewed as reflected in the emergence of post-1945 federations of nations which sponsor international human rights and humanitarian laws.

Yet, can these concepts of cosmopolitanism hold fast in the face of contemporary terrorism? Jihadi movements like Al-Qa'ida have been criticised as 'counter-cosmopolitans' (Appiah 2006: 143). Their doctrine denies plural value, and their action consists too often of brutal and catastrophic attacks in apparent denial of any shared humanity. In turn, states are motivated by terrorism to raise the drawbridge on cosmopolitan comity and to adopt exceptionalism in foreign affairs (described in the chapter by Jason Ralph) and irreconcilable forms of illiberal nationalism at home. Governments become willing to demonise those who reject their values (Thobani 2007) and to proffer for their own purposes a ruthless and violent 'lesser evil' in order to combat the greater evil of terrorism, so that human rights are no longer trumps in the age of terror, even against torture (Ignatieff 2004; Dershowitz 2002). The counter-terrorism world order thus appears to contradict the 'Perpetual Peace' grounded in universal

---

* An earlier version of this chapter was delivered at the Symposium on 'Restrictions of liberty of terror suspects', Israel Defence Institute and ICRC, Jerusalem, 2008.

hospitality as outlined by Kant (1795) and draws closer to an inhospitable 'war all the time' (Walker 2005).

Despite this unpromising landscape, a 'weak' and 'moderate' version of cosmopolitanism (Tan 2004: 1, 10) will be adapted in this chapter as championing the notion of a common shared morality which can apply regardless of nationality and citizenship even in the face of terrorism by one's mortal enemy. The version is 'weak' in that it is not claimed that cosmopolitan liberty delivers equal liberty without borders, but it does demand an equation of liberty for all within borders and at a sufficient level of enjoyment which satisfies international standards. The version is 'moderate' for it is not claimed that cosmopolitanism is the sole normative value of relevance. For present purposes, the core of the applicable morality within cosmopolitanism will remain the universality of human rights. However, the point of this chapter's regard for cosmopolitanism beyond human rights doctrine is to draw out the force of its restraint within a jurisdiction upon state-centric security and also the force of its persuasion to extend mutual respect beyond jurisdictional boundaries. Another helpful feature of cosmopolitanism is to recognise that solidarity demands more than negative respect for universal rights, though allied agendas such as the search for mobilising shared values (such as citizenship) and the impact of broad concepts of collective 'human security' (UN Commission on Human Security 2003; Annan 2005: para. 78) go beyond the scope of this chapter. Instead, it is intended to provide a case study of the cosmopolitan treatment of liberty in the face of terrorism. Its treatment within the United Kingdom will be examined for traces of cosmopolitanism in both internal-facing and outward-facing aspects. A focus on the United Kingdom may be justified by the setting of a prominent counter-terrorism strategy and infrastructure (including laws), the perception of serious threats from aliens and citizens, but at the same time an expressed official commitment to 'put respect for human rights at the centre of our response to the terrorist threat' (Cabinet Office 2009: 5). Whether a mature polity can deliver on this promise provides a good test for the viability of cosmopolitanism in the context of terrorism.

This focus through the prism of cosmopolitanism on the liberty of individuals suspected of terrorism potentially involves consideration of three internal-facing modalities of restriction: police detention following arrest; administrative restrictions on liberty; and detention pending deportation. Then there is the outward-facing incarceration of the enemies of the state.

Internal-facing restraints on liberty

Detention following arrest

Most significant in practical terms for the treatment of liberty within the counter-terrorism powers of the United Kingdom is the power of detention following arrest under s. 41 of the Terrorism Act 2000, by which 'A constable may arrest without a warrant a person whom he reasonably suspects to be a terrorist.' Many extraordinary features flow from this arrest power, but just two will be selected as testing the force of cosmopolitanism.

The first feature is 'reasonable suspicion', the impact of which affects how oppressive is the treatment of 'suspect' communities (Hillyard 1993). Here, the picture is mixed. It was accepted in *Raissi* v. *Commissioner of Police of the Metropolis*[1] that the evidential standard required by the device may fall well short of proof beyond reasonable doubt. Yet, the courts remain willing to examine the facts and to apply standards of sufficiency even to aliens suspected of the most heinous crimes. One such was Lofti Raissi, an Algerian who was arrested in late September 2001 under s. 41 on the basis of information from the FBI which alleged links to one of the 9/11 hijackers and involvement in flight training in Arizona. Also arrested were his brother and wife on the basis of their close relations and physical proximity. The Court of Appeal decided that it was reasonable to suspect complicity on the part of his wife, who had been in Arizona with her husband and had worked at an airline check-in at Heathrow, but the suspicions against his brother did not meet a sufficient standard. Yet, any celebration of British justice should be muted. Lofti Raissi spent five months in detention on the basis of a warrant for extradition to the USA which merely alleged false declarations as to his health and criminal record in connection with his application for a pilot's licence. In other words, the courts did not deliver forceful or speedy justice, and it took until February 2003 for the case to collapse because the American authorities failed at the final deadline to provide sufficient evidence of involvement in 9/11. Even then, he was not formally released from charges until April 2003. His claim to compensation was viewed as viable in *R (Raissi)* v. *Secretary of State for the Home Department* (2008),[2] given that the police had made false representations to the courts and the prosecution had colluded in the use of weak holding charges to deny bail. In summary, some tardy cosmopolitan

---

[1] (2008) [2008] EWCA Civ 1237.   [2] (2008) [2008] EWCA Civ 72.

care for a potentially heinous foreign prisoner was displayed by the courts but not by the executive authorities, and it is particularly contemptible that their abuses should have sullied the device of extradition which seeks to facilitate trust in justice across boundaries.

The next controversial aspect of s. 41 relates to its extraordinary period of detention. Section 41(3) allows for an initial detention period of up to forty-eight hours. The detention period may then be extended for a further five days according to the forms of review and authorisation laid down in Schedule 8 of the Act. Following the successful challenge which arose before the European Court of Human Rights (ECtHR) in *Brogan and ors* v. *United Kingdom,*[3] the authorisation rules set out in Schedule 8 involve an application for a 'warrant of further detention' to 'a judicial authority' and no longer to the Secretary of State. However, faced with the difficulties of international terrorism, the detention period was extended from seven to fourteen days in total by the Criminal Justice Act 2003, s. 306. Next, the detention period was extended to twenty-eight days in total by the Terrorism Act 2006, s. 23. Parliament has since refused on two occasions to extend this period yet further. The proposal was for ninety days in the initial versions of the Terrorism Bill 2005–6, and forty-two days were propounded by the Counter-Terrorism Bill 2007–8. The Home Office has left on the table the lingering threat of the Counter-Terrorism (Temporary Provisions) Bill which promises to revive the forty-two-day period to greet the next outrage (Walker 2009: Chapter 5). It is evident from these extensions of detention that the liberty of foreign terror suspects is severely devalued, even as compared to Irish terror suspects, in whose violent prime the police detention period never exceeded seven days. Yet, there are again indications of a care for transcendental comity and especially for how the treatment of individual detainees is perceived by the communities which identify with them, including even a community as encompassing as the Muslim concept of *Ummah Wahida*. Thus, in the context of Irish terrorism, the courts have already insisted in the cases of *Quigley*[4] and *Ward*[5] upon the right to make representations against further detention. They have also demanded in *Murray,*[6] *Averill*[7] and *Magee*[8] the effective availability

---

[3] (1988) App. nos. 11209, 11234, 11266/84, 11386/85, Ser. A 145-B.
[4] *Re Quigley's Application* (1997) [1997] NI 202.
[5] *Ward* v. *Police Service of Northern Ireland* (2007) [2007] UKHL 50.
[6] *Murray (John)* v. *United Kingdom* (1996) App. no. 18731/91, Reports 1996–I.
[7] *Averill* v. *United Kingdom* (2000) App. no. 36408/97, 2000–VI.
[8] *Magee* v. *United Kingdom* (2000) App. no. 28135/95, 2000–VI.

of legal advice and have ruled against deferments and oversight of consultations in *Brennan*.[9] Above all, the state has recognised that humane treatment is still to be accorded and has insisted upon special safeguards such as oversight of welfare by senior uniformed officers, record-keeping, closed-circuit television, medical checks and the audio and video recording of interviews even before these mechanisms were adopted in quotidian policing (Bennett Report 1979).

Overall, it continues to be questioned whether this special power of arrest should be preserved in force. The police view is that it has proved the most 'critical' provision in successive antiterrorist legislation (Lloyd Inquiry 1996: para. 4.14). Another view is that it is unacceptable as presently designed and executed since it allows excessive intelligence-gathering and oppressive interrogations and detentions, which have caused great damage on balance to the criminal justice system through miscarriages of justice and to communal relations. There is also the drawback of setting lax domestic standards which are taken as a cue by even more repressively minded states, thereby sending all the wrong signals about a cosmopolitan approach to human security against terrorism.

Administrative restraints on liberty

The United Kingdom has frequently resorted to administrative detention in the face of terrorism within the context of colonial conflicts (Simpson 2004; Bonner 2007) and in Ireland (Hogan and Walker 1989; Donohue 2001). Administrative detention has been rarer in Britain itself, at least outside of the World Wars (Simpson 1994). But old habits die hard, and it was revived by Part IV of the Anti-terrorism, Crime and Security Act 2001, which allowed for the detention without trial of certain asylum seekers. The idea that liberty should be afforded to foreign terrorist suspects just because they cannot be convicted by due process became officially unacceptable, and even an adverse report from a Privy Counsellor Review Committee (2003: para. 193) could not persuade the government otherwise (Home Office 2004: Part I, paras. 8, 34; and Part II, para. 31). On the face of it, a more direct challenge to the value of cosmopolitan liberty could hardly be conceived – both liberty and equality were negated by Part IV. However, this damning verdict should be qualified by two provisos.

[9] *Brennan v. United Kingdom* (2001) App. no. 39846/98, 2001–X.

The first is that the policy did reflect an unwillingness to resort to even worse tactics – to return foreign terror suspects to homelands which were likely to inflict torture, in contravention of the ruling of the ECtHR in *Chahal* v. *United Kingdom*.[10]

The second proviso is that Part IV was later condemned as incompatible with the Human Rights Act 1998 by the judicial House of Lords in *A and ors* v. *Secretary of State for the Home Department*.[11] Leaving aside the viability of the derogation notice on which Part IV was dependent, the scheme was defeated on grounds of proportionality because of two factors. One was that Part IV only applied to deportable aliens. Whilst they represented the predominant threat at the time, the existence of what might be called 'neighbour terrorism' (Walker 2008) could not be ignored. The other was that the creation under the legislative scheme in Part IV of a 'prison with three walls' – the absent fourth wall allowing foreign terrorists to choose to depart the jurisdiction (and possibly plot abroad) likewise made no sense. The second challenge to be sustained concerned the discriminatory impact of the detention regime, which could either be taken as a further challenge as to proportionality or could be said to be a challenge under the requirement of Article 15 of the European Convention on Human Rights that there be no inconsistency with other international law obligations (such as Article 14). This condemnation of Part IV very much reflected a cosmopolitan concern for according hallowed values to all categories of person, even alien and unwelcome terror suspects. The Lords' judgment can be contrasted with the more hesitant and procedural-based approach of the US Supreme Court to Guantánamo detainees who have won several stirring legal victories (*Hamdi*,[12] *Rasul*,[13] *Hamdan*,[14] *Boumediene*[15]) but not yet the fundamental recognition that their treatment within the benighted category of 'unlawful enemy combatant' amounts to second-class status compared to US citizen terrorists (Ip 2007).

The Prevention of Terrorism Act 2005 repealed Part IV and provides for 'control orders' (Walker 2007a). A control order is defined in s. 1(1) as 'an order against an individual that imposes obligations on him for purposes connected with protecting members of the public from a risk

[10] *Chahal* v. *United Kingdom* (1996) App. no. 22414/93, Reports 1996–V.
[11] *A and ors* v. *Secretary of State for the Home Department* (2004) [2004] UKHL 56.
[12] *Hamdi* v. *Rumsfeld* (2004) 124 S. Ct. 2633.
[13] *Rasul* v. *Bush* (2004) 124 S. Ct. 2686.
[14] *Hamdan* v. *Rumsfeld* (2006) 126 S. Ct. 2749.
[15] *Boumediene* v. *Bush* (2008) 128 S. Ct. 2229.

of terrorism'. They differ from Part IV in that they can apply to citizens as well as foreigners and that they do not for the most part rely upon a derogation notice. As for the first difference, an increasing number of orders – now the majority – have been issued against British citizens, and insofar as one can claim that equal pain is a cosmopolitan distribution, then there has been an improvement on Part IV. As for the second point, do control orders better respect rights to liberty? There is a strong strand of opinion which contends that outright condemnation of the whole device of control orders should be the preferred path. Yet, that outcome does not appear to be warranted according to the jurisprudence of the ECtHR which, in *Guzzardi* v. *Italy*,[16] did not treat every personal restriction as a loss of liberty under Article 5 of the European Convention on Human Rights.

Much of the litigation about control orders revolves around the processes by which review of the justification of an order is undertaken by the High Court which allows closed hearings, the non-disclosure of evidence, and the appointment of special advocates to test the case on behalf of the absent subject. The House of Lords concluded in *Re MB*[17] and again in *Re AF (no. 3)*[18] that this process is not inherently or necessarily unfair but that a minimum level of disclosure is required sufficient to allow meaningful instructions and challenge. As for liberty, the curtailment of liberty without a fair and open trial (traditionally with a jury) does run counter to traditions in English law. Ever since Magna Carta in 1215, Article 39, English law has specified that life, liberty and possessions cannot be treated adversely 'except by the lawful judgement of his equals or by the law of the land'. However, in *Re JJ*[19] the House of Lords merely placed parameters on the curtailment of liberty by way of curfew conditions in control orders. In that case JJ was subject to an eighteen-hour curfew, in circumstances where 'home' was a one-bedroom flat in which JJ lived alone. His visitors were strictly vetted and limited as were his contacts during the non-curfew period. The court viewed this regime as amounting to conditions rather less favourable than being in an open prison. It was emphasised by Lord Bingham that the line between compliance and non-compliance with Article 5 was not wholly mechanical in terms of just hours of confinement. But Lord Brown took sympathy on the Home Office and advised that sixteen

---

[16] *Guzzardi* v. *Italy* (1981) App. no. 7367/76, Ser. A vol. 39.
[17] *Re MB* (2007) [2007] UKHL 46.   [18] *Re AF (no. 3)* (2009) [2009] UKHL 28.
[19] *Re JJ* (2007) [2007] UKHL 45.

hours would be an acceptable limit. However, the danger of reliance on a mechanical rule was illustrated by the case of *Re AP*[20] where imposed social isolation, amounting to 'internal exile', resulted in the quashing of the control order even though its curfew element did not exceed sixteen hours.

Compared to administrative detention under Part IV, control orders foster a more cosmopolitan approach to liberty. Liberty and other freedoms (such as family life) can be exercised to some degree, and the holistic approach to the social setting of the individual should be welcomed. However, the House of Lords' standards of humanity can be criticised as insufficiently rigorous, and the attitude of the Home Office is grudging. After some early judgments the then Home Secretary, John Reid, reportedly bemoaned that control orders 'have got holes all through them' (Ford 2007: 2). The most recent court output, *AF (no. 3)*,[21] has likewise been labelled by the current Home Secretary as 'an extremely disappointing judgment' (Travis 2009: 4). So, a cosmopolitan approach may be reflected in court decisions but not yet in the heart of government. Parliament's failure to impose any temporal limit on the persistence of a control order is also of growing concern as the system matures. An expiry date (of say, two years per controlled subject) could transform the situation. It would turn a control order into either a provisional charge detention or a provisional deportation detention – either way, the authorities would know they have to act decisively by collecting further evidence for prosecution and not rely indefinitely on control orders.

Liberty and deportation

Much of the focus in counter-terrorism activity since 9/11 has been upon foreigners (Walker 2007b). For those whom the government could not or would not prosecute or control, there were renewed efforts following the end of administrative detention and especially after the July 2005 London bombings to explore new avenues for forced removal. Thus, the nine control orders issued against foreigners were revoked, and they were detained in August 2005 pending deportation (Ford and McGrory 2005: 6). To assuage concerns arising from the *Chahal* decision, assurances as to future treatment have been sought from potential receiving states with records of torture. In total, notices of intention to

---

[20] *Re AP* (2008) [2008] EWHC 2001 (Admin).   [21] See n. 18 above.

deport on national security grounds where assurances from the receiving state are thought to be required were served on twenty-nine individuals (Clarke 2005).

The negotiations to obtain assurances have been pursued with several states, culminating in an agreement with Jordan on 10 August 2005 (Foreign and Commonwealth Office 2005a). Its procedural safeguards require, inter alia, treatment in a humane and proper manner and in accordance with international standards; pre-trial legal assistance; and a prompt, fair and public trial. There is also provision for arranged (but not unannounced) visits by an independent body to be nominated jointly by the United Kingdom and Jordanian authorities but not for consular visits. There is no provision for the recording of interrogations or for regular or independent medical checks. Nor is there any specific guarantee against the death penalty. Similar accords have been settled with Libya (Foreign and Commonwealth Office 2005b), Lebanon (Foreign and Commonwealth Office 2005c), and Ethiopia (Foreign and Commonwealth Office 2008), though arrangements with Algeria are less firm, as related in the case of *Y* v. *Secretary of State for the Home Department*[22] (para. 241).

Is this core device of diplomatic assurances a solution consistent with cosmopolitan liberty? The device raises issues related more directly to humane treatment rather than liberty, but the taking away of liberty has now been frequently perpetrated on the basis that assurances offer legitimacy to the process, and so they are pertinent to this chapter. International law is rightly demanding over levels of protection against torture, the avoidance of which represents the most cosmopolitan of standards. The ECtHR delivered a trenchant warning in *Saadi* v. *Italy*.[23] A deportation to Tunisia would have exposed the applicant to the risk of being subjected to torture or inhuman or degrading treatment. The Court rejected:

> the argument of the United Kingdom Government, supported by the respondent Government, that a distinction must be drawn under Article 3 between treatment inflicted directly by a signatory State and treatment that might be inflicted by the authorities of another State, and that protection against this latter form of ill-treatment should be weighed against the interests of the community as a whole. [para. 138]

As for diplomatic assurances, the weight to be given to assurances from the receiving state depends on the circumstances obtaining at the

---

[22] (2006) (SC/36/2005, 2006).   [23] (2008) App. no. 37201/06, 28 February.

material time. In fact, the Tunisian authorities did not provide such
assurances other than in general terms (paras. 147, 148).

The same cosmopolitan stance was echoed domestically in 2006 with
the Court of Appeal's refusal in *S and ors* v. *Secretary of State for the
Home Department*[24] to endorse the removal of a group of Afghani
hijackers who had been granted discretionary leave to remain, albeit
on the different ground that the Home Secretary's attempt to resurrect
a period of examination was unlawful. This outcome echoed the
compassionate sentiment of Lord Justice Rose regarding Iraqi hijackers
in *R* v. *Abdul-Hussain*[25] when he stated that 'If Anne Frank had stolen a
car to escape from Amsterdam and had been charged with theft, the
tenets of English law would not have denied her the defence of duress
of circumstances on the ground that she should have awaited the
Gestapo's knock at the door.'

The more recent record of the United Kingdom courts on the
acceptance of diplomatic assurances relating to terrorist suspects (all
in the context of extradition) has been variable. If a 'real risk' of torture
is sufficient to avoid deportations (the test laid down in
R (Bagdanavicius) v. *Secretary of State for the Home Department*,[26] it
is hard to see how a piece of diplomatic paper can wholly expunge a
bloody record. Equally, if the courts depict extraordinary rendition into
the jurisdiction as a wholly unconscionable stain upon any subsequent
legal process (as in *R* v. *Horseferry Road Magistrates' Court, ex
p. Bennett*,[27] and *R* v. *Mullen*,[28] so they should find to be a corresponding abuse of process any extraordinary rendition out of the jurisdiction.
In reality, the courts have been more indulgent. On the one hand
assurances by the Russian Federation concerning the future treatment
of Ahkmed Zakayev, a leading Chechen separatist, if he were returned
on charges of murder, soliciting murder, wounding, false imprisonment
and levying war, were rejected (Horsnell and Charter 2003: 15). On the
other hand most other cases have resulted in deportation orders,
including against Babar Ahmad (*Ahmad and anor* v. *Government of
the United States of America*[29]). He has been accused of material
support of terrorism, support of the Taliban and Chechen rebels,
conspiracy to kill (including the possession of plans for attacking US
warships in the Straits of Hormuz), money laundering, solicitation of

---

[24] (2006) [2006] EWCA Civ 1157.   [25] (1999) [1999] Crim LR 572.
[26] (2005) [2005] UKHL 38.   [27] (1994) [1994] 1 AC 42.
[28] (2000) [2000] QB 520.   [29] (2006) [2006] EWHC 2927 (Admin).

funds and conspiracy. The raising of funds for terrorists allegedly arises through websites which Ahmad ran until their closure in November 2001 through Internet service providers in Nevada and then Connecticut. His extradition to the USA was ordered by the Bow Street Magistrates' Court, after a diplomatic note sent to the then Foreign Secretary, Jack Straw, by the US government was produced in court. The note promised that Ahmad would not face the death penalty or be sent to Guantánamo Bay. The decision to extradite was confirmed by the Home Secretary and upheld by the High Court. One may argue that this latter assurance is similar to the death-penalty promise. Thus, it is relatively straightforward for the United Kingdom government to discover whether a rendered prisoner has been sent to Guantánamo or has been tried by military commission – those processes do not occur without official sanction or in secret, unlike torture. Next, in *AS*,[30] the Court of Appeal refused to return the person back to Libya on grounds of the potential for torture. By contrast, misgivings about assurances related to the deportation to Jordan of Abu Qatada, sometimes labelled the most dangerous terrorist in Europe, were dismissed by the House of Lords in *RB and OO* v. *Secretary of State for the Home Department*[31] but await the verdict of the ECtHR in *Othman* v. *United Kingdom*.[32]

One can articulate a number of inherent problems with the device of assurances which cannot easily be overcome even with the best of diplomatic intentions. First, the transfer of the issue into the diplomatic sphere means that human rights are no longer the sole or perhaps predominant issue. The maintenance of cordial relations, through avoiding recriminations or voicing suspicion over troublesome prisoners, will surely mute the reactions of diplomats or politicians to allegations of mistreatment and involve the prioritisation of collective gains over individual protection (as illustrated by *Youssef* v. *Home Office*).[33] In this way: 'The tender arts of negotiation and compromise that characterize diplomacy can undermine straightforward and assertive human rights protection' (Human Rights Watch 2005: 19). Secondly, the very process of agreement-formation betrays the contradictory tacit admission that there is a real risk of ill-treatment which is being condoned as the prevailing position (UN Independent Expert on the Protection

---

[30] *AS* v. *Secretary of State for the Home Department* (2008) [2008] EWCA Civ 289.
[31] (2009) [2009] UKHL 10.   [32] (2009) App. no.8139/09.
[33] (2004) [2004] EWHC 1884 (QB).

of Human Rights and Fundamental Freedoms while Countering Terrorism 2005: paras. 56, 61). Thirdly, given that there is a record of torture
in the receiving state concerned, one might infer a culture or
subculture of torture which will subvert any expressed intended protections (*Chahal* v. *United Kingdom*,[34] para. 103). The linked fourth point
against assurances is that it is not obvious what accountability there
might arise for breach of their promises. There are documented cases
of the failure of assurances, notably in the case of Egypt, as sustained
in *Ahmed Agiza and Mohammed al-Zari* v. *Sweden*.[35] The sending
state may, of course, refuse to render any more prisoners, which may
become an irritant to the receiving state. But one senses that the annoy-
ance of the sending state in being unable to remit troublemakers will
be the greater.

Despite these caveats, the device of diplomatic assurances should
not be utterly discarded, since cosmopolitanism should encourage progressive co-operation between nations. Assurances may serve wider
policy goals of education and standard-setting for foreign states in
transition towards criminal justice reforms. They are signals to affected
minorities that their citizens are both cared for and subject to justice.
Furthermore, it is rightly said to be overly 'dogmatic' to assert that there
can never be any individual circumstances whereby diplomatic assurances can afford sufficient practical protection against breaches of
Article 3 (Lester and Beattie 2005: 569). Nevertheless, as advanced by
the Council of Europe Committee of Ministers (2005), it is submitted
that two conditions should generally be met before assurances can truly
be convincing as serving cosmopolitan purposes. First, the receiving
state should demonstrate sustained and practical legal and political
reforms which instill confidence that their promises can be delivered in
reality. The ratification of international instruments against torture and
subsequent professions of fidelity to them are patently not convincing of
themselves, and there should be evidence of fine deeds as well as
fine words. Secondly, there must be instituted under the guise of diplomatic assurances a degree of intrusion into the receiving state's criminal
justice and penal processes which goes beyond the mechanisms on offer
to date – including effective record-keeping and independent legal and
medical access.

[34] (1996) App. no. 22414/93, Reports 1996–V.
[35] (2005) CAT/C/34/D/233/2003, 24 May 2005.

External-facing restraints on liberty: incarceration as enemy combatants

Tony Blair, whilst prime minister, declared on 12 September 2001 that: 'We ... here in Britain, stand shoulder to shoulder with our American friends in this hour of tragedy and we like them will not rest until this evil is driven from our world' (Jones 2001: 2). One result has been the commitment of British armed forces to the conflicts in Afghanistan and Iraq to a greater extent than any other country except the USA. These overseas operations have inevitably involved the incarceration of 'the enemy', and it is therefore important to plot the rules of engagement and whether a cosmopolitan view of liberty has remained feasible despite these most adverse of circumstances.

As for Afghanistan, the invasion in October 2001 by US forces (supported by the United Kingdom) became a wider mission under the Bonn Conference in December 2001, under the banner of the International Security Assistance Force (ISAF) and authorised by UN Security Council Resolutions (1386, 1413, 1444, 1510, 1563, 1623, 1707, 1776 and 1833). ISAF tasks are delineated in a Military Technical Agreement 2002 between the ISAF Commander and the Afghan Transitional Authority. In 2003, upon request of the UN and government of Afghanistan, NATO took command of ISAF. Within the context of this conflict, the liberty of at least three categories of persons has been disrupted by British armed forces.

In the first category, and arising out of the initial situation of international armed conflict, are prisoners of war under the Third Geneva Convention and also civilian internees under the Fourth Geneva Convention (especially internment under Article 78). Little information has been released about numbers and conditions during that transitional period.

With the establishment of a recognised Afghan government, from 2002 onwards, the British practice has been increasingly to treat the conflict as one which is less than international armed conflict, and so captured persons are treated initially as 'detainees', a category distinct from prisoners of war and internees: 'Detainees are those individuals who, during operations abroad not amounting to International Armed Conflict, are held by UK armed forces because they have committed, or are suspected of committing criminal offences' (Ingram 2006). It follows that the British authorities denied, certainly by 2007 and 2008, that they make any intentional use of US-controlled facilities at Kandahar

Table 16.1 *Individuals detained by conventional UK forces in Afghanistan*

Year	Detained	Released	Transferred to NDS	Deceased	Detainees at year end
Apr. 2006 to Apr. 2007	51	26	22	3	0
Apr. 2007 to Oct. 2007	89	48	38	3	0
Oct. 2007 to Apr. 2008	96	56	39	1	0
Apr. 2008 to Oct. 2008	128	39	88	1	0
Oct. 2008 to 31 Dec. 2008	115	48	67	0	0
Totals	479	217	254	8	0

Source: Ministry of Defence (2009a)

(Browne 2007b) or Bagram Airbase (Taylor 2008), where longer-term internees are held as 'unlawful enemy combatants'. Following this form of detention, there is now a swift transfer to Afghan authorities under a bilateral memorandum of understanding agreed in 2005 (House of Commons Foreign Affairs Committee 2006: Appendix 3). The British policy is that any individual detained by ISAF forces should be transferred to the Afghan authorities 'at the first opportunity and within 96 hours, or released' (Browne 2007b). The agreement includes a prohibition on further transfer to a third country and also the use of the death penalty (House of Commons Foreign Affairs Committee 2006: Appendix 3, paras. 3.2, 6.1). The Afghans may consider criminal procedures, and this resolution appears consistent with British law (*MacDonald*,[36] *Public Prosecutor*,[37] *Mohammed Ali*[38]). Table 16.1 shows the rate of detentions and transfers. It is less certain what happens to those transferred into Afghan hands, given that the transfer is described as being to the National Directorate of Security (NDS) rather than to the criminal justice system.

[36] *Proceedings against Aeneas MacDonald alias Angus MacDonald* (1747) 18 St. Tr. 858.
[37] *Public Prosecutor* v. *Oie Hee Koi and ors* [1968] 2 W.L.R. 715.
[38] *Mohammed Ali* v. *Public Prosecutor* [1968] 3 All E.R. 488.

Though this phase after 2005 involves a move away from humanitarian legal rules, it remains the practice that:

> Arrangements have been put in place to ensure that all those detained by UK Armed Forces in Afghanistan are accurately recorded in terms of the circumstances of their arrest, location, next of kin (where that information is available) and subsequent location on leaving UK custody. International Committee of the Red Cross (ICRC) field workers in Afghanistan will be told of any detention by UK Armed Forces within 24 hours, or as soon as is practical. The National Information Bureau in the Ministry of Defence will submit a report to the ICRC in Geneva every seven days. [Drayson 2006]

Civilians or combatants can be even prosecuted in the United Kingdom provided they are accused of universal crimes such as torture and hostage-taking. It is not the practice to transfer such prisoners for British trial, but those found within the jurisdiction could be tried. An example is the case of Faryadi Zardad (Pook 2005: 10), an Afghan warlord who had relocated to the more serene climes of Streatham.

There have been no major inquiries into British army abuses of the liberty in Afghanistan, but concerns have been voiced about the conditions in which transferred prisoners are held in Afghan custody, and Amnesty International has called for a halt to such transfers (2007).

Turning to Iraq, prisoner-of-war (POW) status under the Third Geneva Convention applied to combatants captured in the initial invasion of 2003. After the establishment of an Iraqi interim government in 2004 (replaced by the Iraqi transitional government after elections in 2005, and then a permanent government in 2006), the Multinational Force, which replaced the US-dominated Combined Joint Task Force 7 in 2004, could impact on liberty in two ways:

> following the detention of any individual by multi-national force Iraq, a decision will be made to either release the individual, transfer him to the Iraqi judicial system (where criminal evidence exists), or to intern him if this is deemed necessary for imperative reasons of security, as permitted under UNSCR 1723. This decision is based on an assessment of the threat posed by the individual and is not related to his nationality. [Browne 2007a]

Security Council Resolution 1723 represented a renewal of Resolution 1546 which, read together with the letters annexed to it, authorised the Multinational Force to detain persons where this is necessary for imperative reasons of security. The numbers of internees held, detained and released by United Kingdom forces at the Divisional Internment Facility in Basra has been substantial, even during the final phase of deployment (see Table 16.2).

The offensive deployment of British forces was effectively terminated at the end of 2008 with the expiry of Resolution 1790 (Brown 2008). The final two internees were then transferred to Iraqi custody pending trial. The legality of their transfer was disputed in *R. (Al-Saadoon and Mufdhi) v. Secretary of State for Defence*,[39] but it was recognised that there remained no viable legal basis for further British detentions in Iraq.

Applying considerations of cosmopolitanism to these two theatres of conflict, one might ask, first, whether there was a recognition of the humanity of 'the other', and then, secondly, whether the procedures applied reflected that recognition.

As regards recognition, one might depict as positive the refusal by the British authorities to follow the American lead and label those whose liberty has been taken away as some new strain of 'unlawful combatant' who fall into a legal 'black hole' (Steyn 2004; Duffy 2005), where they were to remain without any form of recognisable rights in domestic or international law at least until the US Supreme Court began to intervene. The application of the Geneva Conventions and Protocols itself represents a degree of cosmopolitanism which triggers important international standard-setting and oversight and which has eventually exerted influence even within the hostile environment of the US 'War on Terror'.

Since the phase of international conflict has arguably now ended in Iraq, it is even more commendable that the United Kingdom courts asserted further rules of common humanity by finding that the domestic standards of the Human Rights Act 1998 can potentially apply to conflicts abroad. This phase of recognition was sustained with regard to one of the long-term internees, Abdul Razzaq Ali Al-Jedda. He had been detained without trial for three years at the Shaibah Base near Basrah following his visit to Iraq in 2004. His detention was found to be justiciable but, in the event, lawful in *R. (Al-Jedda) v. Secretary of State for Defence*.[40] He could not invoke Article 5 of the European Convention on Human Rights for the purpose of challenging his loss of liberty, even though the detention without trial would be in clear breach in the absence of any derogation under Article 15. The House of Lords reasoned that Article 5 had been qualified by United Nations Security Council Resolution 1546 of 8 June 2004, which, by paragraph 10,

---

[39] (2008) [2008] EWHC 3098 (Admin).   [40] (2007) [2007] UKHL 58.

Table 16.2 *Individuals detained by conventional UK forces in Iraq*

Year	Interned	Released	Bailed	Escaped	Deceased	Transfer to US authority	Transfer to Iraqi criminal justice	Detainees at year end
2003	149	9	0	0	0	0	0	140
2004	230	219	0	1	1	2	124	23
2005	47	21	0	0	0	0	12	37
2006	136	66	0	0	0	0	0	107
2007	77	151	14	11	0	0	3	5
2008	12	11	0	0	0	4	2	0
Total	651	477	14	12	1	6	141	

Source: Ministry of Defence (2009a)

'Decides that the multinational force shall have all the authority to take all necessary measures to contribute to the maintenance of security and stability in Iraq' until the end of the mandated period (31 December 2008). Internment processes were expressly envisaged as part of this authority (though only as specified in an annexed letter of Colin Powell), and they could be implemented without notice of derogation under Human Rights Act 1998. Insofar as there is any conflict between the United Nations Charter and the European Convention, the former prevailed under Article 103 of the Charter. This verdict sanctions an abdication from Article 5 standards but on the explicit condition of clear United Nations authority to override European Convention requirements. In consequence, the British authorities cannot unilaterally establish any detention regime equivalent to Guantánamo Bay but must act within one international law regime or another – United Nations resolutions, the European Convention on Human Rights or the laws of war.

The proposition that English law jurisdiction remains potentially viable was illustrated by a later application by Al-Jedda in *Al-Jedda v. Secretary of State for Defence*[41] that his detention under terms allowed by the Coalition Provisional Authority (CPA) in 2003 became unlawful under Iraqi law following the establishment of the 2006 Constitution. The High Court was again willing to consider the substance of the claim, especially as the British activities enjoyed immunity in Iraqi courts, but found that the CPA regime had survived the coming into force of the Iraqi Constitution. It was therefore willing to assume English law jurisdiction to protect a foreigner in a foreign land, though emphasised that it was the validity of the instruments of the CPA and not Iraqi law which was justiciable.

The extension of domestic norms has been taken a stage further wherever it can be established that there is effective control of territory or facilities by British state forces. The point is illustrated by the case of *R. (Al-Skeini) v. Secretary of State for Defence*[42] which concerned Baha Mousa, who died from physical injuries consistent with severe assaults while held in British military custody in Basrah in 2003. The House of Lords held that his death requires a full investigation which is compliant with Article 2 of the Human Rights Act. Subsequently, the British government admitted to 'substantial breaches' of the European Convention on Human Rights (Norton-Taylor 2008a: 15), and the Ministry of Defence agreed to pay £2.83 million in compensation to the family of

[41] (2009) [2009] EWHC 397 (QB).   [42] (2007) [2007] UKHL 27.

Baha Mousa and nine other men (Norton-Taylor 2008b: 4). Arising from this case, a number of prosecutions were brought under the International Criminal Court Act 2001 for abusive conduct against Iraqi prisoners. Corporal Donald Payne pleaded guilty to the charge of inhumanely treating Iraqi civilians at a court martial of seven soldiers (Evans 2006: 11). The same idea of enhanced human rights standards in circumstances of control within a conflict zone can equally apply to the treatment of soldiers, as required in *R (Smith)* v. *Assistant Deputy Coroner for Oxfordshire*[43] during the coroner' inquiry into the death of a soldier, Private Jason Smith, resulting from heatstroke while sunbathing in camp after returning from patrol in Iraq. As with control orders, disquiet about this cosmopolitan judgment has been expressed by the then Armed Forces Chief of the Defence Staff, Air Chief Marshal Sir Jock Stirrup (Ministry of Defence 2009b).

The same point about grants of cosmopolitan concern in the official manual, but grudging or defective application, applies to internment in Iraq by the British authorities. The following procedures applied on paper:

> All new UK internees have their cases reviewed by the Divisional Internment Review Committee no later than 48 hours after they are apprehended, and then every 28 days thereafter. Cases are also reviewed by the Combined Review and Release Board, a joint UK-Iraqi board, every three months. Individuals held for 18 months have their cases referred to the Joint Detention Committee which is co-chaired by Prime Minister Maliki and the Commander Multi-National Force Iraq. [Browne 2007a]

In addition, 'The International Committee of the Red Cross (ICRC) has regular and open access to our detention facility and all our internees. The facility has also been visited by a team from the Iraqi Ministry of Human Rights' (Ingram 2007). However, whilst perhaps not rivalling the horror stories of Abu Ghraib (Taguba 2004; Schlesinger 2004; Fay 2004), there are serious allegations of abuse against British forces too.

The principal official inquiry in Iraq, the Aitken Report (2008), is a rather brief internal Ministry of Defence inquiry which found that rules forbidding 'deep interrogation' techniques and imposed on the army in 1972 by direction of the prime minister had 'come to be lost' (*ibid.*: para. 19), as a result of which, some of the techniques had revived. After 2005, clearer guidelines were inserted into army

[43] (2009) [2009] EWCA 441.

manuals, though they still do not mention specifically the five techniques of deep interrogation which were also outlawed by the ECtHR in *Ireland* v. *United Kingdom*.[44]

The second inquiry arose when the Secretary of State for Defence announced in May 2008 that there would be a fuller and public inquiry into the death of Baha Mousa. The inquiry has been established under the Inquiries Act 2005 and is chaired by Sir William Gage, a retired Court of Appeal judge (Gage 2009).

Other incidents worthy of further investigation include: nine Iraqis killed in Basrah in 2003 and 2004 (Amnesty International 2004); the abuse of suspected looters in Camp Breadbasket in May 2003 as a result of which Fusilier Gary Bartlam, Corporal Kenyon, Lance Corporal Cooley and Lance Corporal Larkin were imprisoned and dismissed from the army with disgrace (Gillan 2005: 2); and the payment of compensation to many relatives to avert further complaint (Carrell 2004: 1). Two prosecutions for murder, of Trooper Kevin Williams and of Corporal Scott Evans and others, collapsed in 2005 (Evans 2005: 1), but a substantial number of other civil cases are pending relating to the alleged assaults at Camp Breadbasket and at the Shaibah Base.

Even wider judicial inquiries were rejected in *R (Gentle)* v. *Prime Minister* (2008). The claimants were the mothers of British soldiers who had been killed in Iraq. Their deaths had been fully investigated at inquests in the normal way. The claimants argued that the coroner's inquest did not offer a wide enough investigation for the purposes of Article 2 and that an independent public inquiry was required into all the circumstances surrounding the invasion of Iraq by British forces in 2003. The claim was dismissed. Article 2 had never been held to apply to the process of deciding on the lawfulness of a resort to arms. First, the lawfulness of military action had no immediate bearing on the circumstances of particular fatalities. Secondly, the Convention was less suitable as a basis for investigation than the United Nations Charter. Thirdly, the breadth of issues arising in such an inquiry would be forensically unmanageable. Fourthly, the obligation of member states under Article 1 of the Convention was largely territorial. In this case, the deaths occurred in territory within Iraq not effectively controlled by the British army. A non-judicial official inquiry into the invasion of Iraq has been established in July 2009 to consider events from 2001 to 2009 (Chilcot 2009).

---

[44] (1978) App no. 5310/71, Ser. A 25 (1978).

Perhaps the best that can be expected of the force of the principle of cosmopolitanism in external affairs is that it conduces to a willingness to address defaults. To expect that common humanity will always prevail successfully in conflict situations is forlorn fantasy. In that light, the British authorities have shown some degree of respect for the worth of foreign lives, though their reluctance to hold timely inquiries and the casual buying off of victims does suggest a rather dismissive attitude to the particular lives of alien others.

Conclusion

Insofar as there has been a positive story to relate in this chapter about the observance of cosmopolitan ideals by United Kingdom agencies and the avoidance of the depiction that the 'enemy of the moment always represented absolute evil' (Orwell 1954: 31), one might speculate that a couple of factors have been in play. One is the value of experience of terrorism and counter-terrorism, as indicated at the outset of this chapter. Such experience conduces to policies which reflect the need to address the political as well as the military aspects of terrorism. The experiences of Northern Ireland between 1969 and 1975 surely cemented the rejection of a 'war' paradigm for the domestic responses to jihadi terrorism. Yet, hard lessons have sometimes slipped the collective memory, such as revival of deep interrogation in Iraq.

A more effective feature which has aided cosmopolitanism concerns oversight mechanisms which have been enhanced via three devices. One mechanism is the continued appointment of an independent reviewer (Lord Carlisle since 2001) who can give assurance that secretive anti-terrorism agencies and operations observe appropriate standards for the good of all (Walker 2009: Chapter 10). The reviewer has produced insights and factual details not otherwise available, and there is undoubtedly value in the knowledge that security activities are reviewable. However, the review scheme is not perfect. The reviewer is not formally linked to Parliament and has no special powers or resources. Furthermore, not all aspects of special laws or practices are scrutinised. The second mechanism is that Parliament has improved its oversight by engendering detailed and expert debates via select committees, above all by the Joint Committee on Human Rights. These again have provided solid arguments and items of evidence which are cited not only in debates but even by ministers. The third mechanism, about which evidence has already been given in this chapter, concerns judicial oversight. It remains a matter of debate to some as to whether the judiciary have been abjectly deferential in security matters and whether the advent of the Human Rights Act 1998 is therefore futile (Ewing 2004; Ewing and Tham 2008). It is submitted that the better view is that judicial commitment to the priority of human rights has increased in practice and that this attitude has even been applied to terrorism laws though not evenly in all respects (Gearty 2005). Alongside the Human Rights Act, international oversight through the ECtHR remains a striking feature of Western European jurisdictions. That governments can be taken to task for excesses by a court which is beyond most vagaries of the national psyche and polity represents an important and practical instrument in favour of cosmopolitanism. Lord Hoffmann's diatribe against its quality and impact (2009) fails to explain with any conviction where, despite its sometimes lax standard of reasoning, the ECtHR has inflicted unconscionable or impractical outcomes for United Kingdom antiterrorism operatives.

Despite these favourable mechanisms, there remains in apparent opposition to cosmopolitan ideals an official mindset in favour of patriotic security on the basis that it is a rational policy and also delivers political benefits. However, there are some signs from polling on the forty-two day proposal that even the public are becoming sceptical of the worth of the loss of their liberty and suspicious of the motives of politicians (ICM Research 2008). Therefore, we appear destined for the time being to reside in conditions which serve state security rather than cosmopolitan security. In this security state, patriotic policy is generated from above (with ever-increasing budgets) and becomes the organising feature for other sectors of policies such as environmental risk (Cabinet Office 2008) and cultural engagement with minority communities (Department for Communities and Local Government 2007; 2008). At the international level, any global reciprocity on dealing with terrorism via institutional cosmopolitanism (Hutchings and Danreuther 1999; Archibugi 2003; 2009) has been stunted as it is a further feature of the impact of terrorism that institutions such as the United Nations have arguably been weakened after 9/11 by the reassertion of state sovereignty.

References

Aitken Report (2008) *Investigation into Cases of Deliberate Abuse and Unlawful Killing in Iraq in 2003 and 2004*, London: Ministry of Defence.
Amnesty International (2004) *Iraq: Killings of Civilians in Basra and al-' Amara*, London: Amnesty International.

(2007) *Afghanistan: Detainees Transferred to Torture: ISAF Complicity?*, London: Amnesty International.

Anderson-Gold, S. (2001), *Cosmopolitanism and Human Rights*, Cardiff: University of Wales Press.

Annan, K. (2005) *In Larger Freedom*, New York: United Nations.

Appiah, A. K. (2006) *Cosmopolitanism: Ethics in a World of Strangers*, London: Allen Lane.

Archibugi, D. (2003) *Debating Cosmopolitics*, London: Verso.

(2009) *A Global Commonwealth of Citizens*, Princeton: Princeton University Press.

Benhabib, S. (2006) *Another Cosmopolitanism*, New York: Oxford University Press.

Bennett Report (1979) *Committee of Inquiry into Police Interrogation Procedures in Northern Ireland*, Cm. 9497, London: HMSO.

Bonner, D. (2007) *Executive Measures, Terrorism and National Security*, Aldershot: Ashgate.

Brown, G. (2008), *Hansard*, vol. 485, 18 December, col. 1233.

Browne, D. (2007a) *Hansard*, vol. 457, March, cols. 1611–12.

(2007b) *Hansard*, vol. 467, 19 November, col. 468W.

Cabinet Office (2008) *National Security Strategy of the United Kingdom: Security in an Interdependent World*, Cm. 7291, London: HMSO.

(2009) *Pursue, Prevent, Protect, Prepare*, Cm. 7547, London: HMSO.

Carrell, S. (2004) 'Fair price for a life?', *Independent on Sunday*, 1 August.

Chilcot, J. (2009) *The Iraq Inquiry*, www.iraqinquiry.org.uk.

Clarke, C. (2005) *Hansard*, vol. 440, 15 December, col. 167WS.

Council of Europe Committee of Ministers (2005) *Forced Returns, 925th Meeting of the Ministers' Deputies*, Strasbourg: Council of Europe.

Department for Communities and Local Government (2007) *Preventing Violent Extremism: Winning Hearts and Minds*, London: Department for Communities and Local Government.

(2008) *Preventing Violent Extremism: Next Steps for Communities*, London: Department for Communities and Local Government.

Dershowitz, A. (2002) *Why Terrorism Works*, New Haven: Yale University Press.

Donohue, L. K. (2001) *Counter-Terrorism Law*, Dublin: Irish Academic Press.

Douzinas, C. (2007) *Human Rights and Empire*, London: Routledge-Cavendish.

Drayson, Lord P. (2006) *Hansard*, vol. 679, 9 March, col. 149W.

Duffy, H. (2005) *The 'War on Terror' and the Framework of International Law*, Cambridge: Cambridge University Press.

Evans, M. (2005) 'Judge blasts Army as £8m war crimes trial collapses', *The Times*, 4 November.

(2006) 'British soldier admits Iraqi war crime', *The Times*, 20 September.

Ewing, K. (2004) 'The futility of human rights', *Public Law*, 829–52.

Ewing, K. and Tham, J.-C. (2008) 'The continuing futility of the Human Rights Act', *Public Law*, 668–93.

Fay Report (2004) *Investigation of Intelligence Activities at Abu Ghraib*, Washington: Department of Defense.

Fine, R. (2007) *Cosmopolitanism*, London: Routledge.

Ford, R. (2007) 'Terror controls full of holes, says Reid', *The Times*, 25 January.

Ford, R. and McGrory, D. (2005) 'Three-year fight looms to deport extremists held after dawn raids', *The Times*, 12 August.

Foreign and Commonwealth Office (2005a) *Memorandum of Understanding between the Government of the United Kingdom of Great Britain and Northern Ireland and the Government of the Hashemite Kingdom of Jordan Regulating the Provision of Undertakings in Respect of Specified Persons Prior to Deportation*, London: Foreign and Commonwealth Office.

(2005b) *Memorandum of Understanding between the Government of Libya and the Government of the United Kingdom Concerning the Provision of Assurances in Respect of Persons Subject to Deportation*, London: Foreign and Commonwealth Office.

(2005c) *Memorandum of Understanding between the Government of the United Kingdom of Great Britain and Northern Ireland and the Government of the Lebanese Republic Concerning the Provision of Assurances in Respect of Persons Subject to Deportation*, London: Foreign and Commonwealth Office.

(2008) *Memorandum of Understanding between the Government of the United Kingdom of Great Britain and Northern Ireland and the Government of the Federal Democratic Republic of Ethiopia Concerning the Provision of Assurances in Respect of Persons Subject to Deportation*, London: Foreign and Commonwealth Office.

Gage, W. (2009) *The Baha Mousa Public Inquiry*, www.bahamousainquiry.org.

Gearty, C. (2005) 'Human rights in an age of counter-terrorism', *Current Legal Problems*, 58, 25–46.

Gillan, A. (2005) 'Soldiers in Iraq abuse case sent to prison', *The Guardian*, 26 February.

Hillyard, P. (1993) *Suspect Community*, London: Pluto Press.

Hoffmann, Lord L. (2009) 'The universality of human rights', *Law Quarterly Review*, 416–32.

Hogan, G. and Walker, C. (1989) *Political Violence and the Law in Ireland*, Manchester: Manchester University Press.

Home Office (2004) *Counter Terrorism Powers*, Cm. 6147, London: Home Office.

Horsnell, M. and Charter, D. (2003) 'Russian fury as Chechen leader beats extradition', *The Times*, 14 November.

House of Commons Foreign Affairs Committee (2006) *Visit to Guantánamo Bay 2006–07*, HC 44, London: HMSO.

Human Rights Watch (2005) *Still at Risk: Diplomatic Assurances No Safeguard against Torture*, New York: Human Rights Watch.

Hutchings, K. and Danreuther, R. (1999) (eds.) *Cosmopolitan Citizenship*, Basingstoke: Macmillan.

ICM Research (2008) *British Policies Survey*, www.jrrt.org.uk/uploads/ICM%20Poll%20Detention%20of%20Terrorist%20Suspects.pdf.

Ignatieff, M. (2004) *The Lesser Evil*, Edinburgh: Edinburgh University Press.

Ingram, A. (2006) *Hansard*, vol. 451, 7 November, col. 1443W.

(2007) *Hansard*, vol. 457, 19 February, col. 303W.

Ip, J. (2007) 'Comparative perspectives on the detention of terrorist suspects', *Transnational & Contemporary Problems*, 16, 773–871.

Jones, G. (2001) 'We will help hunt down evil culprits, says Blair', *The Daily Telegraph*, 12 September, 2.

Kant, I. (1983) *Perpetual Peace and Other Essays* (orig. pub. 1795), Indianapolis: Hackett Publishing Company.

Lester, A. and Beattie, K. (2005) 'Risking torture', *European Human Rights Law Review*, 6, 565–71.

Lloyd Inquiry (1996) *Legislation against Terrorism*, Cm. 3420, London: HMSO.

Ministry of Defence (2009a) *Statistics on Afghanistan and Iraq Detentions*, FOI request 20090710.

(2009b) 'MOD loses appeal regarding Human Rights Act', www.mod.uk/DefenceInternet/DefenceNews/DefencePolicyAndBusiness/ModLosesAppealRegardingHumanRightsAct.htm.

Norton-Taylor, R. (2008a) 'UK admits breaching human rights convention over detainee death', *The Guardian*, 28 March.

(2008b) 'MoD pays £3m over abuse of Iraqis in custody', *The Guardian*, 11 July.

Nussbaum, M. C. (1997) 'Kant and stoic cosmopolitanism', *Journal of Political Philosophy*, 5, 1.

Orwell, G. (1954) *Nineteen Eighty-Four*, Harmondsworth: Penguin.

Pook, S. (2005) 'Former Afghan warlord given 20 years for crimes against humanity', *The Daily Telegraph*, 20 July.

Privy Counsellor Review Committee (2003) *Anti-Terrorism, Crime and Security Act 2001 Review*, Report, 2003–04 HC 100.

Schlesinger Report (2004) *Independent Panel to Review Department of Defense Detention Operations, Final Report*, Washington: Department of Defense.

Simpson, A. W. B. (1994) *In the Highest Degree Odious*, Oxford: Oxford University Press.

(2004) *Human Rights and the End of Empire*, Oxford: Oxford University Press.

Steyn, J. (2004) 'Guantánamo Bay: the legal black hole', *International & Comparative Legal Quarterly*, 53, 1–15.

Taguba Report (2004) *Treatment of Abu Ghraib Prisoners in Iraq: Article 15–6 Investigation of the 800th Military Police Brigade*, Washington: Department of Defense.

Tan, K.-C. (2004) *Justice without Borders*, Cambridge: Cambridge University Press.

Taylor, Baroness A. (2008) *Hansard*, vol. 703, 29 September, col. 374WA.

Thobani, S. (2007) 'Nationality in the age of global terror' in *Exalted Subjects: Studies in the Making of Race and Nation in Canada*, Toronto: University of Toronto Press.

Travis, A. (2009) 'Civil liberties: secret evidence on terror suspects ruled illegal', *The Guardian*, 11 June.

UN Commission on Human Security (2003) *Human Security Now*, New York: Commission on Human Security.

UN Independent Expert on the Protection of Human Rights and Fundamental Freedoms while Countering Terrorism (2005) E/CN.4/2005/103.

Walker, C. (2005) 'Prisoners of "war all the time"', *European Human Rights Law Review*, 50–74.

   (2007a) 'Keeping control of terrorists without losing control of constitutionalism', *Stanford Law Review*, 59, 1395–463.

   (2007b) 'Foreign terror suspects', *Modern Law Review*, 70, 427–57.

   (2008) '"Know thine enemy as thyself": discerning friend from foe under anti-terrorism laws', *Melbourne Law Review*, 32, 275–301.

   (2009) *The Anti-Terrorism Legislation*, 2nd edn, Oxford: Oxford University Press.

17

Restorative justice and states' uneasy relationship with their publics

JOANNA SHAPLAND[*]

Over the last ten to twenty years, nation states in Western Europe and North America have become somewhat concerned about their publics' reaction to criminal justice (Hough and Roberts 1998; Mattinson and Mirrlees-Black 2000; Judicature 1997). Recent interest in measuring confidence in criminal justice and indeed in developing measures for confidence cross-nationally[1] is a testimony to that concern. Public views on the quality, trustworthiness and legitimacy of criminal justice institutions are newly important, and to be sought, even though governments of nation states vary as to whether they feel that popular views should be mirrored by policy changes.

Several trends have contributed to the perceived need of states to consider public reactions in relation to criminal justice. One is the increasing salience of crime and insecurity politically. Though criminal justice responses to crime are almost certainly now a minor part of states' responses, with crime prevention, controlling social disorder in neighbourhoods and homeland security being dominant trends, criminal justice responses are still seen as a state responsibility and have symbolic importance. Where criminal justice is seen to fail, for example related to major cases such as the Dutroucx case in Belgium, overall citizens' perceptions of government efficacy fall.

---

[*] This chapter has been developed from Shapland (2008), the introduction to a book arising from a series of European seminars organised by Joanna Shapland and Philip Milburn under the auspices of the *Groupe Européen de Recherche sur les Normativités* (GERN: see www.gern-cnrs.com/gern/index.php?id=2) also published in French as Shapland, J. (ed.), (2008) *Justice, communauté et societé civile: études comparatives sur un terrain disputé*, Paris: L'Harmattan.
[1] On some moves to develop cross-national measures of confidence in criminal justice, see the Euro-JUSTIS website at www.eurojustis.eu/index.php.

Another long-term trend is the move to new public management, with its adoption of efficiency, effectiveness and value for money as criteria. Though criminal justice is probably more insulated from social policy management trends than are areas such as health or education, the wind of change eventually reaches the police and thereafter the courts and other criminal justice institutions. Part of the new public management is an emphasis on client/user/public views of quality and accessibility of service,[2] which again puts public perceptions at the forefront.

Political fashions in government are also, in criminal justice, swinging away from professionals' judgements and towards other sources of influence, which may include pressure groups and the media, though clearly some countries, such as the UK, are feeling this trend more sharply in relation to criminal justice than are others (such as Germany, see Groenemeyer 2008). Leaving it to the experts is no longer acceptable in most European countries: experts are not popular, except of course as talking heads on media programmes. Leaving it solely to the professionals has also become unfashionable in certain countries: celebrity comment (and the 'celebrity culture') is acceptable, professionals' comments (and veneration of professional judgement) are less so. Professionals are suspected of having vested interests, particularly when they are legal professionals. The economic doctrine that markets do not work well on professional services – because clients, by definition, find it difficult to judge the quality of the professional's work, compared to the fee charged – has been an important contributor to this unease.[3] Another is the change from venerating professional knowledge and mystique to seeing professionals as potentially out of touch (with the public). The move against professionals in Europe is hardly surprising; America was feeling the twinges of uncertainty about what the public was feeling about the criminal courts in the 1990s and a rash of projects to make courthouses more accountable to users followed (Judicature 1997). These fashions tend to seep across the Atlantic after ten years. Maybe, politicians thought, our own popularity will suffer if the only people involved in criminal justice are politicians,

---

[2] On the modernisation and new public management agenda in e.g. healthcare across Europe and its effects on governance structures and the role of access and quality judgements, see e.g. Hervey (2008).
[3] The principal–agent framework with asymmetric information – see e.g. Rickman *et al.* (1999) for a description of this and how legal assistance has changed in England and Wales to drive risk towards service providers, such as lawyers.

professionals and other experts; we need to bring the discourse about priorities in criminal justice closer to the public.

Populism in criminal justice has clearly been more dominant in some countries than others, with one of the most fervent being the UK. One of the most recent manifestations of it in England and Wales is driving the government's mutedly enthusiastic response to the Casey Report (Casey 2008). The report advocates a series of populist measures, from citizens having more input into neighbourhood policing, to highly visible ways of showing offenders doing community work. The prime minister said, 'We commissioned this frank report because we know how important it is to understand how the public feel about crime and justice. Through this report, people have told us what they want to be done, and we are going to act' (Home Office 2008). The last government's Green Paper in England and Wales on criminal justice is was entitled 'Engaging communities in criminal justice' (OCJR 2009) and covers a range of ways of bringing the public closer, from creating stronger, community-focused partnerships and keeping the public better informed, through to ideas about community prosecutors, community impact statements, involving communities in the selection and deployment of district judges and to restorative justice and greater compensation to victims. The new government seems equally concerned about public views on criminal justice (Ministry of Justice 2010).

The particular focus of disquiet about state–public distance varies. Sometimes it is the judiciary who are seen as too distant, or whose recruitment is perceived as insufficiently reflecting the balance of social, ethnic or religious groups in the population. So, for example, the judiciary have famously been called 'white, male, middle-aged, middle-class' in England and Wales. The adoption of a judicial appointments committee, separate from government, in Northern Ireland was driven by similar concerns (Criminal Justice Review Team 2000). The focus is sometimes on the police and particularly policing priorities between public order and local demands. The police may be seen as not necessarily listening to local views or minimising some forms of crime, such as racially motivated crime or domestic abuse (as in France, Germany and England).

Yet the focus may be less precise and more perceptual: a general feeling that the state has fallen down on its promises to 'deal with crime' or has not succeeded in the 'war on drugs'; that despite governments proclaiming a drop in the amount of crime, people still feel afraid and insecure. Of course, these perceptions may themselves be a result of unrealistic expectations of the capability of state criminal justice agencies, such as the police, to 'deal' with crime. However, if, at the same time, state criminal justice is perceived as distant, then this overall insecurity (which may be driven by other headlines, such as pandemics, terrorism or an uncomfortable awareness that globalisation brings threats as well as benefits) may lead citizens to seek a more local presence for criminal justice or known faces in the neighbourhood.

In the last decade or so, I would argue that, throughout Europe, these concerns have led national governments in Europe and North America to seek to adopt new ways of 'doing justice' in relation to crime and disorder, not necessarily because they are more effective, but because they can be portrayed as bringing justice closer to what governments can portray as local or public concerns. The particular content of these initiatives has tended to vary. It may be local crime prevention or crime reduction partnership programmes, bringing in local democratically elected bodies (local authorities/municipalities/communes) or local voluntary sector bodies. It may be that the police or prosecutors are required to consult more with local representatives before determining their operational priorities, and possibly to feed back to the local populace what they have done. Sometimes, as in France and the Netherlands, criminal justice officials (prosecutors, sometimes courts) have themselves been required to move to be locally situated in offices, reversing, at least temporarily, the move towards centralisation of criminal justice and other social services prompted by efficiency concerns and public expenditure. Sometimes the emphasis has been on developing restorative justice initiatives, whether in policing, at the level of courts' sentencing or during sentence. The development and promotion of restorative justice has been almost a common denominator across nation states in Europe, as well as in North America, whether the traditional legal system has been common law or civil law.

In this chapter I shall be concentrating upon restorative justice – and upon what has happened to those restorative justice initiatives in a number of countries. The initiatives I shall be examining are those where restorative justice has been in close contact with criminal justice. I will argue that what has happened has depended upon national, cultural, deep-seated views, held by both state and citizens, of what justice is and what the state's role should be – and that those are primarily views about what criminal justice should be. Restorative justice, the newcomer, has had to contend with basic ideas about criminal justice. Those ideas are part of the heritage of criminal justice in each country: often deeply held though subconscious, they strongly influence reactions to innovation, localisation and lay people.

Who should governments reach out to?

The first question which needs to be addressed in terms of criminal justice culture – and which determines the boundaries of what is seen as appropriate – is who criminal justice perceives its publics to be. This is one of the great divides. In Anglo-Saxon, common law countries, the answer is relatively uncontentious. It is local communities, meaning local geographical 'neighbourhoods' – though there is not necessarily any enquiry as to whether the neighbourhood actually feels it is a neighbourhood. And hence we have seen advocacy of community policing, community crime prevention, ministers talking about the need for local areas to know about their crime problems and be involved in helping with them and so forth (OCJR 2009).

In France, it is different. As Anne Wyvekens (2008: 30) says:

> The word 'community' is not French at all. One could even say that French people, and French institutional personnel *hate* the word 'community'. They hate it because in French culture it has almost entirely negative connotations. The word 'community' refers to an *ethnic* community – which is viewed, consciously or not, as something not really civilized – but above all it refers to something the French political tradition cannot accept: highlighting and giving importance to what makes people different from each other, while the major national value is equality, republican equality. In France when someone is referring to 'community' the word that is nearly always used is *communautarisme*, as in, for example, *le repli communautaire* – withdrawal into one's own community – i.e. the exact opposite of the major value for the French: that of the Republic, which emphasises unity and equality. [emphases in original]

Milburn (2008) similarly points out that organising criminal justice on the basis of 'community' would be placing an intermediate political entity between the state and the citizen, so negating the important national value of equality of individuals in respect of state action. How then can France have decentralised collective entities, such as local authorities? The answer is that they are seen as elements of the state, not as separate bodies. The result is that French criminal justice is designed such that, notionally, the same product is delivered – equally, to all areas of the country – by professionals. Germany and the

Netherlands hold similar views to France about the dangers of talking about 'community' in connection with criminal justice (Groenemeyer 2008; van Swaaningen 2008).

However, the French have not been immune to these perceived pressure for the state to draw closer to its public. What has happened, though, is that the state has not reached out to 'communities' per se, but to what is called 'civil society' (the collective term for citizens or lay people in the country). The riots in disadvantaged areas in France brought in their train a realisation that there was no equal access to, nor equal delivery of, what were supposed to be state services available everywhere. Hence there was a need to increase state action and state services in these disadvantaged areas. The result was the development of *maisons de justice*: localised delivery points for criminal justice services. Prosecutors were outposted; mediation was developed, initially by community mediators (Wyvekens 2008, see also Crawford 2000a; 2000b). Community justice, no – but what has come to be called 'proximity justice', yes – as long as the state could portray it as still the same service. It would seem to me that this equality is a little fictional – there is still the likelihood of a differentiated service in practice, as the localised service responds to local conditions, through practitioners developing local norms. However, this would not be the same as responding to different 'communities'.

Because proximity justice has been a 'top-down' initiative, it has the potential to be implemented far faster than initiatives which depend upon 'bottom-up' community initiatives from a geographically localised base. It can also, should the state decide so, be more radical, since the state can act by itself, whereas 'community' initiatives require sufficient local coherence and also at least a little collaboration between local criminal justice personnel (used to the previous, national way of doing things), and local actors, residents, community groups etc. The rapid introduction of mediation into the new *maisons de justice* in France, as a result of the funding for mediation, is an example of this rapidity of action – but it is interesting that their continuance was fragile, with criminal justice starting to draw back from the power given to these new, non-criminal justice personnel once the initial impetus for change (too many minor cases swamping criminal justice) had diminished (Wyvekens 2008; Milburn 2008). It is worth charting this process in a little detail.

The parallel mode of 'doing justice' afforded by mediation emerged because the number of minor cases being diverted from prosecution or dropped threatened to cause local disquiet and started to bring traditional criminal justice into disrepute (as has happened several times in Europe, most notably in the Netherlands in the mid 1980s, when prosecutors were not taking to court a substantial proportion of criminal cases: Ministerie van Justitie 1985). Mediators, already working with young people in a social and educational context and in relation to family conflict, were an obvious answer to the overloading of criminal justice (Milburn 2008). The structures set up involved contracts with local authorities. However, mediators were only allowed to take on minor cases, such that mediation was not a threat to traditional criminal justice – and these cases tended to reflect the clustering of problems across the criminal/civil legal divide, as Genn (1999; Genn and Paterson 2001) has also found in England and Wales and in Scotland. In order to resolve these problems in individual cases, mediation needed to access other services (debt, employment, substance abuse, health) – and those coming to mediation services needed to know more about how to acquire access to these services. The result was that in these disadvantaged areas mediation could neither grow its own values and become a system clearly separate from criminal justice (even though it was dealing with cases diverted from criminal justice) nor could it easily respond to the diverse needs of civil society there. Nor were mediators' workloads compatible with the more leisurely time scale suited to neighbourhood conflict (Dignan 2000).

After a while, criminal justice practitioners started to take back this territory, as prosecutors tried to get back to their traditional town-centre offices from the dilapidated suburbs and so the supply of cases from prosecutors diminished. As disquiet diminished, the state decided that what was needed, in order to respond to the diverse range of needs being brought to the centres, was a means to educate the public (civil society) about the state and state services, rather than a means to deliver criminal justice services in a localised manner (Wyvekens 2008). Mediation then had to follow prosecutors back to the centre, where deputy prosecutors were recruited to deal with these minor cases, through encouraging young offenders to provide reparation to victims. Deputy prosecutors could have been people from a social or educational or other social services background – but, because it was seen as important that they had some legal knowledge, the most likely people to be recruited were retired criminal justice personnel, such as police officers or judges (Milburn 2008). The radical experiment had been turned back into state criminal justice – though still with a more restorative and more localised flavour.

Meanwhile, there were also moves in France, as throughout Europe, to develop crime prevention. In France, because of the responsibility of city officials (mayors) for crime prevention in the city, crime prevention became part of urban policies. Partnerships, set up under the Bonne-maison system of a national crime prevention council and local city equivalents, initially concentrated upon policing and local authorities. After a while, criminal justice agents, especially prosecutors, having originally been rather aloof, started also to participate (Milburn 2008). However, local consultation, in France as in Germany, tended to involve local agencies, rather than members of the public. Crime prevention, like *maisons de justice*, seemed loathe to reach out to lay members of the public and discuss priorities with them; instead, they turned to informing local people about state services and interacting with other agencies or the new professionals (mediators, voluntary sector co-ordinators) (Groenemeyer 2008).

So *maisons de justice*, incorporating novel responses to crime (such as mediation) slowly became advice centres; mediators were incorporated into criminal justice professionals; criminal justice professionals relaxed back into interacting with other professionals – none of these difficult citizens or citizen groups. The reaching out by the state did involve a greater range of actors than purely criminal justice ones – and a greater interdisciplinarity in social action in relation to crime – so being in the tradition of deliberative democracy in France. But it ended up being very different from empowering groups or individual citizens to take or formulate their own action.

A similar process has taken place in Germany, where there has been an even greater ethos of professionalisation in criminal justice. There have been innovations in criminal justice in Germany similar to other countries: increased use of mediation; alternative criminal sanctions, particularly for the young; victim support and assistance. But these have been introduced and implemented without reference in Germany to ideas of 'community', but rather in the name of effectiveness, efficiency and modernised services to lay people involved with justice. Germany, like France, turned to existing social organisations to help out the embattled state, rather than create a dialogue with localised geographical neighbourhoods (Groenemeyer 2008). The effect has been a broader use of non-governmental organisations and self-help groups for services parallel to traditional criminal justice, such as victim support, mediation and crime prevention. Even though Germany still strongly sees criminal justice as a professional activity, with no need for lay involvement, it has started to use voluntary sector groups to deliver such services. Mediation, for example, is offered by organisations, such as the Weisser Ring. As in other countries, the use of voluntary sector organisations (which can be held accountable and contracted by the state to provide services) is cheaper and does not threaten state criminal justice power.

In the Netherlands, also with a strong tradition of professionalised criminal justice, the tension and push towards greater interaction with civil society has been in relation to perceived legitimacy, not just better delivery of services. In one sense, this may be an intermediate position between the favouring of 'community' in common law countries and the repulsion of 'community' where it is seen as a threat to equal delivery of services to individuals by the state in civil law countries with a strong state model. Recognition of the threat to legitimacy of state actions in justice, where these are felt to impinge unequally on groups within society, potentially brings in an intermediate source of justice authority such as community. However, in the Netherlands, as Malsch (2008) shows, the tradition of state-based professionalised services has largely remained unchallenged. What has been realised is that if citizens acquire a new role, unwillingly, such as that of 'victim' or 'witness', and that role is insensitively treated by state justice actors, then citizens who are temporarily inhabiting that role (and their associated voluntary groups, such as victim support) will question state actions and potentially the legitimacy of the state as sole provider of justice services. As in France, the political pressure on state criminal justice is to be or to seem less isolationist: pressure for proximity justice, rather than community justice.

So, in terms of improving services to disadvantaged areas, pilot programmes called 'Justice in the Neighbourhood' in the Netherlands have, as in France, seen localisation of prosecutors (see also Boutellier 1997) – but, as in Germany, not necessarily greater participation by individual citizens from those areas. Restorative justice pilots were introduced, both for less serious offences (mediation between adults) and conferencing for slightly more serious offences by young people. But both were diversionary, rather than their products returning to the criminal justice system to be considered by prosecutors or judges as part of a criminal justice outcome (sentence or prosecutorial conditional disposal) (Malsch 2008). Possibly incorporation of restorative justice into criminal justice was seen as too much of a threat to professionalised criminal justice, its products too much of a Trojan horse. Certainly, more recently, restorative justice at the police level has been welcomed in Belgium, with its tradition of separate linguistic community action on social issues, but much more cautiously considered by Dutch police. The Dutch police see restorative policing as potentially a lower-quality product, compared to the provision of a uniform service delivered solely by trained professionals. The Dutch police do not, in contrast to Belgium, want to mediate cases themselves or become strongly involved in mediation, though they do see the possibility of referral of minor cases to trained civilian mediators (van Stokkom and Gunther Moor 2009). Though it may be somewhat of a caricature, it is almost as though Dutch criminal justice realises its flaws and its lack of services, but responds by creating another professionalised service in the social realm, to which difficult cases or groups can be referred.[4] The criminal justice services themselves then do not have to change.

We have seen, therefore, that national criminal justice cultures have been important influences in shaping the image of the groups in civil society which state criminal justice have sought to contact, when they have become concerned that they have become too remote. It is the self-identity of criminal justice, rather than national identity, regional identity, social identity or political identity, which seems to be driving this targeting of potential partners within civil society. Where criminal justice's ethos is unremittingly national, rather than local, it has eschewed trying to deal with interest groups or even geographical localities, in fear that it will be creating different local justice practices. Where criminal justice regards itself as a professional legal forum, then it has found it difficult to interact with lay people and has ended up creating new professional groupings, with the new professions' job being to interact directly with lay people and organisations in civil society.

The difficulty with creating new professionalised services, however – particularly if they are run by non-governmental organisations – is that when funding for justice becomes tight, such schemes can be the first ones cut. It is notable that many pilot projects of restorative justice in the last few years have not been mainstreamed (for example, those in England and Wales and in the Netherlands). Funding has been driven by political priority and when legitimacy of justice wanes as a citizen

[4] As well as mediation services, a similar path has been pursued in the Netherlands for some 20 years in relation to unpaid work done by young offenders who admit vandalism or shop theft offences by the Halt group of schemes. Halt is still run by a set of voluntary organisations, but has gradually become more uniform and now has statutory basis, with referrals from the police as well as the prosecutor (Malsch 2008; van Stokkom and Gunther Moor 2009).

complaint, so does funding. Might it be then that the only initiatives which may continue to be substantially funded are those which prove to be cheaper and easier for state justice?

The managerialist ethos

Reaching out to citizens, whether to geographical units or to victims and witnesses, as we have seen in the case of the Netherlands, brings another tension in its wake. For all European countries, criminal justice is now highly professionalised. Hence, the idea of linking 'community' or even 'civil society' (meaning a group of lay people or even a different set of professionals) with 'justice' can be perceived as very regressive. Justice is thought to demand competent administration, driven by legal values and rules, which is considered as only being able to be undertaken by professionals who are specialists in this area. There is, however, a distinction drawn between professional subject expertise (the 'professionals') and managerial professional expertise (the professional managers with some background in the area). Crawford (2008) has termed this prioritisation of administration, in the context of the United Kingdom, the 'managerialist' ethic. It stresses efficient administration by salaried officials, who are capable of hitting a basket of targets within tight time limits. The targets are of course set within state bodies in a hierarchical process driven by more senior managers and ministers.

On this ethos, justice with a significant community element (which usually requires more time, more persuasion and may be more inefficient, even though more effective in producing lasting outcomes) is then by definition a poorer, less competent, second-choice system – one which may be promoted by political administrations eager to save money, but which should be resisted. Restorative justice, with its bottom-up, inclusive, voluntary nature – where the whole circle of people present at a restorative justice event should discuss until they are able to agree on a conference agreement and so forth – finds it difficult to compress itself into the managerialistic ethos of criminal justice.

Taking an example from our evaluation of three major restorative justice schemes in England and Wales, we have published over the last few years a series of reports on how the schemes developed, the kinds of restorative justice they provided, the views of victims and offenders and reoffending and value for money (Shapland *et al.* 2006; 2007; 2008). The schemes all dealt with cases within criminal justice;

restorative justice was done in addition to criminal justice. The schemes and the evaluation were set up to have two main aims: first, to help victims and to be attentive to victim needs and views and, secondly, to reduce reoffending. As the evaluation has proceeded, since its start in 2001, the emphases and values being expressed by the state about criminal justice have changed slightly. There has been an increasing focus upon preventing reoffending, almost to the exclusion of anything else. Evaluations of all government-funded programmes (not just restorative justice) have been about preventing reoffending – preferably using random controlled trials as the experimental method. Ideas of meeting victim needs, of increasing confidence in criminal justice, of increasing the perceived legitimacy of criminal justice, were still present but have become secondary. The result, in terms of our own evaluation, has been that governmental attention has concentrated upon our last report – on reoffending.

The results from our evaluation do show moderately positive results on reoffending.[5] We have argued that reducing reoffending is a proper aim for restorative justice (Robinson and Shapland 2008), but we have also argued that this focus on reoffending is not normally the prime focus of restorative justice. Restorative justice would see procedural justice and meeting the needs of all participants, especially victims, as key. In fact, there were very positive views expressed by both victims and offenders about restorative justice – they were positive about criminal justice, but they were even more positive about restorative justice (Shapland et al. 2006). But even in this large evaluation, with some 840 restorative justice events (mediation and conferencing) included, facilitators had to squeeze restorative justice into the timescales and reporting frameworks of mainstream criminal justice (Shapland et al. 2006). In order to exist alongside criminal justice, not a very flexible friend, restorative justice was having to meet and, on occasions, outperform on the managerialist ethos set by criminal justice managers for itself. The overall ethos of criminal justice was being superimposed on restorative justice, even though the evaluation was taking place because it

[5] There was a significant decrease in the frequency of reoffending and, for one major scheme, Justice Research Consortium, a significant decrease in the cost of reoffending – so much so that that scheme was value for money: the reduced reoffending paid for the cost of the scheme. However, there was little difference in whether or not people reoffend, though there was no evidence of any significant criminogenic effect of restorative justice, in any of the wide range of groups from different parts of the country at different stages of criminal justice (Shapland et al. 2007).

was recognised that criminal justice by itself was not meeting the needs of citizens, such as victims and witnesses, playing important roles within it.

My critical comments here are not exactly the same as those of restorative justice theorists, such as McCold (2000),[6] who have argued that restorative justice should not come anywhere near criminal justice, because the core values and ideals of restorative justice will necessarily become subordinate to those of criminal justice. The core criminal justice values that have been cited as potentially inimical are, for example, proportionality in sentencing (equal circumstances should produce equal sentences), the dominance of lawyers and an accusatorial stance between victim and offender (mirroring that between prosecution and defence in an accusatorial system). The fears are that the ideal values of criminal justice will trump the ideal values of restorative justice. However, this is not my chief concern. My concern is that the 'ideal' core values of criminal justice (due process, deliberation, giving prosecution and defence their proper say, respect for human rights) are rarely found in the routinised, time-managed current world of the lower courts dealing with the bulk of adult defendants (Sudnow 1964; Carlen 1976). Indeed, defendants are rarely allowed to speak and what is represented as their views tends to be highly managed (McConville *et al.* 1994; Shapland 1981). I would argue that the ideal values of criminal justice are more likely to be found in the procedural justice-rich environment of restorative justice than in the normal procedures of the lower criminal courts (Tyler *et al.* 2007). Hence, my critique is closer to that of Christie (2008), who fears an over-professionalisation of restorative justice. I fear the over-dominance of the managerialist ethic for both criminal justice and restorative justice.

Where a link between 'community' and 'justice' has positive overtones

Though some national criminal justice ideologies, such as that of France, as we have seen, are hostile to localisation, others regard the potential decentralisation of justice to 'communities' positively. The UK, Ireland, the USA and Canada, for example, for different reasons and stemming from their different histories, all see 'community' as a positive attribute when placed alongside 'justice'. It has been important, I think, that these

---

[6] See the discussion on the relation between restorative justice and punishment in Walgrave (2008) for a nuanced account of the considerable disputes in this area.

are all countries where, traditionally, policing has been delivered by police forces which are either local or which emphasise their local roots and values. Policing, worldwide, has tried in the last few decades to move from being entirely activities done by the police to the populace, to activities in which the police seek to form partnerships with the populace to prevent crime and take some burdens – of work and responsibility – from the police.[7] In countries where 'community' is seen as a positive attribute in relation to policing, as Crawford (1997) has shown, citizens have been co-opted into the multi-agency sphere, as potential partners against crime.

In these countries, restorative justice schemes have often been developed locally. Sometimes this has been in co-operation with local criminal justice actors, particularly the police. This was true of the three schemes we evaluated, each of which needed to create formal procedures for referrals and joint working with local criminal justice agencies (Shapland *et al.* 2006).

In Ireland, restorative justice has been developed by the police force, *An Garda Siochana*, as part of its fiercely held mandate to work with local communities and peoples (Mulcahy 2008), which has particularly involved undertaking informal diversion with local young offenders. The result has been, though, that restorative justice has so far been local, but purely diversionary – not trying to deal with adult offending or more-serious offences by young people. It is proving more difficult for restorative justice to break into the highly professionalised territory of the Irish courts.

In Northern Ireland, in contrast, the perceptions of lack of legitimacy of criminal justice to several communities because of the Troubles (both for nationalists and working-class loyalists), have created a different political scenario. Here restorative justice has been adopted as the main statutory measure for young offenders who are being dealt with by the main criminal justice agencies. Court referrals are mandatory on sentencers if the young offender agrees; whilst diversionary prosecutorial referrals are voluntary for both prosecutors and offenders. The results of restorative justice have been evaluated on restorative justice's own terms (Campbell *et al.* 2006), but also on criminal justice terms – with reoffending being a major indicator. Reoffending results, though a little

---

[7] This is of course not applicable to the control of public order, where the police still wish to maintain the upper hand. It has been most demonstrated in the sphere of crime prevention, where citizens are enjoined to work with the police, but has also occurred in relation to minor offences by young people, antisocial behaviour etc.

difficult to interpret (statutory schemes do not allow randomised trials), also seem positive (Lyness 2008; Tate and O'Loan 2009).

However, the political scenario in Northern Ireland has also, after a rather stressful set of negotiations, now seen the state reach out to community restorative justice schemes for them to deal with criminal offences, with proposals for accreditation of these schemes and inspection by state criminal justice inspectors (NIO 2007).[8] This is going much further than just reaching out to local communities. It is agreeing to allow local community agencies, providing they are regulated by the state, to deal with crime themselves. Whether state or community ideals will figure most prominently in these protocols is still very disputed territory.

We can see that the key meaning of 'community' in countries where there is a positive association between the words 'justice' and 'community' has been primarily a geographic localisation, not a different criminal justice service to different social groups, irrespective of place. As in England and Wales, community has meant neighbourhood, whether or not the residents of that neighbourhood do things together or feel any bond with each other. In Northern Ireland, the community restorative justice schemes do each function within one social/political group, which has shared affinity and a shared sense of community – so there is one set of schemes for nationalist communities and one for loyalist communities. However, their prime defining factor is their locality. Each works within a relatively small geographical area for offences committed within and against residents of that small area. They are not resources for the whole of civil society, nor do they generally deal with offenders or victims who come from outside the (small) area.

Similarly, in Canada, special initiatives have tended to be locality-based. The most radical initiatives, where the state has allowed considerable discretionary power in individual cases to pass to local lay people, has been for First Nations peoples (Bartkowiak and Jaccoub 2008). This is because of the political pressure brought by First Nations peoples against the impoverishment of their culture through the imposition of colonialist criminal justice ideas – what is called 'Eurojustice' by First Nations peoples. Though there are now somewhat different criminal justice procedures and local lay judges – and, above all, a greater dominance of traditional justice ideas which feature restorative justice

---

[8] See McEvoy and Eriksson (2008) for a history of the problematic relations between the state and local community restorative justice schemes.

principles – it is notable that these exceptions from state criminal justice are for localities inhabited primarily by First Nations peoples. The same provisions are not available for First Nations peoples living in areas where they are not the majority or in the major cities.

Where 'community' justice is regarded as a potential positive force, it seems therefore to be defined in purely geographical terms, rather than in terms of shared interests, affinity or ethnicity. Nor are such justice initiatives often created without considerable political work by the local groups, nor maintained without obvious continuing local pressure. Both in Northern Ireland and in Canada, community groups have had to argue for and support (and sometimes help to resource) the development of any parallel justice initiatives for those localities (McEvoy and Eriksson 2008; Bartkowiak and Jaccoub 2008). The fragility of the resulting structures and organisations mirrors the relatively short life-span of the *maisons de justice* in France and the pilots in the Netherlands. Such initiatives will only continue whilst the state feels it needs to reach out to that place, or if the group has long-standing commitment to such developments. In other words, though the defining feature of 'community' in terms of new justice developments is locality, it is only if the group also possesses a strong sense of local affinity and culture that such innovations are likely to persist. Otherwise, they are likely to be reabsorbed by state criminal justice agencies and courts.

Does it need a very divided society for this to occur? Not necessarily, but McEvoy and Eriksson (2008: 158) have argued, very perspicaciously I feel, that it is precisely when bridge-building is required between the state and historically estranged groups that 'organic and bottom-up styles of partnership, a willingness from the state in particular to cede some ownership and control, and a commitment on all sides to the development of real relationships based upon trust and mutual respect' can occur. But even if the state gives up some control in order to gain a greater local perception of legitimacy – and acknowledges the local group, there is then a difficulty for the local group as to whether they are seen as still community leaders, or merely as state lackeys. An example can be found in Canada, in the status of the leaders used for state criminal justice procedures (Bartkowiak and Jaccoub 2008). The state seeks to appoint 'community leaders' or 'community representatives'. But these are always state-appointed individuals. The state does not give up its powers to choose judges or criminal justice personnel to local groups. As a result, tensions can emerge about the status and acceptability of these leaders within the local area.

Where 'community' is perceived as causing more concern or being in greater opposition to justice values, initiatives have tended to remain at the peripheries of justice decision making or involve less serious cases (as in France, Germany and the Netherlands). They have not affected the traditional criminal justice path of 'investigation – decision to prosecute – court – sentence', which has remained as the majority response to criminality following the detection of an offender. Where liaison with different groups or communities within that country has become seen as imperative, initiatives have approached closer to key decisions in the traditional path (decentralisation of criminal justice personnel, lay judges) or new, parallel paths have been established (mediation, restorative justice, new forums for determining sentence). Because of the difficulties in interacting with local citizens, it is perhaps no wonder that countries with a stronger nation-state model for criminal justice have created new groups of professionals as easier partners in this difficult, reaching-out enterprise for legitimacy.

Restorative justice's place in initiatives where the state is reaching out

The values of partnership, ceding ownership from state to lay people, and commitment to the development of real relationships, which are characteristic of initiatives to reach out by the state, are also precisely the values of restorative justice. It is unsurprising, I think, that one of the means to which states have turned recently when there has been concern about the relationship between the state and its publics is restorative justice.

So far, localised restorative justice initiatives and restorative justice allied to proximity justice have occurred primarily in relation to youth justice or less-serious offences. However, localisation and difference may become a more prominent characteristic of criminal justice in the future – *if* the state is determined to pull back from its previous 'all-doing, all-determining, taking all responsibility ways' in criminal justice. In an increasingly globalised, multicultural society, trying to prescribe uniform national criminal justice may not be a stable solution. One way of recognising difference and increasing perceived legitimacy is responsibilising others.

However, this is a difficult and often resisted process for states, with the major resistance coming from state criminal justice actors. It is far easier for states (and criminal justice personnel) if justice is delivered by 'us', a small group of state-employed, state-trained, rather similar people.

If it is delivered locally by different kinds of people, 'them', a whole new set of mechanisms of safeguards, training, protocols and partnership agreements tends to have to be set in place. That means work, hard work, for state actors, and such regulatory mechanisms will always fail occasionally – often quite publicly.

I suspect that it is only if states feel at risk or less in control that they will attempt this perilous path of entrusting justice to others. Nonetheless, the overall pressures on states seem to me to be still primarily in the direction of making them feel unsure and needing legitimacy. The factors increasing uncertainty for states include the increasing diversity of their publics with different expectations; their limited resources to meet public expectations of security; the threats posed by cross-national offending (including the Internet-based frauds which affect increasing proportions of their populations); and the need to rely on international instruments for crime control,[9] which take power and prestige away from national criminal justice.

This is likely, however, to be a continuing struggle. We can portray state–civil society relations as a competition for power, legitimacy and popular confidence between the international, national and local levels of criminal justice. In this competition, nation states still have many levers of power, including dominance over policing and normally having the most frequent means of interaction with the media. Justice institutions are also more isolated from globalising pressures than many other areas of social and economic policy and so more able to shrug off pressure for change. The current balance between state criminal justice and the pressure to reach out to civil society, or 'communities', is necessarily a precarious one. We may see more reaching out, as I suspect will occur, or we may see retrenchment into traditional professionalism, as has occurred in parts of mainland Europe.

What may turn out to be key is national criminal justice's own perception of its identity – the extent to which judicial and legal cultures can change. If criminal justice agencies continue to be 'modernised' and made similar in their organisational values to other social policy agencies (such as health or social care, which are likely to continue to be seen as not meeting high public expectations), then criminal justice agencies may continue to perceive themselves as relatively fragile in terms of

[9] International instruments of crime control are increasingly operating in terms of 'ordinary' crime (such as the European Arrest Warrant and cross-national policing of drugs), as well as against war crimes and terrorism (such as homeland security air travel measures and the International Criminal Court).

public confidence. If they are allowed to retreat into judicial isolation, then political pressures to be more relevant are likely to undermine confidence. It is perhaps only if criminal justice can learn to live with, imbue with sufficient justice values, but not monopolise parallel, more local, justice measures which keep justice in touch with its publics that it may find a way to retain legitimacy. We shall continue to live in interesting times.

References

Bartkowiak, I. and Jaccoub, M. (2008) 'New directions in Canadian justice: from state workers to community "representatives"' in J. Shapland (ed.), *Justice, Community and Civil Society: A Contested Terrain*, Cullompton: Willan, pp. 209–34.

Boutellier, H. (1997) 'Right to the community', *European Journal on Criminal Policy and Research*, 5(4): 43–52.

Campbell, C., Devlin, R., O'Mahony, D., Doak, J., Jackson, J., Corrigan, T. and McEvoy, K. (2006) *Evaluation of the Northern Ireland Youth Conferencing Service*, NIO Research and Statistical Series Report No. 12. Belfast: NIO, www.nio.gov. uk/evaluation_of_the_northern_ireland_youth_conference_service.pdf.

Carlen, P. (1976) *Magistrates' Justice*, London: Martin Robertson.

Casey, L. (2008) *Engaging Communities in Fighting Crime*, London: Home Office.

Christie, N. (2008) 'Restorative justice: five dangers ahead' in P. Knepper, J. Doak and J. Shapland (eds.), *Urban Crime Prevention, Surveillance, and Restorative Justice: Effects of Social Technologies*, Boca Raton: CRC Press, pp. 195–204.

Crawford, A. (1997) *The Local Governance of Crime*, Oxford: Clarendon Press.

(2000a) 'Contrasts in victim/offender mediation and appeals to community in France and England' in D. Nelken (ed.), *Contrasting Criminal Justice: Getting from Here to There*, Aldershot: Ashgate, pp. 207–31.

(2000b) 'Justice de proximité: the growth of "Houses of Justice" and victim/ offender mediation in France: a very unFrench legal response?', *Social and Legal Studies*, 9(1), 29–53.

(2008) 'Refiguring the community and professional in policing and criminal justice: some questions of legitimacy' in J. Shapland (ed.), *Justice, Community and Civil Society: A Contested Terrain*, Cullompton: Willan, pp. 125–56.

Criminal Justice Review Team (2000) *Review of Criminal Justice in Northern Ireland: Report*, Belfast: HMSO.

Dignan, J. (2000) *Youth Justice Pilots Evaluation: Interim Report on Reparative Work and Youth Offending Teams*, London: Home Office.

Genn, H. (1999) *Paths to Justice*, Oxford: Hart Publishing.

Genn, H. and Paterson, A. (2001) *Paths to Justice in Scotland*, Oxford: Hart Publishing.

Groenemeyer, A. (2008) 'Crime control in Germany: too serious to leave it to the people – the great exception?' in J. Shapland (ed.), *Justice, Community and Civil Society: A Contested Terrain*, Cullompton: Willan, pp. 63–86.

Hervey, T. (2008) 'The European Union's governance of health care and the welfare modernization agenda', *Regulation and Governance*, 2, 103–20.

Home Office (2008) 'Government responds to Casey report', news story from the Home Office, 18 June 2008, www.homeoffice.gov.uk/about-us/news-casey-report-response.

Hough, M. and Roberts, J. (1998) *Attitudes to Punishment: Findings from the British Crime Survey*, Home Office Research Study No. 179, London: Home Office.

Judicature (1997) Special issue on *Courts and the Community*, March–April 1997, 80: 5, American Judicature Society.

Lyness, D. (2008) *Northern Ireland Youth Re-offending: Results from the 2005 Cohort*, Northern Ireland Office Research and Statistical Bulletin 7/2008, Belfast: Northern Ireland Office, www.nio.gov.uk/.

McCold, P. (2000) 'Toward a holistic vision of restorative juvenile justice: a reply to the maximalist model', *Contemporary Justice Review*, 3, 357–414.

McConville, M., Hodgson, J., Bridges, L. and Pavlovic, A. (1994) *Standing Accused: The Organisation and Practices of Criminal Defence Lawyers in Britain*, Oxford: Clarendon Press.

McEvoy, K. and Eriksson, A. (2008) 'Who owns justice? Community, state and the Northern Ireland transition' in J. Shapland (ed.), *Justice, Community and Civil Society: A Contested Terrain*, Cullompton: Willan, pp. 157–89.

Malsch, M. (2008) 'Lay elements in the criminal justice system of the Netherlands' in J. Shapland (ed.), *Justice, Community and Civil Society: A Contested Terrain*, Cullompton: Willan, pp. 107–24.

Mattinson, J. and Mirrlees-Black, C. (2000) *Attitudes to Crime and Criminal Justice: Findings from the 1998 British Crime Survey*, Home Office Research Study No. 200, London: Home Office.

Milburn, P. (2008) 'How civil society is on the criminal justice agenda in France' in J. Shapland (ed.), *Justice, Community and Civil Society: A Contested Terrain*, Cullompton: Willan, pp. 47–62.

Ministerie van Justitie (1985) *Society and Crime: A Policy Plan for the Netherlands*, The Hague: Ministry of Justice.

Ministry of Justice (2010) *Breaking the Cycle: Effective Punishment, Rehabilitation and Sentencing of Offenders*, London: Ministry of Justice.

Mulcahy, A. (2008) 'Policing, "community" and social change in Ireland' in J. Shapland (ed.), *Justice, Community and Civil Society: A Contested Terrain*, Cullompton: Willan, pp. 47–62.

Northern Ireland Office (NIO) (2007) *Protocol for Community-based Restorative Justice Schemes*, Belfast: NIO, 5 February 2007, www.nio.gov.uk/protocol_for_community_based_restorative_justice_scheme__5_february_2007.pdf.

Office for Criminal Justice Reform (OCJR) (2009) *Engaging Communities in Criminal Justice*, Green Paper, April 2009, Cm. 7583, www.official-documents.gov.uk/document/cm75/7583/7583.asp.

Rickman, N., Fenn, P. and Gray, A. (1999) 'The reform of legal aid in England and Wales', *Fiscal Studies*, 20(3), 261–86.

Robinson, G. and Shapland, J. (2008) 'Reducing recidivism: a task for restorative justice?', *British Journal of Criminology*, 48(3), 337–58.

Shapland, J. (1981) *Between Conviction and Sentence: The Process of Mitigation*, London: Routledge and Kegan Paul.

— (2008) 'Contested ideas of community and justice' in J. Shapland (ed.), *Justice, Community and Civil Society: A Contested Terrain*, Cullompton: Willan, pp. 1–29.

Shapland, J., Atkinson, A., Atkinson, H., Chapman, B., Colledge, E., Dignan, J., Howes, M., Johnstone, J., Robinson, G. and Sorsby, A. (2006) *Restorative Justice in Practice: The Second Report from the Evaluation of Three Schemes*, The University of Sheffield Centre for Criminological Research Occasional Paper 2, Sheffield: Faculty of Law.

Shapland, J., Atkinson, A., Atkinson, H., Chapman, B., Dignan, J., Howes, M., Johnstone, J., Robinson, G. and Sorsby, A. (2007) *Restorative Justice: The Views of Victims and Offenders,* Ministry of Justice Research Series 3/07, London: Ministry of Justice, www.justice.gov.uk/docs/Restorative-Justice.pdf.

Shapland, J., Atkinson, A., Atkinson, H., Dignan, J., Edwards, L., Hibbert, J., Howes, M., Johnstone, J., Robinson, G. and Sorsby, A. (2008) *Does Restorative Justice Affect Reconviction? The Fourth Report from the Evaluation of Three Schemes*, Ministry of Justice Research Series 10/08, London: Ministry of Justice, www.justice.gov.uk/docs/Restorative-Justice.pdf.

Stokkom, B. van and Gunther Moor, B. (2009) 'Pass the buck: restorative policing in the Netherlands' in L. Gunther Moor, T. Peters, P. Ponsaers, J. Shapland and B. van Stokkom (eds.), *Restorative Policing*, Journal of Police Studies, vol. 2009–2/Cahier Politiestudies Cahier no. 11, Antwerp: Maklu, pp. 101–18.

Sudnow, D. (1964) 'Normal crimes: sociological features of the penal code in a public defender office', *Social Problems*, 12, 255–76.

Swaaningen, R. van (2008) 'Sweeping the streets: civil society and community safety in Rotterdam' in J. Shapland (ed.), *Justice, Community and Civil Society: A Contested Terrain*, Cullompton: Willan, pp. 87–106.

Tate, S. and O'Loan, C. (2009) *Northern Ireland Youth Re-offending: Results from the 2006 Cohort,* Research and Statistical Bulletin 4/2009, Belfast: Northern Ireland Office.

Tyler, T. R., Sherman, L., Strang, H., Barnes, G. C. and Woods, D. (2007) 'Reintegrative shaming, procedural justice and recidivism: the engagement of offenders: psychological mechanisms in the Canberra RISE drinking-and-driving experiment', *Law and Society Review*, 41, 511–52.

Walgrave, L. (2008) *Restorative Justice, Self-interest and Responsible Citizenship*, Cullompton: Willan.

Wyvekens, A. (2008) '"Proximity justice" in France: anything but "justice and community"?' in J. Shapland (ed.), *Justice, Community and Civil Society: A Contested Terrain*, Cullompton: Willan, pp. 30–46.

18

Governing nodal governance: the 'anchoring' of local security networks

HANS BOUTELLIER AND RONALD VAN STEDEN

Shedding the structures of hierarchy may seen refreshing (in a normative, positive or symbolic sense), but constitutional authority (manifested in hierarchy) and the 'fiscal spine' of appropriated funds remain the structures within which relational and networked forms are enabled to flourish.

Hill and Lynn 2005: 189

Introduction

The organisation of policing and, in a wider sense, security is undergoing considerable restructuration in Western societies (Crawford 1999; Hughes and Edwards 2002; Crawford *et al.* 2005; Jones and Newburn 2006; Wood and Dupont 2006; Fleming and Wood 2006; Henry and Smith 2007). A key development is that the government is losing its previously taken-for-granted dominance over crime and disorder control under pressure of 'polycentric' or 'networked' agents and agencies. Accordingly, at the local level, police forces and municipalities find themselves in a 'multilateralised' environment of both organisational auspices authorising security and policing *and* providers who supply executive personnel (Bayley and Shearing 2001). These auspices and providers do not necessarily overlap. It is, on the contrary, possible that a municipal authority (public) hires commercial security guards (private) to patrol the streets. Auspices and providers may have become separated. In this manner, the classical distinction between 'the public' and 'the private' has proved problematic (Jones and Newburn 1998; Kempa *et al.* 1999; Johnston 2000). Organisations have become part of 'amorphous' or 'hybrid' assemblages that feature different degrees of 'publicness' and 'privateness' (Dijkstra and van der Meer 2003).

461

There is little controversy about such tendencies. In fact, governments, like the Dutch, overtly assert that 'security is not a matter exclusively for the police. The police need partners and are therefore looking for ways of establishing worthwhile collaboration, for example through community policing' (Ministry of the Interior and Kingdom Relations 2004: 8). This has resulted in the growth of multi-agency working in which the police and local government team up with businesses, non-profit organisations and (groups of) voluntary citizens (Terpstra 2008). To give a few illustrations, various cities have sought to strengthen their relations with citizens who, together with police and municipal services, are actively responsible for safety and security. Other cities have created so-called *Ketenunits* (Chain Units) and *Veiligheidshuizen* (Security Houses) – which we discuss below – that consist of police and judicial services as well as welfare institutions and municipal bodies to promote effective communication and successful action. Elsewhere, there is a flourishing of covenants and other similar contracts (such as funding agreements) that should guarantee long-term partnership. Formalised co-operation has loomed large in the Netherlands. This is partly due to a political tradition – the famous Dutch Polder model – in which conflicts and divisions are offset by the existence of accommodation, co-operation, consensus-building and compromise (Andeweg and Irwin 2002; van Dijk and de Waard 2009).

In this chapter, we will argue for an understanding of urban security governance that draws primarily from the Dutch situation, but has broader implications for assessing multilateral organisational landscapes elsewhere. Modern societies, it is argued, are going through a transition. With the rise of multilateral alliances and institutions, we currently move from a vertically ('top-down') organised world to a more horizontally oriented one wherein the state, the market and civil society interpenetrate – a tendency which has fuelled a blurring of norms, values, interests and working methods. This raises the question of how such governance arrangements can be imagined and managed; or put differently, how can we constitute order in a diffuse and chaotic world? In providing an answer, network theories come to the fore (Boutellier 2007). Discussing and evaluating such theories, this chapter first offers a brief description of Shearing's 'nodal-governance' thesis (Johnston and Shearing 2003; Wood and Shearing 2007) as a framework to capture what is happening to the organisation of local security systems. Central to this framework is the assumption that a state-centred orchestration of governance is challenged by the proliferation of 'public', 'private' and 'mixed' auspices and providers of security. The subsequent section of the chapter explores Loader and Walker's idea of 'anchored pluralism' (Loader and Walker 2006; 2007), rigorously criticising the theoretical and normative assumptions underlying 'nodal governance'. Their perspective fundamentally disagrees with the assertion that the state is 'but one among many' governing nodes. Instead of minimising the state's position, it acknowledges that police and municipal services have a leading role to play. Specifically in the field of policing, the state exercises (symbolic) authority in the sense that public police forces are closely associated with law enforcement, the maintenance of (ontological) security and the constitution of national identities (Loader and Mulcahy 2003; Loader and Walker 2007).

Briefly illustrating a case study of local security policies in the city of Eindhoven, the Netherlands, we describe the faults, failures and ambiguities underlying complex organisational networks. Given such problems, our contention is that governance structures need to be more 'anchored' and 'directed' than nodal theories presuppose. This critique of nodal governance is also in line with Braithwaite's picture of a 'responsive regulatory pyramid' as a good strategy when co-operation between public, private and hybrid organisations fails (Braithwaite 2002). The analogy of his pyramid suggests that the effectiveness of coercive measures held as a last resort – 'speaking softly and carrying big sticks' (Braithwaite 1997) – does not have a corrosive effect on the voluntary and self-regulatory activities informed by persuasion lower down the pyramid. In fact it implies that the effectiveness of ordering in the security field is dependent upon the credible capacity of escalation towards punitive and coercive measures. Only when local safety policies are set up systematically, and backed by solid state presence in the background, are nodal arrangements able to function to their full capacity. Building on Loader and Walker's and Braithwaite's ideas, we revisit the concept of 'anchored pluralism' and seek to restructure and advance some of its theoretical elements by introducing the metaphor of 'team play'. In so doing, we seek to uncover the dynamics that underlie the governance of local security networks. The chapter closes with an attempt to provide some directions for future research.

Nodal governance

Over the past decade, Shearing and colleagues have introduced a new outlook on security and justice under conditions of 'multilateral' or 'polycentric' organisational networks. In so doing, they have created a theoretical approach that gives no *a priori* significance to state co-ordination of these networks. The centralising aspirations of state governance have come under critique (Shearing 2005). Two trends are specifically detectable. First, in line with neoliberal (or 'new public management') strategies, the state has increasingly placed emphasis on deregulation and the outsourcing ('contracting out') of public services: government authorities should be preoccupied with steering, not rowing, activities (Osborne and Gaebler 1992). As such, non-state agencies (businesses, citizens or the non-profit sector) have been activated to provide for collective goods with state agencies serving as regulators 'at a distance' (Clarke and Newman 1997). The normative justification for this is not the weakening or 'hollowing out' of the state (Rhodes 1994), but enhancing its capacities to provide effective and efficient public service provision. Contradictory centralising and decentralising aspirations co-exist and strengthen each other. Secondly, for another and equally important part, Shearing focuses on influential governance initiatives stemming from 'strong' (often corporate and transnational) actors. He lays emphasis on the phenomenon of 'private governments' (Macaulay 1986) engaged in promoting security (Shearing 2006). On this view, marked shifts in property relations have led to a rise in privately owned but publicly used spaces such as shopping malls, airport terminals and leisure parks (Shearing and Stenning 1981) which are strictly governed through corporate security interests and services. In accordance, Johnston and Shearing (2003: 146) speak of a 'new morphology' of security governance overthrowing traditional state-centred visions of domestic ordering functions. State-led orchestration of security and policing seems no more than a 'historical hiccup' (Shearing 2005: 62).

These two observations have led to the advocacy of a 'nodal' theory of governance (Johnston and Shearing 2003; Wood and Shearing 2007). That is, we are witnessing a proliferation of nodes (or organisational sides of security) that leaves open for empirical enquiry whether they are public, private or hybrid in nature; or being more precise, 'nodes' represent 'institutions with a set of technologies, mentalities and resources – that mobilize the knowledge and capacity of members to manage the course of events. Nodes are normally but not essentially points on networks, but networks are a prime means through which nodes exert influence' (Burris *et al.* 2005: 33). A node thus may have a territorial basis such as a shopping mall or (gated) residential area, but it could also be some sort of physical or virtual community like a religious congregation or a group of like-minded strangers populating a chat room in cyberspace (Crawford 2003a; Wall 2007). In this regard, a node is most often, but not necessarily, part of broader relationships with others; 'nodes may not come together to form networks at all' (Wood and Shearing 2007: 26). Subsequently, Wood and Shearing (2007) stress that the purposes and 'mentalities' – that is, the mental and cognitive frames that shape how individuals and organisations see the world and act accordingly (Stenning in Johnston and Shearing 2003: 29) – of nodes may differ greatly from each other in terms of legal conduct. Although we normally think of 'regular' nodes that operate within the ambit of the law, it is equally possible that deviant nodes form 'dark networks' (Raab and Milward 2003) such as mafia syndicates involved in criminal activities. Finally, a node is often a formalised institutional expression (an organisation or a subdivision of an organisation), but may also come as an informal (voluntary) grouping. People can be permanently located in one or more nodes, but they can also switch between boundaries as 'nodes may fall and/or cut across one another' (Button 2008: 15). Van Dijk (2006) even argues that it is possible to take individual persons linked by networks as the basic units of nodalised settings.

Within assorted nodes, security is shaped by complex arrangements of agents and agencies (ranging from the public police to private security companies and active citizens) that constantly interact and struggle with each other. This position, Shearing (2007: 252) argues, 'makes no claim about the relative influence of different nodes in shaping the flow of events at any space-time moment'. The nodal model should be regarded as analytically neutral. Yet, despite such self-proclaimed neutrality, a close reading of Shearing's work reveals subtle claims that verge upon state-sceptic ideas and ideals. In particular, Shearing and his colleagues position themselves as 'left-wing' interpreters of Friedrich von Hayek, a political philosopher who compellingly accounted 'the epistemological limits on human organization and planning' and appreciated markets rather than governments 'as a means of bridging order to complex systems by coordinating diffused knowledge and capacity' (Burris *et al.* 2005: 32). From a Hayekian perspective, social actions should be governed by micro-processes of spontaneously evolving equilibria, not by public bureaucracies lacking the capacity and knowledge to deliver 'intelligent' security services to local communities. Nonetheless, Shearing remains hesitant about neoliberal sentiments leaving things to an unregulated 'free market' as this will inevitably grant better-resourced nodes power advantages over weaker ones (Burris *et al.* 2008: 33). His political agenda therefore is to reshape governance in ways that will benefit poor populations (Shearing and Wood 2003). This is necessary, because the poor are at greater objective risk of becoming crime victims. Furthermore, within a free-market context, security deficits may arise owing to inequalities in access to resources. Consequently, policing budgets should be allocated in such ways as to motivate and enable marginalised groups to specify their own desired security systems, and hence provide them with voice, choice and self-direction in nodal arenas.

Anchored pluralism

Shearing's nodal-governance thesis has been applauded and advanced (Button 2008), but has also met strong criticism in the literature (Loader and Walker 2005). We will briefly discuss such criticisms arguing that, although there is considerable merit in thinking critically about the challenges governance structures pose, the role occupied by the state is still distinctive. Some years ago, Crawford (1999) and Jones and Newburn (2002) took the lead in questioning to what degree current transformations in policing and security should be interpreted as a decisive break with the past – something which is assumed by Shearing and others (Bayley and Shearing 1996; Johnston and Shearing 2003). Instead of understanding the dispersal of policing authorities and providers as something unseen and unheard of, Jones and Newburn choose to locate changes in a wider context of historical processes (see also Rawlings 2003; Zedner 2006). As they observe, taking a long-term view on pluralisation and privatisation, 'policing provision has become less rather than more fragmented. In particular, repeated reorganization over the nineteenth and twentieth centuries has seen a massive decline in the total number of constabularies and bodies of constables' (Jones and Newburn 2002: 136). Thus, while some of the changes are, to a certain degree, undeniable and far-reaching, it is a mistake to easily herald 'a watershed' (Bayley and Shearing 1996: 585) in the evolution and organisation of contemporary crime control. This kind of reasoning tends to overlook consistencies and continuities that still exist in the authorisation and provision of policing. There is no inevitability about the future direction of public–private partnerships and network management that will affect security systems around the world.

In a more recent publication, Jones (2007) questions the practical implications of nodal governance theories. If state agencies have really lost their privileged position, concerns arise about where to locate the responsibility for monitoring and regulating security networks. For example, who would, in the absence of a regulatory state, protect the rights of unpopular (poor) communities and who would take the final decision on a just and fair allocation of policing budgets? Which bodies would serve as a 'last resort' in upholding public order and how is it possible to counter organised crime that cut across local communities without any public police intervention? Indeed, Shearing's line of reasoning 'reveals that the state in fact continues to assume a far from insignificant role in their preferred conception of security' (Loader and Walker 2006: 177). Moreover, as Roberts (2005: 16) points out, the representation of negotiated metropolitan orders (like private governments) does not signal a move, as it were, from public to private 'logics' – namely, from 'command and control' to 'inducement'. The centralised legal order of the state rather permits and encourages the proliferation of autonomous localities (and their 'house rules') to the extent to which they are licensed. Redefined state ambitions in the regulation of society do not, therefore, mean a withdrawal of government institutions per se. We have no reason to assume a paradigmatic shift away from 'vertical' to 'horizontal' modes of governance – let alone that public administration is shrinking or ceasing. Quite the reverse, contemporary political and social engineering in favour of 'smarter' governing capacities have not resulted in deregulation, but rather an expansion in regulatory systems, which straddle the classic public–private dichotomy. As such, public authorities, at least in the field of policing and security, are redrawing and extending rather than withdrawing powers (Crawford 2006a: 471). 'The more hierarchal patterns of governance', as Kooiman (2003: 11) puts it, 'are not yet out of date.'

Reflecting on debates surrounding nodal governance, Loader and Walker (2006: 194) have introduced the concept of 'anchored pluralism' to describe the necessity of state presence in the governance of security. Although they initially deploy this concept in a normative sense, the authors also present relevant analytical clues to identify and assess the distinctive anchoring points states have in steering plural organisational networks. To begin with, Loader and others argue that the state is engaged in crafting social identities through its symbolic power and cultural authority (Loader and Mulcahy 2003). It does so in creating an atmosphere of empathic familiarity and attachment which are inexorably connected with our human senses of safety and security. Public policing represents an 'irreducibly social' good indispensable for the generation of solidarity among people (Loader and Walker 2001). A second point relates to the state's capability to assure an accurate (re)allocation of collective resources by enabling agents and agencies, whether state-based or not, to alleviate feelings of ontological security and anxiety. This can take the form of policing, but we can also think of housing, health services and education. In addition, the state may be concerned with mobilising resources that are able 'to engage in "joined-up" thinking about and "joined-up" funding of the right mix of policies' (Loader and Walker 2007: 185). It encourages channels for deliberation so that policies are being shaped on the basis of democratic participation and consideration of good arguments. This enhances public perceptions of state legitimacy and concerns the very standing of security as a 'thick' social good between organisations and (groups) of citizens with numerous and ostensibly conflicting interests and preferences.

As such, the state stimulates credible commitments among individuals and organisations with whom it develops relationships. Clearly, this is best done in a latent mode wherein the state invests in anticipation and persuasion. Nevertheless, public authorities, including the police, are at all times capable of resorting to overriding (physical) strength as an *ultimum remedium*. 'The ordering and resourcing infrastructure', Loader and Walker (2007: 192) underline, 'needs some kind of coercive underpinning in the final instance for reasons which bear upon effectiveness and reliability of delivery in general without influencing the detailed enforceability of any particular operation.' This assumes state priority in the regulation of nodal security networks. Policing and security cannot be left to the unfettered 'invisible hand' of capitalist economies, because, at a certain stage, these solutions will inevitably derail into eroding the sense of belonging people have to political communities – a downward spiral incurring alienation and, in turn, fuelling the use of ever-more defensive technologies that fracture society into competitive markets and tribes (Loader 2006: 217). In summary, then, the state, in the senses set out before, has a pivotal position in overcoming difficulties of effective partnership working between state, market and civil society agencies. Municipal, police and judicial authorities perform vital cultural and ordering work in 'governing the good of security'. Turning theoretical debates into empirical reality, we would like to illustrate the case of ambiguous and failing local safety politics in Eindhoven, the Netherlands. Drawing on such observations, we suggest that nodal security networks cannot do without state anchoring to function and perform well.

Local safety policies in Eindhoven

The city of Eindhoven is situated in the province of Brabant and is the fifth-largest city in the Netherlands with some 210,000 inhabitants. One of the current authors (Boutellier) was a member of an independent auditing commission evaluating the city's security politics.[1] The establishment of this commission had a tangible reason. For two succeeding years, Eindhoven was rated the most unsafe city in the Netherlands on the 'crime index' published by *Algemeen Dagblad*, a popular Dutch newspaper (with 354,000 subscriptions). In response, its new burgomaster asked the commission to analyse crime figures, judge the policy-making processes and offer advice on how to improve the situation. The commission started in July 2008 and presented its final report *Veel te winnen!* (Much to gain!) in November 2008 (Fijnaut *et al.* 2008). During this time, thirty respondents were interviewed, ranging from the burgomaster to civil servants, from the police chief to street cops and from social professionals to ordinary citizens. In addition, the commission organised ten expert sessions on location. Its members visited the prostitution zone, the football stadium of PSV, the night-life district and other problem areas. Furthermore, the commission studied ninety-five documents of all kinds and initiated a separate research unit to conduct quantitative analyses. The commission's final report covered chapters on actual crime problems and the institutional architecture of crime-related policies. In this regard, they paid special attention to the *Veiligheidshuis* (Security House), a relatively new phenomenon in the Netherlands.

Over the past decade, Security Houses have emerged in several cities throughout the Netherlands. In one building, they represent a physical arrangement of the main parties involved in security issues and crime problems, bringing together the police, municipal bodies and the prosecution service. By early 2009, there were twenty-six Security Houses across the Netherlands, with the government aspiring to create a network of forty houses in forthcoming years. The institutionalisation of Security Houses results from experiments with 'neighbourhood justice' during the 1990s (Boutellier 2001). In certain urban areas, *Justitie in de Buurt* (Neighbourhood Justice) offices were established that aimed for a problem-oriented approach in response to criminal justice matters. These experiments evolved to more integrated organisational networks, which apart from

---

[1] The other members were Joop van Riessen (former chief constable in Amsterdam) and Professor Cyrille Fijnaut (chair).

the prosecution and probation services involve agencies such as mental healthcare, addiction services, social work, victim aid and local municipal authorities. Security Houses focus especially on juvenile delinquency and frequent offenders, though they also tend to concentrate on thematic issues (such as addiction and violence). Case meetings in which representatives of several organisations participate to decide on suitable intervention strategies for individual offenders or specific situations represent a weighty policy instrument. In Eindhoven, the Security House consists of no less than eighteen organisations in the areas of policing, criminal justice, housing, welfare work, child care and community development. As expressed through these new institutions, security policies have genuinely evolved into horizontally organised (or 'networked') arrangements.

After analysing the crime data in Eindhoven, the auditing commission concluded that it would be wrong to underestimate and trivialise the seriousness of security problems. Even though several respondents tended to nuance media reports on crime, statistical resources unequivocally showed that Eindhoven occupies a top-ranking position in relation to crime rates relative to comparable Dutch cities. To give an example, Statistics Netherlands (CBS)[2] registered 150 crimes (of which 10 per cent were violent crimes) per 100,000 inhabitants over the 2005–7 period – a number that ranks just below Amsterdam and Rotterdam, both of which are triple the size of Eindhoven. In addition, the auditing commission thoroughly considered the architecture of Eindhoven's security system. It found that the typically Dutch 'triangle' – an institutionalised tripartite consultation between the burgomaster, the police superintendent and the chief public prosecutor, set up to govern local policing and security policies (Wintle 1996; Ministry of the Interior and Kingdom Relations 2004) – was virtually absent in Eindhoven. None of the three administrators were able to steer local networks effectively.

A major reason for this flaw in the governance of security was the fragmented infrastructure of administrative offices responsible for crime and disorder reduction. On the municipal level, responsibilities were divided among the burgomaster (head of public order) and an alderman (head of 'integrated' safety policy).[3] This alderman chaired the Security

---

[2] See on Internet: www.cbs.nl.

[3] In the Netherlands, the burgomaster (appointed by Royal decree), together with the aldermen, form the executive branch of municipalities. There is a uniform pattern of local Boards (*Colleges van Burgemeester en Wethouders*), with the burgomaster serving as head of public order (see Morlan 1964). The observation that responsibilities for public order were divided among the burgomaster and an alderman makes Eindhoven an exceptional case.

House committee which also included a senior member of the public prosecution service (but not the chief public prosecutor himself).[4] Traditionally, municipal police services, being subdivisions of larger police regions,[5] are headed by one superintendent in the Netherlands. He or she is in charge of daily police work. Yet, in Eindhoven, not one but two police chiefs were heading the force – none of whom had clear tasks and responsibilities. The whole force was essentially divided into six separate departments, each with their own commander, priority settings and annual report. In effect, although the governance 'triangle' should formally take the lead in crime policy issues, the actual political power was in the hands of the Security House committee. This led to the auditing commission's conclusion that Eindhoven suffered from a 'disabled triangle' as a result of a 'burgomaster who shares his core responsibilities with an alderman', a 'very weak position of the public prosecution service' and a 'divided police force' (Fijnaut et al. 2008: 29). Local security policies appeared to float free from any vertically organised anchoring mechanism that might hold the 'family' (Johnston 2007) of agents and agencies together.

As a consequence, in the view of the commission, the governance and enforcement of public order was 'out of hand'. An illuminating example is the management of Eindhoven's night-time economy, the Stratumseind area in particular. This street contains fifty-six pubs and bars located within only 400 metres.[6] It attracts some 40,000 visitors every weekend (starting at Thursday evening) creating a 'social pressure cooker' of potential violence and disorder. Given the nature of the security challenges, such an urban node deserves a thoroughly governed security system composed of public and private organisations, including, among others, the police and judicial apparatus, city supervisors, prevention teams and social workers. In its absence, however, the notion of a 'disintegrated safety policy' might better describe the state of affairs in Stratumseind (and elsewhere). There were a lot of initiatives and projects, with hardly any streamlining and co-ordination. The commission therefore recommended reinstituting a 'vigorous triangle to set

[4] In the Dutch criminal justice system the public prosecution not the police lead in criminal investigations.
[5] The police service in the Netherlands is divided into 25 regional forces (supplemented by a further national force). By contrast, the prosecution office is divided into 19 offices (arrondissementsparketten).
[6] This 'most crowded drinking street of the Netherlands' was a shopping street 20 years ago, indicating a booming emergence of the 'night-time economy'.

ambitious but realistic security policies'; the police, prosecution service and municipality should aspire to reaffirm their command and control over Eindhoven's poorly organised and managed local security networks. The Security House, in this vein, was to be subordinated to the governance triangle, as it constitutes little more than an executive office.

Whether the recommendations will have the intended effect of lowering crime rates or not, the Eindhoven case illustrates how state agencies still need to fulfil an effective and democratically legitimated anchoring function. In this respect, Eindhoven is an atypical case as governance triangles (involving local authorities, police forces and judicial services) seem to function quite well in the Netherlands. The commission's recommendation to organise a clearer division of labour and co-ordination was welcomed as a means to take control over local organisational networks in Eindhoven. After all, in the field of security, the police, in close consultation with the municipality and criminal justice system, remain the *ultimum remedium* when all else fails. They are the ultimate symbolic power that 'brings to mind (and stomach) sensations of order, authority and protection' (Loader 1997: 8), sensations which are prerequisites for the regulation of nodal partnerships, the confirmation of legitimacy and commitment, the mobilisation of 'third parties' and the democratic participation of direct stakeholders. The challenge is to set up local security policies and networks more systematically. What we intend here is to discuss how such configuration of public and private spheres can be depicted or might be imagined. Ideally, as Braithwaite (1997; 2002) sets out, governance arrangements function as a sort of incremental 'regulatory pyramid' with at the base numerous preventative bodies (welfare work, addiction service, youth care, healthcare) and fewer repressive and punishing institutions (police, criminal justice) higher upwards. He is describing this pyramid as a hierarchy of regulatory tools for inducing compliance – ranging from persuasion, inducements or incentives, to sanctions. We now imply that a series of institutions and professionals use different sets of the foregoing tools in their roles as, for example, police officer, youth mentor and social worker. To translate this idea into a governance framework, we will present a 'team-play' metaphor that stresses the highly dynamic environment in which security governance takes place. In so doing, we focus on the organisational assemblages associated with the steering of public–private networks, ultimately having the credible capacity of escalation to formal criminal law when dialogue and co-operation fall short.

Directed governance

One of the central areas in contemporary criminology is how to think practically of a 'virtuous state', facing the task of anchoring and governing nodal security provision. Against the background of Eindhoven's Security House, we present a strategy of directed (self-)governance. Within this strategy, it is crucial to keep in mind that penal law serves as a last resort in reaction to crime and disorder. In the criminal justice response, the sense of right and wrong is confirmed, while the hope of improvement is kept alive. Under present-day circumstances, criminal justice increasingly derives its credibility from its normative position against the background of a declining instrumental function. At the moment that markets and communities occupy a growing proportion of security governance, the position of judicial apparatus has to be carefully stipulated against other actors in the policy field (Boutellier 2004). In addition to guaranteeing a satisfying level of security, criminal justice holds a vital interest in legal equality and legal protection. It has to set adequate normative guidelines for mastering democratically anchored security policies at the local level.

The emergence of networked governance has had a great impact on the context and functioning of criminal justice institutions. Today's criminal justice system operates from an angle of expedience. It intervenes at places where and moments when a line has to be drawn. This trend is not automatically restricted to supervision and order maintenance activities as criminal law has opened up beyond the conventional realm of police and judicial actors. Education, youth care and subsequent welfare organisations also realise that the demand for protection is of growing relevance to their own work, whereas the police and judicial authorities increasingly define themselves in terms of social objectives that are broader than maintaining public order and enforcing the law. Visualising these developments, the governance of security can be thought of as a team (for example, a football team) working outwards in functional lines (Figure 18.1).

The public prosecutor, like a goalkeeper, stands at the deepest end of the field receiving loads of balls (i.e. criminal cases) directed towards him. However, for reasons of overload, the keeper tries to combine forces with a line of 'risk-managing institutions' – institutions of which security is a defining element (in a third line, from the front) – putting the police in a leading position. Connections between the police and private actors (such as contracted security guards, city supervisors and

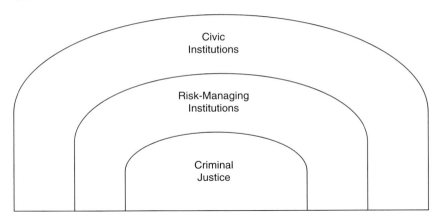

Figure 18.1   Directed governance model.

bouncers) can be bolstered for both reinforcing and preventive purposes. At the same time, 'civic institutions' – institutions of which
security is a secondary element relative to their socialising function –
consisting of, for example, youth care, community work, education and
addiction services surround the 'risk-managing' institutions mentioned
before (constituting a second line). These institutions have a pedagogic
objective in guiding moral consciousness among people, for example
through the deployment of 'contracts' and 'agreements' (Crawford
2003b) in the regulation of antisocial behaviour. Their core tasks are
to support and assist people, instill ethics and correct deviancy. The
forefront players, finally, are everyday citizens and their social activities
(constituting the front line). It is at this crossroad of informal relationship where the government may facilitate civic engagement by reinforcing the 'social web' since face-to-face contacts are arguably much more
effective in correcting intolerable behaviour than the host of surveillance cameras, security staff and police officers populating our cities.
Within the theory of 'anchored pluralism', state agencies bear a crucial
role in facilitating – in 'backing' and 'coaching' to use the team-play
metaphor – the various levels of governance. Explicitly the police are in
a unique position to play the 'libero role' (Boutellier 2005) – free
floating – and serve society with preventative practices as well as
repressive interferences. Their objective is to strike an optimal balance
between firm but fair and restrained action – a practice Kinsey *et al.*
(1986) describe as 'minimal policing'.

Research agenda

Like in many governance debates (most notably those surrounding 'nodal' and 'anchored' positions), the descriptive and normative elements in our team-play metaphor are not always easy to disentangle (Crawford 2006a). By articulating principles of order within a contradictory and contested setting (i.e. thinking of security governance in terms of functional lines), we inevitably move back and forth between empirical findings on the one hand and diagnostic recommendations on the other hand. Nonetheless, the directed governance model outlined above offers a starting point for systematically describing, analysing and evaluating the highly dynamic, contradictory and volatile nature of nodal security arrangements. The Eindhoven case only serves as an illustration of the need for state regulation in the management of networked assemblages – an illustration that calls for more in-depth research. In order to do so, exhaustive data needs to be gathered on the following themes. First, we should address a comprehensive 'mapping' (Dupont 2006) of auspices and providers operating together in security networks. Who are the actors that participate in divergent networks, where do they concentrate, what do they do and how do they relate to one another? In answering the foregoing questions, classification might usefully focus around the lines of risk-managing institutions, civic institutions and social bonds of citizenship. A second and related point is to provide an overview of communications involved in developing, activating and maintaining security networkers. Who is communicating with whom, how frequent are contacts and what is the nature of relationships? Are contacts informal ('old boys' networks') or formal (official meetings, including agendas and minutes)?

Thirdly, the analysis should cover the strategies, technologies, mentalities and practices existing in networked security governance (Stenning in Johnston and Shearing 2003: 22–30; Wood 2006; Wood and Shearing 2007; Button 2008). What are the purposes of actors, what are their deeper considerations and how do they 'problematise' the things which they are supposed to do? Who is designing and implementing policies and who is executing them? What are the physical tools (e.g. weapons, surveillance devices), legal tools (e.g. powers to fine or arrest), symbolic tools (e.g. public respect, authority and legitimacy) and personal tools (e.g. education, training, physique or charisma) actors have (Stenning 2000)? How is a security network really being shaped, sustained and governed? Is there an overriding climate

governing a network or is everything achieved through conflict mediation and consensus-building?

The key question, then, is whether partners are central to co-ordinating
and directing organisational networks. Who is steering at the local level?
Whilst there may not exist a monopoly on coercive force in South Africa,
the country Shearing comes from, it goes much too far to say that in a
European (Dutch) setting 'there are literally no functions performed by
the public police . . . that are not also performed by non-state agencies –
sometimes with state support and other times contrary to the state'
(Singh and Kempa 2007: 303). Public authorities – the police, public
prosecution services and municipalities in particular – continue to serve
an explicitly symbolic and leading function in the Netherlands. A final
point is the democratic prospect of networked governance (Bogason and
Musso 2006; Stenning 2009). The rise of local organisational networks,
predominantly security networks, can offer promises as well as threats to
accountability mechanisms, the meeting of public interests and preferences, and other democratic principles. Although networks come with
opportunities of deliberation, improved flexibility and enhanced effectiveness, we must not turn a blind eye to perils regarding transparency,
equality and (human) rights.

At this point, Crawford (2006a: 469) warns us that:

> the notion of a regulatory pyramid does not address the problem of the
> shifting sands that lie beneath it and the capacity of the pyramid to sink
> deeper into its social foundations; intensifying the extent of regulation,
> lowering the threshold of intervention over behaviour and conduct and
> the formalization of previous informal responses.

Indeed, security-driven policy may have a troublesome flipside of 'defining deviance up' (Krauthammer 1993; van Swaaningen 2002) and 'social
exclusion' (Young 1999; Crawford 2006b). For such reasons, there is a
profound need for cross-national analysis and evaluation. So far, empirical evidence is thin and scattered, and heavily skewed towards Anglo-
Saxon experiences – a position that appears increasingly anomalous in
the light of current shifts in policing and security worldwide (Jones and
Newburn 2006). New empirical explorations should begin to tackle this
shortcoming by drawing detailed comparisons between national and
local jurisdictions, not least to consider the ethical aspects regarding
crime control and security management. Cross-national research
reminds us that it is important to document and understand difference
as well as similarity, and that national and local political contexts

continue to exert a great influence on policy trajectories and (unintended) outcomes (Mawby 1999). Governance – and therefore the 'governance of security' – looks very different across the globe.

Conclusion

Contemporary security policies have propelled in contradictory directions, where alongside the traditional police and criminal apparatus, a plethora of supplementary public as well as private experts have mushroomed in the Netherlands. Unlike what Shearing (2005; 2006; 2007) and his fellow theorists propose, the emergence of such agents and agencies does not imply that the state has lost its priority in the governance of security. Though the state is not always benign (as government bodies have their own professional interests to serve) and sometimes struggles with solving local problems given its remoteness, lack of specific knowledge and limited capacity, markets and communities are still too precarious to take on responsibilities alone. It is only the state that holds the unique position to set binding guidelines so that democratic governance can be guaranteed at the local level. Security policies, as Loader and Walker (2007) stipulate, need to be secured.

Empirically illustrating Loader and Walker's approach, we commented on how security policies in the Dutch city of Eindhoven have evolved over recent years. These comments are not based on scientific research, but on a recently released auditing commission report. Notwithstanding, we think the situation sketched is relevant for academic debates about the governance of security as outlined above. It shows that if a 'vertical' superstructure – in the Netherlands, a triangle of police, municipal and judicial officials – is lacking, submerged security networks of risk-managing and civic organisations start to collapse. A state-based meta-authority is paramount for setting and determining policy agendas, and governing the direction and implementation of policies. Democratically anchored safety policies presume political primacy as a *conditio sine qua non* for widespread commitment.

We imagined the ordering of local security networks in terms of directed governance. In this model, criminal justice is the last anchoring point for good standing between citizens and the potentially threatening world surrounding them (Loader 1997). Penal laws, on the one hand, confirm the legal standard and, on the other hand, promote the development of local safety. Good synergy between the criminal justice service and the police can, in turn, help to reinforce community work. Proper state back-up and assistance stimulates welfare organisations, youth care services and institutions in the field of education to regain space to conduct their normative tasks. Here, the moral consciousness among people can be strengthened (though not superimposed). This, for example, means facilitating volunteer work, advising parents and bringing up children so that the social fabric of civil society keeps running; security problems, after all, start and end with people themselves. Perceived as such, as Skinns (2008: 318) notes, a prominent role of the state is paramount 'because it retains a sense that security is a public good, rather than it being a private good to be purchased by those who can afford it or a matter to be resolved in a fractious manner as a result of parochialism, the exclusion of dissenting voices or those unable to shout the loudest'. Although absolute sovereign state power over crime control policies is an (authoritarian) 'myth' (Garland 1996), undirected nodal governance is destined for confusion and malfunction.

References

Andeweg, R. B. and Irwin, G. A. (2002) *Governance and Politics of the Netherlands*, Basingstoke: Palgrave Macmillan.

Bayley, D. H. and Shearing, C. D. (1996) 'The future of policing', *Law and Society Review*, 30(3), 585–606.

(2001) *The New Structure of Policing: Description, Conceptualization, and Research Agenda*, Washington DC: National Institute of Justice.

Bogason, P. and Musso, J. A. (2006) 'The democratic prospects of network governance', *American Review of Public Administration*, 36(1), 3–18.

Boutellier, J. C. J. (2001) 'The convergence of social policy and criminal justice', *European Journal on Criminal Policy and Research*, 9(4), 361–80.

(2004) *The Safety Utopia: Contemporary Discontent and Desire as to Crime and Punishment*, Dordrecht: Kluwer Academic Publishers.

(2005) *Meer dan Veilig: Over Bestuur, Bescherming en Burgerschap* [*More than Safe: On Governance, Protection and Citizenship*], Den Haag: Boom Juridische Uitgevers.

(2007) *Nodale Orde: Veiligheid en Burgerschap in een Netwerksamenleving* [*Nodal Order: Safety and Citizenship in a Network Society*], Amsterdam: Vrije Universiteit.

Braithwaite, J. (1997) 'On speaking softly and carrying big sticks: neglected dimensions of a republication separation of powers', *University of Toronto Law Journal*, 47(3), 305–61.

(2002) 'Rewards and regulation', *Journal of Law and Society*, 29(1), 12–26.

Burris, S., Drahos, P. and Shearing, C. (2005) 'Nodal governance', *Australian Journal of Legal Philosophy*, 30, 30–58.

Burris, S., Kempa, M. and Shearing, C. (2008) 'Changes in governance: a cross-disciplinary review of current scholarship', *Akron Law Review*, 1, 1–66.

Button, M. (2008) *Doing Security. Critical Reflections and an Agenda for Change*, Basingstoke: Palgrave: Macmillan.

Clarke, J. and Newman, J. (1997) *The Managerial State: Power, Politics and Ideology in the Remaking of Social Welfare*, London: Sage.

Crawford, A. (1999) *The Local Governance of Crime: Appeals to Community and Partnerships*, Oxford: Oxford University Press.

(2003a) 'The patterns of policing in the UK: policing beyond the police' in T. Newburn (ed.), *Handbook of Policing*, Cullompton, Willan, pp. 136–68.

(2003b) 'Contractual governance of deviant behaviour', *Journal of Law and Society*, 30(4), 479–505.

(2006a) 'Networked governance and the post-regulatory state? Steering, rowing and anchoring the provision of policing and security', *Theoretical Criminology*, 10(4), 449–97.

(2006b) 'Policing and security as "club goods": The new enclosures?' in J. Wood and B. Dupont (eds.), *Democracy, Society and the Governance of Security*, Cambridge: Cambridge University Press, pp. 111–38.

Crawford, A., Lister, S., Blackburn, S. and Burnett, J. (2005) *Plural Policing: The Mixed Economy of Visible Patrols in England and Wales*, Bristol: Policy Press.

Dijk, J. van (2006) *The Network Society: Social Aspects of New Media*, London: Sage.

Dijk, J. van and Waard, J. de (2009) 'Forty Years of crime prevention in the Dutch Polder' in A. Crawford (ed.), *Crime Prevention Policies in Comparative Perspective*, Cullompton: Willan, pp. 131–53.

Dijkstra, G. S. A. and van der Meer, F. (2003) 'Disentangling blurring boundaries: the public/private dichotomy from an organizational perspective', in M. R. Rutgers (ed.), *Retracing Public Administration*, Oxford: Elsevier Science, pp. 89–106.

Dupont, B. (2006) 'Mapping security networks: from metaphorical concept to empirical model' in J. Fleming and J. Wood (eds.), *Fighting Crime Together: The Challenges of Policing and Security Networks*, Sydney: UNSW Press, pp. 35–59.

Fijnaut, C., Boutellier, H. and Riessen, J. van (2008) *Veel te Winnen! [Much to Gain!]*, Eindhoven (auditing report).

Fleming, J. and Wood, J. (2006) *Fighting Crime Together: The Challenges of Policing and Security Networks*, Sydney: UNSW Press.

Garland, D. (1996) 'The limits of the sovereign state: strategies of crime control in contemporary society', *British Journal of Criminology*, 36(4), 445–71.

Henry, A. and Smith, D. (2007) (eds.) *Transformations of Policing*, Aldershot: Ashgate.

Hill, J. H. and Lynn, L. E. (2005) (eds.) 'Is hierarchical governance in decline? Evidence from empirical research', *Journal of Public Administration Research and Theory*, 15(2), 173–95.

Hughes, G. and Edwards, A. (2002) (eds.) *Crime Control and Community: The New Politics of Public Safety*, Cullompton: Willan.

Johnston, L. (2000) *Policing Britain: Risk, Security and Governance*, Harlow: Longman.

(2007) '"Keeping the family together": police community support officers and the 'police extended family' in London', *Policing & Society*, 17(2), 119–40.

Johnston, L. and Shearing, C. (2003) *Governing Security: Explorations in Policing and Justice*, London: Routledge.

Jones, T. (2007) 'The governance of security: pluralization, privatization and polarization in crime control' in M. Maguire, R. Morgan and R. Reiner (eds.), *The Oxford Handbook of Criminology*, 4th edn, Oxford: Oxford University Press, pp. 841–65.

Jones, T. and Newburn, T. (1998) *Private Security and Public Policing*, Oxford: Clarendon Press.

(2002) 'The transformation of policing? Understanding current trends in policing systems', *British Journal of Criminology*, 42(1), 129–46.

(2006) (eds.) *Plural Policing: A Comparative Perspective*, London: Routledge.

Kempa, M., Carrier, R., Wood, J. and Shearing, C. (1999) 'Reflections on the evolving concept of "private policing"', *European Journal on Criminal Policy and Research*, 7(2), 197–223.

Kinsey, R., Lea, J. and Young, J. (1986) *Losing the Fight against Crime*, Oxford: Basil Blackwell.

Kooiman, J. (2003) *Governing as Governance*, London: Sage.

Krauthammer, C. (1993) 'Defining deviance up', *The New Republic*, 22 November.

Loader, I. (1997) 'Policing and the social: questions of symbolic power', *British Journal of Sociology*, 48(1), 1–18.

(2006) 'Policing, recognition and belonging', *The Annals of the American Academy*, 605(1), 202–21.

Loader, I. and Mulcahy, A. (2003) *Policing and the Condition of England: Memory, Politics and Culture*, Oxford: Oxford University Press.

Loader, I. and Walker, N. (2001) 'Policing as a public good: reconstituting the connections between policing and the state', *Theoretical Criminology*, 5(1), 9–35.

(2005) 'State of denial? Rethinking the governance of security', *Punishment and Society*, 6(2), 221–8.

(2006) 'Necessary virtues: The legitimate place of the state in the production of security' in J. Wood and B. Dupont (eds.), *Democracy, Society and the Governance of Security*, Cambridge: Cambridge University Press, pp. 165–95.

(2007) *Civilizing Security*, Cambridge: Cambridge University Press.

Macaulay, S. (1986) 'Private government' in L. Lipson and S. Wheeler (eds.), *Law and the Social Sciences*, New York: Russell Sage Foundation, pp. 445–518.

Mawby, R. I. (1999) *Policing across the World: Issues for the Twenty–first Century*, London: Routledge.

Ministry of the Interior and Kingdom Relations (2004) *Policing in the Netherlands*, Den Haag: Police Department.

Morlan, R. L. (1964) 'Cabinet government at the municipal level: the Dutch experience', *The Western Political Quarterly*, 17(2), 317–24.

Osborne, D. and Gaebler, T. (1992) *Reinventing Government: How the Entrepreneurial Spirit is Transforming the Public Sector*, Reading: Addison-Wesley.

Raab, J. and Milward, H. B. (2003) 'Dark networks as problems', *Journal of Public Administration Research and Theory*, 13(4), 413–39.

Rawlings, P. (2003) 'Policing before the police' in T. Newburn (ed.), *Handbook of Policing*, Cullompton: Willan, pp. 41–65.

Rhodes, R. (1994) 'The hollowing out of the state: the changing nature of the public service in Britain', *Political Quarterly*, 65(2), 138–51.

Roberts, S. (2005) 'After government? On representing law without the state', *The Modern Law Review*, 68(1), 1–24.

Shearing, C. D. (2005) 'Nodal security', *Police Quarterly*, 8(1), 57–63.

(2006) 'Reflections on the refusal to acknowledge private governments', in J. Wood and B. Dupont (eds.), *Democracy, Society and the Governance of Security*, Cambridge: Cambridge University Press, 11–32.

(2007) 'Policing our future' in A. Henry, and D. Smith (eds.), *Transformations of Policing*, Aldershot: Ashgate, pp. 249–72.

Shearing, C. D. and Stenning, P. C. (1981) 'Modern private security' in M. Tonry and N. Morris (eds.), *Crime and Justice*: vol. 3, Chicago: University of Chicago Press, pp. 193–245.

Shearing, C. D. and Wood, J. (2003) 'Nodal governance, democracy and the new "denizen"', *Journal of Law and Society*, 30(3), 400–19.

Singh, A. M. and Kempa, M. (2007) 'Reflections on the study of private policing cultures: early and leading themes' in M. O'Neill, M. Marks and A. M. Singh (eds.), *Police Occupational Culture: New Debates and Directions*, Oxford: JAI Press/Elsevier, pp. 297–320.

Skinns, L. (2008) 'A prominent participant? The role of the state in police partnership', *Policing and Society*, 18(3), 311–21.

Stenning, P. C. (2000) 'Powers and accountability of private police', *European Journal on Criminal Policy and Research*, 8(3), 325–52.

Stenning, P. C. (2009) 'Governance and accountability in a plural policing environment – the story so far', *Policing*, 3(1), 22–33.

Swaaningen, R. van (2002) 'Towards a replacement discourse on community safety' in G. Hughes, E. McLaughlin and J. Muncie (eds.), *Crime Prevention and Community Safety: New Directions*, London: Sage, pp. 260–78.

Terpstra, J. (2008) 'Police, local government, and citizens as participants in local security networks', *Police Practice and Research*, 9(3), 213–25.

Wall, D. S. (2007) 'Policing cybercrimes: situating the public police in networks of security within cyberspace', *Police Practice and Research*, 8(2), 183–205.

Wintle, M. (1996) 'Policing the liberal state in the Netherlands: the historical context of the current reorganization of the Dutch police', *Policing and Society*, 6(3), 181–97.

Wood, J. (2006) 'Research and innovation in the field of security: a nodal governance view' in J. Wood and B. Dupont (eds.), *Democracy, Society and the Governance of Security*, Cambridge: Cambridge University Press, pp. 217–40.

Wood, J. and Dupont, B. (2006) (eds.) *Democracy, Society and the Governance of Security*, Cambridge: Cambridge University Press.

Wood, J. and Shearing, C. D. (2007) *Imagining Security*, Cullompton: Willan.

Young, J. (1999) *The Exclusive Society: Social Exclusion, Crime and Difference in Late Modernity*, London: Sage.

Zedner, L. (2006) 'Policing before and after the police: the historical antecedents of contemporary crime control', *British Journal of Criminology*, 46(1), 78–96.

19

From the shopping mall to the street corner: dynamics of exclusion in the governance of public space

ADAM CRAWFORD

Perceptions of security and order increasingly inform how urban spaces are imagined, designed and governed. Drawing on insights from two research studies, this chapter charts the manner in which dynamics of exclusion previously confined to the shopping mall and other examples of 'mass private property' are gradually being extended into the public realm.[1] It outlines the privatisation of public spaces, the emergence of novel forms of spatial exclusion and the growing importance of conditionality as the basis for access to resources, goods and services. Attracting 'good customers', whilst intercepting and deflecting 'flawed consumers', is an increasingly dominant logic of contemporary urban governance. Consideration is given to the politics of behaviour as institutionalised in the British antisocial behaviour agenda and its comparative implications. In particular, the chapter focuses on the ways in which young people as 'non-consumers' are problematised and policed. It is argued that strategies and technologies of 'preventive exclusion' deployed and developed on private property now routinely inform the governance of public spaces. Public streets are being 'reordered' through the banning and dispersal of those who do not conform to the consuming majority or those whose appearance jars with the prevailing vision of an ordered world in which security pervades urban environments. However, the chapter highlights the ambiguous relationship between order and urban consumption suggesting that in certain contexts and at certain times, the logics of security get in the way of, and disrupt, the demands of business, such that urban spaces – particularly in the night-time

---

[1] I am indebted to my colleague Stuart Lister who worked on both these projects for his research assistance and insights. I am also grateful to Sarah Blandy and Phil Hadfield for comments on an earlier draft.

economy – are informed by paradoxical forces that, on the one hand, seek moral cleansing but, on the other hand, generate disorder, antisocial behaviour and a loosening of moral restraint.

'Place as product'

For some, cities are places of difference, excitement, spontaneity, play and even unpredictability, where diverse populations come together, co-exist and interact in uncertain encounters (Sennett 1992). Increasingly, however, the imagining of a city – particularly its urban core – has become bound up with strategies for 'reclaiming' civility, order and security, whilst 'designing out' uncertainty, risk and difference. The pervasiveness of concerns about security and order has led some critics to lament the sameness and sterility that mark many contemporary urban centres (Minton 2009). From Koolhaas *et al.*'s (1995) 'generic city' to Sorkin's (1992) 'variations on a theme park', many urban scholars have sounded a requiem for the city as a place of diversity and bemoaned a farewell to urban civil culture. A central recurring feature of this lament has been the redrawing and blurring of contours of public and private space, in which the privatisation of public space has been a dominant factor and securitisation has been a driving force. De Cauter (2005) evokes this mourning in his description of the 'capsular civilisation', whereby the city has seen the evacuation of the public domain and the 'encapsulation' of artificial ambient spaces entailing minimal communication with the outside in the form of 'an isolated environment of its own' (*ibid.*: 29). There are direct parallels here with Shearing's (1995) 'bubbles of governance' in which discrete zones of privatised urban life are structured around the provision and embedding of security (see also Rigakos and Greener 2000; Johnston and Shearing 2003). These '"fortified cells" of affluence' (Davis 1990) are loosely connected by safe conduits and transits between controlled zones. This process of encapsulation is simultaneously prompted by an 'ecology of fear' (Davis 1990) and an 'ecology of fantasy' (Crawford 1991). On the one hand, perceptions of insecurity demand reassurances and the proactive policing of deviations and deviants. On the other hand, urban spaces evoke a consumer paradise in which the atmosphere is ordered and orderly and there is little place for unplanned spontaneity. De Cauter (2005: 62) describes these two faces of the city as the 'heterotopias of illusion' – including shopping malls, theme parks and department stores – and the 'heterotopias of deviation' – such as prisons, asylums and other

panopticon-like architectures of control. Here, de Cauter draws explicitly on Foucault's earlier thoughts on heterotopias – literally interpreted
as 'other places' that are counter-posed to the unreal space of Utopia.[2]
Heterotopias describe spaces that have more layers of meaning or
relationships to other places than is immediately apparent. What is
insightful from this discussion is the manner in which the heterotopias
of illusion and deviation can be seen to co-exist and become infused
within representations of real urban spaces. As I will demonstrate, this
sometimes takes form in awkward combinations.

As a response to the emergence of privatised out-of-town retail and
leisure outlets, and in part in competition with other cities for new
positions of influence and wealth in the reorganised national and international economy, cities have become a focus of concern. The repositioning of city centres has been an important element in the competition
for inward investment, the generation of local employment and the
regeneration of urban spaces. In the UK, as in North America, the
pressure to re-organise has been acutely felt in old industrial cities
especially where there are nearby large regional shopping centres.
For such cities, regeneration and re-branding have been fundamental
to their urban fortunes. Place has become a product, to be branded and
sold. A central element of this reimagining has been the capacity to
present a city as a 'safe place' to visit, shop and do business. Consequently, concerns about security have become vital components of urban
regeneration that inform 'marketing the urban experience' (Neill 2001).

The preoccupation with regulating urban disorder takes distinct
cultural and local expressions in different cities and across different
jurisdictions. Nevertheless, there are common referents that have been
influenced profoundly by the assumptions informing Wilson and Kelling's (1982) 'broken-windows' thesis. This is particularly evident in the
strategies of local and national governments. It finds expression in the
diffusion, emulation and appropriation of 'zero tolerance'-inspired policies with their focus on policing incivilities and 'civility laws' aimed at
enhancing security and order (Dixon and Maher 2005; Newburn and
Jones 2007; van Swaaningen 2008; Beckett and Herbert 2008; 2010).
Evidently, many municipal governments across Europe, North America
and Australasia have deployed technologies, developed strategies and
trained energies on ordering contested urban spaces. However, any rush

---

[2] Originally outlined in a lecture in 1967, in his later work, Foucault (1977) went on to
elaborate on the panopticon as a paradigmatic heterotopia of modernity.

to conclusions about global policy convergence must be wary that much
of this circulation may be understood more as a matter of 'talk' and
symbolism than reflecting everyday practices (Jones and Newburn
2007). Rather, attention needs to be paid to the manner in which the
reception and adaptation of safety technologies has been conditioned by
their alignment with political struggles and resonance with local cultural
values.

In Britain this concern with urban security has recently taken the
particular, and rather peculiar, form of the 'antisocial behaviour agenda'
and subsequent 'Respect' programme. Tackling 'antisocial behaviour'
has been a central plank of the 'New Labour' political programme in
which the government has sought to frame its relationship with the
electorate increasingly in terms of safety and civility. The first decade
of the twenty-first century saw the proliferation of programmes and new
powers and technologies designed to tackle behaviour defined as 'antisocial' in public places. This 'post-class' *politics of behaviour* (Field 2003)
reflects a preoccupation in which the ambitions of governing and statecraft have narrowed to a focus on individual behaviour as the crucible in
which the fortunes of government are forged. In the face of apparently
uncontrollable flows of capital, goods, people and risks, both municipal
and national governments have re-sighted their energies on the management of public displays of behaviour. Being seen to be doing something
tangible in response to local demands and to assuage public perceptions
via the micro-management of uncivil behaviour have become an increasingly prominent governmental *raison d'être*. An analysis of public policy
pronouncements and initiatives would illustrate abundantly the manner
in which this obsession with the 'politics of behaviour' has engendered a
period of 'hyper-innovation' in the context of 'hyper-politicisation'
(Crawford 2006a). However, this is not the focus of my current argument. Rather, I want to show how the new hybrid tools of regulation
have not only been fostered by government initiatives but have also –
and more fundamentally – been shaped by the appropriation and flow of
technologies from the field of private regulation into the public sphere.

Cross-fertilisation and the private–public divide

In the re-engineering of contemporary cities, 'local growth coalitions'
have played a crucial role, combining municipal authorities and commercial interests in public–private partnerships. As Logan and Molotch
(1987) argue, the 'urban fortunes' of cities – and cities within cities – are

often structured by such 'local growth coalitions'. Cities differ, and by implication, need to be studied (and compared), in terms of the organisation, lobbying, manipulating and structuring carried out by key actors that form growth coalitions. Local community safety partnerships and security networks have become essential components in such coalitions (Crawford 1997). These public–private networks constitute crucial conduits through which control technologies of urban governance have been transferred, adapted and instigated. A number of developments in urban governance and property relations have encouraged a cross-fertilisation of preventive technologies, practices and mentalities of control. Whilst the flow has not been solely one-way (Crawford *et al.* 2005),[3] many of the preventive innovations in governance which first emerged in the private realm, derived from private property rights, have increasingly informed the regulation of public places. A number of formal conduits have facilitated this cross-fertilisation through the development of public–private networks. The first has been a gradual expansion in 'mass private property' (Shearing and Stenning 1981) and its growing role in hosting and structuring key amenities, goods and resources that the public access in everyday life. As a result, there has been a growing rupture between the legal definition of property ownership and its intended use as well as expectations of access. A second factor has been the development of public–private partnerships at the level of urban governance and city administration – including Town Centre Management (TCM) initiatives and policing/security partnerships that have facilitated closer working relations within and between municipal authorities and private businesses.[4] Thirdly, recent years have seen the implementation of Business Improvement Districts (BIDs) as designated areas of town and city centres that are managed through the payment of a levy by local businesses. BIDs explicitly aim to improve the 'trading environment' for businesses by providing additional services. A key element of this management invariably relates to security. Hence, BIDs frequently pave the way for forms of private security and policing. In the UK, BIDs are different from their US counterparts, notably in that UK

---

[3] Public police and organisations such as community safety partnerships – which are largely public sector dominated – are the repositories of considerable local information valued by private businesses. They constitute what Ericson and Haggerty (1997) describe as 'information brokers' for the purpose of private security.

[4] Policy development and lessons have been diffused within networks such as the British Association of Town and City Management (UK) and the International Downtown Association (US).

ADAM CRAWFORD

BIDs levy revenue from business occupiers rather than owners.[5] Finally, we have seen the expansion of privately owned and managed parts of city centres. This most extreme form of privatisation of public space occurs where, in parts of city centres, the land is leased by councils to a private landlord. Such transfers of ownership and management have on occasions been accompanied by compulsory purchase orders and the provision of additional bye-laws to assist governance.

In certain British cities there has been something of a developmental sequence whereby TCM partnerships have spawned BID subsidiaries, often with policing and security agendas (Cook 2010).[6] BIDs represent a more formalised relationship of 'contractualism' between key actors within a defined urban locale in which the nature of the public interest is reconfigured in that 'a different set of norms, professional values and behaviours are brought to bear in defining and resourcing what are determined as the local priorities' (Peel *et al.* 2009: 417). Here, creating an environment conducive to the targeted consumer audience is a key refrain. In the USA, where their growth occurred both earlier and more extensively, BIDs have been dubbed 'malls without walls' (Graham and Marvin 2001). Just as we might see shopping malls as examples of *quasi-public space* whereby public access is provided to private property, so we might understand BIDs as *quasi-private space*, that is 'spaces that are formally owned by the state, by the public, but are subject to control and regulation by private interests' (Mitchell and Staeheli 2006: 153).

Privately owned and managed parts of city centres take the privatisation of public space to a diferent realm, constituting a form of modern 'enclosure' (Crawford 2006b), as a result of which previously public space passes into private hands and becomes subject to private forms of regulation. Often this occurs without the symbols traditionally associated with private property – i.e. gates, walls or even notification. Nevertheless, upon entering such spaces, individuals implicitly 'agree' to be bound by the rules that govern them and the private interests that police and enforce them. Early examples included the Broadgate Centre, London, a thirty-acre site owned and managed by development

<hr />

[5] This model was deemed to fit more closely with the existing system of collecting local business taxation through business occupier rates in England and Wales. However, it does create the potential that occupiers end up paying for longer-term benefits (in business value) that accrue to owners.

[6] By the beginning of 2008 over 60 BIDs had been established across England, Wales and Scotland. Most are in town centres. Coventry One is purported to be the largest BID in the UK and is currently in its second term 2008–13. To date, most ballots have been successful. Details on the range of BIDs are available at www.ukbids.org/BIDS/index.php.

company Broadgate Estates. The Broadgate Centre is patrolled twenty-four hours a day by private security and is aimed specifically at attracting what it describes as 'high-earning people'. Also in London are the Stratford City site (170 acres) being developed for the 2012 Olympics and the seventy acres of land in the King's Cross redevelopment area. In the north of England, Liverpool ONE is being delivered by the Paradise Project, the development vehicle created by Grosvenor (owned by the Duke of Westminster) and its investment partners. The Paradise Project is responsible for regenerating forty-two acres into 1.6 million square feet of shopping. Grosvenor has a 250-year lease from Liverpool City Council, in return for which the city council has secured the renovation of a rundown area, costing almost £1 billion. In a city with a reputation for high levels of crime and antisocial behaviour, presenting the city centre as a safe place has been a key feature of the Liverpool ONE regeneration. Consequently, proactive policing strategies are seen as integral to its success.

For TCM partnerships, BIDs and lease agreements, providing reassurance and presenting a place as safe affords a competitive advantage in luring people, capital, consumers and investors. In Harvey's terms (1989: 157) they are concerned with the 'production of preconditions' by creating a conducive environment for consumption, investment and business profitability. Hence, security as a commodity has been important in establishing a competitive advantage over rival cities within local, national and global economies. Here, the commercial sector has, to some degree, set the agenda from which the public provision of security in urban areas has borrowed. TCMs for example, often ape modes of regulation and policing deployed in privately owned out-of-town shopping centres through the provision of 'city guards', 'street wardens' and city 'ambassadors' to make the city a more attractive and apparently safer place.

Providing 'reassurance' in contested public spaces through visible policing has also been a central feature of recent government initiatives. The introduction of Community Support Officers (CSOs), as a new breed of police officer dedicated to visible patrols and with limited powers has been pivotal in delivering high visibility 'reassurance policing' (Crawford 2007).[7] Reflecting a further blurring of public and private forms of control, CSOs now provide the public police with a

---

[7] There are currently over 16,000 CSOs across England and Wales. Their powers are largely restricted to issuing penalty notices for disorder and to requesting the name and address of a person acting in an antisocial manner.

'commodity' with which to enter the security marketplace and to compete with private and municipal policing providers.[8] Councils and private businesses across England and Wales part-fund CSOs to provide visible patrols. Here we see evidence of both the public policing of private property and public policing entangled in private interests.

Not only has there been an expansion in the private (or hybrid) spaces of consumption, leisure and entertainment, but so too there has been an expansion in market-based modes of control (Crawford 2009a). One of the most important research findings regarding private policing is that the strategies of commercial security tend to differ significantly from those of the traditional police in that they are more instrumental than moral, offering a proactive rather than reactive approach to problem-solving (Johnston and Shearing 2003; Wakefield 2003). They tend to be concerned with loss prevention and risk reduction rather than with law enforcement or the detection and prosecution of offenders. In mass private property the regulatory force of 'membership' and 'access' is a powerful mode of control. If the law is invoked it is often likely to be property or contract law, rather than criminal law. The powers of removal, dismissal and exclusion – whether from a nightclub or shopping mall – are potent administrative tools of policing.

Security as 'positional good'?

In the dystopian image presented by Davis (1990) security is a 'positional good' defined by wealth, access to protective services and membership of secure enclosures. In this context, '"security" has less to do with personal safety than the degree of personal insulation in residential, work, consumption and travel environments, from "unsavoury groups" and individuals, even crowds in general' (*ibid.*: 224). Davis describes the 'obsession with physical security systems' and the 'architectural policing of social boundaries' as constituting a 'zeitgeist of urban restructuring' and a 'master narrative in the emerging built environment movement' (*ibid.*: 223). Accordingly, he pays not as much attention to the less visible and 'softer' forms of exclusion and social control at play in urban environments. This focus on the visible and the symbolic representations

[8] This 'subcontracting' has been stimulated by the short-term nature of initial government funding for CSOs which necessitates that police forces and police authorities increasingly look to external income generation to sustain current commitments to CSO numbers. The Home Office has explicitly sought to encourage matched funding arrangements (Home Office 2006).

of exclusion – in what Davis (1998) calls the 'fortress city' – is to be found elsewhere among critical urban scholars, most notably in discussions about 'gating' where much greater attention has been accorded to the gates and guards (walls and armed security) rather than the processes of governance and control that operate within such spaces (see Atkinson and Blandy 2005; Blandy this volume).[9]

This theme has been picked up also in the context of Los Angeles, by Flusty (1994) who charts the evolving shape and form of what he calls 'interdictory space'; defined as 'selectively exclusionary space' that is:

> commonly designed, built and administered by those affluent enough to do so, and with the wants and sensibilities of the similarly affluent consumer in mind . . . [It] functions to systemically exclude those adjudged unsuitable and even threatening, people whose class and cultural positions diverge from the builders and their target markets . . . In short, difference is fine, so long as it is surrendered at the gate.   [2001: 659]

Contrary to Davis's 'militarisation' thesis, Flusty argues that 'interdictory space' has adapted to become more socially agreeable. He highlights two components through which forms of surveillance and control have become rendered 'publicly acceptable'. These he refers to as including, first, a 'process of naturalisation', whereby 'control becomes so deeply embedded in our daily lives that we simply fail to notice it' and, secondly, a dynamic of 'quaintification' by which forms of control that are too harsh to fade into the background 'are symbolically rehabilitated as both unthreatening and even laudatory' (Flusty 2001: 660). In relation to the latter, he notes the 'ongoing application of a cutely human face to the spaces and technologies of selective exclusion' (*ibid.*: 661). He suggests that, in LA at least, the progression from visible and hard forms of security (as outlined by Davis) to 'quaint policing' constitutes a distinct phase in the development of 'interdictory space'. He concludes that the 'banality of interdiction' is becoming a defining feature of urban spaces.

A dominant characteristic of this banality has been the embedding of forms of security and policing into the design, layout and physical structure of the urban environment. The role of 'architecture' in influencing the flow of events and shaping human interactions has become increasingly recognised (Lessig 1999).[10] Stimulated by 'defensible space' theory (Newman 1972), an array of design practices clustered

---

[9] Low's (2004) analysis of gated communities is a rare exception.
[10] It is, however, hardly new as medieval town planning and Bentham's infamous Panopticon testify.

under the heading of 'crime prevention through environmental design' and situational crime prevention seek to embed control features through the creation of a physical and social fabric that fosters informal policing and removes opportunities for deviancy. This includes 'designing out' crime and disorder features of the physical environment and capitalising upon civilian or 'natural' surveillance. As elsewhere in the field of security and crime prevention, the commercial sector has often been at the forefront of innovations. In this shift from overt forms of disciplinary control to more subtle and nuanced types of social sorting, we see de Cauter's 'heterotopias of illusion' overlaid on 'heterotopias of deviation'.

The power of private property

As the epitome of privately owned spaces to which the public have liberal access with a decidedly public character, shopping malls have been the subject of considerable debate, both in urban studies and criminology. They reflect both the enclosure of erstwhile public spaces and the development of 'commercial clubs' with their own conditions of entry. As such, shopping malls represent a conspicuously symbolic test of the limits of private ownership and the legitimacy of exclusion.

   In the UK, private property vests an almost unqualified common law privilege to exclude or eject strangers arbitrarily, without good reason or objective rational justification. Property law provides owners with powers to exclude derived from trespass, a long-established tort at common law. The owner may give a licence to enter, but once that licence is revoked then the visitor is a trespasser and can be removed without any reason having to be given, let alone without the need to obtain a court order. However, as the Grays (Gray and Gray 1999a) argue, public space, in the sense of space controlled by public authorities, is space that carries a presumption 'for' access, unless and until it is withdrawn. Despite the Grays' convincing arguments that 'The term property is simply an abbreviated reference to a quantum of socially permissible power exercised in respect of socially valued resources . . . [and that] it is beginning to be agreed that the power relationship implicit in "property" is not *absolute* but *relative*: there may well be *gradations* of "property" in a resource' (Gray and Gray 1999b: 12), nevertheless the common law 'has not uniformly incorporated or internalised this understanding of the deep structure of property' (*ibid.*: 13).

This has been reaffirmed in European and British case law. The leading case, *Appleby and ors* v. *United Kingdom*,[11] involved a previously public urban centre – most of the town centre of Washington, Co. Durham, known as 'the Galleries' – that had been privatised in 1987, when Postel Properties purchased it from the Washington Development Corporation. This decision, as required under the legislation, was approved by a government minister. Postel Properties subsequently banned a group of campaigners from protesting within the town centre against the closure of a local playing field. The protestors petitioned the European Court of Human Rights on the grounds of breach of Articles 10 and 11 of the European Convention which relate to interference with the freedom of expression and assembly, respectively. The Court held that the relevant articles do not bestow any 'freedom of forum' for the exercise of those rights and that so long as 'alternative means' for the expression of the rights exist there was no obligation on the British government to interfere with the applicants' exercise of their rights. According to the Court, the applicants were not 'effectively prevented from communicating their views to their fellow citizens'. The Court seems to have agreed with the British government's contention that it was not 'for the Court to prescribe the necessary content of domestic law by imposing some ill-defined concept of "quasi-public" land to which a test of reasonable access could be applied'.

In his dissenting judgment, Judge Maruste argued: 'The old traditional rule that the private owner has an unfettered right to eject people from his land and premises without giving any justification and without any test of reasonableness being applied is no longer fully adapted to contemporary conditions of society.' According to him, public authorities continue to bear responsibility for deciding how the forum created by them is to be used and for ensuring that public interests and individuals' rights are respected. This view appears more in line with developments in other parts of the common law world, where courts have begun to demarcate certain kinds of location as 'quasi-public' spaces to which citizens must be allowed access on a non-discriminatory basis and from which they can be evicted only for good cause. In the US case law, the terminology of 'quasi-public' property has become more commonplace in relation to shopping malls and retail outlets that present themselves as open to the public.[12] This provides some legal protection insofar as

---

[11] Application No. 44306/98, ECHR.
[12] E.g. in the case of *Pruneyard Shopping Center* v. *Robbins* (1980), the Supreme Court held that the mall owners could not claim complete supremacy of property rights and could only limit free speech and assembly so long as the regulations were not 'unreasonable,

eviction and exclusion should be objectively and communicably reasonable. Importantly, the more inclusive the invitation and open the access offered by the mall, the higher the standards for protecting free speech and assembly rights. Nevertheless, US cases such as *Virginia* v. *Hicks*[13] reinforce the extent to which private property, through the judicial process, routinely 'trumps' other kinds of rights and interests.

In Britain, private property remains tantamount to raw exclusive power. This legal position is rendered more problematic by the trend to 'privatise public space' either by transferring ownership – as in the *Appleby* case – or by devolving greater powers to private businesses through developments such as BIDs. The creeping privatisation of public spaces, therefore, raises fundamental questions about the effectiveness of constitutional protection of individual liberties in spaces of 'private government' (Kohn 2004).

From the shopping mall . . . inclusion and exclusion

At their heart, shopping centres embody a tension between the liberality of their inclusive invitation to the general public and their commercial desire to keep out 'undesirables' or at least those that jar with the prevailing image of the place as a safe environment.[14] As citadels of consumption, their imperative is to encourage public access and foster commerce, but also to present the image of a place that is safe and orderly. People and things that detract from the presentation of a safe environment are 'bad for business'. Central to this notion of good order is mobility and free movement (Levi 2008); people and things that get in the way of the circulation of people and goods or that idly loiter without active commercial purpose disrupt orderliness. Consequently,

---

arbitrary, or capricious and the means selected shall have a real and substantial relation to the objective sought' (cited in Kohn 2004: 73).

[13] 2003, 123 S. Ct. 2191. In this case the Supreme Court upheld the right of local governments to enforce laws such as trespass exclusions, asserting that such practices reflect 'legitimate state interests in maintaining comprehensive controls over harmful, constitutionally unprotected conduct'. The case involved the transfer of public housing projects including public streets in the City of Richmond, Virginia, to the Richmond Redevelopment and Housing Authority which enforced its new property rights by writing rules that made it illegal for any person, other than a resident or employee of the housing projects, to enter without a 'legitimate business or social purpose' (Mitchell 2005). Anyone without such a purpose could be served with a 'barment notice'. If breached the individual could be arrested for trespassing.

[14] The discussion that follows draws upon the Nuffield Foundation-funded *Plural Policing* study (Crawford *et al.* 2005).

enticements to 'good customers' within shopping centres are frequently mirrored by subterranean interdictions aimed at the 'unwelcome' or what Bauman describes as 'flawed consumers'. He notes: 'Consumers are the prime assets of a consumer society; flawed consumers are its most irksome and costly liabilities' (2004: 39). Identifying and pre-emptively excluding the 'irksome' thus become a concern of those managing private security. Doing so, in an aesthetically pleasing and consumer-friendly way is the primary challenge.

Responses to this challenge are well illustrated by examples drawn from recent research into the diverse forms of control and policing operating in shopping malls, such as the MetroCentre in Gateshead.[15] Given the commercial imperative to foster free movement of visitors into and within retail complexes, as in Wakefield's (2003: 226) study, the dominant approach to security was based not on filtering and sorting risks 'at the door' – as in the case of bars and clubs (Hobbs *et al.* 2003; Hadfield 2008) – but on the close monitoring and regulation of individuals once inside the premise. An example of this fine balance between open invitation and exclusion was apparent in the MetroCentre's decision in 2004 not to ban all young people under eighteen from the centre after 6.00 p.m. at night (when the shops closed) in response to a number of incidents of disorder and despite police suggestions to adopt such a course of action. To do so, centre managers argued, would adversely affect some outlets where young people spent money; it would get in the way of business.[16] Instead, more nuanced strategies were demanded. One example of this involved security guards asking young people in the centre after a certain time if they had any money on their person. If the young person did not possess significant financial resources (or was unwilling to co-operate), they were likely to be escorted off the premises. Hence, a variety of informal and formal strategies were deployed as the following CCTV operator explains:

[15] MetroCentre, Gateshead, is one of Europe's largest out-of-town shopping and leisure centres, attracting more than 25 million visitors a year and employing over 6,000 people. It was one of the first major shopping centres in Britain to enter into an agreement with its local police authority to finance a team of community beat managers and form a public–private partnership. The contracted police officers adopt the role of 'village bobby' within the communal areas of the MetroCentre, in a vivid example of a 'heterotopia of illusion'.

[16] Interestingly, some shopping malls in the US have begun to implement curfews for youths. E.g. the Mall of America (the largest mall in the US) implemented a 'parental escort policy' for young people under 16 in the evenings (Freeman 1998).

> There's lots of things you can get them on. There's a bye-law which says
> you are not allowed to have more than three people in your group. So if
> there is more than three people 'split up or get out'. You are not allowed
> to have a Ghetto Blaster or radio or anything like that . . . We'll get a
> camera on them and the guard disappears round the corner and they
> don't realise they are being watched and you can get them doing all sorts
> of things. 'Right, let's kick them out.' It's usually only little scrotes! Six
> years up to 15 or 16. After that then it's drink [related problems]. It's just
> the little scumbags really. Rowdy. Not good for the image. So we kick
> them out.

The most routine form of exclusion, therefore, is ejection of perceived
'undesirables' from the premises on the basis of private property rights
asserting a civil trespass order. Those deemed 'not good for the image' of
the centre are 'asked to leave' as a type of pre-emptive exclusion of those
who have no commercial value or who are not seen to 'belong'. One of
the centre's security guards explained:

> The kids, especially in the winter, seem to roam around, they don't do
> anything. We actually have the power to chuck them out if they are not
> taking part in any MetroCentre activities and if they have got no money
> on them, they can't take any part in the MetroCentre activities, i.e.
> cinema, GMX Superbowl, going for a burger. So: 'Get out. You are not
> doing anything here. We don't want you in.' We can actually do that.

The extent to which young people with little or no money to spend are
routinely ejected from, or denied access to, shopping malls is hard to
quantify. However, Wakefield's (2003: 228) somewhat sanguine conclusion that such things generally do not occur is belied by the more robust
practices of preventive exclusion identified in the MetroCentre. Whilst
the liberal enticement to enter and permissive access remain the pervasive commercial credos, the less visible hands of social sorting through
strategies of security remain both evident and a veiled potential.

    At a second-tier, more formal, level 'exclusion notices' were sent by
centre management to individuals' home addresses. These are categorised as being triggered either by a crime-related arrest or an ejection due
to 'disorder'. Formal exclusion notices stated:

> you are hereby given notice that, with immediate effect, the implied
> invitation to enter the MetroCentre is, in your case, withdrawn. That
> means that you are no longer welcome at the MetroCentre and should
> you enter within the period of the ban, one year, you will be considered to
> be a trespasser and will be escorted from the premises. Consideration will
> also be given to taking legal action against you.

Records and images of individuals were kept on file in what was known as the 'rogues gallery' and policed through the extensive CCTV system and the large number of security guards (uniformed and undercover), as well as public police officers contracted to the shopping centre. Security guards in the centre boasted how they often informed those who had been ejected or banned that the MetroCentre had face-recognition technology so that they would be spotted if they violated their ban, although at the time of the research this was not actually the case. It is only when private means of control fail that recourse is made to formal legal (civil and criminal) interventions, as a security manager explained:

> The vast majority of people will take heed of the exclusion orders but the ASBOs are for people who've got no regard at all for exclusion notices or for the law . . . There's a whole range of measures that the magistrates can impose and the one that we're most interested in is keeping them [troublemakers] away from the MetroCentre.

This ambiguity of inclusion and exclusion reflects Young's (1999: 81–8) image of the 'bulimic society' – that ravenously consumes but also spews out; that concurrently absorbs and rejects. At one moment, it assimilates whilst at another point it expels. This social system as bulimia is emblematically represented in the contemporary shopping mall. Developing this analogy, Young notes: 'The very intensity of the forces of exclusion is a result of borders which are regularly crossed rather than boundaries which are hermetically sealed' (2007: 34). This 'precarious-ness of inclusion' captures well the liberal invitation to shop and the associated forces of order through exclusion – the dual processes of 'inviting and uninviting people' which frames such places (Staeheli and Mitchell 2006: 985). Hadfield (2008: 433) illustrates this precariousness of inclusion in the context of the private governance of elite members' clubs in central London, where commercial pressures conspire to demand the exclusion of 'the many' rather than 'the few'. Here, social sorting and stratification operate 'not merely in relation to assessments of *threat*, but also in relation to status entitlement and the *promise* of their potential spending power' (*ibid.*: 437). Rather like gated commu-nities, access to these more exclusive zones is tightly controlled. And whilst the conditions of membership may be more elaborate and intrusive, they provide members with privileges not available to non-members or 'outsiders'. This reinforces the fluid interplay between inclu-sion and exclusion found in diverse types of 'communal spaces' and expressed in different aspirations of community to which they appeal.

In this context, as Kohn suggests, community 'collapses the distinction between public and private. It fulfils peoples' longing for sociability in a context that incorporates the appeals of private life: security, familiarity, identity, and (for some) control' (2004: 193).

The shopping mall constitutes an iconic crucible in which perceptions of safety, commercial imperatives and dynamics of exclusion collide. It also illustrates the manner in which consumerism and enticements to spend can be crimogenic. Crime and disorder may be accepted (and acceptable) by-products of 'doing business'. Security managers at the MetroCentre and police frequently bemoaned the strategy adopted by many retail outlets within the centre in placing tempting and vulnerable goods at the entrance to the shops. While this practice affronted the sensibilities of police and security officers schooled in ideas of opportunity reduction and target hardening by making theft easier and more likely, it was seen as a worthwhile risk for store managers as it provided a crucial way of luring customers into the shop. In a shopping centre where customers are provided with diverse competing outlets in which to spend their money, getting people across the threshold becomes a major achievement. In the calculations of retail managers, the cost of crime is only one factor in a much wider cost equation.

In other ways also, too great a concern for security can be bad for business. Overt forms of security can undermine perceptions of safety. The very pursuit of security can be both self-reproducing in the sense that it requires not only an absence of (sometimes unidentifiable) threats but also a utopian illusion of total safety. The pursuit of security is both insatiable and can be self-defeating, in that symbols of security remind people of their own vulnerabilities to sources of harm. As Zedner notes, it is deeply ironic that quests for security tend to increase subjective insecurity by 'alerting citizens to risk and scattering the world with visible reminders of the threat of crime' (2003: 163).

Managers of commercial outlets and shopping centres are acutely aware of the potential negative implications of intrusive or overly harsh security measures. They are often more aware of the communicative properties and symbolic messages given out by physical and tangible forms of security and associated information. A Northumbria Police Officer working in partnership with the MetroCentre noted this different mentality:

> It's important that we recognise that the MetroCentre have a much greater concern for their image, for the power of PR, and advertising,

than perhaps we're used to dealing with. They want to avoid bad PR at all costs. I think in the past there have been difficulties . . . where we wanted to put up notice boards saying 'look after your valuables, watch where you park in the MetroCentre' and that sort of activity just seems absolutely impossible because you can imagine the negative impact that they would see that having.

An environment that suggests danger through overt security is less likely to constitute a conducive place in which to spend and consume. A senior Security Industry representative highlighted the conundrum presented by selling and delivering security *qua* commodity:

> Two big problems you have when delivering security services are: first, the better you are at it, the less there appears to be a need for it; and the second thing is that it has to be possible, the more you put in security measures, the more restricting it becomes to other people. So it's getting the balance – security must be understood and appreciated, unpredictable but reliable.

There is, thus, a paradox in rendering security simultaneously apparent but non-intrusive; in reassuring users (customers) of protection from unpredictable and unknown risks or unpleasant encounters with 'others' but at the same time offering an aesthetically pleasing, enticing and not overtly hostile environment. Some leisure outlets and retail units prefer not to associate themselves too closely with overt security, for fear that potential customers may be put off by the impression this may give about a place being insecure. For example, MetroLand (a leisure theme park in the MetroCentre) did not have officially titled security officers. Rather, security was a latent function of all employees, albeit some more than others. In part, this is because MetroLand managers were wary of presenting an image of a place where security is necessary as it may make customers feel that MetroLand is an unsafe place:

> We don't have them in security uniforms. We have our own uniforms . . .
> We don't want to look as if we need a high presence of security because that tends to make people think. There's two ways of looking at it. You either feel very secure or you think there's a problem and that's why you've got extra security. [MetroLand Manager]

This echoes with Shearing and Stenning's (1987) analysis of Disney World, where embedded policing takes a particularly 'cute' form. In these and analogous places, features of embedded security constitute core elements of the cultural experience and attraction, encouraging a more pervasive but consensual style of policing. Consequently, designated guards may be replaced (or supplemented) by the dispersal of security arrangements into the fabric of the environment and the occupational responsibilities of all employees.

In places like the MetroCentre, as in Disney World, rules of acceptable behaviour are set out in elaborate 'codes of conduct', backed up by forms of surveillance, monitoring and enforcement, some elements of which are more or less overtly visible than others. They represent a particular type of space in which people are invited to conform to certain defined norms of civility. Here, powers of 'contractual governance' (Crawford 2009a) operate in which the regulatory force of 'membership rules' contain behavioural preconditions. The cornerstone of conditionality is supported by forms of 'preventive exclusion' (von Hirsch and Shearing 2000) on the basis of either an individual's profile or because of some act he or she has committed, as a result of which they are deemed to constitute a 'bad risk'. Preventive exclusion forecloses disruptive behaviour by turning it away.

There are also ways in which private forms of control seek to induce conformist behaviour, often by appealing to instrumental compliance. Private security inscribes incentives for orderly conduct in what Kempa *et al.* refer to as a 'rewards infrastructure' (1999: 206), not only in terms of the goods on offer but also by way of 'experience'. For example, MetroCentre security also participated in 'soft' forms of control through schemes to encourage 'pro-social' behaviour amongst young people, such as the SMART card initiative to promote 'good citizenship'.[17] In a highly instrumental fashion this scheme sought to inculcate a consumerist logic among young people; one of commodity exchange – behaviour for rewards. This is a good example of the potential elision between public values and private concerns, but also the role of private interests in welcoming 'good consumers' whilst preventing security risks.

Codes of conduct: 'no hoodies'

A further example of the finely grained nature of the ambiguous relationship between commercial imperatives and security was apparent in the public furore that accompanied the Bluewater shopping

---

[17] The SMART card initiative was aimed at 7–17-year-old youths and designed to reward good behaviour with points that could be converted into money and used in shops in the MetroCentre. Points could also be removed for bad behaviour.

centre's banning of 'hoodies'. In May 2005, it was reported that managers at the Bluewater shopping centre in Kent had drawn up a code of conduct for the centre which outlined conditions of entry. People contravening it would be asked to leave the complex. The rules outlined the standard of behaviour expected, including not smoking, leafleting or canvassing on site. Guidelines said that intimidating behaviour by groups or individuals, antisocial behaviour and wearing clothing which deliberately obscures the face, such as hooded tops and baseball caps, were not allowed.[18] In addition to banning head coverings (other than those used for religious purposes) and swearing, the code declared that 'groups of more than five without the intention to shop will be asked to leave the centre'.[19] The Bluewater property manager explained the thinking behind the code: 'We're very concerned that some of our guests don't feel at all comfortable in what really is a family environment.' The local police commander added: 'By clearly setting acceptable standards of behaviour, this code will allow staff and police officers to work together in maintaining the quality of experience for guests.'[20]

In the wider media the ban was largely interpreted as an attack on young people. Whilst some commentators noted the irony that the centre, in essence, was banning the wearing of items that were sold in the shops in the centre, others encouraged young people to use their commercial power to boycott the centre. Kathy Evans, Policy Director of The Children's Society was quoted as saying: 'We urge children and young people to use their yearly spending power of £70 million to reverse the ban on so-called "yob" clothing at Bluewater shopping centre.'[21] Given the potential commercial fallout, Bluewater hastily responded by saying it was not a complete ban and it was not solely directed at children. However, they also declared that 22.6 per cent more shoppers went through the doors in the weekend following the ban compared with the same weekend the previous year.[22] Whilst the then prime minister, Tony Blair, endorsed the ban and other centres came out in support – Trafford Centre declared that it had been operating a ban since it opened in 1998 – others preferred not to be associated with such sweeping bans and negative publicity.

[18] http://news.bbc.co.uk/1/hi/england/kent/4534903.stm.
[19] www.msnbc.msn.com/id/7897532/.
[20] http://news.bbc.co.uk/1/hi/england/kent/4534903.stm.
[21] http://news.bbc.co.uk/1/hi/england/kent/4545657.stm.
[22] www.telegraph.co.uk/news/uknews/1490357/Bluewater-profits-from-hoodies-ban.htm.

Exclusion from public spaces

Notable examples of the manner in which dynamics of exclusion from public spaces have become key elements of contemporary urban governance are to be found in a variety of antisocial behaviour interventions that have been introduced in recent years.[23] The capacious definition of 'antisocial behaviour' extends to a wide range of activities, incivilities and crimes. In legislation, it is defined as behaviour that 'causes or is likely to cause harassment, alarm or distress' to others. This broad characterisation is both subjective and context-specific as it rests on the perceptions of others. In this, British developments have parallels with 'civility laws' in the USA (Beckett and Herbert 2008). In the UK, interventions and orders tend to take one of two forms either by targeting identified individuals or by focusing on designated places. In addition to dispersal orders (discussed below), place-based restrictions include curfew orders, designated public places orders (DPPOs)[24] and alcohol-related directions to leave an area.[25] Person-specific restrictions include the antisocial behaviour order (ASBO), a civil order for those aged ten or over which prohibits stated conduct for at least two years – often including bans from designated areas.[26] Breach of the order is a criminal offence with a possible five years' imprisonment. In addition, acceptable behaviour contracts (ABCs) are increasingly widely utilised. These are 'voluntary' agreements and as such do not have direct legal consequences, but may lead to, and inform, an ASBO application. Like ABCs, exclusion from public and private places may be written into or attached to criminal sentences, youth offender contracts and bail conditions. Collectively, these new regulatory tools muddy the traditional distinctions between civil remedies and criminal sanctions and introduce a form of preventive exclusion that seeks to govern future behaviour

[23] This is not to suggest that exclusion from public places is a wholly novel development. There is a long history of public powers to exclude from public space, for example the Riot Act, public order powers and s. 222 Local Government Act 1972 which gives local authorities the right to apply for an exclusionary injunction.

[24] DPPOs were introduced by s. 13 Criminal Justice and Police Act 2001 and give police powers in designated areas in relation to alcohol drinking in public places. Failure to comply with an officer's requests to stop drinking or surrender alcohol without reasonable excuse is an offence.

[25] This grants police powers (under s. 27 Violent Crime Reduction Act 2006) to give directions to leave a locality for up to 48 hours to someone aged 16 or over who is likely to cause or to contribute to the occurrence of alcohol-related crime or disorder in that locality. No prior designation is required.

[26] Introduced by s. 1 Crime and Disorder Act 1998.

rather than regulate past conduct. They also cede considerable discretion and quasi-judicial decision-making authority to non-judicial officers and seek to enlist informal social control, by prompting action by members of the wider community. Echoing the 'broken-windows' thesis, the meaning of acts or omissions derives less from what they are than from what their consequences are or might be, largely due to the ways in which they are interpreted by others. The shift in focus no longer entails a concern to know or account for past or present incidences but rather to disrupt, reorder and steer possible futures.

Rather than review the full panoply of powers and strategies (see Crawford 2009b), I will illustrate the use of two developments with particular implications for the ways in which young people as 'non-consumers' are problematised and policed: the dispersal order and the Mosquito, the former the creation of government and the latter the invention of private enterprise.

The dispersal order[27]

The Anti-Social Behaviour Act 2003 provides police in England and Wales with powers to disperse groups of two or more people from designated areas where there is believed to be significant and persistent antisocial behaviour and a problem with groups causing intimidation.[28] The powers are exceptional in that they are both time-limited and geographically bounded to specific areas that have been authorised for their use. Within a designated zone a police constable or CSO may disperse groups where their presence or behaviour has resulted, or is likely to result, in a member of the public being harassed, intimidated, alarmed or distressed. The officer may direct people in the group to disperse and prohibit anyone who do not reside in the designated area from returning to the relevant locality for a period up to twenty-four hours. No offence is committed if an officer chooses to use the power to disperse. If individuals refuse to follow the officer's directions, however, they will be committing an offence.[29] The Act provides additional powers for police to remove young people aged under sixteen without

---

[27] The discussion that follows draws upon the Joseph Rowntree Foundation-funded research into *The Use and Impact of Dispersal Orders* (Crawford and Lister 2007).

[28] Analogous (although slightly less extensive) powers are available in Scotland. For an analysis of the differences between the legislation in Scotland and England and Wales, and an assessment of the case law development, see Crawford (2008).

[29] Punishable by up to 3 months imprisonment and/or a fine of up to £5,000.

a parent or responsible adult to their home address from the authorised area between the hours of 9.00 p.m. and 6.00 a.m. Although commonly referred to as 'a curfew power', this element of the legislation differs significantly from earlier 'child curfew orders', which remain unused in England and Wales. According to Home Office estimates, between their introduction in January 2004 and April 2006, some 1,065 areas were authorised as dispersal zones across England and Wales (Home Office 2007).

Preventive exclusion

Rather like the ordinances introduced in the USA to deal with gangs, as Levi (2009: 132) highlights, dispersal orders were designed to police the 'doing of nothing', not only to prevent what might happen, the 'doing of something', but also to address the perceived affront to local social order and perceptions of intimidation represented by the visible presence of young people congregating in contested public places. As such, dispersal powers, like forms of exclusion from private property, have a decidedly preventive and pre-emptive logic. They are justified in terms of preventing people from feeling fearful and, hence, discouraged from using public spaces or forestalling an escalation of antisocial behaviour and crime. Rather than sanctioning specific behaviour, what is called into question is 'the failure to reassure' on the part of certain individuals and groups deemed risky. 'Liability for failure to reassure someone in authority about your future conduct', as Ramsay (2008: 120) notes, 'is a legal burden akin to a presumption of guilt. It reverses the onus of proof in respect not of accusations about the past, but of fears about the future'. Not affronting prevailing sensibilities regarding visible representations of local social order becomes a precondition for access to and use of certain urban spaces.

In tandem with other civil preventative orders and antisocial behaviour interventions, dispersal orders seek to govern future behaviour primarily on the basis of exclusion from specific places for a certain (limited) period of time. They constitute a form of 'preventive exclusion' that implies a 'precautionary approach' (Sunstein 2005). Consequently, the 'likelihood' that future acts might cause 'harassment, alarm or distress' and 'preventing' the occurrence of certain behaviours become the touchstones for intervention. People (youths) are judged in terms of what they *might* do. Anticipating and forestalling potential harm constitute a form of temporal and conceptual 'pre-crime' implied in quests for security (Zedner 2007).

In governing the future, however, uncertainty prevails. Whilst the science of 'prediction' has begun to enter the world of governing human affairs, including policing (Harcourt 2007), in reality the scientific knowledge-base for prevention and pre-emption remains too ambiguous to be reliable. In the absence of 'rationalistic' science to inform risk calculations, subjective public perceptions become the volatile basis for this predictive governance. The wide-ranging restrictions attached to ASBOs are a testimony to the precautionary principle in operation. The dispersal order takes this logic further by implicitly clearing certain contested streets of young people as a precaution that they might intimidate others. There is no necessary attempt to induce changes in behaviour by appeals to normative standards or inculcate moral values, merely a command to 'keep out'. Consequently, dispersal powers bypass the agency of the individuals concerned. The precautionary logic of public protection and reassurance takes precedence over attempting to know or understand individuals or their motivations. However, once the individuals have been given a direction to leave a dispersal zone they are treated as wilful and rational actors who either comply with or flout the conditions set down. Their agency becomes crucial to their prospects of criminalisation. A key element of the dispersal order, therefore, lies in the manner in which future conduct is regulated through the discretionary conditions attached to the direction to disperse.

Who is welcome in the city?

In London during the year 2006–7 the majority of the eighty-five dispersal zones were authorised in shopping areas, town-centre locations and around train/bus stations. In these settings, dispersal powers were invariably targeted at identified groups of perceived 'troublemakers'. These groups were routinely informed of the powers and dispersed whilst other people using or visiting the areas were unaffected by, and often oblivious to, the existence of the order. In one city-centre location in the north of England, groups of teenagers were targeted as much for their appearance as anything else. The dispersal authorisation had been prompted by large gatherings of youths known as 'moshers'[30] around the entrance to a shopping arcade. Police managers acknowledged that part of the problem was one of managing the image of places as conducive to

[30] An alternative teenage youth subcultural group that wear black clothes and have a reputation for looking depressed!

business rather than actual levels of crime and antisocial behaviour caused by the youths:

> A lot of this is around the moshers . . . Actually, in terms of their involvement in crime and such, [there are] no issues at all, but they do cause, by their behaviour and the fact that they are gathering in very large groups up and around the [shopping arcade], a great deal of concern for certain groups of people.

A shopkeeper within the arcade identified the wider economic pressures that informed the instigation of the dispersal order:

> It's not about youth, it's not about how people look, it's not even necessarily about how individuals behave, it's about the slow death of the [shopping arcade] . . . The last 15 years has seen a slow succession of owners hiking the rents more and more and have made it even harder for us to survive . . . Now if you take that situation and plonk any mass group outside the front door that reduce the number of people coming into the centre, it's just going to get worse.

It was somewhat incongruous that congregations of pasty-faced teenagers 'hanging around' were being dispersed whilst groups of evening revellers and university students that visited neighbouring bars and clubs – whose drunken antics often took the form of genuine antisocial behaviour – were courted and welcomed. The difference was that the latter came to spend money in the city's burgeoning night-time economy; an accepted by-product of which appears to be the toleration of significant levels of crime and disorder (Hadfield 2006).

This reinforces the inherent messages sent out by dispersal orders concerning who is deemed to be welcome within particular public places and whose presence is regarded as inappropriate, less because of their behaviour and more because of the way others perceive them. It would appear, that dispersal orders fit within a wider trend of urban renaissance in which: 'The culture of respect is manifest largely as a mode of conduct – namely, consumption' and 'the streets are being reclaimed through the exclusion of those who do not conform to this mode of conduct' (Bannister *et al.* 2006: 924). The dynamics of exclusion previously confined to the insides of shopping malls and other examples of 'mass private property' gradually are spilling out into the public realm. The tensions apparent there are now being exposed in public streets where dispersal orders are in operation in commercial areas. The liberality of the inclusive invitation to visit and consume is mirrored in a darker subaltern desire to eject 'failed consumers' and ban 'undesirables'.

There are evident parallels between the British dispersal powers and anti-loitering laws in the USA, such as the Gang Congregation Ordinance enacted in Chicago in 1992. The ordinance had required police to order any group of people standing around 'with no apparent purpose' to move on if an officer believed at least one of them belonged to a criminal street gang. Those who refused to comply promptly with such an order were committing an offence and could be arrested.[31] The ordinance was introduced against the background of a considerable surge in gang-related violence (fuelled by the sale and distribution of crack cocaine) and prompted by a series of public meetings at which residents and aldermen called for legal action to curb gang activities (Levi 2009). By 1995, Chicago police had issued 89,000 dispersal orders under the ordinance and made 42,000 arrests (Harcourt 2007: 51). Most of those arrested were Black or Latino. In a landmark judgment in the case of *Chicago* v. *Morales* (1999)[32] the Illinois Supreme Court struck down Chicago's anti-loitering ordinance, asserting that it was unconstitutionally vague[33] and provided law enforcement officials too much discretion to decide what activities constitute loitering. It was deemed too vague because it proscribes no unlawful conduct in addition to the act of loitering. In delivering the main opinion for the majority, Justice John Paul Stevens declared: 'If the loitering is in fact harmless and innocent, the dispersal order itself is an unjustified impairment of liberty', even if it did reduce crime. He went on to add: 'It criminalized status, not conduct . . . It allows and even encourages arbitrary police enforcement.'

In a dissenting judgment, Justice O'Connor detailed how Chicago might have drafted the ordinance so as to withstand constitutional scrutiny by specifying those that loiter in order to 'establish control over identifiable areas or to intimidate others from entering those areas'. This was taken up by city officials who drafted a new 'dispersal order' which defined gang-loitering in a narrower way to mean 'remaining in any one place in circumstances that would warrant a reasonable person to believe that the purpose or effect of that behavior is to enable a criminal street gang to establish control over identifiable areas, to intimidate others from entering those areas, or to conceal illegal activities' (Palomo 2002: 746). A revised ordinance was passed by the city council in February 2000

---

[31] Chicago Municipal Code 8–4–015 (1992) Gang-Related Congregations. Penalties for violation included a fine of between $100 and $500 or imprisonment up to six months, or both.
[32] 527 U.S. 41.   [33] Under the Due Process Clause of the Fourteenth Amendment.

which restricts enforcement to use in particular 'hot spots' (as defined by the police superintendent) and to specified times periods rather than across the entire city. This narrowing of the powers has been argued by some as threatening to blur an already fading line between the generalised criminal law and more particularised and targeted injunctions with implications for the racialised differential policing of urban spaces (Strosnider 2002). Nevertheless, this revised dispersal power is defined noticeably more restrictively than its British equivalent, as well as being targeted at significantly more serious forms of criminal behaviour.

The Mosquito

An ultrasonic device known as a 'Mosquito' entered the market, providing an apparent technological 'solution' to the perceived problem of loitering youths. The device emits high-frequency screeching sounds that carry over a distance of roughly twenty metres, which are audible only to those under about twenty to twenty-five years of age. Developed by its inventor Howard Stapleton in Merthyr Tydfil, it was first installed outside a Spar shop in Barry, South Wales.[34] Introduced into the British market in 2006, the Mosquito is marketed through a company, Compound Security Systems, which claims to have sold over 3,500 units across the UK in the first year of sales. The product is being marketed in Canada, USA, Belgium, France and the Netherlands. The company's website proudly boasts:

> The Mosquito™ ultrasonic teenage deterrent is the solution to the eternal problem of unwanted gatherings of youths and teenagers in shopping malls, around shops and anywhere else they are causing problems. The presence of these teenagers discourages genuine shoppers and customers from coming into your shop, affecting your turnover and profits. Anti social behavior has become the biggest threat to private property over the last decade and there has been no effective deterrent until now.[35]

The device purports to afford a technological means of dispersing youths regardless of their motivation or behaviour in an impersonal and indiscriminate way. As a mode of control it is unconcerned with and bypasses

---

[34] It was subsequently removed, however, at the insistence of the local community safety partnership.
[35] www.compoundsecurity.co.uk/teenage_control_products.html.

individuals, their motivations or agency. It manages youths as a population group. It does so without any notion of what to say to them, how to
engage and reason with them or even how to socialise them. It lacks any
attempt to inculcate pro-social behaviour or moral values, but instead
emits a droning noise that implicitly says 'go away'. This would appear
to reflect a rather hollow approach to young people on the part of adult
society.[36]

In February 2008, a national campaign entitled 'BUZZ OFF' was
formed to seek a ban on the Mosquito product, led by the Children's
Commissioner, the National Youth Agency and Liberty. At the launch,
Shami Chakrabarti, Liberty's director, posed the following poignant
question:

> What type of society uses a low-level sonic weapon on its children?
> Imagine the outcry if a device was introduced that caused blanket
> discomfort to people of one race or gender, rather than to our kids.
> The Mosquito has no place in a country that values its children and seeks
> to instill them with dignity and respect.[37]

Nevertheless, the device has been enthusiastically embraced by some
retailers and police forces. In a statement issued in response to the above
campaign, the government released a statement saying: '"Mosquito
alarms" are not banned and the government has no plans to do so.'[38]

However bizarre and controversial, in essence, the Mosquito is not new
as a technology of control but rather borrows from and adapts established
strategies deployed in privately managed shopping centres. Often referred
to as the 'Manilow method', many shopping centres have deliberately
played music that is unpopular with young people thereby encouraging
them to move away. It appears that local councils have picked up on this
idea. It was reported in 2006 that the Local Government Association had
compiled a list of such songs for councils to play in trouble spots in order
to move youths on, including Lionel Richie's 'Hello' and St Winifred's
School Choir's 'There's No One Quite Like Grandma'![39]

Like dispersal orders, the Mosquito and analogous strategies are
designed to keep young people on the move, to stop them from loitering
and idly congregating in a 'liquid modern' city (Bauman 2000) that

---

[36] In an interesting adaptation of technology, anecdotal evidence suggests that some young
people record the Mosquito sound on to their mobile phone as a ring tone, so that they
can hear the phone ring without attracting the attention of a teacher!
[37] www.liberty-human-rights.org.uk/campaigns/buzz-off/index.php.
[38] http://news.bbc.co.uk/1/hi/uk/7241527.stm.
[39] According to Matthew Norman in the *London Evening Standard*, 12 June 2006.

celebrates mobility, movement and circulation. In this context, 'doing nothing' whilst simultaneously disrupting the free circulation of people and goods constitutes a threat to 'good order'.

The urban night-time

> They said it changes when the sun goes down.
> Around here.
>
> Arctic Monkeys, *When the Sun Goes Down* (2005)

Commentators who suggest that urban centres are becoming cleansed of disorder and sanitised by forms of zero-tolerance policing and civility laws (Smith 2001; Eick 2006) must, however, confront the fact that the night-time economy, so vital to the fortunes of most British urban centres, constitutes a place in which disorder is an essential by-product of a brand of alcohol-infused consumption, in which normal constraints of social behaviour are loosened. The revitalisation of British city centres in the 1990s was directly coupled to the expansion of the night-time economy, with the alcohol industry playing a pivotal role in this regeneration. Pubs, clubs and other night-time outlets have become important elements of post-industrial urban prosperity by attracting inward flows of capital investment and new consumers. Between 1992 and 2001 there was a 328 per cent increase in the capacity of licensed premises in the West End of London, whilst the number of premises licensed to operate beyond 1.00 a.m. doubled between 1993 and 2001 (Hadfield 2006: 52). This 'progression of a commercial frontier' has been actively facilitated by the local state's deregulatory stance and its encouragement of 'municipal entrepreneurship' (Hobbs *et al.* 2003). The trend towards market-led liberalisation of the retailing of alcohol was further advanced by the Licensing Act 2003, which introduced '24-hour' drinking. It is estimated that in England and Wales alone the licensed trade employs around 1 million people and creates one in five of all new jobs, whilst the pub and club industry presently turns over £23 billion, equivalent to 3 per cent of the UK gross domestic product (Hayward and Hobbs 2007: 448).

The British approach to licensing and regulation has framed alcohol consumption in terms of increasing tourism and economic development rather than disorder (Roberts 2009). As a result, the city at night has become 'a spatial and temporal location where the routine restraints of the day are supplanted by a mélange of excitement, uncertainty and pleasure' (Hayward and Hobbs 2007: 442). In late-night city centres, types of disorder, antisocial behaviour and violence associated with excessive drinking are acted out, heralding new security demands. But order is not the prerequisite for the night-time leisure experience that it is for the day-time shopper. The commercial imperative of the night-time economy is 'the exploitation of hedonism' (Measham and Brain 2005: 275). In the night-time the city centre becomes transformed into a different place in which reordered behavioural norms, interpersonal interactions and instruments of social control both circulate and are normalised. As such, the night-time city centre attracts and is used by different types of consumers. The young patrons of the night-time are attracted and lured by the thrill, risk and hedonistic enjoyment that such 'liminal places' offer. The seductions of the city 'when the sun goes down' are not the cleansed and sanitised spaces of Relph's (1987: 253) 'Quaintspace' or Disney World but the more edgy, carnivalesque qualities of transgression and 'urban excess' (Presdee 2000). As Hobbs *et al.* argue, 'consumers of the night-time leisure experience are encouraged to regard our urban centres as liminal zones: spatial and temporal locations within which the familiar protocols and bonds of restraint which structure routine social life loosen and are replaced by conditions of excitement, uncertainty and pleasure' (2003: 43). This engenders a tense relationship between the market-driven and cultural processes that foster alcohol-related excess and disorder and those forces that seek to exert some form of control and order over the resultant drink-induced problems.

Here consumer culture and security are more ambiguously juxtaposed. Capital accumulation, with its potential crimogenic qualities, may prevail over orderliness. The moral injunctions to comportment, discipline and productivity recede in the face of the alcohol industry's brand of 'marketized liminality' (Hayward and Hobbs 2007: 439). Transgression itself becomes commodified: 'Rather than attempting to curtail the excitement and emotionality that, for many individuals, is the preferred antidote to ontological precariousness, the market chooses instead to celebrate and, very importantly, commodify these same sensations' (Hayward 2004: 173). When the sun goes down, the liberal invitation to spend and consume shifts a gear and takes a different orientation. Order is less the prerequisite that it is in the daytime. Rather, disorder becomes an integral part of the allure of consumption.

These 'crimogenic zones' are not peculiarly British (see Campo and Ryan 2008; Hadfield 2009), albeit they express a particular British cultural phenomena and sensibilities. But ultimately, it is the reality of

consumption rather than the chimera of carnival that prevails. Contrary
to Flusty's contention that cities are becoming places where 'excitement
is unmarred by uncertainty and risks are ultimately riskless' (2001: 664),
the alcohol-drenched urban centres of British cities are far from being
'cozily familiar and candy-coated' places. Nevertheless, there are distinct
control efforts to contain these 'designated zones of patterned liminality'
(Hayward and Hobbs 2007: 443) as discrete micro-districts 'protected'
from other locations in which social norms associated with contemporary city life prevail. This reinforces the point that Young makes about the
permeable and shifting boundaries of contemporary exclusions. The
urban borders that separate rich and poor 'are not islands of isolation:
they are porous vessels in which osmosis of a very calibrated kind occurs'
(Young 2007: 31). Furthermore, in given contexts these 'vessels' must be
understood as determined not only spatially but also temporally.

Conclusion

I have sought to illustrate the manner in which strategies and technologies of 'preventive exclusion' deployed and developed on private property now routinely inform the governance of public spaces. Through
urban 'growth coalitions', public–private partnerships and novel developments in property relations, we have seen a cross-fertilisation and
blurring of public and private modes of regulation and policing.
Commercially oriented strategies that combine dynamics of inclusion
and exclusion now increasingly structure city centres and street corners.
In the process, urban spaces are being 'reordered' through the banning
and dispersal of those who do not conform to the consuming majority
or those whose appearance jars with the prevailing vision of an ordered
world in which security pervades urban environments. However, as
I have sought to highlight, the relationships between inclusion and
exclusion on the one hand and commercial imperatives and security
demands on the other are ambiguous. In specific contexts and at certain
times, the logics of security get in the way of, and disrupt, business
interests. Disorder itself can become both a prerequisite for, and a
by-product of, consumption. Consequently, cities (British cities at least)
remain variegated places in which a culture of consumption both
demands dynamics of finely graded and sometimes porous preventive
exclusion and simultaneously entices disorderliness. It hosts both sani-
tising and de-sanitising impulses. Hence, the shapes taken by contemporary urban exclusions are at once more intense and deeply implicated

by the needs of consumption and yet have permeable and shifting temporal and spatial boundaries rather than solid and fixed contours.

Contemporary efforts to revitalise or 'aestheticise' public space are informed by particular understandings of 'place as product' in which prevailing commercial imperatives and security demands have implications for styles of governance. Forms of preventive exclusion, filtering and conditionality increasingly structure the urban landscape. This increasing dominance of a commercial logic in the branding and governing of urban spaces reinforced an image of youth as problematic and young 'non-consumers' as unwanted. In inferring to young people that they are not welcome in certain essential public places, we may not only be criminalising youth sociability and alienating swathes of young people on the basis of adult's anxieties and assumptions about what young people might do, but we may also be conveying stark messages about the status and value of young people more generally. There are evident concerns that in the haste to create aesthetically pleasing and orderly environments 'flawed consumers' are being pushed to the margins, out of sight and out of mind. In the rush to 'make a difference' and do something about public anxieties, normative questions of constitutional principles, rights of assembly, free movement and expression and proportionality have largely been swept aside. Troublesome, irksome and disturbing behaviour no longer serves as a reminder of the need for a politics of social solidarity and care, but is seen as an outcome of personal choice in which individuals appear as the authors of their own predicament. Containing the social threat they pose and excluding those unwilling or unable to meet the conditions of belonging appear to be becoming the order of the day.

References

Atkinson, R. and Blandy, S. (2005) 'International perspectives on the new enclavism and the rise of gated communities', *Housing Studies*, 20(2), 177–86.

Bannister, J., Fyfe, N. and Kearns, A. (2006) 'Respectable or respectful? (In)civility and the city', *Urban Studies*, 43(5/6), 919–37.

Bauman, Z. (2000) *Liquid Modernity*, Cambridge: Polity Press.

   (2004) *Wasted Lives: Modernity and its Outcasts*, Cambridge: Polity.

Beckett, K. and Herbert, S. (2008) 'Dealing with disorder: social control in the post industrial city', *Theoretical Criminology*, 12(1), 5–30.

   (2010) *Banished: The New Social Control in Urban America*, Oxford: Oxford University Press.

Campo, D., and Ryan, B. (2008) 'The entertainment zone: unplanned nightlife and the revitalization of the American downtown', *Journal of Urban Design*, 13(3), 291–315.

Cauter, L. de (2005) *The Capsular Civilization: On the City in an Age of Fear*, Rotterdam: NAi Publishers.

Cook, I. R. (2010) 'Policing, partnerships and profits: the operation of business improvement districts and town centre management schemes in England', *Urban Geography*, 31(4), 453–78.

Crawford, A. (1997) *The Local Governance of Crime*, Oxford: Clarendon Press.

(2006a) 'Networked governance and the post-regulatory state?: Steering, rowing and anchoring the provision of policing and security', *Theoretical Criminology*, 10(4), 449–79.

(2006b) 'Policing and security as "club goods": the new enclosures?' in J. Wood and B. Dupont (eds.), *Democracy, Society and the Governance of Security*, Cambridge: Cambridge University Press, pp. 111–38.

(2007) 'Reassurance policing: feeling is believing' in A. Henry and D. J. Smith (eds.), *Transformations in Policing*, Aldershot: Ashgate, pp. 143–68.

(2008) 'Dispersal powers and the symbolic role of anti-social behaviour legislation', *Modern Law Review*, 71(5), 753–84.

(2009a) 'Restorative justice and anti-social behaviour interventions as contractual governance' in P. Knepper, J. Doak and J. Shapland (eds.), *Crime Prevention, Surveillance, and Restorative Justice: Effects of Social Technologies*, Boca Raton, FL: CRC Press, pp. 167–94.

(2009b) 'Governing through anti-social behaviour: regulatory challenges to criminal justice', *British Journal of Criminology*, 49(6), 810–31.

Crawford, A. and Lister, S. (2007) *The Use and Impact of Dispersal Orders: Sticking Plasters and Wake-Up Calls*, Bristol: Policy Press.

Crawford, A., Lister, S., Blackburn, S. and Burnett, J. (2005) *Plural Policing: The Mixed Economy of Visible Patrols in England and Wales*, Bristol: Policy Press.

Crawford, M. (1991) 'The fifth ecology: fantasy, the automobile, and Los Angeles' in M. Wachs and M. Crawford (eds.), *The Car and the City*, Ann Arbor: University of Michigan Press.

Davis, M. (1990) *City of Quartz: Excavating the Future in Los Angeles*, London: Verso.

(1998) *Ecology of Fear: Los Angeles and the Imagination of Disaster*, New York: Metropolitan Books.

Dixon, D. and L. Maher (2005) 'Policing, crime and public health: lessons for Australia from the "New York miracle"', *Criminal Justice*, 5(2), 115–43.

Eick, V. (2006) 'Preventive urban discipline: rent-a-cops and neoliberal glocalization in Germany', *Social Justice*, 33(3), 66–84.

Ericson, R. (2007) *Crime in an Insecure World*, Cambridge: Polity Press.

Ericson, R. and Haggerty, K. (1997) *Policing the Risk Society*, Oxford: Clarendon Press.

Field, F. (2003) *Neighbours from Hell: The Politics of Behaviour*, London: Politico's Publishing.

Flusty, S. (1994) *Building Paranoia: The Proliferation of Interdictory Space and the Erosion of Spatial Justice*, West Hollywood, CA: Los Angeles Forum for Architecture and Urban Design.

—— (2001) 'The banality of interdiction: surveillance, control and the displacement of diversity', *International Journal of Urban and Regional Research*, 25(3), 658–64.

Foucault, M. (1977) *Discipline and Punish*, London: Penguin.

Freeman, A. (1998) 'Go to the mall with my parents? A constitutional analysis of the mall of America's juvenile curfew', *Dickinson Law Review*, 102, 481–539.

Graham, S. and Marvin, S. (2001) *Splintering Urbanism*, London: Routledge.

Gray, S. F. and Gray, K. (1999a) 'Civil rights, civil wrongs and quasi-public space', *European Human Rights Law Review*, 3(1), 46–102.

—— (1999b) 'Private property and public propriety' in J. McLean (ed.), *Property and the Constitution*, Oxford: Hart Publishing, pp. 11–39.

Hadfield, P. (2006) *Bar Wars: Contesting the Night in Contemporary British Cities*, Oxford: Oxford University Press.

—— (2008) 'From threat to promise: nightclub "security", governance and consumer elites', *British Journal of Criminology*, 48(4), 429–47.

—— (2009) *Nightlife and Crime: Social Order and Governance in International Perspective*, Oxford: Oxford University Press.

Harcourt, B. (2007) *Against Prediction: Profiling, Policing and Punishing in an Actuarial Age*, Chicago: University of Chicago Press.

Harvey, D. (1989) *The Urban Experience*, Baltimore: Johns Hopkins University Press.

Hayward, K. (2004) *City Limits: Crime, Consumer Culture and the Urban Experience*, London: Cavendish Publishing.

Hayward, K. and Hobbs, D. (2007) 'Beyond the binge in "booze Britain": market-led liminalization and the spectacle of binge drinking', *British Journal of Sociology*, 58(3), 437–56.

Hirsch, A. von and Shearing, C. (2000) 'Exclusion from public space' in A. von Hirsch, D. Garland and A. Wakefield (eds.), *Ethical and Social Perspectives on Situational Crime Prevention*, Oxford: Hart Publishing, pp. 77–96.

Hobbs, D., Hadfield, P., Lister, S. and Winlow, S. (2003) *Bouncers: Violence and Governance in the Night-time Economy*, Oxford: Oxford University Press.

Home Office (2006) *Good Practice for Police Authorities and Forces in Obtaining CSO Funding*, London: Home Office.

—— (2007) *Tools and Powers to Tackle Anti-social Behaviour*, London: Home Office.

Johnston, L. and Shearing, C. (2003) *Governing Security*, London: Routledge.

Jones, T. and Newburn, T. (2007) *Policy Transfer and Criminal Justice*, Maidenhead: Open University Press.

Kempa, M., Carrier, R., Wood, J. and Shearing, C. (1999) 'Reflections on the evolving concept of "private policing"', *European Journal on Criminal Policy and Research*, 7(2), 197–223.

Kohn, M. (2004) *Brave New Neighborhoods: The Privatization of Public Space*, London: Routledge.

Koolhaas, R., Mau, B., Werlemann, H. and Sigler, J. (1995) *S, M, L, XL*, Rotterdam: 010 Publishers.

Lessig, L. (1999) *Code: And Other Laws of Cyberspace*, New York: Basic Books.

Levi, R. (2008) 'Loitering in the city that works: on circulation, activity, and police in governing urban space' in M. D. Dubber and M. Valverde (eds.), *Police and the Liberal State*, Stanford: Stanford University Press, pp. 178–99.

———— (2009) 'Making counter-law: on having no apparent purpose in Chicago', *British Journal of Criminology*, 49(2), 131–49.

Logan, J. R. and Molotch, H. (1987) *Urban Fortunes: The Political Economy of Place*, Berkeley, CA: University of California Press.

Low, S. (2004) *Behind the Gates*, New York: Routledge.

Mayer, C. (2008) 'Britain's mean streets', *Time Magazine*, 2 April.

Measham, F. and Brain, K. (2005) '"Binge" drinking, British alcohol policy and the new culture of intoxication', *Crime, Media, Culture*, 1(3), 262–83.

Minton, A. (2009) *Ground Control: Fear and Happiness in the Twenty-first-Century City*, London: Penguin.

Mitchell, D. (2005) 'Property rights, the First Amendment, and judicial anti-urbanism: the strange case of *Virginia* v *Hicks*', *Urban Geography*, 26(7), 565–86.

Mitchell, D. and Staeheli, L. A. (2006) 'Clean and safe? Property redevelopment, public space and homelessness in downtown San Diego' in S. Low and N. Smith (eds.), *The Politics of Public Space*, London: Routledge, 143–70.

Neill, W. J. (2001) 'Marketing the urban experience', *Urban Studies*, 38(5), 815–28.

Newburn, T. and Jones, T. (2007) 'Symbolizing crime control: reflections on zero tolerance', *Theoretical Criminology*, 11(2), 221–43.

Newman, O. (1972) *Defensible Space: People and Design in the Violent City*, London: Architectural Press.

Palomo, E. (2002) '"The sheriff knows who the troublemakers are. Just let him round them up." Chicago's new gang loitering ordinance', *University of Illinois Law Review*, 729–60.

Peel, D., Lloyd, G. and Lord, A. (2009) 'Business improvement districts and the discourse of contractualism', *European Planning Studies*, 17(3), 401–22.

Presdee, M. (2000) *Cultural Criminology and the Carnival of Crime*, London: Routledge.

Ramsay, P. (2008) 'The theory of vulnerable autonomy and the legitimacy of civil preventive orders' in B. McSherry, A. Norrie and S. Bronitt (eds.), *Regulating Deviance: The Redirection of Criminalisation and the Futures of Criminal Law*, Oxford: Hart Publishing, 109–39.

Relph, E. (1987) *The Modern Urban Landscape*, Baltimore: Johns Hopkins University Press.

Rigakos, G. S. and Greener, D. (2000) 'Bubbles of governance: private policing and the law in Canada', *Canadian Journal of Law and Society*, 15, 145–85.

Roberts, M. (2009) 'Planning, urban design and the night-time city: still at the margins?', *Criminology and Criminal Justice*, 9(4), 487–506.

Sennett, R. (1992) *The Conscience of the Eye: The Design and Social Life of Cities*, New York: WW Norton & Co.

Shearing, C. (1995) 'Reinventing policing: policing as governance' in F. Sack, M. Vob, D. Frehsee, A. Funk and H. Reinke (eds.), *Privatisierung Staatlicher Kontrolle: befunde, konzepte, tendenzen*, Baden-Baden: Nomos Verlagsgellschaft, 70–87.

Shearing, C. and Stenning, P. (1981) 'Modern private security: its growth and implications', *Crime and Justice*, 3, 193–245.

(1987) '"Say cheese!": The Disney order that is not so Mickey Mouse' in C. Shearing and P. Stenning (eds.), *Private Policing*, London: Sage, pp. 317–23.

Smith, N. (2001) 'Global social cleansing: postliberal revanchism and the export of zero tolerance', *Social Justice*, 28(3), 68–75.

Sorkin, M. (1992) (ed.) *Variations on a Theme Park: The New American City and the End of Public Space*, New York: Hill and Wang.

Staeheli, L. A. and Mitchell, D. (2006) 'USA's destiny? Regulating space and creating community in American shopping malls', *Urban Studies*, 43(5/6), 977–92.

Strosnider, E. (2002) 'Anti-gang ordinances after *City of Chicago* v. *Morales*: the intersection of race, vagueness doctrine, and equal protection in the criminal law', *The American Criminal Law Review*, 39, 101–46.

Sunstein, C. (2005) *Laws of Fear: Beyond the Precautionary Principle*, Cambridge: Cambridge University Press.

Swaaningen, R. van (2008) 'Sweeping the street: civil society and community safety in Rotterdam' in J. Shapland (ed.), *Justice, Community and Civil Society: A Contested Terrain*, Cullompton: Willan, pp. 87–106.

Wakefield, A. (2003) *Selling Security*, Cullompton: Willan Publishing.

Wilson, J. Q. and Kelling, G. (1982) 'Broken windows', *The Atlantic Monthly*, March, 29–37.

Wood, J. and Shearing, C. (2007) *Imagining Security*, Cullompton: Willan Publishing.

Young, J. (1999) *The Exclusive Society*, London: Sage.

(2007) *The Vertigo of Late Modernity*, London: Sage.

Zedner, L. (2003) 'Too much security?', *International Journal of the Sociology of Law*, 31, 155–84.

(2007) 'Pre-crime and post-criminology', *Theoretical Criminology*, 11(2), 261–81.

20

Gating as governance: the boundaries spectrum in social and situational crime prevention

SARAH BLANDY

Introduction

This chapter is concerned with crime prevention as part of a broader picture of urban governance.[1] It focuses on residential areas in the UK and specifically on gated developments, a relatively new but fast-proliferating form of housing frequently cited as an exemplar of the current era's 'fortress mentality' (see Blakely and Snyder 1997; McKenzie 1994; and special issues of *Environment and Planning B* 2002 29: 3, *GeoJournal* 2006 66: 1–2, and *Housing Studies* 2005 20: 2). Academic debate has tended to concentrate on analysing the driving forces for gated communities as a particular urban form and on the implications of their recent growth for social exclusion and social cohesion, with less emphasis on whether gated communities are effective in preventing crime or merely cause displacement. The term 'gated community' is usually understood as a form of private residential neighbourhood defined by a physical boundary, as well as by a legal framework which relates only to that neighbourhood and which binds the residents contractually through their property rights (Atkinson *et al.* 2003).

Here it is argued that boundaries and enclosures of all kinds are now established as a key technique of governance in late modernity, the period from the latter half of the twentieth century to the present (Garland 2001). Walls are a visible sign of the current obsession with

[1] The research on which this chapter is based was funded by the British Academy and by the Office of the Deputy Prime Minister. I am grateful to my research colleagues, Rowland Atkinson, John Flint, Stephen Green, Diane Lister, Emma McCoulough and David Parsons, for allowing me to make use of our data and findings. My ideas about boundaries were developed in discussions with Stephen Green and benefited from exchanges at the international colloquium, University of Leeds, 2008. The final version of this chapter owes much to Adam Crawford's careful editing and very helpful suggestions.

boundaries, and can be seen at many scales: the fortified border between Mexico and the USA, the West Bank wall, guarded refugee camps and gated communities. Boundary creation as an instrument of 'the spatial turn in governance' (Perry 2000: 61) must be understood in the context of imperatives and constraints flowing from the neoliberal agenda (see Adam Crawford's chapter in this volume which illustrates the same point in relation to urban public space). Spatial governmentality, or control through the management of space, is oriented to the avoidance of future risk. Techniques which demarcate and differentiate residential areas through boundaries of different kinds – legal, data-driven and physical – are routinely used to address issues of crime and disorder[2] which are now 'enmeshed within a wider framework of community safety which incorporates issues of. . .the environment and housing' (Matthews 2002: 224). Indeed, the Police and Justice Act 2006 has extended the Crime and Disorder Act 1998, which originally referred to strategies for the reduction of 'crime and disorder', to also address 'anti-social and other behaviour adversely affecting the local environment'.

Housing has become an increasingly key arena for the regulation of conduct in the UK (Flint 2006). The discussion in this chapter is illustrated by empirical research into three different forms of enclosure in residential neighbourhoods: privately owned gated communities; alley-gating, a technique in which lanes along the rear of terraced houses are blocked off to deter criminal activity and create private space; and the retro-fitting with walls and gates of council-owned housing estates. Although these examples are from the UK, a wider context is drawn on and the arguments have a broader application. Spatial boundaries in residential areas, whether visible or invisible, can be understood in three complementary ways. First, they exemplify punitive and exclusionary responses to crime, antisocial behaviour and perceptions of insecurity. Secondly, the supposedly inclusionary force of boundaries also furthers the responsibilisation of communities which underpins the British government's agenda for local democratic participation and community cohesion, which is seen as an effective means of countering perceptions of insecurity. Thirdly, boundaries are used to map out geographical areas

---

[2] Disorder is usually referred to as 'antisocial behaviour' in the UK where it is now very much part of the understanding of criminal behaviour, as evidenced by amendments to the original provisions of the Crime and Disorder Act 1998 brought in by the Anti-Social Behaviour Act 2003 which extend its provisions to 'antisocial behaviour'. References to 'crime prevention' in this chapter should therefore be read as including the prevention of antisocial behaviour.

on which particular policy initiatives to reduce crime and antisocial behaviour may be targeted, such as intensive policing, the selective licensing of private landlords, and regeneration initiatives.

This chapter starts by analysing the context of late modernity. The following section then examines recent developments in crime prevention, community safety and planning. Then an analysis of the boundaries spectrum more broadly is presented, drawing on the author's empirical research into gating. The implications of boundaries are discussed in the concluding section.

Features of late modernity leading to boundary techniques

Most social theorists agree that there is something distinctive about the current era of late modernity, produced by huge social and economic changes over the past fifty or so years. Its key features have been identified as: marketisation and commodification; a move away from social inclusion to exclusion (Young 1999); a loss of kinship networks and local communities with a focus on individualism rather than on 'the social' (Rose 1996; Putnam 2000); and a growing awareness of risk (Giddens 1991; Beck 1992); all of which have led to increased insecurity in all aspects of life (Bauman 2001). A parallel trend has been from state government to dispersed governance, in which an increasingly diverse set of agencies have taken on functions previously undertaken by central and local government. In addition, individuals and communities have been encouraged to become actively self-governing, thus making it 'possible to govern without governing *society* – to govern through the "responsibilised" and "educated" anxieties and aspirations of individuals and their families' (Rose 1994: 389, emphasis in original). In policy terms, there has been an obvious shift from welfarism to a new order which 'stresses personal responsibility, rather than collective risk spreading. . .with a harshly enforced, highly moralistic criminal law promising almost total protection against crime, while emphasising how dangerous the world is despite these much-needed measures' (Simon 2007: 23).

The implications of these global trends for residential tenure and forms of housing have been significant. The past twenty or so years have seen the residualisation of the social rented sector (Cowan and McDermont 2006) and the rise of owner-occupation in the UK, against a background of awareness of crime 'as continuous with normal social interaction. . .a routine risk to be calculated' (Garland 2001: 128). It has been suggested that 'in a world that might at times be experienced as threatening and uncontrollable', the private realm of the (owner-occupied) home provides a substitute source of ontological security (Saunders 1990: 361), satisfying that deep psychological need for confidence and trust in the world as it appears to be (Giddens 1991). At the same time, as a result of neoliberal concern with the market and individual wealth, the home has come to be seen as an investment, making owners more anxious about their possessions and keener to defend their property assets. This, coupled with the withdrawal of the state, has created circumstances in which 'protection against risk of crime through an investment in measures of security becomes part of the responsibilities of each active individual' (Rose 2000: 327).

The contingency and insecurity that have become part of everyday life also affect perceptions of residential safety. Individuals may choose to make their own security arrangements, for example by fortifying their homes (Atkinson and Blandy 2007), or by joining a neighbourhood watch association to add a layer of collective security, or even by contributing to the cost of a private security patrol. The decline of community ties since the mid twentieth century, associated with a growing fear of people who are perceived as 'other', also drives the widespread wish to live alongside people 'just like us' (Wilton 1998). Increased mistrust and fear of crime cause those with choice to seek homogeneity in 'more and more finely distinguished "lifestyle enclaves", segregated by race, class, education, life stage, and so on' (Putnam 2000: 209). Withdrawal into the increased protection of a gated community by those housing consumers who are able to afford it represents only a more extreme form of this responsibilised reaction to risk.

Both self-interested market choices and current crime prevention and other social policies generate boundary-creating techniques, with the result that most urban areas are now characterised very visibly by:

> [a] socio-spatial continuum that runs from highly demarcated 'exclusive' areas inhabited by the wealthy, through a range of mixed localities marked by the physical contiguity of better off and low-income social groups, to 'excluded' areas that are also demarcated. [Ellison and Burrows 2007: 300]

Crime prevention, community safety and planning policies

Alongside the deep socio-economic and political changes outlined above, a situational approach to crime prevention was gradually adopted in the UK which aims to prevent 'the act of crime by the direct control of whole populations, categories and spaces' (Cohen 1985: 147). This approach was heavily influenced by Oscar Newman's concept of 'defensible space' which, most importantly for the argument of this chapter, concerns boundary definition. Newman emphasised 'the capacity of the physical environment to create perceived zones of territorial influence' (1973: 51), and was particularly concerned that public space, semi-public space and private space should be clearly and separately demarcated in residential areas. Situational crime prevention (SCP) is based on the concept that '[c]rime is something that can be "designed out" by changing the planning and management of the physical environment' (Cohen 1985: 148). By hardening targets vulnerable to potential offenders in crime 'hot spots', opportunities for crime will be reduced (Sutton *et al.* 2008). The SCP approach is largely embodied in the Home Office-approved police scheme Secured by Design (ACPO CPI 2004a). Established in 1989, Secured by Design echoes Newman (1973) in recommending that there should be 'a buffer zone of more "defensible space" between public and private' in residential areas (ACPO CPI 2004a: para. 2.6).

More recently, there has been a move in the UK to strengthen design-based situational crime prevention principles by adopting 'responsibilisation strategies . . . intimately bound up with appeals to community' (Crawford 1998: 262). This focus is particularly applied to the deprived urban neighbourhoods where problems of crime and disorder are likely to be concentrated, and which are most likely to suffer from a breakdown of informal social control, seen as a strong predictor of disorder and antisocial behaviour (Wood 2004). The government is therefore concerned to enhance the 'collective efficacy' (Sampson and Raudenbush 1999) of residents in deprived areas. These neighbourhoods often coincide with housing estates managed by social landlords, estates which already have clear legal and physical boundaries, making it easier to establish exclusionary and coercive policies as well as attempts to govern in partnership with the community.

The UK crime prevention strategy now follows the principles of crime prevention through environmental design (CPTED). In relation to residential areas, CPTED is closely linked to psychological understandings of how the residents (rather than criminals, as in SCP) experience their surroundings. 'Second generation' CPTED deals with the affective as well as the physical environment (Cozens *et al.* 2005), emphasising territorial control and 'ownership' – not necessarily in the legal sense – at an individual and collective level in residential neighbour-hoods. At an operational level, CPTED builds in assessment of risk by residents into wider community development and regeneration projects. Consultation and participation form an integral part of the process of increasing community cohesion and thus reducing crime and disorder. These efforts to responsibilise communities in relation to crime preven-tion are only one aspect of wider government aims to 'pass power into the hands of local communities, to generate vibrant local democracy in every part of the country and to give real control over local decisions and services to a wider pool of active citizens' (Department of Communities and Local Government (DCLG) 2008: 1; Localism Bill 2010). The move from rowing to steering by the state in late modernity and the develop-ment of the new 'community' approach to crime prevention have had considerable impact on residential areas, regardless of tenure. Partner-ship is another keynote of the new governmentality, in which designing out crime is part of wider risk-calculating crime control strategies (O'Malley 1999). The membership of local Crime and Disorder Reduc-tion Partnerships includes social landlords, along with local authorities and the police, and partnership strategies invariably incorporate com-munity involvement.

These twin concerns of designing out crime in the physical environ-ment and boosting local democratic participation can also be seen in UK planning policies and practice, often resulting in physical boundaries. The government is committed to putting 'planning out crime at the heart of the planning process' (Office of the Deputy Prime Minister (ODPM) 2003: 22). Section 17 of the Crime and Disorder Act 1998 (as amended by Schedule 9 of the Police and Justice Act) requires every local authority 'to exercise its various functions with due regard to the likely effect of the exercise of those functions on, and the need to do all that it reasonably can to prevent, crime and disorder in its area (including anti-social and other behaviour adversely affecting the local environment)'. After a period of uncertainty as to the status of s. 17 in the planning process (see for example, Kitchen 2002), the government's publication *Safer Places* stated definitively that 'crime prevention can be a material consideration in the determination of planning applications' (ODPM/ Home Office 2004: 49). Crime-prevention design advisers, sometimes termed police architectural liaison officers, advise local planning author-ities on crime prevention aspects of planning applications. At the same time, the 'communicative turn' in planning over the past two decades has given greater weight to local community concerns and local participation (Healey 1996), illustrated by the government's emphasis on 'partnership working and effective community involvement' in the planning development framework (DCLG 2005: paras. 15 and 16).

Tensions between these two strands of policy are evident, however. Planning guidance for residential developments favours permeability of the urban environment. Natural surveillance and accessibility, allowing public movement through and around a development, are considered extremely important (DCLG 2006a; DETR CABE 2000). On the other hand, Secured by Design suggests that security in housing developments may be 'compromised *by excessive permeability*' if through-routes are created (ACPO SBD 2009: para. 3.2, emphasis added). As well as crime prevention, these complex and contradictory national planning policies must be taken into account as material considerations by local planning authorities when they consider applications to create physical boundaries around housing developments.[3] Combined with the emphasis placed on creating a sense of neighbourhood identity, these considerations are likely to result in exclusionary gated developments obtaining planning approval.

The next section addresses the boundaries spectrum and its role in current crime prevention policies, examining different types of boundaries which define local residential areas and which are marked out by different techniques: legal, data-driven or physical. Although in practice these different elements are often combined, they are treated separately here for the sake of clarity.

Legal and quasi-legal boundaries

Both state and private interests make use of the law to create boundaries, from the apparently neutral civil law framework which establishes ownership through property rights, to the overtly exclusionary powers of the criminal law. Legal geographers have observed that boundaries:

> signify, they differentiate, they unify the insides of the spaces that they make. *What* they mean refers to constellations of social relational power. And the form that this meaning often takes. . .is *legal* meaning. [Delaney *et al.* 2001: xviii, emphases in the original]

---

[3] Apart from low walls and gates which are exempt from regulation, any new enclosure of private or council-owned property requires development control consent from the local planning authority.

The term 'nomosphere' has been coined for a space in which a particular
legal regime applies, focusing attention 'on the meaning and practical
significance of borders, property lines, thresholds, or gates' (Delaney
2004: 851), and it is used here in relation to a range of nomospheres with
differing legal powers.

Property law creates 'a boundary between public and private power'
(Reich 1964: 771). The exclusionary 'violence' of private property
(Blomley 1994) rests on the common law doctrine of trespass: anyone
who does not have the owner's permission to be on private property is
trespassing, and a proprietor of premises is entitled to use reasonable
force to eject a trespasser. However, the apparently simple binary divide
between public and private property proves more complex in reality
(Blomley 2005), and particularly so when applied to the governance of
urban residential neighbourhoods. For example, the legal entity which
owns a gated development is often made up of the leasehold owners who
on purchase of their dwelling automatically become members of the
residents' management company which owns the freehold.[4] Thus each
owner has two property interests: as individual leaseholder of the dwelling and as collective freeholder of the whole site and its shared facilities.
In contrast, the freehold of social rented housing estates is owned by the
local authority or housing association landlord, while the residents have
tenancies of their individual dwellings.

Property interests in both of these settings are therefore divided
between public and private in complex ways, which can be used to
exclude undesirable people and behaviour and to foster collective
responsibilities and responses to crime and disorder. Private law instruments such as tenancy agreements and leasehold covenants are designed
to control the conduct of all residents, both within their own property
and in the site as a whole, thus taking on a spatial dimension. The legal
documents applicable to social rented estates and to privately owned
gated communities are strikingly similar in their language and content,
creating specific rules for a particular nomosphere. These rules are
potentially exclusionary in effect, as they are enforceable through eviction for breach of tenancy or through forfeiture of the lease.

Quasi-legal contractual governance (Crawford 2003) is an important
technique for the prevention of crime, or more specifically of antisocial
behaviour, and can be seen as part of the boundary spectrum. Acceptable
behaviour contracts (ABCs) draw on the power of law by imitating a

---

[4] In the US these bodies are known as 'homeowners associations'.

legal form, defining in great detail the unacceptable behaviour which the individual promises to cease. Many ABCs also normatively link conduct with place, requiring the signatory not to enter named streets or neighbourhoods. These are exclusionary in effect since non-compliance often results in a more punitive exclusionary measure such as an antisocial behaviour order (ASBO) or eviction from a social rented tenancy. ABCs may also carry inclusionary force in that the resident(s) who complain to the police or social landlord feel that concerns in their area have been taken seriously.

This inclusionary force of contractual governance also underpins the Good Neighbour Agreements which have been adopted by many social landlords. These are intended to promote 'a shared set of community standards and expectations around behaviour' as part of 'a range of other enforcement and preventative measures to address anti-social behaviour' (DCLG 2006b: 3). Although unenforceable, Good Neighbour Agreements mimic the legal form of tenancy agreements and leasehold covenants and apply to a geographically bounded area. The aim is to create a nomosphere in which committed residents abide by a common code of conduct, which typically includes keeping properties and their immediate environment clean, and forbids swearing, dumping rubbish, trespass, graffiti, noise and unruly behaviour.

The Neighbourhood Charters proposed by the former UK government, but not yet enacted, emulate residents' management companies in private sector developments, or tenants' management organisations in social rented housing through which residents' representatives take on a range of responsibilities for their estate. Within a geographically defined neighbourhood, the local democratic organisation (so far undefined) would be empowered to impose fixed penalty notices, apply for ASBOs, and adopt bye-laws to indicate that, for example, 'parking on verges or skateboarding on the street were not acceptable types of behaviour in a particular neighbourhood' (ODPM/Home Office 2005: 22). These legally enforceable bye-laws would encompass both exclusionary techniques and the inclusionary power of boundaries.

Specifically exclusionary legal powers were introduced for social landlords in the Housing Act 1996 and for the police in the Crime and Disorder Act 1998, marking a new type of spatially bounded crime prevention instrument in the UK. These 'two-step prohibitions' (Simester and von Hirsch 2006) define a nomosphere within which specific types of conduct are prohibited, or from which the perpetrator is excluded. Backed by criminal law sanctions, these powers (discussed in

more detail in Adam Crawford's chapter) epitomise the recent turn to
'coercive crime prevention' (Allen 1999, cited in Hughes 2004: 19) and
represent the harshest extreme of the boundaries spectrum.

Data-driven policy boundaries

UK government strategies to reduce crime in impoverished and socially
excluded neighbourhoods rely on data to create differentiated nomospheres, in which particular legal and policy regimes apply. Observing
the shift in crime prevention from a social to spatial approach, Stanley
Cohen accurately forecast that the 'technological paraphernalia [previ-
ously] directed at the individual will now be invested in cybernetics,
management, systems analysis, surveillance, information gathering and
opportunity reduction' (Cohen 1985: 147). Sophisticated technologies
now enable a wide range of data including employment opportunities,
health, crime and disorder, and the provision and condition of housing,
to inform place-based analyses (SEU 1998). Planning authorities, the
police and social landlords, and other agencies map data relating to
crime and other social factors in order to construct local policy
boundaries.

Statistics on crime and disorder allow the governed population to be
divided between active citizens capable of managing their own risks,
including homeowners providing their own security, and disadvantaged
'at risk' lesser citizens (Dean 1999: 167). Such boundaries, albeit sometimes porous, are required so that particular legal measures may be
directed at 'crime hot spots' for example, or to empower citizen participation. Disparate initiatives, policies and types of regulation may apply
in different neighbourhoods. These differential effects are made possible
because: 'regulatory spaces appear as naturally distinct . . . By being
geographicalised, a particular mode of governance avoids being judged
by the standards of a neighbouring but distinct space' (Valverde 1996:
368). Once a particular neighbourhood has been defined by an enclosing
boundary, regulatory initiatives can be targeted there. For example,
official attention once focused on social housing estates now extends
to disorder in residential areas with a high proportion of private tenants.
Measures in the Housing Act 2004 allow local authorities to designate
'selective licensing areas'. Within the boundary, private landlords must
register their properties and submit to particular legal requirements,
including exerting greater control over any antisocial behaviour by their
tenants.

This type of data-driven policy boundary may correspond more with arbitrary administrative criteria than meaningful social or inter-subjective relations, as residents are often unaware of these policy initiatives. Nevertheless, '[r]arely has the neighbourhood enjoyed as high a profile in public policy as it does today' (Lupton 2003: 1). There have been 'almost four decades [of tackling] problems of urban deprivation in England through the designation of area-based initiatives' (Lawless 2006: 1991); but what began as a purely bricks-and-mortar approach has changed to one of community engagement and partnership working, often focused on crime prevention and the reduction of fear of crime through responsibilisation.

Physical boundaries

Three types of gating and enclosure will be discussed here, in different kinds of neighbourhood, illustrating the different forces which all tend towards boundary creation.

Affluent gated communities

Self-interest in the form of responsibilised reaction to risk encourages the affluent to provide residential security for themselves, beyond what the state can provide. The paradigmatic gated community is high status, with a uniformed guard on the gate and secure enclosure symbolically marked by CCTV cameras and deterrent notices: its 'primary concern is to manage space and to separate out different "types" of people' (Garland 2001: 162). The trend towards gated housing developments which are both socially exclusive and deliberately exclusionary began in the USA during the last century but now has a global reach. In addition to being physically enclosed, gated communities have an invisible legal perimeter within which self-governance applies. Legal rules embedded in property ownership ensure that the common facilities are effectively maintained through residents' financial contributions and that market values are not diminished by inappropriate conduct or use of the dwellings by their owners.

In 2002 a national survey of planning authorities in England was carried out, achieving a 93 per cent response rate, which found around 1,000 gated communities (Atkinson *et al.* 2003). The majority of respondent planners, while mindful of their duties under s. 17 Crime and Disorder Act 1998 and of advice from Secured by Design, were concerned about the effect of gating on permeability and social cohesion (*ibid.*). However, very few authorities had a specific policy on gated communities, making it difficult to resist planning applications (see Blandy and Parsons 2004, for an example of this process in practice). Developers are keen to build gated developments which carry a price premium, and are rarely challenged by planning authorities. It is therefore likely that many more enclosed and secure developments have been built in the UK since the 2002 survey. There is a common-sense assumption that gating prevents crime, although this was not borne out by a California study which found no significant differences between gated and non-gated areas, in both high-income neighbourhoods and public housing projects (Wilson Doenges 2000). Police officers interviewed for the UK survey said that gating can give residents a false sense of security which facilitates opportunistic crimes, and that emergency response times to crime calls are slowed by locked gates and security codes (Atkinson *et al.* 2003).

Unlike their American counterparts, very few English private sector gated communities are marketed as providing security from crime (Blandy 2006a). It seems that English purchasers have complex motivations including prestige, convenience and maintenance of property values (Blandy and Lister 2005). Collective efficacy amongst gated community residents is by no means guaranteed, as most residents do not consciously choose a self-governing community (*ibid.*). Although social homogeneity results from the high property values, community life varies widely between gated developments, with some residents reporting genuine neighbourliness and frequent social gatherings while others complained about the lack of community spirit (Atkinson *et al.* 2003). Many gated community residents were also dissatisfied with the legal framework, either wanting more effective sanctions for breaches of covenant or expressing resentment that officious fellow-residents ran the development with 'a rod of iron' (*ibid.*: 30). The legal boundary consisting of collective private property and pre-determined leasehold covenants is therefore not an effective substitute for informally negotiated neighbourhood social norms and sanctions, and in many gated sites has little inclusionary effect.

Gating for lower income owner-occupiers in mixed-tenure neighbourhoods

Physical boundaries in less affluent neighbourhoods may result from developers filling a market niche, from top-down policy or from residents' bottom-up demand, and sometimes from these different drivers in combination.

A small number of low-cost owner-occupied gated communities are situated in deprived areas in the UK, surrounded by rented housing. Some are created when the residents of small private developments, typically with one access road and clear boundaries, apply to their local authority for planning permission to install a fence and gates. Grants are available from the government's Neighbourhood and Home Watch fund to defray residents' costs. Other low-cost owner-occupied gated communities are built by developers, one of whom represented the attitude of marginal owner-occupiers as: 'yes, I will buy on the edge of a council estate or an area of deprivation, but I will want a six foot high wall' (Blandy 2006b: 250). Behind the gates, most residents install additional security measures in their properties but remain fearful of their tenant neighbours (Manzi and Smith-Bowers 2005). There is little evidence that this type of gated community enhances collective efficacy; perhaps at best it produces a 'destructive, negative cohesion. . .[based on] a nervous determination to exclude people seen as outsiders' (Urban Design Alliance 2003, para. 2).

Another type of bounded space in areas of lower-income owner-occupation is created by 'alley-gating', a physical crime prevention technique to provide greater security (Beckford and Cogan, undated). It involves gating off both ends of alleys, the lanes which run along the back of a row of houses, and has been funded and encouraged by national government (Home Office 2006) and promoted by most UK local authorities. Many studies (most recently Haywood *et al.* 2009) have confirmed that alley-gating is effective in reducing (displacing) crime and disorder, and lessening residents' anxiety. Online council guidance about alley-gating almost invariably refers to 'encouraging community spirit by giving a sense of ownership of the alleys', or uses very similar wording to emphasise the link between physical target-hardening and community empowerment.

However, little attention has been paid to the legal aspects of alley-gating. Most alleys are in private ownership, shared between the houses which back onto them, so before gating takes place consent is required from all with a legal right of private access. A 2003 survey established that six of fifteen New Deal for Community programmes[5] had used alley-gating; however, although residents were keen to have their alleys blocked off they were reluctant to pay for the upkeep of this newly privatised collective space (Blandy *et al.* 2004). A case study in one local

---

[5] From 1998 onwards the New Deal for Communities programme targeted 10-year funding at 39 of England's most deprived areas of around 1,000 residents each, around which geographical boundaries were carefully drawn.

authority area found that sixty alley-gating projects had generally improved feelings of ownership, and confidence to confront outsiders. Problems of crime and disorder had been displaced; one resident said of drug dealing that alley-gating had 'squeezed it out of the area'. But in order to achieve their aim of creating so many physical boundaries, the local council weakened the legal boundaries by abandoning their initial requirement of gaining support from at least 75 per cent of the owners whose properties adjoined the alley. Consequently, some residents failed to obey the rules about use of the enclosed collective private space; they left gates open, making the physical boundaries less effective and causing disputes between owners (*ibid.*). The imperative to create physical boundaries to exclude criminals and troublemakers has led to councils tolerating imperfect responsibilisation, which undermines the inclusionary effect of alley-gating.

Retro-fitting of fences and gates to social rented housing estates

The links between gating and governance are yet more obvious in the third type of gating to be considered here, the enclosure of council-owned housing estates. For many years now in North America, 'public housing projects [have used] security guards, gates, and fences to keep out drug dealing, prostitution, and drive-by shootings and regain control of their shared territory' (Blakely and Snyder 1997: 100). There has been a transatlantic drift of this trend to retro-gate rented neighbourhoods, from the USA to other countries including France (Levan 2005). Blakely and Snyder (1997: 102) cite *Washington Post* articles from 1992 of a housing project where local 'government, police and neighbourhood residents are banding together' in the fight against crime. Tenants were initially opposed to fences and gates, but six months later appreciated the reduction in drug dealing and vandalism. Analysis of the 2001 American Housing Survey shows that tenants are now nearly 2.5 times more likely than owners to live in gated communities (Sanchez *et al.* 2005), however these data do not differentiate private tenants from those renting 'in public housing projects, which often have walled and gated design elements' (*ibid.*: 285).

   In the UK, deprived social rented estates often correspond with crime hot spots where various SCP tools including target-hardening initiatives, neighbourhood wardens, concierge schemes and CCTV are already installed. The CPTED crime prevention agenda also incorporates local empowerment and responsibilisation to enhance collective efficacy, as outlined previously. It is hardly surprising that David Blunkett, then Home Secretary, suggested that gating deprived areas would 'make available to the many what is currently available to the few', emphasising that the collective nature of resident self-management leads to identification with the neighbourhood and helps to engage 'people in making decisions, and to reinforce the message that they are part of the solution' (Blunkett 2004). Ron Clarke, formerly head of research at the Home Office and 'the person most closely associated with the development of SCP' (Garland 2000: 9), holds very similar views. Now writing from the USA, Clarke accepts 'possible harms in limiting public access and freedom of movement', but asserts that gated communities

> are not merely for the rich. . .[i]f their development has been encouraged at all by situational prevention, this is in poorer. . .neighbourhoods [where] their benefits may be most obvious and direct. They may strengthen community bonds rather than weaken them, and they might enhance rather than impede informal controls. [Clarke 2000: 103]

Clearly, gated boundaries align well with SCP and CPTED principles. They are also attractive to residents of the areas most likely to suffer from crime and disorder, who understandably hope that physical enclosure will provide security. British tenants and those on lower incomes express more enthusiasm for gated communities than do owners and the better off (Live Strategy 2002). There are no data on how many social rented housing estates have been retro-gated in the UK, but the practice is not widespread so far. The London Borough of Camden, used here as a case study, was an early adopter of retro-gating. In the 1990s tenants of Camden's Cromer Street estate, just south of King's Cross station, were suffering from high crime rates. Following consultation with residents, funding was made available to create gated entrances and to enclose the space between the blocks of flats, leaving one public through-route during daylight hours. Once gates were installed on the estate, tenants were issued with electronic fobs[6] and the tenancy agreement was altered to make giving away the fob a breach of tenancy enforceable through eviction. Disorder and crime dramatically decreased; Cromer Street became a highly sought-after place to live and a national example of good practice (ODPM/Home Office, 2004: 54–5, Annex 1).

Residents (both tenants and long leaseholders) of the London Borough of Camden's other housing estates also look to the Cromer Street

---

[6] A fob is like an electronic car key, programmed for each resident to open the locks necessary to reach their own flat.

estate as a model. Area Forum meeting minutes from various Camden neighbourhoods include frequent requests by residents for fences and gates. Recently, a resident was reported as saying 'gated communities are our only hope', causing the councillor chairing the Local Area Forum to reflect that 'I always believed from the beginning that we shouldn't have people in a prison, basically gated off or behind a fence, but over time I have changed my mind' (Keilthy 2007).

The process which has resulted in the enclosure of several Camden estates repays attention. Undoubtedly a former crime prevention design adviser for Camden, Calvin Beckford,[7] was influential in ensuring that Camden followed Secured by Design guidance; this suggests that regeneration of estates 'provides an opportunity to remove or alter the features of a development that have contributed to crime and anti-social behaviour' (ACPO/CPI 2004b: 3). However, Camden Planning Department's own general guidance states that even where evidence of antisocial behaviour and crime are provided, a gating proposal will be turned down if it would 'have an adverse impact on accessibility [or] on the cohesion and security of the local environment by creating separate residential areas' (London Borough of Camden 2006, para. 16.12). Despite this policy, Camden has apparently readily granted itself planning permission to fence off its own housing estates. When interviewed recently, a current Camden crime prevention design advisor described Camden Housing Department as 'crazy about fencing and gating', which he considers promotes a vicious cycle of displacement of crime and antisocial behaviour, causing residents of nearby ungated estates to demand physically secure boundaries.

Interviews were carried out with residents of the 'Wellspring' estate[8] which was gated in 2006–7. This council-owned estate of 200 flats and houses is not far to the north of the Cromer Street estate. Camden council granted itself planning permission to gate Wellspring in 2004, as a direct result of rising crime and residents' complaints about anti-social behaviour. As Camden housing estates were sequentially retrogated, crime and disorder were excluded from each in turn and moved on to the nearest ungated area:

> I think the worst period was between 2003–05 when they [Camden Council] were closing up all the other estates. All the undesirables came

---

[7] Beckford now works for ACPO Crime Prevention Initiatives Ltd and is a leading supporter of SCP in general and of gating in particular. He also wrote the alley-gating guide previously referred to (Beckford and Cogan, undated).

[8] A pseudonym has been used to preserve anonymity.

here, anything from teenagers with ASBOs to drug takers, you know, burglars and all sorts. It wasn't just displacing – it was *magnifying* the problem. [Interview with leaseholder]

Wellspring residents were vociferous in demanding a secure boundary but additional internal fencing was imposed on them, which now divides the estate into five separate zones, designed to prevent 'inappropriate loitering [and] escape routes used by criminals' (ACPO/CPI 2004b: 3). One tenant said in interview, 'I don't think any of the tenants wanted that at all. They've made it so complicated, it's ridiculous.' Each section of the estate is gated and accessible only to residents of that particular zone. This has reduced informal social contact by making it impossible to walk through the estate, and many long-standing tenants are nostalgic for the community that they feel has thereby been lost. Leasehold owners, who had to contribute towards the cost, now query whether it was worth it. Some residents, both tenants and leasehold owners, consider that problems of crime and disorder have decreased because 'outsiders' are now excluded; others disagree, blaming the council's tenancy allocation system which must by law give priority to homeless and vulnerable people, who allegedly lose their key fobs and allow 'outsiders' to enter.

The internal boundaries at Wellspring seem to have diminished collective efficacy and social cohesion, alongside the desired exclusionary effect. Ironically, the estate is now doubly bounded as it is currently included in a one-mile square dispersal area under the Anti-social Behaviour Act 2003. These exclusionary boundaries have much in common. Smaller dispersal zones focused on a particular hot spot are more likely to result in displacement to a wider area, just as gating one Camden estate had a domino effect on others. Research has shown that 'the need to consult can create pressures to expand the size and focus of dispersal zones' (Crawford and Lister 2007: 30); similarly, residents want their estate protected by a dispersal zone, just as they demand that their estate be retro-gated.

Another Camden housing estate, 'Kelvindene',[9] provides a contrast with Wellspring; it is smaller and located in an area with higher property values. The design of the first enclosure installed there was very unpopular with the residents who had requested it. They felt 'like you're being sectioned off. . .as social outcasts' (interview with tenant). That gate broke soon after its installation and was removed. Further planning

[9] A pseudonym has been used to preserve anonymity.

permission was granted in 2003, and an attractive internal courtyard was created by installing railings and an electronic gate. Restricting access to those who live in Kelvindene has made tenants and leasehold owners feel more secure, and added to their 'community spirit' and sense of 'ownership' of the space enclosed by the fence and buildings. Residents now have 'a sense of pride that, you know, the estate looks better, it is our space because it's quite defined by that gate', said one tenant in interview.

This more successful outcome confirms the view of an experienced landscape architect and urban designer who has worked extensively on such schemes: that about sixty dwellings is the maximum effective size, but this cannot be achieved by artificially dividing up an existing community, as at Wellspring. Although boundary techniques of crime prevention may be demanded by residents of council-owned housing estates, the type of enclosure or a particular design can also be imposed top-down against their resistance, strongly indicating that community participation and empowerment are ultimately less important than containment and exclusion.

The implications of boundaries in crime prevention

This discussion of gating as a form of boundary has highlighted a policy shift in urban governance and crime prevention. Although spatial governmentality is by no means a new phenomenon, in its current form it 'is generally described as a system that provides safety for those who can afford it while abandoning the poor to unregulated public spaces' (Merry 2001: 17). This chapter has argued that, on the contrary, the state is deeply concerned with the regulation of residential areas, and in particular deprived neighbourhoods. Dealing with crime and disorder and, perhaps even more importantly, addressing fear of crime and perceptions of insecurity remain key tasks for government. The technology to collect and manipulate wide-ranging local data enables the state to draw boundaries around targeted areas, to devise specific policies and to work in partnership with other agencies and residents there. Legal and physical boundaries facilitate the governance of differentiated populations and spaces, whether by the state or by responsibilised residents. The three types of gating examined in this chapter illustrate how and why separate nomospheres are created, and now their implications are considered.

Private gated communities offer their residents protective boundaries against a range of problems, both real and imagined. The state's planning development control of these sites is compromised by contradictory guidance; SCP encourages boundaries, while conventional planning principles favour permeability. The resulting exclusionary spaces do not necessarily represent informed choice by purchasers, as the physical and legal boundaries are marketed by developers in an indivisible package. Self-managed neighbourhoods do not inevitably increase collective efficacy or harmony among residents. Further, individual owners in gated communities may 'find to their dismay that the safer they feel inside the enclosure, the less familiar and more threatening appears the wilderness outside, and more and more courage is needed to venture past the armed guards and beyond the reach of the electronic surveillance network' (Bauman 2001: 117). An American anthropological study has confirmed that children growing up in gated enclaves show an exaggerated fear of others and are likely to demand gated housing themselves in the future (Low 2003).

In less affluent residential areas top-down policy concerns add to the drive for boundary creation. Potentially problematic areas of owner-occupation are highlighted through data, and designated for regeneration through community empowerment and by alley-gating. Here the legal and physical boundaries do not always align, so the effect on community cohesion is uncertain. The bottom-up pressure for safe enclosures from residents in council-owned estates is fed by the existence of private gated neighbourhoods as well as retro-gated estates like Cromer Street in the London Borough of Camden. The current emphasis on community involvement in crime prevention leaves planning authorities with little choice but to accede to the demands for gating of social rented housing estates, which in any event would be the logical outcome of SCP. Some retro-gating, or a particularly intrusive form of it as in the Wellspring estate, has been imposed on deprived neighbourhoods. This type of boundary is not based on the partnership paradigm, but is a new form of governmentality targeted at the poor, now segregated into ghettoised spaces (Stenson 2001).

Invisible, data-driven policy boundaries mark out a different type of nomosphere for special attention in terms of more funding and more regulation. Under conditions of late modernity, the 'most visible crime control strategies may work by expulsion and exclusion, but they are accompanied by patient, ongoing, low-key efforts to build up the internal controls of neighbourhoods and to encourage communities to police themselves' (Garland 2001: 17), using techniques based on self-governance through the use of quasi-contracts. Both types of strategy, exclusionary and inclusionary through responsibilisation, require boundaries. Legal means – evictions, injunctions, ASBOs and dispersal orders – are used to exclude criminals and troublemakers, sometimes in conjunction with retro-gating and alley-gating. Demands for ever-larger dispersal areas reflect anxiety about the displacement of crime and antisocial behaviour, echoed by the clamour by residents for retro-gating of social rented estates.

The boundary obsession of late modernity reveals itself in signs and symbols which mark otherwise invisible legal and policy boundaries. Newman (1973) was concerned with what image and milieu conveyed about a particular area, anticipating the broken-windows thesis (Wilson and Kelling 1982) which has had such a pervasive influence in crime prevention stategies. Both SCP and CPTED principles contend that effective boundary-marking reduces crime and disorder. Where there is no physical boundary, visible notices have proliferated in UK residential areas over recent years. Some signs indicate boundaries of private ownership: 'Residents Only', 'Trespassers will be prosecuted', 'Private Road'; while 'Neighbourhood Watch Area' signs are displayed to indicate responsibilised residents co-operating to deter criminals. However, this symbolic boundary-marking can have an ambiguous or contrary effect. CCTV installation or notices pinned to lampposts listing all the local roads included in a dispersal area may suggest a neighbourhood that needs top-down exclusionary governance. The same kind of physical boundary, for example a tall surrounding fence, may symbolise an undesirable high-crime area, or alternatively a prestigious and exclusive gated community. It has become part of the regeneration task to 're-image' stigmatised council estates, symbolically bounded by their recognisable architectural style and physical layout (Hastings and Dean 2003). However, retro-gating may give an estate a poor image. This was the opinion of many Wellspring residents, where the offer of extensive CCTV for the estate had been rejected because it conveyed the message that 'we walk out the front door terrified for our own personal safety' (interview with leaseholder).

The spread of gated residential developments brings closer a genuinely 'capsularised society' as more, and less-penetrable, boundaries are created between different areas and between social groups (de Cauter 2004). For residents of deprived areas, the insertion of an affluent gated community represents an increased risk of crime (Hope 2001). There is little connection between these different populations except for fear and resentment: a London tenant felt that the physical boundary of the nearby wealthy gated community amounted to 'rubbing our noses in it' (Atkinson *et al.* 2003: 31). This effect of boundaries is also apparent where low-cost homeownership, fortified to reassure the purchasers, is established in the midst of social rented surroundings. But even without a physical boundary, nomospheres risk generating bitterness around their edges. For example, residents just outside the policy boundary of an area-based initiative feel unfairly excluded when facilities and housing are upgraded across the road.

In addition to physical and data-driven boundaries, this chapter has underlined how law has been used, not necessarily to blur the distinction between public and private, but to create and strengthen boundaries. A causal connection between legal boundaries and greater community cohesion has yet to be established but the exclusionary power of law has been continuously extended in the UK, as instanced by the development of boundary techniques in less-affluent areas of owner-occupation. Following evidence of the success of alley-gating, the Countryside and Rights of Way Act 2000 gave local authorities powers to close and gate alleyways (including public rights of way) if, following local consultation, it was deemed necessary to prevent crime. Authorities then complained that this process was expensive and resource-intensive. Provisions in the subsequent Clean Neighbourhoods and Environment Act 2005 enable councils to gate a public right of way, overriding any objections, providing the area suffers from *either* crime *or* antisocial behaviour. Thus legal boundaries may be imposed top-down on the basis of expert assessment of local community interests. The control of crime and antisocial behaviour appears to outweigh concerns about privatising public space.

The trends typical of late modernity, including the responsibilisation of individuals and communities, partnership working, target-hardening and exclusion, amassing the information to categorise residential areas (undertaken by commercial organisations as well as by the state and associated agencies), have resulted in boundary creation of varying kinds. Boundaries convey inclusionary and exclusionary force and result from both top-down and bottom-up pressures. Perhaps the last word should go to Oscar Newman who, twenty years on, felt that his theories of defensible space had been misused by SCP. He regretted that 'new developments in the distant suburbs have taken to locking themselves up into gated communities, almost universally' (Newman 1995: 155). The boundaries spectrum, of which gating in all its forms is only one version, can be seen in the current crime prevention strategies, private housing developments, and wider social policies which characterise late modernity.

References

Allen, R. (1999) 'Is what works what counts? The role of evidence-based crime reduction in policy and practice', *Safer Society*, 2, 21–3.

Association of Chief Police Officers/Crime Prevention Initiatives Limited (2004a) *Secured by Design Principles*, www.securedbydesign.com/pdfs/SBD-principles.pdf.

(2004b) *Secured by Design Refurbishments*, www.securedbydesign.com/pdfs/refurbishments.pdf.

Association of Chief Police Officers/Secured by Design (2009) *Secured by Design New Homes*, www.securedbydesign.com/pdfs/newHomes2009.pdf.

Atkinson, R. and Blandy, S. (2007) 'Panic rooms: the rise of defensive home-ownership', *Housing Studies*, 22, 443–58.

Atkinson, R., Blandy, S., Flint, J. and Lister, D. (2003) *Gated Communities in England*, London: Office of the Deputy Prime Minister.

Bauman, Z. (2001) *Community: Seeking Safety in an Insecure World*, Cambridge: Polity.

Beck, U. (1992) *Risk Society: Towards a New Modernity*, London: Sage.

Beckford, C. and Cogan, P. (undated) *The Alleygater's Guide to gating alleys*, http://crimereduction.homeoffice.gov.uk/gating.pdf.

Blakely, E. J. and Snyder, M. G. (1997) *Fortress America*, Washington DC, Brookings Institute and Lincoln Institute of Land Policy.

Blandy, S. (2006a) 'Gated communities in England: historical perspectives and current developments', *GeoJournal*, 66, 15–26.

(2006b) 'Gated communities: a response to, or remedy for, anti-social behaviour?' in J. Flint (ed), *Housing, Urban Governance and Anti-social Behaviour: Perspectives, Policies and Practice*, Bristol: Policy Press, pp. 239–55.

Blandy, S. and Lister, D. (2005) 'Gated communities: (ne)gating community development?', *Housing Studies*, 20, 287–301.

Blandy, S. and Parsons, D. (2004) 'Gated communities in England: rules and rhetoric of urban planning', *Geographica Helvetica*, 58, 314–24.

Blandy, S., Green, S. and McCoulough, E. (2004) *Building Boundaries in NDC areas*, London: Neighbourhood Renewal Unit, Office of the Deputy Prime Minister.

Blomley, N. K. (1994) *Law, Space and the Geographies of Power*, New York: Guilford Press.

(2005) 'Flowers in the bathtub: boundary crossings at the public-private divide', *Geoforum*, 36, 281–96.

Blunkett, D. (2004) *Decentralising Government: Choice, Communities and the Role of Local Authorities*, Speech to New Local Network annual conference, 22 January 2004, www.nlgn.org.uk/public/2004/from-empire-to-community-the-challenge-for-21st-century-governance/.

Cauter, L. de (2004) *The Capsular Civilisation: On the City in the Age of Fear*, Rotterdam: NAi Publisher.

Clarke, R. V. (2000) 'Situational prevention, criminology and social values' in A. von Hirsch, D. Garland, and A. Wakefield (eds.), *Ethical and Social Perspectives on Situational Crime Prevention*, Oxford: Hart, pp. 97–112.

Cohen, S. (1985) *Visions of Social Control*, Cambridge: Polity.

Cowan, D. and McDermont, M. (2006) *Regulating Social Housing: Governing Decline*, Abingdon: Routledge.

Cozens, P. M., Saville, G. and Hillier, D. (2005) 'Crime prevention through environmental design (CPTED): a review and modern bibliography', *Journal of Property Management*, 23, 328–56.

Crawford, A. (1998) *Crime Prevention and Community Safety*, London: Longman.
    (2003) 'Contractual governance of deviant behaviour', *Journal of Law and Society*, 30, 479–505.

Crawford, A. and Lister, S. (2007) *The Use and Impact of Dispersal Orders: Sticking Plasters and Wake-up Calls*, Bristol: Policy Press.

Dean, M. (1999) *Governmentality: Power and Rule in Modern Society*, London: Sage.

Delaney, D. (2004) 'Tracing displacements: or evictions in the nomosphere', *Environment and Planning D: Society and Space*, 22, 847–60.

Delaney, D., Ford, R. T. and Blomley, N. (2001) 'Preface: where is law?' in N. Blomley, D. Delaney and R. T. Ford (eds.), *The Legal Geographies Reader*, Oxford: Blackwell, pp. xiii–xxii.

Department of Communities and Local Government (2005) *Planning Policy Statement 1 (PPS 1) Delivering Sustainable Development*, London: DCLG.
  (2006a) *Planning Policy Statement 3 (PPS3) Housing*, London: DCLG.
  (2006b) *Respect and Housing Management: Using Good Neighbour Agreements*, Housing Research Summary No. 226, London: DCLG.
  (2008) *Communities in Control: Real People, Real Power*, White Paper Cm. 7427, London: DCLG.

Department of the Environment, Transport and the Regions, with the Commission for Architecture and the Built Environment (DETR CABE) (2000) *By Design: Urban Design in the Planning System: Towards Better Practice*, London: DCLG.

Ellison, N. and Burrows, R. (2007) 'New spaces of (dis)engagement? Social politics, urban technologies and the rezoning of the city', *Housing Studies*, 22, 295–312.

Flint, J. (2006) (ed.) *Housing, Urban Governance and Anti-Social Behaviour: Perspectives, Policy and Practice*, Bristol: The Policy Press.

Garland, D. (2000) 'Ideas, institutions and situational crime prevention' in A. von Hirsch, D. Garland and A. Wakefield (eds.), *Ethical and Social Perspectives on Situational Crime Prevention*, Oxford: Hart, pp. 1–16.

(2001) *The Culture of Control: Crime and Social Order in Contemporary Society*, Oxford: Oxford University Press.

Giddens, A. (1991) *Modernity and Self Identity: Self and Society in the Late Modern Age*, Cambridge: Polity.

Hastings, A. and Dean, J. (2003) 'Challenging images: tackling stigma through estate regeneration', *Policy & Politics*, 31(2), 171–84.

Haywood, J., Kautt, P., Whitaker, A. (2009) 'The effects of "alley-gating" in an English town', *European Journal of Criminology*, 6(4), 361–81.

Healey, P. (1996) 'The communicative turn in planning theory and its implications for spatial strategy formations', *Environment and Planning B: Planning and Design*, 23(2), 217–34.

Holder, J. and Harrison, C. (2003) (eds.) *Law and Geography*, Current Legal Issues, vol. 5, Oxford: Oxford University Press.

Home Office (2006) *Operation Gate It*, London: Home Office.

Hope, T. (2001) 'Crime victimisation and inequality in risk society' in R. Matthews and J. Pitts (eds.), *Crime, Disorder and Community Safety: A New Agenda?*, London: Routledge, pp. 13–218.

Hughes, G. (2004) 'Straddling adaptation and denial: crime and disorder reduction partnerships in England and Wales', *Cambrian Law Review*, 35, 1–22.

Keilthy, P. (2007) 'We need fences and gates to bar gangs, estate pleads', *Camden New Journal*, 8 November 2007, www.thecnj.com/camden/2007/110807/news110807_21.html.

Kitchen, T. (2002) 'Crime prevention and the British planning system: new responsibilities and older challenges', *Planning Theory and Practice*, 3, 155–72.

Lawless, P. (2006) 'Area-based urban interventions: rationale and outcomes: the new deal for communities programme in England', *Urban Studies*, 43(11), 1991–2011.

Levan, V. (2005) 'Making public housing safer in France: the gentle rise of situational crime prevention?', *Champ Penal*, http://champpenal.revues.org/65.

Live Strategy (2002) *Telephone Survey into Attitudes Towards Gated Communities in England, for the Royal Institute of Chartered Surveyors* (Unpublished data, on file with author).

London Borough of Camden (2006) *Camden Planning Guidance December 2006*, www.camden.gov.uk/ccm/cms-service/stream/asset/?asset_id=563105.

Low, S. (2003) *Behind the Gates: Life, Security and the Pursuit of Happiness in Fortress America*, London: Routledge.

Lupton, R. (2003) *Neighbourhood Effects: Can We Measure Them and Does It Matter?* CASE paper 73, London: Centre for the Analysis of Social Exclusion, London School of Economics.

McKenzie, E. (1994) *Privatopia: Homeowner Associations and the Rise of Residential Private Government*, New Haven, CT: Yale University Press.

Manzi, T. and Smith-Bowers, B. (2005) 'Gated communities as club goods: segregation or social cohesion?', *Housing Studies*, 20, 345–59.

Matthews, R. (2002) 'Crime and control in late modernity: review essay', *Theoretical Criminology*, 6(2), 217–26.

Merry, S. E. (2001) 'Spatial governmentality and the new urban social order: controlling gender violence through law', *American Anthropologist*, 103(1), 16–29.

Newman, O. (1973) *Defensible Space: Crime Prevention Through Urban Design*, New York: Macmillan.

  (1995) 'Defensible space: a new physical planning tool for urban revitalisation', *Journal of the American Planning Association*, 61, 149–55.

Office of the Deputy Prime Minister (2003) *Sustainable Communities: Building for the Future*, London: HMSO.

  (2004) *Safer Places: The Planning System and Crime Prevention*, London: HMSO.

  (2005) *Citizen Engagement and Public Services: Why Neighbourhoods Matter*, London: HMSO.

O'Malley, P. (1999) 'Governmentality and the risk society', *Economy and Society*, 28, 138–48.

Perry, R. W. (2000) 'Governmentalities in city-scapes', *Political and Legal Anthropology Review*, 23(2), 65–72.

Putnam, R. D. (2000) *Bowling Alone: The Collapse and Revival of American Community*, New York: Simon and Schuster.

Reich, C. (1964) 'The new property', *Yale Law Journal*, 73, 733–87.

Rose, N. (1994) 'Expertise and the government of conduct', *Studies in Law, Politics and Society*, 14, 359–97.

  (1996) 'The death of the social? Re-figuring the territory of government', *Economy and Society*, 25(3), 327–56.

  (2000) 'Government and control', *British Journal of Criminology*, 40, 321–39.

Sampson, R. and Raudenbush, S. (1999) 'Systematic observation of public spaces: a new look at disorder in urban neighbourhoods', *American Journal of Sociology*, 105, 603–51.

Sanchez, T. W., Lang, R. E. and Dhavale, D. (2005) 'Security versus Status? A first look at the census's gated community data', *Journal of Planning Education and Research*, 24, 281–91.

Saunders, P. (1990) *A Nation of Home Owners*, London: Unwin and Hyman.

Simester, A. and von Hirsch, A. P. (2006) 'Regulating offensive conduct through two-step prohibitions' in A. P. von Hirsch and A. Simester (eds.), *Incivilities: Regulating Offensive Behaviour*, Oxford: Hart, pp. 173–95.

Simon, J. (2007) *Governing through Crime: How the War on Crime Transformed American Democracy and Created a Culture of Fear*, Oxford: Oxford University Press.

Social Exclusion Unit (1998) *Bringing Britain Together: A National Strategy for Neighbourhood Renewal*, London: SEU.

Stenson, K. (2001) 'The new politics of crime control' in K. Stenson and R. R. Sullivan (eds.), *Crime, Risk and Justice: The Politics of Crime Control in Liberal Democracies*, Cullompton: Willan, pp. 15–28.

Sutton, A., Cherney, A. and White, R. (2008) *Crime Prevention: Principles, Perspectives and Practices*, Cambridge: Cambridge University Press.

Urban Design Alliance (2003) *Design for Cohesive Communities, Written Evidence Memorandum to the Select Committee on ODPM, Session 2002–3*, London: HMSO.

Valverde, M. (1996) '"Despotism" and ethical liberal governance', *Economy and Society*, 25(3), 357–72.

Wilson, J. Q. and Kelling, G. L. (1982) 'Broken windows', *Atlantic Monthly*, March, 29–38.

Wilson Doenges, G. (2000) 'An explanation of sense of community and fear of crime in gated communities', *Environment and Behaviour*, 32(5), 597–611.

Wilton, R. D. (1998) 'The constitution of difference: space and psyche in landscapes of exclusion', *GeoForum*, 29, 173–85.

Wood, M. (2004) *Perceptions and Experiences of Antisocial Behaviour*, London: Home Office.

Young, J. (1999) *The Exclusive Society: Social Exclusion, Crime and Difference in Late Modernity*, London: Sage.

21

French perspectives on threats to peace and local social order

SOPHIE BODY-GENDROT

What has been learned from almost three decades of urban violence in disadvantaged neighbourhoods? The forms of violence conducted by male youths in such areas are frequently conveyed by the media. Places and potentially violent actors are both perceived as risks. Risks rather than feelings of insecurity are what governments want to anticipate. The questions that our era has to confront were hardly confronted before. The political manipulation of risk, threat and danger linked to unknown youths is made easier when mainstream societies lack markers and the necessary distance to deconstruct the fears impacting on their daily life. All over Europe, since 9/11, a noticeable change has been observed among national and local governments advocating principles of precaution and strict policies of identification, surveillance and repression of 'suspects'. For instance, that the term Muslim has implicitly linked ethnic forms of violence in relegated neighbourhoods and threats of home-grown terrorism in the media rhetoric has allowed 'entrepreneurs' to benefit from such representations producing fears, from the media to the security market itself. A new regime order prevails in Europe giving legitimacy to policies of order at the expense of some people's liberties. Such regime's aims are the securisation of territories and the detection of 'suspects'. But the task being endless, urban governance is taking a leadership role on many aspects, a major one being inclusiveness as a condition of security supported by a preventative approach.

Social order and disorder are deeply intertwined. Unstable city spaces emerge, become sites of conflict and mutate. For residents and space users, threats to public tranquillity in our current context of urban change and global challenges are numerous. What do we mean by threats? What comes to mind are terrorist threats (due to the fascination and rejection that large cities provoke among radical activists), economic insecurity along with an increase of inequalities, class and racial conflicts, fear of crime and lack of bearings (coming from powerlessness and the disarticulation of societies). In other words, such perceptions threaten the commonalities on which the ideal of a city is based.

1 Introduction

The systemic character of violence erupting from one large city after the other, in one form or another cannot be overlooked. This chapter intends to tackle the lack of anticipation for 'what happens' in cities: accidents, catastrophes, collective violence, increasing the perception that 'nothing works'. The questions that our era has to confront were indeed not confronted before, and while solutions seem familiar, the questions are not. For instance, what resources have such global cities to deal with the major risks and threats in our current times of global uncertainty? How do they transmit a sense of order and protection to their residents and users as well as to the hyper-mobile actors on whom they increasingly depend? What co-ordination of actions should be favoured and what level of decision-making? How comprehensive should they be? These are some questions that come to mind when one reflects on the dialectics of safety/unsafety, order/disorder, violence/conflicts, etc. Pondering over twenty-six years of urban unrest in France, this chapter examines the profiles of the producers of a rhetoric of threats and the contexts in which they operate; it analyses then the consequences – that is, the diversity of responses and of scales – before reasserting the role that cities can play in mobilising specific resources when confronted by global threats. My material comes from interviews with local actors in the Parisian Region and in metropolises of the North and the South regions within the frame of conferences organised by the Urban Age Programme at the London School of Economics.[1] It is also provided by hearings I conduct every month as a member of the French National Commission on the Ethics of Security (a Civilian/Law Enforcers Review Board, CNDS).[2]

---

[1] This chapter builds partly on earlier publications (Body-Gendrot 2008a; 2008b).

[2] The CNDS, a 13-member commission, can only be summoned by citizens via a parliamentary member or institutions (e.g. the Children's Defence ombudsman). Currently, the number of cases examined each year averages 170. While the commission has no power to redress harm, it has investigative and hearing powers and it issues statements and recommendations, thus giving visibility to cases of police, border patrols or prison guards' misconducts (such as useless body searches or deliberately tight handcuffing). However, opposition by conservative groups and entrenched interests to CNDS as a counter-power is so strong that CNDS will disappear in 2011.

2 A quarter-century of urban unrest in France

Each society constructs the threats it will confront in a specific manner. The association of male youths and urban threats in current representations is not a completely new phenomenon in France. Since the 1830s, French society has labelled its working-class youngsters 'dangerous classes', in contrast with the hinterland, where closed societies were perceived as more easily exerting control over their youths (Body-Gendrot 2005a). The novels by Honoré de Balzac or by Eugene Sue mention 'murder streets' (*rues assassines*) that were avoided and the proximity of crime and of police stations and prisons. The police were then asked to stop petty delinquents who behaved as if they owned a particular street or a neighbourhood yet, as is currently the case, they hesitated to venture in rough spots. As for justice, the Criminal Code of 1791 ordered that minors under sixteen who had committed a serious crime be locked up and educated until they seemed fit for social reinsertion. The subsequent code of 1810 does not mention a specific treatment for juvenile delinquents. Currently, the 1945 edict, already amended numerous times, placing education before sanction for juveniles, is once more being amended by the conservative government. As for public opinion, *bands of youths*[3] became visible at the beginning of the twentieth century when journalists and novelists evoked *Apaches* perceived as bad boys threatening the order of bourgeois society (Perrot 1979). Then again after the Second World War, *zazous* (zannies) were described as transgressing mainstream order. In the 1950s, *blousons noirs* (black-leather jackets) were also working class and marginalised youngsters, weakly organised, and unstable at times of upheaval – the country becoming more urbanised and socially emancipated. What is novel, then, is the large interest of the media for the ethnicisation and the criminalisation of a minority of youth whose parents or grandparents frequently lived in French former colonies and who are perceived as 'trouble-makers', for justified or unjustified reasons.

What occurred in France during the 1980s and 1990s is related to the progressive autonomy of the issue of a juvenile delinquency formerly linked to immigration.[4] In 1981, the media interpreted the disorders caused by youths in the public housing estates of the banlieue of Lyon, Les Minguettes, as a deficiency in immigrant families' social integration.

---

[3] French researchers, the media, and politicians avoid the term *gang* to differentiate the phenomenon from the American one.

[4] This part draws on Body-Gendrot (2005b).

During those years, dozens of immigrant youths were killed by the police or by exasperated homeowners and marches emanating from the Lyon region, yet started in Marseille, denounced police abuse and racism. They reinforced the links between the banlieue/immigration/youth/violence in the public mind. The French probably understood then that immigrant families were here to stay and that integrating (i.e. assimilating) them in the mainstream would take longer than with prior waves of immigration (frequently Catholic).

The issue of space and of public housing is of major importance in the study of representations. After Les Minguettes (Lyon) in the summer of 1981, other disorders followed in the high-risk zones, usually after real or alleged police misconduct. They attracted more and more media coverage: Vaulx en Velin (Lyon) in October 1990, Montfermeil, Sartrouville, Trappes in the Parisian region, as well as Grenoble at the beginning of the 1990s, Le Mirail (Toulouse) in 1998, then in the Parisian region again, at Grigny (Paris) in 2000, Clichy sous bois the starting point of three weeks of disorders in 2005 and Villiers-le-Bel in 2007.

According to Y.-L. Sapoval, the Head of the *Délégation interministérielle à la ville*, at a debriefing session on the 2005 disorders, juvenile delinquency has grown by 80 per cent in ten years in France (18 December 2006). Whether they are presented as male youths contending with police forces over perceived abuse or as delinquents threatening community life in shared public spaces, those actually involved in the local and circumscribed disorders are a minority of youths. According to a Senate report of 2004, 5 per cent of repeat juvenile offenders account for between 60 and 85 per cent of all offences. The heavily urbanised and industrialised Parisian, Lyon and Marseille regions – on the whole, fourteen out of ninety-six *départements* in metropolitan France – record more offences than the rest of the country. The turfs controlled by the dealers are not quieter than others. The report shows that youths are also more frequently victimised than senior citizens (Sénat 2001–2002).

What is of interest here is the collective and gendered character of urban violence and the confrontation with the symbols of state power.[5] Male youths from one housing estate fighting with youths from another for obscure reasons, most often related to drug or other trafficking, band together as soon as the police arrive. It is not difficult for them to

---

[5] The use of the term 'urban violence' became popular after a section of the French police 'City and Suburbs' was created at the end of the 1980s focusing on issues of contention opposing marginalised youth and police forces.

outnumber police officers, due to the over-representation of youths among public housing residents in the urban sensitive zones – 31 per cent as against an average 24 per cent (Observatoire National des zones urbaines sensibles 2006: 80–2). But one should distinguish the majority of teenagers who are not offenders and who will probably go to college or be available for the labour market in the years to come; those who are petty offenders and occasionally steal and get involved in fights; those who are 'rebels' and intend to trespass whenever the opportunity is given to them and finally those who are about to make a career in organised crime and/or in terrorism (Sicot 2000; Lagrange 2000). Most 'stories' come from the media, government, police, courts, politicians and the hegemonic producers of security technologies and services and not from direct observation or victimisation.

3 Who are the producers of representations related to urban threats?

The media

The difference between our current times and previous ones comes from the revolution in modes of information and communication which have become deregulated and globalised. For centuries, the knowledge of crimes was limited to small territorial entities. Currently, simplistic and populist coverage of crime eventually generates a 'mean-world syndrome'. Images support the views of heavy watchers of TV and the users of the Internet that the world is under siege (Gerbner 1994; Body-Gendrot 2000). There is little relation between the accounts of violence in the media and the real, daily experience of those experiencing violence. Yet due to the binary modes with which reporters relate incidents, to their blurred use of words and heavy resort to identical images coming from their archives, to the entertainment provided by violence (Bok 1998) and to the stereotypes simplifying the reading of isolated events, a simplified presentation of a complex reality leads to narrations making sense for the audience (Balibar 2006). Stereotypes about Muslims are facilitated by the fact that those living in Europe, relative newcomers in segregated neighbourhoods, are not well known. Showing graffiti, scenes of vandalism and of petty delinquency contribute to the easy identification of the areas where they tend to live.

However, there is no correlation between the production of violent images and feelings of insecurity; it is not because the audience sees or reads reports on violent events that it becomes fearful. The media heighten fear of crime only when the audience is already fearful and easily identifies with the message delivered by the medium (Robert and Pottier 1997: 623). No one can deny that the positive role of the media is to report incidents, reveal those involved and the conflicts that would be ignored without them.

Two types of threats come to the forefront of the coverage of urban threats. One is linked to home-grown terrorism and associated in representations with young, male Muslims and potential suicide bombers. The other is also associated with young male Muslim offenders but focuses on the public spaces of marginalised areas in the same large cities. The two types are very different in terms of scope, intent and damages. Yet, the increasing use of the term Islam by the media and what has been made of it since 9/11 explains why the abusive amalgamation of Muslims and bogeymen in the inner cities has been so easy. By juxtaposing events threatening peace in the Middle East and urban incidents in the Western world (like demonstrations opposing young Muslims and young Jews in Western cities after the Gaza events or the number of young Muslims in Western prisons), the media bond the perceptions of threat and danger for the audience. The line dividing internal and external security becomes blurred in many people's minds giving the impression that Muslims are prone to violence and cannot be trusted. Work by Schain (2008) on Muslims and public opinion in France reveals paradoxes. On the one hand, over time, sympathy for all immigrants groups increases, yet a striking gap divides opinions towards European immigrants and North African immigrants, specifically Algerians and to a lesser extent Black Africans, and on the whole, the public opinions are not very optimistic about the ability of the latter to integrate into French society (Schain 2008: 74). On the other hand, compared with their European counterparts, the French have been more accepting of these immigrants. In 2006, 78 per cent of the French public believed that Muslims want to adopt national customs (as compared to 41 per cent of the British and 38 per cent of Germans) and for 72 per cent of them that there is no conflict between devout Muslim practice and living in modern society (as against 49 per cent and 57 per cent in Britain and Germany respectively) (Schain 2008: 20), a thought not shared by law enforcers, as will be seen below.

Political actors

That states would instrumentalise insecurity and fears in order to reinforce order is nothing new. Insecurity is linked to the history of cities. Influential authors such as Michel de Montaigne observed in his *Essays* that what we should fear most is fear itself, this irrational, unjustified, paralysing terror without a name. Thomas Hobbes, as Machiavelli, emphasised that fear springs from the illusion of a danger, sometimes exacerbated by the state. Max Weber, Alexis de Tocqueville, Hannah Arendt, among others, have problematised the state monopoly in the use of violence (or force) as dangerous (Robin 2004).

The instrumentalisation of various fears makes it easier to govern people and it can be manipulated by authorities to mobilise law-abiding citizens on public order and create a social and political consensus. Yet people in need of protection fear the arbitrary use those in power make of it. As observed by Thucydides: 'The strong do what they will, the weak endure what they must.' Some states opt to act on risks without declaring it, via the *savoir-faire* of intelligence services and specialised judges, but others regularly warn the public about active plots and publicise the security measures that they take. CCTV cameras have spread in the developed world. The UK has 4.2 million CCTV cameras, one for every fourteen people (Wykes 2009: 7). After the Leeds-based terrorists were discovered thanks to CCTV cameras, President Sarkozy, much impressed, advocated the increase of CCTVs in cities. These were active at the end of 2009.

Invoking danger, as George Bush did continuously after 9/11, allows an administration to displace worries away from questions that it is unable to answer and to refocus them on security, a regalian domain (Sunstein 2004). According to S. Hoffmann, the Bush administration regularly injected an anxiety-inducing serum into (Americans): differently coloured alerts, the Patriot Act, ethnic profiling, the amalgamation of Saddam Hussein with Al-Qa'ida:

> The purpose of these manipulations has been double: to instil hostility, bellicosity, a fervour for revenge and violent self-protection against external enemies (or 'aliens' ethnic, religious or political groups at home), and to get citizens, properly scared to accept, in the name of the national and personal security, invasions of privacy and reductions of liberties they would not have tolerated if they had not been conditioned to fear.
>
> [Hoffmann 2004: 1029]

The imminent dangers President Bush alluded to in his speeches were founded on weak evidence. Yet, anticipating the question 'what if?' (Mythen and Walklate 2008; Crawford 2010), he would claim that it was his duty not to wait for the next bomb 'which could take the shape of a mushroom'. Vice President Cheney was even more specific, stating that next time it would not be 3,000 deaths the attacks would make but 30,000, 300,000 or even 3 million. Henceforth, according to Jürgen Habermas (in a dialogue with Jacques Derrida), continuous signals have pushed citizens to be on alert, thus fostering a diffuse feeling of anxiety, with no object, meeting the wishes of the terrorists (Borradori 2003). A strategy claiming transparency is, however, dangerous for a democracy. Targeting 'dangerous others' appeals to a punitive populism leaving the targeted very vulnerable against discriminations.

Political parties play on the same rhetoric. However, one should distinguish at which levels the politicians agitating the red flag operate and according to which culture they are able to act as such. 'Suppose we don't act and the intelligence turns out to be right, how forgiving will people be?' Tony Blair exclaimed (quoted in Crawford 2010). Yet national culture makes a difference. Prime Ministers Tony Blair and Silvio Berlusconi or President George W. Bush were more often seen waving the red flag than more cautious German and French politicians. In 2009, the French state acted forcefully to stop local conflicts between youth radicals of Jewish and of Muslim origin fed with images from Gaza brought by satellite TVs or the Internet. In the meanwhile, despite alarming reports relative to potential terrorists' plots, a French bureaucrat, J. Barrot, heading the section Justice, Liberty and Security at the European Community, acted to avoid a stigmatisation of Muslims in general. On the lines of the positions taken by the French state, he wanted to avoid blaming a whole community. His position was that Islam should be seen less as a source of conflict than as a means of integration in Europe.

Law enforcers

In France, policemen in charge of public safety display a wide variety of attitudes and opinions. Yet, as in other countries, when confronted with difficult situations, they tend to develop a binary perception of friends and foes, even if in the field they bring some relativism due to the 'clients' they are familiar with. Exerting surveillance on rough spots where major components of the populations are of Muslim culture allows undercover police, the police intelligence *Renseignements Généraux* (RG), GIR (regional police corps), the anti-riot police (*Compagnies Républicaines de Sécurité*) along with rank-and-file policemen to construct typologies of suspects. For *Renseignements Généraux*, eight criteria determine what a 'sensitive urban zone' is: an important number of immigrant – including polygamous – families; many community organisations; ethnic stores; numerous prayer rooms; non-Western and religious ways of dressing; anti-Semitic and anti-Western tags; school classes made of primo-migrant children who are non-French speakers; the exodus of 'old-stock' French families from the neighbourhood (Smolar 2004a).

These criteria could be denounced as racial profiling in some countries. But who is to complain that some young Muslims with an at-risk profile are continuously under surveillance when the issue of national security is at stake? Due to the 'what if?' approach justifying the precautionary principle, no European government will take risks and then be blamed for them (European Commission 2000). As remarked by sociologist Bonelli, that order and disorder are co-productions is too frequently forgotten. Institutions in charge of security play a role just as important as the populations that they confront (2008: 382). For years, the intelligence police monitored specifically 300 high-risk zones, suspected of more or less pronounced Muslim communitarianism. Mosques, bars, restaurants, Qur'anic bookstores, hallal butchers, long-distance telephone shops, day-care centres, clothes stores perceived as harbouring radical Muslims are thus submitted to undercover surveillance. For a country not recognising officially ethnicity, such approach is paradoxical and borderline in terms of citizenship and human rights.

But the issue of racial profiling and institutional racism are not discussed in France. Although the Council of Europe has required in 2000 that the police develop a more accurate, respectful and sensitive vision of various ethnic and racial groups (Conseil de l'Europe 2000) and in spite of the injunction of the French Ministry of Interior in 1999 that the composition of police forces should be more reflective of the populations they serve, the institution has proven reluctant to open its ranks to second- and third-generation immigrants, and it has chosen to assign this task to private security agencies and to municipal local forces. A French feature, national police focus most of all on order maintenance and the deployment of repressive control. After 2002, with N. Sarkozy's support, it has been resistant to integrating or dialoguing with the communities it supervises. No wonder then that community policing is unpopular among police forces and that the dialogue between run-down areas and the police is so difficult. Neither governments on the Left nor on the Right have been able to counter police unions hostile to reforms enforcing community policing. In other more decentralised countries, change is frequently triggered by pressures exerted by organised minority groups acting from the bottom up and by legitimised anti-discriminatory organisations which, under favourable circumstances, find political allies in the system of decision-making. But in France, another distinction, the national police are insulated from third-party advocates whose issues are not taken up by the mainstream political parties. Since there is no channel by which the problem can be politically recognised, the status quo persists.

How seriously should the threat of terrorism be taken compared with other forms of insecurity, for example coming from road accidents or from food poisoning or even urban violence? According to the International Crisis Group (2006):

> France has a problem with its Muslims and its banlieues which is expressed via riots and terrorism. Paradoxically, the decay of political fundamentalism explains the violence of youth of Muslim/immigrant background. One should worry more about the dangers of the political vacuum around them than about their so-called communitarianism.

It is not unusual for intelligence services to fabricate ad hoc enemies and to increase the potentiality of risks in the eyes of the public, emphasising, in the words of a French prime minister, that 'there is a real continuity between a fundamentalist discourse and terrorist acts' (Smolar 2004a; Body-Gendrot 2007). It could well be that with Islamic extremism, a widespread threat that is alarming governing elites, fascinating the media and fuelling a diffuse fear in the population, including most Muslims in France, the 3,500 members of the French police intelligence have found a way to carve their niche in a very competitive professional environment. At the end of 2008, rather silently, the two services, RG and DST, have merged into DCRI (*Direction centrale du renseignement intérieur*) the goal of which is to provide knowledge gathered from an 'infiltration' in hostile milieux and to anticipate violent expressions of radical Islam.

Why is this lack of accountability to the public tolerated?

According to official reports from *Inspection Générale des Services* (IGS), a body created in 1854, 40 per cent of sanctions targeting public employees apply to policemen, who only make up 8 per cent of them. Policemen receive a warning, a caution, a temporary suspension or an advanced retirement (only 150 cases a year). These sanctions concern all kinds of misbehaviours, like losing their police IDs or vandalising their cars. The internal corps of police officers (*Inspection Générale de la Police Nationale* – IGPN) (also nicknamed boeufs-carottes) have registered a decrease of police violence since 2004 (Mandraud 2008). Police unions are eager to point out that, out of 4 million police interventions a year, only 1,500 have to be examined by IGPN, including 600 for alleged physical abuse. It means one misbehaviour out of 6,000 interventions, which is a very small number but widely commented upon.

Local social order is threatened, nevertheless, by the asymmetry of resources held by the police and the institutions in general versus civil society. Unique to France by comparison with North Europe is both a tendency by judges or prosecutors not to intervene to redress institutional discriminations or to promote minorities' constitutional rights. Policemen's statements are taken under oath. Frequently, cases involving them are closed or dismissed by judges, for lack of proof, a genuine problem. The prosecutors' lack of autonomy from the political sphere makes it unlikely that they will side with the plaintiffs. For victims of police discrimination and their families, the judicial process then seems extremely long. It may take several years and, according to testimonies I heard at the CNDS hearings, it may give them the feeling that policemen or law enforcers in general are above the law. Policemen's capacity to tell the story, the support automatically brought to them by their counsels or their lawyers, their denouncing the plaintiff for obstruction or contempt put young people with few verbal skills in a loser's position. According to the French Criminal Code, contempt is punished by a six-month prison term and a €7,500 fine. It consists of 'any words, gestures or threats . . . addressed to persons discharging a public service mission, acting in the discharge or on the occasion of their office, and liable to undermine their dignity or the respect owed to the office that they hold' (Arts. 433–5). Obstruction is defined as opposing violent resistance to a person holding public authority (Arts. 433–6 of the Criminal Code). It receives the same punishment as contempt. The third offence is assault on an officer, and it is a misdemeanour. Such denunciations from policemen may occur even before the alleged offender is heard by the judge or by the CNDS. All these elements give policemen the last word and discourage citizens from going to court against policemen.

Take a case that the National Commission of deontology on security (CNDS) had to examine in 2007 (CNDS 2008). A witness to police abuse in Toulouse airport filed a complaint after having seen two policemen beating a man on the ground, about to be deported. The scene took place in 2006. The policemen accused the witness of 'slanderous denunciation', two days after the officers were summoned by the CNDS. The judge condemned the witness to write a letter of apology to the two policemen and to give each of them €100, despite the CNDS ongoing investigation. In its annual report, the CNDS denounced unbearable pressures, voluntarily exerted against witnesses in cases of police abuse and called for the attention of the justice minister who remained silent. In January 2008, the head of the national police informed the Commission that the inspection of police corps had launched an investigation of abuse in the police services but there has been no follow-up (Body-Gendrot 2010).

France is frequently sanctioned among the members of the European Council for its lack of respect for human rights. In 2006, the European Court for Human Rights (ECtHR) registered ninety-six decisions including eighty-seven convictions for too-lengthy or unfair judicial procedures. France ranked seventh among the most convicted countries. In 2006, over 2,800 French citizens applied to the ECtHR but between 30 and 50 per cent of the cases were dismissed.

The security market

The prevailing discourse on risks, threats and vulnerability is also supported by those claiming to reduce them with new technologies. In Europe, 1.7 million people work for 50,000 private security firms with a turnover of €15 billion (Mandraud 2008: 9). In France, the sector has expanded rapidly despite its fragmentation. It includes 4,800 firms, 44 per cent of them with less than nineteen employees and the same number with just one. 'All the current security discourse for the last few years has contributed to growing demands on the market' a private researcher remarks. This growth is supported by the progressive withdrawal of the state; private security firms are more and more requested to substitute for institutions (Giolat 2007: VII). Several laws have regulated a market with a dubious reputation in France. The law passed in 2003 supervises the training of the employees; that of 2007 on delinquency requires a professional card from private security employees and a bill on internal security plans to privatise more state missions such as airport security, inmates' transport, etc. In Britain, the phenomenon of privatisation started after 1992 with prisons (11 out of 130), airport security, detention centres (9 out of 11). Britain has more private security employees (250,000) than policemen (141,398), a trend also observed in eight other European countries (including Hungary and

Finland). France has not reached that stage (250,000 public security employees vs. 159,000 private ones), nor has Germany (250,000 vs. 173,000) nor Italy (425,000 vs. 49,166), according to the data circulated at the first European summit on private security (Mandraud 2008). It appears that the closer entrepreneurial firms are to the political sphere, the more they take advantage of this growing market.

4   New 'order' regimes

Disorders, crime and terrorism are perceived as the urban threats of our time. In order to meet this concern, policing and order maintenance occupy a central function in large cities. But cities still need the resources of central states to operate efficiently.

No governments can indeed tolerate lasting disorders. They are perceived by the public and their spokesmen as a proof of institutional weakness. Populist demagogues will blow the issue up at election times and financial and business disinvestment in cities perceived as prone to disorders may follow, along with the exodus of residents, tourists, students etc. Such was the situation in large American cities in the 1960s which emptied to the benefit of suburban areas.

Three strategies of 'order' maintenance converge in Europe. The first strategy aims at securing space without any focus on specific groups; for instance, security measures displayed at airports or at railway stations where very diverse people intersect concern everyone. In his recent Parisian exhibition *Native Land* architect Paul Virilio asserts that for public authorities, traceability now matters more than order and identity correlated to specific territories. Law enforcers are more interested in information contained in massive database than by identity papers with a postal address.

At the same time, space remains a decisive element of police strategy. One of the police's important missions is to contain and assign to specific territories those perceived as potential risks. In most European countries, in high-risk areas, residents want to see the police patrolling the streets and consequently, police chiefs make patrolling visible. Perfunctory and unpredictable interactions make the police an institution distributing definitive and temporary status via their own culture; that is, having diverse expectations according to their 'clients' and the spaces where they are met. If these 'clients' do not behave as expected according to the place where they are – if they run, for instance, instead of remaining seated on the bench where they were – they may be stopped and searched. But, to be fair, it should be said that if youths are on their own turf and if they are not known as offenders, the police are likely to ignore them. The discretionary power of policemen, what Monjardet (1996: 88) called the 'hierarchical inversion' is expressed in response to police perceptions of (potential) disorders.

Stops in neighbourhoods are thus more revealing on police modes of policing, it seems to me, than the race or ethnicity of the individuals who are stopped. At the CNDS, we hear youths complaining of police harassment, of humiliating stops and searches in the grey areas where witnesses will not talk and of their powerlessness at getting a fair treatment. But the confrontational, adversarial identities that these youths develop imply that all encounters with institutions are marked by distrust. Distrust in the police cannot be just explained by a strong ethnic bias on both sides but rather by the daily experiences of adversarial contacts with a police required by the law abiders to multiply 'the stops and searches' and instill a social discipline to the youngsters.

Top-down injunctions transform some of the marginalised urban zones into tinderboxes, calling for continuous surveillance at a heavy cost. In France, national policemen are turned into the wardens of order by the state. Their presence raises disproportionate expectations in comparison with the resources and the training they have received.

The second strategy gives legitimacy to identification, surveillance, deportation and repression of radical individuals and groups perceived as threats to society and hostile to democratic principles. As is well known, modes of distinction and punishment differ according to countries. States submitted to neoliberal pressures and relying on penal populism such as the USA, UK, South Africa and Australia differ from Scandinavian states and from conservative corporate states such as France, Germany and Italy. France displays a remarkable discrepancy between strong beliefs in individual autonomy and in equal treatment and precautionary principles making the lives of 'others' difficult.

This is due in part to French counter-espionage and the Direction of Territorial Safety's (DST) long experience of terrorist attacks during the Algerian war and then with the radical Left and with Corsicans.[6] As early as 1986, terrorist acts were committed in France in the name of the Committee of Solidarity with Arabic and Middle East Political Prisoners. Then in 1995 and in 1996, other attacks were launched on the French territory by Algerian radical Islamists, the GIA. As a consequence,

---

[6] This part draws on Body-Gendrot (2008b).

antiterrorism became a priority for officials in charge of territorial security and in particular, for judges working on these cases. Due to these dramatic events, in 1996 a law was passed. It made 'a plot to commit terrorist attacks' a crime, giving judges tools to prevent such acts from happening, such as prolonged custody in cases of 'association of malefactors in relation with a terrorist enterprise'. The assets of this approach – centralised, flexible, co-ordinated, politically independent – are counterbalanced by the lack of political and judicial supervision over remote, secretive and specialised structures. Field information gathered by the police intelligence or by regular police forces is transmitted to a pyramidal unit of command – for instance, in Paris, to the Police Prefect who also heads the Regional Defence Zone and then co-ordinates the Army, the firemen's brigades, the territorial security branches, the judicial police and other antiterrorist branches. Each head of a sector knows his or her counterparts in other sections in order to enforce co-ordinated actions once an order emanates from the summit. Compared with the US federal fragmentation of antiterrorist units, UCLAT, the French national co-ordinating agency, gathers and exchanges information with Direction of Territorial Security (DST), with the intelligence service (RG), the national antiterrorist section (DNAT) or the office of external security (DGSE) and it relates to the government as well. Some 170 persons have thus been incarcerated since 2004. In 2005, more than a hundred people suspected of terrorism were detained in French prisons.

Strikingly, multicultural countries like the UK and the Netherlands are currently opting for the French repressive posture with nuances of their own. Due to habeas corpus protections, it was only after the London attacks of July 2005, that a former terrorist, Rachid Ramda, was extradited to France and that Abu Hamza, the former imam of the Finsbury Park mosque in North London was convicted for exacerbating hatred. The Europeanisation of antiterrorism policies cannot be denied. The strategy developed in 2005 is based on four diktats: prevent, protect, pursue and respond. Agencies have been either reactivated or created with this aim in mind (see Crawford 2010).

5   Reasserting local public order

How can cities create an effective system of social order? How should local authorities exert their control of power? How to motivate citizens to be part of that process and participate in a co-production of security? These are questions putting large cities at the forefront. In an era of hyperactivity and ambiguity, security as a public good as crucial as freedom is not reducible to the mere activity of the state and this could be the third strategy.

What has changed in the range of threats is the inclusion of the risks of daily life. The current perceptions of security target not only crime but environmental risks and protections as well. What used to be exclusively within states' jurisdiction is now shared by various levels of decision-making and by public and private actors. Urban governance tends to exert a leadership on such issues. More and more European local officials become spokesmen for measures to be taken towards victims, for instance, or towards illegal flux of migrants.

Some Italian cities of the north have been at the forefront in their fight against the feeling of insecurity associated with some neighbourhoods or some categories of people. While some of them have opted for a xenophobic repression against immigrants as in Padova or Milan, others such as Turin or Trieste have developed a more inclusive approach (Bricocoli and Savoldi 2008). For these local authorities, the issue of security is an omnibus issue absorbing problems usually linked to other sectorial policies (such as housing, homelessness, immigration, health, education etc.). The local policies of urban security are somehow residual policies, or mix policies approaching the security issue as a function of social protection, security being perceived as a 'global public good' (Loader and Walker 2007: 234). They reflect a conception of urban governance mobilising a wide diversity of public and private actors committed to the rejuvenation of high-risk spaces which have been abandoned by other policies. In Turin, for instance, territorial maps showing where hot spots are located allow teams to analyse the various problems met by the residents and by the public employees working there. After dialogues with residents and with other institutional partners have taken place, City Hall hires ad hoc agents to examine what can be done with the residents. Then tasks are distributed and the measures are evaluated.

In France, the mayor of Paris, as other mayors, surrounds himself with experts and academics to advise him on what could be done on various issues, including safety. The problem comes from the absence of neighbourhood statistics or of local victimisation surveys which would be too costly. For a question of costs also, it is also difficult for mayors to launch ad hoc measures to confront risks. For instance, what should mayors of touristic resorts do when, in winter time, their locality includes 15,000 residents and in summer 250,000? On what kind of resources can they count and who will provide them? What should they do against hooligans, chronic young offenders or suspicious imams? If the measures they are tempted to take fail, would they be forced to resign, as can be the case in Dutch cities? Whatever the format, the state will need to keep a symbolic role. It is the warden of the legitimacy of laws, and of criminal law in particular. It will also need to keep the leadership whenever, as commonly happens, mayors are reluctant to be accountable on issues of security, especially when their powers and resources remain limited. In France, mayors are more eager to play a preventative role since the national police have given up policing by 'consent'. Unlike the UK, French neighbourhoods are not the focus of the local police decision-making.

How to police is not universal. Police action is triggered by the police leadership, public opinion and police initiatives. The choices made by police chiefs result from institutional arrangements, the acceptance of democratic supervision, the distribution of power in the state apparatus and public expectations relative to safety, tranquillity, police ethics, etc. According to the political scientist, Miller (2008): 'public attitudes about crime are filtered through political structures, just as state formation, electoral systems, democratic control, group representation', and I would add structures of legal and judicial systems. Citizen input is not favoured in France in matters of law and order whether it is to co-operate (perceived as *délation* (telling)) or to act when institutions are dysfunctional and weak. In some countries like the UK and the USA, neighbourhood watch is seen as virtuous by numerous citizens, but not for those who pay heavy taxes to subsidise public servants (including policemen).

As for Paris, it is the only city in France to have an urban police of 'proximity' theoretically (*Police urbaine de proximité* – PUP) with 12,500 men. The PUP do not require citizens to co-produce security. They are ruled by the Police Prefect, himself accountable to the Council of Ministers in practice, and not to the French Ministry of Interior. The name of this police force is fallacious because they are not interested in a dialogue with citizens who complain that 'if they talk, it is mainly with one another, when patrolling'.[7]

Ideally, community policing should reconcile basic police work with specialised counterterrorism. Such expectations are heard in New York or in London. But in Paris, it is very different. Local police chiefs[8] claim insufficient resources to have a good knowledge of the environment

---

[7] Interview of a Parisian police chief by the author (February 2009).
[8] Interview of a Parisian police chief by the author (February 2009).

and admit that there is still a lot of 'unknown unknowns', to quote Donald Rumsfeld in a famous speech (US Department of Defense, 12 February 2002).

French rank-and-file policemen consider that it is not their job but that of the intelligence service in charge of counterterrorism and that the information has to move vertically. They are rarely informed by the DCRI of what or who is suspected. It remains complex indeed to extract information from terrorist networks. A small group of ten people may accumulate 860 different identities, 2,500 SIM cards, etc. Ian Blair, the former Metropolitan Police Service Commissioner had understood that it is only by co-operating with Muslim communities and especially with women and moderate youths that sensitive information might trickle upwards. Both intelligent counterterrorism and ward policing rely on their knowledge of cities and of their social environments.

The lasting issue, then, is one of communication to alleviate security concerns, with police work supported by constructive partnerships (with public housing managers, street-level civil servants, teachers, firemen, public gardeners, nurses, social workers, bus drivers, postmen etc.), municipal employees (street educators, night 'correspondents' whose function is to talk to residents, find out what the issues are and alert the police when street fights or other problems occur), mediators, community organisers, concerned residents, parents, as well as small business owners, transporters, doctors etc. This is not an easy task due to the general distrust characterising collaborative work. Some mayors regularly gather their community councils of prevention; others prefer to work with their wake cells or with other institutions such as public housing management or resource centres.

6   Conclusion: a closer look at the efficiency of the French approach

In the current political context dominated by the precautionary principle, society betrays its lack of trust, relations between people seem risky and marginalised urban places are perceived as no-go areas. These phenomena are more or less similar all over Europe. It is within the states' regalian domain to act on risks, while it is the cities' aim to remain as inclusive as possible in order to contribute to feelings of safety whether one is alone or in a crowd.

While Paris is a generally well-ordered city, problems pile up in some areas where public services are lagging in terms of resources and efficacy.

Residents complain that the police are not visible enough while institutions answer that bands of youths are more violent than before and
that crimes are committed by non-Parisian residents. They also claim
that the justice system is too slow at delivering clear decisions for the
victims. Juvenile court judges answer that the centres taking care of
repeat delinquents are overwhelmed and that there is a crisis in the
recruiting of professionals. Consequently, families with problems hear
institutions quarrelling with one another and not admitting responsibility for their inefficiency. Meanwhile, they do not receive adequate,
tailor-made support. In France, the policies which are criticised as inefficient are national. At the local level, due to some political initiatives and
leadership, the picture is different: mobility does occur, youths from
poor areas do go to college and residents may move out to better places.
Yet, because immigration flux quickly fill the vacant spots in first-entry
places and because economic fluctuations with possible downward
mobility generate anxiety, the perceptions that 'nothing works' prevail,
supported by the service providers themselves eager to keep both their
clients and their jobs. It remains difficult to prove whether a majority of
sensitive urban zones improve, remain the same or decay, the indicators
being too numerous and changing over time. There is still a generous
welfare state in France filling the dual role of philanthropist and of
stretcher bearer, according to economist E. Cohen. The budget allocated
to welfare is twice that of the state at the time of this writing, that is €550
billion. Numerous forms of state redistribution cement the French and
the non-national residents in cities, all of them supporting the public
services (88 per cent of the French have a positive image of the police).
More youths of North African origin, especially girls, reach the middle
classes than was thought.

Risk management induced by the Jihad terrorist threat, and more
generally by more diffuse public disorders, has led to implementing
measures jeopardising civil liberties in all the Western countries. What
these measures have in common is to be very visible, in order to reassure
public opinion on one hand and on the other to be secretive, because
surprise is a weapon; they also combine targeted prevention and specific
repression. They cannot be easily transferred from one country to
another, because public opinion sensitivity, judicial principles and the
organisation of institutions differ. The only standard of their efficiency
comes from the observation, *a posteriori*, that no terrorist attack or
uncontrolled disorders have occurred. In return, authorities allowing
infringements on public liberties take a risk in terms of democratic

legitimacy if no debate has taken place, except some limited and punctual ones, involving intellectual elites.

In addition to social preventative policies, one major factor might also produce public tranquility and social inclusiveness: the time factor. The experience of immigrants in the USA and in Europe reveals that the identity wound caused by cultural uprooting, hurting second generations more than others, does heal gradually. Obviously, the necessary passage of time does not concern attacks generated by geopolitical tensions but it is appropriate to bring it up to explain how essential it is to allow the cicatrisation of the identity wound.

References

Balibar, E. (2006) 'Uprisings in the banlieues', *Lignes*, November.
Body-Gendrot, S. (2000) *The Social Control of Cities? A Comparative Perspective*, Oxford: Blackwell.
    (2005a) 'France: the politicization of youth justice' in J. Muncie and B. Goldson (eds.), *Contemporary Youth Justice*, London: Sage, pp. 48–64.
    (2005b) 'Deconstructing youth violence', *European Journal on Crime, Criminal Law and Criminal Justice*, 13(1), 4–26.
    (2007) 'Police, justice and youth violence in France' in T. Tyler (ed.), *Legitimacy and the Criminal System: International Perspective*, New York: Russell Sage, pp. 243–76.
    (2008a) 'Confronting fear' in R. Burdett and D. Sudhik (eds.), *The Endless City*, London: Phaedon, pp. 352–63.
    (2008b) *La peur détruira-t-elle la ville?*, Paris: Bourin.
    (2010) 'Police marginality, racial logics and discrimination in the *banlieues* of France', *Ethnic and Racial Studies*, 33(4), 656–74.
Bok, S. (1998) *Mayhem*, New York: Addison Wesley.
Bonelli, L. (2008) *La France a peur. Une histoire sociale de l'‘insécurité’*, Paris: La Découverte.
Borradori, G. (2003) *Le ‘concept’ du 11 Septembre. Dialogues à New York avec Jacques Derrida et Jurgen Habermas*, Paris: Galilée.
Bricocoli, M. and Savoldi, P. (2008) *Villes en observation. Politiques locales de sécurité urbaine en Italie*, Paris, Recherches No. 194 du Plan Urbanisme Construction Architecture (PUCA).
Ceaux, P. and Smolar P. (2003) 'Cette circulaire signée Sarkozy qui désavoue la police de proximité', *Le Monde*, 19 February, 7.
Commission nationale de déontologie de la sécurité (2008) *Rapport 2007*, Paris: La documentation française.
Conseil de l'Europe (2000) *European Conference against Racism, Racial Discrimination, Xenophobia and Related Intolerance*, Strasbourg, 11–13 October.

Crawford, A. (2010) 'Regulating civility, governing security and policing (dis)order under conditions of uncertainty' in J. Blad, M. Hildebrandt, N. Rozemond, M. B. Schuilenburg and P. J. V. van Culster (eds.), *Governing Security under the Rule of Law*, The Hague: Eleven International Publishers.

European Commission (2000) *Communication from the Commission on the Precautionary Principle, 2 February*, Brussels: Council of the European Commission.

Gerbner, G. (1994) 'Television violence: the art of asking the wrong questions', *Currents in Modern Thought*, 385–97.

Giolat, F. (2007) 'La sécurité privée se professionnalise pour attirer des candidates à l'embauche', *Le Monde*, 5 June, VII.

Hoffmann, S. (2004) 'Thoughts on fear in global society', *Social Research*, 71(4), 1023–38.

International Crisis Group (2006) *La France face à ses musulmans: émeutes, djihadisme et dépolitisation*, rapport Europe No. 172, 9 March.

Lagrange, H. (2000) 'Sociabilité et délinquance des jeunes', *Cahiers de la sécurité intérieure*, 42, 63–86.

Loader, I. and Walker, N. (2007) *Civilizing Security*, Cambridge: Cambridge University Press.

Mandraud, I. (2008) 'Moins de bavures, plus de petites violences', *Le Monde*, 14 June, 3.

Miller, L. (2008) *The Perils of Federalism*, Oxford: Oxford University Press.

Monjardet, D. (1996) *Ce que fait la police*, Paris: La Découverte.

Mythen, G. and Walklate, S. (2008) 'Terrorism, risk and international security: the perils of asking what if?', *Security Dialogue*, 39(2–3), 221–42.

Observatoire National des zones urbaines sensibles, *Rapport (2006)*, Paris: Editions de la Délégation interministérielle à la ville (DIV).

Perrot, M. (1979) 'Dans la France de la Belle Epoque, les apaches, premières bandes de jeunes' in M. Perrot (ed.), *Les marginaux et les exclus dans l'histoire*, Paris: UGE, 387–407.

Robert, P. and Pottier, M. L. (1997) 'Sur l'insécurité et la délinquance', *Revue française de science politique*, 47(5), 630–44.

Robin, C. (2004) 'Liberalism at bay, conservative at play: fear in the contemporary imagination', *Social Research*, 71(4), 927–64.

Schain, M. (2008) *The Politics of Immigration in France, Britain, and the United States*, New York: Palgrave Macmillan.

Sénat, Rapport Schosteck et Carle (2001–2002) *Délinquance des mineurs, la République en quête de respect* (340).

Sicot, F. (2000) 'Enfants d'immigrés maghrébins. Rapport au quartier et engagement dans la délinquance', *Cahiers de la sécurité intérieure*, 42, 87–108.

Smolar, P. (2004a) 'Les renseignements généraux révisent leur priorité', *Le Monde*, 26 May.

Smolar, P. (2004b) 'Les RG s'alarment d'un "repli communautaire" dans les banlieues', *Le Monde*, 6 July.

Sunstein, C. (2004) 'Fear and liberty', *Social Research*, 71(4), 967–96.

Wykes, M. (2009) 'The English experience: mediating technology and security: violations and vulnerabilities', Paper presented to CRIMPREV WP4 Sixth meeting, University of Porto, 16–17 January.

22

The question of scale in urban criminology*

MARIANA VALVERDE

To govern a problem such as 'urban safety', we first need to visualise it and name it. And any act of visualisation employs a particular scale – whether or not the scale is consciously chosen out of a set, or whether one simply takes up a certain scale without considering alternatives. A crucial insight of recent work on space and governance is that scale-effects pervade all visualisation, not just cartography and other two-dimensional representations. Standing on a mountain top to look down at one's town, for instance, one is using a different scale than that employed in – or as some scholars would put it, constituted by[1] – walking down one's street.[2] Scale is thus a fundamental feature or component of all efforts to render the world in thought.

In empirical social science, particularly in survey-based research, the terms 'scale' and 'scaling' are by no means absent. When researchers ponder whether they should assign numbers to the multiple-choice answers to a question or whether it is best to use qualitative terms such as 'occasionally' and 'frequently', they say they are thinking about 'scaling'. Scaling in this sense is an issue that requires thought because

* This chapter is a shorter version of an article arising from Adam Crawford's invitation to participate in an international colloquium in Leeds in June of 2008. My thanks to Adam and his colleagues for a fruitful discussion, and to Bernard Harcourt for his comments on the original conference paper.

[1] Recent scholarship in critical geography suggests that it may be useful to think of scale not as a grid that exists prior to human use, but rather as the result of human seeing and measuring efforts: social actors 'do not "jump" from one scale to another, but, rather, they actually constitute scale through their social praxis' (Herod and Wright 2002: 11).

[2] Reflections on the important distinction between walking around in a city and examining it from above, either literally from an airplane or imaginatively by means of maps, usually cite Michel de Certeau's influential remarks on the antagonistic 'relation between the itinerary (a discursive series of operations) and the map (a plane projection totalizing observations)' (de Certeau 1984: 7). De Certeau's contrast between embodied seeing and the bird's eye view has parallels in the analyses of the consequences of different techniques of seeing provided by scholars in the science and technology studies field (e.g. Haraway 1991).

even when questions have been written in such a way as to discourage ambiguity and creativity among respondents, anything more complicated than a yes-or-no answer requires paying attention to the implications of how responses are 'scaled'.

The literatures undergirding the present contribution (law and geography, science and technology studies) are also very interested in measurement, but in a rather different manner, since they encourage us to think about how the entities being so carefully measured were invented/discovered in the first place.

Insights from legal geography

Some scalar effects – in the geographers' sense of 'scalar' – have in recent years become apparent to anyone with Internet access. It is no longer news to point out that when we choose a scale we also decide which objects, and which features of those objects, will be visible or invisible, and hence governable.

The zoom feature, however, is the most simple of scalar mechanisms, since it enacts merely quantitative shifts in scale. Even limiting ourselves to cartography, qualitative as well as quantitative distinctions exist: to cite only the simplest of qualitative distinctions, there are 'physical' maps, there are 'political' maps and there are 'demographic' maps. And then there is the question of the choice of projection. Since the earth is not flat, choices have to be made when drawing continents on a flat surface. The traditional projection shows the northern hemisphere as large and important, but some have argued that a more accurate projection would show the global south as much larger.

Recent work in critical geography, science and technology studies, and other fields (Scott 1998; Poovey 1995; Blomley 1994) has amply elaborated the basic insight just outlined – namely, that the choices made by those who draw and use maps are not merely technically convenient. Christian Jacob, one of the pioneers of the critical study of geographical knowledges, reflects a consensus when he writes that a map is 'not a static object' but rather 'a dynamic process whose effects, power, and meanings are to be found at the crossroads of production and reception, of encoding and decoding, of intentions and of expectations' (Jacob 2006: xv).

This insight has been extended beyond geography. In 1987, the influential socio-legal theorist Boaventura de Sousa Santos argued that law can usefully be regarded as a kind of mapping exercise. Like cartography,

Santos argued, law owes much of its flexibility to the fact that any particular place is generally governed not by a single coherent legal system but rather by overlapping legal rules, principles and authorities that do not seem to clash – because they work at different scales. 'Local law is a large-scale legality. Nation-state law is a medium-scale legality . . . The different forms of law create different legal objects upon the same social objects. They use different criteria to determine meaningful details' (Santos 1987: 287).

Santos was then and is still now mainly concerned about 'legal pluralism', particularly in postcolonial contexts, where customary legal principles and institutions persist alongside largely imported legal machineries. One of the ways of describing the relations between local/customary law and colonial law is drawing attention to the very different scales and (literal) perspectives employed and presupposed by the different legal structures. This line of inquiry parallels and complements the historical analyses of colonial knowledge practices undertaken by numerous scholars (e.g. Bernard Cohn, Timothy Mitchell, Paul Rabinow).

I would go further than Santos, and postcolonial scholarship more generally, to point out that even in situations without overtly politicised conflicts of laws and conflicts of cultures, scalar shifts (which in law often overlap with and are enabled by jurisdictional divisions of power) create a complex and not always neatly nested or otherwise co-ordinated situation in which the basic nature of particular problems is constantly being redefined by the simple device of shifting scale.

Let us examine how this works in popular talk about crime first, before going on to examine criminological depictions of 'urban disorder' from the point of view of scale.

The scales of crime

If a gunman who takes someone hostage in a shopping mall does so while shouting 'Long live Al-Qa'ida', this incident will be classified as an example of a world-scale problem. Some will define the problem as 'terrorism'; others, as 'Islamic fundamentalism'; others, as 'the rightful rebellion of the Arab masses against the imperialist West'. But while arguing about the substantive content of the description, law enforcement authorities, criminologists, and media commentators alike will likely assume that a particular *scale* is the appropriate one for visualising and thus beginning to govern this incident – namely, the scale that is rather fuzzily and unhelpfully called 'global'.

By contrast, if the gunman does not say anything, the incident will be classified as a crime rather than as an act of terrorism, and rescaled accordingly. In Baltimore or in Detroit this incident would likely stay at the local level; whereas in Toronto, where our mayor has launched a high-profile campaign to ban 'American' handguns in an effort to rescale the local problem of gun crime and 'responsibilise' the federal government, the incident might be portrayed as another example of the nefarious national consequences of being close to the United States.

The gun example shows the slippery relation between jurisdiction and scale:[3] if Toronto Mayor David Miller is redefining handguns as a matter of one nation having a bad effect on its neighbour, the rescaling of the gun issue quietly performs a politically convenient abdication of jurisdiction over the 'gangs and guns' problem. But the point here is that in order to abdicate jurisdiction the mayor has to first revisualise the problem by shifting scales.

Mayor Miller's campaign to redefine guns as non-Canadian is useful for present purposes because the default scalar setting for most issues pertaining to citizen safety and security is 'the local'. There are exceptions: for example, certain illegal drugs are simultaneously imagined as highly local – as defining the character of particular neighbourhoods or sub-populations – and as transnational. And feminists often talk about violence against women in a resolutely anti-local fashion. But on the whole, garden-variety crime, and therefore urban security in the crime prevention sense of the term, is presented at one scale only – and that is of course 'the local'. This is true both for scholarly criminology and for applied work on crime prevention (see e.g. Crawford 1998).

The point here is not to argue about which scale to use, however, but rather to underline that researchers as well as lay people usually choose a (geographic) scale without a consideration of other choices or a discussion of its pros and cons.

In analysing the implications of the taken-for-granted scale choices made both by popular and scholarly criminology (with 'the local' as the main case study, given its prevalence in urban safety writing) we will proceed by considering what I call the qualitative as well as quantitative dimensions of scale choices. The scalar effects that distinguish one way of seeing urban security from another do not depend only on quantitative shifts such as those achieved by zooming in or out when using Google Earth.

---

[3] I have explored the complex relation between jurisdiction and scale elsewhere (Valverde 2009).

They also depend crucially on the kind of gaze deployed by the (real or imagined) observer. The perspective or standpoint, in other words, constitutes what I think is useful to call the qualitative dimension of scale. As will be seen shortly, in their famous 1982 article on 'broken windows', Wilson and Kelling (1982) use a quantitative scale that is a very popular choice in writing on urban security – the micro-local. But that article uses a qualitative scale that is markedly different from those used in social scientific accounts that are exactly the same in terms of quantitative scale.

Understanding qualitative scale differences might help to explain why the numerous social science critiques levelled at broken-windows criminology have had so little effect. Incommensurabilities of scale (in general) create epistemological heterogeneity – 'dialogue of the deaf' situations. For example, in my empirical research on urban planning disputes, I have observed that neighbours upset about a proposed development are – as long as they continue to speak only on behalf of and about their micro-neighbourhood – impervious to arguments driven by nationwide concerns (the housing crisis, inter-city migration etc.), and are only receptive to global environmental concerns such as global warming if those are translated into local-scale problems (bad air in our neighbourhood). Similarly, 'broken-windows' criminology may be structurally impervious to critiques that come from sources that use a different scale. Arguments about increasing social inequality caused by neoliberal social policies (e.g. Mitchell 2003), which generally cast inequality as nationwide or even global, are unlikely to have an impact on local enthusiasm for proposals to deal with local 'disorderly' people.

To study the qualitative and quantitative workings of the scales used in urban security writings we will undertake a close reading of two of the most cited studies in the field. The first is the seminal article 'Broken windows' published in 1982 by James Q. Wilson and George Kelling. The second is Sampson and Raudenbush's 'Systematic social observation of public spaces' (1999).

The 'broken-windows' scale: the (generic) street corner perceived by the generic eyewitness

Let us thus turn to Wilson and Kelling's seminal article (Wilson and Kelling 1982; Coles and Kelling 1996). The substantive claims made in this article and in the voluminous subsequent literature have been analysed and criticised at great length (e.g. Harcourt 2001). But the *scale* presupposed by the authors has not, to my knowledge, been seriously analysed.

Quantitatively, the scale of broken-windows criminology is local, even micro-local, which is the norm for discourses about urban decay; but there is a particular quality that is related to but not determined by the quantitative element. This can be described initially as follows: the tale about streets in decline is told from an eyewitness perspective (rather than, say, from the perspective of demography), but, unlike much street-corner sociology (Whyte 1988; Duneier 1999; Jacobs 1961), Wilson and Kelling do not actually put themselves in the picture, and do not show us actual locations populated by actual people.

What does one see if one uses this very specific kind of gaze to examine the micro-local environment? The answer is well known:

> A piece of property is abandoned, weeds grow up, a window is smashed. Adults stop scolding rowdy children; the children, emboldened, become more rowdy. Families move out, unattached adults move in . . . Litter accumulates. People start drinking in front of the grocery . . .
>
> [Wilson and Kelling 1982: 32]

The micro-local scale is established partly through the *content* of the prose: individual children and individual weeds (if they actually exist, a question that has to be held in abeyance for now) are the kind of thing that would not appear on city maps, and could only be seen only micro-locally. But the scale is also set partly through the *format* chosen for this passage (Ericson *et al.* 1991).

Formats tend to be hard-wired to specific kinds of outlets. For instance, tabloids share certain format features that remain stable as content changes, since the recognisable format means that their commodity can be instantly recognised by potential buyers and easily distinguished from broadsheets (Ericson *et al.* 1991: 20–5, 149–52). Now, the medium chosen by Wilson and Kelling for their manifesto was the general-interest magazine feature article. As one would expect, the choice of *Atlantic Monthly* (as distinct not only from a refereed journal but also from a television talk show or a front-page news item) shaped the way in which the broken-windows problem was visualised.

Like most feature articles in general-interest magazines, the broken-windows article uses what I call the 'eyewitness' scale. However, there are two ways of using the eyewitness perspective. The first is exemplified in newspaper features: a journalist describes going into market X in city Y and seeing customers buying this or that. The journalist might mention a conversation with shopkeeper A about problem Q, with names and ages being given not because they matter but to lend the article authenticity and verisimilitude. This approach is what one could call the 'actual eyewitness' format.

The second way of using the same kind of highly visual, anecdotal style of conveying information about a situation or problem is to write graphically and concretely, but about generic rather than specific objects and places and persons. In the Wilson-Kelling case, there are neither photographs of actual spaces nor street addresses. What is being represented, then, is a generic street[4] rather than a real place.

Jane Jacobs' tremendously influential *Death and Life of American Cities*, whose insights about urban security were important for broken-windows criminology, is also mainly written from the journalistic eyewitness perspective rather than using social science formats (Jacobs 1961). But the crucial difference between her folksy format and that of Wilson-Kelling is that in keeping with journalistic practice, she either puts herself in the picture as the actual observer – 'Whenever I take my kids to the dentist we walk only along the avenue, never on the side streets' – or else she gives chapter and verse about whose eyes actually saw X or Y event or object (for instance, 'Reverend Smith told me that in his street in Harlem . . .').

By contrast, in the Wilson-Kelling fable, the writing proceeds *as if* the authors are describing what is going on before their very eyes. The reader does not know whether either or both authors ever really saw weeds and rowdy children in close proximity, and if so where.

'Micro-local' does not suffice to adequately specify the broken-windows perspective, therefore. If the same block were being visualised on a city map, that would be a local representation too, but one using a different mode of visualisation (cf. Scott 1998). The original broken-windows thesis, therefore, includes as a central element a certain quantitative *scale* (the micro-local) and a certain qualitative perspective that could be called 'the generic eyewitness gaze'.[5]

---

[4] 'The street' is often generic: 'the Arab street' is nowhere in particular, for instance. 'The street' used in this generic sense is often a synonym for 'the urban' (as when politicians exclaim that 'we must make our streets safe'), but sometimes 'the street' draws a distinction between the everyday and the realm of expertise, as in the powerful legal phrase 'the man on the street'. No inventory of the uses of 'the street' in legal discourse has been compiled, to my knowledge.

[5] The subsequent book *Fixing Broken Windows* (Coles and Kelling 1996) makes minimal use of the generic eyewitness perspective. It is occasionally used, but the book is distinguished by an unusually rich variety of data sources, styles of writing, and knowledge formats – political-theory critiques of civil liberties court decisions, social science analyses of crime data, historical narratives about police governance, popular translations of criminological studies etc.

Tellingly, the article was illustrated not with photographs of actual streets, as is often the case in magazine articles about urban problems, but rather with cartoon-like pencil drawings of generic characters: the hooker, the rowdy youth, the panhandler and the respectable middle-class man in a suit. Composites, ideal types, and stereotypes are the bread and butter of the cartoon format. Indeed, even if the accompanying text did name names and places, the child-like black-and-white cartoons would, independently, send out a clear message that the generic disorderly street is the focus of this article.

Scale slippage: from eyewitness observation to social science data

An interesting feature of the Wilson-Kelling text is that the scale is not completely consistent, even in the short quote cited above. One of the elements mentioned becomes visible only at a scale that is not that of the eyewitness, actual or generic: 'Families move out, unattached adults move in.' A local resident could admittedly see a particular family moving out if the removal van was at the front door when the person happened to go by on the sidewalk. But close attention to grammar reveals that while the window is singular and the abandoned piece of land is singular too, family life is not here visualised one individual family at a time: 'Families move out, unattached adults move in.' This sounds more like a sociological generalisation than an eyewitness observation.

Indeed, the Wilson-Kelling invocation of 'unattached adults' repeats a standard doctrine about urban disorder contained in the original Chicago school text about urban life, the Park and Burgess popular volume *The City*:

> the settler type of population, the married couples with children, withdraw from the center of the city while the more mobile and less responsible adults herd together in the hotel and apartment regions near the heart of the community.   [Park *et al*. 1925: 78]

Standing on a street corner, one could see a broken window; and if one stood there long enough one might see two or three families moving out. But one cannot see census-tract level demographic change. And one certainly cannot see with one's own eyes the moral decline openly invoked by Park and Burgess and less openly triggered by Wilson and Kelling's claim that people moving into downtown are 'unattached'. Whether the traditional nuclear family is in moral crisis or in demographic decline cannot be determined by standing on a street corner and looking.

Crime prevention websites and other popular sources of broken-windows wisdom often exhibit similar scale slippages – from the micro-local to the social scientific, and from the visible physical fact to invisible moral–social phenomena, as if one could see aggregate data as one see pieces of paper blowing about on one's street.

The local as the scale of 'community'

A full genealogy would trace broken-windows criminology back to its origins in Chicago school sociological notions of 'disorganised' or 'pathological' communities.[6] This is not the place for such a genealogy, however, since what concerns us here is simply to show that a certain notion of 'community' that is common coinage within American social science plays a crucial role in enabling urban-security writers such as Wilson and Kelling to collapse different scales.

Tellingly, Wilson and Kelling suddenly deploy 'community' towards the end of the article, when they are discussing responsibility and problem-solving. Having argued that social and physical disorder has a negative effect, on fear of crime if not on crime itself, they then ask: who then needs to take responsibility for disorder? The police should indeed be more concerned with minor disorders, they say; but in the end, 'the essence of the police role in maintaining order is to reinforce the informal control mechanisms of the community itself' (Wilson and Kelling 1982: 34).

This claim imports Durkheim's macro-level theory of national social cohesion into the street corner-perspective. Durkheim's theory was hardwired to the scale of the nation state. The problem of anomie was construed as inherently national (in part by the technique of comparing various data, such as suicide rates, across countries rather than, say, across neighbourhoods). And the solutions too were inherently national:

---

[6] The key influence of Chicago notions of 'disorganised' and 'pathological' communities on late twentieth-century crime prevention writing has been noted by Adam Crawford (1998: 127–8).

teachers (who Durkheim assumed were national-level civil servants) had to replace priests in stimulating social cohesion, national professional bodies had to mediate between individuals and the state, and so forth. Durkheim's theory might well have died as the grandiose vision of a centralised state promoted by Durkheim and later by welfare-state theorists lost popularity, in the 1970s and 1980s. However, the theory was rehabilitated for late twentieth-century crime-prevention purposes via an intermediary that performed a scale shift: the Chicago school notion of 'the community'.

What did 'community' mean, for Chicago school sociology? As is well known, 'community' was and remains a wonderfully capacious term. It could mean a neighbourhood, a city-wide ethnic group or a particular combination of space, class and ethnicity. But while the substantive meaning or referent of 'community' was indeterminate, its scale was fairly narrowly defined. First of all, 'communities' were for the most part urban rather than rural. And, secondly, they were more local than national. Indeed, while 'community' was sometimes a synonym for 'city', communities in the plural were generally identified with specific parts of a city.

It is of course true that some Chicago-trained authors went on to write about phenomena using supra-urban scales; but by and large 'the community' was the object studied. Community could mean the neighbourhood as distinct from the metropolis, or it could mean an ethnic minority as distinct from 'ordinary', unmarked, WASP Americans. Often it referred to a particular combination of place and race, of neighbourhood and identity.

Importantly for our analysis of scale, however, 'community' was not only an indicator of quantitative scale (local rather than national or global) but also of qualitative scale. Ever since the Chicago school, 'community' has also indicated both (a) a focus on civil society rather than the state; and (b) a certain epistemology – as in when we say 'community planning', meaning that lay people should be involved too and not just experts.

The vagaries of the term 'community' in criminology and in law have certainly been noted, inventorised, and critically analysed (Crawford 1997; Cotterrell 1995; Levi 2003). It is not my intention to reiterate these analyses, but simply to note that if 'the local' is the scale of the fuzzy entity that is 'community', then the local will be marked by the same rich ambiguities that scholars have already detected in 'community'.

'Systematic social observation': the desire for replicability and its effects on scale

Sampson and Raudenbush's seminal article begins by acknowledging the importance of direct personal observation of 'disorder'.[7] Rather self-servingly, the discovery of the importance of observing signs of order and disorder is not attributed to the nineteenth-century journalists who alerted the middle classes about 'how the other half lives' with rich accounts of misery and overcrowding – or even to Jane Jacobs' 1950s strolls through Manhattan, a more proximate source – but rather to Chicago-school sociology: 'one of the hallmarks of the Chicago school was its concern with observing public places – not just abstract variables, but the sights, sounds, and feel of the streets' (Sampson and Raudenbush 1999: 604).

The vindication of the sights and sounds – and especially of 'the feel' – of the streets looks like the introduction to an ethnographic study. But no. While courteously acknowledging ethnographic work, Sampson and Raudenbush use a different scale: that which they call 'systematic' observation, described in their subtitle as 'a new *look* at disorder in urban neighbourhoods' (emphasis added). Mentioning Chicago's Albert Reiss as the pioneer of this way of looking, Sampson and Raudenbush state: 'By systematic, Reiss meant that observation and recording are done according to explicit rules that permit replication; he also argued that the means of observation, whether a person or a technology, must be independent of that which is observed' (*ibid.*: 605).

Sampson and Raudenbush do not claim quasi-experimental status for their text; but they do claim to be developing 'ecometric' sociology – which one assumes is for social units what psychometrics is for individuals.[8] This desire to measure in such a way as to make replicability possible leads them: (a) to maximise the number of street blocks surveyed, so as to encompass no less than 196 census tracts; and (b) to classify the non-visible, sociological features of each block carefully according to socio-economic data and information about 'collective efficacy'.

---

[7] The article is ultimately concerned to map the relation between what they call 'disorder' and crime data, but here I will confine my analysis to the way in which they set out to observe and map 'disorder', without entering into the question of how they define crime or the crime–disorder relationship, since the focus of this chapter is ways of seeing the city.

[8] 'Ecometrics' is a curious term, since it unnecessarily imports Chicago biological metaphors about succession of species and so forth into urban data collection projects; 'sociometrics' would have been less ideologically laden.

This dizzying intensive and extensive multiplication of data promotes replicability: the whole point of systematic social observation is to allow for the comparative analysis of variations across a large number of analytically defined ecological areas. Having created fungible abstract categories to describe or rather to classify 'ecological units', replicability becomes possible; and having obtained the massive funding that is required for the collection of vast quantities of observation-based data, replicability is maximised.

But what kinds of things are being counted to generate the replicable measures? Several heterogeneous types of entities are being counted – and shifts in scale are one of the techniques used to paper over this heterogeneity. Let us see how this works.

Scale shifts and the Chicago school: observing moral-legal entities?

A key term used in current-day Chicago urban sociology is 'collective efficacy', which Sampson and Raudenbush measure only at the level of neighbourhoods. Not only is collective life thus posited as a micro-local phenomenon (as if national-level or even city-level collective efficacy were irrelevant, by definition) but the content of this dimension of life is equally impoverished. Micro-neighbourhood efficacy could plausibly include the ability to influence municipal politics. But in keeping with the anti-political stance cultivated by Chicago urban sociology, they specify that collective efficacy 'is conceptualized as relative to the task of maintaining order in public spaces' (Sampson and Raudenbush 1999: 609).[9]

The highly awkward syntax ('is conceptualized as relative to . . .') tells us that the authors, whose writing style is otherwise very clear, are short-circuiting a conceptual problem – or several. Two key assumptions that are contained in and given life by the awkward syntax are:

(a) that every 'ecological unit' has a desire to 'maintain order in public spaces'

---

[9] Adam Crawford notes that Chicago sociology presupposes 'that it is an inherent capacity of communities to mobilise their own resources of social control' (1998: 128) – but it should be added that another equally fundamental presupposition is that 'communities' have a deep collective *desire* to exercise 'social control' and reduce what Chicago sociology would label as 'disorder'.

(b) that the meaning, the content of 'order' can be treated as constant across units.[10]

A critical urbanist (such as Don Mitchell, Nick Blomley, Neil Smith or Sharon Zukin) would here go on at length about the middle-class bias visible in Sampson and Raudenbush's list of 'visual cues of disorder' as well as in the assumption that all communities everywhere want to eliminate 'disorder'. I happen to share their critical stance toward the ideological bias of Chicago-style sociology; but what I wish to show here is something different; namely, how shifts in scale enable and constitute 'systematic social observation' as a way of seeing the city. Therefore, I will briefly analyse the scale effects and contradictions of some of the key 'visual cues' of 'disorder', leaving the question of cultural and class bias somewhat aside.

1 Abandoned vehicles

Any self-styled objective and replicable study of disorder requires consistent coding. However, one can imagine an objective and replicable study whose coding categories are elaborated empirically rather than *a priori* – that is, by ethnomethodologically documenting residents' experiences and definitions. 'Abandonment' is not a condition that can be readily seen by outsiders in poor neighbourhoods where car owners might need to wait some time to earn enough money to pay for car repairs. Whether a car is abandoned (or whether children are rowdy) is not a question that can be reliably decided by an outsider's quick look.

2 'Adults loitering or congregating'

This category is even less consistent than the abandoned vehicle one. That certain persons are adults, and that they are 'congregating', can be determined by looking. However, 'loitering' is a legal category, and to some extent also a common-sense moral judgement (very much like 'prostitution'). Loitering cannot be directly observed (as the efforts of Chicago and then US appeal courts to find more precise wording for gang-congregation ordinances demonstrated). The hybrid category of

---

[10] As Bernard Harcourt has noted, it is curious that in a culturally pluralistic society (today's US), the term 'order', in discussions of urban order/disorder, is still treated as an uncontested quasi-natural condition not only by social conservatives such as James Q. Wilson but also by the new Chicago 'norm-focused scholars' (Harcourt 2001: 134).

'adults loitering' is therefore constructed by means of a sleight-of-hand scale shift from the video-camera perspective to a legal–moral register. The trained observers used by the sociologists no doubt felt that they were seeing 'loitering/congregating'; but they could only see loitering and congregating by means of a Chicago-school scale shift from the physical to the moral or legal.

3 Mixed land use (or 'non-residential land use')

The legal abstraction 'land use' brings into the scale of eyewitness observation the completely different, highly abstract scale of planning law. 'Land uses' did not exist until the early twentieth century: in the nineteenth century, observers noted noisy pubs and foul-smelling factories, but saw them as 'nuisances' (a mixed legal–moral category methodologically similar to 'loitering'), not as inappropriate or abnormal 'land uses' (Valverde 2006). The exceedingly abstract notion of 'land use' imports the abstract 'seeing like a state' scale (Scott 1998) into what is said to be 'direct' observation. In addition, the precise referent of any land use category (including 'non-residential') is determined by the planning law of the relevant jurisdiction, not by a Durkheimian 'collective consciousness'; and, furthermore, land use cannot always be seen from the street.

One could go on analysing the preconditions of Sampson and Raudenbush's coding system – for instance, one wonders what kind of training was provided to research assistants so that their observations of 'prostitution' would have good inter-coder reliability.[11] But our main interest here is not to argue with the authors, but rather to use their article as a case study. And from that perspective, the key point is that the scalar shifts performed (or inherited) by Sampson and Raudenbush have an effect that is also found in qualitative and 'eyewitness' accounts

---

[11] A fuller analysis of the scale of systematic social observation would take up the question of how 'social' disorder is distinguished from 'physical' disorder. This binary opposition re-enacts the basic scalar assumptions of modern rational thought that Bruno Latour has famously deconstructed in his critique of how the natural sciences and the social/human sciences diverged (Latour 1987). But using Latour's critique of the nature/culture binary would not be helpful in this particular instance, since the distinction between 'physical' and 'social' disorder does not do any real work in the Sampson and Raudenbush article – and indeed, a central feature of broken-windows criminal justice and municipal measures is that they deliberately mix the physical (syringes, trash, graffiti) with the human-social (drinking, loitering, congregating), as if the 'modern constitution' that Latour critically studies had never happened.

of urban order and disorder, namely that the detailed description of the tools of systematic observation has the (recursive) effect of making all the entities being counted look as if they are all as solid and visible as a broken bottle. If we are told that a video camera recorded 'loitering', we will end up thinking that loitering is an objectively visible entity.

In sharp contrast to this objectivism, Wilson and Kelling make it clear that observing a broken window is inseparable from contesting what a broken window is; they directly and explicitly engage in the cultural politics that multi-'lifestyle' urban environments constantly experience. This explicit constructionist perspective is much clearer in the subsequent book, which continually highlights rather than suppresses scale conflicts, most notably the conflict between the juridical scale of individual rights and the social-control scale of community 'order' (Coles and Kelling 1996). Sampson and Raudenbush, by contrast, do not discuss why they chose their particular collection of visual cues, and do not justify interpreting these entities as signifiers that always mean disorder.

The objective gaze and SUV citizenship

If replicability is the first component of 'systematic', the second methodological claim that supports the 'systematic' label is objectivity. This is defined here as the strict separation of observer from observed. The authors explain their method (or their methodological desires) by contrasting their approach to the inferior approach chosen by those who explore 'residents' *subjective* perceptions drawn from survey responses' (Sampson and Raudenbush 1999: 605).

Sampson and colleagues may well admit that non-resident researchers also have feelings and prejudices (the highly impoverished content that they appear to give to the philosophically rich term 'subjective'); but they seem to believe that the researchers' subjectivity has been neutralised in a two-step process. The first step is the unspecified 'training' which they mention was provided to the research assistants – which no doubt contributed to the high inter-coder reliability, but which, if their unquestioned use of categories such as 'loitering' and 'mixed land use' is any indication, was unlikely to have counteracted middle-class white observers' culturally specific and distinctly extra-local interpretation of visual cues.

The second step in the elaboration of the scale of systematic observation seems to be more important than the training, since they describe it in loving detail. The trained researchers, we are told, spent countless hours driving down every street in no less than 196 census tracts. Not walking, but driving. And driving not in any old vehicle but in a 'sports utility vehicle' (SUV).

How does the use of an SUV, in the impoverished neighbourhoods that are mainly discussed in the article, affect the scale and hence the findings of the study? Critical urbanist Don Mitchell has written recently about 'SUV citizenship', referring to the symbolic value that SUVs have for middle-class, mainly white, urban or suburban drivers who have no practical need for four-wheel traction or other technical features of SUVs but who feel 'safer' driving down the wild streets of downtown America in a fortress-like SUV (Mitchell 2005). Along similar lines, Jonathan Simon too has written eloquently about the particular gaze (and associated emotional state) deployed by middle-class SUV drivers (Simon 2007: 7). It is clear from both Mitchell's and Simon's observations that an SUV being driven on a mountain road is one entity, but an SUV being driven down a poverty-stricken street in Miami or Chicago is another.

As if to make the SUV stand out even more in poor neighbourhoods, Sampson and Raudenbush told the drivers to go strictly at 5 miles per hour. An SUV driving very slowly, especially if the windows are tinted to facilitate unobtrusive filming, is likely to make passers-by envision either drug dealers or the drug squad, who in many North American cities (and not just on the television programme 'The Wire') tend to use the same oversized, uniformly black, and obviously new vehicles. But nothing is said about the potential effects of unusual vehicles driving unusually slowly on the behaviour of 'street-corner society'.

In addition, the desire to record disorder on videotape dictated that all research be done only during the daytime. Of course all research has temporal limits; but in the case of urban disorder, not collecting data after 7.00 p.m. introduces serious systematic distortions. The limitations of the daytime-only rule are indeed acknowledged, just barely, in noting that not much prostitution was observed: but the effects of this limit on the data collection and subsequent correlations are not analysed.

To conclude the analysis of scale and 'objectivity', then: the video camera in the SUV, operated by a researcher who has been trained to ensure inter-coder reliability and is therefore rigidly prevented from interacting with the observed environment or taking into account local knowledges, is presented as the technology that yields objective and replicable truth about urban disorder. But by neglecting to consider the distortion introduced by a vehicle calling attention to itself by its make and by its slowness Sampson and Raudenbush 'naturalise' their own gaze – a gaze that sees, or rather, *observes* urban 'disorder' by using the scale of outsider videotaping,[12] but which also uses coding categories of notable scalar hybridity.

My analysis is by no means intended to prove that their results are somehow 'invalid'; it is merely intended to demonstrate the limits and internal contradictions of the replicability and objectivity project. I am merely suggesting that the article should have been entitled 'Looking at some Chicago neighbourhoods with (some) Chicago-school methods'.

Conclusions

In this contribution I have limited myself to analysing two influential texts that virtually everybody working on issues of urban order/disorder has read. But in a more complete analysis this would have to be followed by a reflexive analysis, since if my general argument about scales and gazes is correct, my own work too could benefit from a similar analysis. And if the critical gaze were to be turned inward in a reflexive manner, the first thing that I would have to note is that while I claim to be interested only in analysing scale effects and scale shifts within urban safety and urban order discourses, I slip more than once into a political critique of the cultural assumptions made by the authors under consideration, thus slipping from a discussion of method to a discussion of prejudices and politics. However, in my defence, I have tried to clearly indicate when the text changes genre and succumbs to the temptation of political–cultural critique, since what I think is objectionable is the sleight-of-hand by which a scale shift (say, from the physically visible to the realm of moral judgement) is hidden from the reader's view; scale shifts and other sources of inconsistency are not in themselves problematic unless we hold fast to a pre-Einstein notion of objectivity.

It is not coincidental that I happen to think that purity, in choice of scale as in other issues of method, is neither possible nor desirable. There are basic philosophical differences that lead someone like me – trained in continental philosophy and highly influenced by the Nietzschean tradition – to see Rob Sampson's pursuit of methodological rigour as rather

---

[12] Some cultural studies writers would no doubt wax at length about the political implications of videotaping as such, using film-studies terms; but in my view, family members videotaping one another is an activity taking place at a different scale than the concealed videotaping by strangers that was at work in this chapter.

blinkered. In turn, Sampson would no doubt see this chapter as a messy collection of unconstructive observations. In standard American sociology, discussions about basic epistemological issues tend to be seen as idle and useless, since the only epistemological issues that are deemed to be worth talking about are those that fit within the strict limits of the topics already institutionalised under the label '*research* methods'. Discussions not about how to measure but about the character of that which is being measured tend to be dismissed as 'metaphysical' – even though a philosopher would say that it is precisely taking a category such as 'disorder' or 'criminal' for granted that is metaphysical.

But whether or not my analysis is at all audible or visible to people like Sampson, I have tried to show that examining carefully the scale choices made (consciously or not) by observers amounts to more than a debunking operation. It can help us to better understand the limits and the constraints both of our methods and of our basic terms.

In addition, paying attention to scale could help refine comparative analyses: in comparing criminal justice responses to urban disorder across jurisdictions with questions of scale in mind, it may turn out that some of the observed policy differences are not due to political or cultural differences but are instead rooted in the fact that different scales for visualising and managing disorder are assumed to be the correct or normal ones. For example, the fact that Britain has a powerful Home Office whose researchers are constantly generating national-level policies and statistics, added to the legal fact that most law that counts is national, has had the effect of turning British urban disorder into more a national issue than it is in North America, where legal mechanisms are rarely national and where police forces are rarely subject to national policy directives. In turn, as academic observers choose to use one gaze rather than another (the national versus the micro-local, say), their research will tend to impact some state bodies more than others. Of course state agencies can and do perform scale shifts – for example, the Home Office commissions and uses local studies of crime and disorder issues. But scale shifts have their effects too, as when a highly local study is used as an 'example' of 'best practices' rather than as a specifically local narrative.

Overall, then, paying close attention to qualitative and quantitative scales used to produce knowledge of crime and disorder can help to begin clarifying some of the ambiguities and confusions that terms such as 'community' have wrought, not only within the academy but at the policy level as well.

References

Blomley, N. (1994) *Law, Space, and the Geographies of Power*, London: Guilford Press.

Certeau, M. de (1984) *The Practice of Everyday Life*, Berkeley: University of California Press.

Coles, C. and Kelling, G. (1996) *Fixing Broken Windows: Restoring Order and Reducing Crime in Our Communities*, New York: Simon and Schuster.

Cotterrell, R. (1995) *Law's Community*, Oxford: Clarendon Press.

Crawford, A. (1997) *The Local Governance of Crime: Appeals to Community and Partnerships*, Oxford: Clarendon Press.

—— (1998) *Crime Prevention and Community Safety*, London: Longman.

Duneier, M. (1999) *Sidewalk*, New York: Farrar, Strauss and Giroux.

Ericson, R., Baranek, P. and Chan, J. (1991) *Representing Order: Crime, Law, and Justice in the News Media*, Toronto: University of Toronto Press.

Haraway, D. (1991) *Simians, Cyborgs, and Women: The Reinvention of Nature*, New York: Routledge.

Harcourt, B. (2001) *The Illusion of Order*, Chicago: University of Chicago Press.

Herod, A. and Wright, M. (2002) (eds.) *Geographies of Power: Placing Scale*, Oxford: Blackwell.

Jacob, C. (2006) *The Sovereign Map: Theoretical Approaches in Cartography throughout History*, trans. Tom Conley, Chicago: University of Chicago (French edition 1992).

Jacobs, J. (1961) *The Death and Life of American Cities*, New York: Random House.

Latour, B. (1987) *We Have Never Been Modern*, Cambridge, MA: Harvard University Press.

Levi, R. (2003) *The Constitution of Community in Legal Sites*, University of Toronto, Faculty of Law (SJD thesis).

Mitchell, D. (2003) *The Right to the City: Social Justice and the Fight for Public Space*, New York: Guilford Press.

—— (2005) 'The SUV model of citizenship: floating bubbles, buffer zones, and the rise of the purely atomic individual', *Political Geography*, 24, 77–100.

Park, R., Burgess, E. W. and Mckenzie, R. (1925) *The City*, Chicago: University of Chicago Press.

Poovey, M. (1995) *Making a Social Body: British Cultural Formation 1830–1864*, Chicago: University of Chicago Press.

Sampson, R. and Raudenbush, S. (1999) 'Systematic social observation of public spaces: a new look at disorder in urban neighborhoods', *American Journal of Sociology*, 105(3), 603–51.

Santos, B. de Sousa (1987) 'Law: a map of misreading: toward a postmodern conception of law', *Journal of Law and Society*, 14(3), 279–302.

Scott, J. (1998) *Seeing Like a State*, New Haven, CT: Yale University Press.

Simon, J. (2007) *Governing through Crime*, Oxford: Oxford University Press.

Valverde, M. (2006) 'Taking "land use" seriously: toward an ontology of municipal law', *Law, Text, Culture*, 9, 34–59.

   (2007) 'Genealogies of modern states: Foucaultian reflections', *Economy and Society*, 36(1), 159–78.

   (2009) 'Jurisdiction and scale: legal technicalities as resources for theory', *Social and Legal Studies*, 18(2), 139–57.

Whyte, W. F. (1988) *City*, New York: Anchor.

Wilson, J. Q. and Kelling, G. (1982) 'Broken windows: the police and neighbour-hood safety', *The Atlantic Monthly*, March, 29–37.

INDEX

Aas, Katja Franko xi, 2–3, 7, 8, 28–9
abandoned vehicles, observations of
    579
ABCs (Acceptable Behaviour
    Contracts, UK) 526–7
aboriginals, in Canada *see* First Nations
    peoples
Abu Qatada 423
accountability
  of European agencies 395
  for international crimes 150, 151–4,
    161–2
  of international criminal justice
    system 121–2, 135
  of police forces, in France 554–5,
    555–6
ad hoc tribunals *see* international
    criminal tribunals
administrative detention, in United
    Kingdom 417–20
adult sentencing, in Canadian youth
    justice system 342–3,
    346–9
adults, loitering/congregating by
    579–80
Afghanistan
  detentions and transfers by UK
    forces in 425–7
  ISAF mission in 425
aggression, crime of
  excluded from ICC Statute 89
  ICC efforts for codification of
    59–60
  as international crime 119
Ahmad, Babar 422–3
Ahn, S.-H. 268
Aitken Report (UK) 431–2

Al-Jedda cases (House of Lords UK and
    England and Wales High
    Court) 428–30
Al-Qa'ida, UN sanctions regime against
    53, 55
Al-Skeini case (House of Lords UK)
    430–1
alley-gating 531–2, 539
anchored pluralism (Loader and
    Walker) 463, 467–8
Andenaes, J. 254
Anderson, J. E. 16
Andreas, P. 59
Anglophone societies
  penal policies in 24–5
    convergence with Scandinavian
      societies 251–2, 252–6, 271
    and exclusionary criminal justice
      approaches 261–5, 271–2
    penal excess in 251–2, 256–8
  welfare state restructuring in 261–3
Annan, Kofi 109
anti-loitering laws, in United States
    507–8
antisocial behaviour interventions
    (UK) 486, 502–3, 520
  acceptable behaviour contracts
    (ABCs) 526–7
  dispersal orders 503–4, 504–5, 505–6
antiterrorism legislation/strategies
  cosmopolitanism rejected in
    413–14
  European 559
  in France 558, 562
  and human rights 29–30, 131–2
  UN role in 55–6
  of United Kingdom

Brants, Chrisje xi, 19–20, 90,
        93, 104
Broadgate Centre (London) 488–9
'broken windows' criminology, scales
        used in 570–1, 571–4,
        574–6, 581
Brown, M. 196
Browne, D. 427, 431
Bryman, A. 148
'bulimic society' 497
bureaucracy see civil service
Burgess, E. W. 574–5
Burrows, R. 522
Burundi, requests for establishment
        of a war crimes tribunal
        by 49
Bush, George H. W. 44, 332
Business Improvement Districts
        see BIDs
Butler, Robin 253
'BUZZ OFF' campaign (UK) 509

Cambodia, Extraordinary Chambers 49
Camden (London), gated housing
        estates in 533–6
Campbell, M. 353
Canada
    criminal justice system in 308–9,
        312–13
    human rights of prisoners in 177, 188
    imprisonment rates in 26, 304–5,
        305–11, 312, 313–14, 326
        pre-trial detention 316–17
        provincial level 317–19, 322
        for youth 331, 336, 337–8, 343–7,
            352, 353
    judiciary in 309
    neoliberalism in 322–6
    penal cultures in 322, 327
    penal policies in 26–7, 305, 326, 333
        and political economy 304–5,
            312–22, 326–7
        transnational transfer from
            United States to 351–2
    punitiveness in
        increases of 322–6, 327, 332
            rhetoric 333–4, 334–6, 336–7,
                338, 339–40, 350, 351

Quebec opposition to 338–9, 350–1,
        352
    restorative justice schemes in 453–4
    victims' movements in 309
    youth justice system in 26–7
        adult sentencing and transfer to
            adult courts 342–3, 346–9
        sentencing policies 341–2, 344–6,
            346–9
        Young Offenders Act 332–3,
            333–6
        Youth Criminal Justice Act
            (2003+) 336–46, 349–51
capital punishment see death penalty
capitalist societies, political economies
        of 221–4
cartography 568
Casey Report (UK) 264, 441
Catholicism, in Spain 288
Cauter, L. de 484–5
Cavadino, Michael xi, 23–4, 193, 216,
        217, 221, 235, 304–5, 312,
        326–7, 357, 361
CCTV camera surveillance, use of 551
Certeau, Michel de 567
chance-oriented egalitarianism 365
Cheney, D. 552
Chevigny, P. 226
Chicago School of sociology
    on communities 575–7, 578
    on urban life 574–5
        and disorder 578–9
        'feel of the streets' 577
children's hearing system (Scotland)
        277–8
Christie, N. 451
cities see urban areas
citizenship, global 124–5
The City (Park et al.) 574–5
civil service
    in corporatist societies 207, 227–8
    in neoliberal societies 207–8, 227–8
civil societies, and nation-states 456
Civitas 202
Clarke, Ron 533
CNDS (National Commission on the
        Ethics of Security, France)
        546

federal systems/states 231–2
  and criminal justice systems, Canada
    308–9, 312–13
Fekete, L. 401
Findlay, Mark xii, 20–1, 97
Finland
  penal policies in 260, 261, 270–1
  prison conditions in 259
Finlay, A. 261–2
First Nations peoples (Canada)
  imprisonment rates of 318
  restorative justice schemes for 453–4
'first-past-the-post' systems
        see majoritarian electoral
        systems
Fixing Broken Windows (Coles and
        Kelling) 573
'flawed' consumers (Bauman) 495
Flusty, S. 491, 512
foreigners
  deportation of, in UK antiterrorism
        legislation 420–4
  imprisonment of, in European
        countries 235
forgiveness, as part of restorative
        justice 159–61, 162
formats 572
Foucault, Michel 215, 218, 484–5
France
  antiterrorism legislation/strategies in
        558, 562
  community-based policing in 561–2
  criminal justice reforms in 446
    crime prevention 446
    mediation 444–5
    proximity justice 443–4
  human rights in, ECtHR
        condemnations of 556
  imprisonment of foreigners in 235
  policing in
    accountability of 554–5, 555–6
    racial profiling 553
  private security sector in 556–7
  restorative justice approaches in
        30–1
  terrorism threats in 554, 558
  urban security governance in 33–4,
        560–1, 562–3, 563–4

urban unrest in 547–9, 549–50,
        552–4
  Welfare state in 563
  youth justice system in 547
Friedland, M. L. 309
Friedrichs, J. 133
Frontex (European Border Control
        Agency) 394–5, 399, 401,
        404–7
functional-equivalence approaches, in
        comparative criminal
        justice research 10
funding, of criminal justice reforms
        448–9

Gaeta, Paola 42
Garland, D. 6, 10, 327–8, 529, 537
gated communities 7, 519
  for the affluent 529–30, 536–7,
        538–9
  for lower-income owner-occupiers
        530–2, 537, 538, 539
  in public housing estates 532–6
  rules of 526
  and urban security governance 32–3,
        490–1, 536–7
Geertz, C. 14
gendered violence, in Spain 284
generic eyewitness perspectives 573–4
Genn, H. 445
genocide 117
Gentle case (House of Lords, UK) 432
geography
  critical 567, 568
  and scales 568
Gerber-Stellingwerf, L. 52
Germany
  criminal justice reforms in 446–7
  human rights of prisoners in 169–70,
        171
  ICC supported by 73
  reform of prison laws in 169
Giddens, Anthony 2
global citizenship 124
  and international criminal justice
        124–5
Global Counter-Terrorism Strategy
        (UN General Assembly) 56